DEFAULTED SECURITIES

THE GUIDE FOR TRUSTEES AND BONDHOLDERS

January 2018

JAMES E. SPIOTTO, AUTHOR

CONTRIBUTORS:
ANN E. ACKER
LAURA E. APPLEBY
MARLA CHERNOF COHEN
M. JOEL LAUB
STEPHEN R. TETRO II
FRANKLIN H. TOP III

ISBN: 978-0-692-06046-9

Table of Contents

"The law ought not make trusteeship so hazardous that responsible individuals and corporations will shy away from it."

Judge Learned Hand

Dabney v. Chase Nat'l Bank, 196 F.2d 668, 675 (2d Cir. 1952)

Preface to *Defaulted Securities: The Guide for Trustees and Bondholders*

One commentator on the indenture trustee's role in finance observed: "... [i]t is noteworthy that there has been so little written upon it in the fifty years during which this field of law has been developing. Indeed, the comparatively few cases which deal with the subject leave many of its problems altogether untouched." You may conclude this is a recent statement, but in fact it was made in 1928 in a *Harvard Law Review* article and later in a book by Louis S. Posner, *Liability of the Trustee under the Corporate Indenture*. However, many an indenture trustee, legal scholar and judge might well agree that the remark remains true today. In the 1980's, the American Bankers Association ("ABA") Corporate Trust Committee shared Mr. Posner's concerns expressed over 50 years earlier, and the Committee requested that I create a book setting forth the role of the indenture trustee based on the Trust Indenture Act of 1939 and the evolving case law as well as the best practices of various indenture trustees as demonstrated over the years. Since I had practiced in the area for about 20 years, chaired an annual Practising Law Institute program for trustees and bondholders, their counsel and advisors since 1980, regularly made presentations at the ABA Corporate Trust Workshops and at the Cannon Financial Institute, we agreed it would be a task worth pursuing. From this effort came the book *Defaulted Securities: The Prudent Indenture Trustee's Guide*, published by the ABA in 1990.

Now, almost 30 years later, indenture trustees, their counsel and advisors, and legal scholars have, by their gentle suggestions for updates and their continuing requests for the book long out of print, indicated that a new volume on the ever-developing role of the trustee and bondholders in defaulted bond situations would be both welcomed and helpful. Further, developments in the financial markets and the expanded use of trustees for security issuances in the years since the publication of the ABA volume have provided ample additional material for a new book. Also, since 1990, additional, more developed structured financial products such as securitizations, CDO, CLO, RMBS, CMBS, ABS, MBS, SIV and derivatives have become a focus of trustees and bondholders.

As has been recognized in bankruptcies, workouts and litigations over the past 28 years involving these newer products as well as some older ones, there still is a demand for a clear and concise explanation of the role of the indenture trustee and bondholders as well as the role of the securitization trustee and investors/certificateholders in time of distress for these financings. Further, the need for coordination, communication and understanding between indenture trustees and bondholders or securitization trustees and investors/certificateholders in defaulted securities situations increasingly has become more critical and desired.

The intent of this new book is not only to update the prior version but also to develop a guide for indenture trustees, bondholders, certificateholders and investors so that together the trustees and holders can maximize the recovery for all, having learned from the past for the betterment of the future. The views expressed herein have been developed from the wisdom of the trustees, holders and their counsel and advisors. In particular, trustees have benefited from the collective knowledge of members of the ABA Corporate Trust Committee guided by the skilled judgment of Cristeena G. Naser, the recently retired Vice President and Senior Counsel to the Center for Securities, Trust & Investment of the ABA as well as her successor, Tab Stewart, along with the numerous trustees we have had the pleasure of working with or observing in a defaulted securities situation. Further, from the holders' perspective, the insurance companies, funds, banks, and institutional investors that we have represented in a variety of financings have helped shape the guide for bondholders, certificateholders and investors. The individual trustees and holders who have made this invaluable contribution are far too numerous to list here as are the over 400 troubled securities issues I have been involved in, but many of them are referred to in the text and footnotes that follow.

The purpose of this book is to provide a guide to be considered and reviewed by current and future generations of trustees or holders as well as their counsel and advisors. In recent years, I have served as an expert witness in cases involving trustees and holders and have observed that judges have expressed a keen interest in background and reference resources on the topic of the respective roles of the trustees and holders. Also, it is intended that this book assist courts, rating agencies, government regulators and others in understanding and considering issues relating to trustees in corporate and municipal financing. The ABA book was helpful but is not as current as one would desire. This new book recognizes that being effective in default situations for trustees and holders begins with acceptance of the trusteeship and the decision to invest, respectively, based on documentation and structure that are workable and designed to accomplish the purpose of the transaction. The book begins with a review and analysis of these basics because the knowledge of the documents, their provisions and terms will be vital to successfully navigating the troubled waters of default. From this background flows the role of the trustees and holders, checklists and consideration of conflicts, forms of communication, rights, remedies, workouts, settlements, amendments, bankruptcies, litigations, trust instruction proceedings and court approval and direction as effective means of resolving defaulted securities. Traditional bonds, notes, debentures with and without collateral, subordination, exchange offers along with more recent products of asset-backed securitizations, derivatives and other more esoteric structurings will be reviewed and analyzed as to the developed case law and experience. Hopefully, this book will provide an explanation, or statement of the appropriate practice or action that will help resolve future disputes and financially-troubled situations or at least point the way toward that goal. If the book achieves this end, then it is a tribute to those who have shown all of us the way over these many years.

I would like to thank the partners, attorneys and staff at Chapman and Cutler LLP. In particular, I would like to recognize the contributions of Ann Acker of Chapman Strategic Advisors LLC and Laura Appleby, Marla Chernof Cohen, M. Joel Laub, Stephen Tetro and Franklin Top of Chapman and Cutler LLP, whose insights and input were invaluable. I am grateful to Isabella Bankowski, Rebekah Alm and Tricia Bonarek who processed more drafts of this book than they probably ever thought possible. Leah Mayes was our patient and knowledgeable proofreader. Finally, Nancy Linder skillfully and creatively managed the publication process.

This book, in reality, was a community effort by and for trustees, holders and their respective professionals who over the years have shared their wisdom and experience for the benefit of all. It is intended that this book will be updated as often as needed.

Of course, we again want to thank you, the reader, for your continued time, efforts, and comments, which are appreciated and valued, and with that input, we can continue to make this book and its updates of service to you and the financial markets.

James E. Spiotto
Chapman Strategic Advisors LLC
Chicago, Illinois
January 2018

Preface to *Defaulted Securities: The Prudent Indenture Trustee's Guide* (1990)

Forty years ago, a banker could spend an entire career in a corporate trust department and never experience a defaulted issue. To the corporate trust officers of that era, defaults were nightmares that rarely translated themselves into reality. However, the 1970's brought the default of the Penn Central Railroad Company and the end to the relative tranquility that characterized the corporate trust business. Succeeding years have meant an increasing number of complex defaulted issues that corporate trust officers have had to confront.

Four years ago, a group of corporate trust officers, who had taken an active role in the work of the American Bankers Association Corporate Trust Subcommittee, approached me at the National Corporate Trust Workshop about writing a manual regarding the administration of the defaulted trust account. They indicated their belief that, because of the extensive writing and lecturing I had done in the area, the compilation of such a manual could be accomplished speedily. In what would prove to be sheer naiveté, I agreed that this project would take a matter of months. Four years later, we are the proverbial older but wiser. Fashioning a text that would be useful, that synthesized the lessons of the defaults of the past, and that was worthy of the corporate trust and legal community, as well as the investing public, was not an easy task.

The rising default rate for both tax-exempt and corporate debt has increased the likelihood that a corporate trust officer will be faced with default, bankruptcy or workout. The legal principles and practical rules which ought to govern the performance of an indenture trustee in a troubled situation had not been assembled in one text, and indenture trustees had called for a manual to supplement the fine body of work available with respect to corporate trust administration and management generally.

This book is designed for the corporate trust officer and its counsel who are experiencing a default situation for the first time. The goal is to provide a basic, understandable discussion of the issues presented by a default and the areas which should be of concern to the indenture trustee and its counsel. Both the rules of law and the teachings of experience are stressed. Moreover, given the likelihood that more and more transactions in any corporate trust officer's portfolio may go into default, the volume is designed to provide a general background by which indenture trustees can examine proposed trusteeships at their inception. In particular, it is hoped that this text will assist an indenture trustee in reviewing draft indentures to determine whether a given transaction is one which warrants its attention and which contains adequate default and remedies provisions.

It also was the intent of the American Bankers Association that this book aids the legal profession, including corporate trust counsel and class action attorneys for bondholders, in understanding the role, duties and responsibilities of an indenture trustee in a default situation. Further, the American Bankers Association hoped that this text would assist the judiciary, currently laboring over troubling issues, by presenting a coherent statement of the custom, practice and understanding in the industry of the scope of the duties and responsibilities of indenture trustees. Ideally, such could assist in obtaining decisions which are based on a clear understanding of the nature of the corporate trusteeship.

Further, given the growing involvement of institutional investors and their analysts in the resolution of defaulted issues, the manual should provide aid to this growing constituency in realistically appraising what indenture trustees can and cannot do. The acute concerns of this audience have been made clear to me as I have spoken with institutional investors and participated in discussions with analysts, including the Society of Municipal Analysts, of which I am a member. Defaults can best be dealt with where there is cooperation between the indenture trustee and the major holders, not when they are working at cross-purposes. It is hoped that this text will assist to bring these groups closer together.

Chapters I through VI treat the general nature of the corporate trusteeship, the trust indenture, and pre-default considerations. Chapters VII through X involve an examination of defaults, the role of the indenture trustee when faced with a default, and the threshold issues which confront an indenture trustee for a defaulted issue. Chapters X through XVII discuss the basic remedies available to the indenture trustee and the common problems facing an indenture trustee when the obligor of its issue is in bankruptcy. The last portion of the book deals with out-of-bankruptcy workouts, exchange offers, and substantive areas of the law which have been emerging as avenues of recovery and sources of liability for indenture trustees. At the end of many chapters, forms are included where helpful.

It is hoped that this book will be a useful tool for indenture trustees. If the manual is successful, this result is a tribute to those who have shown me the way over many years. At the risk of an unintentional omission, I would like to thank a number of individuals who assisted me tremendously. First, I acknowledge the great contribution of the American Bankers Association whose suggestions and criticisms strengthened the book. In particular, I pay tribute to the group of corporate trust officers who had the perseverance to read the final draft, to suggest changes, and to question positions: Tim Crane of Manufacturers Hanover Trust Co., Tony Guthrie of Citizens & Southern National Bank, Ruth Keeth of the Idaho First National Bank, Jack Kruger of Continental Bank, N.A., Terry McRoberts of Security Pacific National Bank, Jeff Powell of the

First National Bank of Chicago, and John Soldati of Citizens & Southern National Bank. Their continuing efforts on behalf of the industry should be saluted. Moreover, I wish to express appreciation to Bob Landau, whose wisdom and guidance have assisted me and countless others over the years. I look forward to a continuing association with him.

I would be remiss if I did not thank the many helpful corporate trust officers who provided valuable help to me as a young lawyer and taught me so much about the corporate trust business. I particularly would like to mention Roland K. Weber of LaSalle National Bank, one of those corporate trust officers who helped educate me regarding corporate trust. This was no minor feat.

The students I have taught during the past twelve years at the American Bankers Association National Corporate Trust Workshop, the Cannon Financial Institute, and the Practising Law Institute consistently have challenged me with their insightful questions which have helped give focus to the manual.

I also am grateful to the members of the firm and all the lawyers at Chapman and Cutler. I especially appreciate the work of the attorneys, paralegals and secretaries of our Special Litigation, Bankruptcy and Workout Group, who have suffered through drafts of this volume in an effort to make it a better product and to make a contribution to the corporate trust community. In particular, I would like to thank my partner, Ann Acker, for her dedication and perseverance as principal editor of this book. I also am indebted to my partner, James R. Richardson, for his thoughtful contributions with regard to municipal default issues. My thanks to the Special Litigation, Bankruptcy and Workout Group word processors, who, under the leadership of Valerie Cervantes, have typed more versions of this text than they originally thought humanly possible. Certainly, the accounting concepts and the tax issues discussed in the following pages would not be as understandable or precise without the generous help of Ken White, a partner at Ernst & Young in Chicago, who has been a guiding light for many an indenture trustee in the storm of default. It goes without saying that the patience of my family as I struggled through the various stages of the writing process was remarkable and truly made this manual possible.

Of course, I would like to thank you, the reader. With your time, effort, and continuing comments, we will, through the years, attempt to make this book of better service to you and to financial markets generally.

James E. Spiotto
Chicago, Illinois
April 1990

I. Role of the Indenture Trustee Generally

A. Historical Overview

The role of an indenture trustee in debt financing in the United States is unique in many respects. While the common law recognizes the use of the trustee to hold collateral or protect the rights of others, indenture trustees in England did not hold collateral or even act on behalf of public debtholders. Historically, in Canada, the use of indenture trustees was limited to protection of rights, covenants and obligations.

In the United States, the use of indenture trustees evolved from basic common law roots regarding paying agents and the ability to hold or act on behalf of others. The turning point in the use of indenture trustees came in the middle of the 1800s, when the United States Supreme Court was asked to review the issue of whether certain bondholders of a mortgage railroad bond issue could foreclose on the mortgage absent 100 percent of the holders.[1] The Supreme Court held that, absent all the bondholders, the mortgage could not be foreclosed, since each bondholder should be present to defend his own claims and protect his own interests.[2] This brought about the necessity of having an entity hold the mortgage for the benefit of the bondholders. At first, the railroads thought it wise to appoint one of their employees to act as the holder of the mortgage for the benefit of the bondholders. However, such appointment became a career-threatening position when there was a default and the bondholders were demanding action by the indenture trustee to foreclose on the mortgage property held by the trustee's employer. The practical difficulties of this arrangement led to the common-sense approach of obtaining the services of an independent, sophisticated institution that could act for the benefit of others. There arose the use of an indenture trustee to take action on behalf of the holders, to hold the collateral if any was granted and, upon default, to protect the rights and interests of the holders as a prudent person would do with regard to that person's own property.

The next stage in the development of the indenture trustee came during the early part of the 1900s. During the 1920s and 1930s, given the financial turmoil of those times and perhaps the uncertainty with respect to an indenture trustee's role, there were instances when indenture trustees did not cover themselves with praise and glory. One case in particular is representative of failure to act in the best interest of holders.[3] There, the bank serving as the indenture trustee was also a lender. The bank as lender liquidated the obligor, thereby paying off the obligor's

---

1 *Nashville and Decatur R.R. Co. v. Orr*, 85 U.S. 471 (1873).

2 *Id.* at 474–75.

3 *Drueding v. Tradesmen's Nat'l Bank and Tr. Co.*, 319 Pa. 144, 179 A. 229 (1935).

loans from the bank. After the bank had been paid off, the bank as indenture trustee gave notice to the holders of existing defaults. Obviously, there was no ability for further action by the indenture trustee on behalf of the holders since there were no assets available to pay the holders of the securities. The court's conclusion was not surprising, nor was the court's impatience with the indenture trustee. The cases that arose out of the 1920s and 1930s brought about the Trust Indenture Act of 1939 ("TIA") and, pursuant to Congressional investigation, a groundswell of popular support for an independent, qualified and compensated indenture trustee to protect the rights of the holders.

An accurate understanding of the role of the indenture trustee is important to both the trustee and the bondholders for whom it acts. There is no benefit to any of the parties if the actions of the bondholders and their trustee are not coordinated and focused. The reality of the default situation is that bondholders and their trustee can expedite the resolution and increase the likelihood that the most favorable result will be obtained by working together as opposed to taking different approaches and courses of action.

It is against this historical backdrop that the role, duties and responsibilities of the contemporary indenture trustee have been defined. There are many different ways of describing what an indenture trustee is. The basic definition of its duties and responsibilities will flow from the fact that its origins arose out of the necessity of having someone, in the time of default, capable of either holding collateral and realizing thereon, or taking actions on behalf of a disparate group of public debtholders in an effort to maximize the recovery and return. A more recent development is the role of the trustee under a pooling and servicing agreement, which is different from the role of an indenture trustee. The trustee in a pooling and servicing agreement, which is associated with various types of securitizations and structured financings, is the legal nominee for trust assets as well as, among other things, the distributor of payments and notices. An understanding of the appropriate role of the trustee will assist bondholders working with the trustee to achieve the best result in the case of default.

B. Nature of the Indenture Trustee's Duties and Responsibilities

A trust indenture is a unique sort of document, and the trustee acting thereunder has unique duties and obligations. Over the years, various courts have characterized the role of the corporate trustee in different ways. A corporate trustee has, from time to time, been characterized as a fiduciary,[4] an agent,[5] a contracting party[6] or a combination of the above.[7] The trustee in a securitization and derivative transaction under a pooling and servicing agreement, as will be discussed in Chapters XVI and XVII by contrast, simply agrees to perform certain duties related to the holders.[8]

At times, various courts have combined the above approaches in attempting to rationalize how an indenture trustee should act. As a practical matter, as will be discussed in this chapter, the indenture trustee by and large has been viewed as the party who has contracted for specified duties and responsibilities prior to default; and, upon default, the indenture trustee is the party who, in the nature of a fiduciary, will take such action as is reasonable and prudent under the circumstances to protect the rights and interests of the holders. Many times, in the eyes of the court or a jury in a court proceeding, the trustee will be viewed as the face of the faceless bondholders or as the legal representative of the trust in which the bondholders invested.

Holders should understand that this notion of a post-default fiduciary does not mean that, in the case of the hopelessly insolvent obligor, where there are no funds to pay any money to the holders, the indenture trustee should pile expense upon expense, wasting its own funds in attempting to obtain a recovery that is not possible. Such action would not be prudent or indicative of a wise representative of the bondholders. Likewise, the indenture trustee must consider taking appropriate action when the indenture trustee knows there should be a recovery, and when taking such action will be compensated by the recovery to be obtained. In the case of defaults, the indenture trustee's duties and responsibilities are not normally delineated with the brightest of lines. Experience, judgment and practical wisdom normally lead the indenture trustee to the right decision to the benefit of the bondholders. This chapter will analyze how courts have treated indenture trustees and how courts have developed the standard by which the conduct of a corporate trustee is to be judged.

---

4 *York v. Guar. Tr. Co.*, 143 F.2d 503 (2d Cir. 1944), *rev'd*, 326 U.S. 99 (1945).

5 *First Tr. Co. v. Carlsen*, 129 Neb. 118, 261 N.W. 333 (1935).

6 *Hazzard v. Chase Nat'l Bank*, 159 Misc. 57, 287 N.Y.S. 541 (N.Y. Sup. Ct. 1936).

7 *Dunn v. Reading Tr. Co.*, 121 F.2d 854 (3d Cir. 1941).

8 *See* Georgette C. Poindexter, *Subordinated Rolling Equity: Analyzing Real Estate Loan Default in the Era of Securitization*, 50 EMORY L.J. 519, 538 (2001).

As early as the mid-nineteenth century, courts were treating the corporate trust relationship as unique. Today, the corporate trustee is to be judged by rules gleaned from statute and case law. It is important to note that, at least in certain stages of the corporate trust relationship, the corporate trustee is by no means identical to the ordinary fiduciary. A clear understanding by debtholders of the duties and obligations of the indenture trustee today must be premised upon an understanding of the history of the role of the trustee.

C. The 1858 Decision in *Sturges v. Knapp* and the Development of the Prudent Person Rule

It is frequently said that the nature of the trust created by a mortgage to secure a bond issue is different before and after default. The trustee's duties are passive until some default by the obligor occurs.[9] After default, the duties of an indenture trustee become proactive and more fiduciary in nature — this is the very origin of the prudent person rule. Such rule finds its source in the Vermont case of *Sturges v. Knapp*.[10] In that case, authored by Chief Judge Redfield, the mortgage executed by a railway company to secure payment of bonds contained no provisions concerning the rights and duties of the trustee, either before or after foreclosure. Although the document at issue was quite different from the sophisticated indentures of today, the *Sturges* case gave rise to certain general principles that continue to govern the conduct of indenture trustees. The trustee in *Sturges* foreclosed on the mortgaged property, took title to the property and leased the property to another railroad. A majority of the bondholders sued to void the lease on the ground that the trustee had no power to enter into the lease. In upholding the action taken by the trustee, Judge Redfield referred to the duties of the indenture trustee prior to default as executory and silent (basically prescribed by the language of the indenture, whether extensive or sparse). However, the court defined the role of the indenture trustee after default as follows:

> [A]fter the forfeiture occurs, either by non-payment of interest, or principal, or both, as in the present case, the duties of the trustees become, not only active and responsible, but critical and delicate. It not only is not a dead, dry trust, but it is one of the most active and momentous responsibility.[11]

The court then described the powers and the duties of the trustee after default. According to Judge Redfield, they are not limited by the language of the indenture but are "to be estimated by the surrounding circumstances, and what a prudent owner would esteem reasonable under these

---

9 Quindry, BONDS AND BONDHOLDERS §§ 205, 211 (2d ed. 1934); Leonard A. Jones, THE LAW OF BONDS AND BOND SECURITIES § 1030 (4th ed. 1935); *Northampton Tr. Co. v. Northampton Traction Co.*, 270 Pa. 199 (1921); *Colo. and S.R. Co. v. Blair*, 214 N.Y. 497 (1915).

10 *Sturges v. Knapp*, 31 Vt. 1 (1858).

11 *Id.* at 54–55.

circumstances."[12] This legal analysis parallels the development of a "prudent person" rule for personal trustees and general fiduciaries.[13]

D. Later Developments

The nature of the trustee after default was defined in similar fashion in other cases. For example, in *Merrill v. Farmers' Loan & Trust Co.*, the court stated that the general rules of the law of trusts are applicable to the trustee upon default, and the duties of the trustee are rendered active.[14] Although the above-cited precedent existed and was extensively followed prior to 1939, there was no uniformity regarding the powers and duties of trustees. In part, this was due to the method of financing in which the terms of indentures were tailor-made to the specific transaction. At least one commentator has concluded that the role of the corporate trustee developed more from the terms of specific indentures than from the law of trusts or any established body of law.[15] The patchwork quilt of case law did not produce a clear and uniform standard for indenture trustees in early days.

E. Early Use of Exculpatory Clauses

The diversity of viewpoint alluded to regarding the basic nature of the corporate trust relationship resulted in a lack of uniformity in judicial decisions defining the post-default responsibility of corporate trustees. The tendency of some courts to imply duties on the part of the trustee above and beyond those specifically set forth in the indenture induced trustees prior to 1939 to include provisions in the instruments relieving them from liability for losses to bondholders.[16] These exculpatory clauses generally provided that the trustee was not required to take notice of any default unless notified of the existence thereof by a specified percentage of the bondholders, and was under no duty to take any action until it had been furnished with a written demand by the bondholders and a tender of indemnity. Furthermore, the trustee was exempted

---

12 *Id.* at 58.

13 *Harvard College v. Amory*, 9 Pick. 446, 461 (Mass. 1831).

14 *Merrill v. Farmers' Loan & Tr. Co.*, 24 Hun. 297 (N.Y. 1881). *See also Lyman v. Stevens*, 123 Conn. 591 (1937); *Chicago Title & Tr. Co. v. Chief Wash Co.*, 368 Ill. 146 (1938); *Hoffman v. First Bond & Mortg. Co.*, 116 Conn. 320 (1933); *Nay Aug. Lumber Co. v. Scranton Tr. Co.*, 87 A. 843 (Pa. 1913).

15 V. Brudney and Wm. Bratton, BRUDNEY AND CHIRELSTEIN'S CORPORATE FINANCE, 166 (3d ed. 1998).

16 References to "bondholders" in this work should be interpreted as applicable to noteholders, debentureholders and certificateholders unless it is clear that the language is only applicable to holders of long-term secured debt. The TIA uses the term "indenture security" to describe the securities issued under a TIA-qualified indenture. 15 § 77ccc(11). When the term "holder" is used, it is intended to cover holders of various types of debt securities and investor interests in a trust represented by an indenture trustee unless a more restrictive meaning is clear from the language of the document creating the trust and the trustee.

from liability for loss to bondholders arising from any fault other than the trustee's gross negligence or bad faith. The practical result of these provisions was the creation of the troublesome cases of the 1920s and 1930s. It was ultimately determined to be unfair, unreasonable and likely futile to expect a diverse and uncoordinated group of bondholders to be able to become aware of a default, know what to do, find other holders and direct and indemnify the indenture trustee.

One of the most frequently referenced decisions upholding the trustee's right to rely on an exculpatory clause is *Hazzard v. Chase National Bank of City of New York*.[17] In *Hazzard*, debentureholders sued the corporate trustee for permitting the substitution of collateral securities that later became worthless. The indenture provided that the company could substitute for securities withdrawn any other securities plus documentation as to the earnings, but not the value, of the substituted collateral. The trustee accepted both the substituted securities (stock in a holding company) and the necessary documentation as replacements for the original collateral securities. The holding company went into bankruptcy and the substituted securities became worthless. Meanwhile, the original collateral had retained substantial value. The trust indenture provided that the trustee would be liable only for acts resulting from gross negligence or bad faith. The court ruled that, if judged by the standard of care imposed on a common law trustee, this trustee would be guilty of negligence. However, the court dismissed the case since the indenture trustee had little in common under the terms of the indenture with a trustee under the common law, and the court could not determine that the indenture trustee had been guilty of gross negligence or bad faith. The court indicated its dissatisfaction with the state of the law: "The entire system, however, should be changed by legislation so as to provide more adequate compensation to the trustee, and the imposition of a duty of active vigilance akin to that placed upon ordinary fiduciaries."[18]

F. The Reaction to *Hazzard*

The financial collapse of 1929 and the resultant loss to investors triggered a series of federal statutes, including the Securities Act of 1933 ("Securities Act" or "1933 Act") and the Securities Exchange Act of 1934 ("Securities Exchange Act" or "1934 Act"), which established the Securities and Exchange Commission ("SEC") and authorized the SEC to investigate protective and reorganization committees and to submit a report to Congress. The SEC commenced an investigation of the field of corporate trusteeships, conducted extensive public hearings and

---

17 *Hazzard v. Chase Nat'l Bank*, 287 N.Y.S. 541 (N.Y. Sup. Ct. 1936) (gross negligence requires willful or reckless disregard of the rights of the bondholders).

18 *Id.*

reviewed over 400 indentures. In 1936 the SEC delivered its Report to Congress on the activities of indenture trustees.[19] In its Report, the Commission noted:

> "[The indenture trustee] has been invested with power to certify securities; to supervise the deposit and the withdrawal of collateral and application of funds; to take action upon default; and, in short, to do everything upon which the protection and enforcement of the security of a bondholder depends.
>
> "Both in law and practice, this reliance of the security holder upon the trustee for protection of his investment is complete. It is a matter of common knowledge that purchasers of securities seldom examine the terms of the trust indenture, although they are legally bound by its terms. Even if they did examine the indenture, the significance of its elaborate provisions would appear only to specialists. In some instances, indeed, it is so drafted that vital provisions apparently escape the notice of highly trained investment agencies. Reliance for adequacy of the security underlying the bonds, notes or debentures, is placed by the investor upon the reputation of the issuer, the underwriting bankers and the trustee. And for honest, faithful and efficient operation of the provisions of the indenture, reliance is placed upon the trustee as representative of the security holders under the terms of the indenture . . .
>
> "But an examination of the provisions of modern trust indentures and their administration by trustees will show that this reliance is unfounded. It will show that typically the trustees do not exercise the elaborate powers which are the bondholders' only protection; that they have taken virtually all of the powers designed to protect the bondholders, but have rejected any duty to exercise them; and that they have shorn themselves of all responsibilities which normally trusteeship imports. The 'so-called trustee' which is left is merely a clerical agency and a formal instrument which can be used by the bondholders when and if enough of them combine as specified in the indenture . . .
>
> "Nevertheless one basic, fundamental fact cannot be overlooked: the trustee is the only agency avowedly designed for the protection of security holders during the entire life of the security. Furthermore, under the modern trust indenture it alone is capable of effective action . . . On these facts the trustee

---

19 *See* SEC Report on the Study and Investigation of the Work, Activities, Personnel and Functions of Protecting and Reorganizing Committees, Part VI (1936) ("SEC Report").

> should not be allowed, through indenture provisions never seen by the beneficiary, and which would not be understood if they were seen, to whittle away at the number of his express duties until they are practically non-existent, and to surround itself with exculpatory clauses which leave it harmless, despite inactivity or negligence . . .
>
> "The basic problem is to refashion the trust indenture for the purpose of according greater protection to investors. That entails prescribing certain minimum standard specifications for the conduct of trustee and issuer thereunder. As in the case of other contracts involving persons not capable nor in a position to protect themselves, the contents of the trust indenture can no longer be left to the conventions of the issuer, the trustee or the underwriter.
>
> "This means that a more proper balance between the interests of investors and requirements of issuers can be had only by enlarging the definition of the trustee's duties in those cases where its failure to take swift and positive action leaves the investors without effective protection of their interests. The contrary desires of issuer, trustee and underwriter must be made to bow to the insistent demands of investors and of the public interest in such cases."[20]

The SEC declared that the trust indenture should be refashioned to impose full fiduciary duties upon the corporate trustee. "[T]he trustee can no longer be allowed to be nothing but a stakeholder . . . It must be transformed into an active trustee lest the interests of investors be neglected both prior to and subsequent to default."[21] To attain this end, the SEC recommended the enactment of uniform legislation by Congress to transform trustees "into active trustees with the obligation to exercise that degree of care and diligence which the law attaches to such high fiduciary position."[22]

G. The Role of the Trustee under the TIA

Thereafter, a series of conferences was held with committees representing the American Bankers Association, the Investment Bankers Association and a number of institutional purchasers of debt securities. Through these conferences and a series of Congressional hearings, the legislation called for by the SEC evolved into the TIA. The purpose of the TIA as defined by a committee report of the House of Representatives was in part to "assure that the security holders

---

20 *Id.* at 2–6.

21 *Id.* at 20–22, 67–70, 110.

22 *Id.* at 110.

will have the services of a disinterested indenture trustee, and that such trustee will conform to the high standards of conduct now observed by more conscientious trust institutions."[23]

Moreover, the report stated that the TIA's goals included providing full and fair disclosure not only at the time of the original issue of the bonds, notes, debentures and similar securities but also throughout the life of such securities and to provide machinery whereby such continuing disclosure may be made to the security holders and whereby they may get together for the protection of their own interests.[24]

The TIA itself notes that it is contrary to the public interest when:

> "the trustee does not have adequate rights and powers, or adequate duties and responsibilities, in connection with matters relating to the protection and enforcement of the rights of such investors; when, notwithstanding the obstacles to concerted action by such investors, and the general and reasonable assumption by such investors that the trustee is under an affirmative duty to take action for the protection and enforcement of their rights, trust indentures (A) generally provide that the trustee shall be under no duty to take any such action, even in the event of default, unless it receives notice of default, demand for action, an indemnity, from the holders of substantial percentages of the securities outstanding thereunder, and (B) generally relieve the trustee from liability even for its own negligent action or failure to act."[25]

The statute attempts to remedy this situation by providing that all indentures required to be qualified thereunder must meet certain specific standards.[26] A basic knowledge of the provisions of the TIA will assist the trustee in performing its duties. Also, a basic understanding of the TIA by the holders will assist in understanding the action to be taken by the trustee, what actions a trustee may take and the limitation on the role of trustee in a default situation and prior to default.

---

23 *See* H.R. REP. NO. 1016, 76th Cong., 1st Sess. 25 (1939).

24 *Id.*

25 *See* TIA § 302(a)(2).

26 The TIA was amended in 1990 by the Trust Indenture Reform Act of 1990 ("TIRA"), Pub. L. 101–550, Title IV, § 401, 104 Stat. 2721. For a summary of the key provisions, see Appendix I to this chapter. For an exhaustive analysis of the TIA as amended, see The Committee on Trust Indentures and Indenture Trustees, American Bar Association Section of Business Law, *Annotated Trust Indenture Act*, 67 BUS. LAW 977 (2012) and the Committee's HANDBOOK FOR INDENTURE AND TRUST INDENTURE ACT INTERPRETATION (American Bar Association 2017) and Elizabeth D. Lauzon, Annotation, *Construction and Application of Trust Indenture Act of 1939 (TIA)*, 15 U.S.C.A. §§ 77aaa *et seq.*, 80 A.L.R. Fed. 2d 329 (2013).

The TIA embodies the distinction between the duties of the trustee pre-default and post-default.[27] A qualified indenture under the TIA shall automatically provide that, prior to default, the trustee shall not be liable except for the performance of such duties as are specifically set out in the trust indenture.[28] However, as set forth above, in order to be qualified under the TIA, a trust indenture shall be deemed to provide that, in the event of default, the trustee shall exercise its rights and powers as a prudent person would under the circumstances.[29]

The provisions of the TIA authorize certain powers and impose certain duties and responsibilities on trustees who serve under indentures required to be qualified under the TIA. The trustee is held to a good faith standard unless such standard is expressly excluded.[30] The common law that existed before the TIA remains applicable to non-TIA transactions.[31] It is clear that the TIA and its rules are inapplicable to issues that are exempt from the TIA or issues that were closed prior to its effective date (1939).[32] That said, and as noted above, the trustee's pre- and post-default standard of care codified by the TIA has become the marketplace standard for drafting most indentures, not just those qualified under the statute.

Moreover, Section 323 of the TIA states that the rights and remedies provided thereunder are in addition to those that exist under the securities laws or otherwise in law or equity, and Section 326 of the TIA provides that states may regulate trust indentures so long as the regulation

---

27 This distinction is often applied to non-TIA indentures and the trustees that serve under them. *See, e.g, Eldred v. Merchants Nat'l Bank of Cedar Rapids*, 468 NW 2d 221 (Iowa 1991).

28 *See* TIA § 315(a)(1); *Elliott Assocs. v. J. Henry Schroder Bank and Tr. Co.*, 838 F.2d 66 (2d Cir. 1988).

29 *See* TIA § 315(c). The exact nature of the indenture trustee's post-default duties under the TIA has been the subject of much legal writing and analysis. As noted, prior to the TIA's adoption, the SEC had recommended in the SEC Report that, post-default, indenture trustees "be transformed into active trustees with the obligation to exercise that degree of care and diligence which the law attaches to such high fiduciary position[s]." Although an early draft of Section 315(c) of the TIA used the term "fiduciary," the TIA as adopted did not specifically use the term "fiduciary" but rather used the "prudent person" standard post-default. Whether this is a distinction without a difference is the subject of analysis in Steven L. Schwartz and Gregory M. Sergi, *Bond Defaults and the Dilemma of the Indenture Trustee*, 59 ALA. L. REV. 1037, n 185 (2008) (noting judicial trend to view the indenture trustee as a limited fiduciary after default).

30 *See* TIA § 315(d)(2).

31 *E.F. Hutton Sw. Props. II, Ltd. vs. Union Planters Nat'l Bank*, 953 F.2d 963 (5th Cir. 1992); *In re Med. Capital Secs. Litig.*, 2012 WL 12142396 (C.D. Cal. Feb. 7, 2012).

32 *Friedman v. Chesapeake and Ohio Ry. Co.*, 261 F. Supp 728 (S.D.N.Y. 1966), *aff'd*, 395 F.2d 663 (2d Cir. 1968), *cert. denied*, 393 U.S. 1016 (1969); *Haas v. Palace Hotel Co.*, 101 Cal. App. 2d 108 (Cal. Ct. App. 1950), *cert. denied*, 342 U.S. 813 (1951). *See also Ret. Bd. of the Policemen's Annuity and Benefit Fund of the City of Chicago v. The Bank of N.Y. Mellon*, 775 F.3d 154 (2 Cir. 2014) (TIA does not apply to RMBS certificates issued under pooling and servicing agreement.)

does not conflict with the TIA.[33] As a result, some limited additional pre-default duties may apply. For example, New York state law imposes two pre- and post-default extra-contractual duties on indenture trustees: first, an indenture trustee must avoid conflicts of interests and second, an indenture trustee may be liable for failure to perform basic, non-discretionary tasks.[34] This rule becomes an issue when New York is the governing law under the indenture. The indenture trustee owes no other duties, fiduciary or otherwise, to the holders prior to a default.[35]

Holders should recognize that, although the trustee polices compliance with certain terms of the indenture, the operation of the TIA does not always create an active monitor before an event of default. The nature and extent of the duties of the trustee before default will vary with each indenture, because pre-default, the scope of the trustee's duties is as defined in the contract, and the indenture defines the scope of the powers of the indenture trustee. Thus, the bondholder should be familiar with the terms of the indenture before coming to a conclusion on the powers and duties of the indenture trustee. The indenture trustee has the power to perform those pre-default acts authorized by the express terms of the indenture or by necessary implication. Some indentures provide that no implied duties or covenants on the part of the trustee shall be read into the indenture, and such language has been upheld.[36] Language to the effect that the trustee has no obligation to perform any implied duties may be helpful. However, every indenture trustee has seen situations where it has felt it necessary to act beyond the scope of the specified duties and powers expressly set forth in the indenture. The right of the trustee to exercise such implied powers is discussed below. It should be noted that, if the actions the trustee feels compelled to take are an extreme departure from the terms of the indenture, and time permits, consideration could be given to seeking court approval of such action.

H. Implied Powers of the Indenture Trustee

An evolving area of the law is that grey, pre-default area with which trustees and bondholders are all too familiar. It has been said with regard to pre-default duties that to regard the corporate trustee as a mere stakeholder is to understate its responsibility; to treat the trustee

---

33 *LNC Invs., Inc. v. First Fidelity Bank,* 935 F. Supp. 1333 (S.D.N.Y. 1996).

34 *U.S. Tr. Co. v. First Nat'l City Bank,* 394 N.Y.S.2d 653 (1977) (citing § 323 of TIA and holding that the TIA does not abrogate an indenture trustee's common law, pre-default duty of loyalty), *aff'd,* 410 N.Y.S.2d 580 (1978); *Beck v. Manufacturers Hanover Tr. Co.,* 218 A.D. 2d, 632 N.Y.S.2d 520 (1995). *Dresner Co. Profit Sharing Plan v. First Fidelity Bank,* No. 95, 1996 WL 694345 (Dec. 4, 1996); *Williams v. Cont'l Stock Transfer & Tr. Co.,* 1 F. Supp. 2d. 836 (N.D. Il. 1998); *Philip v. L.F. Rothschild & Co. Ins.,* No. 90 C 0708, 1999 WL 771354 (S.D.N.Y. 1999); *AG Capital Funding Partners v. State St. Bank and Tr. Co.,* 896 N.E.2d 61 (N.Y. 2008).

35 *Elliott Assocs.,* 838 F.2d at 71.

36 *See Meckel v. Cont'l Res. Co.,* 758 F.2d 811, 816 (2d Cir. 1985).

as though it were an ordinary trustee is to overstate the extent of its duties and to subject it to a standard of conduct not required by the nature of the trust.[37] While the TIA embodies the concept of a pre-default trustee with simply contractual obligations, the duties and powers of an indenture trustee prior to default are circumscribed by the contract, but not to the extent that trustees are stymied in their efforts to protect holders. The courts have long held that the law does not imply any duties on an indenture trustee that are inconsistent with those provided for in the trust indenture.[38] Courts are reticent to imply duties in regard to a relationship that has been carefully negotiated by sophisticated parties.[39]Any implied covenants must be derived directly from the language of the indenture.[40] Indenture trustees have duties that are expressly declared in the instrument itself, as well as those incidental duties the law imposes upon the trustee as a necessity in bringing to fruition those obligations that the indenture expressly defines.[41] One court has expressed this concept by drawing a distinction between the limitations that a trust indenture may place on a trustee's duty and the trustee's duty to discharge whatever obligations it does assume with absolute single-mindedness of purpose.[42] Another court, when faced with an attempt to expand the pre-default duties of the indenture trustee by a resort to the implied covenant of good faith and fair dealing, noted that unless the indenture trustee has deprived holders of a right or benefit specifically provided to them in the indenture, there is no violation of the implied covenant.[43]

---

37 L. Posner, *Liability of a Trustee Under the Corporate Indenture,* 42 HARV. L. REV. 198, 200 (1928-29).

38 *See Hazzard v. Chase Nat'l Bank,* 287 N.Y.S. 541 (N.Y. Sup. Ct. 1936). "The trustee should be held accountable for failing to carry out its duties properly, but there is no basis for holding . . . that the trustee owes to each holder duties or obligations not specifically spelled out in the contract or required of it by statute or regulation." *Dell'oca v. The Bank of N.Y. Tr. Co., N.A.,* 159 Cal. App. 4th 531, 71 Cal. Rptr. 3d 737 (Ct. of App. 2008) (quoting *Landau & Krueger on Corporate Trust Administration*).

39 *See Metro. Life Ins. Co. v. RJR Nabisco, 716* F. Supp. 1504, 1519 (S.D.N.Y. 1989).

40 *Gardner and Florence Call Cowles Found. v. Empire, Inc.,* 589 F. Supp. 669 (S.D.N.Y. 1984), *vacated on other grounds,* 754 F.2d 478 (2d Cir. 1985).

41 2 R. Bowers, THE LAW OF BONDS AND BOND SECURITY § 1050 (4th ed. 1935). *Cf. Marine Midland Tr. Co. v. Allegheny Corp.,* 28 F. Supp. 680 (S.D.N.Y. 1939) (obligation to maintain stated minimum ratio of collateral imposed on obligor when indenture was construed as a whole and read in light of certain correspondence).

42 *Dabney v. Chase Nat't Bank,* 196 F.2d 668, 671 (2d Cir. 1952), *cert. dismissed,* 346 U.S. 863 (1953). But see *Elliott Assoc,* 838 F.2d at 73 ("[W]hile *Dabney* stands for the proposition that a trustee must refrain from engaging in conflicts of interest, it simply does not support the broader proposition that an implied fiduciary duty is imposed on a trustee to advance the financial interests of the debentureholders during the period prior to default.").

43 *Lorenz v. CSX Corp.,* 1 F.3d 1406, 1415 (3d Cir. 1993) ("The covenant, however, cannot be used to insert new terms that were not bargained for."). *See also AMBAC Indem. Corp. v. Bankers Tr. Co.,* 573 N.Y. Supp. 2d 204 (S. Ct. N.Y. 1991); *Eldred v. Merchants Nat'l Bk.,* 468 N.W.2d 221 (Iowa 1991).

I. Implication of the Prudent Person Rule

It is clear that courts in applying the prudent person rule, both prior to and after the adoption of the TIA, were concerned about protection of the rights of the security holder. An indenture trustee who fails to record a mortgage promptly and protect the security of the holders would be liable, even though the indenture had exculpatory language.[44] The delay in notice to the holders of a default while the company liquidates to pay the indenture trustee bank debt is actionable.[45]

Generally, indenture trustees have been protected when they reasonably rely on the terms and conditions of the indenture. For example, in a case involving whether or not the indenture trustee could be held liable by the bondholders for redemption of the bonds consistent with the terms of the indenture prior to default, the court held that the contractual provisions regarding redemption applied regardless of arguments by the bondholders concerning the necessity of other provisions.[46] It is clear that, post-default, such literal reading of the terms of the indenture will not be followed and more expansive duties will be imposed.

Whenever the indenture trustee in good faith believes that the language of the indenture is unclear and that it may be subjecting itself to criticism or possible liability, given its interpretation of its powers and duties, it may seek direction and guidance from a court of competent jurisdiction. This is the traditional concept in personal and corporate trust law of seeking direction and instruction from a court when there is a legitimate dispute and controversy over interpretations, powers or duties of the trustee.[47] Resort to the court should be viewed by bondholders not as obstructionist but as a traditional way for the trustee to determine the appropriate course of action, satisfy its obligations and protect the bondholders, and provide notice of the issue to be decided and an opportunity to be heard for the bondholders.

J. Duties of an Indenture Trustee and Compensation

It is clear from the legislative history of the TIA and from the cases that abounded prior to its enactment that, in order to have a proactive, sophisticated and competent indenture trustee, the indenture trustee must be well compensated.[48] There should be no risks to the indenture

---

44 *Benton v. Safe Deposit Bank*, 236 N.Y.S. 36 (N.Y. Sup. Ct. 1926).

45 *Drueding v. Tradesmen's Nat'l Bank and Tr. Co.*, 319 Pa. 144 (1935).

46 *Meckel v. Cont'l Res.*, *supra* note 36; *Elliott Assocs. v. J. Henry Schroder Bank and Tr. Co.*, *supra* note 36.

47 *See, e.g.* MINN. TRUST CODE, ch. 501C; N.Y. CPLR § 7701; CAL. PROB. CODE § 17200.

48 Of course, in addition to compensation, the proactive indenture trustee will need funds available to preserve the collateral and to exercise appropriate remedies, if necessary. This requirement is discussed further in Chapter IX.

trustee for taking those actions that the indenture trustee's contractual or fiduciary duty mandates in order to protect the holders. It is clear from the very language of the TIA that the purpose of the indenture trustee is to ensure that the security holders will have the services of a disinterested indenture trustee, and that such trustee will conform to the high standards of conduct now observed by the more conscientious institutions. Inadequate compensation was clearly recognized as one of the factors that caused indenture trustees to lack interest and appropriate capacity to go forward in protecting the interests of the holders. Certainly no indenture trustee should be required to risk its own assets and funds to protect the rights and interests of holders under the terms of an indenture. As a result, as set forth in Chapter VIII, the direction of holders to the indenture trustee to take a specified action must be accompanied by indemnification, including of the indenture trustee's fees and expenses. Consequently, the indenture trustee's compensation should include acceptance fees and annual fees, as well as extraordinary fees upon default, that are sufficient not only to appropriately compensate the indenture trustee, but also to allow the indenture trustee (generally a bank) to hire professional and well-compensated trust officers and to hire outside advisors such as counsel or accountants who, during such tense and demanding periods, will devote the time and energy necessary to obtain an appropriate result. The ability of the indenture trustee to have its fees and expenses paid in bankruptcy will be discussed in Chapter XI.

Appendix I
The TIA

A. Summary of Key Provisions of the TIA

The essential purpose of the TIA is to ensure that every indenture to which the TIA applies is deemed to contain the minimum standards imposed by the act and conforms to the requirements of the TIA. In general, the legislation intended to accomplish three basic purposes:

1. The establishment of certain minimum standards with respect to specified acts and duties of the obligor and trustee to which all indentures must conform (accomplished by mandating that certain provisions are deemed included in each qualified indenture, thus becoming an essential part of the contract);

2. The imposition of minimum standards of responsibility and accountability for trustees under indentures and the elimination of broad exculpatory provisions; and

3. When securities are in default, the regulation or the elimination of conflicting relationships between the trustee and the obligor and between the trustee and underwriters for the obligor.

B. TIA Requirements

A brief synopsis of the TIA requirements is as follows:

Section	Topic
310	Persons eligible for appointment as indenture trustee and the definition of conflicts of interest that disqualify an indenture trustee if the indenture securities are in default (as such term is defined in such indenture)
311	Preferential collection of claims against obligor where trustee is a creditor of the obligor
312	Bondholder lists and access of holders thereto

Section	Topic
313	Report to bondholders by indenture trustee regarding the trust and qualification of indenture trustee
314	Reports by obligor: (a) financial reports to indenture trustee and holders; (b) evidence of recording indenture and need for continual refiling; (c) evidence of compliance with conditions precedent; (d) certificates of fair value regarding release of property; (e) recitals as to basis of certificates or opinions; (f) other requirements of compliance with conditions and covenants
315	Duties and responsibility of the indenture trustee: (a) prior to default, only duties specifically set forth in the indenture; reliance on certificates and opinions; examination of evidence required by § 314 of TIA; (b) notice of default to security holders, required and discretionary; (c) upon default, the prudent person duties; (d) no exoneration of indenture trustee for willful misconduct; (e) undertaking for costs of suit
316	Directions and waivers by bondholders; prohibition of impairment of any holder's right to payment[49]
317	Special powers to sue for the whole amount of principal and interest and to file proofs of claim for all holders; paying agents hold funds in trust for holders.
318	Provisions deemed included (duties imposed by Sections 310–317) shall control in case of inconsistency

49 This provision and its scope have been the focus of a number of court decisions. *See* discussion in Chapter XV.

C. TIA-Imposed Provisions

The prescribed provisions under the Trust Indenture Act include:

Section	Provisions
310	(a) No obligor or party directly or indirectly controlled by the obligor shall serve as trustee. (b) Upon the occurrence of a default, as such term is defined in the indenture, but exclusive of any period of grace or requirement of notice, nine enumerated relationships constitute a conflict. Relationships include creditor of or trustee under another indenture of obligor (with certain exceptions) and underwriter for the indenture securities. Conflicts generally require resignation within 90 days, and such resignation is not effective until a successor is appointed. There is a strict prohibition at all times against the obligor or its affiliates acting as trustee for its own securities.
311	This section governs the trustee who is a creditor of the obligor, which is a conflict under Section 310(b). With certain exceptions, the trustee must set aside any funds received on its loans three months prior to default for possible sharing with the indenture security holders.
312	The indenture trustee must preserve the list of holders required to be provided by the obligor every six months. Procedures permitting three or more holders desiring to communicate with other security holders are described.
313	A mandatory annual report to holders is required if there is a change as to, among other things, the trustee's eligibility and qualifications, the creation or material change to any of the provisions of Section 310(b) (conflicts), amount of advances that may constitute a prior lien above a certain amount, changes to debt owed to trustee individually, property in the trustee's possession, release of trust property or any action that materially affects the indenture securities.
314	Among other things, the obligor must provide to the indenture trustee an annual certificate with respect to compliance with the conditions and covenants of the indenture. This is to be furnished by the principal executive officer, financial officer or accounting officer.

Section	Provisions
315	This section describes the duties and responsibilities of the indenture trustee and incorporates the distinction between pre- and post-default duties and standard of care. Section 315(e) of the TIA allows a provision to the effect that all parties thereto, including the security holders, agree that a court may require in any suit for enforcement of any right or remedy under the indenture or against any trustee, an undertaking for the costs of such suit and that such court may in its discretion assess reasonable costs including reasonable attorneys' fees against any party litigant in such suit having due regard to the merits and good faith of the claims or defenses made by such party litigant, provided such provisions do not apply to suits instituted by holders of more than 10 percent in principal amount of the securities outstanding or suit for enforcement of payment of principal or interest after their respective due dates expressed in such indenture.
316	With respect to directions and waivers by bondholders, the holders of at least a majority in principal amount of the indenture securities may direct the conduct of any proceeding or the exercise of any power under the indenture. The obligor may set a record date for the purpose of determining holders entitled to vote or consent. The right of a holder to receive payment of principal and interest when due shall not be impaired or excepted without consent.
317	The indenture trustee is authorized, in the event of default, to recover judgment as trustee of any express trust for the whole amount of principal and interest remaining unpaid on the securities. Further, the indenture trustee is authorized to file a proof of claim or other papers necessary or desirable in any judicial proceeding in order to have the claim of the trustee and the holders allowed. The paying agent holds funds in trust for the benefit of the banks and indenture trustee.

II. Role of the Indenture Trustee Prior to the Closing of the Transaction

A. Introduction

It should always be kept in mind by holders that, while the indenture trustee may, in its sole discretion, review the documentation to make sure that the trust can be administered effectively and that the rights and interests of the bondholders are properly protected, including the bondholders' receipt of the benefit of the bargain, it is not the duty or responsibility of the indenture trustee to perform a pre-closing review in order to accomplish these results. The present structure of the financing and the compliance with the disclosure contained in the prospectus or official statement should be the duty of others involved in the transaction. If, by failure to properly structure or orchestrate the securities offering, the rights and interests of the bondholders are not properly protected, the indenture trustee should not be held liable.

In any party's consideration of the role of the indenture trustee, it is important to recognize that the indenture trustee has certain rights that are either implied or expressed, are permissive in nature and are not requirements subjecting the indenture trustee to liability. These powers include the ability of the indenture trustee to take action in order to insure that it is not involved in a security offering that will turn out to be a significant problem. Such a problem could drain corporate trust assets and manpower and impair the continued effective operation of the corporate trust department. At times, lawyers seeking to find a deep pocket in a default situation will seize upon some strained notion of fiduciary duty that will thrust upon the indenture trustee the duty to make sure that everything was right. The indenture trustee should not be held accountable or liable for the structure of the financing or the wording of the documents. Nevertheless, the indenture trustee should review the indenture and determine that it is consistent with the trustee's general operating procedures and that the trustee can effectively accomplish the duties and responsibilities of the trustee set forth in the indenture.

If the transaction structure does not work, that is not and should not be the responsibility of the indenture trustee. If the transaction was fatally flawed from the beginning, on account of the documentation, the feasibility of the project or the structure of the cash flows, that is and should remain the responsibility of others. The indenture trustee is merely the policeman of the rights and interests of the bondholders upon default. Prior to default, the indenture trustee has specifically described duties, liabilities and certain other implied rights which it, as the trustee, in its sole discretion, may appropriately exercise. While certain conscientious and professional indenture trustees perform numerous tasks in order to insure that they do not become involved in unfavorable situations, those efforts should not be interpreted as an obligation for them or other indenture trustees. It is the holders who, in essence, make the investment decision, and in connection with flawed transactions, for liability they should look to and rely on the parties who structured the financing, not the trustee.

B. Function of the Indenture Trustee Pre-Closing

Prior to accepting a transaction, the indenture trustee should satisfy itself that there are no state law issues, particularly with regard to holding collateral, that would preclude the trustee from serving.[50] The duties of the indenture trustee, prior to default, are those circumscribed by the terms of the indenture. However, from a practical standpoint, prior to closing, if possible, the trustee should interject itself into closing issues to the degree necessary to insure that the trust created by the documents can be effectively administered. In other words, while it is not the responsibility of the trustee to see to it that the transaction is a "good deal," it certainly makes practical sense for an indenture trustee to review the documents prior to closing to satisfy itself that the transaction, at least from the trustee's operational standpoint, is clear and workable. In particular, the indenture trustee will want to make sure that any provisions requiring administration on its part are clear, unambiguous, understood and capable of compliance.[51]

The indenture trustee, and, indeed, the bondholders, should keep in mind that an underwriter generally does not consider that it is its job to insure that all possible provisions for protection of the bondholders are included in relevant documents. Similarly, indenture trustees and bondholders should not assume that it is the goal of bond counsel or underwriter's counsel to provide for protection of the bondholders throughout the documents. Typically, bond counsel is opining with respect to the tax status of the bonds and/or the validity or enforceability of the obligations created, compliance with applicable law, or the perfection of liens on the collateral. Underwriter's counsel may be concerned about compliance with the applicable securities law but

---

50 Some states prohibit the exercise of trust powers by a non-resident trust company, particularly where property within the state is pledged as security. Further, the federal government imposes certain restrictions on foreign-owned or controlled banks. For example, the Federal Aviation Administration ("FAA") requires that the owner trustee in an aircraft financing must qualify as a U.S. citizen or U.S. resident alien. Similarly, the trustee of a ship mortgage must be organized under the laws of the United States or a state.

51 If the transaction is particularly complicated, the indenture trustee may request a flow chart from bond counsel, or from counsel to the issuer or the transaction, documenting the way the transaction is to work. This will assist the indenture trustee in the development of an accurate "tickler system" post-closing. A tickler system is a calendar-based alert system that follows the requirements of the indenture, the TIA and other applicable rules and that, periodically, before the event, notifies the trust administrator of the upcoming event. Further, a checklist of key provisions in the documents requiring action by the indenture trustee should be developed.

not necessarily with protecting the bondholders to the fullest. There may very well be no one at the table who has put the bondholders' interests first. It therefore makes practical sense for an indenture trustee to be certain prior to assuming a trusteeship that, if the trusteeship is accepted, the indenture trustee will be able to function under the terms of the documents in order to comply with the stated duties and to protect the rights of the bondholders.

C. Check of Participants to Transaction

The indenture trustee certainly does not want to assume the role of a rating agency or credit agency in terms of conducting "due diligence" on the participants to a proposed transaction.[52] However, it is sound practice to make informal requests for information regarding the credit standing and reputation of the potential obligor. Furthermore, it is also sound practice to run a check of the participants to the transaction through the appropriate channels in the bank. This will not only reveal any obvious problem participants, but will also uncover any possible conflicts of interest which have to be disclosed. If the professionals involved are unknown to the indenture trustee, it is wise to look into their standing in the business community. The common-sense practice of conducting an internet search to locate any pending lawsuits or SEC investigations involving the participants should be adopted. Moreover, the frequently relied-upon "smell test" should not necessarily be abandoned. If the parties to the transaction sound wrong and look wrong, chances are this may be a matter in which the corporate trust department does not want to become involved.

D. Examination of the Indenture and Related Documents

As referred to above, it is important that the indenture trustee determine that, regardless of what the deal is, the deal works from an operational perspective. Unfortunately, the typical practice provides the indenture trustee with the closing documents a short time before the scheduled closing, which can create problems when the indenture trustee attempts to raise questions or provide comments with respect to the documents. It is sound practice for the potential indenture trustee to notify the participants to the proposed transaction early on that it will require final drafts of the documents within a reasonable period of time prior to closing so that such documents can be examined by the appropriate parties. Once the documents are in the possession of the indenture trustee, the indenture trustee must walk a fine line. It would be unusual for the indenture trustee to demand changes to the substance of the underlying financial transaction. The trustee certainly does not want to interject itself into the transaction by suggesting substitute provisions. On the other hand, the indenture trustee will want to make sure

---

52 An indenture trustee has no liability to debentureholders because it failed to do an independent credit analysis before accepting the trusteeship. *In re Am. Cont'l Corp.*, 794 F. Supp. 1424 (D. Ct. Ariz. 1992).

that the documents are in such form that will permit it to exercise its duties pursuant to the transaction. Where possible, it is wise for the indenture trustee to have its in-house counsel or, if need be, experienced outside counsel review the documents to determine that they work from the indenture trustee's standpoint.

E. Review of Security and Adequacy of Granting Clauses, If Any

In a secured issue, there typically is a granting clause at the beginning of the indenture. The indenture trustee should check to make sure that the legal description in the granting clause is the same property covered by the title insurance policy and any related security documents and that is represented to be conveyed or assigned in the prospectus or official statement. The definitions of "trust estate," "mortgaged property," "permitted liens" or "encumbrances," "excepted property" and "prior liens" should be provided for in the indenture. Counsel's opinion should reflect the security interest conveyed to the indenture trustee. The priority of the lien should be in accordance with the representations made to the holders of the securities in the prospectus or the official statement. If there are mortgages or UCC statements that need to be filed, the trustee should insist upon evidence of perfection.[53] While recording of a mortgage or security instrument should be the responsibility of company counsel, evidence of perfection plus a legal opinion addressed to the trustee regarding the same should be in the file of the trustee.[54]

In order to secure repayment of the debt evidenced by the indenture, an indenture trustee may be given a lien upon and security interest in certain real property and personal

---

53 In *AG Capital Funding Partners v. State St. Bank & Tr. Co.*, 842 N.E. 2d471 (N.Y. 2005), where there had been a failure to file and deliver the additional secured indebtedness registration statement ("ASIRS") and where the court ruled that the allegations of the indenture trustee that the underwriter had assumed that duty stated a claim, the court quoted from an affidavit stating it was not the custom and practice for the indenture trustee to make such filings. The decision assumed, without deciding, however, that the trustee had the duty to make sure the ASIRS was delivered.

54 *See Harriet & Henderson Yarns, Inc. v. Castle*, 75 F. Supp. 2d 818 (W.D. Tenn. 1999), where the court held that the indenture agreement imposing a duty on the indenture trustee to hold a security interest on behalf of the holders of debentures did not impose a duty on the trustee to perfect those security interests and that the requirement of the obligor to furnish the indenture trustee with an opinion of counsel as to proper recordation and filing of a security interest did not impose a duty on the indenture trustee to review the filing and effectiveness of any lien intended to be created by the indenture or to insure that the liens were perfected for the benefit of the debentureholders.

But see *Bank of N.Y. v. Sheff*, 854 A.2d. 1269 (Md. 2004), in which there was a failure to file a required financing statement. In the bankruptcy of the issuer, the indenture trustee settled with the issuer and then sued issuer's counsel for failure to file. That suit was dismissed in part because issuer's counsel did not owe a duty to the bondholders and due to the expiration of the statute of limitations.

property used or useful in connection therewith. The lien and security interest granted to the indenture trustee may be granted under the indenture, a mortgage or a deed of trust. The mode of conveyance will very likely depend upon the law of the state in which the real property is located. In certain states, a deed of trust can be used and has certain advantages since it can be foreclosed upon by a trustee sale under a power of sale clause with limited court proceedings.

No matter what form of conveyance is used, the description of the "mortgaged property" in the indenture is of great importance. While a mortgage may automatically cover fixtures, it does not cover personal property. Therefore, not only must the land be accurately described, but the personal property used or useful in connection with the real property must also be adequately and accurately described. Upon foreclosure, it is important for the mortgaged property to be taken over as an operating unit. Anything essential for usability or viability should be included in the term "mortgaged property." In the case of a mortgage on a healthcare facility, a restaurant or any other operating business, it is essential that all personal property useful in connection with the business be described. For instance, all hospital beds, refrigerators, dishwashers, washing machines, cooking apparatus, furniture, floor coverings and other items essential to the use of the property must be adequately described. Following the legal description of the real property in the mortgage, there should be a general catchall enumeration of the common items necessary for the mortgage to function as a security agreement that complies with the terms of the Uniform Commercial Code ("UCC"). A separate financing statement may be prepared and filed (or the mortgage itself can also function as a financing statement) in the appropriate offices.

The UCC governs the perfection of non-possessory security interests in most states. The UCC requires the filing of a financing statement in order to perfect the security interest of most personal property. When the proper filing is accomplished, the security interest created by the security agreement is then perfected. The necessity for filing and the place of filing are determined by the kind of personal property collateral involved. Filing is required to perfect a security interest in inventory, accounts, general intangibles, equipment, crops, timber, mineral rights and fixtures. Local rules and practices should be checked to determine the place of filing and the content of the financing statement. The UCC has certain exceptions in which no filing is required for perfection. Typically, the perfection of excluded transactions is governed by state or federal law other than the UCC.[55] For instance, most states require that a notation of the security interest in a motor vehicle be placed on the title certificate for such motor vehicle. Likewise, a

---

55 Significantly, Article 9 of the UCC may not apply to the creation, perfection, priority or enforcement of a security interest of a state or a governmental unit of a state. § 9-109(c). However, the law of the state should be consulted to determine the existence or scope of the exception for governmental transfers.

mortgage on a sailing vessel may be perfected by the recording of a ship mortgage containing certain required information in the applicable U.S. Coast Guard Vessel Documentation Office and an aircraft mortgage must be registered with the FAA's aircraft registry. The indenture trustee should be aware of the requirements for filing continuation statements with the appropriate office, when necessary, to continue the effectiveness of the original filing. If the security for the bondholders requires an interest in a license or the transfer of an interest in contracts that typically are not assignable, the transaction must deal with these issues to the satisfaction of counsel for the trustee.

F. Review of Covenants

Every indenture should have at least one covenant, namely, the payment of principal, premium, if any, and interest on the securities. Care should be taken that these key provisions are identically described in the accompanying debt instrument. Typically, the indenture will contain covenants the breach of which will immediately trigger an event of default. Events of default include the failure to pay principal when due and the filing of an involuntary bankruptcy or similar insolvency proceeding. Virtually every indenture has other covenants that are the agreed-upon responsibilities of the obligor and the breach of which will, under certain circumstances with notice, become events of default under the terms of the indenture. Other general covenants include maintenance of office or agency for payment of the securities, payment of taxes and other claims against the obligor; maintenance of the property of the obligor; annual statement of compliance with the terms of the indenture by the obligor; and maintenance of corporate existence. Such covenants include provisions relating to the ratio of assets to indebtedness, permitted indebtedness, maintenance of books and records, the inspection of books and records by the indenture trustee, and maintenance of insurance. Other restrictive financial covenants include a negative pledge, a limitation on encumbrances, a limitation on the debt of the obligor, a restriction on the dividends of the obligor, and limitations on sale-leaseback and other lease obligations. In secured indentures, there can also be obligations for after-acquired property and further assurance of the recording of the liens, warranty of title and perfection of the security interest. If the issuer is a special purpose entity, there should be a covenant by the issuer not to declare bankruptcy and covenants relating to maintaining its independent corporate identity. As you can see, some covenants are "occurrence" covenants that are triggered possibly sometime during the life of the indenture and some that are "maintenance" covenants that must be maintained during the life of the indenture. To the degree that the official statement or prospectus given to the holders indicates such covenants are a part of the transaction, such should also be in the indenture, but the indenture trustee is not responsible for assuring the disclosure and the indenture are in agreement.

G. Remedial Provisions and Trustee Article

Every indenture should provide for effective remedies upon the failure of the obligor to comply with the terms and conditions of the indenture. Also, the indenture should provide for a clear and unambiguous definition of what constitutes a default or an event of default that triggers the ability to exercise remedies. The remedies will vary based upon the nature of the obligations and the obligor. Prior to closing, the indenture trustee should assure itself that the remedy section is adequate to permit the trustee to protect the rights of the holders if such action is ever needed. If the intent is to make the right to the payment of postpetition interest a priority over the payment of principal in the event of default, this should be spelled out, especially if the issue contains different tranches of lenders. In general, the indenture should provide for events of default; for acceleration of the maturity, including acceleration upon the direction of a certain percentage of the holders, and rescission or waiver of acceleration or default upon the direction of a certain percentage of the holders; language requiring acceptable indemnification of the trustee to accompany any direction; and provisions regarding collection of the indebtedness by the trustee as the trustee of an express trust. Further, there should be a limitation on the rights of holders to institute lawsuits, which limitation should require notice and demand upon the indenture trustee before institution of any suit on the indenture in order to prevent duplication and multiplicity of suits; and a provision regarding application of money collected, mandating that the first dollars collected from the exercise of the remedies will be applied to the indenture trustee's fees and expenses. There will be certain required provisions under the TIA, including the holder's right to sue on and receive past-due principal or interest payments; a provision on the reservation of rights resulting from delay or omission in exercising of remedies; and a provision that rights and remedies are cumulative. In secured issues, there should be a provision with regard to foreclosure on the collateral, a waiver of appraisement and other laws so that the indenture trustee need not obtain an appraisal before foreclosure or bidding at the foreclosure sale, a provision for the appointment of a receiver, and a corresponding provision granting the obligor's consent to such appointment. A covenant forbidding the impairment of collateral is helpful in that it may permit the indenture trustee to take action before serious harm is done. Except under extremely rare circumstances, the indenture trustee should not agree to subordinate its fees and expenses. Otherwise, the indenture trustee will find that, should recovery be less than sufficient to pay outstanding principal and interest in full, the indenture trustee will have been working as a volunteer for no compensation.

H. Execution, Delivery and Recording of the Indenture and Other Documents

The indenture trustee should see to it that it has a complete set of executed closing documents. It is safe to assume that if the indenture trustee does not receive a document upon the conclusion of the closing, the indenture trustee may very well never see that document appropriately executed. Upon the occurrence of an event of default, it is extremely embarrassing for an indenture trustee to have to inform its holders that it is missing a crucial document. If the closing is conducted remotely with the simultaneous release of previously escrowed documents, this same insistence on receipt of all appropriately executed documents should apply.

I. Necessary Opinions and Certificates

The indenture trustee should assure itself that it has received all necessary opinions and certificates. These include the opinion of bond counsel as to the tax-exempt status of the bonds if the transaction is tax exempt. The indenture trustee should also obtain the opinion of company counsel that the company is, in fact, authorized to enter into the transaction;[56] that the transaction does not violate any contractual or other obligations of the company, and that the transaction is binding, valid and enforceable on the company according to the terms of the documents. Further, an opinion of company counsel should be obtained, stating that all conditions precedent to the issuance have been fulfilled. It is helpful to receive an opinion with respect to the disclosures given in each respective transaction. Opinions should be directed to the indenture trustee and should indicate that the indenture trustee may rely on such opinions. In the alternative, the indenture trustee should receive a reliance letter with respect to such opinions. Frequently, incumbency certificates and certificates of compliance are given. A resolution of the obligor authorizing the issuance of the bonds certainly must be obtained.

An opinion of counsel should be obtained with respect to the real and personal property covered by the mortgage and/or security agreement. Such opinion should be obtained along with title insurance. In addition to the nature and scope of the review and examination, a pre-closing security opinion should state:

(1) The form of the mortgage and the acknowledgments thereto comply with all applicable laws of the state in which the real property is located.

(2) The legal descriptions contained in the mortgage are legally sufficient descriptions of such property for the purpose of creating and maintaining the lien purported to be created by the mortgage.

(3) The mortgage has been filed and recorded in appropriate filing offices.

---

56 It should be noted that a state trial court in Washington issued a troubling unpublished ruling that seemed to indicate that the indenture trustee may have a duty to conduct an independent investigation as to whether the issuer, under state law, had the authority to issue bonds or appoint a trustee. *Trimble v. Holmes Harbor Sewer Dist.*, No. 01-2-00751-8 (Island County Wash. Super. Ct. 2003). To date, this opinion does not appear to have been widely cited or followed.

(4) Upon such recording and filing, the mortgage constitutes security for the indebtedness and a valid first mortgage lien on the real property described in the mortgage, and a first perfected security interest in all personal property described in the mortgage, including any accounts, contract rights, general intangibles and proceeds described as being mortgaged or assigned.

(5) No approval, authorization or consent from any court or any federal, state or local governmental authority or regulatory body is necessary to the validity, legality or effectiveness of the mortgage instrument or, if required, such has been obtained.

J. Review of Any Guaranty by a Subsidiary of the Debt of Its Parent Corporation

When a subsidiary corporation guarantees its parent's obligations, that guaranty is referred to as an "upstream guaranty." An upstream guaranty is typically used when the parent needs extra capital but the subsidiary's guaranty is needed to provide extra protection to the parent's lender. The upstream guaranty may be secured or unsecured. An upstream guaranty may be attacked as a fraudulent transfer because only a portion, or none of the total business benefits that result from the financing transaction and the entire guaranty transaction, go to the guarantor. Courts use a variety of tests to determine whether an upstream guaranty is valid. One such test is the "benefit" test. Courts frequently require that there be a benefit to the subsidiary guarantor so that the transaction fulfills a corporate purpose of the guarantor and is an authorized act and not a fraudulent transfer. Therefore, it is important that substantial, traceable benefits flow from the parent corporation to the subsidiary guarantor. It is also useful for the guaranty itself to state that it is being given in consideration of certain direct and indirect benefits to the subsidiary guarantor. It is important for the trustee to be aware that if any of the terms of the transaction are modified during the life of the issue, the guaranty will need to be reaffirmed.

K. Receipt of Original Documents

As set forth above, it is important for the trustee to leave the closing room or virtual closing in receipt of all appropriately executed closing documents, which will have been escrowed, in either physical or electronic form. It is important to receive original documents, if such is possible. Should litigation arise or the authenticity of documents be called into question, it is always helpful to have "original documents" in paper or electronic form.

L. Registration Statement and Qualification of the Indenture

If the securities in question are to be distributed publicly, absent some exception, they must be registered pursuant to the provisions of the Securities Act. The issuer files a Form S-1, the registration statement under the Securities Act of 1933.[57] A copy of the indenture typically is filed as an exhibit to the registration statement. This filing makes the issue qualified. Some trustees follow a practice of reviewing for consistency the sections of the registration statement summarizing the indenture provisions. In order for the SEC to obtain necessary information with regard to the indenture trustee, the TIA requires that a form T1 be completed.[58] Among other things, Form T1 requires information with respect to other issues of the obligor for which the bank serves as a corporate trustee and information with respect to the corporate trustee bank's eligibility and financial status. The TIA requires that all indentures, with certain specified exceptions, be submitted to the SEC for qualification along with the issuer's registration statement under the Securities Act.

Ordinarily, the provisions of the TIA do not apply to, and the submission of the indenture and form T1 is not required with respect to, the following securities:

1. Securities Other Than Debt Security

Any security other than a note, bond, debenture or evidence of indebtedness, certificate of interest or participation in, temporary certificates for or guaranties of the foregoing;[59]

2. Certificates of Interest in Securities with Different Rights and Privileges

Any certificate of interest or participation in two or more securities having substantially different rights and privileges or a temporary certificate for any such certificate;[60]

---

57 If a security is not required to be registered under the Securities Act and no exemption is applicable, an application for qualification of the indenture is to be filed with the SEC by the issuer. TIA § 307(a).

58 5 FEDERAL SECURITIES LAW REPORTS (CCH) ¶ 43.101.

59 *See* TIA § 304(a)(1).

60 *See* TIA § 304(a)(2). As will be discussed in Chapter XVI, this section was the basis for the Second Circuit's holding that RMBS certificates governed by a pooling and servicing agreement are exempt from the provisions of the TIA. *Ret. Bd. of the Policemen's Annuity and Benefit Fund of the City of Chicago v. Bk. of N.Y. Mellon*, 775 F.3d 154 (2d Cir. 2014).

3. Securities Act Exemption

Securities exempt under the Securities Act, and therefore under TIA, include government securities and bank securities, insurance policies, certain interests in employee benefit plans, commercial paper, securities that are part of a completely intrastate issue, and securities of:

(a) charitable, non-profit organizations;

(b) savings and loan and similar institutions;

(c) common carriers; and

(d) a bankruptcy trustee or receiver;[61]

Also exempt are securities in private placement transactions exempt under Section 4 of the Securities Act;[62]

4. National Housing Act

Any security issued under a mortgage indenture as to which a contract of insurance under the National Housing Act is in effect;[63]

Any security issued under a mortgage or trust deed indenture as to which a contract of insurance under Title XI of the National Housing Act is in effect;[64]

5. Foreign Government Issuer

Any note, bond, debenture or evidence of indebtedness issued or guaranteed by a foreign government or any of its subdivisions or instrumentalities;[65]

6. Guaranty—Exempt Security

Any guaranty of any security exempted from the provision of the TIA;[66]

---

61 *See* TIA § 304(a)(4).
62 *See* TIA § 304(b).
63 *See* TIA § 304(a)(5).
64 *See* TIA § 304(a)(10).
65 *See* TIA § 304(a)(6).
66 *See* TIA § 304(a)(7).

7. Securities Not Issued under Indenture

Securities that are not issued under an indenture, provided that the exemption is not applied within a period of 12 months to more than $5,000,000 aggregate principal amount of securities of same issuer. Securities that are exempt and those which are issued under exempt transactions under the other paragraphs of TIA Section 304 are excluded in computing the aggregate amount;[67] and

8. Aggregate Amount Not Exceeding $10,000,000

Any security that has been or is to be issued under an indenture which limits the aggregate principal amount of securities at any time outstanding to $10,000,000 or less, provided that the exemption is not applied within a period of 36 consecutive months to more than $10,000,000 aggregate amount of securities of the same issuer. However, securities that are exempt and those which are issued under exempt transactions under other paragraphs of TIA Section 304 are excluded in computing the aggregate amount.[68]

Although the disqualification of the trustee for a conflicting interest is not measured until the occurrence of a default, it is prudent at the time of acceptance to determine if there are any possible conflicts that will become problematic in the event of default and to flag the file accordingly. (See Chapter VI for a further review of potential conflict of interest situations).

---

67 *See* TIA § 304(a)(8).

68 *See* TIA § 304(a)(9).

III. Post-Closing Considerations Prior to Default

A. Introduction

On closing a transaction, the indenture trustee begins its trusteeship. The trustee should be assured in the beginning that the flow of funds and the establishment of the accounts pursuant to the terms of the financing documents have been and can be accomplished. It is important prior to closing to make sure that the practical realities of the situation are well in hand. If the indenture trustee's computer system cannot accomplish the flow of funds for the accounting set forth in the indenture, there should be appropriate changes to ensure that the terms of the indenture can be implemented. Too often, documents are the result of a mere markup of a previous transaction used for a different indenture trustee and not enough attention is paid to operational concerns. Counsel for underwriters for the transaction should prepare a flow of funds chart in order to demonstrate how funds should be used. In addition, there should be clear delineation in the language of the indenture as to how funds will be applied pursuant to its terms.

For example, there should be no guesswork or choice involved as to how a deficiency in the principal and interest account will be funded from other accounts. At times, indenture trustees have been asked to pick among various accounts and, unfortunately, a guaranteed investment contract or other high yield investment has been cashed only to discover a shortfall at the end of the day. Current market practice by indenture trustees is to eliminate all discretion with respect to investment issues by requesting a direction or standing order. In talking about post-closing considerations prior to default, it is important that the structure of the transaction, the flow of funds (known as the priority of payment) and, in essence, the chronology of events (when the tickler system is utilized) be well in hand.

B. Tickler System

It certainly is a truism that, upon default, a trustee is judged by hindsight. Therefore, the procedures used in the acceptance of an account and the general administration of that account prior to and after default may be subject to careful scrutiny. An electronic tickler system, as defined on page 20 in note 51, informing the indenture trustee on a timely basis of all the duties and obligations of the obligor and the indenture trustee under the indenture and applicable law should be established. It is likely that the corporate trust department will have in place its own procedures designed to create a reliable system, and such procedures must be complied with. As soon as possible after the closing, the indenture trustee should establish within this tickler system all actions that have to be taken in connection with the administration of the indenture, including all dates on which interest, principal and sinking fund payments are to be made, and should provide for notice of redemption dates, as well as the time by which notices, certificates, SEC filings and opinions must be supplied or, if applicable, actions under the TIA must be taken. UCC continuation statements (normally filed every five years) should also be noted and diaried. This is particularly important if the transaction documents place the responsibility for filing continuation statements on the indenture trustee. However, even if another party to the transaction is required to file the continuation statement, the tickler will remind the trustee to check to see if the continuation statement indeed has been filed.[69] It may be advisable to give a copy of the tickler information to the obligor if it is not a frequent debt issuer to sensitize it to the requirements of the transaction. Current market practice is to place the primary responsibility for UCC filings on the issuer or a related party, not the indenture trustee.

Since the tickler system is part of any early warning detection system of a default, it is important that the tickler system evidencing compliance with the terms of the indenture be set up immediately after closing. Failure to set up a file and a tickler system on a timely basis can be fatal to proper default administration. Some indenture trustees have developed the practice of providing a modified tickler list to the obligor and other parties to the transaction. In this way, other parties will be aware of the obligor's responsibilities on a timely basis. Other indenture trustees use the tickler system in a fashion to provide notice of key events to the obligor prior to the occurrence of such events. These various efforts clearly are not mandated by indentures. Nevertheless, as a matter of good practice, they constitute evidence to demonstrate the reasonableness of the trustee's actions and provide notice to the obligor of its duties and obligations.

C. Continuing Conflicts Checks

If the bank has a lending relationship with the obligor, there must be frequent checks to ensure that there is no default problem that would trigger the applicability of Sections 310 and 311 of the TIA under qualified indentures. Such checks can be done without breaching any confidential relationships, state or federal privacy statutes, or a firewall separating the commercial and trust sides of the bank. There is a genuine need for both sides of the bank to assure themselves that the bank is not facing a potentially embarrassing and expensive situation. Consideration may be given to obtaining a waiver by the obligor of any privacy issues. Many banks require quarterly checks and some large financial institutions even require a bimonthly conflict check for each file. A conflict check also should be performed in conjunction with the

---

69 *See Becker v. The Bank of N.Y. Mellon Tr. Co., N.A.*, 2016 WL 1178072 (E.D. Pa. Mar. 23, 2016).

consideration of the annual report, which may, under certain circumstances, need to be given to security holders under the TIA, to ensure the bank's continued eligibility and qualification to serve as a trustee under the indenture should a default arise. This frequently requires verification of the bank's capital and surplus.

The indenture trustee need not take action with respect to qualification under the TIA until an event of default occurs under the indenture; as a result, careful supervision and monitoring of conflict situations become important. The TIA makes the indenture trustee's relationship between the bank, as lender, and the obligor, as borrower, a conflict and, accordingly will require the resignation of the indenture trustee upon a default. Not only are conflict checks important, but failure to have a routine method of assuring a corporate trust officer that there is no conflict will place the bank in a very difficult situation if a default should occur. Without proper preparation, the identification of a successor trustee and an expeditious method of qualifying the indenture without a successor, banks may face grave problems in the event of a default.

D. Review Committee in Bank

A corporate trustee should establish a committee to review the administration of corporate trusteeships. This committee should meet frequently and review, in particular, troubled accounts and defaulted accounts. While it is probably appropriate to keep minutes of such meetings, the bank should be aware that, unless the minutes are drafted and maintained by trust counsel, such minutes are not privileged and can be subject to discovery in any litigation arising out of the trust relationship. Therefore, care should be taken with respect to the preparation of the minutes.

E. Communication with Obligor

Any communications with the obligor should be carried on in a serious, businesslike manner. While it is certainly wise to develop a good working relationship with the obligor, never put anything in writing that you do not wish read to a judge or a jury. Communication should be formal and comply with the terms of the trust indenture. At all costs, avoid any language that indicates that you as indenture trustee are less than serious about pursuing the remedies under the documents or that you are communicating to the obligor because of some disgruntled holders. Moreover, it is helpful when communicating a particular request or demand to the obligor that the indenture trustee include language reserving all other rights and remedies under the trust indenture. All written communication with the obligor should be carefully kept in a correspondence file or electronic folder for the transaction. Keeping detailed notes with respect to any verbal discussions with the obligor, while not required, may be advisable. It is helpful to memorialize not only what the obligor said to you, but what you said to the obligor and the date of such statement. Be aware, however, that such notes are discoverable in any litigation and that electronic communications can never really be "deleted." Consequently, care should be taken not to include anything in such notes that would present the bank in a less than favorable light. In particular, disparaging references to the obligor should be avoided. If a serious issue is presented, the matter could be memorialized in a memo to trust counsel seeking legal advice. Check with in-house or outside counsel on an appropriate procedure or protocol.

Any notes and all written communication should be objective in nature and free from subjective judgments or observations. If there are personality conflicts within the corporate trust department, they should not be visited upon the corporate trust file. If one disagrees with the subjective determinations of a fellow corporate trust officer, those disagreements, which are, in reality, personal likes and dislikes, are not objective facts to be placed in the file. It is also helpful to confirm in writing conversations with the obligor or promises which the obligor makes to the trustee. This provides an appropriate paper trail to demonstrate the continued creditability of the obligor or its inability to meet its promises in the terms of the indenture.

F. Communication with Bondholders

In addition to the annual report that is required under certain circumstances, it may be appropriate for the indenture trustee to communicate with the bondholders during the course of the administration of the issue. All such communication should be written in a straightforward and understandable manner. Communications to bondholders should be neither overly pessimistic nor unduly optimistic. The indenture trustee should recognize that the bondholders may make investment decisions after receiving the statements made to the holders. Accordingly, statements made should be statements of objective fact, not a subjective guess, projection or estimate. If any subjective statement is required to be made under the circumstances, it should be clearly labeled as such. The communication should direct the holder to consult with its own investment and tax advisors. This is not a dodge of any responsibility by the indenture trustee but a helpful reminder to holders of the limits of the indenture trustee's role and that the holders' advisors should be the parties providing advice. The indenture trustee should recognize that a market in the securities probably exists, whether or not notice of default has been provided. Great difficulties will result if an indenture trustee does not provide prompt notice of an event of default and a secondary market purchaser buys a security at a premium only to find out that a default had existed. Not only do the indenture and the TIA require prompt notice of default known to the trustee (within ninety days of the occurrence of such default), but prudence requires appropriate communication to the holders of the defaulted bonds.

Communication with bondholders prior to an event of default but after it is apparent that a potential source of trouble exists may cause problems for an indenture trustee. If, prior to a default, the obligor decides to take action that will impair the rights and interests of the holders, the trustee may determine under the circumstances that it is appropriate and prudent to inform the holders of this event so that they and others may not suffer any harm from the impending problem. However, care should be taken that the potential default is in fact an absolute certainty. Many times, a company has expressed to an indenture trustee a possible inability to make an interest payment when, shortly thereafter, the situation changes or the company decides it is more appropriate to make the payment. The trustee would find itself in an unenviable predicament in the event it gave notice of a potential interest payment default, causing the price of the securities on the secondary market to plummet and holders to sell their securities only to find that there was no problem as the interest payment was made on time. Any such notice should be undertaken only after careful review of the indenture provisions relating to events of default and notice thereof and with the advice of counsel, as such has ramifications to the marketplace and possible negative impact on the obligor. Reminding holders in the letter that the indenture trustee gives no investment advice and that holders should consult their own legal and financial professionals is wise and consistent with the role of the indenture trustee. This reminder is designed to direct the holders to the appropriate parties for advice. Further discussion of communication with bondholder is contained in Chapter V, along with sample letters and notices.

G. Monitoring Compliance: Certificates and Opinions

Prior to default, the indenture trustee must make sure that certain requirements of the issuer under the indenture are complied with, including delivery of insurance policies, certificates and financial records and the filing and perfection of mortgages and other security interests. Prior to default, the indenture prescribes the duties of the indenture trustee, and the indenture trustee monitors compliance with certain indenture provisions. Prior to default, the indenture trustee may rely in good faith on appropriate officers' certificates and opinions of counsel. The indenture trustee must examine the officers' certificates to determine if the form of certificate conforms with the requirements of the indenture.[70] This duty to examine the certificate does not require the indenture trustee to look beyond the numbers presented and make its own calculations.[71] Prior to default, the indenture trustee may rely on an opinion of counsel so long as it conforms to the requirements of the indenture.[72] Pre-default, the trustee's obligation is to

---

70 *Semi-Tech Litigation, LLC v. Bankers Tr. Co.*, 450 F.3d 121 (2d Cir. 2006); *In re Med. Capital Sec. Litig.*, 2012 WL 12142396 (C.D. Cal. Feb. 7, 2016).

71 *Peak Partners, LP v. Republic Bank*, 191 Fed. Appx. 118 (3d Cir. 2006) (the indenture trustee was not required to recalculate the net interest figure reported by the obligor and to reconcile that amount and the amount that was actually available for distribution).

72 *Cruden v. The Bank of N.Y.*, 957 F.2d 961 (2d Cir. 1992) (the trustee's good faith is not put into question merely by virtue of the fact that the opinion relied upon may have been wrong).

monitor compliance, which frequently may be accomplished with the receipt and review of certificates and opinions. When an issue does begin to slip into trouble, an indenture trustee may be wise to examine the totality of the situation and to assess its duties in light of the purpose for which the indenture provisions were drafted, including principles of good faith and fair dealing. However, it has been held that the indenture trustee has no pre-default duty to examine an obligor's financial condition even following receipt of reports indicating a likely need to restructure long-term debt or to take advantage of the right to inspect the obligor's books and records.[73]

H. Use of Watch Lists and Problem Reviews

Any account that, in the judgment of the trust officer, warrants careful review should be put on a watch list for monthly or periodic reports. The trustee should internally discuss whether counsel needs to be contacted. These pre-default situations are very sensitive and are often fraught with peril for the indenture trustee. Therefore, it is important that experienced personnel in the bank and counsel be consulted. Careful action and planning during a troubled pre-default period can significantly ease the difficulties of default administration. If a trust auditor is reviewing a trust account in which an event of default has occurred, advice of counsel should be sought concerning the nature, scope and format of the audit. Likewise, if the trust auditor discovers a default or problem before a report is generated, counsel should be consulted as to the nature and extent of the report. While all files should be accurate and complete, they need not contain any misguided statements that could be interpreted as some type of confession. Counsel may well direct that all reports and writings on the matter be addressed to counsel at counsel's request in anticipation of litigation in an effort to maintain and preserve confidentiality and privilege over those discussions. Bank personnel should use caution when creating any writing in light of its probable discovery.

I. Implication of Assuming Additional Duties

Any duties assumed by the indenture trustee that are specifically set forth in the indenture should be performed with care. Although it is tempting to rely upon a strict reading of the indenture prior to an actual default and for the trustee to hesitate to take any action prior to that time, there are no reported cases in which an indenture trustee has been held liable for a good faith attempt to take action to protect its holders in a troubled situation prior to default. Certainly the implied power of a trustee would clearly authorize such action, even though the

---

73 *Magten Asset Mgmt. Corp. v. The Bank of N.Y.*, 15 Misc. 3d 1132(A), 2007 WL 1326795 (N.Y. Sup. May 8, 2007) (indenture provided "trustee in its discretion may make such further inquiry or investigation into such facts or matters as it may see fit"); *Dresner Co. Profit Sharing Plan v. First Fidelity Bank*, 1996 WL 694345 (S.D.N.Y. Dec. 4, 1996).

indenture does not make it mandatory. However, in order not to been seen as setting a precedent if action is taken prior to a default, indentures frequently include a provision stating that permissive rights of the indenture trustee are not to be taken as mandatory duties.

J. Information in Troubled but Non-Default Situations

As set forth above, the type of communication that should be given to holders by the indenture trustee in problematic non-default situations is a sensitive issue. Initially, the indenture trustee should examine the indenture to determine whether or not there are specific requirements with respect to pre-default communication. The indenture trustee should be careful in any troubled situation to avoid giving investment advice about the securities in question in its communications to holders. Several principles apply to pre-default communications to holders. The Securities Act and, in particular, Section 10b-5 of the Securities Exchange Act require the indenture trustee and the obligor to be accurate, uniform and not misleading in their communication to bondholders. In other words, if you tell one holder, you must tell all. Pre-default, it is often helpful to have the company itself prepare a letter setting forth the problems faced by the company for a mailing by the indenture trustee.[74] In the mailing, the indenture trustee can specifically disclaim any responsibility for the communication. Thus, it is the company's statements, and not the trustee's, upon which bondholders rely. During this stage, understandably, telephone or e-mail communications or in-person meetings with holders are fraught with risk. One cannot communicate to large institutional holders what one would not communicate to small holders. Discussion with holders must be uniform and clear and must be handled by a designated, responsible person at the bank. Any communication, whether written or oral, at the pre-default stage can subject the indenture trustee to liability to the company if the tone is too inflammatory and to the holders if the language is misleading. Therefore, great care must be taken in any such communication. As noted above, the best communication to holders is in a writing provided to the indenture trustee for distribution to holders and is an objective statement of the important facts, which is distributed to all known holders and is available to all holders upon request. The understanding of holders that for good reason the indenture trustee cannot have substantive one-off conversations with individual holders will avoid unnecessary disputes.

---

74 It has been held that the requirement of Section 314 of the TIA to the effect that annual reports the obligor is required to file with the Securities and Exchange Commission also be filed with the indenture trustee (1) does not create a duty on the part of the trustee to assure that the information contained in any report filed is true and accurate and (2) merely requires that any report delivered to the indenture trustee should be forwarded to the registered holders whatever reports are actually filed. *Racepoint Partners, LLC v. J.P. Morgan Chase Bank, N.A.*, 14 N.Y.3d 419, 902 N.Y.S.2d 14 (2010).

K. Supplemental Indentures

Almost every indenture should and does provide for a mechanism allowing the indenture to be supplemented or modified with or without the approval of the bondholders. Generally, modification of the indenture without the consent of the holders is only proper when it is to correct an ambiguity, does not adversely affect the rights of the holders or gives additional security to the holders. At times, in a pre-default situation, the indenture trustee will be confronted with a request by the obligor to execute a supplemental indenture. In most circumstances, an indenture trustee will seek approval of the holders for any supplemental indenture, but it is advisable for the indenture trustee to seek the advice of counsel to help navigate the sometimes complicated amendment process. An indenture trustee has been held to assume liability for any damages arising out of an improper modification of the indenture.[75]

L. Redemptions

At times, a redemption under the terms of the bond issue may be seized upon as a solution to a pre-default troubled situation. Care must be taken to determine whether the indenture really provides for such redemption or whether or not a bona fide event of default needs to exist before such redemption can take place. Central to such a determination by the indenture trustee is the disclosure that was made to the holders with respect to the possibility of redemptions prior to maturity. Such complications probably do not exist when there is a bona fide declared event of default and the indenture permits or requires acceleration or redemption upon such declaration. However, it would not be unusual to hear allegations of manufactured default where, in a low interest rate environment, the effect of default is to permit redemption of a high interest rate issue. The indenture trustee must comply with the notice provisions set forth in the indenture in connection with any redemption of the indenture securities.[76] Similarly, an indenture trustee for convertible securities has only those duties specifically set forth in the indenture and is not required to negotiate the conversion price or determine if conversion is in the best interest of holders.[77] The requirement that notice be provided to holders means registered holders of the securities. Where securities are held by the Depository Trust Company in the name of its nominee, the indenture requirements does not require notice to beneficial holders as the duties of the indenture trustee pre-default are strictly as defined in the

---

75 *Myers v. Am. Nat'l Bank and Tr. Co.*, 277 Ill. App. 378 (1934).

76 *Meckel v. Cont'l Res. Co.*, 758 F.2d 811 (2d Cir. 1985); *N.Y. State Med. Care Facilities Fin. Agency v. The Bank of Tokyo Tr. Co.*, 216 A.D. 2d 126, 629 N.Y.S.2d 3 (1995).

77 *Browning Debenture Holders Comm. v. DASA Corp.*, 560 F.2d 1078 (2nd Cir. 1977); *Elliott Assocs. v. J. Henry Schroder Bank and Tr. Co.*, 838 F.2d 66 (2d Cir. 1988); *but see Broad v. Rockwell International Corp.*, 614 F.2d 418 (5th Cir. 1980) (state law could impose a fiduciary duty on an indenture trustee to require the option for holders to convert into common stock rather than cash).

indenture.[78] As will be discussed in Chapter XII, there are specific rules governing notices relating to municipal issues.

---

78 *Raymond James & Assocs. v. The Bank of N.Y. Tr. Co.*, 2008 WL 4279629 (D. Ct. M.D. Fla Sept. 18, 2008).

IV. Analysis of Types of Default

A. Know Your Defaults

A default is the failure of the obligor to comply with specified terms of the indenture. In the following pages, the most common types of default will be discussed along with the distinction between default and events of default. Typically, a default is an event that, after the passage of a stated period of time (a "cure period"), can ripen into an event of default. In virtually every indenture, the failure to pay principal, the failure to pay interest after the passage of time, the voluntary bankruptcy of the issuer, an order by the court for relief under the bankruptcy law against the issuer that remains unstayed and in effect for 60 days, and the breach of any covenant under the indenture and the continuation of such breach for 30 days after notice are events of default.[79] An understanding of what constitutes a default and the default/event of default distinction is important. The occurrence of a default may preclude certain activity by the indenture trustee or by the obligor, and the existence of an event of default as defined in the indenture transforms the nature of the trusteeship to the active role discussed in previous chapters. Furthermore, the occurrence of an event of default triggers the ability of the indenture trustee to enforce the remedies provided under the particular indenture and changes the indenture trustee's standard of care. Under unusual circumstances, the indenture trustee may take action prior to an event of default to protect the rights and interests of the holders. For example, the negotiation of a lease of substantial assets of the obligor at a below-market rate contrary to the terms of the indenture may be acted upon prior to the execution of the lease.[80] Of course, reference should be made in any particular case to the specific terms of the indenture. Often, there are provisions unique to the particular transaction with which the indenture trustee must be familiar. The indenture trustee may decide to institute an action for a temporary restraining order or preliminary injunction to preserve the status quo (compliance with the indenture) pending a determination of a suit for specific performance (a lawsuit to require the obligor to perform that obligation that is in default).

---

79 *See* Corporate Debt Financing Project, *Commentaries on Model Debenture Indenture Provisions, 1965, Model Debenture Indenture* Provisions *All Registered Issues, 1967, and Certain Negotiable Provisions Which May Be Included in a Particular Incorporation Indenture,* AM. BAR FOUND. 1971 ("MDI") § 501; *American Bar Association Model Simplified Indenture* ("MSI") § 6.01, available in HANDBOOK FOR INDENTURE AND TRUST INDENTURE ACT INTERPRETATION, (American Bar Association 2017); *Mortgage Bond Indenture Form,* AM. BAR FOUND. 1981 ("MBI") ¶ 9.01.

80 *Guardian Tr. Co. v. White Cliffs Portland Cement & Chalk Co.*, 109 F. 523 (5th Cir. 1901).

It is important for bondholders to recognize that indenture defaults will be defined in the documentation and construed carefully. In *Savings Bank of New London v. New York Trust Company*,[81] bondholders sued the corporate trustee for permitting a railroad mortgagor to discontinue its railway without notifying them. The plaintiffs, however, could find no provisions specifying the discontinuance of the railroad as a default or event of default. The court thus dismissed the complaint, since the trustee could act on various remedies only in the case of an event of default as defined in the indenture.

B. Default in Payment of Principal or Interest

A default in the payment of principal or interest is the dreaded monetary default, which any indenture trustee should be able to recognize because it typically is the paying agent. Generally, a failure to make a payment of principal on the securities when the same becomes due is immediately an event of default. A default in the payment of an installment of interest on securities is treated somewhat differently. As a company may suffer a temporary cash crunch, a 30-day cure period provides a method of ensuring reasonable compliance. When the interest becomes due and payable, and the non-compliance continues after a grace period, the default in the payment of any installment of interest on the securities ripens into an event of default.[82] Care should be taken since some forms of financing and their respective indentures do not provide for the 30-day grace period. Normally, failure to pay principal and interest requires no notice to the obligor to become an event of default.

C. Involuntary Bankruptcy

The entry by a court having jurisdiction of a decree or order for relief in respect of the company in an involuntary case, or appointing a custodian for the company or any substantial part of its property, or ordering the winding up or liquidation of its affairs, and the continuance of such decree or order unstayed and in effect for a grace period of generally 60 consecutive days is normally an event of default.[83] Should the company consent to the entry of an order for relief against it in an involuntary case, it is an immediate event of default.

While the obligor obviously has no control over whether or not its creditors will institute an involuntary bankruptcy or other proceeding for the restructuring of its debt or reorganization of the debtor company, the pendency of such an action clearly creates a situation in which the indenture trustee should be able to proceed with remedies under the terms of the indenture. As will be discussed in Chapter XI, the indenture trustee normally is not a party that institutes a

---

81 *Savings Bank of New London v. N.Y. Tr. Co.*, 27 N.Y.S.2d 963 (N.Y. Sup. Ct. 1941).

82 *See* MDI § 501(1)–(2); MSI § 6.01; MBI § 9.01(A) and (B).

83 *See* MSI § 6.01(4) and (5).

bankruptcy action against an obligor. However, there are cases and circumstances under which the institution of an action under the Bankruptcy Code is the only way to protect adequately the rights and interests of the holders against the improper transfer or conversion of property by other creditors.

The reason for a grace period in connection with an involuntary bankruptcy is that there have been cases in which certain creditors have alleged that the obligor was insolvent and such creditors have initiated the proceeding, only to have the court determine that the debtor was not insolvent and that the involuntary petition was not filed in good faith. The grace period is a reflection of the fact that such involuntary petitions may not always be filed in good faith or well founded; rather than allow other creditors to proceed with action that may be difficult to rescind or unwind, it is more appropriate to provide a reasonable grace period to see if the involuntary petition is dismissed.

D. Voluntary Bankruptcy

The commencement by the company of a voluntary case; the institution by the company of proceedings to be adjudicated a bankrupt or insolvent; the consent by it to the institution of a bankruptcy or insolvency proceeding against it; the filing by it of a petition or answer or consent seeking reorganization, arrangement or relief under the Bankruptcy Code or any other applicable federal or state law; the admission by it in writing of its inability to pay its debts generally as they become due; or the taking of corporate action by the company in furtherance of such action is an event of default.[84] The filing of a voluntary bankruptcy proceeding does not require any waiting period to ripen into an event of default.

No grace period applies in connection with a voluntary bankruptcy. If the debtor chooses to seek protection under federal bankruptcy laws or other applicable federal and state laws, or admits in writing its inability to pay its debts, it places its assets with a court or trustee for the benefit of creditors. This could be an immediate threat to creditor interests. As a result, no reason exists to provide for a grace period. The indenture trustee should be enabled to take all actions necessary for the benefit of the holders under the terms of the indenture and the powers of the indenture trustee to protect the rights and interests of the holders. In taking actions under the indenture, however, the indenture trustee must be mindful of the automatic stay of actions against debtors in bankruptcy proceedings (discussed in Chapter X below).

---

84 *See* MDI § 5-1.

E. Breach of Covenants

The breach of any covenant or failure of the obligor to perform any condition provided for in the indenture will lead to a default. When the default does not involve the payment of principal or interest, the default sometimes is referred to as a "covenant" default. It is customarily provided that an event of default shall not occur for breach of such covenant until the expiration of a stated period of time after either the indenture trustee or a specified percentage of the holders has notified the obligor in writing of the breach of the covenant or condition or a specified percentage of holders has directed the indenture trustee to give the notice.[85] Whether or not an event of default occurs under this provision is based upon whether notice has been given. This section provides some leeway to holders who desire to have the obligor cure the breach before the event of default is actually declared. Of course, the indenture trustee must exercise this discretion with great prudence.

Sometimes the obligor attempts to negotiate with the indenture trustee, such as requesting that the indenture trustee not give notice of the default since the default will be cured in a short period of time. As such negotiations drag on, many times it becomes clear that prompt notice of default is in the best interest of both the indenture trustee and the holders, and the continuing delay serves no useful purpose. One argument obligors sometimes make should be noted. Many times the obligor will state with regard to a covenant default that providing notice of the default within the time period will cause an event of default to occur under the indenture, which will trigger a cross-default on other debt instruments of the obligor. This will thereby prevent the obligor from curing not only the indenture default but all other debt obligations. Consequently, the obligor will have no other alternative but to seek relief in bankruptcy, even though the covenant default was not significant in the obligor's opinion and there was no failure of the obligor to make payment when such payment was due. While hindsight is always accurate and care should be exercised by the indenture trustee, the inclination of most indenture trustees is to provide the notice and commence as soon as possible the running of the grace period. If the default of the covenant is as inconsequential as the obligor claims, this fact can be explained to holders and other creditor groups. If it is more significant, the indenture trustee acted appropriately in providing the notice.

F. Default Impairing or Affecting the Security or Ability to Pay

Some indentures provide that the obligor is obligated to refrain from taking any action that, while not specifically prohibited by the indenture, would impair the security for the issue. Such actions include the transfer of pledged revenues to other than the intended bondholders

---

85 *See* MSI § 6.01.

prior to a scheduled interest or principal payment, or the contention by a municipality that the pledge of revenues or the underlying contract is invalid. Further, under certain indentures, the indenture trustee has the power to institute and maintain proceedings to prevent any impairment of the trust estate or acts that are unlawful or in violation of the indenture.[86] Such would also include failure to discharge lien obligations that are senior or prior to the relevant securities. Unless the breach of the senior debt constitutes an event of default under the indenture securing junior obligations, the holders of the junior securities might be unable to take steps to protect their equity in the property until it has been substantially dissipated. The same is also true of unsecured obligations that contain cross-default provisions, so that a failure to pay principal or interest on the senior security is a default under the junior indenture. It is most helpful that the trust power of the indenture trustee to protect the trust estate and to prevent impairment of the rights and interests of the holders, as the trustee deems appropriate or as properly directed by the holders, be recognized in the indenture.[87]

G. Failure to Supply Necessary Documents

Failure to supply required documentation (financial reports, insurance certificates, certificates of compliance, etc.) after notice and lapse of time is an event of default.[88] This type of default, along with the covenant defaults encompassed by section E above, are sometimes referred to by the inexperienced as "technical defaults." This term has no meaning, however, as a default is a default regardless of whether it is monetary in nature. While accountants, corporate officers and insurance companies may be late in supplying appropriate reports and certificates, there may also be a serious problem that prevents such reports and certificates from ever being issued. It is important once such a default has occurred that notice be given to the obligor of its failure to supply such necessary documentation, and also that the indenture trustee inquire as to the reason why such report or certificate has not been given. In a number of instances, indenture trustees have inquired of auditors why the annual report has not been provided or the accountant's certificate was late, only to find that the accountants are no longer comfortable giving a clean opinion or stating that the obligor is a "going concern." It is to the benefit of the indenture trustee to be aware of these matters as soon as possible. Care should be taken that, when such a default occurs, it is followed by prompt inquiry into why the required documents cannot be provided. It is also true, especially with regard to insurance certificates and compliance certificates, that a number of obligors may simply not keep track of these obligations. A letter prior to the due date informing the obligor of the necessity of supplying such required certificate

---

86 *See* MBI § 9.20.

87 Note that § 315(c) of the TIA provides that in case of default, the indenture trustee shall exercise the rights and powers "vested in it *by such indenture*" (emphasis added).

88 *See* MBI § 9.01(c); MDI § 501(3).

or report, and letters to the obligor after the due date inquiring why such has not been provided to the obligor, can be helpful in assuring prompt compliance with documentation requirements. Notice of the default not only makes common sense but is required in most indentures in order for the grace period to begin running. This notice normally is required in writing, specifying that it is a notice of default. The indenture trustee should provide to the obligor prompt notice of default after its occurrence.

H. Failure to Submit SEC Filings to the Indenture Trustee

The TIA and the language of many indentures require that the obligor file with the indenture trustee copies of reports the obligor is required to file with the SEC. Indentures often impose a time limit requiring, for example, that the company file the report with the trustee within fifteen days after the company files such report with the SEC. The issue of whether an obligor that has failed for whatever reason to file a report with the SEC has breached the terms of an indenture by failing to deliver such report to the trustee has been widely litigated. In *The Bank of New York v. BearingPoint, Inc.*,[89] the court found that the obligor had an independent obligation under the indenture to deliver the SEC reports to the indenture trustee. As a result, the court held that a notice of default setting forth the failure of BearingPoint to deliver timely SEC reports to the trustee was sufficient to evidence the existence of the default and, with the passage of time, supported an acceleration of the indebtedness. This decision proved to be controversial and a number of courts have held that Section 314 of the TIA simply was intended to require the obligor to provide the trustee with reports that are filed with the SEC, not to create an independent obligation. Thus the court in *United Health Group, Inc. v. Wilmington Trust Co.*[90] held that Section 314(a) of the TIA clearly identifies which reports must eventually be forwarded to the trustee and does not independently impose any particular timetable for providing such reports to the indenture trustee. The court in *Affiliated Computer Servicers, Inc. v. Wilmington Trust Co.*[91] rejected the holding in *BearingPoint* and agreed with the reasoning of the 8th Circuit that Section 314(a) simply requires the obligor to provide copies of reports that are actually filed with the SEC. This position has been taken by other courts as well.[92]

---

89 *The Bank of N.Y. v. BearingPoint, Inc.*, 13 Misc. 3d 1209, 824 N.Y.S.2d 752 2006 WL 2670143 (Sept. 18, 2006).

90 *United Health Grp., Inc. v. Wilmington Tr. Co.*, 548 F.3d 1124 (8th Cir. 2008).

91 *Affiliated Computer Servs., Inc. v. Wilmington Tr. Co.*, 565 F.3d 924 (5th. Cir. 2009).

92 *See RacePoint Partners LLC v. J.P. Morgan Chase Bank N.A.*, 902 N.Y.S.2d, 14, 14 N.Y.3d 419 (N.Y. 2010); *Cyerbonics, Inc. v. Wells Fargo Bank N.A.*, 2007 WL 1729977 (S.D. Texas June 13, 2007); *Finisar Corp. v. U.S. Bank Tr. Nat'l Assoc.*, 2008 U.S. Dist. LEXIS 65329 (N.D. Ca. Aug. 25, 2008), *aff'd* 2010 U.S. App. LEXIS 16660 (9th Cir. Aug. 6, 2010).

I. Misrepresentations

Proven material, untrue representations and warranties of the obligor relating to the issue constitute an event of default. This event of default may be specifically negotiated by the parties to the indenture. Normally, an indenture trustee becomes aware of material, untrue representations and warranties of the obligor by discovering that the holders did not receive the benefit of the bargain. Many times, the indenture trustee becomes aware of proven untrue representations and warranties of the obligor either through the SEC or by the institution by third parties of successful security fraud litigation against the obligor and others. This provision regarding proven material, untrue representations and warranties is normally an automatic event of default with no grace period, since the obligor usually has no ability to cure.

J. Judgments

A judgment against the obligor over an amount that remains unsatisfied after a grace period is an event of default that may be negotiated by the parties to the indenture.[93] The indenture trustee may be the last to know of the entry of a significant judgment against the obligor. Unless the indenture trustee is informed in writing of such a judgment or acquires actual knowledge of it, the indenture trustee has no duty to discover such a breach. Holders of the securities or officers of the obligor may inform the indenture trustee of the existence of such a judgment, which information the indenture trustee should confirm with the clerk of the appropriate court. Provisions for a default based upon an order for the payment of money in excess of a certain amount require continuation of the judgment or an order unsatisfied in effect for a certain number of consecutive days without a stay of execution. The grace period varies from 30 to 90 days, and the amount varies based upon the materiality of the amount to the obligor and its business enterprise.

K. Sinking Fund Payments

Failure to make reserve or sinking fund payments is an event of default if negotiated by the parties to the indenture. Since failure to make the sinking payment may be caused by a temporary deficiency in cash flow, there normally is a grace period to allow the obligor to obtain additional cash flow or borrow funds to the permitted extent in order to make the sinking fund payment before an event of default will occur. Notice of default to the obligor is normally required if there is a grace period, in order to trigger commencement of the grace period.

---

93 *See* MDI § 5-1.

L. Default under Other Debt Instruments

A default by the obligor in respect of its indebtedness (other than the indenture securities) may result in a default under the indenture if so negotiated by the parties.[94] Many indentures provide that a default under any bond, debt, note or other evidence of indebtedness of the obligor, other than securities evidenced by the indenture or under any indenture or other instrument under which evidence of indebtedness has been issued, becomes a default under the indenture after expiration of the applicable grace period under that indenture (a "cross-default") and then becomes an event of default. A default under other debt securities may not come to the attention of the indenture trustee unless representatives of the obligor, holders or others bring it to the indenture trustee's attention, or the default becomes known to the indenture trustee through periodic financial filings (10-Q and 10-K). The indenture trustee should not be charged with any knowledge other than actual knowledge of default on other indebtedness of which the indenture trustee is informed by either the obligor or holders of the securities, or by documents presented to the indenture trustee pursuant to the terms of the indenture (annual report, certificate of no-default, etc.).

M. The Distinction Between Defaults and Events of Default Is Extremely Important

Most remedies are triggered upon the event of default as opposed to upon a default which, remaining uncured after lapse of time, ripens into an event of default. Frequently, only an event of default and not a default, is a defined term in indentures, and references therein to a matured or unmatured event of default use the language "the occurrence and continuance of an event of default or an event which, after notice or lapse of time for both, would become an event of default." The nonexistence of a default is a usual condition precedent in indentures for certain freedom of action by the company, such as issuance of additional bonds, withdrawal of trust monies, release of trust estate assets, voting and receipt of income from pledged securities, consolidations, mergers, etc.

As set forth above, indentures frequently provide that defaults in the payment of principal, voluntary bankruptcy of the obligor and voluntary liquidation by the obligor are of such a nature that there can be no prompt cure; therefore, no grace period is needed, and they become events of default upon their occurrence. Defaults in regard to nonpayment of interest, compliance with other covenants, reporting requirements, involuntary bankruptcy or money judgments normally have a grace period before ripening into events of default, at which point certain remedies can be taken.

---

94 *Id.*

Since, under most indentures, the applicability of the prudent person standard of care depends upon occurrence of an event of default, it follows from the strict interpretation of the language of most indentures that:

(1) The trustee becomes immediately subject to that standard upon a default in the payment of principal or the institution of voluntary bankruptcy proceedings by the obligor;

(2) The trustee generally becomes subject to the standard upon the expiration of 30 days after a default in interest or covenant defaults with notice that remain uncured for 30 days (or longer period if the grace period in the indenture so provides); and

(3) The trustee may be able to avoid the standard altogether as to other defaults to the extent it determines in good faith not to give notice to the obligor, unless the bondholders themselves thrust the standard on the trustee by giving such notice or requiring the trustee to give such notice.

Section 315(c) of the TIA requires that the indenture trustee exercise in the case of default the same degree of care and skill as a prudent person. The term default is to be defined in the indenture. Many indentures define default to mean the occurrence and continuation of an event of default. It should be noted that some indentures define a default that after notice, lapse of time or both would become an event of default as an unmatured event of default. This definition would require the prudent person standard to be applied as of the time of the default for breach of the term of the indenture and not as of the date, if applicable, when the default would ripen into an event of default. Accordingly, the indenture trustee should use care in reviewing the terms of the indenture both prior to closing and upon the occurrence of default to see precisely when, under the terms of the indenture, the prudent person standard will begin. Generally, the prudent person rule under most indentures begins upon the event of default, which is defined as a default consistent with the requirements of the TIA. As a practical matter, the indenture trustee may very well consider that the prudent person rule governs its conduct upon an occurrence of failure of the obligor to comply with the terms of the indenture. While the indenture trustee may not be obligated under that standard, using it as a general rule will provide the best protection for the indenture trustee and holders of the securities.

N. Knowledge of Default

The problem of knowledge arises principally in connection with the performance by the obligor of its non-monetary covenants. It has been held that knowledge by the trustee of a default involving a breach of covenant by the obligor may not be assumed without proof.[95] Nor does the duty of a prudent administration require the trustee to discover defaults at its peril. Courts generally have recognized that corporate trustees cannot be expected to employ experts to make a continuous first hand investigation of the obligor's activities to determine if a default has occurred.[96] The TIA provides for the trustee to be furnished with certain periodic reports, certificates and opinions. Prior to an event of default, the trustee may conclusively rely upon certificates or opinions furnished to it subject only to its duty not to act in bad faith and to examine such documentation (without investigation as to facts) to determine whether it conforms to requirements of the relevant indenture.[97] The absence of bad faith requirement suggests that even a statement of no default, fair on its face, may not be absolute protection to the trustee where the statement omitted reference to interest payments.[98] The certificate should be viewed in the context in which it is presented, and the trustee should have the discretionary right to look behind the facts of the certificate if the trustee so chooses. The trustee must be sure that the facts stated therein are complete on their face.[99] If the certificate is from officers of a company that may be defaulting, this factor may prevent the trustee from reasonably relying on the certificate alone, especially where the indenture provisions regarding the content of the certificate are not complied with.[100] Counsel's opinion, particularly counsel to the obligor, may be helpful, but if such opinion is qualified, it is of little real assistance to the trustee, particularly where the trustee does not or cannot actually rely upon it.[101] A situation may arise, then, where there is a dispute between the trustee and the obligor as to whether a default has occurred under terms of the indenture. This could result from different opinions of counsel on the proper interpretation or application of a particular indenture covenant. In some instances, obligors have been known to refuse to provide additional information beyond the no-default certificate, even though the indenture trustee has reasonable grounds to believe that such may be inaccurate. In these situations, the trustee may consider the possibility of instituting a declaratory judgment action

---

95 *In re Pittsburgh Terminal Warehouse & Transfer Co.*, 69 F. Supp. 289 (W.D. Pa. 1946).

96 Sav. *Bank of New London v. N.Y. Tr. Co.*, 27 N.Y.S.2d 963 (N.Y. Sup. Ct. 1941).

97 See TIA § 315(a)(2); *Cruden v. Bank of N.Y.*, 957 F.2d 961 (2d Cir. 1992).

98 *See, e.g.*, *Chem. Bank & Tr. Co. v. Prudence-Bonds Corp.*, 207 F.2d 67 (2d Cir. 1953), *cert. denied*, 347 U.S. 904 (1954) ("Prudence-Bonds").

99 *Id.*

100 In *Shawmut Bank N.A. v. Kress Assocs.*, 33 F.3d 1477 (9th Cir. 1994), the court found that the ability of the trustee to rely on the basis of a requisition certificate was dependent upon the face of the document containing reasonable detail and that "land and building" did not satisfy the criterion.

101 *Prudence-Bonds* at 78–79; *E.F. Hutton Southwest Properties II, Ltd. v. Union Planters Nat'l Bank*, 953 F.2d 963, 973 (5th Cir. 1992) (trustee entitled to rely on advice of counsel).

against the obligor, seeking judicial determination of whether a default has in fact occurred or whether it is entitled to information in addition to the certificate to determine such.[102]

O. Waiver and Estoppel Considerations

There may be an attempt by the obligor to work out or cure the default and a request may be made to the indenture trustee to refrain from sending the formal notice to the obligor, which notice will begin the running of the grace period. In addition, there may be an attempt to obtain the agreement of the indenture trustee to extend the grace period. Even after an event of default occurs, the obligor may attempt to obtain a moratorium on the exercise of remedies by the trustee or bondholders. At this time, the coordination between the trustee and bondholders may prove advantageous. It may be that the trustee, in conjunction with the bondholders, believes that it is in the best interest of the bondholders to permit the obligor to try to work out its problems. However, extreme care must be taken to document the position of the indenture trustee and the bondholders that there is no waiver of defaults or remedies in any extension of the grace period or moratorium on the exercise of remedies.

---

102 *But see Harris Tr. and Sav. Bank v. E-II Holdings Inc.*, 962 F.2d 636 (7th Cir. 1991) (dismissing declaratory action of trustees), *cert. denied*, 502 U.S. 866 (1991). More recently, it has become common for indenture trustees to seek court direction either by declaratory judgment, interpleader or the use of certain state statutes with respect to proposed action. Such will be discussed in Chapter IX.

V. Communications to Holders, Obligor and Others by Trustee in the Event of Default

A. Introduction

Among the decisions an indenture trustee must make upon occurrence of an event of default, and one that is of great importance to holders is when to communicate the default to the holders (and thereby to the market and the public) and what to state in that communication. The obligor may argue that communication of the event of default or a default in compliance with the terms of the indenture will be the one act that brings the obligor to collapse. Generally, however, upon occurrence of an event of default, notice is required to be given to the holders under the terms of the indenture. Section 315 of the TIA specifically prohibits withholding notice of default in the case of the nonpayment of principal, interest or sinking fund installment. In addition, since the holders of the securities vary from the very sophisticated to "moms and pops" without expertise in the securities market, an indenture trustee receives a variety of inquiries during the life of a trust concerning compliance, the status of trust funds and accounts, and general information concerning the obligor's business and compliance with the terms of the indenture. Section 313 of the TIA sets forth the information that must be reported to the holders on an annual basis. Many analysts of corporate and municipal securities look to the indenture trustee as a quick resource for updates on the status of the indenture securities. Indenture trustees feel uncomfortable giving accurate but sensitive information concerning various facts surrounding the indenture and compliance therewith that has not been generally communicated to all the holders, the industry or the marketplace. While there is significant debate regarding whether holders and analysts should obtain information on an individual basis as opposed to group communications, it appears the problem could be solved by having an appropriate mechanism such as an information web site. This web site, available to holders, could collect and hold all communications from the indenture trustee including notices, communications to and from the obligor, certificates by professionals retained by the obligor concerning the status of the trust accounts, balances in various funds, compliance with the indenture, and annual statements of the obligor. If the matter is in litigation, key court filings and orders could be included. This type of trustee web site for investors or other key parties already is in place for many securitization transactions.

B. Obligation of the Trustee to Provide Notice of Default to the Bondholders

Pursuant to Section 315(b) of the TIA, the indenture trustee is required to give the holders notice of all defaults known to the indenture trustee within 90 days after the occurrence of the default.[103] However, an indenture qualified under the TIA is deemed automatically to provide (unless it is specifically stated that such provision is excluded) that, except in the case of default in the payment of the principal or interest or in the payment of any sinking fund installment, the indenture trustee shall be protected in withholding such notice so long as the board of directors, the executive committee or trust committee of directors and/or responsible officers of the indenture trustee, in good faith, determine that withholding such notice is in the interest of the holders. (A form of notice of default to the bondholders can be found in Appendix V-A.) Further, as noted, Section 313 of the TIA governs the annual report, which must be filed by an indenture trustee under a qualified indenture. The indenture trustee under a TIA-qualified indenture must, among other things, report no less frequently than every twelve months any action taken by the indenture trustee in the performance of its duties that it has not previously reported which materially affects the securities except for notice of default withheld under the above-referenced Section 315. Further, under Section 313(a)(3), the indenture trustee must, on an annual basis, set forth the character and amount of any advances made by the indenture trustee that aggregate more than half of 1 percent of the principal amount of the indenture securities outstanding. Moreover, under Section 313(b)(2), in the case of advances by the indenture trustee to preserve the trust estate, the indenture trustee must give notice within 90 days of making any such advances if the amount of advances remaining unpaid aggregates more than 10 percent of the principal amount of the indenture securities outstanding.

The prior requirements evolved from historical situations in which trustees advanced their own funds to cure the obligor's default. In one case, the officers of an insolvent trustee were held individually liable to bondholders for the action of the indenture trustee in advancing its own funds to meet interest due on the bonds without notice to the bondholders, thereby, in effect, concealing the existence of the obligor's default.[104] The trust officers were held liable for any decline in the value of the mortgaged property between the time the interest payment default occurred (when the trustee should have notified the bondholders) and the time when the bondholders, upon learning of the trustee's concealment, could have obtained control of the mortgaged property. The matter of unannounced advances by the indenture trustee has been the subject of frequent litigation involving the indenture trustee's assertion of a lien against the trust

---

103 *Policemen's Annuity and Benefit Fund of City of Chicago v. Bank of Am., N.A.*, 907 F. Supp. 2d 536 (S.D.N.Y. 2012) (but see *Retirement Bd. of the Policemen's Annuity and Benefit Fund of the City of Chicago v. Bank of N.Y. Mellon*, 775 F.3d 154 (2d Cir. 2014) (holding RMBS securities governed by pooling and servicing agreements exempt from requirements of TIA)). If the indenture trustee's lack of knowledge of the default is due to failure to examine certificates as required by the indenture, it has been held that failure to comply with the notice requirement is not excused. *In re Bankers Tr. (Semi-Tech)*, 353 F. Supp. 2d 460 (S.D.N.Y.), *aff'd*, 450 F.3d 121 (2d Cir. 2006).

104 *First Tr. Co. v. Carlsen*, 129 Neb. 118 (1935).

estate for such advancement senior to the claim of the bondholders. It seems clear that the indenture trustee cannot claim a lien for its advances to meet interest payments unless the bondholders are notified.[105] Occasionally, lack of notice has also been held to defeat the indenture trustee's claim for advances related to the mortgage property, such as rents or taxes.[106] There is a clear distinction, however, between advances to meet interest obligations, which tend to conceal the existence of a serious default from the bondholders, and advances related to the preservation of the security itself or legal fees incurred in furtherance of the trustee's duties. In *First Trust Co. v. Ricketts*,[107] the indenture trustee's lien for advances was defeated as to interest, but upheld as to taxes and insurance, notwithstanding the failure to notify the bondholders. Nevertheless, it is helpful to keep bondholders informed of significant advances being made so they can evaluate the economics of the situation, including whether it is reasonable to continue such advances. Frequently, prior to declaring a default, without direction from the holders a trustee will avoid advancing funds for the protection of collateral or trust assets, and the trustee has no obligation to advance monies for principal or interest. More often, an event of default will be declared and the indenture trustee will work with bondholders and their counsel to craft an agreed-upon solution.

Because most investors hold their securities in street name, often the registered security holder will be Cede & Co., the nominee of the Depository Trust Company ("DTC"). DTC maintains custody of securities for its participants and their customers through its affiliated nominee, Cede and Company.[108] Cede and Company is the registered holder of the securities, often the only registered holder on the indenture trustee's records. The participants, typically institutional and brokerage firms, in turn represent their customers, banks, brokers or other nominees, who in turn represent the beneficial holders of the securities. Particularly in transactions that are held by numerous and diverse holders, the indenture trustee may find it actually difficult to reach the beneficial holders with a communication. In order to assist communications reaching the beneficial holders of the securities, Section 313(c) of the TIA requires that reports compiled thereunder also be delivered to such holders who have transmitted their names to the indenture trustee for this purpose within the last two years and, under certain circumstances, names on bondholder lists compiled pursuant to Section 312 (list of holders provided by the obligors).[109] Bondholders, especially beneficial holders, who desire to

---

105 *Klein v. Dunn*, 337 Pa. 480 (1940).

106 *Marshall & Ilsley Bank v. Guar. Inv. Co.*, 213 Wis. 415 (1933).

107 75 F.2d 309 (8th Cir. 1934).

108 For a helpful explanation of the role of DTC see National Association of Bond Lawyers, *Demystifying DTC: The Depository Trust Company and the Municipal Bond Market*, March 2017 available at www.nabl.org ("Demystifying DTC").

109 TIA § 313(c).

receive reports and other communications promptly from the trustee should provide contact information.

Section 315(b) provides that notices of default are to be distributed in the manner and to the extent provided in Section 313(c). Upon receipt of a notice from the trustee, DTC posts the notice where it can be accessed by the participants. DTC also posts legal notices it receives to its Legal Notice System ("LENS") service, where the notice can be accessed by all LENS subscribers. Prospective users must register for the LENS service.[110] The indenture trustee should consider obtaining the DTC position list that should disclose the DTC participants for the transaction. The indenture trustee should also consider sending a hard copy of the notice to this list. To the extent the beneficial or nominee holders contact the indenture trustee and wisely make their identity known, the indenture trustee should consider maintaining a list of those holders and using it for notice and communication purposes.

C. Risks of Noncommunication to Holders vs. Alleged Damage

The bondholders are entitled to prompt notice if their security or their investment is threatened. The trustee should be prompt in notifying them of any serious default, and notice should be given to the holders pursuant to the terms of the indenture.

Whether or not to give notice of default may be a delicate decision. Notice will have an impact on: (1) the obligor who may be able to cure the default, except for the perceived loss of public confidence upon public notice of default, and (2) the value of the bondholders' bonds that may drop once the default is made public. Some authorities may argue that the safest course is to notify bondholders since the TIA does not appear to give a basis for holding the trustee liable for notifying bondholders. Further, failing to provide notice may put the trustee in a difficult position, especially if a seemingly slight default turns into a substantial one. A decision to withhold notice must be made by high-level officers, the board of directors, the executive committee or the trust committee of directors and/or responsible officers of the trustee. Any default, other than a few days' delay with a report or other minor infraction, should be reviewed immediately by a committee of responsible officers up to the board of directors or its equivalent. In addition, an opinion of counsel and an investigation into the facts are presumed. A negligent failure to notify may subject the trustee to liability for any reduction in value of the trust estate that results from the non-notice.

Once an event of default has occurred, it may be more useful for the indenture trustee to attempt to obtain an accurate list of the actual beneficial holders of the issue. It should be noted that most indentures provide that the direction and instruction to the indenture trustee shall be

---

110 *Demystifying DTC*, p. 13.

made by the holders, normally defined as the registered holders. Since registered holders generally will not provide direction or instruction unless directed by the beneficial holder and because in some situations the actual registered holders are not as effective in promptly passing on the notices of default or other communications as would be desirable, it is helpful for the indenture trustee to develop a list of beneficial holders so that the communication can be sent directly to beneficial holders as well. This will enable these beneficial holders to direct the trustee. As previously noted, beneficial holders will be well advised to consider providing contact information to the indenture trustee.

In certain proceedings instituted by indenture trustees, courts have entered orders that require registered holders or nominees that act on behalf of others to disclose to the indenture trustee or other representative the names and addresses of the party for whom they act so that the indenture trustee can develop a list of beneficial holders for the purpose of communication. Sometimes these orders also provide that the nominee who refuses to provide to the indenture trustee the names of the beneficial holders shall thereafter be responsible and liable to the beneficial holder for any claims, and that the indenture trustee is thereby absolved of any liability to the beneficial holder. If the nominee fails to give the indenture trustee the name and address of the beneficial holder, then the beneficial holder may only look to the nominee for any claim or cause of action. Such an order has been effective in opening and enhancing the avenues of communication to the beneficial holders in a bankruptcy situation.[111]

D. Nature of Communication to Obligor and Holders

Although true throughout the administration of a trust, it is particularly important after default that all communication with the obligor, particularly notice of default, be businesslike and conform to the terms of the indenture. (A form of notice of default to the obligor without acceleration can be found in Appendix V-B. A form of notice of default with acceleration can be found in Appendix V-C.) It is not unreasonable to expect that such letters will become exhibits in litigation or may be scrutinized by third parties. Such letters should not be threatening, but all requirements of the indenture should be met, including addressing the proper recipient and directing the proper manner of delivery.[112] As indicated previously, care must be taken to indicate that the letter does not amount to a listing of all possible defaults, an election of remedies

---

111 *See In re Southland Corp.*, 124 B.R. 211 (Bankr. N.D. Tex. 1991); *In re St. Therese Care Ctr., Inc.*, 1991 WL 217669 (Bankr. D. Minn. Oct. 23, 1991); *In re Tenn-Fla Partners*, 1993 WL 151346 (Bankr. W.D. Tenn. Apr. 29, 1993); *In re Pioneer Finance Corp.*, 246 B.R. 626 (Bankr. D. Nev. 2000).

112 Sometimes an obligor changes its business address without formally amending the indenture to change the notice provision. The notice provision in the indenture should always be followed, but where a newer address is known by the trustee the trustee should likewise send the notice to the new address.

or waiver of other provisions not complained of. The holders should likewise be addressed in a businesslike fashion. An attempt should be made to make the communication readily understandable, while complying with requirements of the indenture. Only facts should be communicated to the holders; speculation has no place in bondholder letters. Further, it is clear that the indenture trustee should not give legal, tax or investment advice, and the holders should be advised to consult with their own legal or other advisors. The letter of an indenture trustee to the holders cannot be overly optimistic or overly pessimistic. It should be objective to the degree that the obligor makes a statement on the subject of the default, and the obligor's statement can be attached or specifically quoted. The indenture trustee should consider periodic communication with the holders. The holders should be apprised of efforts by the indenture trustee to protect the rights and interests of the holders, so that they may then provide direction, instruction and indemnity to the indenture trustee if they desire that the trustee take some particular action. Periodic communication is a critical means of insuring cooperation and understanding on the part of the holders and their counsel. Bondholders also should utilize businesslike language in corresponding to the indenture trustee. Rude or accusatory language could be misinterpreted in any litigation against the obligor and probably will not enhance the opportunity to establish a good working relationship between the trustee and the inquiring holders or improve the timing or quality of the desired result.

E. Need for Uniform Communication

One of the basic principles governing communications to bondholders is the necessity for uniform communication.[113] Prior to enactment of the TIA, it was not unusual for trustees to keep large holders and institutions informed of the progress of the default, while neglecting to inform the small holders. That is unacceptable. What the trustee communicates to one holder should be communicated to all. This is true not only of written communication, but also of telephone conversations with the trustee. It is most important that specific people in the corporate trust department be assigned to a transaction as needed. If one person cannot handle the volume of bondholders' telephone calls on a troubled bond issue, designated trust officers should share the responsibility. Such calls should not be handled by clerical personnel or by someone without a clear understanding of what should be communicated. A record of each such communication indicating the person who contacted the trustee and the date, time and summary of the

---

113 This principle is modified in the case of the dissemination of material, non-public information with regard to an obligor. The receipt of such information by a holder may be conditioned upon the execution of a non-disclosure agreement ("NDA"), which typically requires that the recipient refrain from trading in the subject debt. There necessarily will be a distinction between the information provided to holders executing the NDA versus the holders who prefer to remain non-restricted.

conversation is imperative for the protection of the trustee. Some trustees have a prepared statement that is read to each holder that calls and inquires as to the status of the issue. Any questions of the holders are noted and the answers are considered for inclusion in the prepared written statement, if appropriate. The prepared written statement can be sent periodically to the registered and beneficial holders known to the trustee. The record may be maintained in electronic form and should also contain a summary of what the representative of the trustee said to the holder. Obviously, special situations may lead to a need for sophisticated forms of communications. For example, in the Washington Public Power Supply System default, Chemical Bank initiated a hotline which provided a recorded status report to the largely retail holders and was available by a toll-free number. While this was an unusual situation, it reflects an example of the requirements to provide uniform communication to holders. More recently, notably in the airline and *Lehman* bankruptcy cases and in residential mortgage-backed securities litigation, trustees have established public web sites devoted to specific defaulted issues where notices from the obligor and the trustee, significant events and court filings are posted. Some indenture trustees have chosen to communicate with holders exclusively in writing so that all holders receive the same information. Even if a holder calls or e-mails, the holder simply receives the latest version of the communication. Of course, simple questions of objective fact such as payment amount or date should be able to be answered by phone or e-mail.

One approach that has been found useful by indenture trustees is to provide periodic reports in writing to the holders concerning the status of the defaulted matter. These reports can be posted online as well as mailed to known holders. In response to telephone or other inquiries by holders, the trustee can then refer the holder to the facts as set forth in the last communication to the holders. Thus, those who make an oral inquiry will be made aware of the updated status as of the last periodic report, and no individual will have more information than that included in the last communication to all holders.

F. The Frequency and Detail

While reports are required to be given annually under TIA-qualified indentures, it is not unusual in a default situation to provide information far more frequently. Holders become concerned if there is no communication from the trustee; therefore, it is imperative that fairly regular reports be given. The degree of detail will vary with the nature of the default. While minute detail is not necessary for every garden-variety default, care should be taken that all material facts are revealed to the bondholders.

A communication to holders could be governed by the rule of reason. An indenture trustee should inform the holders of those facts that the indenture trustee believes in good faith are material and relevant to the default or defaults presently existing. Generally, notices of default to the holders have the following structure subject to the unique requirements of the relevant indenture:

(1) it should contain a specific statement that the obligor has failed to comply with the specified section of the indenture, describing precisely the failure or non-compliance with the terms of the indenture;

(2) the indenture trustee should inform the holders that notice of the default has been given to the obligor, if such is required, in order to commence the beginning of the grace period and should inform the holders of when, if the default remains uncured, it will ripen into an event of default (as noted above, certain defaults automatically become events of default while others, pursuant to terms of the indenture, require notice, lapse of time and the continuation of the default in order to ripen into an event of default);

(3) the holders should be informed of their right under the indenture to accelerate and the percentage of principal of the outstanding securities necessary to give the notice of acceleration;

(4) the indenture should set forth the requisite percentage necessary to provide such a notice and should state that the notice must be addressed to both the indenture trustee and the obligor;

(5) it may be advisable for the indenture trustee to state that the holders may accelerate and that, if they do accelerate, such does not necessarily assure them that payment will be made given the troubled financial condition of the obligor; rather, it merely means that, as a legal matter, all principal and interest are immediately due and owing, and suit can proceed for the full amount of principal plus accrued interest;

(6) the indenture trustee should inform the holders that, pursuant to the terms of the indenture, if it so provides, a requisite percentage of holders, normally 50 percent or more, may direct and instruct the indenture trustee to take action, if such holders provide the indenture trustee with appropriate indemnity satisfactory to the trustee, and if the request of the holders is neither contrary to the law nor deemed by the indenture trustee to be adverse to the rights and interests of all the holders;[114]

---

114 In transactions that provide that holders of less than a majority of outstanding principal amount may direct the indenture trustee, it is possible that the indenture trustee could receive conflicting directions from two or more groups who hold the requisite percentage. In such case, the indenture trustee may consider seeking direction from a court of competent jurisdiction as to how to proceed. Further, an effort can be made to have holders modify their direction to eliminate the conflict.

(7) the indenture trustee should inform the holders if counsel to the trustee has been retained and the identity of such counsel;

(8) the indenture trustee may also desire to make a statement as to the name, address and contact person at the obligor to whom inquiries may be directed;

(9) the indenture trustee may want to advise the holders that the indenture trustee will provide such additional information and communication as the indenture trustee deems appropriate under the existing circumstances; and

(10) finally, a notice should end with a statement that the trustee is not providing investment, tax or legal advice.

In preparing the notice of default, the trustee should consider whether there is any other relevant information that the trustee should communicate to the holders in addition to the straightforward notice of failure to comply with the terms of the indenture, such as whether the obligor has filed a petition under the federal bankruptcy laws or creditors of the debtor have filed a petition under the federal bankruptcy law, or if lawsuits have been instituted against the obligor. Generally, the indenture trustee will communicate objective facts to the holders and not the subjective merit of any action taken by third parties. Any such notice should be reviewed by trustee's counsel (in-house or outside counsel) prior to sending or posting.

G. State and Federal Laws Relating to Communications

The indenture trustee should be aware that certain state and federal laws govern the production of documents and communication of matters with respect to default. Basic laws of libel, slander and tortious interference with business relationships must be kept in mind in communicating with and about the obligor. The indenture trustee should also be aware that applicable state privacy statutes may, under certain circumstances, preclude the production of information and documents to third parties and the giving of testimony, unless pursuant to subpoena with notice.[115] Moreover, the Federal Right to Financial Privacy Act[116] provides that customers of financial institutions are entitled to notice of any government requests for their financial records and to the opportunity to challenge the request. The SEC, for example, was enjoined from violating this act in *Hunt v. United States Securities & Exchange Commission*.[117]

---

115 *See, e.g., Illinois Banking Act,* 205 ILL. COMP. STAT. 5/48.1.

116 12 U.S.C. §§ 3401–3422 (2016).

117 520 F. Supp. 580 (N.D. Tex. 1981).

H. E-mails and Telephone Calls from Analysts and Purported Holders

The indenture trustee necessarily must be careful when persons purporting to be holders or analysts seek information on the status of the default. If the analyst has no particular connection to the transaction, it obviously is inappropriate for the indenture trustee to reveal confidential non-public information to such an analyst. Moreover, care must be taken to determine that purported holders are in fact holders before confidential information is disclosed to them. Before such information is disclosed, the holder should be informed that the information is non-public, and the holder should seek advice of its counsel regarding appropriate treatment. An indenture trustee who requires proof of holder status is not being overcautious, since non-holders have been known to attempt to obtain facts by posing as holders. It is sometimes appropriate for the indenture trustee to request that the party making an inquiry and claiming to be a holder send a letter or statement to the indenture trustee representing and warranting that it is a holder and identifying the registered holder or nominee for its holding. The indenture trustee may then inquire of the nominee whether or not it knows it represents that party so that the indenture trustee can identify the chain of ownership from DTC to the DTC participant to a nominee, if any, to the beneficial holder. Ultimately, the indenture trustee can use such information in establishing a list of registered and beneficial holders. Many times, indenture trustees have had the holders provide a certificate of ownership, which provides not only certification of ownership but also an indication of the nominee and registered holder. While the need to supply such information may be a temporary inconvenience, beneficial holders should take comfort in efforts of the indenture trustee to avoid discussion with unauthorized persons.

I. Sensitivity of Non-Public Information

As previously mentioned, typically the execution of a NDA will be a condition precedent for the receipt of non-public information by a holder. This is particularly true when the information is of such a nature that its public disclosure could damage the trust estate or violate applicable law.[118] The NDA often contains provisions for the burn-off of the non-disclosure restrictions with the passage of time or release of the information by the obligor.

J. Communications to Other Participants to the Transaction

Once a notice of default has been made public in accordance with the indenture requirements, it may be necessary for the indenture trustee to notify and communicate with the issuer, credit enhancer or rating agency with respect to the matter. Obviously, the issuer, particularly in conduit financing, will be disturbed about a default in a security it has issued and

---

118 Examples include borrower information in residential mortgage-backed securities transactions or material prepared for litigation.

will require a report as to the seriousness of the situation. A credit enhancer, who has obligations triggered by an event of default and who may ultimately stand in the shoes of the holders if required to pay the principal and interest on the bonds, likely will request and should receive information with respect to the matter. Finally, rating agencies who learn of the default will contact the indenture trustee as their basic source of information. It is wise for the indenture trustee to respond to such requests for information quickly, accurately and factually.

A corporate action is an event with respect to a public company that affects the debt issued by the company. It may involve a request for direction and instruction to the indenture trustee. In such a case, the proposed action will be set forth in a communication from the indenture trustee, the form of which will be reviewed by DTC. DTC transmits the communication to its participants, who in turn transmit the communication to their broker-dealers and to nominees. Ultimately, the communication is received by the beneficial holders of the debt security. Then, each beneficial holder considers the subject matter of the direction and instruction. If it deems the action appropriate, the beneficial holder will send the executed direction and instruction back through the same channel in reverse order for signatures by the nominee, DTC participant and DTC as the registered holder. This method, although cumbersome, does ensure proper respect for the chain of ownership.

K. Role of the Securities and Exchange Commission

It may be that the SEC will begin an investigation of the default after it becomes known. The rules governing SEC investigations are set forth at 17 C.F.R. § 203.1, *et seq.*, and apply to investigations of corporate and municipal bond issues. An SEC investigation commences with the formal order of investigation. This order in a general way describes the scope of the investigation, sets forth the names of SEC staff members who will conduct the investigation, and grants such members the right to issue subpoenas and interrogate witnesses. If an indenture trustee receives a subpoena with regard to an ongoing SEC investigation, the indenture trustee should request a copy of the formal order initiating the investigation, which order the SEC is obligated to supply to the indenture trustee. In reviewing the formal order, the indenture trustee can be apprised of the allegations and the nature of the investigation and, in responding to the subpoena, can better protect the rights and interests of the holders of the relevant security for which the trustee acts. Subpoenas can be issued to the target of the investigation or to third parties who are believed capable of supplying information regarding the target. Typically, subpoenas issued initially pursuant to a formal order of investigation request production of documents. Under bank privacy laws of some states, the indenture trustee is obligated to inform the "customer," which may be interpreted as referring to the obligor or, if the subpoena is directed to a specific bondholder, the bondholder. After an opportunity to object, if there is no court order preventing production, then the indenture trustee should proceed with production.

After the documents have been produced, the SEC will determine whether or not it wishes to take a statement from a witness with regard to the documents. An indenture trustee must rely upon the allegations set forth in the formal order to determine whether or not the indenture trustee or others are the target of the investigation. More likely than not, the target of the investigation will be the obligor.

Since there will be expense involved in complying with the subpoena, particularly electronic discovery, the holders should be informed of the receipt of the subpoena, the need for response and that the cost will be borne by the trust.[119] The indenture trustee should consult counsel about the procedures to be followed regarding the production under a subpoena and whether the investigation is so confidential that notification to holders should not be given. When a default occurs, it is appropriate for the indenture trustee to issue an internal document preservation notice so that all relevant papers and e-mails are retained. Documents produced to the SEC should be number stamped so that the indenture trustee can maintain a record of what is produced. Documents withheld under claim of the work-product doctrine, attorney-client privilege or some other privilege should be described in an index but not produced. If confidentiality is not requested by the indenture trustee for the documents produced, the documents will be available to the general public and litigators in any related litigation by means of the Freedom of Information Act ("FOIA").[120] If confidentiality is requested under the FOIA, the documents must indicate on their face that such confidential treatment is requested and the name of the party requesting such treatment. Furthermore, a letter setting forth this fact should be sent to the SEC at the time of production, with a copy to the SEC FOIA officer. Both the letter and the documents must specify that information for which confidential treatment is requested. The issue of whether such confidentiality is warranted will not be ruled upon until a request to review the documents is made because documents generally are not produced during the formal investigation. No request to review the document under the FOIA will be considered until the SEC investigation is closed. (Forms of the required FOIA letters can be found in Appendix V-D-1 and 2.)

Generally, the prudent indenture trustee should have no fear of the SEC and its investigation into a defaulted issue. While the SEC normally will not state to a party that it is not a target of an investigation or that the SEC does not intend to accuse an indenture trustee of improper action, the practical result is that the indenture trustee, the bondholders and the SEC should all be on the same side. There are, however, a few cases where an indenture trustee either

---

119 A trustee of any type of corporate trust should always know how fees and expenses of the trust and trustee are to be paid in the event of a problem. This issue is discussed in more detail in Chapters VII and XI.

120 5 U.S.C. § 552 (2016).

has failed to act in a prudent manner or has taken action contrary to the best interest of the holders in violation of the rules and regulations of the SEC and federal securities law, which may lead to an adversarial relationship between the SEC and the indenture trustee. As a practical matter, little is to be gained from an adversarial relationship, and most investigations where the indenture trustee is the target are situations that can be resolved quickly and reasonably between the indenture trustee and the SEC.

L. Documentation of Communication

As stated above, all verbal communications in a default situation with bondholders, obligor, issuer, credit enhancer or rating agencies should be memorialized by the indenture trustee either by letter, e-mail or memorandum to the file. The indenture trustee should be aware that all such communications are discoverable and, therefore, they should be written professionally and prudently. Such letters and memoranda provide a paper trail to document the prudent actions taken by the indenture trustee. When in doubt about the content of such a writing, the trustee should consult with counsel.

Appendix V-A
Form of Notice of Default to Bondholders

[Date]

Re: ____ (the "Bonds")

Dear Bondholders:

_____________________ is Trustee (the "Trustee") for the certain __________________ issued in the principal amount of $___________ (the "Bonds") and issued pursuant to an Indenture between ________________, a _____________ corporation (the "Company"), and the Trustee dated as of ___________ (the "Indenture").

As you are aware pursuant to the terms of the Indenture, the Company entered into a ________________________________.* We as Trustee have conducted a review of the compliance of the Company with the terms and conditions of the Indenture and ___________________.* Pursuant to Section ____ of the Indenture, we as Trustee are writing this letter to inform you, the Bondholders, of the certain matters relating to the above-cited Bond issue and to notify you, the Bondholders, of certain defaults under the terms of the Indenture and ___________________.*

I. Existing Defaults

The review by us as Trustee indicates that the Company has failed to comply with the terms of ____________________* and the Indenture in that:

1. The Company has failed to comply with the requirements of Section ____ of the Indenture and Section _____ of the ______________________,* which require that ________________________________.

2. The Company has failed to comply with the requirements of Section _____ of the _____________________________.*

3. The Company has failed to make required repayments to Debt Service Reserve Fund as required pursuant to Section _____ of the _____________.*

---

* List relevant operative document such as trust agreement, indenture, loan agreement or pooling and servicing agreement, etc.

4. The Company has failed to make the required interest and principal payments in the amount of ______________ interest and ______________ principal due on __________________ and has failed to supply sufficient funds to make the payments as required by Section _____ of the ________________.*

Other defaults may exist under the Indenture and the Trustee reserves all rights with respect thereto.

II. Notice of Default to Company and Consideration of Resolutions

On ____________________________ we as Trustee gave notice to the Company of the above-cited defaults and demanded that all defaults be immediately cured. Pursuant to Section _____ of the ______________________________,* the failure of the Company to comply with the terms and conditions of the ______________________,* including the items listed above, constitutes an Event of Default if not cured within __ days of the date of this notice, provided the Trustee, in its sole discretion, does not agree, in writing, to an extension of the applicable "grace period." An Event of Default under the ________________________* constitutes an Event of Default under the Indenture pursuant to Section _____.

III. Acceleration

Upon the occurrence and continuation of an Event of Default, Section _____ of the Indenture provides that the Indenture Trustee (or holder of not less than 25 percent in aggregate principal amount of the Bonds then outstanding with an indemnity to the Trustee) may declare the principal amount of all the Bonds to be due and payable immediately by notice in writing to the Company and upon such declaration such principal shall become immediately due and payable. You as holders of the Bonds should realize that a Notice of Acceleration simply results in the principal of all the Bonds becoming immediately due and payable as a legal matter, but it does not in any sense assure such payment. We as Trustee have not as of the date of this letter sent a Notice of Acceleration to the Company and we are proceeding to consider whether such Notice of Acceleration is presently in your best interest.

IV. Direction by Holders

Section _____ of the Indenture provides that the holders of a majority in aggregate principal amount of the Bonds at the time outstanding shall have the right, at any time, by an instrument or instruments in writing executed and delivered to the Trustee, to direct the time, method and place of conducting all proceedings to be taken in connection with the enforcement

---

* List relevant operative document such as trust agreement, indenture, loan agreement or pooling and servicing agreement, etc.

of the terms and conditions of this Indenture, provided that such action is legal, appropriate and in the best interest of all holders, and there is sufficient indemnity provided to us by such holders.

V. Additional Information

Bondholders with questions may contact ______________________.

Prior to any distribution to Bondholders, funds held under the relevant Indenture may be used first for payment of the fees and costs incurred or to be incurred by the Trustee in performing its duties, as well as for any indemnities owing or to become owing to the Trustee.

The Trustee reserves all rights under the relevant Indenture. Please be aware that the Trustee may conclude that a specific response to particular inquiries from individual Bondholders is not consistent with equal and full dissemination of information to all Bondholders. Bondholders should not rely on the Trustee as their sole source of information. The Trustee makes no recommendations and gives no investment, legal or tax advice. Each Bondholder should seek investment, legal, tax and other advice from its own advisors based on such Bondholder's particular circumstances.

Recipients of this notice are cautioned that this notice is not evidence that the Trustee will recognize the recipient as a Bondholder. Under the Indenture, the Trustee is required only to recognize and treat the person in whose name a Bond is registered on the registration books maintained by the Trustee as a Bondholder.

In our capacity as Trustee, we will continue to monitor developments in this matter and inform you as we deem appropriate.

Very truly yours,

______________________________________,

as Trustee as Aforesaid
By:
Title:

Appendix V-B
Form of Notice of Default to Company Without Acceleration

[Date]

[The Company]

Re: ________________________________ (the "Bonds")

Ladies and Gentlemen:

______________ is Trustee (the "Trustee") for the ____________ (the "Bonds") pursuant to an Indenture between ____________________ and the Trustee dated as of __________________ (the "Indenture").

Pursuant to the terms of the Indenture, ____________________, a ____________ corporation (the "Company"), entered into a ______________________________.

The Company is required to comply with the terms of the ________________. We hereby give you written notice of the following defaults:

1. The Company has failed to comply with the requirements of Section ____ of the [Applicable Document]* in that __________________.

2. The Company has failed to comply with the requirements of Section ____ of the [Applicable Document]* with regard to the ______________.

3. The Company has failed to make required repayments to the Debt Service Reserve Fund as required pursuant to Section ____ of the ______________* in that the Company failed to deposit __________ in the Debt Service Reserve Fund on __________ and each month thereafter as required by Section of the [Applicable Document].*

4. The Company has failed to make the required interest and principal payments due on __________ in the amount of __________, and has failed to supply

---

* List applicable document such as trust agreement, indenture, loan agreement or pooling and servicing agreement, etc.

sufficient funds to make the payments as required by Section ____ of the [Applicable Document].

This is a Notice of Default. The Trustee hereby requests and demands that all existing defaults be cured immediately. Pursuant to Section ____ of the [Applicable Document],* the failure of the Company to comply with the terms and conditions of the [Applicable Document]* within _____ days of our written notice constitutes an Event of Default. Pursuant to Section ____ of the ____________________, the failure of the Company to make the required deposits to the Interest Fund and Bond Fund, as noted in item 4 above, are Events of Default. Events of Default under the [Applicable Document]* constitute Events of Default under Section ____ of [Applicable Document].* The defaults noted above have already become, and continue to be, Events of Default. Unless these matters are cured forthwith, the Trustee will take all action the Indenture Trustee deems appropriate under the circumstances.

The foregoing is not an exhaustive summary of defaults that exist under the [Applicable Document]* and the Trustee reserves the right to supplement this information including as the Trustee obtains knowledge of any additional defaults. Nothing contained herein shall be deemed to waive, limit or alter any or all of the rights, claims and causes of action of the Trustee, all of which are reserved. This is not an Election of Remedies.

Very truly yours,

____,

as Trustee as Aforesaid
By:
Title:

---

* List applicable document such as trust agreement, indenture, loan agreement or pooling and servicing agreement, etc.

Appendix V-C
Form of Notice of Default to Company with Acceleration

[Date]

[The Company]

Re: ________________________________ (the "Bonds")

Ladies and Gentlemen:

____________________ is Trustee (the "Trustee") for the ______________________ (the "Bonds") pursuant to an Indenture between ______________________ and the Trustee dated as of ____________________ (the "Indenture").

______________, a ______________ corporation (the "Company"), is in default for payment of principal and interest pursuant to the terms of that certain [Applicable Document]* and ___________________, having failed among other things to pay interest and principal due on and after ______________, despite repeated written requests to do so. The Company is similarly in default under that certain [Applicable Document],* dated as of _________________, executed by the Company. The principal balance outstanding is $______________, with accrued and unpaid interest as of ______________ in the amount of $______________, together with fees and expenses incurred by the Trustee.

This is a Notice of Default and Acceleration. Pursuant to Section _____ of the [Applicable Document].* As a result of the foregoing, the Trustee hereby declares all sums due under the aforesaid [Applicable Document]* to be due and payable and demands payment forthwith. Pursuant to this Notice of Default and Acceleration there is now due and payable the sum of $______________ as of ______________, plus interest accrued from and after such date and fees and expenses incurred by the Trustee. In addition, the [Applicable Document]* provides that interest continues to accrue at the default rate of ________.

---

* List applicable document such as trust agreement, indenture, loan agreement or pooling and servicing agreement, etc.

Please be advised that unless there is paid to the Trustee all sums due to it under the terms of the aforesaid [Applicable Document]* forthwith, the Trustee will exercise its rights pursuant to the terms of the Indenture including, but not limited to, its right to foreclose all collateral held for the payment of such sums; will seek a judgment in the aggregate amount due and unpaid; and will request public sale of all such security to satisfy such judgment. Nothing contained herein shall be deemed to waive, limit or alter any or all of the rights, claims and causes of action of the Trustee, all of which are reserved. This is not an Election of Remedies.

Very truly yours,

____________________________________,

as Trustee as Aforesaid

By:

Title:

Appendix V-D-1
Form of Freedom of Information Act Letter to the SEC

[Date]

FOIA CONFIDENTIAL TREATMENT REQUESTED
Mr./Ms. _______________
Securities and Exchange Commission
Division of Enforcement
450 5th Street, N.W.
Room 5029
Washington, D.C. 20549

Re: In the Matter of _______________; File No. _____

Dear Mr./Ms. _______________:

Pursuant to the subpoena heretofore directed to _______________ and based upon our conversations with the Commission, we are forwarding to you a disk containing documents numbered _____ through _____.

If you have any questions concerning this information, do not hesitate to contact us. We wish to inform you that this information is being produced pursuant to process. It is not to be released by the Securities and Exchange Commission to any other party relative to the Freedom of Information Act. Specifically, the undersigned claims that the information it is producing is immune from such disclosure under Title 5, United States Code, Section 552(b)(4), as commercial or financial information that is privileged or confidential.

Very truly yours,

Appendix V-D-2
Form of Letter to Freedom of Information Act Officer

[Date]

FOIA CONFIDENTIAL TREATMENT REQUESTED
Freedom of Information Act Officer
Securities and Exchange Commission
450 5th Street, N.W.
Washington, D.C. 20549

Re: In the Matter of ______________; File No. _____

Dear Sir/Madam:

We represent ____________________________. Pursuant to our letter of this date to Mr./Ms. ____________, we have produced certain information. In that letter, a copy of which is attached hereto as Exhibit 1 and is incorporated herein, ______________________ claims this information is immune from disclosure pursuant to the Freedom of Information Act under Title 5, United States Code, Section 552(b)(4), as commercial or financial information that is privileged or confidential. The purpose of this letter is to inform you of this request for confidential treatment as required by 17 CFR § 200.83.

If you have any questions concerning the foregoing, do not hesitate to contact us.

Very truly yours,

VI. Conflicts of Interest, Sharing Requirements and Successor Indenture Trustee

A. Conflicts of Interest under the TIA

It is well established under the common law that, pre-default, the duties of an indenture trustee are strictly defined and limited to the terms of the indenture.[121] In addition, under the common law of the state of New York, which governs many indentures, it is clear that the indenture trustee must nevertheless refrain from engaging in a conflict of interest.[122] The enactment of the Trust Indenture Act of 1939[123] ("TIA") as amended by the Trust Indenture Reform Act of 1990[124] ("TIRA") is instructive in analyzing relationships that could lead to complications for the indenture trustee. The criteria for determining conflicts embodied in the TIA are not exhaustive. As discussed in Chapter XI on the Role of the Indenture Trustee in the Reorganization of the Obligor and Chapter XIX on Theories of Liability That Have Been Raised Against the Indenture Trustee, there are fact patterns not anticipated by the TIA that have led to claims of conflict. Further, for non-TIA debt issues, the provisions of the TIA merely are instructive. Nevertheless, a review of the conflict provisions of the TIA is helpful in analyzing the most frequent problem areas.

Prior to the enactment of the TIA, courts rarely penalized an indenture trustee for having a relationship with the obligor except where there was clearly established self-dealing and bad faith on behalf of the indenture trustee. As originally enacted, the TIA set forth nine relationships that would be considered disabling conflicts and preclude an institution from serving as trustee or, if the relationship arose post-closing, would require the immediate resignation of the indenture trustee. Prior to 1990, the TIA did not preclude the indenture trustee from also acting as lender to the obligor. At least one court specifically found that, prior to default, the mere fact that the indenture trustee might have a relationship with the obligor as lender did not necessarily give rise to a material conflict of interest.[125]

---

121 See Chapter I *supra.*

122 *United States Tr. Co. v. First Nat'l City Bank,* 57 A.D.2d 285, 394 N.Y.S.2d 653 (1st Dep't 1977), *aff'd* 45 N.Y.2d 869, 410 N.Y.S.2d 580, 382 N.E.2d 1355 (1978); *Beck v. Manufacturers Hanover Tr. Co.,* 218 A.D.2d 1, 632 N.Y.S.2d 520 (1st Dep't 1995).

123 15 U.S.C. §77aaa *et seq.*

124 Pub. L. No. 101-550, tit. IV, 104 Stat. 2713 (1990).

125 *Mintener v. Mich. Nat'l Bank,* 324 N.W.2d 110 (Mich. App. 1982).

While maintaining all of the prohibited relationships of the original TIA (and adding that of creditor to the list of forbidden relationships), TIRA modified the time that the indenture trustee would be disqualified on account of a conflicting interest from any time during the life of the transaction to after the occurrence of a default.[126] Thus, pre-default, when the role of the indenture trustee is deemed essentially ministerial, the fact patterns outlined in the TIA are not deemed disqualifying.

Another modification introduced by TIRA was that, if an indenture is qualified under the TIA, then certain provisions under Sections 310(b) (the disqualification of the indenture trustee) and 311 (preferential collection of claims against the obligor) of the TIA will automatically be incorporated into the indenture. A practice followed by many indenture trustees is to flag the trust file if one of the prohibited relationships exists that may be triggered in the event of default. This is particularly true where the indenture trustee is also lender. In such circumstances, it is a good practice also to flag the commercial file from the inception of the acceptance of the trusteeship. Accordingly, where the bank on the commercial side has a relationship with the obligor, if any problem arises, there can be appropriate communication between the commercial and trust departments as to next steps. If a material conflict does arise, the indenture trustee can then proceed to resign and have a successor appointed. This is not to suggest that the establishment of a wall between the departments may not be appropriate. However, given the structure of the TIA after TIRA, it will be necessary to determine the conflict of interest and the status of certain commercial loans at the bank.

B. Checklist as to Conflict of Interest under the Trust Indenture Act of 1939 as Amended by TIRA

1. Whether the indenture trustee is a trustee under any other securities or certificates of interest or participation in any other securities of that obligor.[127]

    a. Under the TIA, there is an exemption for indenture securities only collateralized by securities issued under such other indenture (identical interests since the value of the collateral trust notes is fully dependent on the collateral of the security).

---

126 15 U.S.C. § 77jjj(b). "Default" means default as defined in the indenture, exclusive of any period of grace or requirement of notice. An exception to determining conflicts as of the time of default is the trustee acting as its own or an affiliate's trustee. This always is prohibited regardless of the absence or existence of default. 15 U.S.C. § 77jjj(a)(5).

127 *See* TIA § 310(b)(I).

b. There is an exemption for indentures covering obligations of real estate companies where the obligor has no substantial unmortgaged assets and if each indenture is secured by wholly separated parcels of real estate.

c. There is an exemption for indentures that specifically exclude another specifically described indenture from the operation of the disqualification provisions (*pari passu* provision).

d. There may be situations that may not fit under any of the above specific exemptions where no material conflict of interest may exist given the structure of the transaction and the duties of the respective indenture trustees.

e. Indenture trustees should be alert to certain situations: (i) where the obligor under the indenture is a guarantor of another issue under which the bank also acts as indenture trustee; (ii) where an obligor is merged into or acquired by another obligor for whom the bank acts as indenture trustee; or (iii) where the obligor of one indenture issue is an affiliate of the obligor of another.

2. Whether the indenture trustee or any of the bank's directors or executive officers is an obligor on the indenture securities or an underwriter for such an obligor or has any relationship with either the obligor or the underwriter.[128]

a. Where the trustee or principals of the trustee are also the obligor or the underwriter, the possibility of a conflict is present.

b. In any lending situation to the obligor, a potential conflict may occur. The same may be true with regard to any lending relationship with an underwriter.

---

128 *See* TIA § 310(b)(2).

3. Whether the trustee is an affiliate of either the obligor or the underwriter.[129]

   a. A conflict exists when the indenture trustee is directly or indirectly in control[130] of or is controlled by or in common control with the obligor or an underwriter for the obligor.

   b. Care should be taken to ascertain whether any such "control" relationship exists indirectly and, in such situations, the definition of "control" should be somewhat expansive.

4. Whether there are any interlocking officers and directors of the indenture trustee and obligor or between the indenture trustee and underwriter.[131]

   a. Under the TIA, more than one interlock between the indenture trustee and the obligor or indenture trustee and underwriter of one obligor or one executive officer is prohibited; however, one additional interlock is allowed when the trustee has more than nine directors.

   b. A conflict is present as to the indenture trustee if, in addition to subparagraph a above, any other of the trustee's directors or executive officers is a director, officer, partner or representative either of the obligor or the underwriter for the obligor who is currently engaged in the business of underwriting.

   c. One individual may be a director or executive officer of the trustee and a director or executive officer of the obligor so long as that person is not an executive officer of both.

---

129 *See* TIA § 310(b)(3). Accordingly, the SEC would not provide a no-action letter where a subsidiary of a trustee would have the status of underwriter of the guaranty of the obligor. *Baxter Labs., Inc.*, SEC No-Action Letters, [1971–1977] 71–72 Fed. Sec. L. Rep. (CCH) Dec.,¶ 78, 575 (Nov. 12, 1971).

130 TIA §§ 310(b)(3) and (7) use the word "control." According to the legislative history, "[t]he words 'whether by agency, stock ownership or otherwise', which appeared in Sections 310(b)(3) and 310(b)(7) of the Senate Bill, have been eliminated as unnecessary, in view of the opinion of the Supreme Court on April 17, 1939, in *Rochester Telephone Corporation v. U.S. and the Federal Communications Commission* [59 S.Ct. 754]." H. COMM. REP. No. 1016 (1939), 76th Cong., 1st Sess., p. 47.

131 *See* TIA § 310(b)(4).

5. Whether there is any ownership of the indenture trustee's voting securities.[132]

   a. Under the TIA there is a conflict if the obligor or any partner or executive officer of the obligor owns more than 10 percent of the voting securities of the indenture trustee or if any such person or persons collectively own more than 20 percent of such securities.

   b. A conflict also exists under the TIA if an underwriter of the obligor or any director, partner or executive officer or any combination of these persons owns 10 percent or more of these voting securities.

   c. Even if the obligor or underwriter or any director, partner or executive officer does not have control of the trustee's voting securities, a conflict may exist under the TIA.

6. Whether the indenture trustee owns any of the obligor's voting securities.[133]

   a. A conflict exists if the indenture trustee beneficially owns or holds as collateral for an obligation that is in default: (i) 5 percent or more of the voting securities of the obligor; (ii) 10 percent or more of any other class of the securities other than securities under the indenture; or (iii) 10 percent or more of any class of securities of the underwriter for the obligor.

   b. The bank's ownership of voting securities and the collateral it holds for any obligation should be flagged on the commercial side and on the trust side in order to prevent such a conflict of interest in a default of a commercial loan.

7. Whether the indenture trustee owns voting securities of an affiliate of the obligor.[134]

   a. The indenture trustee has a conflict under the TIA if it beneficially owns or holds as collateral for an obligation in default 5 percent or more of the voting securities of an affiliate (control person) of the obligor, known by the trustee to be such.

---

132 *See* TIA § 310(b)(5).

133 *See* TIA § 310(b)(6).

134 *See* TIA § 310(b)(7).

b. If the indenture trustee owns or so holds that same interest in a person, though not in control of the obligor, but who holds 10 percent or more of the obligor's securities, there is a conflict under the TIA.

c. At the inception of an issue, the relationships between the obligor and its major shareholders and the bank should be explored to determine if any potential conflicts may exist.

8. Whether the indenture trustee owns securities of the parent of the obligor.[135]

a. If the indenture trustee beneficially holds or owns collateral security for an obligation in default 10 percent or more of any class of security of any person who, to the trustee's knowledge, owns 50 percent or more of the voting securities of an obligor, a conflict exists.

b. At the inception of the acceptance of the trusteeship, both the commercial and trust accounts of the parent of the obligor should be flagged as to this possible conflict situation.

9. Whether the indenture trustee holds securities in another trust capacity.[136]

a. There is a conflict of interest under the TIA if the indenture trustee owns, in its capacity as executor administrator, testamentary or inter vivos trustee, guardian, committee or conservator or any similar capacity, an aggregate of 25 percent or more of the voting securities or of any class of securities of the obligor or any other person listed in subparagraphs 6, 7, and 8 of Section 310(b).

b. The trust indenture may provide that if the securities bring the indenture trustee's holdings above the 25 percent limit, in its capacity as executor, testamentary trustee of an estate that includes them, and the holdings of the estate itself are less than the limit, the conflict will not be triggered until two years after the acquisition of the described holding.

c. Under other provisions of the TIA, the indenture trustee, on a yearly basis, is to make a determination of its compliance with the TIA. In exempt issues, it may be helpful to have a periodic review of any

---

135 *See* TIA § 310(b)(8).

136 *See* TIA § 310(b)(9).

conflicts of interest that may arise over holdings of a security in a trust capacity.

d. It should be noted that even if a conflict exists, the trustee still may serve in such ministerial capacities as transfer agent, registrar, custodian, paying agent, escrow agent or depository, provided no other potential or real conflict exists.

10. Whether the indenture trustee is a creditor of the obligor.[137]

As noted, TIRA added Section 310(b)(10), which section provides that a trustee has a conflicting interest if the trustee shall be or shall become a creditor of the obligor. Such creditor relationship was not specifically set forth as a conflict under prior law. Under Section 303(10) of the TIA, "indenture trustee" is defined to mean each trustee of the indenture to be qualified and each successor trustee. Thus, whether or not a conflict exists is to be determined by examining the lending relationship of the bank that serves as trustee. The definition does not appear to include the parent of the trustee as lender.

Moreover, the time period during which the "underwriter" conflict is measured is reduced to one year prior to the time the determination is made. Under prior law, the relevant time period was three years. Further, in structured financing, where the trustee and the notes or certificateholders look to a collateral pool for payment and the issuer does not have liability for the ultimate pledge, there may be a lack of a practical conflict if each trust looks to its own specific collateral for payment. Of interest is the effect of the language in Section 310 of the Trust Indenture Act of 1939, 15 U.S.C. § 77jjj(b):

> "For the purposes of this subsection, an indenture trustee shall be deemed to have a conflicting interest if the indenture securities are in default (as such term is defined in such indenture, but exclusive of any period of grace or requirement of notice) and—
>
> (1) such trustee is trustee under another indenture under which any other securities, or certificates of interest or participation in any other securities, of an obligor upon the indenture securities are outstanding or is trustee for more than one outstanding series of securities, as hereinafter defined, under a single indenture of an obligor, unless—

---

137 *See* TIA § 310(b)(10).

(A) the indenture securities are collateral trust notes under which the only collateral consists of securities issued under such other indenture,

(B) such other indenture is a collateral trust indenture under which the only collateral consists of indenture securities, or

(C) such obligor has no substantial unmortgaged assets and is engaged primarily in the business of owning, or of owning and developing and/or operating, real estate, and the indenture to be qualified and such other indenture are secured by wholly separate and distinct parcels of real estate . . . .

For purposes of 'paragraph 1' of this subsection, and of section 316(a) of this title, the term 'series of securities' or 'series' means a series, class or group of securities issuable under an indenture pursuant to whose terms holders of one such series may vote to direct the indenture trustee, or otherwise take action pursuant to a vote of such holders, separately from the holders of another such series; Provided, That 'series of securities' or 'series' shall not include any series of securities issuable under an indenture if all such series rank equally and are wholly unsecured."[138]

Section 310 of the TIA, by its specific terms, limits a conflict among series of securities to those instances in which any series *votes separately* from the other series to direct the trustee. If, under the terms of an indenture, the senior notes under each of the series provide direction to the trustee, the conflict of interest that could confront a trustee representing multiple series within a

---

138 The SEC granted the application for a finding that the trusteeship of a trust company under eighteen indentures covering eighteen series of first mortgage collateral bonds of an obligor was not likely to involve a material conflict of interest so as to make it necessary to disqualify the trust company, where each series of bonds was secured by its own collateral, a default in one series constituted a default in all series, and each series had a proportionate interest in any surplus of collateral. *Prudence-Bonds Corporation*, FSLR SELECTED RELEASES [1940–1972], SEC Docket 41–44 Fed. Sec. L. Rep. (CCH) ¶75, 432, Trust Indenture Act Release No. 28 (Mar. 9, 1944). Further, a no-action letter was granted holding that the serial issuance of a company's first mortgage bonds would not be deemed a series of securities where each series is secured on an equal and ratable basis by a certain mortgage and deed of trust, the indenture provides that holders of at least a majority in aggregate outstanding principal amount of bonds may direct the trustee in the exercise of its duties under the indenture and to the extent any such direction affects holders of bonds issued under one or more but less than all outstanding series, such direction may be authorized by at least a majority in aggregate principal amount of the affected series. *Tucson Electric Power Co.*, SEC No-Action Letters, [1983-2003] Fed. Sec. L. Rep. (CCH) ¶76,160 (Jan. 8, 1992).

single indenture and receiving conflicting directions under the terms of the indenture does not exist.

Under the provisions of the TIA, if an indenture trustee has or acquires a conflicting interest as described above, within 90 days after ascertaining that it has such a conflicting interest, assuming such conflicting interest has not been cured or otherwise eliminated, such trustee is either to eliminate such conflicting interest or, except as set forth below, to resign and the obligor shall take prompt steps to have a successor appointed pursuant to the terms of the indenture.[139] Any resignation of an indenture trustee becomes effective only upon the appointment of a successor trustee and such successor's acceptance of such appointment.[140]

C. When a Trustee Is Not Required to Resign upon a Default

Section 310(b) of the TIA provides that, except in the case of a monetary default, upon a default in the payment of the principal of or interest on any indenture security, or on the payment of any sinking or purchase fund installment ("Monetary Default"), the indenture trustee shall not be required to resign as provided by Section 310 if there is a non-monetary default so long as such trustee shall have sustained the burden of proving, on application to the SEC and at the opportunity for hearing thereon, that (i) the default under the indenture may be cured or waived during a reasonable period and under the procedures described in such application, and (ii) a stay of the trustee's duty to resign will not be inconsistent with the interest of holders of the indenture securities. The filing of such application shall automatically stay the performance of the duty to resign until the SEC orders otherwise.

D. Trustee as Lender: Sharing Provisions

Section 311 of the TIA prevents a bank that is both a creditor and an indenture trustee from being favored by the obligor as lender by means of an elaborate sharing provision. Section 311 of the TIA provides that where the bank that is indenture trustee is a creditor of the obligor, directly or indirectly, secured or unsecured within three months prior or subsequent to a monetary default (unless it is cured), the bank must set apart and hold in a special account for the benefit of the bank individually and for the holders of the bonds an amount equal to any and all reductions in the amount due and owing upon any claim as creditor with respect to principal and interest after the beginning of such three-month period prior to the monetary default. It must also set apart all property received in respect of any claim as creditor, either as security therefor or in

---

139 §77jjj(b)(i). Similarly, OCC Interpretative Ruling 12 C.F.R. 9.100 provides that a national bank may act both as indenture trustee and as a creditor until 90 days after default if the bank maintains adequate controls to manage the potential conflicts of interest.

140 §77jjj(b).

satisfaction or composition thereof, after the beginning of such three-month period and set apart an amount equal to the proceeds of such property if it should have been disposed of.

Section 311 is not intended to affect the right of the bank to retain for its own account: (1) payments made on account of any such claim by any person other than the company who is liable thereon; (2) the proceeds of any bona fide sale of such claim by the bank to a third person; (3) distributions made in cash, securities or other property in respect of claims filed against the company in bankruptcy or receivership or in proceedings for reorganization pursuant to the Federal Bankruptcy Code; (4) payments or realization for its own account upon any property held by it as security for such claim if such property was so held prior to the beginning of the three-month period; and (5) realization or payment for its own account to the extent that the claim was secured simultaneously with its creation by any property held by it as security for such claim even if the secured claim was created within the three-month period. If such claim was created after the three-month period and such property was received as security simultaneously with the creation thereof, the bank must sustain the burden of proving that at the time such property was so received, the bank had no reasonable cause to believe that a default would occur within three months. The bank is not precluded from receiving payment on any claim against the release of any property held as security for such claim to the extent of the fair value of such property. Section 311 goes on to describe in great detail the method for accounting of the funds and property held in the special account and the apportionment thereof. Generally, Section 311 requires the trustee and holders to realize the same percentages from the distribution in bankruptcy. The funds in the special proceeds accounts are to be used to adjust upward the holders' share of distribution until it equals the combined percentage return to the bank as lender.

Not only is the preferential payment of bank claims precluded by statute, it is also contrary to the common law. In *Dabney v. Chase National Bank,*[141] a bankruptcy trustee brought an action against the indenture trustee to compel an accounting under the indenture. The defendant trustee in this case collected a loan owed to it by the debtor at the time the trustee had reasonable grounds to believe the debtor was not solvent or was in imminent danger of insolvency. The court held that the trustee was liable for the difference between the amount of the loan it collected and the value of the claim of the trustee as representative of the debentureholders. The court held that it is the duty of a trustee not to profit at the possible expense of its beneficiary. It is part of the trustee's obligation to give its beneficiary its undivided loyalty, free from any conflicting personal interest. The court held that the provisions of the indenture cannot relieve the trustee of its duty to discharge obligations under the indenture with

---

141 196 F.2d 668 (2d Cir. 1952), *cert. dismissed*, 346 U.S. 863 (1953).

absolute singleness of purpose, free from conflicts of interest. The court in *Dabney*, under common law principles, looked back more than six years to hold the trustee liable to account to the holders. Given the harshness of the common law, Section 311 can, to a degree, be viewed as a safe harbor from the results of *Dabney*.

It should be clear that no indenture trustee wants to find itself in this type of Section 311 dilemma with the commercial side of the bank. Therefore, a conscientious indenture trustee that is also a lender, if it has knowledge of a troubled situation, will resign as indenture trustee before any of the provisions of Section 311 are triggered. A practice followed by many banks is to flag the trust file and the commercial file from the inception of the acceptance of any indenture trusteeship in which the commercial side of the bank has a relationship with the obligor. Then, if any problem arises, there can be appropriate communication between the commercial and trust departments. If a potential for material conflict does arise, the indenture trustee can then resign and have a successor appointed. It is important that an indenture trustee have a good working relationship with another qualified indenture trustee who may act as a successor in times of difficulty to assist in the timely transfer of responsibility.

E. Finding the Successor Trustee and the Mechanics of Documenting the Succession

It is in the best interest of the indenture trustee who must resign because of a default situation to obtain as a successor an indenture trustee experienced in handling default and bankruptcy situations. Ultimate recovery by the bondholders, and therefore their reaction to the way the matter was handled, is directly related to the skill utilized by the successor indenture trustee in administering the default. There are certain corporate trust departments that have developed a well-known expertise in this area. It is wise to begin your search for a successor trustee with one of those experienced successor trustees. The bondholders also may express a preference for certain institutions. A retiring indenture trustee will be constrained in its selection by the requirements of the indenture which set capital and surplus requirements and often a principal place of business location for a qualified trustee. If, however, in the case of a massive default it is impossible to obtain an indenture trustee in the designated state, court orders have been obtained permitting an out-of-state institution with the requisite capital and surplus requirements to serve as successor indenture trustee. Sometimes the documents evidencing the succession will be prepared by the resigning indenture trustee and its counsel; other times, the successor trustee will insist on its own documentation. A supplemental indenture, if such can be obtained, is most helpful to the successor trustee in the case of a secured transaction since it clearly confirms the rights and interests of the successor trustee in the trust estate. Any succession agreement, regardless of form, should contain a clear and complete statement of the transfer of all trust funds, rights, powers and claims to the successor, and a representation by the successor trustee of its qualification to serve as successor indenture trustee and necessary corporate authorization to enter into the agreement. The succession agreement should contain the appointment by the obligor of the successor trustee and the acceptance by the successor trustee of the appointment. Most importantly, the document should recite and confirm the transfer of the trust powers and collateral, if any. Moreover, to the extent possible, the obligor should be a party to this agreement. Appendix VI-A is a list of the documents frequently drafted regarding a succession.

Often, the transfer agency and registrar duties are also transferred and such should be embodied in the succession document. This document should provide that the company will give notice of the succession to the holders and should indicate the applicability of the original indenture, except as modified. If a bankruptcy has not taken place and there is collateral involved, it may be wise to record the instrument of succession. If the matter is in bankruptcy, in the case of a secured transaction, it is extremely helpful to have the bankruptcy court bless the succession and find that: (1) it is proper for the successor indenture trustee to serve; (2) the rights, claims and powers of the retiring trustee are fully vested in the successor trustee; and (3) the recording of any necessary documents is appropriate. It is also helpful to obtain officers' certificates from both the company and the retiring trustee describing the defaults of which they are aware and an opinion of company counsel indicating compliance with the terms of the original indenture.

Given the provisions of the TIA that the indenture trustee who is also a lender must promptly find a successor trustee upon the occurrence of the default, is incumbent upon the indenture trustee to devise mechanisms to ensure that a prompt succession will take place. One approach that can be taken is to have already designated, formally or informally, the successor trustee. This may include preapproved documentation regarding the succession. In fact, it may even be advisable to have such documentation prepared, executed and held in escrow, thereby allowing for these documents to be released upon the occurrence of the default and for the resignation of the trustee to be conveyed to the escrow agent.

F. Indemnification of Successor Indenture Trustee

In a default context, the successor indenture trustee is stepping into an extremely challenging situation. Obviously, no financial institution would assume such a difficult and time-consuming job if it was not certain of being paid for its time and expenses. While most indentures generally provide a promise on the part of the company to pay the fees and expenses of the indenture trustee, if a company is not paying its debt service, it certainly is not going to worry about the fees and expenses of the indenture trustee. Therefore, the successor indenture trustee will need an assured source of payment for such on a regular basis. Although, as will be discussed in Chapter XI, it may be possible under certain circumstances in a bankruptcy of the obligor for the indenture trustee to obtain some of its fees and expenses for contributing to the reorganization of the company or as part of the payment of the indenture trustee's contract claim, there is no assurance that such will be paid in total. Therefore, typically a successor indenture trustee will not assume that role without an adequate indemnity agreement from the retiring trustee. Such indemnity agreement will provide for the orderly transfer of the trusteeship's books, records, and information and will contain a promise by the retiring trustee to pay the fees and expenses of the successor indenture trustee, including its consultants', advisors', and counsel fees within a short period of time if not received from the obligor.

Generally, the fees of the successor trustee will include extraordinary fees arising out of default administration in addition to its regular annual administration fee. The agreement should make it clear that the successor trustee has the discretion to employ such counsel, experts, advisors or professionals that it needs with respect to the administration of the trusteeship and that the fees for these consultants will be paid by the retiring trustee. Moreover, the retiring trustee will indemnify the successor trustee and hold it harmless against any and all loss that may have been caused directly or indirectly by any action or omission of the retiring trustee during its tenure or as a result of the acceptance of the successor trusteeship by the successor trustee.

Indemnification will not take place for damages that arise out of the misconduct or negligence of the successor trustee. A point for negotiation is whether such will be limited to willful misconduct or gross negligence. The length of the indemnity should be sufficient to cover any possible claims that may arise down the road and certainly should extend to a period after the conclusion of any bankruptcy proceeding. The agreement may provide that if the successor trustee feels, in its sole discretion, it must resign as successor trustee, it can assign and transfer the benefits of the agreement to a qualified third indenture trustee.

In a situation where there are large institutional holders or an already existing bondholder group, the larger organized bondholders can be helpful to the retiring trustee in obtaining or supporting a successor trustee or providing a direction with the requisite percentage of securities outstanding under the indenture to direct the trustee to appoint a certain successor or to appoint a successor trustee pursuant to the specific terms of the indenture. From the bondholder perspective, cooperation and assistance with the retiring trustee in appointing a qualified and experienced successor trustee is in the best interests of all, and in the default situation will aid in maximizing an appropriate recovery or resolution of the default. In some cases, large institutional holders or the organized bondholder groups have facilitated the obtaining of a successor trustee by acknowledging that the lien of the successor trustee for reasonable fees and expenses is senior to payment on bonds. *See, e.g.,* Letter and Direction and Appointment of Wells Fargo Bank Northwest N.A. as Successor Trustee for the Delta Airlines 9.50% Senior Secured Notes, Oct. 2005.

G. Common Indenture Provisions Governing Resignation and Successor Indenture Trustees

The TIA provides and most indentures include the provision that no resignation or removal of the indenture trustee or appointment of a successor trustee is effective until the acceptance of an appointment by the successor trustee. That means an indenture trustee cannot resign and leave the holders unprotected. If the resigning trustee is unable to secure a successor trustee and feels compelled to resign, the common indenture language provides that within 30 days after giving a notice of resignation, the resigning trustee may petition a court of competent jurisdiction for the appointment of a successor trustee. Of course, a common provision permits the holders of a majority in principal amount of the outstanding bonds to remove the trustee. The issue of the selection and indemnification of the successor trustee in such circumstances is often thrust upon the holders. Many indentures provide that if the trustee resigns or is incapable of acting, the company can appoint a successor trustee until a new trustee has been appointed by the holders. Ultimately, it is the holders who should choose or approve their fiduciary since the company's choice may not be in the best interest of holders, especially given the circumstances that brought about the resignation.

H. Possible Claims of Successor Indenture Trustee Against Prior Indenture Trustee

Unfortunately, one of the obligations of the successor trustee is the sensitive task of reviewing the performance of the retiring trustee to determine whether or not there is a possible claim on behalf of the holders against the retiring trustee. Such claims typically arise in situations where the bank was not only the original trustee but also a lender and where events took place that benefited the bank to the detriment of the holders. For example, in *United States Trust Company v. First National City Bank*,[142] the successor indenture trustee brought an action against the original trustee on the ground that it had favored its own interest as individual creditor of the obligor over the interests of the debentureholders it had a duty to represent. In that case, the court held that a complaint filed by the successor indenture trustee stated a cause of action against the original trustee, because its redelivery of stock within four months prior to default constituted property received by the defendant as security for its individual creditor claim and was thus subject to the sharing requirements of the indenture and Section 311 of the TIA. Further, the court sustained the complaint on the theory that regular quarterly interest payments due on a grid note issued under a revolving credit agreement that was entered into by the defendant as agent for itself and three other banks, and which provided that the four banks agreed to make loans to the obligor, was a payment subject to the sharing requirements of the indenture and Section 311. In addition, the court refused to dismiss the allegation against the original trustee

---

142 394 N.Y.S.2d (App. Div. 1977).

that, with respect to funds the defaulting obligor had on deposit in general deposit accounts with the defendant and with three other banks, pursuant to revolving credit agreements, the banks' exercise of setoff against balances to reduce the amount owed under the revolving credit agreement came within the sharing requirements of the indenture and Section 311.

It must be clear in the indemnity agreement referred to above that the cost of such efforts will be paid by the retiring trustee even though it is the cost of litigating the rights of the holders against the indemnitor. It should be noted that a successor indenture trustee who discovers that the retiring trustee has, within three months of the date of default, received as lender a significant paydown or collateral for antecedent debt should consider appropriate methods of ensuring protection of the holders. Such measures include determining whether the default that has occurred is a monetary default which will trigger Section 311 liability and sharing on the part of the retiring trustee. In this regard, if a non-monetary default has occurred within three months of that date, and if the retiring trustee received as lender a significant paydown or collateral, then the successor trustee should consider the question of acceleration in order to trigger a monetary default and thereby provide for the holders the benefits of Section 311 and its sharing provision. For example, a retiring trustee as lender may have received a significant cash paydown or collateral less than 90 days from the date of the filing of a bankruptcy. The voluntary bankruptcy of the obligor is an immediate event of default but is not a monetary default that will trigger Section 311. Accordingly, the successor indenture trustee should consider whether or not, given the seriousness of the situation, it would be prudent to accelerate immediately by application to the bankruptcy court or by notice to the obligor, in order to obtain the benefits of Section 311. An indenture trustee that is also a lender, when faced with this situation, should consider acceleration in order to discharge its duty to holders even though such acceleration may be contrary to the best interest of the bank.

I. Mergers and Acquisitions of Indenture Trustees and Obligors

Sometimes a lender is aware of the potential conflict at the time it becomes an indenture trustee. There are other situations, however, in which the indenture trustee has no ability to foresee the problem. One example of this is the situation in which a bank acting as indenture trustee is acquired or merged into another bank that is the indenture trustee for another debt security of the same obligor qualified under the TIA. Problems will occur when both trust departments are merged. Some have attempted to set up a trust company independent from the merged bank as a means of avoiding the conflict. Likewise, if one obligor of a debt security issued under the TIA acquires or merges with another obligor for which the same bank acts as indenture trustee on a qualified issue of debt securities, there would be a conflict if the original obligor assumes the obligations under the acquired company's debt securities. The situation, however, becomes more difficult when it is not a straightforward acquisition, but rather is an acquisition by the subsidiary of the obligor or by a parent of the obligor. Such affiliate relationships are not *per se* prohibited under the TIA, and generally the rationale for not prohibiting such affiliated relationships is that holders purportedly look only to the entity that is the direct obligor and not elsewhere. The indenture trustee that acts in this capacity for both subsidiary debt instruments and holding company debt instruments, however, may clearly have a potential conflict. Absent a guaranty, such indenture trustee may still have a problem to the extent that the indenture trustee of the holding company may, for equitable reasons, need to trace the proceeds of that issue down into the subsidiary where it also acts as an indenture trustee. Such a potential conflict means that care should be exercised in accepting and continuing to serve as indenture trustee for affiliated obligors. For this purpose, an affiliate means a corporation or entity that is owned or controlled by the other entity for which the indenture trustee acts. The one possible exception to the merger conflicts is where the indentures have specific language that provides that the debt under such indentures is treated as *pari passu* and the trustee may act under their terms. If, in fact, at the time of the issuance of the securities there is contemplated a merger either of banks or of obligors, such *pari passu* treatment can be provided for in the documents and the problem can be avoided.

In addition to problems created by mergers, a series of problems have been created by companies selling plants or facilities to other companies that have either conduit financing debt or separate subsidiary public debt issues where the acquiring company assumes the obligation to pay that indebtedness while it remains the primary obligation of the transferor company. That assumption of obligation may trigger a conflict if the indenture trustee on the original security is also indenture trustee on the public debt instruments that are not in parity with the acquiring company. The charts set forth in Appendices VI-C and D indicate conflicts created by the merger of the obligors, by the merger of banks and by the assumption by a new obligor of debt for which the indenture trustee also acts as indenture trustee.

Appendix VI-A
Documents Typically Drafted to Evidence Appointment of Successor Trustee

Re: Company Name, Name of Issue

DOCUMENTS RELATING TO APPOINTMENT FOR SUCCESSOR TRUSTEE FOR DEBENTURE ISSUE

1. Name of Retiring Trustee
2. Company Name
3. Name of Successor Trustee

#1 First Supplemental Indenture dated as of _______________ between Company, Retiring Trustee as Original Trustee and Successor Trustee or, in the alternative, a Tri-Party Agreement among Company, Retiring Trustee and Successor Trustee.

#2 Company Officers' Certificate evidencing the authorization of certain officers to execute the First Supplemental Indenture or Tri-Party Agreement and Resolution of Company relating thereto.

#3 Opinion of Company's counsel to Successor Trustee as to Effectiveness of Transfer.

#4 Letter to Security holders whose names and addresses are known to Retiring Trustee to be sent to such holders informing them of its resignation as Trustee for the above-cited Security Issue and the appointment of Successor Trustee and the execution of the First Supplemental Indenture or Tri-Party Agreement to this effect.*

#5 Letter of Transmittal of Company to Successor Trustee enclosing the relevant documents.

#6 Letter of Retiring Trustee to Successor Trustee regarding the orderly transfer of trusteeship, books, records and information; status of issue; and representation that there is no known default, or setting forth known defaults.

---

* Similar documentation would evidence resignation for a debenture note or bond issue except that, in a secured debt issue, transfer of interest in collateral must be documented.

#7 Proposed Officer's Certificate of Retiring Trustee regarding Indenture, First Supplemental Indenture or Tri-Party Agreement to be submitted to Successor Trustee after the execution of documents.

#8 Company's proposed Resolutions of the Board of Directors relating to the First Supplemental Indenture or Tri-Party Agreement.

#9. Notice of Resignation and Appointment of Successor Indenture Trustee for the Security Issue.

#10 Secretary's Certificate of Company evidencing the authorization of certain officers to execute the First Supplemental Indenture or Tri-Party Agreement and Resolutions of Company relating thereto.

#11 Agreement between Retiring Trustee and Successor Trustee relating to the transfer of the trusteeship.

#12 Letter of Resignation of Retiring Trustee.

#13 Incumbency Certificates of Retiring Trustee and Successor Trustee.

#14 Form or Court Order, if necessary, if Successor Trustee does not meet all requirements of Indenture, if there is a possible conflict or if necessary to confirm transfer of collateral.

Appendix VI-B
Conflict of Interest – Assumption of Debt or Assets

Conflicts arise when ownership of a plant is transferred between Company A and Company B and each company uses the same Indenture Trustee.

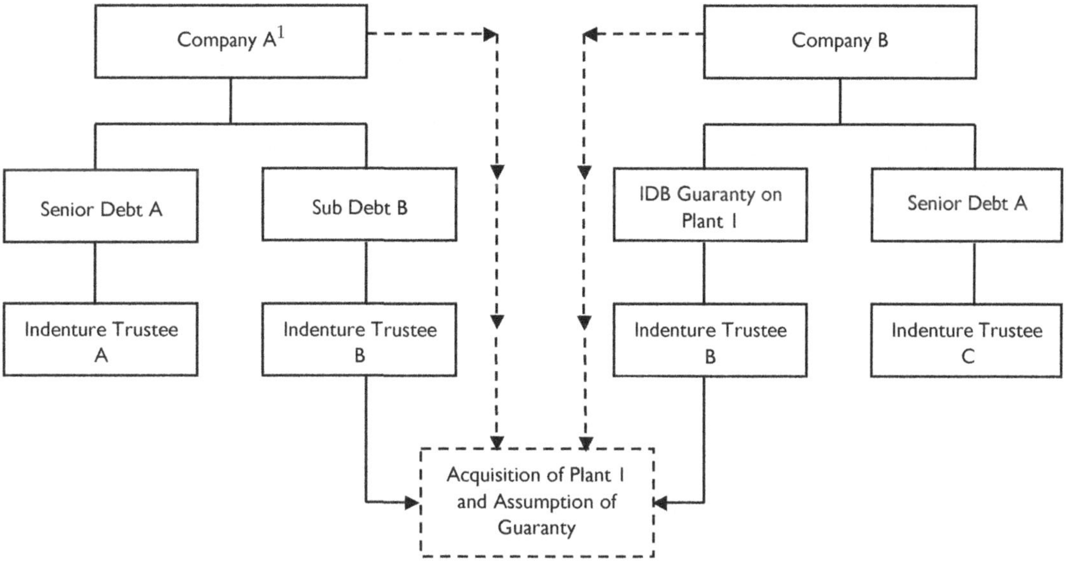

1 Company A acquires Plant 1 and assumes the guaranty, which creates a conflict of interest for Indenture Trustee B in the non-*pari passu* Subordination Debt B.

Appendix VI-C Conflict of Interest – Merger of Banks

Conflicts arise when two banks merge and combine their trust functions in the new "Merger Bank." The issuer (Company A) is now faced with a situation where the Indenture Trustee of both senior and subordinated debt is one and the same.

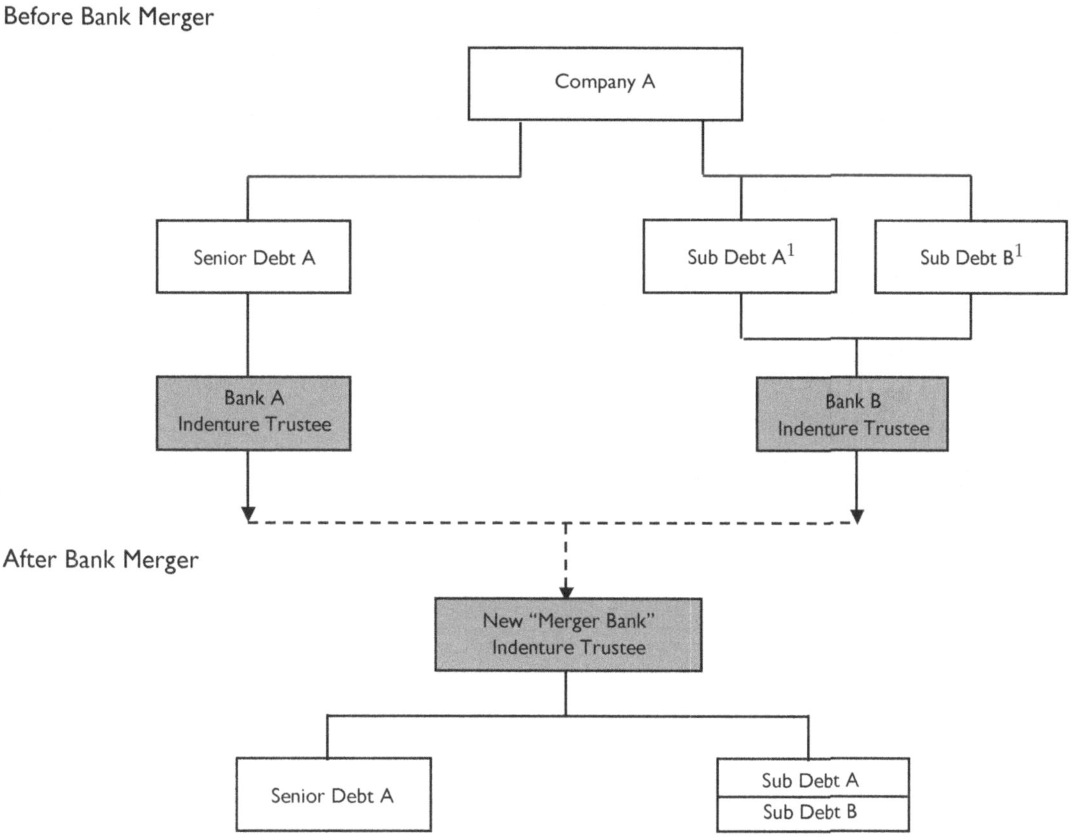

1 Subordinated Debt A and B are both *pari passu* by the express language of the Indenture. No pre-merger conflict exists between senior and subordinated debt issues, but that situation changes with the new "Merger Bank."

Appendix VI-D Conflict of Interest – Merger of Obligors

Conflicts arise when two companies merge and consolidate their operations into a new legal entity called "Merger Co." Prior to the merger, there were no problems since there were two separate companies. After the merger, the same indenture trustee is acting for senior and subordinated debt of the same obligor. the indenture trustee must now be alert to corporate merger and acquisition, which can cause conflict.

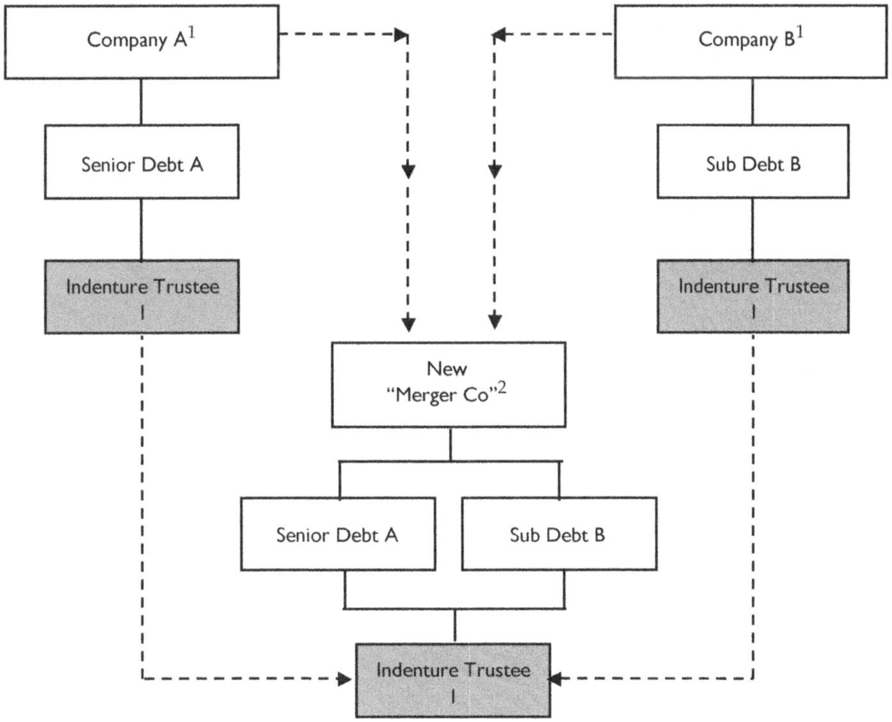

1 Prior to merger, Company A and B are separate and distinct corporations, and there is no conflict for Indenture Trustee 1.

2 Post-merger, new "Merger Co" is the obligor on old Company A Senior and old Company B Subordinated Debt, both of which have the same indenture trustee.

VII. The Three Phases of Default and Checklist of Considerations

A. Introduction

It is important for both the indenture trustee and the bondholders to understand the phases of activity through which an indenture trustee must proceed in order to achieve an appropriate resolution of the default. Obviously, the timing of the phases will depend upon the particular circumstances surrounding the default. If the situation is one that is fast breaking and seriously eroding, phases one through three may occur quite quickly, possibly within the same day. If there is more time, because the indenture trustee or the bondholders were capable of spotting either the default or trouble ahead of time, the indenture trustee or the bondholders may have a period of days, weeks or months in between each phase in order to achieve the desired result. It is most important that the indenture trustee, in considering the three phases of default, recognize that time is of the essence and that a quick but reasoned process is preferable to an unduly prolonged process to obtain a result. After discussing the phases of default, this chapter will present a checklist of considerations once an indenture trustee is aware of the default. This checklist will refer to other chapters in order to provide a full exposition of the matters covered. The purpose of the checklist is to provide the indenture trustee with a quick reference to the types of problems that should be considered during the various phases of a default.

Before venturing into a discussion of general default considerations and remedies, it is helpful to review the three phases of default and the activities that occupy the indenture trustee during these three phases.

B. Phase One: Gathering of All Documents and Perfected Security or Additional Security

When faced with a default, the indenture trustee should quickly verify and re-confirm that all documents that should be signed are signed, and that all documents that should have been recorded are recorded. Special attention should be paid to whether appropriate continuation statements of UCC filings have been made. It may be possible to obtain additional security during this period of time, although the indenture trustee should be aware that others may challenge the pledge of new collateral during this period on preference grounds or other avoidance theories, should the obligor file a chapter 11 proceeding within 90 days or even a year of the additional pledge.[143]

The indenture trustee, on being notified or learning of the existence of the default, should review the indenture and related documents to insure that the indenture trustee has all required documentation, is aware of all existing defaults and is aware of the process the documents require be followed to assert rights on behalf of holders. The one default coming to the attention of the indenture trustee may not be the only existing default under the terms of the indenture. The indenture trustee should thus examine the indenture to be sure that, in giving notice to the obligor and to the holders, all defaults that are known or that should be known by the indenture trustee are the subject matter of such notice. It is extremely embarrassing for an indenture trustee to provide notice to the holders of a default stemming from failure to provide an insurance certificate, no-default certificate or annual report, and yet fail to inform the holders that the obligor is in bankruptcy or that the obligor has failed to make sinking fund payments for the past two years. Once the indenture trustee learns of a problem with regard to compliance with the indenture, the indenture trustee should make sure that all problems capable of being discovered are discovered and properly noticed. The indenture trustee should review the indenture to determine whether the default occurring also triggers a cross-default in any other transaction document. The notice of default should contain language confirming that the notice may not contain an exhaustive list of defaults and that the indenture trustee reserves the right to supplement the information as it obtains knowledge of any additional defaults or events of default. At this time, the indenture trustee should welcome the input of interested holders.

There have been a number of examples in which an indenture trustee that did not have certain documents, including annual reports of the obligor, certificates of insurance and accountant's certificates, was able, once a default was known, to obtain missing documentation in order to complete the indenture trustee's file and to gain a better understanding of the current situation. In a different example, an indenture trustee, after reviewing its file and learning facts necessary to apprise it of the situation, was able to obtain additional collateral, which ultimately became the true source of repayment to the holders. While a beleaguered obligor at the time of a monetary default typically does not have enough money to pay its creditors, earlier problems such as failure to provide financial statements, failure to provide certificates of insurance or failure to provide default certificates may provide an opportunity for the indenture trustee to discuss with the obligor ways of providing assurance to the holders that payment will be made.

---

143 *See* Chapter X on preferences, generally a payment or pledge made during the 90-day period prior to a bankruptcy filing or a year if the preferred creditor has insider status.

It is during phase one, after reviewing the documents and obtaining, if necessary, any and all supplementary documentation or collateral, that the indenture trustee can obtain additional information concerning the status of the obligor's compliance with the terms of the indenture and the obligor's financial condition, in order better to assess what actions the indenture trustee should take in the following phases.

C. Phase Two: Attempts to Refinance, Workout and Settle All Problems

After the indenture trustee is satisfied that its file is in order, the indenture trustee should obtain as much financial information as it can with respect to the obligor and determine, with the assistance of counsel, accounting experts or financial advisors, if necessary, whether or not a refinancing or workout is possible. It simply makes sense for the indenture trustee to explore this possibility prior to the institution of available remedies. Particularly if the indenture trustee has been able to identify large beneficial holders or an organized group of holders that have the requisite percentage of outstanding securities of the issue to direct, instruct and indemnify the trustee under the terms of the indenture, it will be prudent to determine their views or the appropriate direction of the requisite holders with respect to a workout or action to be taken.

The indenture trustee should explore all possible means of resolving the default, without compromising any of the rights or potential remedies open to the indenture trustee and the holders. Many times obligors will tell the indenture trustee that it just needs a brief rest from the demands of creditors and that a moratorium or forbearance agreement would be in the best interests of all parties. By and large, the absence of payment by the obligor is in fact a moratorium until a court order can be obtained to force the obligor to make payment if the obligor is capable of doing so. Hindsight is far clearer and probably harsher on moratoriums than would be expected in the initial stages of a default. Normally, indenture trustees do not enter into moratorium or forbearance agreements without being directed, instructed and indemnified by the holders. Much of what happens during this phase and beyond may be dictated by a group or groups of actual holders and their counsel, who may seek to lead the negotiations with the obligor to control the outcome. All will benefit from a spirit of cooperation between the indenture trustee and the holders.

D. Phase Three: Acceleration, Foreclosure Litigation, Collection of Debt

After the indenture trustee has its file in order, has obtained financial information from the obligor and has satisfied itself that a refinancing or workout is not possible, the indenture trustee must resort to the exercise of remedies. Such should really be looked upon as a last resort and may be used as a last resort if the indenture trustee has been careful to preserve all of its rights and remedies throughout the administration of the default. Ideally, the exercise of remedies will have been discussed with and directed by the requisite percentage of holders under the terms of the indenture. In the following pages, general principles governing the administration of a default, non-bankruptcy remedies and bankruptcy remedies will be summarized.

E. Checklist of Considerations Once an Indenture Trustee or Bondholder Is Aware of a Default

1. Type of Default and Its Effects (See, *e.g.*, Chapter IV)

a. Defaults in the Payment of Principal and Interest

Usually indentures provide a grace period for default in payment of interest but not for defaults in the payment of principal.[144]

b. Defaults Affecting or Impairing the Security of the Issue

Some indentures provide that the obligor is obligated to refrain from taking any action that, while not specifically prohibited by the indenture, would impair the security for the issue, such as a transfer of pledged revenues to other than the intended debtholders prior to scheduled interest or principal payments or the contention of the municipality that the pledge of revenues or the underlying contract is invalid.[145]

c. Defaults Other Than a and b above of Covenants Contained in the Indenture

1) Failure to supply required documentation (financial reports, insurance certificates, certificates of compliance, etc.).[146]

2) Default under other indentures, agreements or similar instruments of debt of the obligor.

3) Proven material, untrue representations and warranties of the obligor relating to the issue.

4) Insolvency, bankruptcy, receivership or incapacity of the obligor.[147]

5) Judgments against the obligor over a certain amount, which remain unsatisfied after a grace period.

---

144 *See* MDI §§ 501(1) and (2); MBI §§ 9.01A and B; and MSI § 6.01.

145 *See* MBI § 9.20.

146 *See* MBI § 9.01C; MDI § 501(3); and MSI § 4.03.

147 *See* MDI §§ 601(4) and (5); MBI §§ 9.01D and E; and MSI § 6.01.

6) Failure to make reserve or sinking fund payments.

d. Whether Default or Events of Default Exist and the Requirement of Notice to the Obligor for the Commencement of the Grace Period

2. Time Is of the Essence

a. All security and additional security should be perfected or acquired, if necessary.

b. All covenants and obligations of the obligor under the indenture should be reviewed to determine if there are any other existing defaults.

c. Preservation of collateral and protection against further erosion.

1) Prevent any withdrawal of trust funds.

2) Prevent authentication of new securities, but not the transfer of existing securities.

3) Take actions necessary to preserve, protect, maintain and insure the collateral pledged to the trust for the benefit of the holders.

3. Investigation by the Indenture Trustee or Bondholder into the Nature and Extent of Defaults under the Indenture

a. Communication with the obligor (see, *e.g.*, Chapter V).

b. Businesslike tone and type of communication of a trustee investigating whether defaults exist.

c. Notice to the obligor, if required, of the existence of the default, requesting that it be immediately cured, and the form of such notice.

d. No waiver by the trustee or holder of any rights under the indenture.[148]

e. Inspection and analysis of records of obligor and others.

1) Hiring of experts to analyze the books and records and to trace the use of funds.

2) The necessity of an identified paper trail to prove any theory of equitable subordination or constructive trust.[149]

---

148 *See* MBI §§ 9.14 and 9.15.

149 *See Fosdick v. Schall*, 99 U.S. 235 (1879); *Virginia Ry. & Power Co. v. Davis*, 284 F. 479 (4th Cir. 1922), *cert. denied*, 260 U.S. 746 (1923). *See also* 11 U.S.C. § 510.

3) Availability of records under the public records laws.

4) Examination of Debtor under Section 341 of the Bankruptcy Code.

4. Actions to Be Taken in the Bankruptcy Proceedings (See, e.g., Chapters X and XI)

a. File appearance.

b. Institute complaint to lift or modify automatic stay and for adequate protection.[150]

c. Object to use of cash collateral where questionable liens of other creditors are sought to be approved or proposed in cash collateral order that contains provisions unfavorable to trustee or holders.

d. Institute adversary proceedings.

1) Request monetary judgment for any unliquidated or disputed claims.

2) Request specific performance.

3) Request lift stay to permit foreclosure of security for issue.

4) Request other legal or equitable relief.

e. Petition for sale of property or collateral (judicial and non-judicial).

f. File proof of claim in bankruptcy.

g. Consider joining creditors' committee if unsecured.

h. Negotiate plan treatment of bondholders, ideally with significant input from bondholders.

i. Monitor, appear and file papers in bankruptcy proceedings to the extent relevant to the rights of the holders.[151]

i. Where appropriate, urge necessary action upon the debtor in possession or reorganization trustee.[152]

---

150 *See* 11 U.S.C. §§ 362(d) and (e); *see In re Cont'l Airlines, Inc.*, 154 B.R. 176 (Bankr. D. Del. 1993), *appeal dismissed as moot* 91 F.3d 553 (3d Cir. 1996).

151 *See Bitker v. Hotel Duluth Co.*, 83 F.2d 721 (8th Cir. 1936), *cert. denied*, 299 U.S. 577 (1936); *In re Int'l Power Sec. Corp.*, 119 F. Supp. 31 (D.N.J. 1954).

152 *In re Multiponics, Inc.*, 436 F. Supp. 1072 (E.D. La. 1977), *aff'd*, 622 F.2d 731 (5th Cir. 1980).

5. Use of Non-Bankruptcy Remedies (See, e.g., Chapter IX)

a. Acceleration of principal and interest.

b. Institution of lawsuit.

1) Request monetary judgment.

2) Request specific performance.

3) Request foreclosure of security for issue.

4) Request other legal or equitable relief.

c. Sale of trust estate collateral (judicial and non-judicial).

d. Use of supplemental indentures to cure or waive defaults (with consent of holders).

e. Acceptance of defaults with court approval in unusual situations.

f. Consideration of securities fraud actions, ideally brought by holders.

g. Acknowledgment of debt and consent to judgment.

h. Right to entry.

i. Rescission of acceleration and waiver of default.

6. Communication with Holders (See, e.g., Chapter V – C, D, E, F, G and H; Chapter XI – F and O; and Chapter XV - C)

a. Communicate in light of nature of holders (public vs. institutional).

b. Tell one, tell all the holders.

c. Establish form of notice of default by indenture trustee.

1) When notice should be given (at very least within 90 days of the occurrence of the default).[153]

2) What type of information in addition to notice of default should be communicated to the holders.

a) Remedies.

---

153 *See* TIA §§ 313(a) and 315(b); MBI § 10.02; and MSI § 7.05.

b) Rights of holders, including right to accelerate issue and right to direct indenture trustee.

c) Pertinent facts objectively stated.

d) Trustee's right to payment of fees and expenses (charging lien).

3) Existing litigation, insolvency of obligor and other extenuating circumstances.

4) Informing holders of their rights under the indenture, including right to instruction and indemnity under certain circumstances and the requirements for acceleration by the trustee or the holders.

5) The requirement of notice to the holders and the problem of protecting holders with regard to the trading of defaulted securities during pendency of the default and prior to notice to the public.

6) Publication of notice of default.

a) Form.

b) Extent.

c) The problem of separate communications to individual holders (large, as compared to small, holders; sophisticated, as compared to unsophisticated, holders).

7) Whether certain communications by indenture trustee are subject to Section 14(a) and (d) of the Securities Act.

a) Whether debt instrument is altered.

b) Whether a new security is being offered to cure default.[154]

7. Formation of Holder Committee (See, e.g., Chapter VIII – B, C, D and E; and Chapter XI – F, H and J)

a. Discussions with interested parties on the formation of the holders committee.

b. Statements to the holders and notice of defaults.

---

154 *E.H.I. of Fla., Inc. v. Ins. Co. of N. Am.*, 652 F.2d 310 (3d Cir. 1981).

c. Mechanisms holders may employ to join together (organized holder groups or committee) and the role of the indenture trustee. Retention of counsel.

d. Confidentiality issues.

e. The use of debtholders' meetings to discuss default and possible viable alternatives.

   1) Indenture provisions to allow such meetings and formation of such committees.

   2) Whether obligor should be present for part of meeting, and role of indenture trustee at such meetings.

   3) Use of debtholders' meetings in relationship to a bankruptcy proceeding of obligor.

   4) Role of counsel and issues of privilege.

f. Filing requirements under Bankruptcy Rule 2019.

8. Release of the Names and Addresses and Holdings of Holders by the Indenture Trustee (See, e.g., Chapter I, Chapter V – B, C, D, E, F, G and J)

a. The requirements of Section 312(b) of the Trust Indenture Act.

b. Use of section in light of prevalence of holdings through DTC.

c. The holders' right to privacy.

d. Question of indemnity to the indenture trustee for release of lists.

e. Options in compliance with Section 312(b) of the Trust Indenture Act:

   1) Turnover of all names and addresses of the registered holders by the indenture trustee.

   2) All mailings to be done by the indenture trustee and no actual release of the names to the other holders and with disclaimer by trustee as to content.

   3) DTC participant to forward communication to its customers.

   4) When the indenture trustee may refuse to turn over names and addresses or to do a mailing.

f. SEC and problem of proxy statements.[155]

g. Provisions in the indenture to allow reasonable procedures for release of names.[156]

9. The Problem of the Dual Role of a Bank Having a Relationship with an Obligor as Lender and Indenture Trustee or as Indenture Trustee on More Than One Issue (See, e.g., Chapter VI)

a. Conflicts of interest and the requirements of Section 310(b) of the TIA.

b. Whether there can be communication between the commercial department and the corporate trust department.

c. Pari passu debt vs. senior subordinated structure.

d. Preferential collection of claims against the obligor.[157]

e. Provisions in the indenture to prevent and remedy a conflict-of-interest situation.[158]

10. Compensation, Expenses and Advances by the Indenture Trustee or a Holder (See, e.g., Chapter I; Chapter V – B; Chapter VIII – E and I; and Chapter XI – Q)

a. Whether the indenture trustee or holder should ever use its own funds.

1) Authorization by the indenture.[159]

2) Authorization by other holders.

b. Whether the indenture trustee should make periodic charges against trust funds held by the indenture trustee.

1) Necessary indenture provisions.[160]

2) Authorization of holders and/or holder committee.

---

155 *See E.H.I. of Fla., Inc. v. Ins. Co. of N. Am.*, 652 F.2d 310 (3d Cir. 1981).

156 *See* MBI § 11.02.

157 *See* TIA § 311. *Cf. Dabney v. Chase Nat'l Bank,* 196 F.2d 668 (2d Cir. 1952); *Morris v. Cantor,* 390 F. Supp. 817 (S.D.N.Y. 1975); *U.S. Tr. Co. v. First Nat'l City Bank,* 394 N.Y.S.2d 653 (1977), *aff'd,* 45 N.Y.2d 869 (1978).

158 *See* MBI §§ 10.08 and 10.13.

159 *See* MBI § 10.07.

160 *See id.*

c. Notice to holders of all charges against trust funds or advances made by the indenture trustee for its fees and expenses.[161]

d. Indemnity from holders or holder committee.

e. Advances to protect the mortgaged property.

1) When advances are authorized by the indenture.[162]

2) When the indenture trustee should advance its own funds to protect mortgaged property or security and the rights and interests of the holders.

f. Role, if any, of court for approval of fees and expenses.

1) In bankruptcy proceedings including plan provisions.[163]

2) In foreclosure proceedings.

3) In actions for approval and direction.

11. The Indenture Trustee in an Obligor's Bankruptcy Proceeding (See, e.g., Chapter X and Chapter XI)

a. When and whether the indenture trustee should ever institute bankruptcy proceedings.[164]

---

161 *See* TIA § 313; MBI § 11.03A(2).

162 *See* MBI §§ 10.07 and 14.11.

163 *See In re AMR Corp.*, 497 B.R. 690 (Bankr. S.D.N.Y. 2013); *In re Adelphia Comm'ns Corp.*, 441 B.R. 6 (Bankr. S.D.N.Y. 210); but *see Davis V. Elliot Mgmt. Corp.* (*In re Lehman Bros. Holdings Inc.*), 508 B.R. 283 (S.D.N.Y. 2014). Further, see discussion of effect of *Baker Botts LLP v. ASARCO LLC,* 135 S. Ct. 2158 (2015), on such provision in Robert J. Keach and Brady C. Williamson, *The Boomerang Effect, Is There a Contract Exception to ASARCO (and if Not, What Then?)*, 97 AM. BANKR. INST. J., Apr. 2016. The issue of the payment of indenture trustee's fees in bankruptcy has often been the subject of litigation. One court has declined to approve the payment of an indenture trustee's fees and expenses as part of a settlement separate from the plan process. Transcript of Record, *In re Caesars Entm't Operating Co., Inc., et al.*, Case No. 15-0145 (Bankr. N.D. Ill. Oct. 31, 2016), ECF No. 6167. Such fees ultimately were paid as part of a confirmed plan. ECF No. 6334. A bankruptcy court has ruled that the trust indenture is a contract for the payment of fees and expenses that satisfies the exception to the "American Rule" that each litigant pays its own fees and places the indenture trustee outside the *ASARCO* circumstances. *In re Nortel Networks Inc.*, Case No. 09-10138 (KG) (Bankr. Del. Mar. 8, 2017), ECF No. 18001 (unsecured notes).

164 The Bankruptcy Code authorizes the award of attorneys' fees upon dismissal of an involuntary petition. 11 U.S.C. § 303(i); *DVI Receivables XIV LLC v. Rosenberg*, 779 F.3d 1254 (11th Cir. 2015).

b. Notice to holders of default/insolvency of the obligor and filing proof of claim on behalf of all holders.

c. Filing proof of claim for trustee and holders.

The indenture trustee is authorized to file proof of claim on behalf of all holders.[165]

d. Creditors' committee—the question of whether an indenture trustee or holder should become a member.

1) Sophisticated, as compared to unsophisticated, holders and whether the indenture trustee should be involved in a creditors' committee.

2) The case law problem of an indenture trustee being on a creditors' committee and thereby being a fiduciary with two masters: creditors and the holders of the issue.[166] The problem first was decided in the 1980s by a bankruptcy court in *In re Charter Company*.[167] The court noted that even though the indenture trustee is not eligible to vote on the reorganization plan, it may serve on the creditors' committee. The current practice is to appoint indenture trustees to creditors' committees, sometimes with *ex officio* status, particularly since beneficial holders may not want to be restricted because of the confidential information received by committee members.

e. Cooperation and coordination between various indenture trustees and security holders of a bankrupt or insolvent obligor.

f. Protection of the interests of all holders of the security; the balance of protection of rights and interests for the holders as compared to making an investment decision for such holders.

1) Normally, the indenture trustee cannot vote on a plan of reorganization or debt adjustment.[168]

---

165 *See* TIA § 317(a); *In re Randolph-Wells Bldg. Corp.*, 197 F. Supp. 327 (E.D. Ill. 1961); MBI § 9.09.

166 *See Woods v. City Nat'l Bank & Tr. Co.*, 312 U.S. 262 (1941). *See also In re Wickes Cos. Inc.*, No. LA-826658-WL (Bankr. C.D. Ca. May 13, 1982) (order allowing the indenture trustee to serve on the official creditors' committee). Over time, the appointment of an indenture trustee to an official committee has become routine.

167 *In re Charter Co.*, 42 B.R. 251 (Bankr. M.D. Fla. 1984); *In re McLean Indus. Inc.*, 70 B.R. 852 (Bankr. S.D.N.Y. 1987).

168 *In re Allied Owners' Corp.*, 74 F.2d 201 (2d Cir. 1934).

2) Under what circumstances an indenture trustee should object to a plan of reorganization or debt adjustment proposal. Section 1109(b) of the Bankruptcy Code provides the indenture trustee may petition and be heard.[169] Objections should be made when it is clear the plan is grossly inadequate or unjustifiably impairs the holder's claims.[170]

3) Under what circumstances holder should object to plan of reorganization or municipal debt adjustment.

g. The Bankruptcy Code provisions for experts and compensation (see *e.g.*, Chapter XI – Q and K).

1) Whether an indenture trustee or bondholders should seek, under the Bankruptcy Code, an order for the appointment of:

a) An examiner.[171]

b) A trustee.[172]

2) Under what circumstances an indenture trustee may have its fees and expenses and the fees and expenses of its advisors[173] paid out of the bankrupt estate as an administrative expense.

---

169 11 U.S.C. § 1109(b).

170 *See York v. Guar. Tr. Co.*, 143 F.2d 503 (2d Cir. 1944), *rev'd on other grounds*, 326 U.S. 99 (1945); *In re Portland Elec. Power Co.*, 97 F. Supp. 903 (D. Ore. 1947); *Rothschild v. Jefferson Hotel Co.*, 56 F. Supp. 315 (E.D. Mo. 1944).

171 11 U.S.C. § 1104(c).

172 11 U.S.C. § 1104(a).

173 11 U.S.C. § 503(b)(4).

VIII. Initial Decisions upon the Occurrence of a Default

A. Use of Experts and Attorneys

When confronted with a material default, the indenture trustee should consult with in-house counsel and explore the necessity of retaining outside counsel to advise the indenture trustee with respect to the default. In terms of fulfilling the prudent man standard with respect to post-default administration, a decision to seek the advice of outside counsel is difficult to fault and, depending on the volume of other matters being handled by in-house counsel, may be necessary. Most indentures provide protection for any action taken, suffered or omitted by the trustee in good faith and in reliance on written advice or opinion of counsel. Experienced indenture trustee counsel may advise the indenture trustee that, given the particular nature of the problem, other consultants need to be retained. It may be that accounting help will be required to review the financial records of the obligor. If mortgage-backed securities or securitizations are involved, experts experienced in determining mortgage loan or servicing defaults may be appropriate. Once the indenture trustee has retained counsel, the indenture trustee should consider whether all other consultants should be in the employ of and report to counsel. In that way, the results of their advice and investigation are covered by the attorney-client privilege and the work product doctrine and should only have to be disclosed voluntarily. There can be a significant difference in results if competent and experienced counsel is retained immediately upon default or even when a default appears imminent.

B. Conference Call with Known Holders

Assuming that the default is material and not merely a covenant default that can easily be remedied, serious thought should be given to holding a conference call with known beneficial holders of the debt securities. Determining the make up of the universe of such beneficial holders may be difficult. Notification of a proposed call and request for beneficial holders to identify themselves to the indenture trustee may be sent out through DTC channels (and posted on electronic bulletin boards). Ample time should be allowed to permit dissemination of the notice through the DTC system. The notice could be accompanied by a holder information sheet to be returned to the indenture trustee in which the beneficial holders represent the amount of the holdings they own or over which they have investment authority. Upon receipt of the completed form, the beneficial holder could be supplied with the dial-in number for the holder conference call. Most telephonic services will provide the host with a list of the phone numbers that dial into a call, and such list should be obtained and retained by the indenture trustee. While the holders likely will appreciate being informed of the default, the circumstances surrounding the default, and proposed next steps, they may be concerned about receiving material non-public information that could restrict them from trading. Consideration should be given as to what information can be shared with all holders since it will be subject to disclosure to the market generally. This disclosure ideally would be made by the obligor in the form of an appropriate filing with the SEC or otherwise. During the call the next steps proposed to be taken can be discussed and the holders should be reminded of the ability of a majority to direct, instruct and indemnify the indenture trustee. The indenture trustee may wish to inquire whether there are holders who would consent to be restricted and wish to obtain material non-public information. The participation by restricted holders who are fully informed of the status of the default and are able to direct the actions of the indenture trustee may be of assistance to the indenture trustee in determining a course of action.

C. Debtholder Meetings

The decision of whether or not to hold an in-person debtholder meeting is a difficult one. Certainly, there is no question that under certain circumstances, a debtholder meeting can be helpful to communicate to anxious holders the facts surrounding the default, to demonstrate the concern, actions and efforts of the indenture trustee to remedy the default and to permit productive discussion. The televised meeting held in connection with the Washington Public Power Supply System massive municipal default in which many holders were "retail" and not institutional was an effort to reach holders in order to communicate the steps being taken by an indenture trustee in a difficult situation. However, even more than a debtholder conference call, a debtholder meeting can also provide a network for dissident holders to meet and unite against the action of the indenture trustee or the majority. There are more than a handful of examples where a debtholder meeting has turned nasty and unproductive. Moreover, unless such a meeting is well organized with a specific agenda, a debtholder meeting can degenerate into a forum for heaping abuse on all the participants to the transaction. On the other hand, if you have an issue in which there are few holders, many of whom are sophisticated investors, a debtholder meeting may be preferable to a conference call to discuss the course of action which the indenture trustee intends to take. In any event, should the indenture trustee determine that a holders meeting is warranted under the circumstances, the indenture trustee must be thoroughly prepared with regard to the facts and the options available to the holders, so that the meeting will be of real benefit to the holders.

The indenture trustee should maintain at the entrance of the meeting place a sign-in list for all holders or their representatives. (A sample holder registration sheet can be found in Appendix VIII-A.) If someone is a registered holder, its name, address and holdings should be checked. If, as is more likely the case, someone is a beneficial holder, a certificate of beneficial interest should be signed. (A form of such a certificate can be found in Appendix VIII-B.) It may be difficult to exclude representatives of the obligor from the meeting. It is better practice to admit the obligor for a general session, to exclude non-holders from any confidential statements of the obligor and to exclude everyone except holders from substantive discussions of actions and remedies. The movement of people can be facilitated by different-colored name tags and separate seating sections for holders and representatives of the obligor.

If the indenture trustee has a specific course of action in mind, a debtholder meeting is an opportunity to obtain direction and instruction from the holders, and a form of direction should be available for execution (by registered holders or pursuant to certificates of beneficial ownership) at the meeting. If confidential strategies are to be discussed at the meeting, it is also wise to obtain a confidentiality agreement from the participants at the meeting, so that the position of all the holders will not be jeopardized. As is the case with a debtholder conference call, there likely will be reluctance on the part of holders to obtain information that will restrict them for a long period of time. The indenture trustee should be prepared to discuss how the information will be made public.

Do not be disappointed, however, if you throw a party and no one comes. At one debtholder meeting called by an indenture trustee with respect to an issue that was in default, for instance, only one large institutional investor appeared at the well-noticed meeting. The indenture trustee should be sure that the debtholder meeting is called for a legitimate purpose under the indenture and is not an improper proxy solicitation by some holders. The SEC has recognized this distinction in "no-action" letters.[174]

D. Debtholder Committees: Cooperation and Interface

Depending on the nature of the indebtedness and the default, a debtholder committee may be a helpful tool in achieving a resolution acceptable to all the holders. Generally, such committees find the source of their authority in a written agreement based upon the provision in the indenture that permits a majority of the holders to execute an instrument in writing directing the trustee to act.[175] If there are certain experienced holders who have the time and inclination to work with the trustee and to direct and instruct the trustee with respect to certain action, a

---

174 *See, e.g., First Mortgage Investors*, SEC No-Action Letters, [Washington Service Bureau] (July 28, 1975).

175 The indenture or other operating document will provide the requisite percentage of principal amount of securities outstanding to direct the trustee to take action. This amount for direction is normally 50 percent of the outstanding securities, not including securities held by the obligor for treasury or investment purposes. However, there may be certain circumstances where the indenture may require a higher or super-majority.

debtholder agreement executed by a majority of the holders, appointing those holders as agents to do all things necessary and proper to enforce the rights of the holders, will empower said committee to act on their behalf. The nature and extent of the powers of the holder committee are to be found in the actual holder agreement, and the committee will be held to be vested with all the powers enumerated in the instrument together with such incidental powers as may be required to enable the committee to carry out those express powers.[176] A debtholder committee has the right to sue on behalf of the holders it represents, if such constitute a majority of the holders.[177] (A form of agreement appointing certain debtholders to serve as a committee and empowering such holders to act on behalf of the undersigned debtholder can be found in Appendix VIII-C.) While debtholder committees with the authority to effect a resolution on behalf of all holders occasionally were used in the past, it is more and more unlikely today that holders will surrender their ability to determine the outcome of a default to other holders regardless of their experience level. This is particularly true if holders believe the execution of a debtholder agreement would adversely impact their ability to transfer the securities at an appropriate time.

E. Direction and Instruction and Indemnity of Holders

Section 315 of the TIA provides that an indenture to be qualified under the TIA shall automatically be deemed to provide protection to the indenture trustee with respect to any action taken or omitted to be taken in good faith in accordance with the direction of the holders of not less than a majority of principal amount of the outstanding securities.[178] To the extent possible, all of the relevant existing facts and circumstances should be disclosed to holders at the time such holders give their directions, instructions and indemnity. However, in obtaining direction, instruction and indemnity, the indenture trustee should not guess what the future may hold, promise the impossible or attempt to be clairvoyant or to possess other supernatural powers. We should all practice the art of the possible and not the superhuman.

---

176 *Carter v. First Nat'l Bank*, 98 A. 77 (Md. App. 1916); *Bullard v. City of Cisco, Tex.*, 290 U.S. 179 (1933).

177 *Royal Oak Drainage Dist. v. Keefe*, 87 F.2d 786 (6th Cir. 1937).

178 *See* TIA § 315(d)(3).

Qualified indentures are deemed to include a provision giving the holders of a majority in principal amount of the securities outstanding the right to direct the time, method and place of conducting any proceeding or any remedy available to the indenture trustee or of exercising any trust or power conferred upon the indenture trustee under the indenture.[179] As a result, a prudent trustee, if it is about to embark on action that may be subject to criticism, may request the direction and instruction of the majority of the holders to so act. Moreover, a frequent provision in indentures provides that:

> the Trustee shall be under no obligation to exercise any of the rights or powers vested in it by this Indenture at the request or direction of any of the Bondholders pursuant to this Indenture, unless such Bondholders shall have offered to the Trustee reasonable security or indemnity against the costs, expenses and liabilities which might be incurred by it in compliance with such direct request or direction.[180]

Before exercising remedies or taking action against the obligor in a situation where the recovery is questionable and the source of the indenture trustee fees and expenses is not free from doubt, a wise trustee will seek the written direction, instruction and indemnity of a majority of the holders. A form of such direction, instruction and indemnity is attached as Appendix VIII-D. The form direction attached is designed to provide strong protection to the indenture trustee. It may be that the directing holders will desire a different form of direction. The form of direction and instruction that the indenture trustee agrees to accept should be carefully reviewed by counsel to the indenture trustee to determine whether it is sufficient under the circumstances. Frequent requests by holders include a provision that the agreement to indemnify is limited to that holder's respective pro rata share of those delivering similar direction letters and excludes payment for claims incurred as a result of the willful misconduct or gross negligence of the indenture trustee. In addition, holders sometimes request that the trustee first use funds in its possession that are available for distributions otherwise payable to the holders prior to relying upon any indemnity provided by holders. This is sometimes referred to as an "internal" indemnity. Whether or not such language will be acceptable to the trustee in connection with a direction and instruction will depend on all the facts and circumstances. It may be that an "external" indemnity, the direct promise of the holder to indemnify and hold the indenture trustee harmless from the holder's own funds, will be required. If a favorable result can be achieved through the efforts of the indenture trustee, then direction, instruction and indemnity will help strengthen the resolve of the indenture trustee and unify the effort. If no benefit can be

---

179 *See* TIA § 316(a)(1).

180 *See, e.g.*, MBI § 10.03. In addition, a typical indenture will provide that an indenture trustee is not required to risk its own funds in taking action under the indenture.

achieved from further action, given the dire financial condition of the obligor, then a direction, instruction and indemnity is useless and should not be sought except to confirm that no action should be taken. The indenture trustee should probably not demand an indemnity for any action that would be normal, customary or required. The excessive use of indemnities can have a negative effect on the coordination between the indenture trustee and the bondholders.

F. Relationship with Credit Enhancers and Large Holders

A prudent trustee will identify from its investigation any large institutional holders of a defaulted issue and will attempt to communicate with such holders on their views with respect to the matter. Of course, the indenture trustee will not favor one holder over another, but, from a practical standpoint, it may be that the financial resources and power of a large institutional investor can be utilized in a manner that will benefit all the holders. Such an institutional holder should be informed about the actions proposed to be taken by the trustee and should be consulted with on a regular basis. The indenture trustee certainly should abide by all notice provisions in the indenture and relevant agreements with respect to insurers and credit enhancers. If the transaction includes a type of credit enhancer, which can be an insurer, who will pay the principal and interest on the securities arising out of the default, the indenture trustee should be cooperative with such credit enhancer, as it will likely step into the shoes of the bondholders after these payments are made or may, under the terms of the indenture, be empowered to direct the indenture trustee. While the indenture trustee, bondholders and credit enhancer should work together to maximize value, the party who actually suffers the loss should have the ultimate say. To the degree the credit enhancer is directing the exercise of remedies, it should make sure that the indenture trustee and bondholders understand if they will suffer any loss. If the credit enhancer is requesting the indenture trustee to take action that appears to depart from the terms of the indenture, suitable indemnification should be sought. If the credit enhancer is seeking a court determination with respect to a resolution of the default, the indenture trustee should cooperate in such proceeding so that it too will obtain the benefit of the court order. The basic premise of cooperation and full information flow to the credit enhancer is that the credit enhancer will pay principal and interest on the debt. If the credit enhancer questions this basic premise and seeks to rescind or nullify such obligation, then cooperation and information flow can and should be restricted because the indenture trustee may need to take action against the credit enhancer to enforce its obligations under the indenture.

G. Time Records of Indenture Trustee for Default Administration

Once a transaction goes into default, the time records of the indenture trustee are crucial for several reasons. First, the indenture trustee will be seeking compensation for its extraordinary administrative fees and expenses arising out of the default either from the proceeds of recovery or, if possible, out of the bankruptcy estate. In either event, care must be taken to document the tasks performed by the indenture trustee. Such records must be detailed; a description that the indenture trustee spent its day working on "x" file is not sufficient. (A form of a daily time record of an indenture trustee working on a defaulted issue can be found in Appendix VIII-E. However, the indenture trustee likely has an electronic timekeeping system.) Detail should be provided as to the date and time spent in segments of an hour (*e.g.*, 1/10 or 1/4) and in the description of what service or activity was performed. Such a chronology, if carefully prepared, can be helpful in justifying the actions of the trustee. Keep in mind that such time records may be discoverable by adverse parties so that, while detailed, the time records should not reveal the strategy or litigation plans of the indenture trustee or read like a confession of problems or wrongdoing.

H. Release of Holder Lists

Section 312 of the TIA requires the obligor to furnish to the indenture trustee at least every six months all information in the obligor's possession or of any of its paying agents as to the names and addresses of indenture security holders. The indenture trustee is to provide an annual report to indenture security holders, the contents of which is set forth in Section 313 of the TIA. This report deals with the items referred to in Chapter III and is to be delivered by the indenture trustee to all registered holders of the securities, to all holders of the indenture securities whose names and addresses have been furnished to the indenture trustee by the obligor, as set forth above, and to such holders of indenture securities as have within the two years preceding such transmission filed their names and addresses with the indenture trustee to receive the annual report.

Section 312 of the TIA also governs communication by holders with each other and their ability to obtain holder lists. If three or more holders of the securities inform the indenture trustee of their desire to communicate with other holders, and if they can establish proof that they have been holders for six months or longer, the indenture trustee must either provide a debtholder list to such holders or, upon payment of costs by them, mail copies of the information to all security holders known to the trustee. If the indenture trustee, after reviewing the information sought for distribution by the holders, determines that the mailing of such information would not be in the best interests of the holders, it must, within five days of receiving the materials, file the same with the SEC together with the trustee's reason for objecting to the mailing. The SEC will determine whether or not such mailing is appropriate. These rules must be complied with. For example, a proposed dissemination by objecting debentureholders of a letter requesting written support of their position on an approved offer of compromise and settlement in a bankruptcy case without application to the indenture trustee would constitute a violation of Section 312 of the TIA.[181] Likewise, the indenture trustee should not be asked to be the arbiter of competing proxy

181 *In re W.T. Grant Co.*, 6 B.R. 762 (Bankr. S.D.N.Y. 1980).

solicitations by warring factions of holders. (A form of indemnity for disclosure of a debtholder list to a holder can be found in Appendix VIII-F.) As a practical matter, given the widespread use of DTC and the likelihood that the nominee of the Depository Trust Company, Cede & Co., will be the registered holder of the vast amount of debt securities, the ability to obtain a list of such holders is of limited utility. A more frequent use of Section 312(b) of the TIA is a request by certain holders to the indenture trustee to circulate a communication to all holders. Providing such communication directly to the DTC participants (in addition to DTC itself) will make it more likely that the beneficial holders will receive the document. In litigation or bankruptcies in which it is important that beneficial holders receive notices or ballots, the court may enter an order requiring DTC participants or brokers to pass on the material to the beneficial holders.

I. Compensation, Expenses and Advances Generally

Most indentures provide that the trustee is entitled to reasonable compensation for acting as trustee and that such is the obligation of the obligor. Further, the indenture typically provides that the obligor will indemnify the trustee for any liability incurred or damage suffered by it other than any liability resulting from its own gross negligence or willful misconduct. The indenture should provide that the trustee is permitted but not required to make advances to preserve the trust estate to pay taxes or insurance or for other purposes. All of these items, including all expenses and disbursements of the trustee, should be payable by the obligor on demand, with interest in the case of any funds advanced by the trustee. The language of the indenture should be clear and beneficial to the indenture trustee. Any advance by the trustee for fees or expenses or to preserve the trust estate should be at a market interest rate or its equivalent. The indenture trustee should have a lien superior to the rights of the holders for repayment of advances, including a lien on any funds collected for payment on the debt. If the indenture is a secured indenture, the trustee is usually given a lien on the trust estate prior to that of the holders to assure payment of its compensation, expenses and advances. Such expenses and advances include the cost of attorneys and advisors. However, as noted above, in a default situation it may be unrealistic to expect payment from the obligor, and so an understanding with a majority of the holders should be arrived at with regard to payment of the trustee's fees and expenses. If the indenture trustee will have to exercise its "latch-on" rights (the superior lien or right to receive payment on funds collected), the indenture trustee must be aware of such, directing any payment or recovery so that the funds reach the indenture trustee directly. Many indenture trustees desire to be the exchange agent or disbursement agent in any bankruptcy or debt restructuring, in order to ensure protection of their rights to receive such payment based on "latch-on" rights. Larger holders may object to such exercise of the latch-on rights since it will diminish the holders' net recovery. Such matters have been viewed by bankruptcy courts as intercreditor matters not subject to the bankruptcy courts' jurisdiction. In some situations, the larger holders have directed and indemnified the indenture trustee to take action and have even advanced funds to the indenture trustee themselves, reserving the right to recover payment of such advances from the indenture trustee's latch-on rights and senior claim for fees and expenses so that the cost and expense of the indenture trustee's actions are borne equally by all holders pro rata.

J. Record Keeping

As referred to above, it is imperative that, after default, the files of the indenture trustee be well documented. Records of all conversations with holders and with the obligor should be available. At the same time, since these may have to be produced to the opposition party or to dissident holders, records should be prepared with that in mind. You don't want to put in writing what you don't want read to a judge or jury. Memoranda regarding any actions the indenture trustee believes in hindsight it should not have taken or reflecting any problems with the transaction from the indenture trustee's standpoint do not belong in the general file but should be communicated to counsel in a manner that is privileged and confidential. Even counsel's files are not always protected from discovery, in the event of an "advice of counsel" defense[182] or since a dissident holder may be successful with the argument that counsel to the trustee is in effect that holder's counsel, and the holder is entitled to all such records. Therefore, both the indenture trustee and indenture trustee's counsel must keep the possibility of prodcution in mind when creating any writing.

K. Internal Investigation

Before initiating any remedies or taking any action, the indenture trustee should conduct an internal investigation of the manner in which the account has been handled. Typically, the corporate trust department will have in place protocols for default scenarios. Usually, a senior business head in the corporate trust department should be aware of what has transpired and of the state of the file. Often, administration of a defaulted issue is transferred to a default management group and the bank's law department should be notified. Any involvement of the bank on the commercial side should be explored before any actions are begun. Any audit of the trust file and any problems discovered should be kept confidential given the anticipation of litigation. Any trust audit post-default should be coordinated with counsel and possibly directed to counsel as privileged and confidential. Confessions should be restricted to religious experiences and have no place in the trust file post-default.

---

182 In litigation against the trustee, if the indenture trustee defends its action based upon "advice of counsel," the other party to the litigation may argue waiver of the attorney-client privilege and the right to obtain communications between the indenture trustee and its counsel.

L. Staffing the Default Administration

Default administration is not for amateurs. A senior corporate trust officer should be assigned to the file, if possible. It is probably a good idea to have the senior officer work alongside a more junior trust officer, so that the senior officer is not the total repository of knowledge with respect to the issue. Moreover, the experience with default administration will prove invaluable for a young trust officer in administering new files and in review of incoming transactions. Default administration is serious business that requires top-priority attention and the best and the brightest of the corporate trust area. Mistakes in administering a defaulted account can cost the corporate trust department its profits for years to come. Successful handling of a default might even be a profitable venture. As stated, some larger banks create a default administration group for these reasons. Similarly, institutional holders such as banks, insurance companies and funds, with a large position in the defaulted debt, will want to assign an experienced person to the credit. Many of such institutional holders have developed workout or special asset groups whose focus is dedicated to obtaining the best recovery possible under the circumstances.

M. Request by Majority Holders to Direct the Retention of Counsel

It is not unusual for a majority of holders to request the indenture trustee to retain counsel of the holders' choice in connection with the administration of the default. Obviously, this approach is influenced in part by the expectation that the fees and expenses of such counsel, who otherwise would be retained by the holders individually, will be paid by the obligor or through other avenues available to the indenture trustee such as contractual and latch-on rights. Unless there are valid reasons for the indenture trustee to oppose the retention of counsel of the debtholders' choice, there is little to be gained by refusing to honor such request if it is made in conjunction with an acceptable direction, instruction and indemnity. Particularly if the issue is greatly troubled and litigation or bankruptcy is anticipated, accepting counsel of the debtholders' choice removes the ability of holders to second-guess the strategy selected by the indenture trustee. It may be that the holders' choice of counsel is a firm well known and acceptable to the indenture trustee. At the same time, questions may develop in the course of the default administration in which the indenture trustee requires legal advice regarding its rights and duties from a law firm strictly devoted to representing the indenture trustee's interests. It is not unusual then for the indenture trustee to agree to counsel of the debtholders' choice with the understanding that the indenture trustee will retain separate independent counsel for the purpose of advising the indenture trustee on corporate trust issues, where necessary. Bondholders should recognize that this is a necessary expense. In such instances, however, care must be taken to coordinate the roles of the law firms so that there is no unnecessary duplication of effort. If the distinct roles of the law firms are not clearly understood, it is possible that there will be objections to compensating such law firms either by the obligor, through the charging lien or otherwise. In an ideal situation, the two law firms can coordinate their efforts and actually produce a more efficient and better result for all the holders. If this is the procedure to be utilized, it will be important that all the beneficial holders are aware of the retentions and will not be surprised by the fees and expenses.

Appendix VIII-A
Form of Meeting Sign-in Sheet

FORM OF MEETING SIGN-IN SHEET

_______________ (the "Debentures")

DEBENTUREHOLDER REGISTRATION SHEET

MEETING OF ________

(PLEASE PRINT)

Holder: ____________________ Registered ☐ Beneficial ☐

Address: ____________________ Phone: ____________________

Name of Registered Holder, DTC Participant, Broker or Nominee (as applicable):

____

Principal Amount of Debentures Held: $ ____________________

Person Attending: ____________________

Relationship to Registered or Beneficial Holder*: ____________________

Signature of Person Attending (Registered or Beneficial Holder or Representative):

____

HOLDER NUMBER: ____________________

Witness: ____________________

* Circle applicable one and explain relationship.

Appendix VIII-B
Form of Certificate of Beneficial Interest

FORM OF CERTIFICATE OF BENEFICIAL INTEREST

CERTIFICATE OF OWNERSHIP

__________________ (the "Bonds")

INSTRUCTIONS FOR USE OF THIS FORM

If you desire to give the following Certificate of Ownership for the above issue, please return this form promptly to __________________ and fill in all information in the spaces provided as to the Bond(s) you hold either as registered holder or as beneficial holder as of ____________ and date and sign this form in the appropriate spaces. Signatures of corporate officers, fiduciaries and other representatives must be notarized; all other signatures must be witnessed. If the Bond(s) are held in the name of more than one person, all holders must sign. Signatures must correspond with the name or names as shown on the face of the Bond(s) or the name(s) of the actual beneficial holders. If you have any questions, please call ______________________ of ______________________ at __________________.

CERTIFICATE

The undersigned hereby certifies that as of ______________________ the undersigned is a registered holder or beneficial holder of the following Bond(s). If the undersigned is a nominee for another person, please specify on the reverse side the name, address and amount held for each beneficial holder

(Please Print)

Print Name and Address of Holder (Please fill in)	Bond(s) Owned (Attach additional list if necessary)	
	Serial Number(s)	Principal Amount
______________________	______________	______________
______________________	______________	______________
______________________	______________	______________
______________________	______________	______________
If Bond(s) are registered in a name other than the holder shown above, please provide name of registered holder.	TOTAL	
______________________		
______________________		

TAX IDENTIFICATION OR SOCIAL SECURITY NUMBER: ______________________

The undersigned hereby authorizes the Trustee to release the undersigned's name, address, telephone number and amount of holdings to other interested Bondholders:

☐ Yes ☐ No (Please place an "X" in the appropriate box)

Sign Here: ____*
Signature(s) of Registered or Beneficial Owner(s) of Bond(s)

PLEASE PRINT
NAME(S): ________________________________ DATED: ________________________________
____

ADDRESS: ________________________________
____

Must be signed by registered or beneficial holder exactly as name(s) appear(s) on the Bond(s) or by person(s) authorized to become registered holder(s) [beneficial holders]. If signature is by attorney, executor, administrator, trustee, agent or guardian or others acting in a fiduciary capacity, please set forth full title.

(If held individually)
STATEMENT OF WITNESS

I, the undersigned, hereby certify that I know the aforesaid holder(s) and that such person(s) executed this Certificate of Ownership in my presence or acknowledged to me that said person(s) executed this Certificate of Ownership. I hereby state that I am twenty-one (21) years of age or over.

____
Signature of Witness

(If held as corporation, fiduciary or representative)

________________, being duly sworn, deposes and says that he/she has legal authority to execute the foregoing Certificate of Ownership on behalf of ______________ and consents to the release of such beneficial owner's name to ________________.

Subscribed and sworn to before me this _____ day of ________________, 20__.

____
Notary Public

or

SIGNATURE GUARANTEED
MEDALLION GUARANTEED
COMPANY INC.

____
Authorized Signature
X0002011
NYSE, Inc. Medallion Signature Program

* By executing this Certificate of Ownership, the person signing represents and warrants that it is a person or entity who is or represents the holder, registered or beneficial as so indicated, and is fully authorized to take such action.

Appendix VIII-C
Form of Bondholder Committee Agreement

WHEREAS, the undersigned has in his possession (a) Bond(s) secured by the Trust Indenture by and between [Obligor] and [Trustee], dated [date]; and

WHEREAS, the Indenture, Section __, permits a majority of the Bondholders of the Bonds outstanding to execute an instrument in writing, directing and instructing the Trustee to take certain actions on behalf of all Bondholders; and

WHEREAS, the undersigned having reviewed the letters dated [dates] from [Trustee] concerning the status of this bond issue and the actions and directions [Bondholder representatives] have previously given to [Trustee], the undersigned hereby ratifies, confirms and approves of those directions,

NOW, THEREFORE,

The undersigned BONDHOLDER(S) hereby nominate(s), constitute(s) and appoint(s) [Bondholder Representatives as a Committee—a group of individual holders acting as a committee or a specific major bondholder] as their agents to do all things necessary and proper to enforce the rights of the undersigned BONDHOLDER(S); and

FURTHER, the undersignd empowers the said Bondholder Representatives to receipt for payment of any and all sums due to the undersigned for and on behalf of the undersigned; and

FURTHER, the undersigned agrees to deposit said Bond(s) with the agents so named, when required to receive any benefits due or accruing to the undersigned in connection herewith; and

FURTHER, the undersigned represents and warrants that it is a person who is or represents the Bondholder(s) and is fully authorized to take such action.

DATED this __ day of _________, 20__.

Bond Number(s)

_________ ____

_________ ____

_________ ____

BONDHOLDER(S) Name & Address

or: _______________ to _______________, inclusive

Appendix VIII-D
Form of Direction and Instruction and Indemnity Agreement

**DIRECTION, INSTRUCTION, CONSENT
AND INDEMNITY ("DIRECTION") BY
BONDHOLDER(S) OF __________ (THE "BONDS")
TO ________________, AS TRUSTEE**

The undersigned hereby represents and warrants that the undersigned is a beneficial holder or has the power to act as agent for or give a direction on behalf of the beneficial owner of the aggregate principal amount of the Bonds in the principal amount shown below issued pursuant to a Trust Indenture dated as of _______________ (the "Indenture"). To the extent required, the undersigned directs, instructs and empowers _______________ (Registered Holder or DTC Participant) and _______________ (broker or nominee) for the beneficial holder to provide to the Trustee, as defined below, any document required by the Trustee to confirm the direction, instruction and other matters set forth herein or pursuant to this document. The undersigned hereby directs, instructs and empowers _______________, as Trustee ("Trustee") to proceed with and take all actions the Trustee deems necessary to protect the interest of the Bondholders as outlined in the letters dated ________ and ________ from the Trustee, the enclosures thereto or as listed below ("Letters of the Trustee"). The undersigned hereby acknowledges and consents to the use of payments on the undersigned's Bonds, as received by the Trustee, and to pay the Trustee's fees, costs and expenses, including attorneys' fees and other professional fees, damages or liabilities incurred by the Trustee in following this direction and instruction in accordance with the resolution outlined in the Letters of the Trustee and hereby consents to receive payment on the undersigned's matured Bonds solely in accordance with the terms set forth in such letters and hereby waives any other sum due and owing from _______________.

The undersigned further represents and warrants that this Direction has been duly authorized, executed and delivered on its behalf and constitutes its legal, valid and binding obligation enforceable in accordance with its terms.

The undersigned hereby indemnifies and holds harmless ______________________, individually and as Trustee, and its respective employees, agents, attorneys, representatives, successors, assigns, officers, directors, members, insurers, subsidiaries, owners and affiliates from any and all losses, costs, damages, expenses, fees (including reasonable attorneys' fees and expenses), court costs, judgments, penalties, fines, suits, disbursements, claims, demands, causes of action, damages or liabilities, either asserted or unasserted, whether or not now known, suspected or claimed, incurred by or asserted against _______________, individually and/or as Trustee, in connection with or resulting from the Trustee's acceptance of or reliance upon this Direction ("Indemnified Items").

The undersigned does hereby execute this document pursuant to the terms of the Indenture, including Section __, and does hereby direct and empower the Trustee to take all actions the Trustee deems appropriate regarding the collection on the undersigned's Bonds and to take the action referred to in the Letters of the Trustee, including but not limited to the institution of litigation. The undersigned acknowledges the duties and responsibilities of the undersigned to the Trustee pursuant to Sections ____ and ____ of the Indenture given the direction and instruction contained herein. The undersigned hereby approves and adopts all actions and positions taken by the Trustee as outlined in the Letters of the Trustee dated ___________ and ___________ and any action the Trustee may take pursuant to this Direction, Instruction, Consent and Indemnity (or the direction, instruction, consent and indemnity of a majority of holders).

The undersigned hereby directs, instructs and empowers you, as Trustee, to take the following actions:

[list the specific actions to be taken]

This Direction may be combined with similar letters of direction executed by other Holders for purposes of the direction contained herein; all of which taken together shall constitute one and the same instrument. The parties intend to be bound by signatures transmitted by any regular method of communication, including by telecopier and electronic mail.

[Name of Beneficial Holder or Agent for the Beneficial Holder]

By:____________________________________
Name:
Title:

Aggregate Face Amount of the Bonds Beneficially Owned or over Which the above-Signed Entity Has the Power to Direct on Behalf of the Beneficial Owner

$______________

Address for Notices:

Attention:
E-mail Address for Notices:

Acknowledged and Agreed:

DTC Participant, Broker or Nominee (as applicable to demonstrate actual beneficial ownership):

____

INSTRUCTIONS FOR THE USE OF THIS FORM

If you desire to give the above-stated Direction, Instruction, Consent and Indemnity, please return this form promptly in the enclosed envelope and fill in all information in the spaces provided as to the Bonds you hold and date and sign this form in the appropriate spaces. Signatures of corporate officers, fiduciaries and other representatives must be notarized; all other signatures must be witnessed. If the Bonds are held in the name of more than one person, all holders must sign. Signatures must correspond with the name or names as shown above on the face of the Bonds, if registered.

As a holder of the Bonds, the undersigned directs and instructs the Trustee to take the actions as above described and further agrees to indemnify the Trustee and hold it harmless from any loss, cost, expense or charge (including the expenses of counsel to the Trustee) arising from, related to or incurred or suffered as a result of acting pursuant to this direction and instruction.

_____________ (the "Bonds") (Please print)			
Print Name and Address of Holder (Please fill in)	Notes (Attach additional list if necessary)		
	Number(s)	Series	Principal Amount
If Bonds are registered in a name other than the holder shown above, please provide name of registered holder:	________________ ________________ ________________ ________________ ________________	________________ ________________ ________________ ________________ ________________	________________ ________________ ________________ ________________ ________________
			Total $

TAX IDENTIFICATION OR SOCIAL SECURITY NUMBER: ____________________________

SIGN HERE: ____

PLEASE PRINT

X____________________________________ DATED: ____________________

Address ___________________________

X____________________________________ DATED: ____________________

Address ___________________________

Signature(s) of Owner(s)

Must be signed by registered holder(s) exactly as name(s) appear(s) on the Bond(s) or by person(s) authorized to become registered holder(s). If signature is by attorney, executor, administrator, trustee or guardian or others acting in a fiduciary capacity, please set forth full title

(If held individually:)
STATEMENT OF WITNESS
I, the undersigned, hereby certify that I know _________________, the foregoing holder(s) and that such person(s) executed this Direction, Instruction, Consent and Indemnity in my presence or acknowledged to me that said person(s) executed this Direction, Instruction, Consent and Indemnity. I hereby state that I am twenty-one (21) years of age or over.

____
Signature of Witness

(If held as corporation, fiduciary or representative:)
__________________________, being duly sworn, deposes and says that he/she has legal authority to execute the foregoing Direction, Instruction, Consent and Indemnity on behalf of ____.
Subscribed and sworn to before me this ____ day of ______________, 20__.

____
Notary Public

Appendix VIII-E
Form of Daily Time Record of Indenture Trustee

Name of Trust Officer		Trust Name	Trust Number
DATE	TIME (MINUTES)	DETAIL	
5-1-2017	60	Review with special trust counsel form of status letter to holders	
5-1-2017	15	Speak with John Jones, bondholder, regarding status and memo to file	
5-1-2017	120	Conference call with creditors' committee members regarding issue of objecting to proposed asset sale	
5-2-2017	180	Travel between New York and Boston (round-trip) to attend meeting with obligor re: plan negotiation	
5-2-2017	180	Attend meeting with obligor re: plan negotiation	
5-5-2017	60	Meeting of senior public debt trustees to plan strategy re: recoveries	
5-5-2017	15	Coordinate with company and operations regarding requested authentication of bonds	
5-5-2017	120	Meet with special trust counsel and appraiser regarding value of collateral	
5-6-2017	60	Read opinion of bankruptcy court regarding issue of equitable subordination of bank debt	
5-7-2017	10	Call special counsel regarding opinion and discuss impact on plan process	
5-8-2017	300	Prepare for testimony as witness and appear as witness in court on hearing to lift the automatic stay	

Appendix VIII-F
Form of Indemnity for Release of Bondholders List

[Date]

[Name of Indenture Trustee]
[Address of Indenture Trustee]

Attention: Corporate Trust Department

Re: [Description of Security Issue] (the "Bonds")

Gentlemen/Ladies:

The undersigned hereby represents and warrants that the undersigned is a beneficial holder of the Bonds of the above-captioned issue in the amount stated below and as such is duly authorized to give this letter as a holder of the Bonds. The undersigned hereby authorizes, directs and empowers ___________________, as Indenture Trustee, to release to ____________ a list of holders of all of the Bonds as of ______________. The undersigned hereby agrees to indemnify and hold _______________, individually and as Indenture Trustee, its respective officers, agents, employees, attorneys, representatives, successors, assigns, directors, subsidiaries and affiliates ("________"), harmless from and against any loss, liability, costs, expenses (including reasonable counsel fees and expenses), claims, demands and causes of action that may be incurred by, imposed upon or asserted against ______________ individually and as Trustee as a result of or in connection with the release by ______________, as Indenture Trustee, of the Bondholder list pursuant to the terms of this letter. This letter should be read in conjunction with similar letters received from at least two other holders of the Bonds.

[Name of Beneficial Holder or Agent for the Beneficial Holder]

By:_____________________________________
Name:
Title:

Aggregate Face Amount of the Bonds Beneficially Owned or over Which the above-Signed Entity Has the Power to Direct on Behalf of the Beneficial Owner

$______________

Address for Notices:

Attention:
E-mail Address for Notices:

Acknowledged and Agreed:

DTC Participant, Broker or Nominee (as applicable to demonstrate actual beneficial ownership):

____

IX. Non-Bankruptcy Remedies

A. Introduction

Upon the occurrence of default, as the indenture trustee moves from the investigatory stage in phases one and two, into, if necessary, the accusatory stage in phase three, it must consider what remedies would be appropriate under the circumstances. Remedies should fit the circumstances the indenture trustee faces given the particular default. For example, failure to provide an insurance certificate or failure to provide an accountant certificate may not warrant an immediate acceleration of principal and interest, a foreclosure or other more drastic remedies. Instead, the failure to comply with covenants requiring documents to be presented to the trustee is more fittingly the subject matter of a suit for specific performance if the failure, after appropriate notice, has continued. However, there are times when such a failure to provide documentation is merely the first indication of a deeper and more critical problem. In such cases, certain remedies of a more serious nature may be not only warranted but necessary to protect the rights and interests of the holders. It goes without saying that the wishes of the holders must be taken into consideration. For that reason, holders should consider responding to notices of default from the indenture trustee with a direction and instruction and indemnity to the indenture trustee and coordinate such direction with constructive discussion with the indenture trustee as to the proper remedy to be taken. Holders consulting, coordinating and ultimately directing and indemnifying the indenture trustee is the preferred method of obtaining the best result under the circumstances. If the holders do not step forward to communicate with and direct the indenture trustee, then the indenture trustee as a prudent person will have to take the action it deems appropriate. The following descriptions of certain non-bankruptcy remedies provide a summary of what can be accomplished with the use of each remedy. It should be noted that any decision by the indenture trustee to exercise or refrain from exercising any such remedy should be made in consultation with all applicable in-house and outside counsel. This chapter will conclude with a discussion of some practical issues that may impact the exercise of non-bankruptcy remedies.

B. Acceleration

One of the most powerful remedies the trustee may exercise is the remedy of acceleration. Acceleration means to declare the entire principal amount of the securities outstanding immediately due and payable. Principal and interest may be accelerated upon the occurrence of an event of default. The indenture trustee and a certain percentage of the holders as provided under the indenture, normally 25 percent, are empowered to accelerate.

One reason for acceleration may be a stepped-up interest rate. The indenture may provide that, upon acceleration, all overdue principal and interest may earn an increased interest rate as permitted by law.[183] Acceleration is also necessary in order to obtain a deficiency judgment or judgment for principal and accrued interest against the obligor.

In reality, acceleration may have little immediate effect. An obligor who is unable to pay a principal or interest installment will probably be unable to pay the full amount of the issue outstanding. Moreover, as will be discussed below, acceleration may tie the hands of the indenture trustee in certain workout scenarios. Normally, a much higher percentage of the holders (usually 50 percent or more) is required to rescind the acceleration than to accelerate (25 percent or less). Given a large public debt issue with thousands of holders, it may be difficult, if not impossible, to locate 50 percent of the holders, let alone obtain their consent for rescinding an acceleration if a non-accelerated resolution is found. It may be that, depending on all factors, acceleration should not take place immediately.

Acceleration is not necessary for the filing of a proof of claim in bankruptcy, or for seeking an appropriate non-accelerated remedy from a court (such as specific performance and other equitable remedies).[184]

Further, acceleration is not necessary if the intended remedy is a lawsuit to enjoin the impairment of security, the transfer of certain assets or the enjoining of certain actions.[185] As set forth above, acceleration may decrease the ability of the obligor to cure the default. The waiver or annulment of the effect of acceleration in publicly held issues is difficult to achieve and normally requires a higher percentage of holders than does acceleration.[186] However, if, under all the circumstances, the indenture trustee believes it should attempt to obtain a judgment for the full amount of principal or interest so that it can become a judgment lien creditor, or if other trustees for securities of the obligor have accelerated their debt, the indenture trustee may very well wish to follow this action.

---

183 *Thompson v. Getz*, 178 F.2d 325 (1st Cir. 1949) (where the court utilized the statutory rate for post-maturity interest because the interest would only be owed "from the date hereof to maturity"); *Guar. Tr. Co. v. Henwood*, 86 F.2d 347 (8th Cir. 1936), *cert. denied*, 300 U.S. 661 (1937).

184 *Oster v. Buildings Dev. Co.*, 213 Wis. 481, 252 N.W. 168 (1934); *Van Wezel v. McCord Radiator & Mfg. Co.*, 20 N.Y.S.2d 91 (N.Y. City Ct. 1939); *Maynard v. Elliott*, 283 U.S. 273 (1931).

185 *Guardian Tr. Co. v. White Cliffs Portland Cement & Chalk Co.*, 109 F. 523 (C.C.D. Ark. 1901) (trustee entitled to bring action before grace period expires to protect assets); *Marine Midland Tr. Co. v. Allegheny Corp.*, 28 F. Supp. 680 (S.D.N.Y. 1939) (trustee may obtain preliminary injunction to preserve status quo pending determination of specific performance lawsuit); *see also Knickerbocker Tr. Co. v. City of Kalamazoo*, 182 F. 865, 869 (C.C.D. Mich. 1910); MDI § 503; MBI § 9.20; RMSI § 6.01.

186 *See* MDI § 502; MBI § 9.02; MSI § 6.02.

Whether the indenture acceleration provision applies only to acceleration in preparation for foreclosure depends upon the language of the document.[187] Of course, as previously noted, acceleration is not without its perils. It has been held that an indenture trustee lost its right to unearned future interest when it elected to accelerate debt, and the election to accelerate the debt could not be rescinded if the borrower reasonably and detrimentally relied upon the acceleration and paid in full the accelerated amount before the scheduled maturity.[188] As will be discussed further in Chapter XI, acceleration in the event of a bankruptcy filing raises unique issues. Specifically, bankruptcy can complicate the right of an indenture trustee to a make-whole or prepayment penalty, the charge payable to compensate a lender for lost interest when a loan is paid prematurely by the debtor before maturity. Many indentures currently provide that the bankruptcy of the borrower constitutes an event of default that automatically results in acceleration without any action by the indenture trustee. Further, even without such a provision, the filing of a bankruptcy petition renders all of a petitioner's outstanding debts due and payable.[189] In the bankruptcy context, indenture trustees typically assert the right to a make-whole as part of the claim due the holders. However, unless the indenture clearly and specifically provides for a prepayment premium notwithstanding automatic acceleration of the debt due to a bankruptcy event of default, the trend appears to result in the denial of the make-whole tied to prepayment.[190] The reasoning includes the idea that acceleration advances the maturity date so there is no prepayment.[191] Until this matter is finally determined or the industry settles on language that is accepted as preserving the make-whole in bankruptcy, indenture trustees can expect to spend time and effort on this issue in the event of bankruptcy.

C. Suit to Recover Judgment

The indenture trustee may initiate a lawsuit for past-due principal or interest on the debt.[192] The lawsuit may be filed for a missed principal or interest payment or upon the

---

187 *Brady v. UBS Fin. Servs., Inc.*, 06-CV-0282, 2006 WL 2901824 (N.D. Okla. Oct. 10, 2006).

188 *Coca-Cola Bottling Co. of Portland, IN v. Citizens Bank of Portland*, 582 N.E.2d 184 (Ind. App. 1991).

189 *HSBC Bank USA, Nat'l. Ass'n v. Calpine Corp.*, 2010 WL 3835200 (S.D.N.Y. Sept. 15, 2010).

190 *See, e.g., U.S. Bank NA v. Am. Airlines Inc. (In re AMR Corp.)*, 485 B.R. 279 (Bankr. S.D.N.Y. 2013), *aff'd*, 730 F.3d 88 (2d Cir. 2013).

191 *But see Delaware Tr. Co. v. Energy Future Intermediate Holding Co. LLC (In re Energy Future Holdings Corp.)*, 842 F.3d 247 (3d Cir. 2016), where the court distinguished between a redemption premium and a prepayment premium, noting a premium based upon redemption would be unaffected by the acceleration of a debt's maturity.

192 If an action to recover a judgment is filed in federal court based on diversity of citizenship of the parties' jurisdiction, the trustee should be aware that there are limits to that jurisdiction based upon its own citizenship. If the indenture trustee is a party in its own name to a lawsuit in the federal court, it is the citizenship of the indenture trustee and not the citizenship of the holders that is

accelerated debt if acceleration has taken place. The initiation of a lawsuit for the payment of principal and interest does not assure collection, and in some circumstances the indenture trustee should be aware that the filing of such a lawsuit may push the obligor into bankruptcy. If the indenture trustee is faced with a defaulted municipal issue, there are additional complications. While sovereign immunity is a possible defense to suits to compel the payment of money from a municipal body, courts have generally held, given statutory waivers of sovereign immunity or implied waiver by entering into the debt obligation, that debtholders' rights to commence an action for payment of their debts should not be restrained.[193] A money judgment against a municipality is complicated by the fact that, generally, courts on public policy grounds do not allow the seizing of municipal property to pay debt obligations, as it would disrupt local government.[194] Likewise, in the absence of specific statutory authority authorizing the seizure of private property to satisfy a judgment on a defaulted municipal bond, there can be no remedy directly to the property held by the residents or inhabitants of the municipal body.[195]

The indenture should contain language which permits the indenture trustee in its own name, as trustee of an express trust, to institute a judicial proceeding for the collection of the sums due and unpaid, to foreclose the mortgage, to prosecute such proceeding to judgment, and to enforce the same against the company, municipality or obligor under the issue without the requirement of having possession of the bonds, notes or other evidence of indebtedness. The purpose of such provisions is to allow the indenture trustee to collect a deficiency judgment in a mortgage foreclosure action or to obtain a judgment on an unsecured issue. Without such provisions, defenses can be raised as to the power of the indenture trustee to proceed to collect and enforce the judgment.[196] The power of the indenture trustee to sue for the collection of principal and interest has sometimes been broadly construed. For example, a suit by an indenture trustee of senior debt to enjoin a corporate debtor from amending the subordination provisions of

---

determinative for diversity of citizenship purposes. *LMP Ninth Street Real Estate, LLC v. U.S. Bank Nat'l Ass'n, et al.*, 2016 WL 6068302 (M.D. Fla. Oct. 17, 2016).

193 Compare 17 McQuillin, The Law of Municipal Corporations § 49.02 (3d ed. 1982), with *Flushing Nat'l Bank v. Mun. Assistance Corp.*, 40 N.Y.2d 731 (1976); *State v. City of Lakeland*, 154 Fla. 137 (1943) (some courts have held a contractual municipal debt obligation is a waiver of sovereign immunity); *Grant Constr. Co. v. Burns*, 92 Idaho (1968); *Williams v. North Las Vegas*, 91 Nev. 622 (1975).

194 *See Delta Cty. Levee Improvement Dist. No. 2 v. Leonard*, 516 S.W.2d 911 (Tex. 1974), *cert. denied*, 423 U.S. 829 (1975); *Meriwether v. Garrett*, 102 U.S. 472 (1880) (if there are funds not held for a municipal purpose such as a "rainy day" fund, then those funds may be seized or levied under certain state laws); *see also Nat'l Surety Corp. v. Friendswood Indep. Sch. Dist.*, 433 S.W. 2d 690, 694 (Tex. 1968).

195 *See Merritt-Chapman & Scott Corp. v. Pub. Util. Dist.*, 319 F.2d 94 (2d Cir. 1963), *cert. denied*, 375 U.S. 968 (1964).

196 *See* TIA § 317(a)(2); MDI § 503; MBI § 906; *Cont'l Bank & Tr. Co. v. First Nat'l Petroleum Tr.*, 67 F. Supp. 859 (D.R.I. 1946); *Browning Debenture Holders' Comm. v. DASA Corp.*, 454 F. Supp 88 (S.D.N.Y. 1978), *aff'd*, 605 F.2d 35 (2d Cir. 1978); *MacKay v. Randolph Macon Coal Co.*, 178 F. 881 (1910).

a junior indenture that prohibited payment if there was a default on the senior debt was found to be authorized as an action to collect principal and interest.[197]

D. Suit to Obtain Specific Performance

The indenture trustee may initiate a lawsuit to obtain an order requiring the obligor to comply with the terms of the indenture. Such an action is called an action for specific performance. As set forth above, there is no need for acceleration if the performance sought does not require the payment of all principal and accrued interest. In the municipal context, a suit for specific performance may take the form of a mandamus action, whereby the indenture trustee seeks a writ from a court of competent jurisdiction requiring the performance of a particular specified ministerial duty by an officer of the government body charged with levying taxes. There are practical problems in mandamus actions such as vacancies in office or resignation by municipal officers. Such events remove the benefit of any mandamus because the holders do not have the right to cause the court to have such vacancies filled. Mandamus actions sound simple and easy, but the municipality and its taxpayers may fight a long time before bondholders are paid. For example, in 1929 the California Supreme Court ordered a recalcitrant irrigation district to levy a tax to pay on defaulted bonds. Forty years later, the bondholders had yet to receive any money and were still fighting in court.[198]

Specific performance is a less drastic remedy than involuntary bankruptcy, which is available to an indenture trustee facing a debtor who refuses to live up to its financial obligations. This less extreme remedy is sometimes utilized where, because of various considerations including preference concerns or the junior status of the debt, an immediate bankruptcy by the obligor would not be in the best interest of the holders.

E. Foreclosure

An indenture that is secured by a mortgage on real estate or other collateral should specifically provide the right of the indenture trustee to proceed with the judicial action for foreclosure. Generally, indentures provide for automatic acceleration upon the sale of the mortgaged property.[199] An indenture trustee has considerable discretion as to the institution and continuation of a foreclosure action.[200] The indenture trustee should consider the appointment of a receiver to manage the trust property during the litigation if there is sufficient income to justify

---

197 *Fleet Nat'l Bank v. Trans World Airlines, Inc.*, 767 F. Supp. 510 (S.D.N.Y. 1991).

198 *Water Users Ass'n v. Bd. of Dirs.*, 34 Cal. App. 3d 131 (Cal. Ct. App. 1973).

199 MBI §§ 9.04B and 9.05.

200 *Van Wezel v. McCord Radiator & Mfg. Co.*, 20 N.Y.S.2d 91 (N.Y. City Ct. 1939); *Chicago Title & Tr. Co. v. Chief Wash Co.*, 368 Ill. 146 (1938).

such expense and if the obligor has demonstrated gross incompetence. The indenture should provide the right of the indenture trustee to have a receiver appointed and paid for and the specific waiver of the obligor to object to such appointment.[201] While indenture language may provide for the automatic appointment of a receiver at the request of the indenture trustee, some courts will require the indenture trustee to establish the elements necessary for the appointment of a receiver under state law (*e.g.*, waste, dissipation of assets, lack of equity in the property).

The trustee should have the right to bid in the outstanding indebtedness (or credit bid) at a foreclosure sale in the event there is no bid that is appropriate for the mortgaged property. The absence of such a provision in the indenture has, on certain occasions, prevented the indenture trustee from being able to protect the first mortgaged property from being sold for an inadequate price.[202] Some states, such as Indiana, Michigan, Iowa and Colorado, recognize no implied right of the indenture trustee to bid in at the foreclosure sale.[203] If the indenture trustee finds no provision to bid contained in the indenture and no authority under state law, the trustee can attempt a receiver sale with a peg bid or the right of the receiver to reject unreasonably low bids.

A bondholder or an indenture trustee may petition the court to set an upset bid or to peg the bid at a certain level in order to protect against an inadequately low sale price. It is helpful for the indenture trustee to have a realistic appraisal of the fair market value of the property on a quick-sale basis. This appraisal can be used in presenting to the court the amount at which bidding should begin (*i.e.*, the upset-bid price).

Some courts have held that if economic conditions are depressed, an indenture trustee who bids at the foreclosure sale may have to hold and manage the property until such time as the market value is restored and the property can properly be sold.[204] An indenture should provide that a trustee who bids at a foreclosure sale may manage and operate the property through either itself or its agents and receive compensation for doing so without being guilty of improper delegation of duty.[205] The indenture should also provide for the waiver (to the degree permitted by law) of appraisement, valuation, stay and redemption rights of the obligor.[206]

In a foreclosure action, there are various methods and arrangements to protect the mortgaged property from being wasted and the sale price at the foreclosure sale from being

---

201 MBI § 9.08.

202 *Christ v. Collins*, 211 Ind. 474 (1937); *see also* MBI § 9.05B.

203 *Cf. Nay Aug Lumber Co. v. Scranton Tr. Co.*, 240 Pa. 500 (Pa. 1913) (trustee has implied power to bid at a foreclosure sale); *Werner, Harris & Buck v. Equitable Tr. Co.*, 35 F.2d 513 (10th Cir. 1929).

204 *See Hoffman v. First Bond & Mort. Co.*, 116 Conn. 320 (1933).

205 *See Himmel v. Straus*, 288 Ill. App. 566 (Ill. Ct. App. 1937).

206 MBI § 9.19.

inadequate. First, given the nature of the property, there should be adequate advertisement and, if necessary, use of a court-appointed and approved broker. Depending on the estate being foreclosed, a data room, which may be electronic, can be established subject to suitable confidentiality. Advertisement can be in the form of a professionally prepared bid book, with a sealed bid being made to the receiver or sheriff and an auction by bid at the time of sale if all sealed bids are rejected. Advertisement should be more than a legal notice. Notice should be provided in regional or national trade publications. Consideration should be given to a possible bid book mailed to the regional or national operators and owners of such facilities. All sales materials may be approved by the court as to accuracy and completeness. The indenture trustee should make no representation or warranty as to the mortgaged property. The decree of foreclosure can make specific findings of fact which may be referred to as representations. In addition, in some states, title insurance can be obtained, which may facilitate the ability to have a successful foreclosure sale.

Second, as referred to above, the indenture trustee or other party holding the mortgage should request the court to set a peg-bid price or upset bid after a hearing as to the value of the property to ensure a fair starting bid.[207] If an unreasonably low bid is made and accepted, the trustee should object to such a sale and request a new sale with an appropriate upset bid.

Third, if possible, all sales should be confirmed by the court to ensure that neither the obligor nor the holders will later object to the adequacy of the sale price. In addition, a confirmation of sale is necessary in order to obtain a deficiency judgment.

The indenture should provide that the bondholders or the indenture trustee may advance money to protect the mortgaged property prior to and during foreclosure. Such advances should earn interest. During foreclosure, it will be necessary to pay for insurance, real estate taxes, repairs and maintenance of the property.[208] All sales and actions of the indenture trustee should, if possible, be approved and confirmed by the court. The indenture trustee can foreclose a mortgage without making the bondholders a party.[209]

Upon completion of a foreclosure sale, the indenture trustee must complete and file an Internal Revenue Service ("IRS") Form 1099A [Acquisition or Abandonment of Secured Property]. This form requires the indenture trustee to list the balance of principal outstanding, the fair market value of the property, the borrower and the description of the property.

---

207 *Palmer v. Bankers' Tr. Co.*, 12 F.2d 747 (8th Cir. 1926).

208 *See* MBI § 10.07; *Baydrop v. Second Nat'l Bank*, 120 Conn. 322 (1935) (trustee should be compensated for extraordinary services and expenses in a foreclosure).

209 *White v. MacQueen*, 360 Ill. 236 (1935); *Chicago Title & Tr. Co. v. Exch. Nat'l Bank*, 19 Ill. App. 3d 565 (Ill. Ct. App. 1974).

With respect to certain properties, it is important that the indenture trustee conduct an environmental audit before taking title or proceeding with foreclosure if the obligor has not already done so. The indenture trustee should avoid taking title, ownership or control of the property directly and should always receive the proceeds of a sale based on its mortgage lien security. Special purpose entities, typically LLCs, can be created to hold the foreclosed property still subject to the lien or mortgage of the indenture (the lien or mortgage can be in the nature of a purchase money lien or mortgage). Attached as Appendix IX-A is a list of some considerations regarding holding title to foreclosed property. This is of particular relevance to residential mortgage-backed securities ("RMBS") portfolio foreclosed properties.

Many times a straight legal foreclosure sale brings no interested parties. The above-referenced procedures are designed to increase the chance of having a successful foreclosure sale and to prevent the indenture trustee from becoming title owner and operator of such a facility. Ownership and operation by the indenture trustee are to be avoided, since the protection of court approval and supervision is generally lacking, and the liabilities, environmental and otherwise, can be significant.

An indenture trustee should carefully consider all of the benefits and detriments to foreclosing on collateral, including the one form of action rule discussed in Section T. One indenture trustee had foreclosed its mortgage on a development financed with commercial development revenue bonds issued by a municipal authority. At the time of the foreclosure, there were monies in the bond reserve fund. After foreclosure, the appraiser, who had originally valued the property at over one million dollars, indicated the cost of repair exceeded the potential value of the property. The indenture trustee discontinued advancing monies from the reserve fund to pay for operating deficits and for repairs because it determined that no value could be realized from the property. Reasoning that the fund was the one source from which bondholders could recover their losses, the indenture trustee petitioned under Minnesota state statute for instructions regarding the administration of the trust. It requested that the court instruct the indenture trustee to forego making further advances to fund operating deficits, declare that the indenture trustee had no obligation to any tenant to fund repairs or operating deficits, and authorize the indenture trustee to disburse the proceeds in the fund to the bondholders. The court noted that the indenture trustee had the option to foreclose or not. It held that the trial court correctly determined that the indenture trustee, having foreclosed and purchased the property, became the owner with rights and liabilities under the lease and that it was not entitled to rescission of the foreclosure sale because it bought the building with notice of the defects and operating deficit. Moreover, the court held that having denied rescission, the trial court was also justified in refusing to authorize the disbursement of the fund because as owner the indenture trustee was exposed to possible liability to the tenants and to the city. The court held that the petition for instructions gives the court supervisory control to protect the indenture trustee when the meaning of the trust instrument is in doubt. The court held that it could exercise its equitable authority to protect beneficiaries against the trustee's inefficiency, incompetency or neglect. The court affirmed the trial court's order requiring the bank to continue to fund operating deficits and emergency repairs until further order of the court.[210]

F. Sale of Non-Real Estate Collateral

Some states provide for non-judicial power of sale by the holder of a mortgage. Such sale is usually by public auction, after publication, for a specified period of time.[211] Care should always be taken in proceeding to exercise the power of sale absent a judicial foreclosure. There is a definite benefit of having court approval, confirmation of the sale and sale price or, if necessary, rejection of all bids at a foreclosure sale.[212] The indenture trustee should generally avoid a non-judicial sale, given this lack of protection coupled with the normal result that the mortgage holder (in this case the trustee) must bid and own and operate the property. Each state has adopted a form of Article 9 of the UCC, which provides for the foreclosure of security interests. The indenture trustee may, for its protection and the protection of its holders, structure the sale in conjunction with a court action to determine liens and approve the elements of the UCC sale. Attached as Appendix IX-B is a possible timeline for the UCC foreclosure sale process.

G. Suits by the Indenture Trustee for Interpleader or Instructions

When the facts facing the indenture trustee present it with uncertainty as to how to administer the trust or distribute funds, there are several judicial avenues available to assist in the decision-making process. These avenues may consist of (1) interpleader actions, (2) declaratory judgment actions or (3) trust instruction proceedings. In an interpleader action, the indenture trustee may ask a court to determine ownership rights in certain property it holds as trustee, such as a construction fund. A declaratory judgment action may be brought by the indenture trustee to have a court determine a contested legal issue between the obligor and the holders, including whether certain conduct by the obligor violates the terms of the indenture. In several states, there are statutory provisions for trust instruction proceedings whereby an indenture trustee can have a court determine whether certain proposed action by the indenture trustee is fair and reasonable and consistent with applicable law and the indenture.

---

210 *First Tr. Co., Inc. v. Union Depot Place Ltd. P'ship*, 476 N.W.2d 178 (Minn. App. 1991).

211 MBI § 9.04A.

212 *Rospigliosi v. New Orleans, M. & C. R.R.*, 237 F. 341 (5th Cir. 1916); *Provident Life & Tr. Co. v. Camden & T. Ry. Co.*, 177 F. 854 (3d Cir. 1910); *Kitchen Bros. Hotel Co. v. Omaha Safe Deposit Co.*, 126 Neb. 744 (1934).

Where, for example, there is a dispute as to whether a securities fraud settlement is payable to investors who were record holders on the date the trust came into possession of funds or investors who held earlier, an interpleader action is appropriate.[213] Likewise, an interpleader by the indenture trustee is proper when faced with competing claims of noteholders and the Federal Deposit Insurance Corporation.[214] While a request for instructions by the indenture trustee may sometimes be brought as a declaratory judgment action,[215] as noted, some states have specific statutes permitting trustees to request instructions as to the proper interpretation of a governing trust instrument or whether a settlement affecting bondholders is fair and reasonable.[216] By giving notice to the affected parties of such a proceeding, the order has been held to be binding *in rem* upon the trust estate and upon the interests of the beneficiaries. This *in rem* feature distinguishes the trust instruction proceeding.[217] Where there is collateral involved, a suit for instructions can be combined with a request for court approval of a uniform commercial code foreclosure sale that would be binding on the holders.

H. Other Lawsuits

A detailed overview of other causes of action available to the indenture trustee will be set forth in Chapter XVIII. The Trustee should examine the language of the indenture, the applicable governing law and whether, given the considerations, any other causes of action exist and should be pursued, such as breach of contract, breach of implied covenants of good faith and fair dealing, tortious interference with contractual relationships, common law fraud, negligent misrepresentations, negligence of claims against officers and directors, lender liability claims, and RICO or causes of action enforcing or attacking the effectiveness of subordination.[218] If the indenture trustee determines that it will only be pursuing a claim based upon the debt, the holders should be informed in an appropriate communication so that they can take the action they deem appropriate subject to the no-action clause, discussed below.

---

213 *U.S. Tr. Co. of N.Y. v. Alpert*, 10 F. Supp. 2d 290 (S.D.N.Y. 1998); *U.S. Tr. of N.Y. v. Jenner, aff'd*,168 F.3d 630 (2d Cir. 1999); *U.S. Bank v. ILDA, LLC*, 2014 WL 4290543 (S.D.N.Y. Aug. 29, 2014).

214 *The Bank of N.Y. v. First Millennium, Inc., et al.*, 607 F.3d 905 (2d Cir. 2010).

215 28 U.S.C. § 2201 *et seq.*

216 *See, e.g.*, Minn. Trust Code, § 501C; N.Y. CPLR § 7701; Cal. Prob. Code § 17200. It has been held that a Section 77 proceeding is not removable to federal court. *Blackrock Fin. Mgmt. Inc. v. The Segregated Account of AMBAC Insurance Corp.*, 673 F.3d 169 (2nd Cir. 2012).

217 *In the matter of the Trusteeship Created by Am. Home Mortg. Inv. Tr. 2005-2*, 2014 WL 3858506 (S.D.N.Y. July 24, 2014). *See, e.g.*, Minn. Trust Code § 501C.0201.

218 *U.S. Bank Nat'l Ass'n v. U.S. Timberlands Klamath Falls, L.L.C.*, 2004 WL 1699057 (Del. Ch. July 29, 2004) (causes of action of trustee to be found in language of indenture).

The indenture must be reviewed to determine the standing of the indenture trustee to bring the lawsuits referred to here. "If an Event of Default occurs and is continuing, the Trustee may pursue any available remedy by proceeding at law or in equity to collect the principal of, premium, if any, or interest on the Bonds or to enforce the performance of any provision of the Bonds, this Indenture, the Facility Lease Agreement or the Guaranty" has been construed to preclude the indenture trustee from pursuing the bondholder's tort claims, including securities fraud claims.[219] Similarly, language empowering the trustee to bring "all rights of action ... under this Indenture or any of the Bonds" did not include individual tort claims on behalf of the noteholders.[220] However, a broad grant of authority to the indenture trustee "to protect and enforce its rights and the rights of the holders of the Bonds ... in the enforcement of any other legal or equitable right as the Bond Fund Trustee, being advised by counsel, shall deem most effectual ..." has been held to provide authority to the indenture trustee to bring a 10-b5 securities fraud claim.[221] The trustee's consideration of other causes of action will be discussed further in Chapter XVIII.

I. Acknowledgment of Debt and Consent to Judgment

In some situations, the more efficient remedy is to have the obligor acknowledge the debt and the default and consent to the judgment of a monetary amount or specific performance to be effectual after an agreed-upon period for curing the default. This remedy saves time, money and effort. It can be used when the obligor believes it will shortly be able to cure the default and satisfy the judgment but needs time, not litigation, to accomplish this. When utilizing such technique, preliminary legal research should be performed as to the enforceability of such an agreement in the particular jurisdiction of the obligor, and the jurisdiction enforcement will be sought. A form of the documentation may be found at Appendix IX-C.

---

219 *Regions Bank v. Blount Parrish & Co., Inc.*, 2001 WL 726989 (N.D. Ill. June 27, 2001) (language does not give the trustee the power to protect all rights of the bondholders).

220 *Cont'l Bank N.A. v. Caton*, 1990 WL 129452 (D. Kan. Aug. 6, 1990) ("no carte blanche assignment of the bondholders' claims arising from the common law or the securities law") and *Premier Bank v. Tierney*, 144 F. Supp. 2d 877 (W.D. Mo. 2000) ("nowhere permit the trustee to pursue the bondholders' freestanding tort claims against. . . directors"); but *see Cortlandt St. Recovery Corp. v. Hellas Telecomms.*, 996 N.Y.S.2d 476 (N.Y. Sup. Ct. 2014) *aff'd as modified*, 37 N.Y.S.3d 505 (N.Y. Sup. Ct. App. Div. 2016) ("Trustee may pursue any available remedy to collect payment" conferred standing on trustee to pursue, for the benefit of *all noteholders* on a *pro rata* basis, not only breach of contract claims, but also fraudulent conveyance, unlawful corporate distribution, and unjust enrichment claims. The trustee was not asserting claims for particular injuries unique to individual noteholders.).

221 *In re Wash. Pub. Power Supply Sys. Sec. Litig.*, 623 F. Supp. 1466, 1483 (D. Wash. 1985), *aff'd on other grounds*, 823 F.2d 1349 (9th Cir. 1987).

J. Right to Entry

An indenture may allow the indenture trustee in a mortgage issue to enter the premises of the obligor to proceed to operate those premises.[222] Generally, however, indenture trustees are reluctant to exercise the right to entry without judicial approval, and such reluctance is well founded.[223] Even though the right to entry is contained in the indenture, not every court will automatically permit the indenture trustee to so enter. In any event, given the developing case law in the area of lender and environmental liability, an indenture trustee would be foolhardy to attempt to exercise the right without a court order.

K. Right to Select Members of the Board of Directors or to Appoint Consultants

Some indentures provide that, upon default, the holders or the indenture trustee have a right to select the majority of the board of directors or a certain number of directors. This provision is normally found in a private placement issue. Care should be taken in exercising this option so that the holders or indenture trustees are not determined to be control persons or insiders and are not subjecting themselves to claims of lender liability.

Certain municipal issues, especially revenue bond issues for municipal utilities, provide for certain consultants to confer with the municipal body regarding the rates or taxes to be charged and give those consultants the power to approve decreases in rates and to recommend increases in rates. Such provisions, so long as they are not an improper delegation of a municipal unit's powers, are helpful in structuring a workout or resolution of a defaulted revenue bond issue. Consideration should be given in structuring a revenue bond issue as to the use of such provisions. Care must be taken to ensure that the consultant is not deemed to be the trustee's consultant, and that rates are set by the consultant and not by the trustee.

L. Supplemental Indentures

Almost every indenture provides and should provide for a mechanism of allowing the indenture to be supplemented or modified with or without the approval of the bondholders. Modification of the indenture without the consent of the holders is only proper when it does not affect the rights of the holders or if such modification gives additional security to the holders.[224] If the indenture trustee is involved, the supplemental indenture should not be executed without

---

222 *See* MBI § 9.03.

223 *See Baydrop v. Second Nat'l Bank*, 120 Conn. 322 (1935); *In re Bastanchury Corp.*, 62 F.2d 537 (9th Cir. 1932).

224 MBI §§ 13.01 and 13.03. *See SNB Stabfund Kommanditgesellshaft Fur Kollective Kapitalenlagen v. NuCo2 et al.*, 12 C 1482 (S.D.N.Y. May 21, 2012), ECF No. 25.

the approval of the holders or in compliance with the specific provision in the indenture allowing for such execution without the approval of the holders. An indenture trustee assumes liability for any damages arising out of an improper modification of the indenture.[225] In most circumstances, an indenture trustee will seek approval of the holders for any supplemental indenture except those specific, well-defined, undisputed areas where the amendment is to correct an ambiguity, gives additional security or benefit to the holders, and does not impair any of the rights and interests of the holders.[226] Supplemental indentures have been successfully used with the approval of the holders in order to resolve a defaulted issue.[227] As will be discussed in Chapter XV, some argue that collective action clauses, whereby a certain percentage of holders can agree to action that binds all of the holders, should be authorized in the United States to permit modification of material terms of the indenture or execution of substantive supplemental indentures.

M. Rescission of Acceleration and Waiver of Default

Sometimes the obligor, after being informed of the acceleration of an issue, may be able to cure the default that caused acceleration, but may not be able to get the required approval of the bondholders to rescind the acceleration. Indentures should provide—before either sale of the collateral or entry of a final judgment or decree against the obligor—that acceleration can be rescinded and annulled if the obligor pays all amounts due and owing absent acceleration, plus all fees and expenses of the indenture trustee, if all defaults have been cured or waived, and if a majority of the holders approve the rescission of acceleration.[228] If rescission of acceleration is the appropriate remedy given the ability of the obligor to provide assurance of continued compliance with the indenture, the trustee may (if the required percentage of holders cannot be identified or found) seek instructions from a court of competent jurisdiction.

N. Acceptance of Default

Widely held public issues may make it impossible to get the requisite percentage of holders to direct certain action to resolve a defaulted issue. Circumstances may be such that the above remedies are inappropriate and it is in the best interest of the holders to accept the default. Examples include destruction of the collateral by earthquake or where the credit enhancer

---

225 *See Myers v. Am. Nat'l Bank & Tr. Co.*, 277 Ill. App. 378 (1934).

226 *Marine Midland Tr. Co. of N.Y. v. Alleghany Corp.*, 28 F. Supp. 680 (S.D.N.Y. 1939).

227 *See In re Sharon Steel Corp.*, 1981 SEC No-Act. LEXIS 3664 (May 12, 1981) (solicitation by issuer of consent by noteholders to supplemental indenture not a violation of federal securities law); *see also Sharon Steel Corp. v. Chase Manhattan Bank*, 691 F.2d 1039 (2d Cir. 1982), *cert. denied*, 460 U.S. 1012 (1983).

228 *See* MBI § 9.03.

becomes insolvent and is liquidated. Court approval of acceptance of the default may be in the best interest of the obligor, the indenture trustee and the bondholders.[229]

O. Application of Proceeds

The indenture should have an appropriate provision regarding disbursement of funds that are collected pursuant to the exercise of remedies. Indenture language should provide that funds flow first to pay the cost and expenses of the indenture trustee without limitation, then to the holders and, if there is any surplus, to the company or obligor. Funds collected for holders who cannot be located cannot be paid as a windfall to known owners.[230] Usually any surplus of money collected that cannot be distributed because the holders are not known or cannot be located is paid either to the state or to the obligor.[231]

P. Whether Any Remedy Can or Should Be Taken

It bears repeating that, in considering remedies, the indenture trustee should be aware that, at times, it may be in the best interest of the holders to be patient and not to proceed immediately to litigation or other remedies. Complete liquidation or acceleration of debt may not always be in the best interest of the obligor and may adversely affect the obligor's ability to resolve its problems. A forced sale or acceleration may actually impair the security of the holders and cause the bondholders to recover less.[232] To the degree possible, input from the holders should be sought and notice should be given to holders of any circumstance that makes action at this time problematic or unwise.

---

229 *See Chase Nat'l Bank v. Manila Elec. Co.*, 40 N.Y.S.2d 385 (N.Y. Sup. Ct. 1943) (no distribution of sinking fund or foreclosure due to default since foreign troops occupied the mortgage property); *N.J. Nat'l Bank & Tr. Co. v. Lincoln Mortg. Title Guar.*, 148 A. 713 (N.J. Ch. 1930) (requirement that acceptable mortgages be placed as collateral was impossible given the default rate during the Depression). *See also Groseclose v. Merchants Nat'l Bank & Tr. Co.*, 335 N.Y.S.2d 652 (N.Y. Sup. Ct. 1972) (where court, in response to minority bondholders' lawsuit, ordered trustee to foreclose mortgage even though the majority of bondholders consented to acceptance of default).

230 *See Mayer v. Chase Nat'l Bank*, 233 F.2d 468 (2d Cir. 1956), *cert. denied*, 352 U.S. 841 (1956).

231 *See R.M. Smythe & Co. v. Chase Nat'l Bank*, 291 F.2d 721 (2d Cir. 1961) (surplus money from bonds not presented for payment was paid over to New York comptroller as abandoned property rather than being distributed as windfall pro rata to holders who had presented bonds for payment).

232 *See Lyman v. Stevens*, 123 Conn. 591 (1937).

Q. The Ability of the Indenture Trustee to Represent the Holders in Litigation and the Settlement Thereof

1. Introduction

In general, an indenture trustee as representative of all holders has the power to represent bondholders in an action to protect the rights of such holders under the indenture, and the resolution of such action by settlement or trial will bind all the bondholders.[233] This can take place in the bankruptcy court or another court of competent jurisdiction.[234] For example, in *Redmond v. Commerce Trust Company,*[235] the obligor had been adjudicated bankrupt on a voluntary petition, and the indenture trustee applied to the bankruptcy court for leave to sue the trustee in bankruptcy and the bankrupt in order to test its powers, as indenture trustee, to sell the trust's security. This application was allowed.

Subsequently, the indenture trustee, the trustee in bankruptcy and the obligor entered into a settlement of their controversies. As part of the settlement, the indenture trustee agreed not to make any distribution of the trust fund without approval of the bankruptcy court. The settlement agreement provided that it was not valid until approved by order of the court, which approval was obtained.

In a later action, bondholders alleged that the indenture trustee had no power or authority to enter into such an agreement, and that the agreement was not binding on the bondholders. Following the well-established rule that once an event of default had occurred under the trust indenture, the indenture trustee was authorized to act as a reasonably prudent person would in the situation, the *Redmond* court found that the trustee was authorized to act on behalf of the bondholders. Furthermore, the court recognized that state law empowered the trustee of an express trust to sue in its own name without joining the beneficiaries. The court concluded, therefore, that where it is reasonably prudent to compromise claims so filed, the indenture trustee may do so. In addition, the court held that where a court of competent jurisdiction approves the compromise as fair and equitable, the compromise is binding upon all of the bondholders.

---

233 *Carey v. Brown,* 92 U.S. 171 (1875); *Shaw v. Little Rock and Fort Smith Ry.. Co.,* 100 U.S. 605 (1880) ("Shaw"); *First Nat'l Bank of Cleveland v. Shedd,* 121 U.S. 74 (1887) ("Shedd"); *Busch v. City Tr. Co.,* 101 Fla. 392, 134 So. 226 (1931); *Redmond v. Commerce Tr. Co.,* 144 F.2d 140 (8th Cir. 1944), *cert. denied,* 323 U.S. 776, *reh'g denied,* 323 U.S. 819 (1944).

234 *See In re Bd. of Dir. of Telecom Argentina,* S.A., 528 F.3d 162. (2d Cir. 2008).

235 144 F.2d 140.

2. Absent a Showing of Unfairness, Power of the Majority Should Not Be Defeated by a Small Minority

Courts have long recognized the general rule that a minority of bondholders should not be allowed to defeat a settlement that a court determines is fair and in the best interest of all holders.[236] In *Shaw,* which involved the exchange of bonds for stock in a railroad corporation, an arrangement was confirmed by court order, but certain dissenting bondholders sought reversal of that confirmation. In rejecting the bondholders' arguments, the court stated:

> The trustee of a railroad mortgage represents the bondholders in all legal proceedings carried on by him affecting his trust, to which they are not actual parties, and whatever binds him, if he acts in good faith, binds them . . .
>
> * * *
>
> The trustees had an undoubted right to commence these suits when they did, and it is apparent from the whole record, that all their proceedings, both before and after the sale, were in the interest of their beneficiaries generally, since one hundred and eighty in number, representing, in the aggregate, $8,000,000 out of the $8,500,000 of the bonds outstanding, accepted the result and exchanged their bonds for stock in the new Corporation. To allow a small minority of bondholders, representing a comparatively insignificant amount of the mortgage debt, in *the absence of any pretense even of fraud or unfairness, to defeat the wishes of such an overwhelming majority of those associated with them in the benefits of their common security, would be to ignore entirely the relation which bondholders,* secured by a railroad mortgage, *bear to each other.*[237]

Similarly, in *Palmer v. Bankers' Trust Co.,*[238] the court upheld the denial of two petitions filed by a minority bondholder to intervene in proceedings reviewing the plan of reorganization. Eighty-four percent of the bondholders involved requested the trustee to support the plan before the district court. The court concluded that the trustee had a duty under the mortgage to support the majority view, stating:

> The general rule in such cases is that the trustee, being a party to the suit, represents all the bondholders, and that the latter will not be permitted to intervene unless a showing is made that the trustee is not unexceptionable; for

---

236 *Shaw,* 100 U.S. at 611–12; *Palmer v. Bankers' Tr. Co.,* 12 F.2d 747 (8th Cir. 1926); *Shedd.*

237 *Shaw,* 100 U.S. at 611-612 (emphasis added).

238 12 F.2d at 754–55.

> example, that the trustee has or is representing a financial interest in the litigation opposed to that of the bondholders, that the trustee is conspiring with someone to bring about unfair results, and that the trustee is guilty of fraud or is not acting in good faith.[239]

The court further stated:

> While a court of equity will not allow minority bondholders to be disregarded or unfairly treated in a reorganization plan, yet, on the other hand, it will not lend its aid to a scheme by a minority bondholder of holding up a fair reorganization plan, solely as a means for obtaining greater value or more favorable terms for his bonds than are to be given by the plan to the great majority of the bondholders.[240]

3. Courts Have Approved Class-Action Settlements over Minority Bondholders' Objections

Courts have approved settlements supported by indenture trustees in class actions over minority objections.[241] In *Centerre,* holders of 16.65 percent of the outstanding bonds issued for the Martin Luther King, Jr. Bridge objected to the acceptance by a bondholder committee of a tender offer of $550 per $1,000 bonds, which bonds had been in default for over 12 years. The tender offer was made by a public corporation for the purposes of acquiring and ultimately discharging the outstanding bonds as well as conferring jurisdiction over the bridge to Missouri and Illinois so that the bridge could be properly repaired and maintained. All outstanding bonds needed to be discharged for the deal to be successful. The corporation intervened in a lawsuit pending from 1974, seeking declaratory judgment approving its tender offer, and certain dissenting bondholders intervened. The action was certified as a non-opt-out class action under Missouri law.

The trial court found that the tender offer price was a "fair and equitable settlement of the rights of all bondholders" and approved the agreement. The intervening minority bondholders appealed, and the Court of Appeals affirmed after modifying the claims period. The Court of Appeals' affirmation included that: (1) the trial court properly exercised its equitable powers to approve the settlement; (2) the non-opt-out class was proper; and (3) the bondholders' interests were identical and, therefore, there was no conflict of interest.

---

239 *Id.* at 752.

240 *Id.* at 754.

241 See *Centerre Tr. Co. v. Jackson Saw Mill Co.,* 736 S.W.2d 486 (Mo. Ct. App. 1987); *Rievman v. Burlington No. R.R. Co.,* 118 F.R.D. 29 (S.D.N.Y. 1987).

In *Rievman*, Judge Carter of the Southern District of New York approved the settlement of a dispute between defendant Burlington Northern and holders of two of its bond issues, resulting in the substitution of collateral securing those bonds, over the objection of dissenting minority bondholders. In *Rievman*, a class action under Rules 23(b)(1)(A) and 23(b)(2), the court approved a settlement allowing for the substitution of assets securing the mortgages on two bond issues, and for payment of certain sums to bondholders. Fifty-three percent of the bondholders approved the settlement; possibly 5 percent opposed. The court considered a variety of factors in finding the settlement fair, reasonable and adequate, including: (1) the terms of the settlement against the costs and likely award of future litigation; and (2) the adequacy of the sum paid to the bondholders in comparison to the premium the bonds carried in the market.

In addition, the Ninth Circuit Court of Appeals concluded that in a case brought by the bond trustee and a class of bondholders, individual bondholder consents were not necessary before an indenture trustee entered into a settlement which, by its very nature, would alter the rights of the bondholders to receive principal and interest on their securities. In the *WPPSS* case,[242] three groups of bondholders appealed the district court's order approving a class action settlement of various claims brought by, among others, Chemical Bank as indenture trustee for all of the holders of certain bonds issued to finance two nuclear power plants to be constructed by the Washington Public Power Supply System ("WPPSS"). The bonds were issued in the original aggregate amount of $2.25 billion, but the bond proceeds fell dramatically short of the amount necessary to finance construction of the nuclear power plants, and construction was halted.[243] Shortly thereafter, Chemical Bank, as indenture trustee, brought an action alleging securities fraud, negligence and other claims under state and federal law as well as breach of contract claims against various defendants primarily arising out of allegations of material misrepresentations or omissions in the prospectuses issued in connection with the offer and sale of the bonds.

After trial began, a global settlement was reached involving the payment of approximately $687 million in cash to the bondholders, which settlement was approved by the district court. On appeal to the Ninth Circuit, a group of bondholders asserted that Chemical Bank, as indenture trustee, could not compromise their right to enforce the payment of their bonds under the terms of the indenture and Section 316(b) of the TIA.[244] The Ninth Circuit disagreed, stating as follows:

---

242 *Class Plaintiffs v. City of Seattle*, 955 F.2d 1268 (9th Cir. 1992), *cert. denied*, 113 S.Ct. 408 (1992).

243 955 F.2d at 1274.

244 *WPPSS*, 955 F.2d at 1281.

> We do not read section 11.5 [of the indenture] so strictly. While section 11.5 [of the indenture] does affirmatively grant to individual Bondholders the "absolute and unconditional right" to bring claims against WPPSS for payments on their bonds without needing the consent of Chemical Bank or other Bondholders, we do not construe this language to take away from Chemical Bank the power to settle or compromise Bondholders' claims against WPPSS, in performance of its duties under section 11.4 [of the indenture] to bring suit for all sums due in connection with the bonds, on the ground that the Bank has not obtained universal Bondholder consent. Such a reading of section 11.5 [of the indenture] would allow a single dissenting Bondholder, by withholding consent, to deny Chemical Bank the ability to universally settle or compromise Bondholders' claims against WPPSS as a whole, an interpretation which we find to be incongruous.[245]

The court went on to hold that, in the absence of any express language in the indenture to the contrary, Chemical Bank as indenture trustee was authorized to settle or compromise the claims of the bondholders, provided it exercised reasonable prudence in accordance with its fiduciary duties.[246]

Inherent in an indenture trustee's power to commence litigation is the power to settle litigation. The best interest of the trust may require that assets of the trust not be wasted on continued litigation that will not result in increased recovery to the holders of the certificates. These powers are discretionary[247] and must be exercised with "reasonable prudence."[248]

---

245 *Id.*

246 *Id.* at 1282.

247 RESTATEMENT (SECOND) OF TRUSTS: POWER TO COMPROMISE, ARBITRATE AND ABANDON CLAIMS § 192 cmt. A.

248 *See In re Bank of N.Y. Mellon*, 127 A.D.3d 120 (N.Y. App. Div. 1st Dep't 2015); RESTATEMENT (SECOND) OF TRUSTS: POWER TO COMPROMISE, ARBITRATE AND ABANDON CLAIMS § 192 cmt. a (1959); *see also IBJ Schroder Bank & Tr. Co.*, 271 A.D.2d 322, 322 (1st Dep't. 2000). *Id.* at § 192 (*See In re Application of IBJ Schroder Bank & Tr. Co.*, Index No. 101530/1998, at 6 (N.Y. Sup. Ct. N.Y. County Aug. 16, 2000) (holding that 'the trustee's *decision* to compromise the . . . action is within the scope of the trustee's powers, is reasonable and prudent, and is entitled to judicial deference') (emphasis added). Nor should the Court consider whether the Settlement is, in fact, the *best* settlement, or the *best* resolution for all Trust Beneficidaries. *See id.* (refusing to 'invalidate the proposed settlement merely because certain beneficiaries believe a greater recovery might be obtained if the . . . action is submitted to an expensive and unpredictable litigation').).

The court in the *Delta* bankruptcy, *In re Delta Air Lines, Inc.*, 370 B.R. 537 (Bankr. S.D.N.Y. 2007), recognized that an indenture trustee has the ability to settle a court proceeding, noting:

> Implicit in the authority to commence proceedings to remedy defaults is the power to negotiate and agree upon settlements, subject to the power to direct in writing by a majority in amount of the Bondholders. This basic postulate has been recognized by the courts. *See In re Smart World Tech., LLC,* 423 F.3d 166, 174–75 (2d Cir. 2005) (power to sue conferred by Bankruptcy Code "presumably includes the derivative power to settle suits") . . . *Evans v. Tucker,* 101 Fla. 688, 135 So. 305, 309 (1931) (citing "general rule" that the right to compromise is an incident to the power to sue and collect); *Codman v. Dumaine,* 249 Mass. 451, 144 N.E. 408, 411 (1924) (the power to sue and be sued carried with it as a necessary incident the power to compromise); *Fantham v. City of Lincoln,* 75 Neb. 502, 106 N.W. 666, 667 (1906) ("The power to compromise grows out of, and is incident to, the power to sue and be sued.") [249]

Importantly, the *Delta* court references the right of a majority of holders to direct the action of the indenture trustee. This right is always subject to the specific requirements of the indenture. Holders should consider coordinating with and directing the trustee to petition a court of competent jurisdiction to consider approval of a proposed settlement that is believed to be appropriate and acceptable under the circumstances. The court may consider the reasonableness and fairness of the settlement and enter an order binding all holders and thereby prevent wasteful continued litigation or continuing a default situation with no other prospect of resolution of the default.

R. Restrictions on Rights of Individual Holders to Bring Suit – No-Action Clauses

In order to expedite any remedies taken by the indenture trustee, there should be provisions in the indenture that the trustee may enforce rights and remedies under the indenture without possession of the bonds.[250] Holders have the right pursuant to Section 316(b) of the TIA to sue on their securities for past-due interest or principal without requesting the indenture trustee or any other party to take action.[251] However, in order to prevent a multiplicity of lawsuits, some indentures provide in a no-action clause that debtholders can only file suit against the obligor (except for overdue principal and interest on their individual securities) after such holders have: (1) obtained approval to take such action from a certain percentage of holders of

---

249 370 B.R. at 548

250 *See* MBI § 9.10; *Title & Tr. Co. v. Sec. Bldgs. Corp.*, 129 Ore. 262 (1929).

251 TIA § 316(b). *See Mayo v. Fitchburg L. & S.T. Ry.*, 269 Mass. 118 (1929).

the principal amount of the debt (normally 25 percent); (2) directed and requested the trustee to take such action and indemnified the trustee for its satisfaction for costs, expenses and liability for such action; and (3) waited an appropriate time for the trustee to take action (normally 60 days).[252] Under certain circumstances, courts have held that such limitation of the right to sue should be strictly construed against the issuer.[253]

Based upon the language of the indenture, bondholders have been required to comply with the no-action clause in connection with fraudulent conveyance actions and RICO cases.[254] In addition, it has been held that the no-action clause can apply to suits against non-parties to the indenture to the extent the claims are common to all bondholders.[255] No-action clauses do not apply to suits to collect unpaid principal or interest.[256] Further, a no-action clause does not apply to suits against indenture trustees.[257]

The exception to the application of the no-action clause where a claim against the indenture trustee is concerned is rooted in common sense. The other exception regarding the payment of principal and interest finds its source in TIA Section 316(b), which protects the holder against non-impairment of its right to payment. However, as set forth in the previous section, courts have approved class action settlements by indenture trustees that bind all holders.

---

252 *See* TIA § 316(b); *Quirke v. St. Louis-S.F. Ry. Co.,* 277 F.2d 705 (8th Cir. 1960), *cert. denied,* 363 U.S. 845 (1960); *see also Friedman v. Chesapeake & Ohio Ry. Co.,* 261 F. Supp. 728 (S.D.N.Y. 1966), *aff'd,* 395 F.2d 663 (2d Cir. 1968), *cert. denied,* 393 U.S. 1016 (1969); *Schallitz v. Starrett Corp.,* 82 N.Y.S.2d 89 (N.Y. Sup. Ct. 1948); *Walnut Place LLC, et al. v. Countrywide Homes,* 951 N.Y.S.2d 84 (N.Y. Sup. Ct., N.Y. Cty. 2012).

253 *See, e.g., Watts v. Missouri-Kansas Texas R.R. Co.,* 383 F.2d 571 (5th Cir. 1967) (clause strictly construed against issuer), *cf. Cruden v. Bank of N.Y.,* 957 F.2d 961 (2d Cir. 1992) (clause strictly construed against bondholders).

254 *Feldbaum v. McCrory Corp.,* 1992 WL 119095 (Del. Ch. June 2, 1992) (applying New York law); *Victor v. Riklis,* 1992 WL 122911 (S.D.N.Y. May 15, 1992).

255 *Akanthos Capital Mgmt. v. CompuCredit Holdings Corp.,* 677 F.3d 1286 (11th Cir. 2012) (applying no-action clause to suit against officers and directors).

256 TIA § 316(b); *UPIC & Co v. Kinder-Care Learning Centers, Inc.,* 793 F. Supp. 448 (Bankr. N.D. Ill. 1994); *Great Plains Tr. Co. v. Union Pacific RR Co.,* 492 F.3d 986 (8th Cir. 2007).

257 *Howe v. Bank of N.Y.,* 783 F. Supp. 2d 466 (S.D.N.Y. 2011); *R.J. Capital v. Lexington Capital Funding III, Ltd.,* 2011 WL 3251554 (S.D.N.Y. July 28, 2011), *Royal Park Invs. SA/NV v. HSBC Bank USA, Nat'l Ass'n,* 109 F. Supp. 3d 587 (S.D.N.Y. 2015); *Blackrock Core Bond Portfolio v. U.S. Bank Nat'l Ass'n,* 2016 WL 796848 (Feb. 26, 2016). However, the no-action clause would apply to suits against a servicer in a securitization transaction. *Ellington Credit Fund, Ltd. v. Select Portfolio Servicing Inc.,* 837 F. Supp. 2d 162 (S.D.N.Y. 2011). But, where the no-action clause only refers to suits with respect to the indenture, the no-action clause has been held to leave a security holder free to pursue independent claims involving rights not arising from the indenture agreement. *Quadrant Structured Prods. Co. v. Vertin,* 992 N.Y.S.2d 687 (Ct. App. 2014).

Recent discussions have explored the scope of Section 316(b). One district court, in reviewing an exchange offer that issued new notes to qualified institutional buyers but not to other noteholders, held that there was no violation of Section 316(b) since the exchange offer did not leave the plaintiffs with no practical ability to receive payment, nor did it force the plaintiffs to relinquish claims outside of bankruptcy court protections. Further, the exchange offer did not dispose of assets or amend the indenture or guaranty.[258] A more narrow interpretation of Section 316(b) was adopted by another district court.[259] Rather than focusing on the practical ability to receive payment, the court interpreted Section 316(b) as protecting only the holder's legal right to receive payments of principal and interest. This latter view is similar to the Second Circuit's decision in *Marblegate*.[260] The court in *Marblegate* also adopted a narrow reading of Section 316(b), holding that the provision only precludes non-consensual amendments to the indenture's core payment terms as opposed to factors that might affect the holders' practical right to collect. A dissent to the majority opinion was filed,[261] and it remains to be seen how the law on this issue will develop. However, the majority opinion is consistent with some earlier cases.[262]

---

258 *Waxman v. Cliff Nat. Res., Inc.*, 2016 WL 7131545 at *7 (S.D.N.Y. Dec. 6, 2016).

259 *Cummings v. Chesapeake Energy Corp.*, Case No. 16-C-00647 (W.D. Okl. Feb. 8, 2017), ECF 62.

260 *Marblegate Asset Mgmt. LLC, et al. v. Educ. Mgmt. Fin. Corp., et al.*, 846 F.3d 1, 14–17 (2nd Cir. 2017).

261 846 F.3d 17.

262 *See YRC Worldwide Inc. v. Deutsche Bank Tr. Co.*, 2010 WL 2680336 (D. Kan. July 1, 2010); *Magten Asset Mgmt. Corp. v. Northwestern Corp.*, 313 B.R. 595 (Bankr. D. Del. 2004).

The impact of Section 316(b) on exchange offers is discussed in Chapter XV. Unlike United States issues, sovereign debt often has a collective action clause that allows a super-majority (generally 66-2/3 or 75 percent of the outstanding debt securities) to approve modification of principal, interest, maturity, collateral and other provisions and drag along the other holders without their specific consent.[263] In 2015 an attempt was made to amend Section 316(b) similar to what the *Marblegate* court would later rule, by adding language to a federal transportation bill,[264] but the amendment was not included in the final text of the bill.[265]

Sometimes the trustee may waive the provisions of the no-action clause to the extent applicable to allow a holder as a class representative to proceed to enforce rights and remedies that are more appropriately raised and litigated by the holder (*e.g.*, security fraud claims, misrepresentations made to the holder, settlement discussions and approval of a workout or negotiated sale by the holder). The trustee should be sure that such actions of the holder are not contrary to the law and do not adversely affect the rights and interests of other holders.

S. Statute of Limitations

To be effective, remedies must be timely. The law recognizes this by setting limitations of time periods in which actions must be brought after the event causing the complained-of harm or injury. Actions that are brought after the time period will be barred and dismissed. Statutes of limitations are those time periods set by law to bring an action. These periods vary by state and

---

263 *In re Board of Dirs. of Multicanal S.A.*, 307 B.R. 384 (Bankr. S.D.N.Y. Mar. 12, 2004). *But see NML Capital, Ltd. et al. v. The Republic of Argentina*, 699 F.3d 246, fn. 15 (2012) (the Argentina FAA Bonds, which were the subject of a decade-long dispute between the sovereign and certain dissenting bondholders, did *not* contain a collective action clause).

264 "For purposes of this subsection, the right of a holder of an indenture security to receive payment of the principal of and interest on such indenture security is impaired or affected only when the terms of the indenture governing such indenture security are amended to reduce the specified principal amount or interest rate or to extend the maturity date of such indenture security. The right of a holder of an indenture security to institute suit to enforce payment of the principal of and interest on such indenture security is impaired or affected only when the indenture governing such indenture security contains (or is amended to contain) provisions preventing the holder from commencing an action at law or in equity to enforce payment. Nothing in this subsection shall be construed as requiring the consent of all holders of an indenture security to any amendment to an indenture or to any action, including, without limitation, an action undertaken by an obligor, except as specifically provided in this subsection."

265 Max Frumes, Angelo Thalassinos and Sarah Gefter, "The Mysterious Shelved Amendment To The [sic] Transportation Bill That Would Divide Billionaires," available at Forbes.com/sites/maxfrumes/2015/12/04/the-mysterious-shelved-amendment-to-the-transportation-bill-that-would-divide-billionaires/#6981c7784427. *See* further discussion in Chapter XV of TIA § 316(b) and the collective action clause.

type of action. Generally, securities fraud actions under state or federal law must be commenced within one to three years; breach of contract actions run three to ten years (depending on whether the contract is in writing); actions for fraud are three to ten years; actions for professional malpractice are one to five years. The indenture trustee should consult with counsel promptly after a default concerning which causes of action are available and which statutes of limitations apply. It is important for the indenture trustee to keep all available options open and to file all actions necessary within applicable statutes of limitation.

Occasionally, peace will be more profitable to the holders than war. The indenture trustee may consider entering into a tolling agreement whereby the potential target agrees with the trustee to postpone the necessity of filing suit and waives any defense to untimely suit including the statute of limitations. Such agreements may be subject to attack on grounds that statutory limitations are jurisdictional and cannot be waived by the parties to an action. Consequently, after the running of the statute of limitations, the court loses jurisdiction. While this argument may have some appeal at first blush, generally, tolling agreements are accepted by courts as being effective to preserve the cause of action (at least by contract).

Sometimes obligors request the indenture trustee to agree to abstain from taking action for a set period of time in order to proceed with a workout or debt restructuring. These agreements are generally referred to as moratorium or standstill agreements. Moratorium agreements should only be entered into in extremely compelling and unique situations and upon the advice of counsel and, ideally, with input from holders. Generally, indenture trustees patriotically maintain that the only thing they waive is the American flag.

T. Setoff and the One Form of Action Rule

The equitable remedy of setoff has been recognized in the law and is appropriate under certain circumstances. Many times, bankers look to compensating balances as a means of obtaining a banker's lien on that which is in the bank's possession, believing the bank can then use setoff as a way of obtaining recovery. In order to have the ability to set off, especially under the Bankruptcy Code, there must be mutuality of debt and obligations.[266] Typically, this requirement will preclude setoff of the operating account of an obligor by an indenture trustee. This principle also raises questions regarding the ability of the indenture trustee to use funds in the debt service reserve and sinking fund accounts of an obligor. The counterargument the indenture trustee may raise is that such bond funds are trust funds and not the property of the obligor. The right of setoff must be exercised in good faith, and failure to meet this obligation can

---

266 11 U.S.C. § 553.

cause the bank to be liable for damages for improper setoff. The indenture trustee should be aware of cases holding setoffs improper.[267]

Care must be taken by the indenture trustee if the law of California is applicable to its indenture. California has established the so-called "one action rule." Under California law, when a bank sets off a debt from a borrower's account, the one form of action rule requires the lender to exhaust its security before proceeding against the borrower for any deficiency.[268] Other states have similar one form of action or foreclosure first rules.[269] Others even bar deficiency judgments after non-judicial foreclosures.[270]

U. Practical Considerations

While each default situation presents its own unique challenges, a number of considerations are often relevant. Is there the possibility of a consensual resolution of the default and should a forbearance while a workout is being discussed be entered into? Does the indenture trustee need the assistance of a financial advisor to proceed with remedies or consider a workout? Is there a third party, such as an insurer or other credit enhancer, who controls the exercise of remedies and should be consulted? Will there be funds (trust funds or otherwise) to pay for the costs of the exercise of remedies? How active do the bondholders desire to be in the resolution of the default? Will there be a majority of holders available to direct, instruct and indemnify the indenture trustee with respect to the actions taken? Is it likely that the securities will change hands during the default situation, presenting the indenture trustee with a different constituency? How best can the indenture trustee coordinate with the control parties so that the indenture trustee does not subject itself to liability but, rather, is carrying out the wishes of those with the economic interest? Is a court-approved settlement the best approach? Is the one form of action rule implicated? All of these questions should be considered within the context of the indenture trustee's carefully controlled protocols and in conjunction with the advice of its in-house and/or outside counsel and other advisors.

---

267 *See Smith v. Mark Twain Nat'l Bank,* 57 B.R. 373 (Bankr. E.D. Mo. 1986), *aff'd in part, rev'd in part,* 805 F.2d 278; *Navajo Tribe v. The Bank of New Mexico,* 700 F.2d 1285 (10th Cir. 1983); *Bank of Am. v. Daily,* 152 Cal. App. 3d 767 (Cal. Ct. App. 1984).

268 *See* The California Civil Procedure Code § 726(a); *Sec. Pac. Nat'l Bk. v. Wozab,* 51 Cal. 3d 991 (1990).

269 *See* Idaho Code § 6-101; N.J. Stat. § 2A: 50-2; Nev. Rev. Stat. § 40.430; Or. Rev. Stat. § 86.735; Utah Code § 78-37-1.

270 For example, Arizona, California, Colorado, Kentucky, Louisiana, Maine, Maryland, Montana, Oklahoma and Pennsylvania.

Appendix IX-A
Considerations Regarding Method of Holding Title to Foreclosed Properties

I. Statement of the Issues

- The relevant documents for RMBS or other secured transactions frequently provide that, upon foreclosure or deed in lieu or similar disposition of mortgaged property, where the trust takes ownership of the mortgaged property ("Foreclosed Properties"), the name of the record owner on the Foreclosed Property would be in the name of the Trustee as the legal representative for the trust.
- As recent litigation by certain cities in the RMBS cases and other litigation related to Foreclosed Properties generally has indicated, there is a misperception that the Foreclosed Property is actually owned by the bank as opposed to being trust property held solely for the benefit of the trust in the name of the trustee under the terms of the relevant documents and managed by the servicer.
- One way of possibly avoiding confusion, if not distortion, of the true ownership of the Foreclosed Properties held for the benefit of the trust is to look at an alternate way of having the Foreclosed Properties listed as far as record title holder.
- There are a number of different ways in which banks have chosen to show record title ownership in a name (as nominee, designee or agent) other than the precise name of the trustee for the trust.

II. Possible Vehicles for Holding Foreclosed Property in a Name Other Than That of the Trustee

A. Use of Co-Trustee

- Generally, pooling and servicing agreements for RMBS transactions provide that there may be co-trustees or separate trustees appointed to act for the trust for the purposes of meeting legal requirements of any jurisdiction or any mortgaged property.
- Generally, these provisions require the depositor and the net interest margin securities ("NIMS") insurer and possibly others to be involved in the approval and implementation of such actions, including approval by the master servicer, the NIMS insurer and the depositor.

- While there is precedent in various transactions, including corporate bond relationships relating to aircraft, vessels, railroads and utilities (especially as to the eligibility of the trustee to hold the collateral under the applicable law), to have a co-trustee to hold certain property, there are additional considerations concerning eligibility and the more complicated process of implementing the appointment of a co-trustee which requires the cooperation of the depositor, the master servicer, the NIMS insurer and possibly others.

B. Use of Agents or Custodians

- There are also typically provisions in pooling and servicing agreements allowing for the trustee to exercise any trusts or powers under the relevant documents and perform any duties directly or by or through agents or custodians and such arrangements generally provide that the trustee shall not be responsible for any misconduct or negligence on the part of any such agent or custodian appointed by it with due care.
- Implementation appears possible pursuant to the general terms providing for trust powers to be carried through by an agent or custodian, and there would have to be appropriate implementation documents consistent with the transaction documents to provide the notice and implementation of such a process.

III. What Is the Best Type of Entity to Act as Custodian or Agent (Nominee or Designee) for the Trustee with Regard to Ownership of Foreclosed Property by the Trust?

A. Use of Limited Liabilities Corporation by Banks and Structured Vehicles for Real Estate Owned

- With regard to real estate owned and other structured vehicles, banks have used the limited liability corporation ("LLCs") as a structure to hold real estate in a capacity separate and distinct from the bank or moneyed interest.
- While trusts and master trusts could be used for this purpose, generally banks in other circumstances have used the LLC since it should be simpler and does not raise questions of possible regulatory requirements that certain trusts might involve, especially the need for a named trustee, all of which weighs in favor of the use of LLCs.

B. Issues Relating to Formation and Use of LLC

- There are a number of issues relating to the use of a limited liability corporation. They include:

  (1) whether you have set up one LLC for each trust or use a series of LLCs;

(2) the use of any LLC is only as good as making sure the separateness of the LLC is maintained, such as no commingling of funds, separate organizational documents and operations, and clear distinction of assets and liabilities;

(3) the bank as trustee could be the organizing member of the LLC for the benefit of the trust and the trustee;

(4) since different RMBS or secured trusts have different beneficiaries, there probably should be at least one separate LLC for each RMBS or secured transaction or distinct group of beneficiaries in order to prevent commingling of trust relationships;

(5) there will be issues with regard to the LLC qualifying in each state and, to avoid an LLC having to qualify in numerous states, series LLCs by state may be desirable (there may be a decision to use a separate series LLC for each state where the trust has mortgaged property); and

(6) the benefit of the use of series LLCs is you do not have to duplicate the formation documents and operational documents each time you create a new series; you just create a separate designation similar to the master trust concept.

IV. Implementation Issues of Taking Foreclosed Property in RMBS and Other Secured Transactions Currently Naming the Trustee as Record Owner or in the Future and Having a Designated Agent or Custodian for the Trustee to Hold the Foreclosed Property in Its Name

- With regard to implementation of the substitution of LLCs in connection with the Foreclosed Property already in the name of the trustee, there are issues regarding transfer tax liability in each state. There may be exceptions in various states for placing substitute ownership in the name of an affiliate or agent or custodian, but this needs to be reviewed on a state-by-state basis.
- Banks in other situations have chosen to do a cost-benefit analysis as to the cost of any transfer tax or transfer of the prior existing property to a LLC to determine whether it makes economic sense.
- Coordinating with the specific RMBS or secured transaction documents is important, as is making sure the servicer recognizes, either on a going-forward basis or if it is to be applied to current Foreclosed Properties, that the name of the LLC is to be substituted for the trustee and as the record owner for Foreclosed Property. (Form documentation, notice and implementation can be developed to facilitate this.)

- While the LLC structure may provide a different name of ownership of the Foreclosed Property, caution is always given that someone might claim, because of lack of separateness, given the structure of the transactions or other reasons, that the ultimate owner is the bank as trustee. However, the bank as trustee is a step removed and basic trust law provides that the bank as trustee is really the trust and not the bank. Therefore, if one were going to pierce the ownership of the LLC, doing so should relate to the trust, as the ultimate owner.
- Implementation would be based on trust by trust, property by property, which has a cost-benefit analysis issue and obviously some time and effort will be required.

Appendix IX-B
UCC Foreclosure Sale Process – Possible Timeline

Prior to filing the complaint to determine liens and approval of UCC sale, notice and procedure	• Pre-Filing — determine whether there is any benefit to sales effort to identify a stalking horse bid for all or most of company's assets at price acceptable to indenture trustee (to the extent possible pursuant to direction of holders) or develop a stalking horse from the pre-filing sales effort below
Prior to filing date	• Establish information/data room for potential purchasers (if not already done; if so; then court approval of process and sufficient information provided)
Filing date	(i) File complaint to determine lien, judgment on amount due and UCC/foreclosure sale and approval of sale and process (j) File motions for approval of sale, schedule, notice of sale and process to establish sale procedures
1–10 days from the filing date	• Hearing on order for approval of scheduling final hearing on sale and schedule for UCC sale and approval of sale notice and sale procedures • Obligor or indenture trustee to identify to court that there is a stalking horse or identified purchaser for private sale or potential purchasers or targets for public auction sale and, if necessary, approve form of confidentiality letter as part of sale procedures and establishment of data room and sale information • Mailing of UCC notice of sale and solicitations for bids to potential targets (with draft confidentiality letter) (if not already done; if done prior to filing, the court approval of that process) • Form of asset purchase agreement ("APA") and bid form presented to court for approval in connection with bidding procedures

By 2–10 days from the filing date	• Financial advisors or representatives of the indenture trustee or holders' representative ("Trust Representative") to receive qualification (financial capacity) of bidders who have expressed interest in bidding
By 15–25 days from the filing date	• Contact and negotiation by Trust Representative and investment banker engaged by the court for sales purposes to deal with potential sale candidates
25–35 days from the filing date	• Bids due on sale - Obligor, if applicable, and Trust Representative in consultation with bondholders, if possible, have right to reject bids non-conforming with bidding purchases and form contract or to negotiate discrepancies - Earnest money due - Trust Representative in connection with bondholders has the right to reject any and all bids below cash payout of loans and right to bid in
By 27–37 days from the filing date	• Auction sale date • Court hearing approving auction sale • Filing of affidavit of obligor, if applicable, sale agent (receiver) or investment banker for sale as to notice and sale effort demonstrating reasonableness of sale and the designated winning bid and rationale for acceptance by Trust Representative in consultation with the holders, if possible; also post-filing brief on legal basis for sale and affidavit of proof of liens and security interest of indenture trustee or collateral agent and amount due on loans
By 27–40 days from the filing date	• Entry of order approving sale
By 30–40 days from the filing date	• Closing on sale of assets
By 50–60 days from the filing date	• Close case

Appendix IX-C
Form of Acknowledgment of Debt and Consent to Judgment*

This ACKNOWLEDGMENT OF DEBT AND CONSENT TO JUDGMENT (the "Acknowledgment") dated as of ____________________, by ____________________, a ____________________ corporation (the "Obligor"), is submitted to ____________________, as trustee, and its successors and assigns (the "Trustee"); under a Trust Indenture dated as of ____________________ (the "Indenture"). All terms used herein and not defined herein shall have the same meanings assigned to them in the Indenture and the hereinafter defined Loan Agreement, and all other financing documents (collectively the "Financing Documents"), unless otherwise expressly provided or unless the context otherwise requires.

WITNESSETH:

WHEREAS, on ________________________ (the "Obligor") issued its Debentures, Notes or Bonds (the "Bonds") pursuant to the Indenture;

WHEREAS, the Bonds were issued for the purpose of financing the Obligor or for acquiring, constructing or financing the operation or maintenance of the Collateral (the "Collateral") and for the cost of acquiring and renovating a property (the "Project") in the City;

WHEREAS, pursuant to the Indenture, Mortgage or Collateral Agreement by and between the Obligor and the Trustee dated as of ____________ ("Indenture" or "Security Agreement," as applicable), the City loaned the net proceeds it received from the sale of the Bonds to the Obligor;

WHEREAS, the Bonds were purchased by the Bondholders for whom the Trustee acts;

WHEREAS, to secure the repayment of the Bonds the Obligor executed and delivered to the Trustee the Indenture or Security Agreement, and an Assignment of Revenues, Leases and Rents (as applicable), dated as of ____________________ (the "Pledge of Revenues");

WHEREAS, pursuant to the Indenture all monies and investments, including without limitation the Security Agreement and Pledge of Revenues (as applicable), are held under the Indenture as security for the Bonds;

WHEREAS, on __________________, interest was due on the Bonds in the amount of $__________ and the Obligor was obligated to make payment in a like amount;

WHEREAS, the Obligor failed to make payment pursuant to its obligations under the Indenture and Security Agreement;

WHEREAS, on ____________________, the Obligor received a notice from the Trustee of the occurrence of an Event of Default under the Indenture;

WHEREAS, the Obligor has heretofore acknowledged that it has failed to comply with its lawful obligations under the Security Agreement or Pledge of Revenue (as applicable) with respect to the Bonds and the Indenture, thereby creating an Event of Default under the Indenture;

WHEREAS, the Bondholders, as owner of the Bonds, are now lawfully entitled under the Indenture to direct the Trustee to accelerate the payment of the Bonds in accordance with the terms of the Indenture; and

WHEREAS, the Obligor has offered to acknowledge the indebtedness due and owing to the Trustee by the Obligor and to consent to the entry of a Decree of Foreclosure and Sale or such other transfer, assignment or conveyance of the rights and interests of the Obligor in the Collateral as the Trustee shall desire, with the understanding that the Obligor will waive all of its rights, claims and interests in any appraisement, evaluation, redemption, stay, extension or exemption law or so-called moratorium laws now or hereafter enacted and to evidence the same has entered into a Settlement Agreement, dated as of ____________________ (the "Settlement Agreement");

NOW, THEREFORE, in consideration of the covenants, undertakings and promises as set forth above and in the financing documents, and due to the defaults set forth above and other good and valuable consideration, the receipt of which is hereby acknowledged, the Obligor acknowledges, consents and agrees as follows:

(a) The Obligor acknowledges that unless specifically modified herein, the terms and provisions of the Indenture, Security Agreement and Pledge of Revenues, as applicable, remain in full force and effect.

(b) The Obligor does hereby acknowledge, confess and stipulate that it owes and will owe to the Trustee (i) the full amount of the principal of all outstanding Bonds, (ii) all interest accrued and unpaid on such outstanding Bonds at the rate set forth in the Bonds until the date of payment, (iii) the amount of any fees (including attorneys' fees), expenses, costs and advances incurred by or on behalf of the Trustee in connection with the Collateral and the Financing Documents, (iv) any amounts necessary to pay or discharge any liens or encumbrances prior to or on a parity basis with the Indenture, Security Agreement or Pledge of Revenues, together with (v) interest on such amounts until paid at the rate equal to ____ percent (__%) per annum.

(c) The Obligor does hereby acknowledge, confess and stipulate that it is in default of the terms of the Financing Documents and does hereby waive the issuance and service of process and does consent to entry of and does confess judgment against the Obligor in favor of the Trustee for the amount stated in Paragraph (b) above and does consent. to the entry of a decree of foreclosure against the Obligor's interests in the Collateral and does hereby release all errors and waives all right to appeal as to any judgment entered pursuant to the above.

(d) To the full extent permitted by law the Obligor hereby covenants and agrees that it will not at any time insist upon or plead, or in any manner whatsoever claim or take any advantage of, any stay, exemption or extension law or any so-called "moratorium law" now or at any time hereafter in force, nor claim, take or insist upon any benefit or advantage of or from any law now or hereafter in force providing for the valuation, appraisement or marshalling of the Collateral, or any part thereof, prior to any sale or sales thereof to be made pursuant to any provisions contained in the Financing Documents, or any power granted to the Trustee, or to any decree, judgment or order of any court of competent jurisdiction, or after such sale or sales claim or exercise any rights under any statute now or hereafter in force to redeem the property so sold, or any part thereof, or relating to the marshalling thereof, upon foreclosure sale or other enforcement of the Financing Documents. To the full extent permitted by law, the Obligor hereby expressly waives any and all rights of redemption from any trustee's sale or any sale under any order or decree of foreclosure of the Indenture, Security Agreement or Pledge of Revenues (as applicable), on its own behalf, on behalf of all persons claiming or having an interest (direct or indirect) by, through or under the Obligor and on behalf of each and every person acquiring any interest in or title to the Collateral subsequent to the date hereof, it being the intent hereof that any and all such rights of redemption of the Obligor and of all other persons are and shall be deemed to be hereby waived to the full extent permitted by applicable law. To the full extent permitted by law, the Obligor agrees that it will not, by invoking or utilizing any applicable law or laws or otherwise, hinder, delay or impede the exercise of any right, power or remedy herein or otherwise granted or delegated to the Trustee, including without limitation the enforcement or foreclosure of the Indenture, Security Agreement or Pledge of Revenues (as applicable) or the delivery of possession thereof immediately after such sale to the purchaser at such sale, but will suffer and permit the exercise of every such right, power and remedy as though no such law or laws have been or will have been made or enacted; and the Obligor, for itself and all who may at any time claim through or under it, hereby waives to the full extent that it may lawfully do so the benefit of all such laws, and any and all right to have the assets subject to the lien of the Collateral marshalled upon any foreclosure or sale. To the extent permitted by law, the Obligor hereby fully and absolutely waives and releases all rights and claims, if any, the Obligor may have in and to the Collateral as a homestead exemption or other exemption under and by virtue of any act of __________ now existing or that may hereafter be passed in relation thereto.

(e) The Obligor understands and agrees that this Acknowledgment is hereby executed and delivered in the STATE OF __________ and that any action, causes of action, claims, controversies, damages and demands which the Trustee may have arising or to arise, directly or indirectly, from or by reason of this Acknowledgment or the Security Agreement, Indenture or Pledge of Revenues (as applicable) shall be litigated in the courts, either state or federal, for the STATE OF __________ or any other federal or state court that the Trustee in its sole discretion determines as acceptable for its purposes. It is understood and agreed to by the Obligor that the Consent to Judgment entered against the Obligor shall be entered in the courts, either state or federal, for the STATE OF __________ or any other federal or state court that the Trustee in its sole discretion determines as acceptable for its purposes. It is further agreed and understood by the Obligor that it waives any and all objections it may have to venue or jurisdiction of the United States District Court for __________ as the court that should enter the Consent to Judgment which is contemplated and permitted by this Acknowledgment or any other federal or state court that the Trustee in its sale discretion determines as acceptable for its purposes.

(f) The Obligor understands and agrees that in any action instituted by the Trustee to obtain entry by a court of the Consent to Judgment referred to in Paragraphs (c), (d) and (e) above, the Obligor does hereby waive any and all notice required of such action, does hereby waive any right to appear or be represented by counsel other than as set forth herein and does hereby waive the issuance of service of process and does hereby confess and consent to the judgment as set forth above in any of the courts set forth in Paragraph (e) above. The Obligor further agrees that the interest on such judgment shall be equal to __________ percent (___%) per annum.

(g) The Obligor does hereby agree and does hereby authorize the Trustee to file an Appearance and Consent to Judgment substantially in the form attached which is authorized by this Acknowledgment. There is attached hereto and incorporated herein a signed Appearance and Consent to Judgment to be filed in any court proceedings contemplated by Paragraphs (f) and (g) above as determined by the Trustee.

(h) The Obligor acknowledges and stipulates that this Acknowledgment and the entry of the judgment permitted hereby are not intended to be nor shall be construed to be a waiver of any rights of the Trustee under the Financing Documents or an election of remedies, and if the Trustee should in its discretion elect to have a judgment entered under this Acknowledgment, then the Trustee is still free to pursue any and all other remedies available to it pursuant to the terms of the Financing Documents.

(i) The Trustee acknowledges and stipulates that this Acknowledgment and the entry of judgment permitted hereby are not intended to be and shall not be construed to be a waiver of any rights of the Obligor under the Financing Documents and, except as specifically set forth herein, are not intended to create any further rights or remedies in addition to the rights and remedies provided to the Trustee under current law, the Settlement Letter and the Financing Documents.

(j) The Obligor acknowledges that prior to its execution of this Acknowledgment, it was adequately represented by counsel and understood the effect of this agreement and the execution of it.

(k) The complete or partial invalidity, illegality or unenforceability of any provision hereof at any time, whether under the terms of then applicable law or otherwise, shall not affect (i) in the case of partial invalidity, illegality or unenforceability, the validity, legality or enforceability of such provision at such time except to the extent of such partial invalidity, illegality or unenforceability, or (ii) the validity, legality or enforceability of such provisions at any other time, or of any other provisions hereof at that or any other time.

IN WITNESS WHEREOF, the Obligor has executed this Acknowledgment as of the day and year first above written.

______________________________,
the Obligor

By: ______________________________
Its: President
Printed Name: ____________________

ATTEST:

By: ______________________________
Its: ________________________ Secretary
Printed Name: ____________________

RECEIVED BY:

______________________________,
as Trustee

By: ______________________________
Its: Attorney-in-Fact
Printed Name: ____________________

DATE:

____________________, 20__

STATE OF ____________________)
) SS.
COUNTY OF ___________________)

Before me, the undersigned, a Notary Public in and for said County and State, on this day personally appeared ____________________ and ____________________, on behalf and as President and Secretary, respectively, of ____________________, a _______________ corporation, known to me to be the persons whose names are subscribed to the foregoing instrument, and acknowledged to me that they executed the same for the purposes and consideration therein expressed, and as the act and deed of said corporation.

Given under my hand and seal of office on this the ______ day of __________, 20___.

____
Notary Public in and for the State of
____

My Commission Expires: ____________________

STATE OF ____________________)
) SS.
COUNTY OF __________________)

Before me, the undersigned, a Notary Public in and for said County and State, on this day personally appeared ______________, attorney-in-fact of ______________, a ____________ banking association and trust company, whose name is subscribed to the foregoing instrument, and acknowledged to me that the same was the act of the said ___________________, and that he/she executed the same as the act of such banking association and trust company, as such attorney-in-fact for the purposes and consideration therein expressed, and in the capacity therein stated.

Given under my hand and seal of office on this the _____ day of _________, 20___.

____
Notary Public in and for the State of
____

My Commission Expires: ___________________

______________________________, as	)
trustee under a Trust Indenture dated as of	)
______________________ from the City of	)
______________________,	)
	)
Plaintiff,	)
	)
v.	)
	)
______________________,	)
	)
Defendant.	)

APPEARANCE AND CONSENT TO JUDGMENT

Defendant, ______________________________, by its duly retained and authorized attorney, enters a voluntary and general appearance in this action and does submit to the jurisdiction of this court for all purposes and hereby consents to the entry of a judgment in this action against ___________________________ in the amount of (i) the full amount of the principal of all outstanding Bonds, (ii) all interest accrued and unpaid on such outstanding Bonds to the date of judgment, (iii) the amount of any fees (including attorneys' fees), expenses, costs and advances incurred by or on behalf of Plaintiff, as trustee, and of the Obligee in connection with the Collateral and the Financing Documents as defined in the Acknowledgment of Debt and Consent to Judgment dated as of ____________, (iv) any amounts necessary to pay or discharge any liens or encumbrances prior to or on a parity basis with the Indenture, Security Agreement or Pledge of Revenues (as applicable), together with (v) interest on such amounts until paid at the rate of interest equal to _____ percent (_____%) per annum.

[Name of Obligor]

By: ______________________________

One of Its Attorneys

AGREED TO:

[Name of Obligor]

By: ______________________________

Its Vice President

* ______________________________

This form Acknowledgment of Debt and Consent to Judgment refers to a secured debt issue and can be modified for use in connection with an unsecured debt issue. All references to Collateral and Financing Documents should be deleted, as well as all references to foreclosure with respect to the Collateral. It should be noted that not all states provide for or allow the use of an Acknowledgment of Debt and Consent to Judgment. Therefore, local law and practice should be checked to determine if an Acknowledgment of Debt and Consent to Judgment is viable in the jurisdiction in which its use is planned.

An Acknowledgment of Debt and Consent to Judgment is sometimes, however, an efficient remedy when used in connection with a settlement or forbearance agreement whereby the debtor is given a specific time to cure an existing default. An Acknowledgment of Debt and Consent to Judgment can save time and money where the primary obligor believes it can cure the existing default but merely needs time to accomplish such.

X. Bankruptcy Code Primer for Indenture Trustees and Bondholders New to the Bankruptcy Arena

A. The Bankruptcy Reform Act of 1978

In response to the difficulties corporations and municipalities were experiencing in the 1960s and early 1970s, Congress as part of the Bankruptcy Reform Act of 1978 (the "Bankruptcy Code")[271] created new Chapters 7, 9 and 11 to deal with bankruptcy liquidation, municipal debt adjustment and corporate reorganization, respectively. In the following pages, a brief overview of these statutes by way of background will be provided for the corporate trust officer or neophyte bondholder.

B. Initiation of Proceedings under Chapters 7, 9 and 11

1. Chapter 9 (Municipalities)

A Chapter 9 proceeding for the adjustment of the debt of the municipality may be filed only by the municipality.[272] In such a case, the debt of the municipality is adjusted, not eliminated. Only a municipality may be a debtor under Chapter 9, and only a municipality may file a petition under Chapter 9. Creditors of a municipality cannot institute involuntary proceedings.[273] Chapter 9 is the exclusive chapter under which municipalities can file. Chapters 7 and 11 are not available because municipalities are not debtors under such chapters. Before a municipality is able to institute a proceeding under Chapter 9, it must be specifically authorized to be a debtor under such chapter by state law.[274] This is not as simple and clear as it may seem, and advice of counsel should be obtained as to whether a municipality is authorized to file a Chapter 9 proceeding and what process, if any, is required to obtain such authorization. What the indenture trustee or bondholder needs to know about Chapter 9 is discussed in more detail in Chapter XII of this book.

---

271 11 U.S.C. §§ 101–1330 (2010).

272 *See* 11 U.S.C. § 109(c).

273 *See* 11 U.S.C. §§ 303 and 901(a).

274 *See* 11 U.S.C. § 109(c). See discussion of the various state laws in Chapter XII *infra*.

2. Chapters 7 and 11 (Corporations and Business Entities)

A Chapter 7 proceeding is essentially a liquidation. Conversely, a Chapter 11 case is a proceeding for reorganization of the debtor, and the ideal is for the debtor to emerge from the case as an operating entity with a different debt structure.[275]

A Chapter 7 or Chapter 11 proceeding may be instituted by the debtor (voluntary) or by three creditors of the debtor (involuntary). No involuntary petition may be filed against a farmer or corporation that is not a monied business or commercial corporation (not-for-profit corporation).[276] Three creditors holding claims against a debtor, not contingent as to liability, in the aggregate of at least $15,775 in excess of the value of any lien securing the claims may file a petition if the debtor against whom the order for leave is sought is a person or entity entitled to benefits under Chapter 7 or 11. An indenture trustee may be counted as such a creditor.[277]

C. Dismissal of Petition

If it can be shown to the bankruptcy court that a petition was filed by a municipality not in good faith or not meeting the requirements of Chapter 9, that petition may be dismissed. Similarly, a bad faith filing under Chapter 7 or 11 of the Bankruptcy Code should be dismissed. Single-asset entities or special purpose corporations (represented to be "bankruptcy proof") may be subject to charges of bad faith filing if the petition is an attempt to interfere with the exercise of remedies or to benefit other parties who are not the debtor. If a debtor in a Chapter 11 proceeding continues to operate at a loss or diminution of the estate with an absence of a reasonable likelihood of rehabilitation, or if a debtor is unable to effectuate a plan or delays unreasonably in formulating a plan, a Chapter 11 proceeding may be dismissed or converted to a Chapter 7 case. Generally, the court may dismiss or convert a Chapter 11 proceeding to a case under Chapter 7 for any grounds that are in the best interest of the creditors and the estate.[278] Appendix X-A provides an Overview of the Reorganization Process (Chapter 11).

---

275 There have been Chapter 11 proceedings, however, where a debtor has proposed a liquidating plan of reorganization.

276 *See* 11 U.S.C. §§ 301 and 303.

277 *See Caplin v. Marine Midland and Grace Tr. Co.*, 406 U.S. 416 (1972). The Third Circuit has held that a fully secured creditor may participate in the filing of an involuntary proceeding if the other petitioning creditors' unsecured claims aggregate to the required amount. *See Paradise Hotel Corp. v. Bank of Novia Scotia*, 842 F.2d 47 (3d Cir. 1988); *In re Fox*, 1994 WL 484596 (N.D. Ill. Sept. 2, 1994).

278 11 U.S.C. § 1112(b)(1); *Shulkin Hutton, Inc., P.S. v. Treiger (In re Owens)*, 552 F.3d 958 (9th Cir. 2009).

D. The Automatic Stay

1. Effect of Stay

Under Section 362 of the Bankruptcy Code, the filing of a petition under Chapter 7, 9 or 11 operates as an automatic stay of any action to collect a debt from the debtor, create a lien on the debtor's property or take possession of the debtor's property. In essence, any action after the filing of the petition where one creditor would attempt through such action to be preferred over other similarly situated creditors is prohibited. (The exception in Chapter 9 of the Bankruptcy Code with respect to pledged municipal special revenues or revenues subject to a statutory lien and the statutory and constitutional basis mandating payment of principal and interest will be discussed in Chapter XII.) In other words, upon the filing of a petition, a creditor is precluded from taking any steps to exercise remedies absent a court order providing relief from the stay.

This restriction includes a secured creditor. The purpose of the automatic stay is to avoid harassment of the debtor and to permit an orderly reorganization or liquidation of the estate. Section 362(a)(1) stays virtually all judicial and quasi-judicial activity against the debtor. Section 362(a)(2) bars the enforcement of a judgment. Subsections 362(a)(3), (4) and (5) prohibit any act to obtain possession of the property of the estate or to create or perfect a security interest against the property of the debtor or the estate. Subsections 362(a)(6) prohibits any act to collect a debt from the debtor and subsection 362(a)(7) prohibits setoff. Given the sweep of Section 362, creditors frequently argue that the section does not apply because the property in question is not property of the estate.[279] However, it is important to separate fact from fiction.

2. Lifting the Stay

A creditor may petition the court for relief from the automatic stay and, after notice and hearing, the court may either continue, modify conditions of or terminate the stay.[280] A creditor will file an application for relief of the stay because he believes the collateral is declining in value and the mere passage of time is jeopardizing his position. Section 362 permits the court to grant relief from the stay: (1) for cause including lack of adequate protection (which will be discussed later), or (2) if the debtor does not have any equity in the property and the property is not necessary for an effective reorganization. This provision is one of the strongest protections conferred on secured creditors. Likewise, holders of liens on "single asset real estate" receive certain protections pursuant to Section 362(d)(3).[281] For example, if the debtor is not making payments to the secured creditor, the bankruptcy court shall grant relief from the stay to allow a

---

279 *Rodger v. County of Monroe (In re Rodgers)*, 333 F.3d 64 (2d Cir. 2003).

280 11 U.S.C. §§ 362(d) and (e).

281 "Single Asset Real Estate" is defined under 11 U.S.C. § 101(51B).

creditor secured by an interest in such single asset real estate to institute actions against the debtor unless, the later of 90 days after the bankruptcy filing or 30 days after the court's determination that the debtor is a single asset real estate entity, the debtor has filed a plan that has a reasonable possibility of being confirmed within a recoverable time.

3. Adequate Protection

Adequate protection is not defined in the Bankruptcy Code but examples are given in Section 361: cash payments necessary to compensate for any decrease in value; additional or replacement liens to compensate for a decrease in value; resumed debt payments or any other means that will result in the realization of the indubitable equivalent of the creditor's interest in its property. Courts can be creative in ordering adequate protection. For example, in the *Delta Airlines* bankruptcy, the court ordered the debtor airline to follow and comply with a plan to maintain the aircraft serving as collateral as a form of adequate protection. The requirement of adequate protection seeks to ensure that, while a creditor's remedies may be suspended or abrogated by the automatic stay, the value of its secured position as it existed at the commencement of the case is protected throughout the case.[282]

The interest to be protected by Section 362(d)(1) is the creditor's interest in the property, which is measured by the value of the lien, and not by the amount of the debt. In the case of *United Sav. Ass'n v. Timbers of Inwood Forest Assocs.*,[283] the United States Supreme Court held that the adequate protection provisions of the Bankruptcy Code do not require periodic postpetition payments of interest or lost opportunity cost to unsecured or undersecured creditors (where the value of the collateral is less than the debt) in order to compensate them for the delay occasioned by a Chapter 11 reorganization proceeding, and their interest does not accrue postpetition. The fully secured creditor (where the value of the collateral is more than the debt) should be entitled to interest accruing postpetition.

A sufficient equity cushion existing between the amount of the indebtedness owed and the value of the property securing such indebtedness may provide the creditor adequate protection against a decrease in value during the automatic stay.[284] Where there is no evidence that the value of the property is declining during the automatic stay, this alone may prevent relief from the stay even where the equity cushion is minimal. Periodic cash payments to the secured creditor as necessary to compensate for any decrease in value of the property during the stay

---

282 *In re Helionetics, Inc.*, 70 B.R. 433 (Bankr. C.D. Cal. 1987).

283 484 U.S. 365 (1988).

284 *Pistole v. Mellor (In re Mellor)*, 734 F.2d 1396 (9th Cir. 1984); *In re Swedeland Dev. Grp., Inc.*, 16 F.3d 552 (3d Cir. 1994); *In re Franklin Equip. Co.*, 416 B.R. 483 (Bankr. E.D. Va. 2009); *In re AMR*, 490 B.R. 470 (S.D.N.Y. Apr. 3, 2013).

have been held to provide adequate protection. Where the value of the property will not decrease during the period of the automatic stay, adequate protection is provided by the payment of taxes and insurance.

4. Relief from Stay for Other Than Lack of Adequate Protection

Relief from the stay provided for in Section 362(d), which applies only to the stay of an act against property, may be based upon lack of equity in the property accompanied by a lack of need for the property for an effective reorganization.[285] The reference to an effective reorganization requires relief from the stay if there is no reasonable possibility of a successful reorganization within a reasonable period of time. The lack of equity test is most relevant in liquidation cases where rehabilitation is not being sought and where, if there is no equity to be realized for junior interests, there is no reason to continue the stay. The stay may also be lifted for "cause."

In a creditor's request to lift the automatic stay with respect to a secured claim, the creditor should seek to establish that the estate is being grossly mismanaged, that necessary repairs to its collateral are not being made, that insurance premiums and taxes are not being paid, that the debtor is not complying with state and local laws, that the collateral is not essential and that the debtor is not likely to reorganize or liquidate under Chapter 11.

Since the automatic stay covers the property of the debtor, it generally does not preclude a suit against a guarantor or the drawing upon a letter of credit. However, the automatic stay may prevent application of a debt service reserve fund[286] to pay principal or interest without leave of court.

5. Timing of Sections 1110 and 1168: Relief from Stay for Aircraft Equipment, Vessels and Rolling Stock Equipment

Under Sections 1110(a)(2) and 1168(a)(2) of the Bankruptcy Code, a secured party with a purchase money security interest in equipment defined therein, or a lessor or conditional vendor (including an indenture trustee) of aircraft equipment and vessels or rolling stock, respectively, as defined, may take the possession of such equipment in compliance with the terms of the financing documentation 60 days after the order of relief granting the bankruptcy petition, unless the debtor agrees to perform all obligations on and after that date under the financing documents and cures the default (other than the bankruptcy and insolvency). Sometimes the parties will

---

285 *In re Indian Palms Assoc. Ltd.*, 61 F.3d 197 (3d Cir. 1995).

286 *See In re Hernando Healthcare Inc.*, 157 B.R. 701 (Bankr. M.D. Fla. 1993); *In re CS Assocs.*, 121 B.R. 942 (Bankr. E.D. Pa. 1990); *see also In re United Airlines*, 438 F.3d 720, 727 (7th Cir. 2006).

agree, subject to the payment of acceptable consideration, to extend the time within which the debtor must agree to perform all obligations.

E. Debtor's Use, Sale or Lease of Property

From a debtor-in-possession's point of view, the ability to use and dispose of property is essential to a business reorganization. From a secured creditor's position, this power poses a threat. On the one hand, a creditor realizes that a successful rehabilitation may result in a full return to him. On the other hand, he is concerned that the debtor-in-possession might consume his collateral in an unsuccessful reorganization attempt. Where the property is relatively liquid, such as accounts receivable, inventory or cash, this concern is acute. Section 363 of the Bankruptcy Code gives the debtor-in-possession or the trustee the power to use, sell or lease property of the estate in the ordinary course of business without notice or hearing except if such property constitutes cash collateral. The use, sale or lease of cash collateral requires either the consent of the entity having an interest therein or court authorization. As will be explained further in Chapter XI, a hearing on the debtor's use of cash collateral will take place early in the proceedings. Particularly if the indenture trustee is a secured creditor of the estate, the indenture trustee will want to ensure it is receiving adequate protection for that use of cash collateral. The use, sale or lease of estate property other than in the ordinary course of business also requires consent or court authorization. Section 363 does not apply to a Chapter 9 proceeding (the Bankruptcy Code does not provide for jurisdiction over the government and affairs and revenues of the municipality) but would be applicable to a private corporation in a conduit municipal financing. The sale can be subject to or free of existing liens. Use may cause depreciation of collateral. Where the collateral is cash, its use may be tantamount to consumption unless it is used to purchase other property having equal value. What safeguards are afforded the creditor with an interest in such property?

1. Adequate Protection

The court must condition or prohibit the debtor's use, sale or lease of property from diminution in value of the collateral at the request of an entity with an interest therein as necessary to adequately protect the requesting entity. Adequate protection here has the same meaning as in a hearing on relief from the automatic stay as described in D above. A common form of adequate protection is for the security interest to attach to the proceeds of the sale or a replacement lien to attach to new collateral including that generated during the bankruptcy.

2. Cash Collateral

The debtor has the burden of establishing that his use of cash collateral will be such that adequate protection is provided to the creditor's interest in the property. The debtor is required to obtain a court order approving the use of cash collateral at which the issue of the adequate protection to the secured lender is the primary focus. Section 363(c)(4) provides that the debtor is required to segregate and account for any cash collateral in the debtor's possession.

3. Sales Free of Liens

Such sales can occur only in one of five situations: (a) applicable non-bankruptcy law would permit a sale of such property free of the interest; (b) the entity with the interest consents; (c) the interest is a lien on the sales price greater than the aggregate value of the lien; (d) the interest is in bona fide dispute; or (e) the entity could be compelled in a legal or equitable proceeding to accept a money satisfaction of such interest.

4. Ineffective *Ipso Facto* Clauses

An "*ipso facto*" clause is one that limits or terminates a debtor's rights as a result of the filing of the bankruptcy proceeding or the debtor's financial condition. With respect to an executory contract or unexpired lease, an attempt to terminate or modify the debtor's interest in property of the estate by the use of *ipso facto* clauses (namely, provisions that state that, in bankruptcy, the debtor has no right to use, sale or possession of property) will be ineffective with respect to executory contracts or unexpired leases pursuant to Section 365(e)(1). Under the Bankruptcy Code, the mere fact that a debtor files for relief under the bankruptcy laws should not be used against the debtor to claim that such executory contract or unexpired lease has been breached.[287]

F. Obtaining Postpetition Credit (Debtor-in-Possession Loans)

A debtor is required to seek court permission to use "cash collateral" or to borrow money in a bankruptcy proceeding. After the debtor has obtained permission to use cash collateral, the debtor will likely seek to obtain credit under Section 364 of the Bankruptcy Code, generally early in the proceeding and often as part of the "first-day" motions. Typically, a creditor who has already lent a large amount of money to the debtor will consider providing postpetition financing. Often, such creditor advances funds postpetition to protect its interest in the company, determining that an immediate liquidation would result in a substantial loss to the lender.

---

287 In what has been described as an "outrageous" decision (Richard Broude, *Executory Contracts and Unexpired Leases in Bankruptcy,* C867 AB1-ABA 471, 2008 WL4924926), one court has held that as an indenture is subject to the provisions of Section 365 as an executory contract, no acceleration by unsecured creditors was allowed on account of an *ipso facto* clause for the sole reason of the filing of a bankruptcy proceeding. *In re Texaco,* 73 B.R. 960 (Bankr. S.D.N.Y. 1987). It is generally agreed that an indenture is *not* an executory contract. *See In re AMR Corp.,* 730 F.3d 88 (2d Cir. 2013) ("AMR") (indentures are not executory contracts).

Section 364 authorizes the lending of money to the debtor-in-possession. Unless the court orders otherwise, a debtor may obtain unsecured credit and incur unsecured debt in the ordinary course of its business, allowable as an administrative expense under Section 503(b). If the debtor is unable to obtain unsecured credit allowable under Section 503(b)(1) as an administrative expense, the court after notice and hearing may authorize the obtaining of credit or the incurring of debt: (i) with a priority over all administrative expenses of the kind specified in Section 503(b) (*i.e.*, wages, taxes, compensation of professionals, etc.) or 507(b) (claims arising from insufficient adequate protection); (ii) secured by a lien on property of the estate that is not otherwise subject to a lien; (iii) secured by a junior lien on property of the estate that is subject to a lien; or (iv) obtain credit secured by a lien equal or senior to that of a prior lien on the property of the estate under certain circumstances.[288] Although subsection (a) authorizes unsecured borrowings, they are not routinely available from lenders or creditors.

G. Safe-Harbor Protections for Certain Contracts

Under the Bankruptcy Code, certain categories of contractual agreements are excluded from the scope of the automatic stay imposed by Section 362. Section 362(b)(6) provides that the stay does not bar the right under a security agreement or arrangement forming a part of a commodity contract, forward contract or securities contract to offset or net out termination value, the payment amount or any other transfer obligation. Section 362(b)(7) contains a similar exclusion relating to repurchase agreements. Sections 362(b)(17) and 362(b)(27) contain similar provisions applicable to swap agreements and master netting agreements, respectively. Further, there is no prohibition from terminating securities contracts,[289] commodities or forward contracts,[290] repurchase agreements,[291] swap agreements[292] or master netting agreements[293] because the debtor has filed a bankruptcy petition. The non-debtor party, which may be a corporate indenture trustee, has the ability to declare the bankruptcy filing an event that terminates the contract. These contracts will be discussed further in Chapter XVII. The purpose of these safe harbors is generally to protect the sanctity of the financial markets from the bankruptcies of market participants.

---

288 *See In re Colter, Inc.*, 53 B.R. 958 (Bankr. D. Colo. 1985).

289 11 U.S.C. § 555.

290 11 U.S.C. § 556.

291 11 U.S.C. § 559.

292 11 U.S.C. § 560.

293 11 U.S.C. § 561.

H. The United States Trustee

Under Section 307 of the Bankruptcy Code, the United States Trustee ("U.S. Trustee") may raise, may appear and may be heard on any issue in any case or proceeding under the Bankruptcy Code, but it may not file a claim. An official committee for unsecured creditors is required in all Chapter 11 cases and typically is appointed by the United States Trustee at a first-day meeting of creditors. However, in limited situations, additional committees may be appointed to represent other constituencies, such as bondholders or noteholders, if the U.S. Trustee thinks it appropriate. Actual committee membership is left to the discretion of the U.S. Trustee. It is not unusual for the U.S. Trustee to take an active role in the negotiation of a cash collateral order with a view to protecting the rights of all creditors, particularly if official creditors' committees have not been appointed at the time of the negotiation of the order. The U.S. Trustee will review fee applications filed in the case and has been known to object to applications that it believes are excessive. The U.S. Trustee may also request the appointment of a trustee or examiner in appropriate cases.

I. The 1111(b) Election to Be Treated as a Fully Secured Creditor

Section 1111(b) is designed to allow an undersecured creditor to be treated as a fully secured creditor in a Chapter 11 proceeding. Because the creditor surrenders any claim to a deficiency when he elects the 1111(b) option, he is likely to make the election in circumstances in which he believes the court has undervalued the collateral and in which he believes the collateral will appreciate substantially during the period following confirmation. If the creditor wishes to be able to object to a plan of reorganization, the election should not be made, since one would give up the ability to vote against the plan as an unsecured creditor. The indenture trustee of a leverage lease transaction should consider a Section 1111(b) election only if directed by the holders and if assured that the property has greater value than would be generated by continued involvement as a secured creditor with a deficiency claim.

J. Notice, List of Creditors and Proof of Claim

Under Chapter 9, notice must be given of the commencement of the case, of an order for relief under Chapter 9 and of any dismissal of the case under Chapter 9. Such notices must be published once a week for three successive weeks in at least one newspaper of general circulation published in the district in which the case was commenced and in such newspapers having general circulation among bond dealers and bondholders as the court designates.[294] Under both Chapter 9 and Chapter 11, in order to vote on any plan of adjustment or plan of reorganization and to be counted as a creditor, a party who has a claim against the debtor (corporate, municipal

---

294 11 U.S.C. § 923.

or business entity) must either file a proof of claim under Section 501 or be listed as a creditor in the list of creditors filed by the debtor under Sections 521(1) and 924. Pursuant to Sections 925 and 1111(a), any claim that appears in a list of creditors filed by the debtor in a Chapter 9 or 11 proceeding will be deemed to be a filed proof of claim under Section 501 except in the case of a claim that is listed as disputed, contingent or unliquidated. The indenture trustee should carefully review the schedules and make sure the proof of claim filed reflects the full amount owed to the indenture trustee and bondholders and all claims or cause of action that can be asserted. The proof of claim should be filed as soon as possible by the indenture trustee, who should reserve the right to amend such proof of claim. The amount due holders on their debt securities is included in the indenture trustee's proof of claim. Of course, if a bondholder contends it has an additional unique, separate and independent claim against the debtor, the bondholder can file its own claim. To the degree the bondholder's claim is duplicative of the indenture trustee's claim, the debtor likely will move to strike the bondholder claim.

K. Assumption, Rejection or Assignment of Executory Contracts and Unexpired Leases

A municipality or corporate debtor subject to court approval may assume or reject an executory contract or unexpired lease of the respective municipality or corporate debtor subject to certain specific provisions of the Bankruptcy Code.[295] Legislative history suggests that executory contracts are those in which performance remains due to some extent on both sides. Under this view, notes, bonds and contracts under which the only outstanding obligation is repayment on the one side and some ministerial act such as surrender of the note or cancellation of a lien on the other do not constitute executory contracts.[296] *Ipso facto* clauses, that is, clauses terminating or modifying an executory contract or unexpired lease or any right or obligation under such contract or lease on account of insolvency or bankruptcy, are unenforceable in bankruptcy. These include clauses that accelerate the payment of obligations in the event of insolvency or bankruptcy.

If a municipality or corporate debtor desires to assume such an executory contract or unexpired lease, it must cure any default that may exist except for defaults that are caused by reason of the institution of the bankruptcy proceeding or the financial condition of the debtor at the time of the pendency of the bankruptcy proceeding.[297] If the municipality or corporate debtor decides not to cure the existing default, the municipality or corporate debtor may still

---

295 11 U.S.C. § 365.

296 *In re Zenith Lab, Inc.*, 104 B.R. 667 (Bankr. D.N.J. 1989); *In re PWS Holding Corp.*, 2002 WL 32332066 (Bankr. D. Del. Jan. 30 2002); *In re AMR Corp.*, 730 F.3d 88, 106 (2d Cir. 2013 (citing cases)); H.R. REP. NO. 95-595, 95th Cong., 2d Sess. 347.

297 11 U.S.C. § 365(b).

assume the executory contract or unexpired lease if it provides adequate assurance that any such default will be promptly cured and provides adequate assurance that future performance under the contract or lease will be complied with.[298] A corporate debtor must assume or reject an unexpired lease of nonresidential real property under which the debtor is the lessee within 120 days after the order for relief, by the date of the entry of an order confirming a plan or prior to the expiration of the 120-day period (which may be extended for 90 days for cause) or the lease shall be deemed rejected and the nonresidential real property surrendered to the landlord.[299] A Chapter 9 or 11 debtor may assume or reject an executory contract or unexpired lease at any time before confirmation of the plan except that, upon request, the court may order the debtor to determine within the specified period of time whether to assume or reject it. In a Chapter 7 proceeding, if a trustee does not assume or reject an executory contract or unexpired lease of the debtor within 60 days after the order for relief or such additional time as the court may fix, such contract or lease is deemed rejected.[300] The debtor may not assume or assign an executory contract to borrow money, for debt or equity financing or for financial accommodations to or for the benefit of the debtor.[301] If a contract or lease is rejected, the creditor has a claim for damages arising out of the rejection. It should be noted that, in a Chapter 9 case, a lease to a municipality will not be treated as an executory contract or unexpired lease for purposes of Section 365 (executory contracts) or Section 503(b)(6) (real estate lease damage limitations) of the Bankruptcy Code solely by reason of its being subject to termination in the event the debtor fails to appropriate rent.[302]

L. Ability of a Municipality or Corporate Debtor to Set aside Transfers and Liens (Preferences and Fraudulent Conveyances)

The debtor can avoid transfers, including transfers of security interests, that would be avoidable by a judicial lien creditor on the property of the debtor as of the date of the petition. Such an actual or hypothetical creditor would have the status granted either by having a writ of execution against the property of the debtor unsatisfied as of the date of the petition or by being a bona fide purchaser of real property of the debtor as of the date of the petition.[303] However,

298 11 U.S.C. §§ 365(b)(1)(B) and (C).

299 11 U.S.C. § 365(d)(4). If the court grants an additional 90 days for cause, it may grant a subsequent extension only on prior written consent of the lessor.

300 11 U.S.C. § 365(d)(1).

301 11 U.S.C. § 365(c).

302 11 U.S.C. § 939. The obligation under Section 929 is treated as a debt financing and not an executory contract that can be rejected.

303 11 U.S.C. § 544.

under Chapter 9, the transfer of property of the debtor to or for the benefit of any holder of a bond or note, on account of such bond or note, cannot be set aside as a preference.[304]

1. Statutory Liens

Any statutory lien, such as a mechanic's, warehouseman's or tax lien, that can be placed on the debtor's property after commencement of a proceeding under Chapter 11 can be avoidable if (1) such is triggered upon commencement of a proceeding; (2) it is not perfected or enforceable on the date of filing of a petition; (3) it is for rent; or (4) it is a lien of distress for rent. Once an involuntary petition in bankruptcy has been filed against an insolvent taxpayer, the government's rights as a recorded tax lien holder under the federal insolvency statute[305] close and are no longer governed by that statute, and its priority rights are governed by the Bankruptcy Code. As will be discussed in Chapter XII, under Chapter 9, municipal bankruptcy, a prepetition statutory lien granting a creditor an interest in certain taxes or revenues of the municipality is effective postpetition and cannot be terminated by the filing of a Chapter 9 petition.

2. Preferences

Under Section 547 of the Bankruptcy Code, the debtor may avoid any transfer, including the transfer of a security interest, made to or for a creditor on account of an antecedent debt within 90 days before the filing of a petition, if such transfer would give the creditor more than he would otherwise receive in a liquidation of the bankruptcy estate under Chapter 7. The preference period is extended to one year if the creditor is an insider (such as a director, officer or major shareholder of a corporate debtor; a general partner of a debtor; or the relative of a general partner, director, officer or person in control of a debtor). The trustee is prevented from avoiding payments made in the ordinary course of business of debts incurred in the ordinary course of business according to ordinary business terms during the 90-day preference period. Such language has been interpreted as including interest payments on long-term debt.[306] A voidable preference does not occur if the transaction was intended and, in fact, was a substantially contemporaneous exchange for new value given to the debtor.[307] A preference does not occur if the transfer was in payment of debt incurred in the ordinary course of business or financial affairs of the debtor.[308] A voidable preference does not occur upon the transfer of a perfected

---

304 11 U.S.C. § 926.

305 31 U.S.C. § 3713.

306 *See, e.g.*, *In re Magic Circle Energy Corp.*, 64 B.R. 269 (Bankr. W.D. Okla. 1986); *Fidelity Savs. & Inv. Co. v. New Hope Baptist*, 880 F.2d 1172 (10th Cir. 1989).

307 11 U.S.C. §§ 547(c)(1), (c)(3) and (c)(4).

308 11 U.S.C. § 547(c)(2).

security interest in inventory or receivables except to the extent of any net reduction in the excess of the secured claim over the value of the security.[309] As will be discussed in Chapter XII, payments to municipal bondholders within 90 days of filing a Chapter 9 petition are not preferences in a Chapter 9 proceeding.

3. Fraudulent Conveyance

A conveyance of property made prepetition by a debtor may be avoided for "active" fraud or "constructive" fraud. A fraudulent conveyance is a transfer of the interest of the debtor (a) that was with the actual intent to hinder, delay or defraud any entity to which the debtor was indebted, or (b) where less than reasonable equivalent value was received by the debtor, where the debtor was insolvent or with unreasonably small capital or where the transfer caused all of the debtor's debt to exceed the debtor's ability to pay. The debtor may avoid fraudulent transfers made within two years before the filing of the petition,[310] which can under certain circumstances include a foreclosure sale.[311]

The debtor may avoid fraudulent transfers made within two years before the filing of the petition.[312] It has been stated that a leveraged buyout can constitute a fraudulent conveyance under certain circumstances.[313] Such a legal determination would mean, in some cases, that parties obtaining collateral as part of the leveraged buyout would have to give up that collateral. The leveraged buyout as a fraudulent conveyance issue arises because the purchaser acquires the funds necessary for the acquisition through borrowings secured directly or indirectly by the assets of the company being acquired, and the proceeds are used in essence to pay the old stockholders. The lender who provides the funds is looking primarily to the future operating earnings of the acquired company or to the proceeds from future sales of assets of the company rather than to any other asset of the purchasers to repay the borrowings used to make the acquisition. A leveraged buyout generally results in the substitution of significant amounts of new debt in the place of equity in the corporation's capital structure. In transactions where banks or other institutional lenders provide the major portion of the debt financing, this new debt is

---

309 11 U.S.C. § 547(c)(5).

310 11 U.S.C. § 548.

311 *Durrett v. Wash. Nat'l Ins. Co.*, 621 F.2d 201 (5th Cir. 1980).

312 11 U.S.C. § 548.

313 *See U.S. v. Gleneagles Inv. Co.*, 565 F. Supp. 556 (M.D. Pa. 1983), *aff'd*, 803 F.2d 1288 (3d Cir. 1986), *cert. denied*, 483 U.S. 1005 (1987); *Kupetz v. Wolf*, 845 F.2d 842 (9th Cir. 1988); *In re Kaiser Steel Corp.*, 87 B.R. 154 (Bankr. D. Colo. 1988); *Wieboldt Stores, Inc. v. Schottenstein*, 94 B.R. 488 (N.D. Ill. 1988); *In re Bachrach Clothing Inc.*, 480 B.R. 820 (Bankr. N.D. Ill. 2012); *In re Tousa, 680* F.3d 1298 (11th Cir. 2012).

likely to be senior secured debt. Thus, a leveraged buyout can adversely impact existing creditors of the company by reducing the assets available for the satisfaction of their claims.

4. Postpetition Acquisitions

Property acquired by the debtor after commencement of the case is not subject to any lien resulting from any security agreement entered into prior to commencement of the case.[314] In other words, a prepetition lien on inventory or accounts receivable does not include postpetition accounts receivable and inventory since the debtor is treated as a new, separate legal entity. There is an exception to this, namely, if in a Chapter 11 or 7 proceeding, the interest is included in the security agreements as "proceeds, product, offspring, rents, or profits" of property covered by the security agreement before commencement of the case, or if, in a Chapter 9 case, the interest is subject to a statutory lien or special revenues in Chapter 9.[315]

Any action to avoid transfers under Section 544, 545, 547, 548 or 553 must be commenced within a specified period of time.[316] The avoiding powers under Sections 544, 545 and 549 are subject to general applicable law that permits "perfection of an interest in property to be effective against an entity that acquires rights in such property before the date of perfection" and "are subject to the right of a seller of goods. . . in the ordinary course of such seller's business, to reclaim such goods" under certain circumstances.[317]

M. Setoffs

A creditor may offset a mutual debt owing by such creditor to the debtor that arose before the commencement of the case against a claim of such creditor against the debtor that arose before the commencement of the case.[318] Although not defined in the Bankruptcy Code, the term "mutual debt" has been construed to mean that the debts are in the same right and between the same parties standing in the same capacity. Section 553 prohibits the setoff of claims against the debtor that were transferred to the creditor by an entity other than the debtor either after the commencement of the case or during the 90 days preceding the petition while the debtor was insolvent. Section 553(a)(3) restricts the setoff of a debt owed to the debtor by a creditor that was incurred within 90 days before the filing of the petition while the debtor was insolvent for

---

314 11 U.S.C. § 552(a).

315 11 U.S.C. §§ 552(b) and 928(a).

316 Generally, such action may not be commenced after the earlier of (1) the later of entry of the order for relief or one year after the appointment or election of the first trustee pursuant to Section 1104 or 1163 or (2) the time the case is closed or dismissed. 11 U.S.C. § 546(a).

317 11 U.S.C. §§ 546(b)(1)(A) and (c)(1).

318 11 U.S.C. § 553(a).

the purpose of obtaining a right of setoff against the debtor. This provision is intended to discourage the practice by which a debtor increases its deposits in its account with a lender bank for the purpose of preferring the bank over other creditors through setoff of these accounts.

N. Administrative Claims

As among unsecured claims, the costs of administration are paid first. Such administrative expenses include the necessary costs of preserving the estate, *i.e.*, wages, salaries or commissions for services rendered after commencement of the case, taxes incurred by the estate and compensation of officers as permitted by the court and of professionals as permitted by the court.[319] Even in the case of a secured claim, the debtor can recover a surcharge for the cost and expense of maintaining the collateral.[320]

O. Plan of Adjustment for Municipalities or Reorganization for Corporations

A municipality must file a plan of adjustment of its debt either with the petition or at such later date as the court may fix.[321] In a Chapter 9 proceeding, only a municipality, and not a creditor, can file a plan of debt adjustment. The municipality may modify the plan at any time prior to confirmation, provided such modification is consistent with the requirements of Chapter 9. The debtor in a Chapter 11 proceeding has the exclusive right to file a plan until 120 days after and to obtain acceptances 180 days after the date of the order for relief. The 120-day period may not be extended beyond a date that is 18 months, and the 180-day period may not be extended beyond a date that is 20 months, after the date of the order for relief. Thereafter, any party in interest may file a plan. The unique features of and procedures applicable to a prepackaged plan are discussed in Chapter XV.

P. Contents of the Plan

The plan may provide among other things for the sale of property of the estate, either subject to or free of any lien; cancellation or modification of any indenture or similar instrument; extension of a maturity date or a change in an interest rate or adjustment of debt or other term of outstanding securities; or issuance of securities of the debtor for existing security; and it may impair any class of claims, secured or unsecured.[322] The plan shall include the following: (a) designation of the classes of claims that exist, specifying any class of claim or interest that is not impaired under the plan; (b) a statement of the treatment of any class of claims or interest that

---

319 11 U.S.C. § 503.

320 11 U.S.C. § 506(c).

321 11 U.S.C. § 941.

322 11 U.S.C. § 1123.

is impaired under the plan; (c) a statement providing for the same treatment for each claim or interest of a particular class unless the holder of a particular claim or interest agrees to less favorable treatment of such claim or interest; (d) a statement of a means for the execution of a plan such as the sale of property, the transfer of property, the satisfaction or modification of any lien, the cancellation or modification of any indenture or similar instrument, the curing or waiving of default, the extension of a maturity date, an adjustment of debt, the change of interest rate or other terms of outstanding securities or the issuance of new securities; (e) a statement, if appropriate, of the settlement or determination of any disputes between parties; and (f) the assumption or rejection of any executory contracts or unexpired leases.

A claim or interest is impaired under the plan unless it remains unaltered as to its legal, equitable or contractual rights and any default that caused the acceleration of the indebtedness is cured; and, in addition, the original maturity of such claim or interest is reinstated as such maturity date existed before the default and any damage suffered by the holder of such claim or interest as a result of reasonable reliance by such holder on such contractual provisions or such applicable law is appropriately compensated and, after curing the default, the equitable, legal and contractual rights of the holder of the claim or interest are not altered or modified.

Q. Classification of Claims and Claim Decision Tree

The plan should classify the claims or interest against the debtor. Each class of claims should contain only those claims or interests that are substantially similar to the other claims or interests of such class. Debtors sometimes attempt to classify public debt with other creditors more favorably inclined to the debtor in order to prevent a separate class of public debtholders who would vote against the plan. The indenture trustee should be alert to improper classification of public debt claims. The general breakdown of the classification of claims and treatment in a plan of reorganization can be found in Appendix X-B. A claim decision tree to determine a claim consideration under a Chapter 11 plan of reorganization can be found in Appendix X-C.

R. Postpetition Disclosure and Solicitation

Acceptance or rejection of a plan may not be solicited after the commencement of a Chapter 9 or 11 proceeding from the holder of a claim or an interest unless at the time of or before such solicitation there is transmitted to such holder the plan or a summary of the plan and a written disclosure statement. This disclosure statement must be approved by the court after a notice and hearing and be determined by the court to contain adequate information to enable creditors to make a decision as to whether to vote in favor of or against the proposed plan of reorganization. After approval of the disclosure statement, the plan and the disclosure statement are sent to the creditors to vote to accept or reject the plan. Many times there is a distribution agent for distribution of the disclosure statement, plan and ballots and to employ a voting tabulation agent for reviewing and counting the ballots. The indenture trustee or its counsel should review the distribution and voting procedures to make sure that the appropriate ballot, disclosure statement and plan are effectively sent to the holders of the indenture securities and that the vote tabulation procedure will capture the votes from security holders' ballots. Most indentures provide that the indenture trustee is not authorized to vote in respect of the claims of the security holders.[323] Accordingly, to the degree possible, the procedures should be structured so that voting on the plan is "passed through" to the holders of the debt. Of course, if for some reason this is not possible, the trustee should bring the problem to the court's attention and obtain an order to avoid injustice to the holders, including allowing the trustee to cast a ballot for them.

Adequate information is defined in the Bankruptcy Code as "information of a kind" and in sufficient detail, as far as is reasonably practicable in light of the nature and history of the debtor and conditions of debtor's books and records, that would enable a hypothetical reasonable investor, typical of holders of claims or interests of the relative class, to make an informed judgment about the plan.[324]

S. Acceptance of the Plan

A holder of an allowed claim or interest may vote to accept or reject a plan. Creditors of a class are deemed to have accepted the plan if two-thirds in allowed amount of the class and more than one-half in number of creditors of the class of those creditors voting vote to accept the plan.[325] Exceptions to this rule are in the case of a class that is not impaired and if there is a "cram down." A cram down consists of a determination by the court that the plan does not discriminate unfairly and is fair and equitable with respect to each class of claims and interests that is impaired under and has not accepted the plan.[326] At least one class of creditors of impaired claims has to accept the plan to have the court confirm the plan in a confirmation hearing.[327]

T. Confirmation of the Plan, Hearing and Requirements

After notice to all interested parties, the court shall hold a hearing on confirmation of a plan. A party in interest, a creditor who is a member of an impaired class, may object to the

---

323 *See, e.g.*, Revised Model Simplified Indenture Section 6.10 set forth in the HANDBOOK FOR INDENTURE AND TRUST INDENTURE ACT INTERPRETATION (American Bar Association 2017), at 20.

324 11 U.S.C. § 1126(c).

325 11 U.S.C. §§ 1126(c) and 1129(a)(8)(A).

326 11 U.S.C. § 1129(b)(1).

327 11 U.S.C. §§ 1129(1)(10) and (b)(1).

confirmation of the plan. The court shall confirm a plan only if it meets the specific requirements of Chapter 9 or 11, including being proposed in good faith and not by any means forbidden by law, and if at least one class of claims has accepted the plan or the court has determined that the plan does not discriminate unfairly and is fair and equitable with respect to each class of claims or interests that is impaired under and has not accepted the plan.[328] In addition to the above requirements, the court shall confirm the plan if it is in the best of the creditors and is feasible.[329]

U. Modification of a Plan

The proponent of a plan in a Chapter 11 proceeding may modify the plan at any time prior to confirmation, provided such modification otherwise meets the other requirements of Chapter 11. In addition, the plan may be modified at any time after its confirmation but before substantial consummation, provided not only that such modification meets the other requirements of Chapter 11, but also that the court, after notice and hearing, confirms such a plan as modified. A municipality in a Chapter 9 proceeding may only modify a plan before confirmation, provided the modification otherwise meets the requirements of Chapter 9 and takes effect upon filing.

V. Effects of Confirmation and Discharge

The provisions of a confirmed plan bind the debtor and any creditor whether or not a proof of claim is filed by such creditor, such claim is allowed or such creditor has accepted the plan. With respect to a Chapter 9 proceeding, the municipality is discharged of all debts that the plan provides are to be discharged upon: (1) confirmation, (2) deposit of the consideration with the disbursing agent and (3) determination that any security to be issued is valid and binding on the debtor as provided in the plan.[330]

W. Continuing Jurisdiction and Closing the Case

The court may retain jurisdiction over the case for such period of time that is necessary for the successful implementation of the plan. Upon the completion of the court's administration of the case, the case will be closed and the court shall have no continuing jurisdiction.

X. Plan of Reorganization and Implementation

The basic options and methods of treating claims in a Chapter 11 plan of reorganization are generally depicted in Appendices X-B and X-C. The purpose of these appendices is to depict

---

328 11 U.S.C. §§ 1129(a)(2), (a)(3), (a)(8), (a)(10) and (b).

329 11 U.S.C. §§ 943 and 1129.

330 11 U.S.C. § 944(b).

the basic structure, flow of cash and assets, and treatment of secured and unsecured claims in a plan of reorganization, which clearly indicates administrative claims must be paid in full first. Appendix X-D shows the basic structure of the reorganized company and the distributions to secured, unsecured and equity claims. In this appendix, notes, secured or unsecured, are used to pay the secured claims, and notes and possibly equity are paid to unsecured claims. Equity will be given whatever is necessary to preserve tax benefits and the remaining value of the company after treatment of creditors.

Appendix X-E demonstrates the basic structure of a liquidating trust. A liquidating trust may be used in a plan of reorganization where the ongoing business will not survive and, in effect, the plan of reorganization is the liquidation of the company. The assets are placed into a liquidating trust to be sold. The creditors who have a security interest in those assets held by the trust may be given the secured notes, and the unsecured creditors receive either notes from the liquidating trust or a certificate of beneficial interest. The equityholders would receive a certificate of beneficial interest junior to any received by the creditors. In any plan process, the allocation of cash to the classes of claims based upon the priorities and funds available is a necessary ingredient of implementing any plan of reorganization.

Appendix X-F sets forth the priorities of claims under Chapter 11 of the Bankruptcy Code. Appendix X-G depicts the allocation of cash to classes of Chapter 11 claims based upon priorities. This appendix generally shows that filed claims, less the contested and disputed claims, which will ultimately be either eliminated or determined, will result in allowed claims.

A general depiction of a plan of reorganization and the initial distribution of debtors' assets on the effective date of a Chapter 11 plan is shown in Appendix X-H-a, which shows secured notes going to bank secured claims (Class 6) and unsecured claims (Class 7) and subordinated notes going to subordinated claims (Class 8), while the priority claims, such as administrative claims (Class 1), priority claims (Class 2), tax claims (Class 3), secured claims (Class 4) as well as small claims (Class 5), receive cash from the distribution fund. Appendix X-H-b deals with a liquidating trust and indicates that the remaining assets are certificates of beneficial interest that go to the equityholders. This assumes that the Chapter 11 debtor is not an ongoing entity that will have its assets sold and liquidated. Allowed claims will be paid under certain specific priorities in a Chapter 11 proceeding, which are depicted in Appendix X-I.

Appendix X-J depicts the treatment of unsecured and secured claims under a plan of reorganization. This chart shows the reorganized company distributing consideration through an estate administrator either to the unsecured claims account, which would be distributed to allowed unsecured claims, or to a reserve account where money would be held until undetermined or contested claims are resolved, a claim is either eliminated or treated as an allowed unsecured claim, and funds from the reserve account are transferred to the unsecured claim account. In addition, payment may be made directly by the reorganized company to the secured lender as a priority payment or, if there is a deficiency claim, it will be made by the estate administrator.

Appendices X-K and X-L show cash distribution and liens post-confirmation for a plan of reorganization and a plan of reorganization with a liquidating trust. The reorganized company pays cash and transfers assets to a distribution fund, and the fund distributes to allowed unsecured claims and reserves appropriate amounts for undetermined claims. Once claims have been resolved, either determined or eliminated, the funds allocated to undetermined claims in the reserve account are transferred to the fund for allowed unsecured claims. Generally, the secured lender claims will be dealt with directly by the reorganized company either by maintaining the liens on the respective collateral or by transferring cash or other consideration to the secured lender for its claims. The distribution of funds through a liquidating trust follows basically the same priority and scheme as that of a plan of reorganization for an ongoing business.

The purpose of these appendices is to show, in a schematic, graphic form, some of the basic structures, claims, treatment and flow of consideration contained in a plan of reorganization.

Y. Chapter 15

The Bankruptcy Code contains a special chapter, enacted in 2005, based upon the Model Law on Cross-Border Insolvency formulated by the United Nations Commission on Insolvency Trade Law. Chapter 15 is designed to encourage cooperation between the United States and other countries with respect to cross-border insolvency matters. Cases instituted under Chapter 15 are intended to be ancillary to cases brought in the debtor's home country unless a bankruptcy case is brought under another chapter of the United States Bankruptcy Code (*i.e.*, Chapter 7 or Chapter 11). An important distinction is the difference between a "foreign main proceeding" or a "foreign non-main proceeding." A proceeding will be designated "main" if it is pending in the country where the debtor has the "center of its main interests," or "non-main" if the debtor has an establishment (any place of operations where the debtor carries out a nontransitory economic activity) in such country.[331] Upon the recognition of a main proceeding, certain provisions of the United States Bankruptcy Code automatically apply without further order of court, including the automatic stay, Section 361 (adequate protection), Section 363 (sale, use and lease of property) and Section 552 (postpetition effect of security interest), which protect the debtor and its property located within the United States. In a non-main proceeding, the court has discretion to

331 11 U.S.C. § 1517(b).

grant the necessary relief and assistance in furtherance of Chapter 15, including suspending the right to transfer assets and entrusting U.S. assets to the foreign representative. Several decisions have denied Chapter 15 petitions seeking recognition as a foreign main proceeding in the winding-up of hedge funds where proceedings were commenced in the Cayman Islands. Both courts ruled that because the funds had little or no contact with the Caymans other than a certificate of incorporation, they could not qualify as a main proceeding.[332] Important factors are the location of the debtor's headquarters, the location of those who manage the debtor, the location of the debtor's primary assets, the location of the majority of the debtor's creditors and the jurisdiction whose law would apply to most disputes.[333]

Z. Bankruptcies Involving Aircraft Equipment and Vessels and Rolling Stock

There are special provisions of the Bankruptcy Code relating to aircraft equipment, vessels[334] and rolling stock.[335] These provisions are designed to protect the lessors, lenders and conditional sellers of these special types of equipment by limiting the ability of the Chapter 11 debtor to remain in possession of such equipment without curing defaults and making the required payments. Being a holder or serving as trustee for financings secured by such equipment can be challenging in a bankruptcy situation. Attached as Appendix X-M is a summary of special considerations applicable to these cases, and Appendices X-N through X-P illustrate certain types of structures typically seen.

AA. Tax Considerations

Chapter 11 obviously has significant tax consequences for the debtor. Major issues typically include the possibility of sheltering cancellation of debt income and the effect of the restructuring on net operating loss carryforwards.[336] Creditors and shareholders also face tax consequences in a Chapter 11 proceeding, particularly regarding their ability to recognize losses incurred or the need to recognize noncash income.[337] Where debt has changed hands during a Chapter 11 case, the non-par subsequent purchaser may face the possible recognition of its gain.

---

332 *See, In re Bear Stearns High Grade Structured Credit Strategies Master Fund,* 389 B.R. 325 (S.D.N.Y. 2008) and *In re SPhinX, Ltd.,* 371 B.R. 10 (Bankr. S.D.N.Y. 2007).

333 *Morning Mist Holdings v. Krys,* 2013 U.S. App. LEXIS 7608 (2d Cir. Apr. 16, 2013).

334 11 U.S.C. § 1110.

335 11 U.S.C. § 1168.

336 In some cases, the tracking of equity or debt of a debtor is restricted by court order (a claims-trading order) in an effort to preserve net operating loss carryforwards due to a concern that such trading may result in a "change of control" of the debtor.

337 Deborah Paul, *The Taxation of Distressed Debt Investments,* 64 TAX LAW. 37 (2011).

As a general rule, the plan will contain disclaimers by the debtor as to tax consequences, so the debtholders must be reminded to consult their own tax advisors on tax issues.

Appendix X-A
An Overview of the Corporate Reorganization Process

Bankruptcy

Analyze the Company's Financial Condition

- Preparation of Debtor Projections
- Review of Debtor Projections for the Following:
  - Optional cash flow for distribution
  - Business strategies for core assets
  - Credit and other financial technologies
  - Proceeds from sale of non-operating assets (non-core)
  - Corporate general and administrative expenses and capital expenditures
- Compare Operating Results to Similar Industry Trends
- Liquidation Analysis and Going Concern Value:
  - Assess and value collateral
  - Determine perfection of security interests
  - Determine distribution to secured and unsecured holders
  - Value litigation, notes receivable and non-core assets
- Review NOL Carry Forwards and Any Cash Flow Benefits

Identify Legal Considerations

- Joint or Separate Plans
- Adequate Protection
- Analysis of Corporate Structure and Assets
- Substantive Consolidation
- Officer and Director Liability and Indemnity
- Classification of Claims by Debtor
- Determination of Amount of Claims of the Debtor
- Preferences, Fraudulent Conveyances and Piercing the Corporate Veil
- Determination of Causes of Action
- Postpetition Operation and Closing Costs, Liabilities and Claims
- Net Operating Losses and Tax Liabilities

Analyze Claims and Priority of Claims

- Identify debtor's administrative, priority, secured and unsecured claims
- Analyze cash flow from non-bankrupt subsidiaries and beneficiaries to debtors
- Analyze legal issues such as substantive consolidation

continued on next page

continued from previous page

Structure the Plan

↓

- Negotiate Plan with Debtors, Creditors' Groups and Committees
- Items to Consider:
  - Cash payments to certain creditors (ability to pay)
  - Capture increasing value of reorganized company for creditors:
    - Debt instruments:
      - Exchangeable preferred stock
      - Common stock
      - Warrants
  - Equity fix to generate credit and business with contractors
  - Escalating interest and dividend rates
  - Exchange portion of debt for equity
- Mechanics for Sharing in Upside of Business:
  - Common stock and warrants
  - Provisions for exchange and / or redemption
  - Contingent cash payments based on operating performance
- Project Creditor's Positions:
  - Restrict new debt and equity issuances to avoid dilution
  - Restrict level of capital expenditures and business expansion
  - Limit secured debt, layering of debt and dividends
  - Board of directors representation
- Management Incentives to Return Business to Optimal Levels:
  - Performance-based incentives

↓

Plan Approval Process

- Indenture Trustees and Other Creditors File Proofs of Claim on or Before Bar Date as Set by the Court
- Preparation of the Plan and the Disclosure Statement
- Plan and Disclosure Statement Are Filed
- Hearing on the Adequacy of the Disclosure Statement and Approval by the Court
- Distribution of the Plan and Disclosure Statement to All Creditors Who Have Filed Claims
- Approval of the Plan by 2/3 of the Amount of Claims and 50 Percent of the Number of Creditors in Each Class
- If All Other Bankruptcy Code Requirements Are Met, Then the Court Will Confirm the Plan (May "Cram Down" on Junior Creditors)
- Upon Confirmation, the Debtor Is Discharged from All Prepetition Debts Except as Provided in the Plan

↓

Distribution

Appendix X-B
Chapter 11 Classification of Claims

Class	Type of Claim	Possible Treatment
Class 1	Administrative Claim (priority and tax claims may be classified separately)	Must be paid in full upon confirmation (tax claims within six years of assessment)
Class 2	Fully Secured Claims (if any)	Payment in full or cure all defaults and provide assurance of future performance
Class 3	Secured Claims (which have collateral value less than debt outstanding)	Secured claim for value of collateral with market rate terms
Class 4	General Unsecured Claims (trade debt and deficiency claim on Class 3 unsecured portion)	Cash, notes or equity, or a combination of all
Class 5	General Unsecured Claims, for example $10,000 or less (or claims above $10,000 that reduce claim to $10,000)	Set recovery of a fixed amount of cents on the dollar
Class 6	Senior Public Debt	Cash, notes or equity (same as Class 4) plus the benefits of subordination
Class 7	Banks and money borrowed: creditor entitled to benefits of subordination (could be Class 3 deficiency claim)	Cash, notes or equity (same as Class 4) plus the benefits of subordination
Class 8	Public Subordinated Debt	Cash, notes or equity (same as Class 4) minus payment on subordination to the degree it is effective
Class 9	Security Fraud Claims of Class 7	Depends on amounts of cash, notes and equity available after satisfying lower numbered classes
Class 10	Security Fraud Claims of Class 8	Depends on amounts of cash, notes and equity available after satisfying lower-numbered classes
Class 11	Equity Interests	Depends on equity available after satisfying lower-numbered classes

Appendix X-C
Claim Decision Tree and Consideration Provided under Chapter 11 Plan of Reorganization

Is the claim. . .

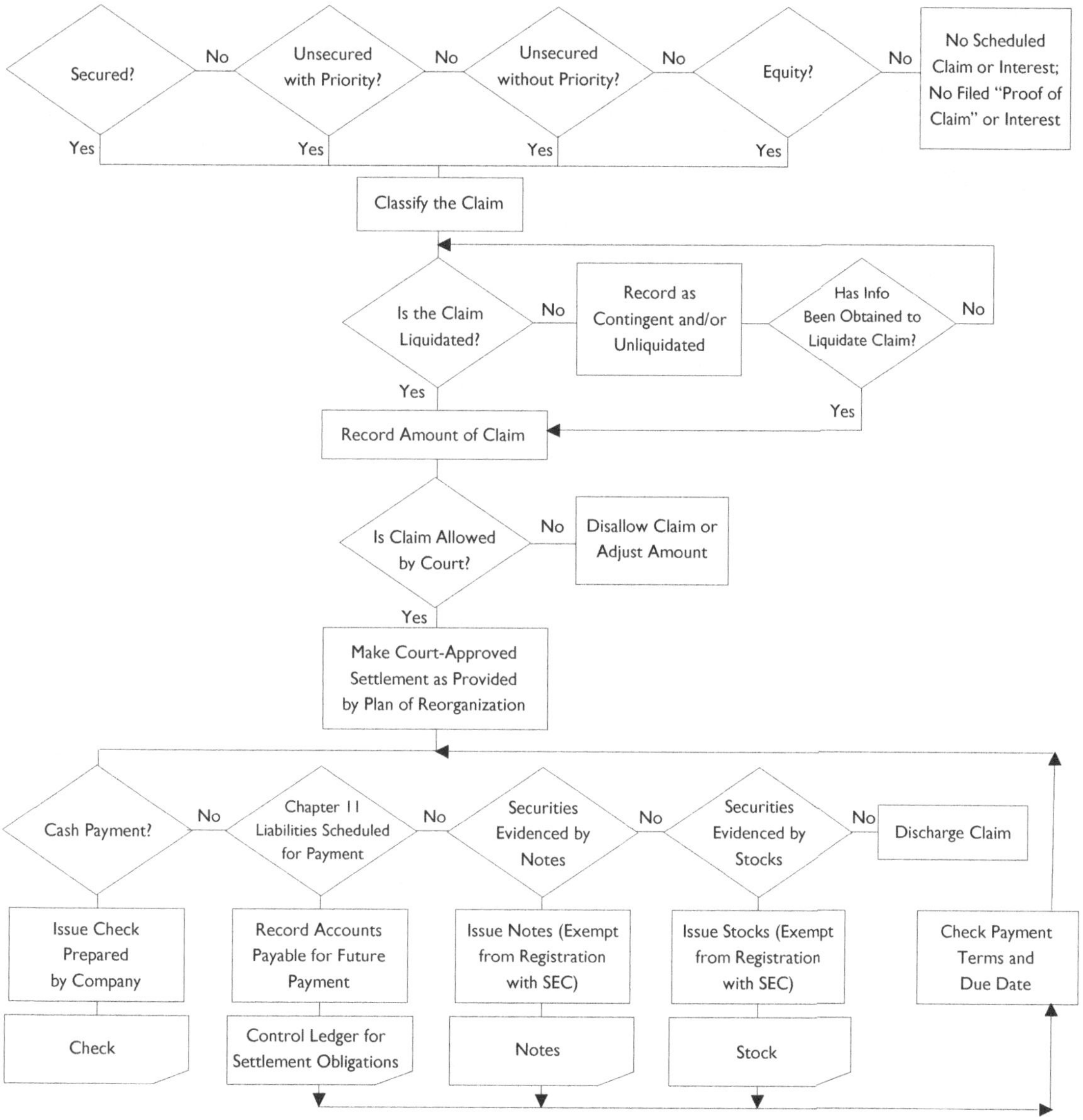

Appendix X-D
Basic Structure of Restructured Debt of a Reorganized Company

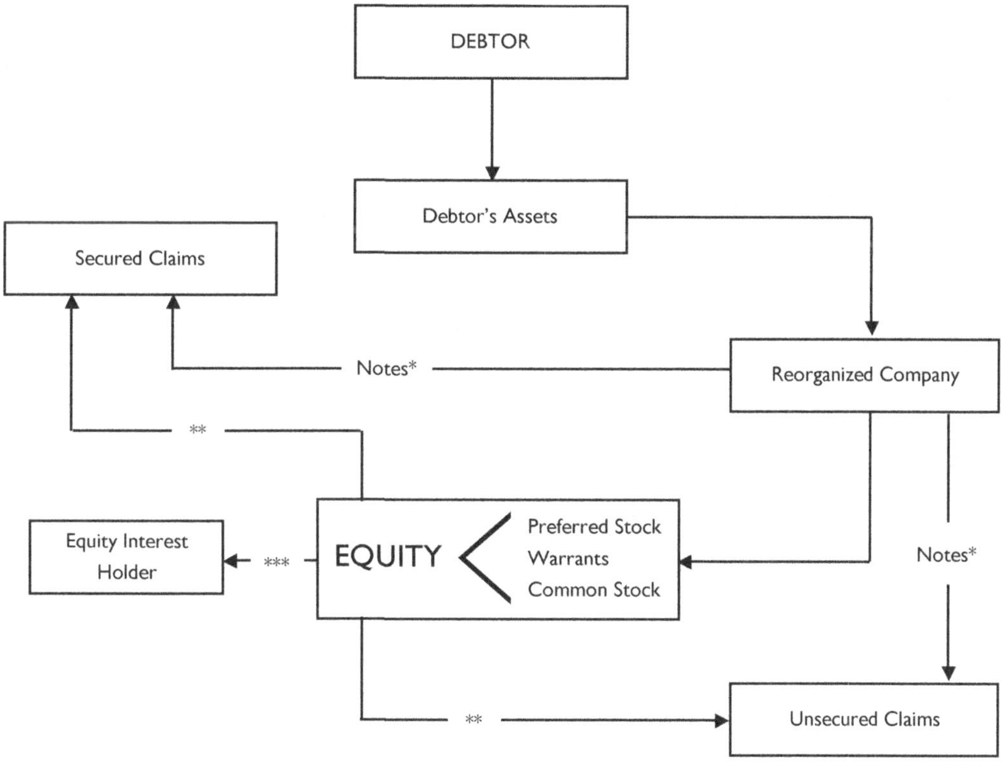

* Notes may be secured or unsecured.

** Equity interest to compensate for loss of value or risk given the reorganization.

*** To extent necessary to preserve tax benefits and remaining value of company after treatment of creditors.

Appendix X-E
Basic Structure Liquidating Trust

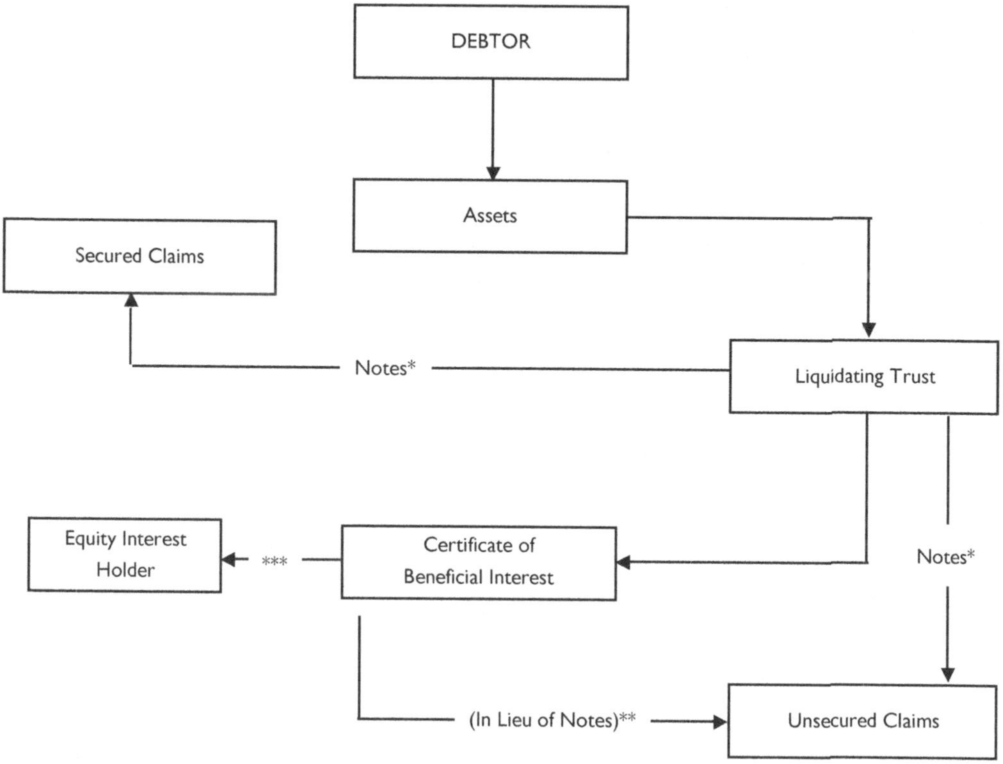

* May be secured or unsecured in relation to prepetition priority and security interest.

** In lieu of or in addition to notes and in the amount determined fair and equitable (more than liquidation value).

*** To extent of the remaining value after treatment of the creditors and/or negotiated value.

Appendix X-F
Priorities of Claims under Chapter 11 of the Bankruptcy Code

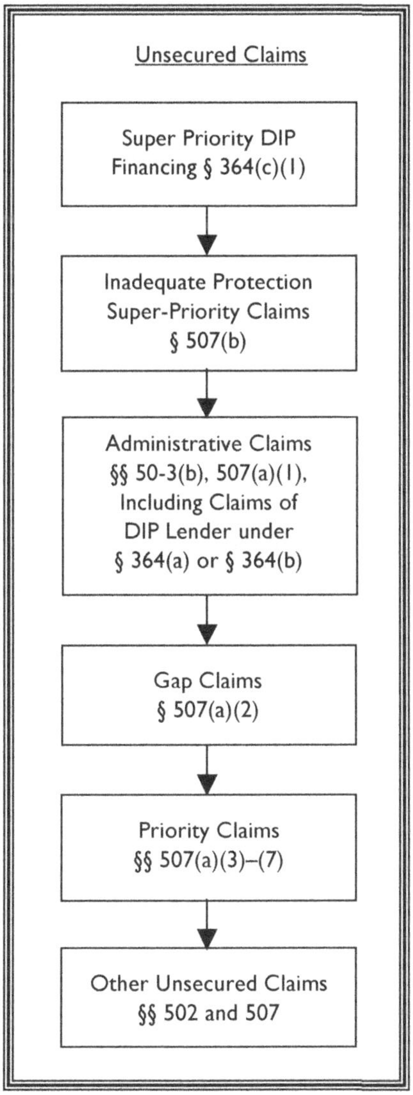

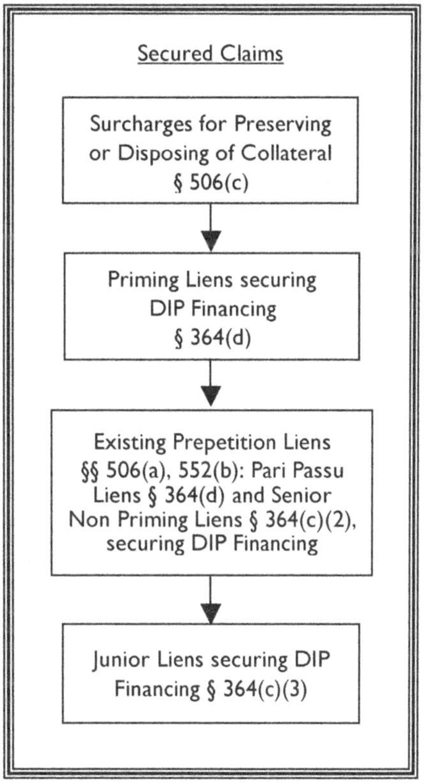

Gap claims arise in an involuntary case during the period after the petition has been filed but prior to the entry of an "order for relief." An order for relief is entered if the petition is uncontroverted or, if it is controverted, when the court finds that the case is a proper involuntary case.

Below gap claims certain other unsecured claims are entitled to priority in a specified order.

Appendix X-G
Allocation of Cash to Classes of Chapter 11 Claims Based upon Priorities and Funds Available after the Plan Effective Date

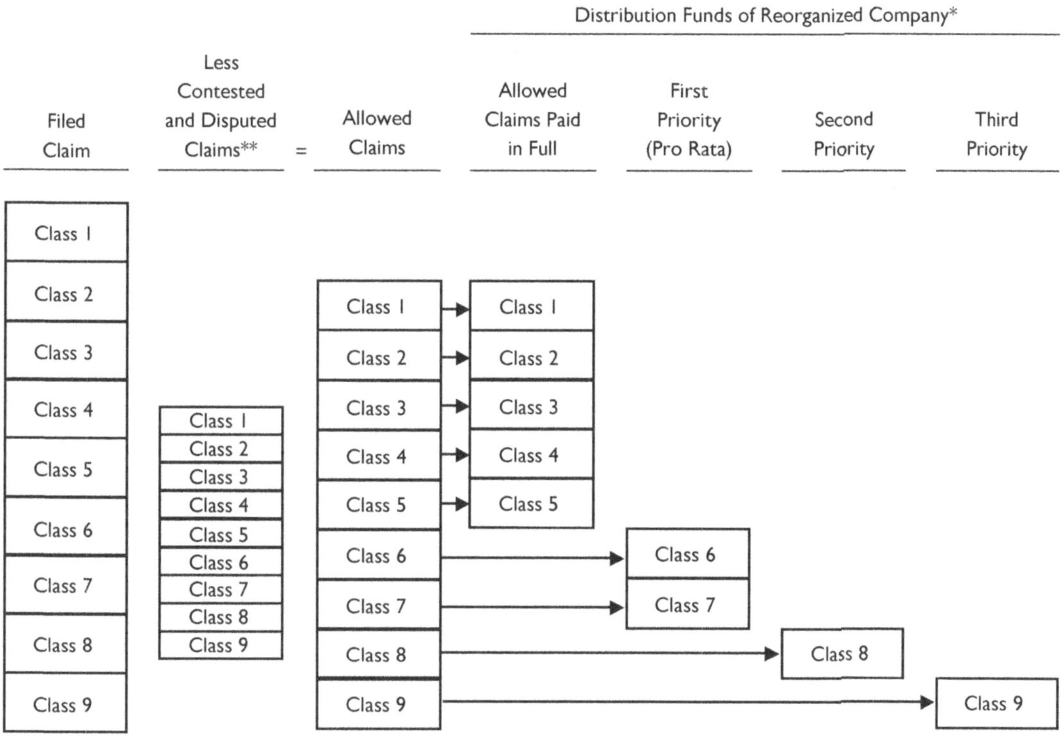

Class 1 – Administrative Claims
Class 2 – Priority Claims
Class 3 – Tax Claims
Class 4 – Secured Claims
Class 5 – Small Claims
Class 6 – Bank Lender and Senior Public Debt Claims in separate class or sub-class
Class 7 – Unsecured Claims including Public Debt but in separate class or sub-class
Class 8 – Subordinated including Subordinated Public Debt Claims but in separate class or sub-class
Class 9 – Equity

* Proceeds of liquidation of non-performing or non-core assets and operational cash flow from reorganized company.

** As part of the reorganization process, contested and disputed claims are resolved so that claims at issue are either eliminated or determined to be allowed claims.

Appendix X-H-a
Initial Distribution of Debtor's Assets on Effective Date of Chapter 11 Plan

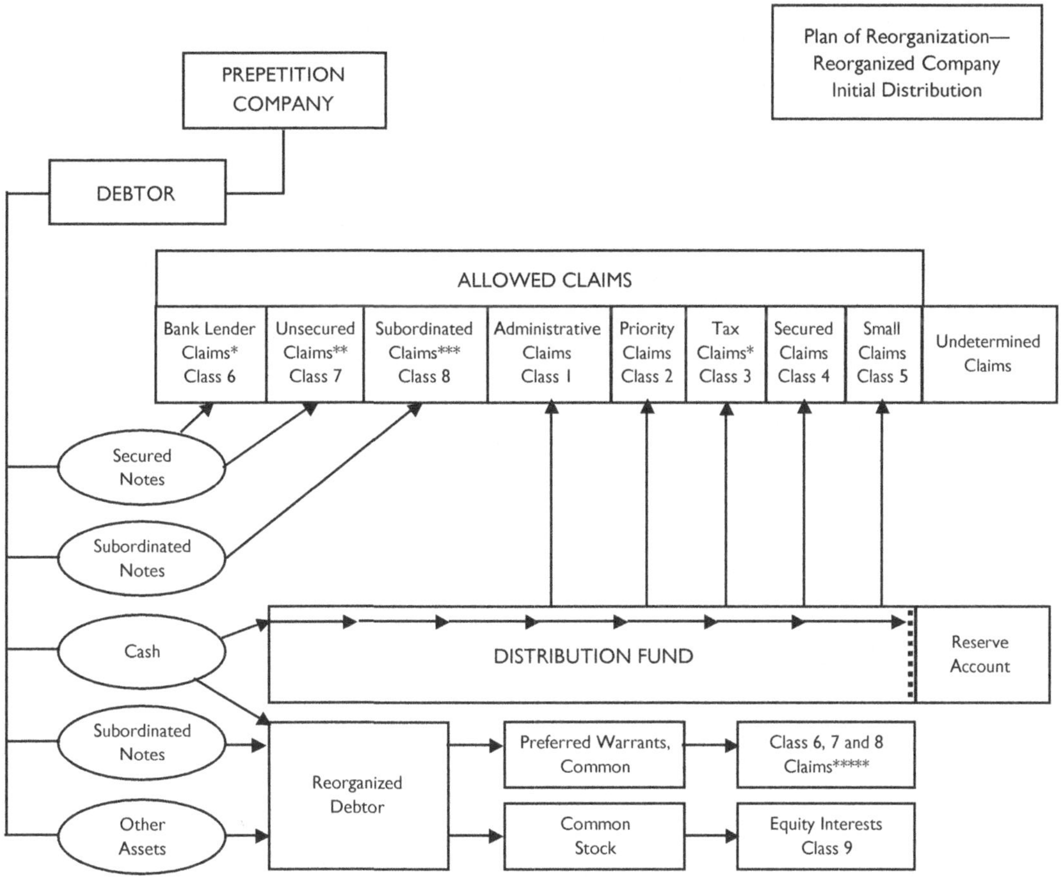

*	Class 6 Claims will retain their notes.
**	One new note will be issued to the estate administrator for the benefit of holders of Allowed Class 7 Claims.
***	One new note will be issued to the estate administrator for the benefit of holders of Allowed Class 8 Claims.
****	Classes 6 and 7 will have a lien depending on their prepetition priority on all or certain assets of the reorganized company.
*****	Class 6, 7 and 8 Claims will have an interest in the reorganized company's equity to the degree necessary to compensate for risk or loss in value due to reorganization.

Appendix X-H-b
Initial Distribution of Debtor's Assets on Effective Date

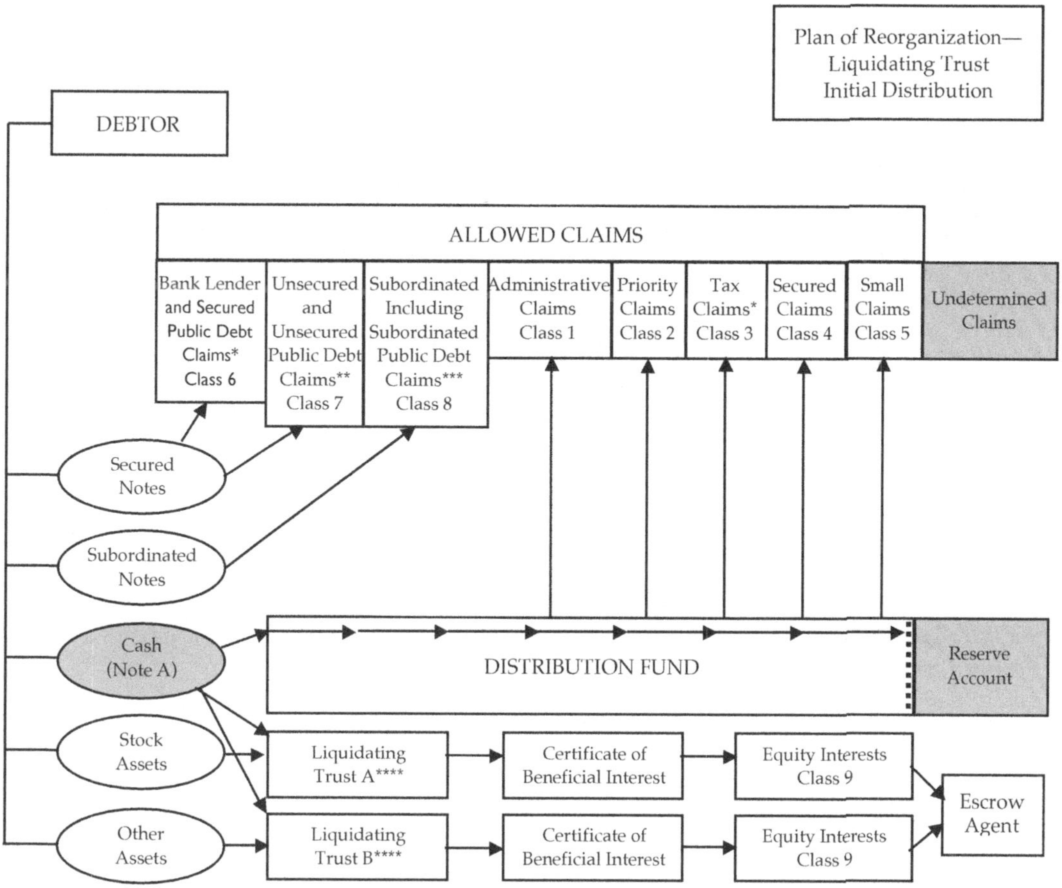

* Class 6 Claims will retain their notes and secured banker lenders and secured public debt should be in separate classes or sub-classes given the difference in debt instruments that are not similar as to term and, most likely, as to collateral.

** One new note will be issued to the estate administrator for the benefit of holders of Allowed Class 7 Claims.

*** One new note will be issued to the Estate administrator for the benefit of holders of Allowed Class 8 Claims.

**** Class 6 and 7 Claims will have a first lien on all liquidating trust assets. the general unsecured claims and unsecured public debt claims should be in separate clasess or or sub-classes given the difference in terms of the debt.

Note A: Cash could also be distributed to Classes 6, 7 and 8.

Appendix X-I
Absolute Priority

Schematic of Payment – Debt/Equity

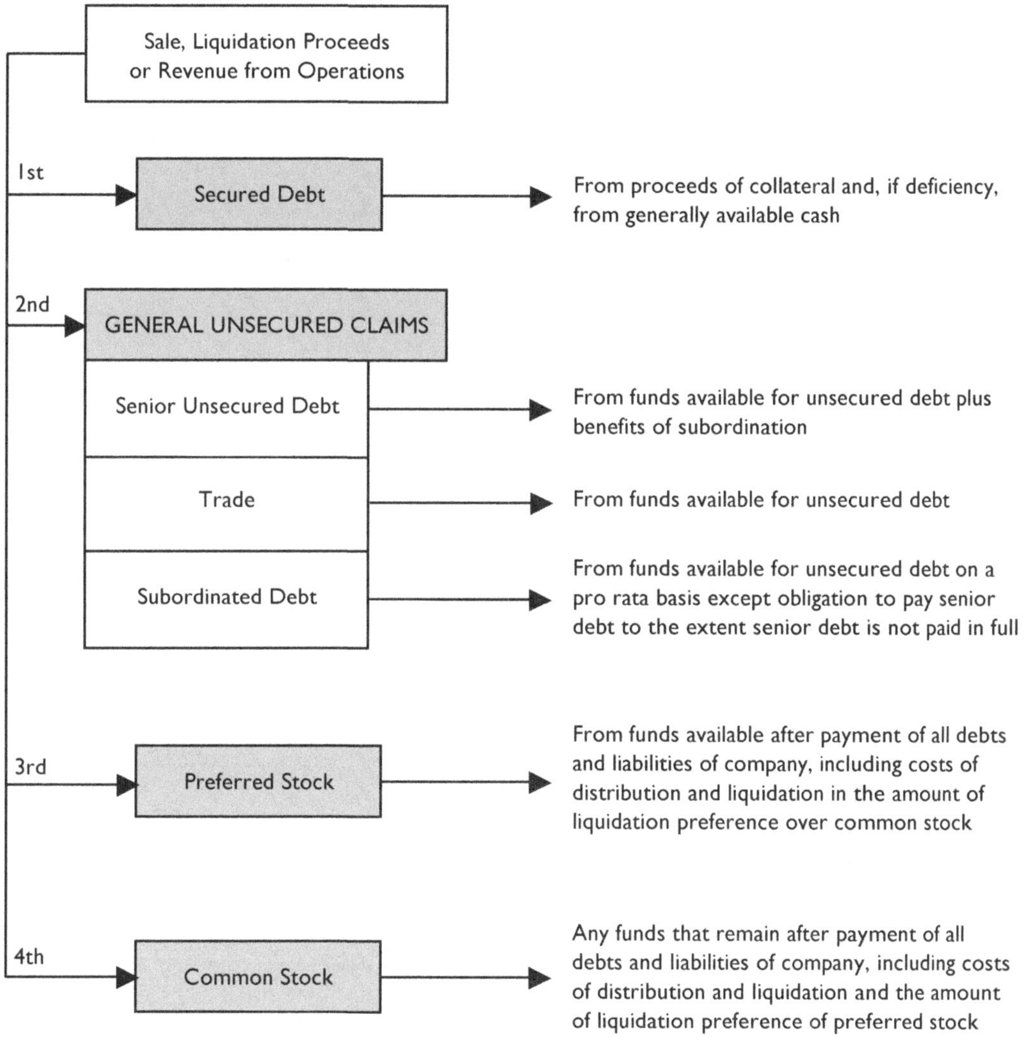

Appendix X-J
Treatment of Unsecured Claims and Secured Lender Claims under Plan of Reorganization

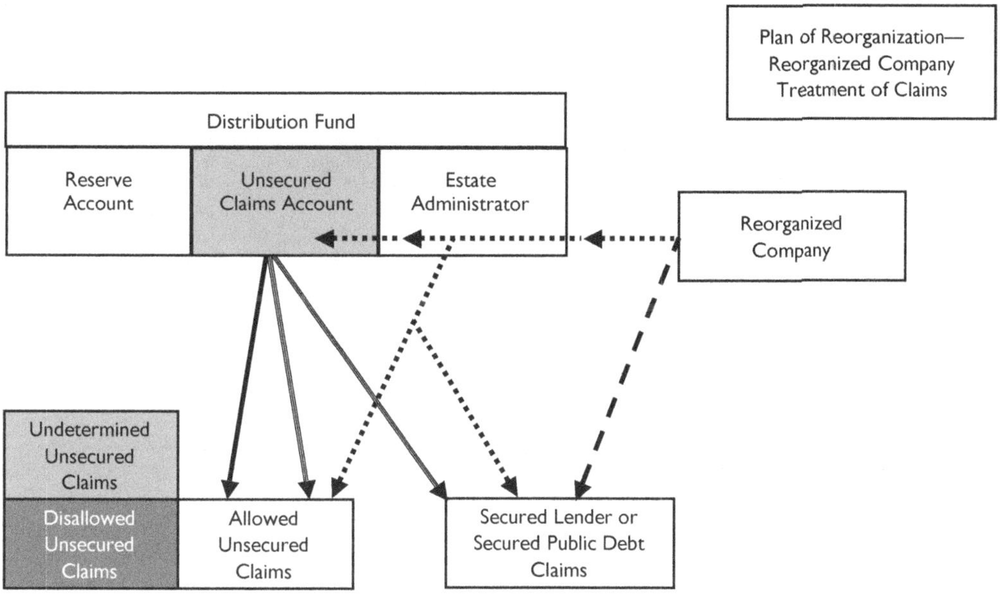

⟶ Partial payment of claim upon allowance

– – → Priority payment or liens to Secured Claims to the extent of the value of pre-confirmation collateral

·······→ Pro rata notes or payment to Allowed Claims and to reserve for Unsecured Claims not yet determined (from liquidation of assets or cash flow of operations) and to Secured Lender to extent of Unsecured Deficiency Claim

⟹ Upon disallowance of Unsecured Claim pro rata distribution of amounts previously reserved in Unsecured Claims Account for such Unsecured Claim and to Secured Lender to extent of Unsecured Deficiency Claim

Appendix X-K
Cash Distributions and Liens Post-Confirmation of Plan – Reorganized Company

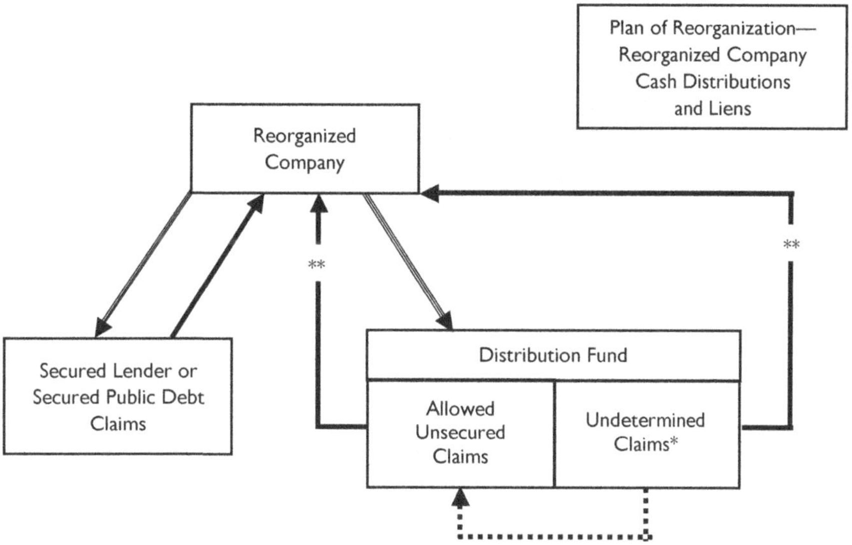

→ Liens

⇒ Distributions

⋯→ Transfer of distribution consideration from allocation for undetermined claims to allowed claims based on determination of allowed or disallowed.

* Undetermined claims may become allowed unsecured claims.

** Unsecured claims may have junior lien for reorganized debt or unsecured debt.

Appendix X-L
Cash Distributions and Liens of Liquidating Trust

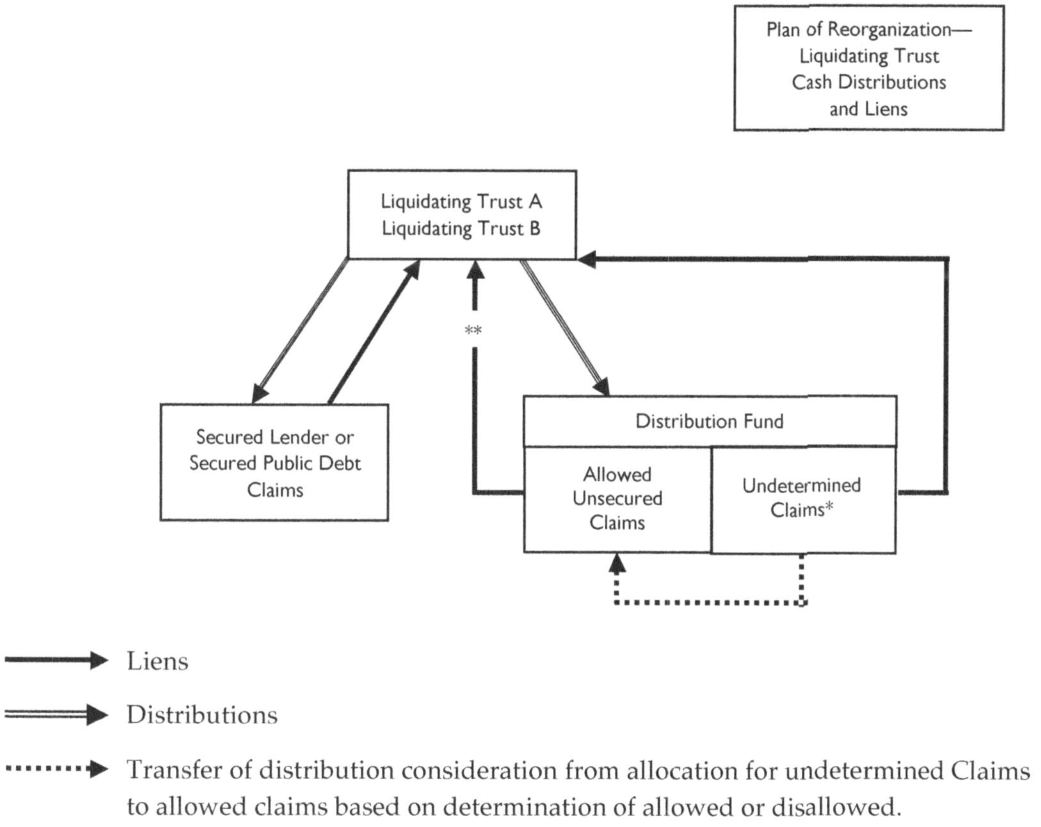

* Undetermined claims may become allowed unsecured claims.

** Unsecured claims may have junior lien for reorganized debt or unsecured debt.

Appendix X-M Special Consideration Applicable Where Trust Collateral Involves Aircraft, Vessels or Railcars

A. Pre-Bankruptcy Considerations

1. *Pre-Workout Agreements.* Use pre-work out agreements where airline, shipping line or railroad requests negotiation by creditors of one or more transactions for efficiency and coordination of benefits and to make sure the borrower waives and releases any claims or cause of action against creditors — just to be safe rather than sorry.

2. *Assurances of Maintenance Condition of Collateral.* Obtain, if possible, current maintenance records and status. Documents should provide for this and also can be amended for maintenance reserves or scheduled (block time) maintenance which, if not commenced and completed, requires cash payment to a reserve fund. Assure the possible return of collateral with half-life or at least some green time left. Stop the return of fully used aircraft, vessels or railcars.

3. *Create a Cash Reserve.* Obtain cash funding from the borrower for a reserve for costs and expenses of returned aircraft, vessels or railcars, including needed maintenance and storage, or hold back from payment to set up reserve. Even better, is there additional collateral to be given to assure payment?

4. *Clarify or Establish Return Conditions.* Negotiate return conditions for any aircraft, vessels or railcars returned and negotiate payments and return conditions for use in bankruptcy (even though such agreement may not be binding in bankruptcy).

5. *Make Sure Maintenance Records and Configuration Are "Standard" (Airlines).* If airline does not follow the Manufacturer's Maintenance Program ("MMP"), negotiate "C" check to MMP as a new return condition or as part of any future heavy maintenance. To the extent possible, reject unique configuration of aircraft and insist on the return to "standard." It could be time-consuming and costly to deal with "special cases" for configuration and maintenance records.

B. Upon Filing of a Bankruptcy

1. *Object to any claims-trading order* that impairs security holders' right to deal freely with their securities:

(a) The true value of net operating loss ("NOL") is a legal fiction in the industry where profits are currently rare and hard to come by.

(b) "Property of the Estate" jurisdiction does not extend to restricting public debt trades.

(c) Trading of secured claims does not offset NOL.

2. *All core equipment should be subject to § 1110(a) (aircraft equipment or vessels) or § 1168(a) (rail equipment) election or the airline, shipping company or railroad should promptly lose the benefit of continued use of equipment* — no game of blink or using § 1110(a) (aircraft equipment or vessels) or § 1168(a) (rail equipment) elections for less than all equipment needed:

(a) If the airline, shipping company or railroad fails to make § 1110(a) or § 1168(a) election for the equipment it needs before 60 days after the date of the order for relief under Chapter 11, the debtor deserves to have the aircraft equipment, vessel or rail equipment creditors exercise § 1110(c) or § 1168(c) rights.

(b) Any failure to timely fulfill § 1110(a) or § 1168(a) obligations should be met with § 1110(c) or § 1168(c) demand for the return of the related equipment.

(c) Section 1110(b) or § 1168(b) stipulation should only be used where there is also provided:

- interim payments,
- reservation of rights (including right to terminate continued use),
- continued and sufficient maintenance of aircraft equipment, vessel or rail equipment,
- proper maintenance records, and
- provisions for the condition in which the equipment is to be returned and the location and logistics of the return (commonly known as return conditions).

All of the above should be favorable for the respective aircraft equipment, vessel or rail equipment creditors. Violations of the stipulation by the debtor should give rise to the right of the creditors to demand the immediate return of the collateral.

(d) Any continued use of the aircraft equipment, vessel or rail equipment must be predicated on the condition of adequate protection, which is stipulated and court ordered as a condition of continued use of Section 363(e). See Chapter XI.J.3 for further discussion of issue relating to lifing the stay of adequate protection.

3. *Use pre-workout agreement and obtain a release and waiver of claims and causes of action by the airline, shipping company or railroad.*

4. *Retain experts to manage supervision of aircraft equipment, vessel or rail equipment maintenance and remarketing.* An airline maintenance program and an aircraft's maintenance status are highly technical and require advice of competent advisors.

5. *Promptly establish priority of payment in debt structures:*

(a) EETCs[338] typically provide for first payment to A Tranche.

(b) Consider acceleration of debt before distribution to PTC and ETC certificateholders to avoid different amortization provisions.

(c) Notice must be provided to owner trustee, owner participant and lower debt tranche (if necessary) and of equity interest of remedies to be taken.

6. *Make sure control is not lost to liquidity provider in EETC and others in enhanced transactions:*

(a) If there is a liquidity provider or the aircraft equipment, vessel or rail equipment in a transaction is not subject to a § 1110(a) or § 1168(a) election, then make sure the debtor is making sufficient payment to pay off the liquidity provider (as you go or before the 18-month time bomb explodes — generally the document provides if there is a default in paying obligations due the liquidity provider for 18 months the liquidity provider takes control of the foreclosure, disposition and resolution of the collateral).

(b) Creative methods have been used for the controlling tranche holders provide funds to take out the Liquidity Provider.

7. *Reserve rights to administrative expense claim for use of aircraft, vessels or railcars:*

---

338 Enhanced equipment trust certificate. Attached for illustrative purposes as Appendices X-N, X-O and X-P are diagrams of a typical PTC/ETC transaction and EETC transaction and operation of the EETC waterfall. While figures A and B reference an aircraft transaction, similar structures can be used for vessels and railcars.

(a) If aircraft equipment, vessel or rail equipment is not subject to a § 1110(a) or § 1168(a) election, then the debtor should be required to agree that any interim payments that are less than contract are partial payments, that Section 365(d)(10) is applicable and that there is an administrative expense claim for full contract payment at the end of the case. If not, then why should the airline, shipping company or railroad be allowed to continue to use the aircraft equipment, vessel or rail equipment?

(b) Any "maintenance burn" from the use of equipment postpetition should be subject to a § 503(b) claim as an agreed and allowed administrative expense claim and the debtor airline, shipping company or railroad should be required to agree to the § 503(b) claim for maintenance burn.

(c) If the airline, shipping company or railroad will not agree to (a) and (b) above, then either take the respective aircraft equipment, vessel or rail equipment or reserve the right to assert later administrative expense claims.

(d) At least obtain agreement with the debtor, shipping company or railroad on the orderly return of the aircraft equipment, vessel or rail equipment and acceptable return conditions (required location; all records; spare parts with aircraft equipment, vessel or rail equipment and related engines, if applicable, installed and assembled in working condition).

8. *Monitor all motions and orders as to how they can affect the rights of the creditors:*

(a) Watch out for a DIP financing order that gives DIP lenders a lien on the debtor's interest in the equity of aircraft equipment, vessel or rail equipment, or contract rights.

(b) The excessive allowance of administration claims to others can threaten necessary payment to aircraft equipment, vessel or rail equipment creditors.

(c) The excessive allowance of unsecured claims can reduce deficiency claim recovery for aircraft equipment, vessel or rail equipment creditors.

(d) Watch for and object to related matters that may now affect others but can be used as a precedent against you.

9. *Preserve all rights and claims:*

(a) "It's Not over until It's Over" — early waiver of claim or causes of action can be fatal to full recovery or fair treatment and recovery.

(b) Only a final resolution of all claims should address any waiver or release issues.

(c) Resolve all issues at once and beware of the death of a thousand cuts.

10. *Obtain the continued cooperation of the debtor in the remarketing of the returned aircraft equipment, vessel or rail equipment and in providing continued financial and operational information:*

(a) In any stipulation of Section 1110(b) or Section 1168(b) or adequate protection, there should be a continuing obligation even after return to provide documents or information about the aircraft equipment, vessel or rail equipment necessary for the remarketing of the aircraft equipment, vessel or rail equipment. In addition, there should be an obligation for the debtor to provide continuing operational and financial information.

(b) Even if there is no § 1110(b) or § 1168(b) stipulation or adequate protection stipulation, the continued cooperation agreement is a necessary predicate for any restructuring.

11. *Receive prompt and full disclosure of fleet plans for aircraft equipment, vessel or rail equipment and transactions terms:*

There should be full disclosure by the debtor airline, shipping company or railroad of its fleet plan for the airline equipment, vessel or rail equipment (preferably at the start of the case or within 60 days from the petition date with updates on changes). This is necessary to evaluate whether the debtor ultimately will seek to retain the relevant aircraft or whether the creditor should begin considering where to place the aircraft upon its eventual return. Further, any restructuring or agreements on aircraft should be fully and publicly disclosed. This is especially necessary when there are public debt transactions and the public trading of securities.

C. Restructuring or Reinstatement Should Be a Final Resolution

1. It is normally better to reinstate than restructure but if the prepetition documents do not provide all the benefits needed, they should be improved.

2. There is always a price for retrading a deal.

3. A final resolution will provide a real penalty for a failure to consummate so that the debtor and others are not confused into believing that retrading might be better.

4. No issue should be left open. No one will have the patience, energy or goodwill to fight over issues that should have been resolved in the restructuring.

D. Key Provisions for Restructured Transactions

1. *Final Deal.* It should be a final, binding agreement that resolves all issues and cannot be retraded (no future rejections, amendments, administrative issues or claims to fight about); however, the equipment creditors should be able to revoke if there is a material adverse change in the condition or plans of the debtor.

2. *Priority of Payment.* Any priority of payment issues among debtholders should be resolved and clear — especially in terms of how the money will be paid.

3. *Security Deposits of Additional Collateral.* Additional collateral or security deposits should be considered to provide assurance of future performance.

4. *Continuation of the Benefits of the Original Deal.* Unless otherwise required, consider financing leases or mortgages for public debt transactions versus operating leases to ensure full payment of the debt. However, operating leases and assumed residual value may provide assurance of full payment. Generally, operating leases require a supervising adult (technical advisor).

5. *Cross-Default and Cross-Collateralization.* In multiple-equipment transactions, require cross-default (avoid a cherry picking § 1110(a) or § 1168(a) election in any future bankruptcy) and cross-collateralization (avoid loss of value to airline, shipping company or railroad before debt is paid in full).

6. *Control and Direction.* The continued and future control in the "controlling party" should be clear and the use of a designated representative as a "coordinating party" should be considered. Future more elaborate maintenance provisions may require airline, shipping company or railroad technical consultants to sign off on required compliance. Going forward, security holders may select a holder or holders to be the "designated control party" for certain matters.

7. *Maintenance Reserve or Maintenance Assurance Payments or Contracts.* The maintenance condition of an aircraft may constitute a significant component of the aircraft's value. The restructured transaction should assure continued and sufficient "standard" maintenance by either a reserve or maintenance assurance contractor with an acceptable third-party provider or maintenance assurance payments at scheduled maintenance times (*e.g.*, designated hours or cycles or calendar date per aircraft or engine, vessel or rail equipment and

determined cash payment for failure either to initiate or complete maintenance on time). It is important to create economic incentives and obligations to maintain equipment at determined levels and to have easily transferable maintenance records and standard maintenance programs. There should be a provision for continued cooperation of the airline, shipping company or railroad in the remarketing or sale of any returned equipment.

8. *Improved Return Condition.* Require at least half-time condition and "C" check to manufacturer's maintenance program for aircraft equipment and standard maintenance schedule of manufacturer for vessel and rail equipment if the airline, shipping company or railroad does not follow that standard, and make sure that back-to-birth records in useable and readable form are available and must be provided. The return conditions should address the logistics and location of the aircraft's return.

9. *Provide Quick-Take and Unwind Provision If Airline, Shipping Company or Railroad Fails to Perform Plus a Penalty.* The airline, shipping company or railroad should agree that failure to consummate a plan of reorganization consistent with the restructuring of the transaction would allow, at the equipment creditors' option, a quick return and unwind of the restructuring and an administrative claim or cash payment of a significant predetermined amount both to deter a retrade and to compensate for the costs.

10. *Deregistration and Repatriation of Aircraft Equipment, Vessel or Rail Equipment.* If there is foreign registration or use of the aircraft equipment, vessel or rail equipment, there should be a clear provision that, upon demand, the foreign registration will be terminated and the aircraft equipment, vessel or rail equipment will be returned to an acceptable location. The provision should require the continued cooperation the airline, shipping company or railroad.

11. *Use of Court Approval of Fairness and Bar Order.* In any public debt transaction, Section 316(b) of the TIA and case law will require that non-consenting holders' interest can only be impaired (as to certain matters, including principal and interest payments) after a fairness hearing with notice by a court of competent jurisdiction. In addition, the court order should bar any third party, including non-consenting securitytholders, the owner trustee or the owner participant from instituting suit or interfering with the settlement and restructuring.

12. *Continued Financial and Operational Information.* The debtors should agree to provide to the aircraft equipment, vessel or rail equipment creditor continued and up-to-date financial information and operational information on the airline, shipping company or railroad.

13. *Resolution of Administrative Claims for Rejected Aircraft Equipment, Vessel or Rail Equipment.* Any restructuring of a deal involving multi-aircraft equipment, vessels or rail equipment where some items have been returned and others are being retained should resolve all

administrative claims for returned aircraft equipment, vessels or rail equipment and determine that there will be no more rejection or abandonment of aircraft equipment, vessel or rail equipment or, if so, it should specify the administrative claims or how they then would be calculated.

Appendix X-N
Diagram of PTC/ETC Transaction

Typical PTC*/ETC** Transaction

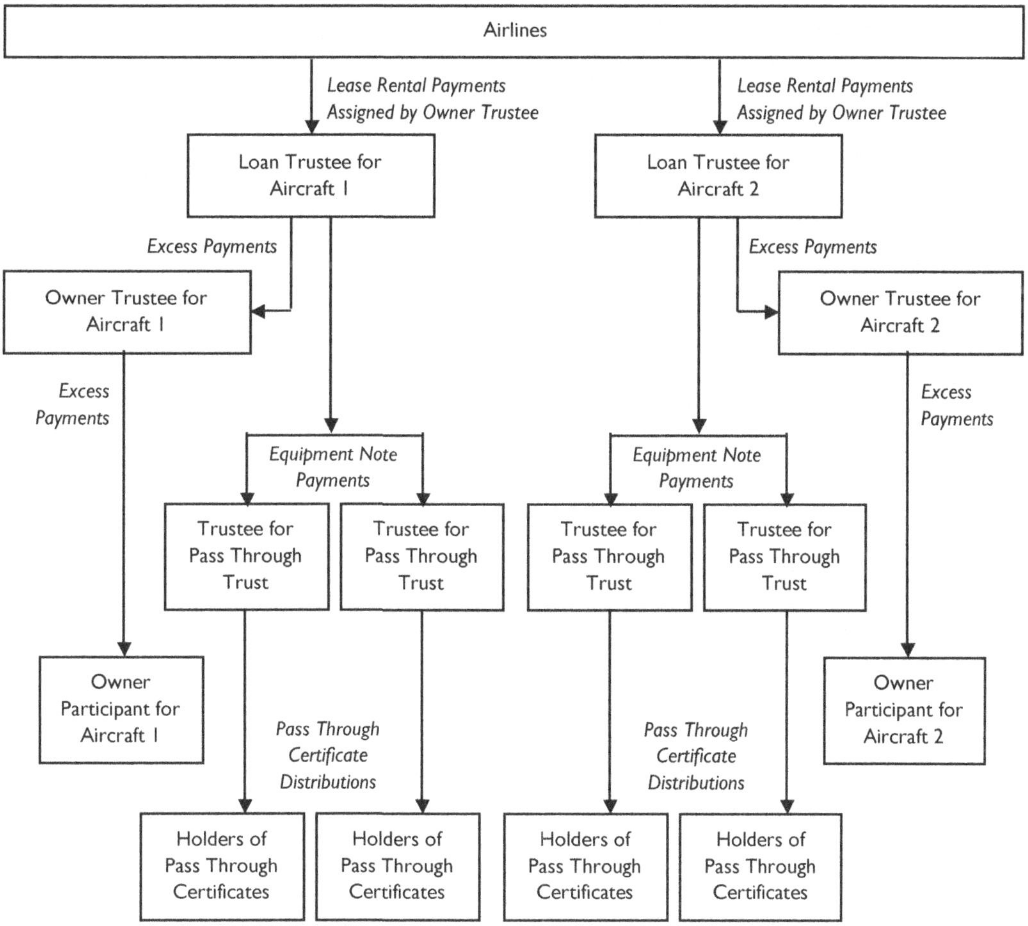

* Pass Through Trust Certificate

** Equipment Trust Certificate

Appendix X-O
Structure of an EETC Airline Transaction

Typical Airline EETC Transaction

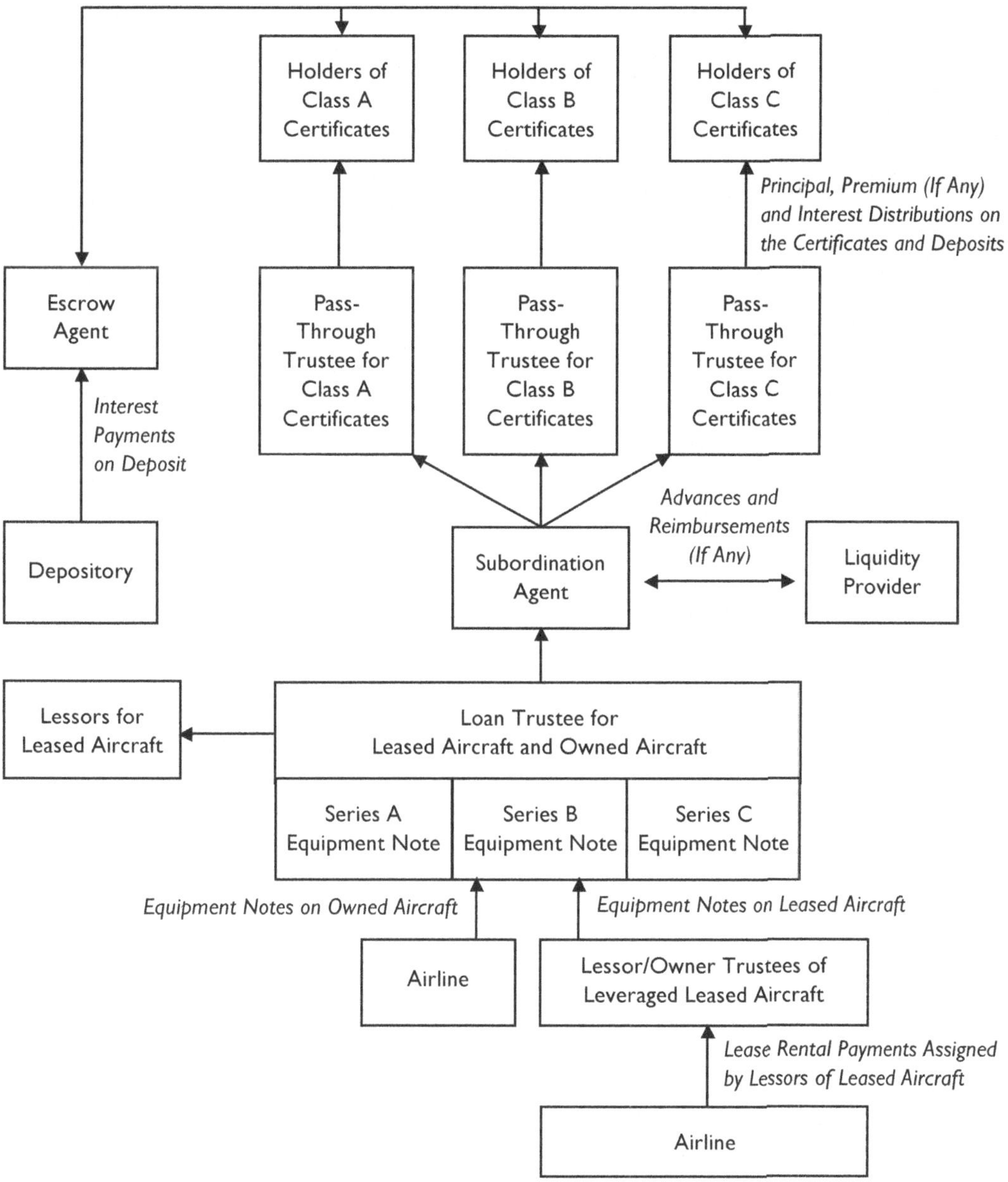

Appendix X-P
Diagram of the EETC Waterfall

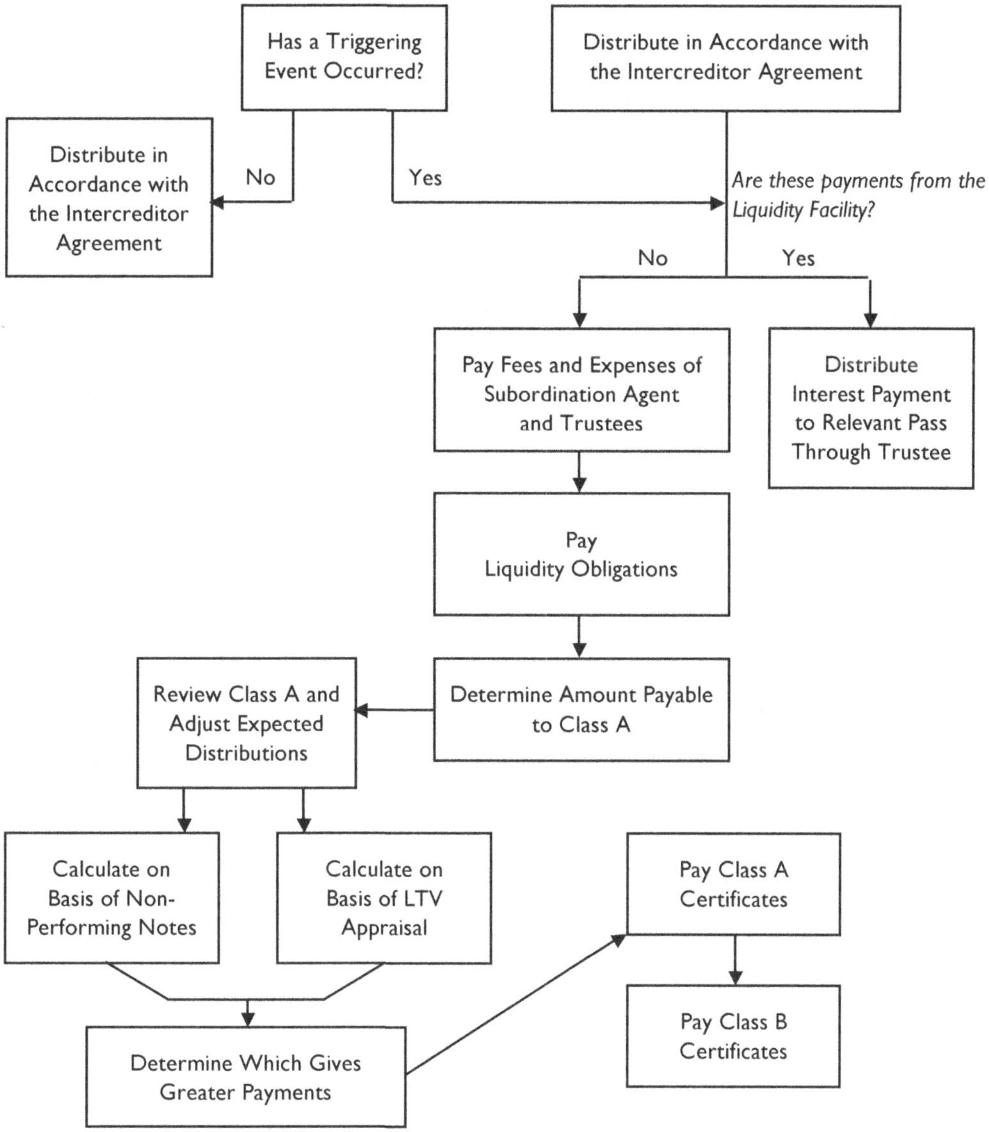

XI. Role of the Indenture Trustee in the Reorganization of the Obligor

A. Introduction

In the following pages, issues of particular importance to indenture trustees in a corporate reorganization will be reviewed in detail. It is helpful for a good working relationship with holders that holders appreciate these issues and the basis for the position of the indenture trustee.

B. Interrelationship between Non-Bankruptcy Remedies and the Bankruptcy Proceeding

The non-bankruptcy remedies outlined in Chapter IX herein may not be exercised by the indenture trustee once a proceeding in bankruptcy has been filed, absent some relief from the automatic stay by order of the bankruptcy court or pursuant to applicable law, such as the payment of special revenues under Chapter 9 or the liquidation, termination or acceleration of swap agreements under Chapter 11. The rationale is that the filing of a petition in bankruptcy freezes all individual attempts to collect obligations due and owing from the debtor and consolidates all such efforts in the bankruptcy court, where the goal is a coherent plan of reorganization or liquidation that will deal with all competing creditors of the debtor. Section 362(a) of the Bankruptcy Code stays the exercise of contractual remedies against the debtor, including those possessed by the indenture trustee.

C. Ability of Indenture Trustee to Institute Proceedings

As set forth in Chapter X herein, an involuntary petition in bankruptcy may be instituted by three petitioning creditors. Section 303(b)(1) of the Bankruptcy Code specifically provides that an indenture trustee representing holders may be one of the petitioning creditors. However, in practice, it would be an extremely unusual situation in which an indenture trustee would want to be one of the petitioning creditors.[339] Typically, holders are not going to benefit from the bankruptcy experience and, given the sensitive nature of the decision to initiate bankruptcy proceedings, an indenture trustee should consider such filing a last resort. Some holders who have just acquired their debt securities, assumedly at a low price, have been known to institute involuntary Chapter 7 cases against their obligors. This has been done at times in the face of ongoing negotiations by the obligors with majority holders to accomplish debt restructurings

339 Improperly initiating an involuntary proceeding may give rise to a claim for damages by a debtor against such petitioning creditors.

outside of bankruptcy. The wisdom of such filings is still being debated. In any event, the indenture trustee will want to be sure that a majority of holders supports the action to be taken by the indenture trustee.

D. Necessity and Ability to Accelerate Debt; Make-Whole Payments

Indenture language that provides the voluntary bankruptcy filing by the obligor will automatically accelerate the debt has been upheld.[340] Because indentures are not executory contracts,[341] the *ipso facto* clause ban found in Section 365(e)(1) of the Bankruptcy Code does not render such provisions unenforceable. If an indenture does not contain such automatic acceleration language, the indenture trustee still can pursue a claim for the full amount of the debt. Although the automatic stay prevents an indenture trustee from delivering a notice of acceleration after the institution of a bankruptcy proceeding by the obligor, such will not prevent the indenture trustee from asserting a claim for the full amount of the principal and interest outstanding. For claims purposes, the indebtedness under an indenture is accelerated by the filing of the debtor's Chapter 11 case and a proof of claim can be filed for the full amount of the debt.[342] For the purpose of Section 311 of TIA and to obtain a monetary default to trigger a sharing provision with a prior trustee who is a lender, the indenture trustee should consider either lifting the automatic stay or sending a notice of default and acceleration acknowledging the bankruptcy and automatic stay and stating the notice is to permit assertion of a claim against third parties, which claim has no effect on the estate.

Automatic acceleration language can complicate the ability of the indenture trustee to successfully make a claim for a make-whole payment. The specific language of the indenture is determinative. Where a make-whole payment was due upon voluntary prepayment by the debtor but the filing of a bankruptcy petition triggered automatic acceleration of the debt, certain courts have held that no make-whole payment is required.[343]

Courts that have examined the issue first focused on whether the documents specifically provide for the payment of a make-whole in the event of an automatic acceleration because of

---

340 *In re AMR Corp.*, 730 F.3d 88, 100 (2d Cir. 2013), *cert. denied* ____ U.S. ____, 134 S. Ct. 1888 (2014).

341 *Id.* at 106.

342 *In re Manville Forest Prods. Corp.*, 43 B.R. 293 (Bankr. S.D.N.Y. 1984), *aff'd in part, rev'd in part,* 60 B.R. 403 (S.D.N.Y. 1986).

343 *In re AMR Corp.*; *In re MPM Silicones, LLC*, 531 B.R. 321 (S.D.N.Y. 2015); *but see In re School Specialty, Inc.*, 2013 WL 1838513 (Bankr. D. Del. Apr. 22, 2013).

bankruptcy. In the bankruptcy court *Energy Future* decision,[344] where there was no reference in the automatic acceleration provision to the payment of the "Applicable Premium," and the court examined other cases in which the payment of a make-whole had been denied:

> "Comparing the relevant language in the governing Indenture with language from other cases compels the conclusion that the Indenture does not provide for a make-whole premium following a bankruptcy acceleration.
>
> - *Calpine*: In the case of an Event of Default specified in clause (10) or (11) of Section 6.01 [which includes a bankruptcy filing], ***all outstanding Notes will become due and payable immediately without further action or notice.*** (Romanowicz Decl., Ex. 2 § 6.02 ¶ 1, *In re Calpine Corp.*, No. 05-60200, 2007 WL 950090 (Bankr. S.D.N.Y. 2007) (Dkt. No. 3481-4), overruled by *HSBC Bank USA, N.A. v. Calpine Corp.*, No. 07-3088, 2010 WL 3835200 (S.D.N.Y. Sept. 15, 2010) (emphasis added)); *HSBC Bank USA, N.A. v. Calpine Corp.*, No. 07-3088, 2010 WL 3835200, at *4-*5 (S.D.N.Y. Sept. 15, 2010) (Calpine II).
> - *Premier*: In the case of an Event of Default specified in clause (j) [commencement of a voluntary bankruptcy case] . . . of § 6.01 hereof, with respect to Premier . . . *all outstanding Notes will become due and payable immediately without further action or notice.* (Romanowicz Decl., Ex. 3, at 73 (§ 6.02 ¶ 2), *In re Premier Entm't Biloxi LLC,* 445 B.R. 582 (Bankr. S.D.Miss.) (Dkt. No. 6-1 to -3) (emphasis added)); *In re Premier Entm't Biloxi LLC,* 445 B.R. at 626-632.
> - *Momentive*: If an Event of Default specified in Section 6.01(f) or (g) [which includes a bankruptcy filing] with respect to the Company occurs, *the principal of, premium, if any, and interest on all the Notes shall ipso facto become and be immediately due and payable without any declaration or other act* on the part of the Trustee or any Holders. (Romanowicz Decl., Ex. 5, at 92, *In re MPM Silicones, LLC, et al.*, No. 14-22503 (Bankr. S.D.N.Y. June 18, 2014) (Dkt. No. 464-1) (emphasis added)); *Momentive,* 2014 WL 443635, at *13-14.

---

344 *In re Energy Future Holdings Corp.*, 527 B.R. 178, 193–194 (Bankr. D. Del. 2015) (applying New York law). Significantly, there was no reference to *prepayment*, but rather, *optional redemption* in the make-whole language.

> - *Solutia*: If an Event of default specified in 6.01(7) occurs with respect to the Company or any Subsidiary Guarantor [which includes filing a bankruptcy petition] *the principal of and premium, if any, and accrued interest, if any, on the Notes then outstanding shall become and be immediately due and payable without any declaration or other act* on the part of the Trustee or any Holder. (Romanowicz Decl., Ex. 4, at 11/70 (§ 6.02 ¶ 1), *In re Solutia*, 379 B.R. 473 (Bankr.S.D.N.Y.2007) (Dkt. No. 4211-1 to -2) (emphasis added)); *In re Solutia Inc.*, 379 B.R. at 4.88.
>
> In each of these cases, the court found no make-whole obligation was created by acceleration provisions substantially similar to the language before the Court. The Court agrees with the holdings in these cases and finds that the acceleration provision in the Indenture does not include clear and unambiguous language that a make-whole premium (here the "Applicable Premium") is due upon the repayment of the Notes following a bankruptcy acceleration. Because the Indenture does not specify that the Applicable Premium is owed after automatic acceleration, the Applicable Premium is not owed."

The district court affirmed the decision of the bankruptcy court, ruling there was no right to a premium. However, the Third Circuit reversed, holding that the make-whole in this case was payable in the event of redemption, not prepayment. In explaining the distinction, the court stated that "*prepayments* cannot occur when payment is now due by acceleration of the debt's maturity."[345] However, *redemption* of a debt security may occur "at or before maturity."[346] The court held that a premium tied to redemption is unaffected by acceleration of a debt's maturity by reason of the bankruptcy filing. According to the Third Circuit, "by avoiding the word 'prepayment' and using the term 'redemption', they [the drafters] decided that the make-whole would apply without regard to the notes' maturity."[347]

A number of trustees faced with an indenture providing for a make-whole premium have, in the alternative, sought to lift the automatic stay to rescind the acceleration caused by a bankruptcy filing. The automatic stay can only be lifted if "cause" is established.[348] Much attention has now been directed at developing indenture language that will be deemed sufficient

---

345 *In re Energy Future Holdings Corp.*, 842 F.3d 247, 259 (3d Cir. 2016).

346 *Id.*

347 *Id.* at 260.

348 11 U.S.C. § 362(d)(1).

to support a make-whole enforceable in bankruptcy.[349] The discussion by the Third Circuit in *Energy Future* where the premium was deemed a redemption premium and the indenture did not specifically nullify the make-whole obligation upon acceleration presents a good roadmap. It will be interesting to see the approach taken by other courts of appeal. In any event, a bondholder will want to have a clear understanding of the nature of the applicable premium of any debt security it is acquiring.

E. Pursue Third-Party Guarantors

Some transactions may include a separate guaranty of payment by a non-debtor third party. Upon a bankruptcy filing by the issuer of the debt, the indenture trustee should consider the advisability of proceeding immediately to collect on a third-party guaranty. If any terms of the underlying transaction had been modified subsequent to the execution of the guaranty, it would be important in any enforcement action that the guarantor had reaffirmed the guaranty. The automatic stay of Section 362 of the Bankruptcy Code, which prohibits action to recover from the debtor or its property on a prepetition debt, does not typically apply to a claim against a non-debtor. However, some courts have held the automatic stay to apply to non-debtor guarantors in unusual circumstances. These have been defined as situations "when there is such identity between the debtor and third-party defendant that the debtor may be said to be the real party defendant and that a judgment against the third-party defendant will in effect be a judgment or finding against the debtor."[350] Some courts have utilized Section 105 of the Bankruptcy Code to enjoin suits against a non-debtor guarantor if such relief was deemed necessary to ensure a successful reorganization.[351] In litigation arising out of the bankruptcy of the Caesars Entertainment Operating Company, the Seventh Circuit Court of Appeals examined litigation brought by certain indenture trustees against the debtor's principal owner and guarantor. The court held that Section 105(a) of the Bankruptcy Code would permit the stay of litigation if it could be shown that the injunction would enhance the prospects for a successful resolution of the disputes attending to the bankruptcy.[352] Thus, the efforts of the indenture trustee to proceed against the third-party guarantor while the bankruptcy is pending may not be successful depending upon the circumstances. As a general rule, the indenture trustee should not be questioned over a decision to pursue such guarantor and to incur the related expense. Conversely, the indenture trustee that simply assumes an action against the guarantor must wait

---

349 *See* Ferve Ozturk, "Seeing the Future Clearly: The Make-Whole Decisions in EFH," XXXV ABI J. 44, Apr. 2016.

350 *Queenie, Ltd. v. Nygard Intern.*, 321 F.3d 282 (2d Cir. 2003); *A.H. Robins Co., Inc., v. Piccinin*, 788 F.2d 994 (4th Cir. 1986).

351 *Willis v. Celotex Corp.*, 978 F.2d 146 (4th Cir. 1992).

352 *In re Caesars Entm't Operating Co., Inc.*, 808 F.3d 1186 (7th Cir. 2015).

for another day without input from the holders could be subject to criticism, especially if the guarantor's ability to pay is significantly reduced in the interim. Holders with strong feelings about the wisdom of pursuing the guarantor and the timing of the action should clearly communicate this to the indenture trustee.

F. Notice and Communication to Holders

It is extremely important, upon the institution of a bankruptcy proceeding involving the debtor, that the indenture trustee give notice of such event to the holders. This is particularly true if a payment date is approaching, but notice must be given regardless of the next payment date. The notice should briefly describe the events surrounding the filing; what actions the indenture trustee is taking in the bankruptcy; that the indenture trustee will file a proof of claim in the bankruptcy for the amount due; that the indenture trustee will continue to monitor the bankruptcy and keep the holders informed as it deems appropriate; when the first meeting of creditors will occur; the bar date on filing proofs of claim if one is set and what, if any, action needs to be taken by the holders at that time; the ability of holders to file additional proofs of claim; and the ability of holders of a majority of the principal amount of securities outstanding to direct, instruct and indemnify the action of the indenture trustee in bankruptcy or to join the creditors' committee. Throughout the course of the proceedings, the holder should receive periodic reports with respect to the progress of the bankruptcy. If, as will be described below, the indenture trustee is a member of the creditors' committee, the indenture trustee will not be able to communicate all information in its possession because certain information must be held in confidence. However, the holders should be given the general status of the matter. It is particularly important in these notices with respect to major and complicated bankruptcies that the holders be aware that the indenture trustee cannot predict when the bankruptcy will be concluded and what form of payment the holders will receive. The indenture trustee may consider whether, under the circumstances, it should obtain court approval of any letter sent to the holders regarding a plan of reorganization.[353] Section 1145 of the Bankruptcy Code provides for an exemption from the securities law for such court-approved communications. In addition, some courts have held an indenture trustee and its counsel in contempt for communication with holders about a plan without court approval. While such decisions were clearly wrong (the indenture trustee should be able to communicate with the holders at all times), care should be taken in such communication.

---

353 *See In re Portland Electric Power Co.*, 97 F. Supp. 903 (D. Or. 1974); *In re Glen Sheridan Realty Tr.*, 90 F.2d 466 (7th Cir. 1937).

G. Service List and Necessary Court Filings

As soon as possible after the filing of a petition, the indenture trustee should enter an appearance in the bankruptcy and follow the local procedure for being included on the electronic service list. Generally, Bankruptcy Rule 2002 provides for notice to indenture trustees for various matters. The indenture trustee and its counsel should begin monitoring the case filings on ECF or PACER, the Public Access to Court Electronic Records service, which allows users to obtain case and docket information online. An experienced bankruptcy practitioner will tell you that many significant events with respect to the future progress of the case, particularly with regard to postpetition financing and use of cash collateral, take place immediately after the filing of a petition by the debtor. It will be helpful to be aware of the filings being made in the crucial first hours and days of the case without waiting to be included on the debtor's service list. During this period, the indenture trustee may be contacted by holders who intend to be active in the case, and this may be a good opportunity to discuss coordination of efforts.

H. Creditors' Committee Membership and Status Thereon: Who Should Serve?

As discussed in detail in prior chapters, the indenture trustee upon the occurrence of an event of default assumes the role of a prudent person vis-à-vis its holders. The fact that the indenture trustee in a bankruptcy context has a heightened responsibility for its holders has created some concern with respect to that same trustee's serving on the creditors' committee. One court had expressed the fear that the indenture trustee would become a fiduciary with two masters, as a member of the creditors' committee owes a fiduciary duty to all creditors in the proceeding.[354] However, given the fact that many plans of reorganization are hammered out at the creditors' committee level and that the rights of holders could be negatively impacted by the indenture trustee's absence from the negotiating table, historically a number of indenture trustees sought court orders permitting them to serve on creditors' committees.[355] Some time ago, the issue was decided by one bankruptcy court which noted that, even though the indenture trustee is not eligible to vote on a plan of reorganization, it may serve on the creditors' committee.[356] Subsequently, it was noted that indenture trustees often serve on creditors' committees.[357]

---

354 *See Woods v. City Nat'l Bank & Tr. Co.*, 312 U.S. 262 (1941).

355 *See, e.g., In re Wickes Co., Inc.*, Case No. LA826658-WL (Bankr. C.D. Cal. May 13, 1982) (order allowing the indenture trustee to serve on the official creditors' committee), and *In re Nucorp Energy, Inc.*, No. 82-03106-K11 (Bankr. S.D. Cal. Oct. 12, 1982) (order permitting the indenture trustee to so act).

356 *See In re Charter Co.*, 42 B.R. 251 (Bankr. M.D. Fla. 1984). *See also U.S. Tr. Co. of N.Y.*, SEC No-Action Letters, 1985 WL 54208 (Mar. 25, 1985).

357 *In re McLean Indus. Inc.*, 70 B.R. 852 (Bankr. S.D.N.Y. 1987); *see In re Enron Corp.*, 279 B.R. 671 (Bankr. S.D.N.Y. 2002), where the initial committee included three indenture trustees, and *In re Lehman*

The appointment of the indenture trustee as an ex officio member without any voting power or voice to raise issues at committee meetings can be a concern. In some situations, the inability to vote or to raise issues has presented a problem for the indenture trustee. Indenture trustees should attempt to be regular members and not ex officio to the degree possible. A form of bylaws for a creditors' committee which is sensitive to the indenture trustee's position can be found in Appendix XI-A. Sometimes an institutional holder may wish to serve on the creditors' committee. Because of the likelihood of postpetition sales of debt securities by institutions or the varying views of holders depending on whether or not they were par purchasers, the United States Trustee's office frequently looks favorably on the committee appointment of the indenture trustee who is likely to be able to serve for the duration of the case and can represent all the holders. A sensitive situation can arise when an institutional holder also wishes to be on the creditors' committee and, given the size of the case, the United States Trustee must choose between the indenture trustee and the holder. Occasionally, in a large case, a separate committee of debtholders will be appointed.[358] More often than not, if there is a question of adequacy of representation on the unsecured creditors' committee, debtholders can be added to the existing committee.[359]

The receipt by the indenture trustee as a member of the creditors' committee of confidential information that cannot be disclosed to holders is a sensitive matter. The issue is ameliorated somewhat by the requirement in the Bankruptcy Code that the committee provide access to information to creditors who hold the same type of claims.[360] While a committee will not be required to disclose confidential and non-public information, the committee should take into account the creditor's willingness to be bound by confidentiality agreements or trading orders.[361]

Bros. Holdings Inc., 508 B.R. 283 (S.D.N.Y. 2014), where the committee included two indenture trustees.

358 *See In re Beker Indus. Corp.*, 55 B.R. 945 (Bankr. S.D.N.Y. 1985).

359 *In re Pub. Ser. Co. of N.H.*, 89 B.R. 1014 (Bankr. D.N.H. 1988) (where indenture trustee was an *ex officio* member).

360 11 U.S.C. § 1102(b)(3); *In re S&B Surgery Center, Inc.*, 421 B.R. 546 (Bankr. C.D. Cal. 2009) (in case that involved more than 200 unsecured creditors with over $36 million in unsecured claims, the indenture trustee would be required to establish and maintain an internet website to provide non-confidential information to unsecured creditors).

361 *In re Refco*, 336 B.R. 187 (Bankr. S.D.N.Y. 2006); *In re MF Glob. Holdings Ltd.*, 2012 WL 734195 (S.D.N.Y. Mar. 6, 2012).

Inevitably, the holders who have a real economic stake in the outcome of the case may desire to serve on the committee that will negotiate the plan of reorganization.[362] Sometimes holders will opt for membership in an informal or *ad hoc* committee with similarly situated holders to share the expense and strengthen the impact of their position. This status requires compliance with Bankruptcy Rule 2019 but does not require the member to assume duties to other creditors or to cease trading unless it receives confidential information.[363] However, membership on an official committee, although placing the holder at the table where the plan is being discussed, does impose certain requirements. Traditionally, orders have been entered in bankruptcy cases permitting an institutional committee member whose representative receives material non-public information to continue to trade in the securities of the debtor if a "Chinese wall" is established, screening the committee member from other employees of the holder.[364] Concern over the risks of receipt of material non-public information was heightened after the bankruptcy court ruling in the *Washington Mutual* bankruptcy with respect to potential inequitable conduct and temporary insider status by noteholders involved in settlement talks who traded in the debtor's securities, albeit at the end of a lock-up period.[365] Since the *Washington Mutual* decision, holders have been especially careful to insist on the entry of orders permitting trading by an official committee member upon the establishment of trading orders.[366] Further, before holders, not committee members, have begun to engage in settlement negotiations, orders have been entered providing that such holders are not temporary insiders and that trading pursuant to blocking procedures is permitted.[367]

---

362 Richard L. Kuersteiner, James O. Johnston, Richard L. Wynne and Lance Miller, *Your Bond Issuer Has Filed for Bankruptcy? A Survey of the Trips, Traps, and Opportunities that Await Corporate Bondholders in a Chapter 11 Case,* Ann. Surv. Bankr. Law (2008).

363 *Id.*; Matt Porcelli, *Bankrupting the Inside Job: Alternatives to the Washington Mutual Approach to Policing Creditor Committee Insider Trading,* 9 N.Y.U. J.L. 295 (2012).

364 *See, e.g., In the Matter of Federated Department Stores,* 1991 WL 79143 (Bankr. S.D. Ohio 1991); Daniel Sullivan, *Big Boys and Chinese Walls,* 75 U. Chic. L. Rev. 533 (2008).

365 *In re Wash. Mut. Inc.,* 461 B.R. 200 (Bankr. D. Del. 20199), *vacated in part* 2012 WL 1563880 (Bankr. D. Del. Feb. 24, 2012).

366 *See, e.g., In re Caesars Entm't Operating Co., Inc.,* Case No. 15-01145 (N.D. Ill. Feb. 18, 2015), ECF No. 583. COLLIERS HANDBOOK FOR CREDITORS' COMMITTEES contains a series of forms for the treatment of confidential information.

367 *See, e.g.,* Order in Aid of Settlement Discussions, *In re Vitro, S.A.B. de C.V.,* Case No. 11-33335 (Bankr. N.D. Tex. Jan. 26, 2012) ECF No. 311; Stipulation and Agreed Order Appointing Mediator, *Motors Liquidation Co. GUC Tr. v. Appaloosa Inv. Ltd. P'ship,* Case No. 12-09802 (Bankr. S.D.N.Y. June 27, 2013), ECF No. 241; Order Appointing Mediator, *In re Residential Capital, LLC,* Case No. 12-12020 (Bankr. S.D.N.Y. July 31, 2013), ECF No. 2538.

I. Proof of Claim

The indenture trustee is authorized to file a proof of claim on behalf of all holders. This language is contained in most indentures,[368] and is a requirement of Section 317(a) of the TIA. Great care must be taken by the indenture trustee in filing the proof of claim. Given the trend in recent cases to set a bar date shortly after the institution of the case, the indenture trustee should promptly prepare and file a proof of claim before the bar date. The indenture trustee should make certain that the claim is filed for the full amount of principal and premium due, if any, plus all interest,[369] fees and expenses that have accrued and will accrue. The proof of claim should contain a specific reservation of the right to amend the proof of claim. Furthermore, if related entities of the obligor have also filed bankruptcy petitions, it may, under certain circumstances, be wise for the indenture trustee to file a proof of claim in those other cases to the degree the proceeds of the debt issue may have been misappropriated and used by the other entities. The official form of proof of claim for a debenture issue can be found in Appendix XI-B, along with a form of addendum in Appendix XI-C. A claim for a secured bond issue would include a description of the collateral and attach key security documents. Specialized proofs of claim involving securitization and derivatives will be provided in later chapters.

While some indenture trustees inform their holders that the indenture trustee only will be filing a proof of claim for principal, interest, premium, if any, and expenses, a very defensible position, the indenture trustee may consider all claims and causes of action against the debtor and its affiliates in preparing a proof of claim. Many experienced trustees contend that any legitimate claim or cause of action arising under the indenture against the debtor or its affiliates (those who own or control the debtor or those whom the debtor owns or controls) should be included or at least reserved in the indenture trustee's proof of claim. If the guarantor of the issue goes into bankruptcy, a protective proof of claim should be filed even if the obligor is current and there are no defaults. If the obligor is a holding company, the indenture trustee should consider filing proofs of claim in the subsidiary bankruptcies or asserting claims against non-bankrupt

---

368 *See, e.g.*, MBI § 909.

369 While as a matter of form the proof of claim may contain a request for payment of default interest, it is payable under special circumstances. Bankruptcy Code Section 506(b) provides that an *oversecured* creditor is entitled to interest on its secured claim pursuant to the terms of its contract. Under these circumstances, there is a rebuttable preemption in favor of the contract default rate. *In re Residential Capital, LLC.*, 508 B.R. 851 (Bankr. S.D.N.Y. 2014). No court has adopted a bright-line rule that contract default rate should be refused in all insolvent debtor cases. *See In re Madison 92nd St. Assoc., LLC,* 472 B.R. 189 (Bankr. S.D.N.Y. 2012). Thus, in the *Res Cap* case, an oversecured creditor was granted postpetition contract default rate interest after the court balanced the equities, including the potential effect on the terms and credit available for high-risk borrowers. 508 B.R. at 861.

subsidiaries for any proceeds of the public debt issue wrongfully diverted to the subsidiaries. As discussed in Chapter XVIII, the standing of an indenture trustee to maintain a security fraud action against the obligor has not been subject to consistent treatment by the courts, but claims of constructive trust or equitable lien may be possible against third parties and reserved in the proof of claim. Well in advance of the bar date, the indenture trustee should notify the holders that it will be filing a proof of claim against the obligor/debtor for the principal, premium, if any, interest and expenses due under the indenture. If the indenture trustee expects to assert additional claims, the holders should be notified so they can direct and instruct the indenture trustee as they deem appropriate. Further, the holders should be informed that, if they have individual claims against the debtor in addition to the principal and interest due on their debt, they should file claims asserting such prior to the bar date. Importantly, if the indenture trustee will not be asserting any claims arising under the securities or other laws, the indenture trustee can alert the holders before the bar date. Again, it is advisable for the holders to consider coordinating with the indenture trustee as to possible claims that the trustee should assert or reserve in the proof of claim as well as providing direction and instruction to the trustee on asserting such claims.

J. Actions to Be Taken in the Case for the Benefit of the Holders

There are certain steps that the indenture trustee can and should take in the bankruptcy proceeding to attempt to protect the rights of the holders. Even if the securities for which the indenture trustee serves are fully secured and the holders would benefit from a quick liquidation, it is unrealistic to think that, in the present climate, the bankruptcy judge will permit liquidation early in the case. More likely than not, the bankruptcy court will give the debtor an opportunity to attempt a reorganization. Therefore, at least for some period of time, there are a number of key areas requiring vigilance by an indenture trustee and the holders in a Chapter 11 bankruptcy of the obligor:

1. Use of Cash Collateral and Extension of Credit

In the first days or weeks of the case, the debtor, often in conjunction with the banks that have been funding the debtor prior to the petition, will attempt to obtain an order permitting the debtor to use cash collateral and to obtain postpetition funding. Extreme attentiveness must be used in reviewing the applications and any proposed orders since the lending banks may be attempting through the use of such proceeding to validate prepetition liens, to obtain postpetition collateral for certain prepetition advances or to prime the secured position of the indenture trustee. If such a scheme is proposed, it would be appropriate for the indenture trustee to object to such orders. At the very least, the cash collateral or debtor-in-possession financing orders should contain language reserving the right of the indenture trustee to challenge the lien of the banks or any other creditors until there has been full disclosure and sufficient time to review the facts.

2. Review of All Sales

The indenture trustee must carefully review any application for the sale of property of the debtor pursuant to Section 363 of the Bankruptcy Code to determine whether or not the indenture trustee has any interest in the collateral. If the indenture trustee does have an interest in the collateral and the indenture trustee determines the sale is in the best interest of the holders, the indenture trustee must make certain that all liens attach to the proceeds of the sale. All sales should be for the best price possible. Sales of assets in depressed markets should be avoided as well as sales of parts at a depressed value in relation to the whole business. Generally, in bankruptcy the cash-bleeding operations should be closed or sold if possible. The jewels of the operation should not be sold unless necessary. Appendices XI-D and XI-E are graphic portrayals of issues raised by such sales and likely timeline.

3. Adequate Protection and Motion to Lift the Stay

If the securities for which the indenture trustee serves are secured, the indenture trustee may attempt to file a motion to lift the automatic stay to foreclose on the collateral. It may be difficult to achieve this goal early in the proceedings. Defaults with respect to aircraft equipment, vessels and rail equipment must be cured and paid within 60 days of the order of relief or the indenture trustee who is the owner trustee or lessor should be entitled to obtain possession.[370] In any event, if the debtor is using collateral of the indenture trustee in the reorganization, the indenture trustee may seek to have adequate protection payments made to the holders. The principles of adequate protection include, among others, no erosion in value, the payment of taxes and insurance, cash payment for current interest, replacement liens or other adequate protection so that there is no diminution in value during the course of the proceeding. The ruling by the bankruptcy court in the *Continental Airlines* bankruptcy must be carefully considered. In that case, at the conclusion of the confirmation hearing, the court held that it would have been necessary for the indenture trustees' for secured equipment certificates to have sought relief from the automatic stay in order to be entitled to adequate protection for market value decline.[371] The debtor proceeded to consummate the plan of reorganization. The district court dismissed the appeal of the trustees as moot without reaching the merits. The Third Circuit in a 7-6 decision held that the district court properly dismissed the appeal under the doctrine of equitable

---

370 11 U.S.C. §§ 1110 and 1168. *See also* Appendix X-M for Special Considerations Applicable Where Trust Collateral Involves Aircraft, Vessels or Railcars

371 *In re Cont'l Airlines, Inc.,* 154 B.R. 176 (Bankr. D. Del. 1993).

mootness, while describing the trustees' arguments on the merits as "interesting and challenging."[372] Since the bankruptcy court decision was never reversed, it has become fairly typical practice for the indenture trustee to seek the alternative relief of lifting the automatic stay and of adequate protection. Again, it is in the best interest of the holders to cooperate and coordinate with the indenture trustee to assure the most efficient and effective result in obtaining adequate protection and lifting the stay as necessary.

4. Examination of Subordination Provisions

An indenture trustee should examine the status of its securities and determine whether they are senior or subordinated debt. An indenture trustee should review the indenture to determine if the payment of the trustee's fees and expenses has been subordinated. Further, the indenture should be reviewed to determine if the payment of postpetition interest under a plan has been given any priority.[373] It is important if one serves as indenture trustee for subordinated debt to determine whether or not there are factors that would militate against the application of the subordination language, particularly inequitable conduct on the part on the senior creditors, and whether Section 510(c) of the Bankruptcy Code providing for equitable subordination is applicable.[374] An indenture trustee for senior debt should immediately put the subordinated debtholders on notice of its claim to the benefits of subordination. These concerns are essentially intercreditor disputes, and some may argue that the bankruptcy court should not interject itself in these matters. Generally, however, the bankruptcy court will not have jurisdiction over intercreditor issues relating to subordination matters.

5. Coordination with Institutional Holders

More and more frequently, large institutional holders are filing their own appearances, retaining counsel and participating in reorganization proceedings. The indenture trustee should, of course, encourage such participation and, to the degree possible, coordinate with the institutional holder and its counsel so that the indenture trustee and the holder, who should have similar goals, are not working at a cross-purpose. In some cases, where institutional investors control the entire issue, institutional holders may desire to have their own counsel appear and represent their interests in the bankruptcy proceeding or represent the indenture trustee as well.

---

372 *In re Cont'l Airlines*, 91 F.3d 553, 557 (3d Cir. 1996).

373 *U.S. Bank N.A. v. T.D. Bank, N.A.*, 569 B.R. 12, (2017).

374 *See infra* Chapter XIII on the effectiveness of subordination.

6. Review Status of Bond Funds

Particularly where there is a debt service payment due postpetition, the indenture trustee may consider its ability to apply moneys in the debt service reserve fund to such payment. It has been held that because the debtor has a reversionary, albeit inchoate, interest in the fund, the indenture trustee should move to lift the automatic stay to permit the interest payment to be made.[375] However, although the debtor has a reversionary interest in the debt service reserve fund, the debtor cannot use the money in the fund for other purposes until the bonds are paid. Thus, a plan that provides for the use of the bond reserve fund to pay administrative expenses should not be not confirmable.[376] Where a debtor makes a draw on the construction fund postpetition for prepetition work, the funds to which the debtor would otherwise be entitled are subject to setoff by the indenture trustee under 11 U.S.C. § 553(a), which permits setoff if a creditor's claim against the estate and the estate's claim against the creditor both arose before the filing of the debtor's bankruptcy case.[377]

K. Participation in the Plan Process

To the degree possible, the indenture trustee should be involved in negotiating the plan of reorganization.[378] In particular, the indenture trustee should be sure that its security holders have been placed in an appropriate classification for purposes of voting on the plan of reorganization. As noted above, if the debtor does not classify the public debt claim separately, the indenture trustee should argue for separate treatment. Further, the indenture trustee should be certain that the method of distribution under the plan comports with the requirement of the indenture. Attempts by the obligor to distribute directly to the holders should be recognized as a method of defeating the rights of the indenture trustee under the indenture to a first claim to such distribution for payment of fees and expenses. If there has been appropriate coordination and communication with the holders, they should support the payment of the indenture trustee's reasonable fees and expenses.

---

375 *In re Hernando Healthcare Inc.*, 157 B.R. 701 (Bankr. M.D. Fla. 1993).

376 *In re Cent. Med. Ctr., Inc.*, 122 B.R. 568 (Bankr. E.D. Mo. 1990).

377 *In re United Airlines, Inc.*, 438 F.3d 720 (7th Cir. 2006).

378 Similarly situated indenture trustees may coordinate their efforts in a bankruptcy case, even with respect to actions to be taken on their collateral, without running afoul of the antitrust laws. *United Airlines, Inc. v. U.S. Bank N.A. and The Bank of N.Y. as Indenture Trustees*, 406 F.3d 918 (7th Cir. 2005), *enforced* 409 F.3d 812 (7th Cir. 2005).

L. Bankruptcy Settlement by the Indenture Trustee to Bind Bondholders

Most indentures contain language prohibiting the impairment of the holder's right to payment of principal of and interest on the security without the holder's consent. Indeed, the TIA specifically prohibits such impairment.[379] However, this provision does not prevent the indenture trustee from agreeing to settle a claim in bankruptcy agreed to by a majority of holders subject to bankruptcy court approval. Upon default, the indenture vests in the indenture trustee alone the power to exercise the bondholders' remedies subject to instruction by a majority in principal amount of bondholders. Implicit in the authority to commence proceedings to remedy defaults is the power to negotiate and agree upon settlements in bankruptcy, subject to the power to direct in writing by a majority in principal amount of the bonds.[380] In bankruptcy situations, where contractual rights are already impaired, non-impairment clauses are moot.[381]

M. Plan Provisions

There are a number of key provisions to a plan from the perspective of an indenture trustee. These provisions can be found in Appendix XI-F. In negotiating or reviewing a plan, the indenture trustee should consider:

1. Definitions

All terms including the indenture and indenture trustee are properly described and the amount of the claim for principal, interest and expenses is reflected in the definition. All key terms should be defined. The indenture trustee's claim should be defined as an allowed claim or the dispute identified.

2. Classification

The indenture trustee claim should be classified separately unless there is sufficient justification for classification with other claims. The subordination of claims should be reflected in the classification or in the treatment provided the subordination is effective.

---

379 TIA § 316(b). *See* discussion in Chapter XV.

380 *In re Delta Air Lines, Inc.*, 370 B.R. 537 (Bankr. S.D.N.Y. 2007), *aff'd*, 374 B.R. 516 (S.D.N.Y. 2007), *aff'd*, 309 Fed. Appx. 455 (2d Cir. 2009), *cert. denied*, 558 U.S. 1007 (2009); *In re Bd. of Dirs. of Telecom Argentina, S.A.*, 528 F.3d 162 (2d Cir. 2008). In non-bankruptcy situations, Section 316(b) may prevent a settlement absent agreement of all the holders. See discussion in Chapter XIV.

381 *Id.*; *In re Residential Capital, LLC*, 497 B.R. 720 (Bankr. S.D.N.Y. 2013); *UPIC & Co. v. Kinder-Care Learning Ctrs.*, 793 F. Supp. 448 (S.D.N.Y. 1992).

3. Treatment

The treatment of the indenture trustee's claim should be clear and understandable. The disclosure statement should clearly inform the holders of the value to be received.

4. Method of Distribution

The method of distribution should be reasonable and practically possible. All distributions to the holders should be made through the indenture trustee unless holders have good reason to object and arrangements have been made for the payment of the indenture trustee's fees and expenses. If the indenture trustee acts as distribution agent, provision must be made in the plan for compensation of the bank as distribution agent and protection of the bank for its actions post-confirmation, especially if the indenture has been discharged and the indenture trustee has been released as part of the plan and confirmation order. There should be no distribution unless there has been a proper tender of the securities for cancellation. Appendix XI-G is the transmittal letter from holders for receipt of plan distribution.

The claim resolution process should not be allowed to delay distribution of some, if not all, consideration to public debtholders. Most indentures provide that the holder for distribution purposes entitled to the full distribution is the holder of the security at the time of the distribution record date, and not previous holders. This should be clearly spelled out in the plan and disclosure statement. Any compromise or settlement of claims of public debtholders other than for principal and interest should be clearly disclosed and passed on by the court. There are serious jurisdictional objections to releasing any claim against non-debtor parties such as revolver banks accused of a lender liability claim in the absence of consent and consideration for such release.[382] However, liability under Section 311 of the TIA may be resolved in a plan given the language of the statute.

5. New Securities

The terms and the method of issuance of the new securities should be set forth in the plan. If the old indenture trustee is to remain indenture trustee on the new securities, such should be disclosed. New securities should have a legend on them indicating the issuance pursuant to a plan as opposed to a registered offering. Fractional shares of securities should be resolved by either a fractional share pool or rounding up or down. Such fractional share or securities pool could be the first source of payment of the indenture trustee's latch-on rights before such funds are used to pay the holders or for the debtor's benefit. The use of a fractional share pool or

---

382 *In re AOV Indus., Inc.*, 792 F.2d 1140 (D.C. Cir. 1986); *In re Monroe Well Serv., Inc.*, 80 B.R. 324 (Bankr. E.D. Pa. 1987).

rounding up or down should be part of the plan that is confirmed and so ordered by the bankruptcy court.

6. Board of Directors

The name, background and affiliation of each member of the reorganized company's board of directors shall be set forth in the disclosure statement.

7. Proof of Claim

The plan should provide that the indenture trustee's proof of claim shall survive and proofs of claim filed by holders that are duplicative should be stricken to the extent they are covered by the trustee's proof of claim. Holders may object to a provision that restricts their proof of claim for matters not covered by the indenture trustee's proof of claim.

8. Release, Discharge, Surrender and Cancellation of Claims

The plan should provide that the claims of the holders and indenture trustee shall be discharged upon surrender of the old security and issuance of consideration under the plan. Also, the plan should provide that upon its confirmation, the indenture is discharged and released except for the right of the indenture trustee to receive payment under the terms thereof (latch-on rights) of its fees and expenses. Sweeping releases of an indenture trustee *qua* trustee by the debtor under the plan may be problematic.[383] The law regarding the ability of the bankruptcy court to approve non-consensual third-party releases as part of a plan continues to evolve. In the case of *In re Master Mortgage Investment Fund, Inc.*,[384] the court applied a five-factor test to determine whether a debtor's release of a non-debtor is appropriate: (1) an identity of interest between the debtor and the non-debtor such that a suit against the non-debtor will deplete the estate's resources, (2) a substantial contribution to the plan by the non-debtor, (3) the necessity of the release to the reorganization, (4) the overwhelming acceptance of the plan and release by creditors and interest holders and (5) the payment of all or substantially all of the claims of the creditors and interest holders under the plan.

---

383 For example, in the Modified Third Amended Joint Chapter 11 Plan of Lehman Brothers Holdings Inc. and Its Affiliated Debtors, No. 08-13555 (Bankr. S.D.N.Y. Dec. 5, 2011), ECF No. 22973, the indenture trustees who served as members of the unsecured creditors' committee would be released parties *solely* in that capacity (1.136). Further, the plan specifically provided the release did not extend to any action taken prior to the commencement date or to acts or omissions that constituted willful misconduct or gross negligence.

384 *In re Master Mort. Inv. Fund, Inc.*, 168 B.R. 930 (Bankr. W.D. Mo. 1994).

Citing this case, the bankruptcy court in the *Washington Mutual* case declined to approve the indenture trustees' release under the plan as originally proposed.[385] According to the *Washington Mutual* court, there was no identity of interest between the indenture trustees and the debtor. The trustees had not contributed cash or anything else of tangible value to the plan or to creditors, nor had they provided an extraordinary service that would constitute a substantial contribution to the plan or case. Moreover, because the indenture trustees were creditors' committee members, the release provisions appeared to the court to be duplicative. When the plan was finally approved, revised release provisions had been consensually agreed to by the holders of claims to the extent that they affirmatively elected to grant such releases and were entitled to receive a distribution under the plan. While some courts have simply held that non-consensual non-debtor releases are impermissible under the facts of the case,[386] other courts have followed the *Master Mortgage* analysis of the circumstances supporting third-party releases.[387] In any event, the indenture trustee being released must inform its holders of what is taking place. Since many indentures contain provisions indemnifying the indenture trustee for costs and claims asserted against it, there is a basis for finding that a release benefits the estate by reducing potential unliquidated claims. This may be subject to the facts of a specific case and to the balancing of interests of all parties concerned. Likewise, bondholder groups and committees, especially when they support and direct the trustee to support the plan, should seek to obtain a release in the plan as outlined above for all actions related to participation in the plan process.

Non-consensual release of claims against the indenture trustee by holders in a plan is also problematic. The release of the indenture trustee by holders must be clearly communicated

---

385 *In re Wash. Mut., Inc.*, 442 B.R. 314 (Bankr. Del. 2011).

386 *See* discussion in *Cont'l Airlines,* 203 F.3d 203, 212 (3d Cir. 2000) (citing *Master Mortgage* but not adopting test).

387 *In re Zenith Electronics Corp.*, 241 B.R. 92 (Bankr. D. Del. 1999); *In re Wash. Mut., Inc.*, 442 B.R. 314 (Bankr. D. Del. 2011) (third-party releases against non-debtor would be effective only with respect to those parties that affirmatively consented to releases by voting in favor of plan and not opting out of release); *see also In re Millennium Lab Holdings II, LLC*, Case No. 16-110-LPS (D. Del. Mar. 20, 2017), ECF No. 48 (holding *Stern v. Marshall* precluded a bankruptcy court from entering a final order granting non-consensual third-party releases of non-bankruptcy claims, even as part of a confirmation order; proposed findings of fact and conclusions of law must be submitted to the district court). Significantly, *Master Mortgage, Washington Mutual* and *Continental* predated *Stern v. Marshall,* 131 S. Ct. 2594 (2011). The *Millennium* case has been remanded to the bankruptcy court for further proceedings. Whether *Millennium* is followed by other courts remains to be seen. However, where there is adequate disclosure of and the requisite consent by holders to the release of an indenture trustee under a plan of reorganization, plans containing such a release continue to be confirmed. *See, e.g.*, Fourth Amended Joint Plan of CHC Group Ltd. and Its Affiliated Debtors, *In re: CHC Group Ltd. et al.*, Case No. 16-31854 (Bankr. N.D. Tex. Feb. 16, 2017), ECF No. 1701.

to the bondholders. In the matter of *In re Lower Bucks Hospital*,[388] the indenture trustee had failed to timely file a continuation statement prepetition. Postpetition, because of issues regarding perfection, there was an agreement between the indenture trustee and the debtor to a secured claim less than the outstanding principal amount. The plan contained a bondholder release of the indenture trustee. Although the trustee had sent various communications to its holders regarding the plan and settlement, the trustee's communication did not reference potential claims against the trustee or the nature of the release. Moreover, the release was not highlighted or emphasized in the disclosure statement. Accordingly, the Court of Appeals held the bankruptcy court did not abuse its discretion in finding that the third-party release in the plan was not adequately disclosed to bondholders affected thereby and in declining to approve the release. Accordingly, any release by holders of the indenture trustee must be adequately described in the disclosure materials, including the nature of the claims being released and the possible value of such claims. Further, the release should ideally be explained in a holder communication.

9. Identification of Impaired and Unimpaired Claims

The public debt claim should be identified as impaired or unimpaired. As noted above, only an impaired class can vote. If a secured creditor is fully secured, has no deficiency claim and is unimpaired under the plan, then the secured creditor does not vote and is deemed to have accepted the plan.

10. Retention of Jurisdiction

If any matter relating to public debt is not resolved in the plan, the court should retain jurisdiction if such resolution is necessary for appropriate treatment of public debt. For example, the court could retain jurisdiction over any determination as to the fairness of the distribution of the special proceeds account under Section 311 of the TIA.

11. Tax Issues

Certainly, it would be unusual for the indenture trustee to offer an opinion on the tax ramification of a particular plan or restructuring, but the indenture trustee should be sensitive to the matters and alert holders that there may be tax issues that may impact distributions or securities they may receive that should be reviewed by their tax advisors. Further, the debtor should be encouraged to disclose the general tax ramifications and intended results.[389]

---

388 *In re Lower Bucks Hospital*, 571 Fed. App. 139 (3d Cir. 2014).

389 In the early days of the bankruptcy case, the debtor may seek to have an order entered limiting transfers of equity interests and claims against the debtor to preserve net operating losses. *See, e.g.*, *UAL Corp. v. State St. Bank and Tr. Co.*, Case No. 03 A 0061 (Bankr. N.D. Il. Feb. 24, 2008).

N. Holders Vote on and Objection to the Plan

Normally, the indenture trustee cannot vote on a plan of reorganization except for the indenture trustee's claim for fees and expenses. Many beneficial holders of debt securities are not record holders of the securities. Frequently, bankruptcy court orders provide that the debtor is authorized to send master ballots to the record holders of the securities. Such master ballot agent in turn will distribute approved materials plus a beneficial holder ballot to the beneficial owners the agent represents. The beneficial owner ballot either will be returned to the master ballot agent for inclusion in the master ballot or, if the beneficial holder ballot has been prevalidated, will be delivered directly to the debtors' voting agent.[390] An indenture trustee should object to a plan of reorganization when the plan clearly is grossly inadequate or unjustifiably impairs the bondholders' claims. If inequitable treatment is provided by a plan, the objection of the indenture trustee should be no surprise. In public debt issues where there are only small holders, the indenture trustee may be the only one organized and competent to represent the interests of the holders. If the plan does not reinstate the securities, the indenture trustee should insist the plan discharge both the indenture and the indenture trustee. If the securities are to be reinstated, care must be taken that all defaults are cured and all the provisions of the indenture, including the fees and expenses the indenture trustee has incurred in the course of the bankruptcy, are to be paid before the debtor can be allowed to treat the securities as if no default had taken place.

O. Accrual of Interest and Tax Liability Without Payment

It is not uncommon for a corporate debtor, during the pendency of its Chapter 11 proceeding and even before instituting the Chapter 11 proceeding, to have accrued an interest expense on its books and records while never making payment of such interest to the holders of the debt securities. Thereafter, the plan of reorganization and the disclosure statement may have failed to indicate or clearly point out that the company intended to take a deduction for the accrued interest on the debt securities, even though the interest was not paid, and that the distribution to the debtholders under the plan of reorganization was less than the principal face amount of the debt securities. This position, taken by more than one debtor, has left the indenture trustee post-confirmation with the dilemma of having to file a IRS Form 1099B. This form is an information return, showing the name and address of each recipient and the gross proceeds

---

390 *See, e.g., In re AMR Corp., et al.*, in the United States Bankruptcy Court for the Southern District of New York, Order (I) Approving Notice of Disclosure Statement Hearing; (II) Approving Disclosure Statement; (III) Establishing a Record Date; (IV) Establishing Notice and Objection Procedures for Confirmation of the Plan; (V) Approving Solicitation Packages and Procedures for Distribution Thereof; (VI) Approving the Forms of Ballots and Establishing Procedures for Voting on the Plan; and (VII) Approving the Form of Notice to Non-Voting Classes under the Plan, June 7, 2013, ECF No. 8614.

received, even though, under the circumstances described, no income in the form of interest payments was ever received by the indenture trustee or the holders of the debt securities. Sometimes, given the actions of the debtor and the omission or unclear statements in the plan and disclosure statement, the holders may be faced with income attributable to them, even though they have not received the benefit of such interest payments. Indenture trustees, post-confirmation, have had to fight the method and manner in which the debtor treated an interest expense while not paying such interest, and the theory that the payment of far less than the face amount of principal on the debt securities would or could include a payment of interest that has been accrued but unpaid. Obviously, from the debtor's position, it receives a tax benefit by receiving the interest expense without having to pay the interest, and it generally pays no more to the debtholders than it would have paid if it was not able to accrue the interest. The indenture trustee should carefully consider this issue in connection with a proposed plan and a disclosure statement. The indenture trustee should make sure that the disclosure statement adequately sets forth the tax liability that creditors, including public debtholders, face. This includes subsequent income attributable to interest that was not paid but which accrued on the books of the debtor. In the alternative, the indenture trustee can have the court, at the confirmation hearing, make a determination of whether any accrual of interest and any payments, as is set forth in the plan, could be attributable as income to the debtholders. Since a debtholder, depending upon its basis, may be recognizing a loss on the distribution of the consideration under a plan of reorganization, the debtor many times argues that there is little or no income actually recognized and taxable. However, there is no doubt that the accrual of an interest expense without the payment of interest to the debtholders is to the detriment of the debtholders while it is to the benefit of the company. The investment decisions faced by the debtholders can benefit from clear and accurate disclosure in the plan of reorganization or an appropriate determination by the court as to the reasonableness and fairness of the accrual of interest without payment attributable as income to the debtholders.

P. Compensation to the Indenture Trustee in Bankruptcy

There are several avenues available to the indenture trustee to collect its fees and expenses incurred in bankruptcy. Appendix XI-H sets forth the sources of indenture trustee compensation in bankruptcy. Typically, the indenture under which the indenture trustee is acting will give the indenture trustee the contractual right to payment of its "reasonable fees and expenses," which include attorneys' fees, from the borrower. This right is not eliminated but is complicated when the borrower is in a proceeding under the Bankruptcy Code. As mentioned previously, the proof of claim filed by the indenture trustee should include its contractual claim against the debtor for fees and expenses.[391] Whether or not the claim for fees will be allowed may be judged on whether the expenditures were prudent based upon the then-existing circumstances, not based upon hindsight.[392] Further, the contract claim includes the reasonable fees and expenses of the indenture trustee for defending its fees.[393] The chief concern is the method of collection of this contract claim. Such claim often will be of the same classification as the claim in chief and very likely will not be paid 100¢ on the dollar. Further, if the issue is unsecured, postpetition fees and expenses may not be covered by the claim.[394]

More problematic is the ability of an indenture trustee to be compensated for its fees and expenses from the bankruptcy estate on a priority basis. Compensation can be accomplished if the indenture trustee meets the challenging "substantial contribution" test of Section 503(b) of the Bankruptcy Code.[395]

To the degree an indenture trustee makes a substantial contribution to a case, it is entitled to an allowance of its fees and expenses pursuant to Section 503(b)(3) of the Bankruptcy Code. However, some courts have not allowed such a claim to include actions taken solely for the benefit of the indenture trustee's own holders. These actions would include the routine day-to-day administration of the securities during the bankruptcy (the transfer and registrar function, providing lists of holders and other requested services).[396] If possible, the indenture trustee

---

391 The Eighth Circuit's decision in *In re Flight Trans. Corp. Secs. Litig.*, 874 F.2d 576 (8th Cir. 1989), held that an indenture trustee retains its contractual rights to compensation and reimbursement for attorneys' fees when the issuer or obligor of the underlying securities enters bankruptcy. In that case, the court determined that the indenture trustee was not entitled to compensation or reimbursement for attorneys' fees under Section 503(b) of the Bankruptcy Code for making a substantial contribution, which will be discussed below, merely because it acted as a prudent person under the TIA. *Id.* at 583. However, the court recognized the indenture trustee's right to pursue a separate contractual claim for its fees and expenses. *Id.*

392 *In re Nortel Networks Inc.*, Case No. 09-10138 (KG) (Bankr. Del. Mar. 8, 2017), ECF No. 18001.

393 *Id.*

394 The extension of the contract claim to include postpetition fees and expenses has been questioned where the claim is unsecured. *In re Glob. Indus. Tech.*, 344 B.R. 382 (Bankr. W.D. Pa. 2006).

395 *See In re Worldwide Direct, Inc.*, 334 B.R. 112 (Bankr. D. Del. 2005).

396 *See In re Northwestern Corp.*, 365 B.R. 453 (Bankr. D. Del. 2007), where the court found that the indenture trustee did not make a substantial contribution under Section 503(b) because the services it performed primarily benefited the underlying security holders. The court focused on the fact that the indenture trustee opposed the plan of reorganization ultimately confirmed by the court. *See also In re Gillette Assocs.*, 101 B.R. 866 (Bankr. N.D. Ohio 1989) (expenses primarily benefited trustee and objections increased cost of case). In *In re Mich. Gen. Corp.*, 102 B.R. 554 Bankr. (N.D. Tex. 1988), the court held that prepetition expenses may not be recovered pursuant to Section 503(b) because prior to the date on which the bankruptcy petition is filed, no bankruptcy estate exists to which the indenture trustee can substantially contribute. *Id.* at 559. Furthermore, the court held that the

should attempt throughout the case to demonstrate to the court and other case participants the necessity of input from the indenture trustee and that the actions being taken by the indenture trustee are for the success of the reorganization. The Bankruptcy Code's specific references to the payment of indenture trustees' fees and expenses are limited to the provisions that authorize the estate to reimburse the indenture trustee for necessary expenses,[397] reasonable attorneys'[398] fees and reasonable compensation[399] where it has made a substantial contribution to the case. As noted, this can be a difficult standard to meet given the indenture trustee's principal responsibility to its holders.

In order to minimize this burden and to resolve contested issues through negotiation, many cases simply have provided for the payment of indenture trustee's fees and expenses as part of the plan of reorganization. The articulated justification for such plan provisions is the language in the Bankruptcy Code that permits a plan to contain "any other appropriate provision not inconsistent with the applicable provisions of this title."[400] Relying upon this language, a number of bankruptcy courts have approved the payment of the indenture trustees' fees.[401] Detailed discussion of the payment of fees bargained for under a plan of reorganization may be found in several cases.[402]

The acceptance of this approach has not been universal.[403] In an appeal from the bankruptcy court decision, the district court in the *Lehman* bankruptcy ruled that a plan of reorganization cannot bypass the Bankruptcy Code by permitting permissive plan payments. According to the district court, payments for fees must meet the substantial contribution test.[404]

---

indenture trustee could not recover any expenses after the confirmation of the plan of reorganization because the plan rejected the indenture contract. *Id.* Applying the "substantial contribution" standard, the court disallowed certain fees incurred during the case claimed by the indenture trustee's counsel, including (1) fees relating to a determination of whether the indenture trustee was properly removed as trustee of the indenture; (2) fees relating to services found to be duplicative; and (3) fees relating to certain legal research issues. However, the court did ultimately award the indenture trustee $46,845.50 under Section 503 for compensation and reimbursement of attorneys' fees.

397 11 U.S.C. § 503(b)(3)(D).

398 11 U.S.C. § 503(b)(4).

399 11 U.S.C. § 503(b)(5).

400 11 U.S.C. § 1123(b)(6).

401 *See, e.g., In re ARM Corp.*, 497 B.R. 690 (Bankr. S.D.N.Y. 2013) (creditors' committee included indenture trustees); *In re Worldwide Direct*, 334 B.R. 112 (Bankr. D. Del. 2005).

402 *In re Adelphia Commc'ns Corp.*, 441 B.R. 6 (Bankr. S.D.N.Y. 2010).

403 *See, e.g., In re Cty. of Orange*, 179 B.R. 195 (Bankr. C.D. Ca. 1995).

404 *In re Lehman Bros. Holdings Inc., et al.*, 508 B.R. 283 (S.D.N.Y. 2014); Motion for Certificate of Appealability Denied, 2014 WL 3408574 (S.D.N.Y. 2014). But as noted, for example, the plan ultimately approved in the *Caesars* case provided for the payment of indenture trustee fees and

The viability of providing for payment of fees and expenses in plans will continue to be analyzed by the courts.[405] The importance of a satisfactory resolution of the indenture trustee's fee issue has been underscored by the United States Supreme Court decision holding that an estate may not compensate professionals for fees incurred in defending fee applications.[406]

In the situation in which the indenture trustee's claim is fully secured, the indenture trustee may assert a claim under Section 506(b) of the Bankruptcy Code for its fees and expenses, including those incurred postpetition.

Success at the foregoing sources of payment will be increased by careful time records that segregate the nature of the tasks being performed for the holders in particular and the case in general. As set forth above, to the degree the indenture trustee is not paid under a substantial contribution theory under Section 503(b) of the Bankruptcy Code, it may be entitled to compensation under its indenture agreement as a contractual claimant even if the claim is unsecured, so long as the debtor and others are in agreement. Finally, the indenture trustee has its latch-on rights based upon the provision in the indenture for payment of the indenture trustee's fees and expenses prior to any distribution to holders.

Q. Standards for Fee Applications under Section 503(B)

As set forth above, under Section 503(b) of the Bankruptcy Code, reasonable compensation for professional services rendered by an attorney for a creditor, an indenture trustee, an equity security holder or a committee representing creditors may be awarded if there has been a substantial contribution to the Chapter 11 case. Courts have struggled to formulate the proper measure for determining the reasonableness of a particular fee award where an indenture trustee is concerned. It has been held that "substantial contribution" requires more from an indenture trustee than satisfactory performance as indenture trustee and fulfilling its obligations to its holders.[407] Rather, the test is whether the services substantially contributed to a successful result for the debtor's estate and its creditors.[408] If the services benefit only its holders, the request of the indenture trustee for payment of fees and expenses as a substantial contribution

---

expenses. *See* note 163 *supra*. Similarly, in the CHC Group Ltd. Plan, the postpetition fees and expenses of both the secured and unsecured indenture trustees were to be paid. Fourth Amended Joint Plan of CHC Group Ltd. and the Affiliated Debtors, *In re CHC Group Ltd., et. al.,* Case No. 16-31854 (Bankr. N.D. Tex. Feb. 16, 2017), ECF No. 1701.

405 See Jeffrey Chubak, "Nixing Permissive Plan Payments Effectively Repeals § 1129(A)(4)," 33 Am. Bankr. Inst. S. 18 (July 2014).

406 *Baker Botts LLP v. ASARCO LLC,* 135 S. Ct. 2158 (2015).

407 *In re Flight Transpo. Corp. Sec. Litig.,* 874 F.2d 576 (8th Cir. 1989).

408 *Id.*; see also *In re Worldwide Direct, Inc.,* 334 B.R. 112 (Bankr. D. Del. 2005).

claim may be denied. This test of a causal connection between the work performed and benefit to all parties in the case must be considered when evaluating a substantial contribution claim.

R. Rule 2019

Rule 2019 of the Federal Rules of Bankruptcy Procedure provides that every group or committee representing more than one creditor or security holder shall file a verified statement setting forth the names and addresses of the creditor or security holder, the nature and amount of the economic interest and the time of acquisition of the economic interest unless it is alleged to have been acquired more than one year prior to the filing of the petition. Rule 2019 has been amended to specify that an entity is not required to file a statement solely because of its status as indenture trustee.[409] If the indenture trustee is a member of a creditors' group or committee, the indenture trustee should confirm that a Rule 2019 statement for the committee has been filed.

S. Timeline

The bankruptcy process can be extremely time consuming and often requires a substantial commitment of resources for the indenture trustee. The Bankruptcy Timeline attached as Appendix XI-I sets forth merely the minimum times required by the Bankruptcy Code.

---

409 Rule 2019(b)(2).

Appendix XI-A
Form of Bylaws for the Creditors' Committee

Official Creditors' Committee ("Committee")

(Case No. ____________________)

MEMBERSHIP

A. The Committee shall be known as the ____________ unsecured creditors' committee and is referred to in these Bylaws as the "Committee." Members of the Committee are those designated by the United States Trustee ("U.S. Trustee") for the bankruptcy court having jurisdiction over the Chapter 11 case entitled ____________________ ("Bankruptcy Court").

B. Each Committee member shall designate not more than [two] individuals to act as its representative(s) on the Committee. Each member's representatives may be assisted by counsel, but solely at the expense of the applicable member, with the understanding that ____________, as indenture trustee, has the right to payment of its reasonable fees and expenses, including attorneys' fees, under the terms of the indenture and applicable law. These Bylaws are not intended to interfere with any existing rights of the indenture trustee to payment of its fees and expenses. The Committee members and their respective representatives are identified on <u>Exhibit A</u> to these Bylaws. All references to "members" of the Committee shall mean only those entities identified on <u>Exhibit A</u> to these Bylaws, acting through their representatives, as designated from time to time in accordance with these Bylaws.

C. Any member of the Committee may designate an alternate or alternates to attend Committee meetings, provided that such alternate is an employee of or attorney for the creditor represented by such member and that such designation is made in writing; any such alternate shall be deemed a member of the Committee for all purposes of the meetings in the absence of the member.

D. Any creditor represented by a member may designate a substitute for such member by writing addressed to the Chairman of the Committee; any such substitute shall thereupon become a member of the Committee for all purposes, subject to the approval of the Committee.

E. If a member resigns from the Committee, and that member or the creditor represented by that member does not or does not wish to designate a substitute, the Committee shall make recommendations to the Bankruptcy Court for a substitute to replace the resigned member. If feasible, the substitute shall represent interests similar to those of the resigned member. During the period after the resignation and prior to the approval of the substitute, the total membership of the Committee shall be those members remaining after the resignations. A member that no longer holds any unsecured claim (including, without limitation, because the claim is paid in full, released or transferred by sale, participation, grant of an option or other method) shall promptly notify in writing the Chair and Committee counsel of such transfer. Upon receipt, Committee counsel shall forward notice of such transfer to the remaining members of the Committee. Upon consummation of the payment, release or transfer of such claim(s), the member shall resign or shall be deemed to have resigned from the Committee. No member shall have the right to transfer its membership in the Committee.

There shall be a single Chair of the Committee, who shall be elected from among the representatives of the Committee members by a majority vote of the Committee, and who shall serve until the earlier of resignation, removal or dissolution of the Committee at the conclusion of the case.

As authorized by the Committee, the Chair or the Committee's professional advisors shall speak for the Committee in reporting the Committee's non-confidential decided position to other parties-in-interest in this proceeding and to the press, if appropriate. Committee counsel and other professionals retained by the Committee shall be authorized to act on the advice and instructions of the Chair issued in accordance with these Bylaws. The Chair shall have the authority to sign documents on behalf of the Committee as appropriate in order to implement decisions of the Committee.

The Chair, once elected, may be removed, with or without cause, by affirmative vote of at least two-thirds of the members. Upon removal of the Chair, the Committee shall immediately elect his or her successor.

If the Chair resigns his or her position from the Committee, then the Committee shall immediately elect his or her successor.

The Committee may elect a Vice-Chair who may exercise the duties if the Chair is not available to perform his or her duties.

QUORUM

A quorum shall consist of a majority of the voting members of the Committee.

MEETINGS

No meeting shall be held unless a quorum is present.

Regular meetings shall be held from time to time on dates and at locations set by announcement at a meeting or on at least three business days' notice of the time and place by telephone, fax, e-mail, mail or other similar means of communication, provided, however, that any telephonic notice shall be confirmed in writing by mail, or other similar means of communication.

Special meetings may be called by the Chair on at least 48 hours' notice by telephone, fax, e-mail or mail to each member, provided that in an emergency the Chair may call a meeting on shorter notice. To the extent feasible, the primary purpose for the special meeting shall be set forth in the notice.

Meetings shall be held in person or by telephone conference call, and so long as each member may hear the remarks of each other member then any member present by telephone shall be deemed to be present in person.

ACTION BY COMMITTEE

A. Action by the Committee at a meeting requires the affirmative vote of a majority of those voting. No member may vote at a meeting except in person by its named representative, alternate or counsel. Votes will be by secret ballot upon the request of any member of the Committee. Each member shall have a single vote.

B. In an emergency, action may be taken by the Committee without a meeting, provided that the Chair or Committee counsel determines that such procedure is necessary and appropriate. In such cases votes must be obtained by polling members on the issue by telephone, e-mail or fax. Polling may be conducted by the Chair or the Chair's designee or Committee counsel. Such a vote is effective if a good faith effort is made to reach and consult with each member of the Committee or his or her alternate with respect to the proposed action and, if prior to the taking of such action, at least a majority of the Committee approves the action. The Chair or the Chair's designee or Committee counsel shall provide prompt notice of any such action to each member who has not given approval, which notice shall be in writing or confirmed in writing.

C. Matters brought to the Committee shall be handled in accordance with the following procedures:

1. Each matter brought to the Committee for action shall be reviewed by the Chair or by Committee counsel.

2. The following matters shall be taken to the full Committee for consideration either at the next regularly scheduled meeting or by polling or telephone conference call:

a. Matters that the Chair determines raise such significant and controversial issues that they should be discussed by the full Committee;

b. Matters that do not require a response prior to the next regularly scheduled meeting and that are not routine or administrative in nature; and

c. Matters considered under paragraph 3 below, where the requisite vote has not been obtained.

3. All matters that require a response prior to the next regularly scheduled meeting (other than matters falling under paragraph 2a above), or that are routine or administrative in nature, shall be resolved in the following manner;

a. If a matter falls within the purview of an existing operating subcommittee and the subcommittee has been delegated authority to act upon the matter presented, then the Chair of the subcommittee shall confer with the subcommittee and dispose of the matter. Any such action by a subcommittee shall be by a majority vote.

b. If a matter falls within the purview of an existing operating subcommittee, but the subcommittee has not been delegated authority to act upon the matter presented, then an Executive Committee consisting of the Chair and Vice-Chair (if one has been elected by the Committee) of the full Committee and the Chair of the affected subcommittee shall, with the assistance of Committee counsel, confer and dispose of the matter. Any action by an Executive Committee so constituted must be by a majority vote.

c. If a matter does not fall within the purview of any existing operating subcommittee, then an Executive Committee consisting of the Chair and Vice- Chair (if one has been elected by the Committee) shall, with the assistance of Committee counsel, confer and dispose of the matter. Any action taken by an Executive Committee so constituted shall be by a unanimous vote.

d. If a matter is purely legal or procedural in nature, Committee counsel shall be empowered to act on the matter after obtaining the approval of the Chair or, in the Chair's absence, the Vice- Chair. All such actions shall be reported to the Committee.

e. Without prior Committee action or consent, the Chair, with the advice of the professionals for the Committee, shall be empowered to consent to or otherwise act on relatively minor matters between meetings, which may include (i) requests by a party-in-interest for the entry of court or other matters involving amounts not greater than $100,000 in the aggregate for all such matter during such period and (ii) other matters not readily susceptible of monetary evaluation that, in the judgment of the Chair, upon advice of Committee counsel, are considered to be in the normal course of business and not significant (including not significant to the interests of unsecured creditors generally), including, without limitation, such matters raised by court-filed applications. This authorization is for convenience purposes and it is not the intention of this authorization that all such relatively minor matters be handled without consultation of the Committee. The Committee shall be advised promptly of any matters so acted on by the Chair, and the Chair or its designee shall use its reasonable best efforts to do so within two business days after such action. Notwithstanding the foregoing, no such action shall be taken by the Chair if it can reasonably be expected to have precedential effect.

In special, unexpected emergency situations, actions may be taken by the Chair on behalf of the Committee without a meeting, provided, however, the Chair determines, after consultation with the Committee's professionals, that such action is absolutely vital to the interests of the Committee and action is required before the Committee can be called together for a meeting or polled, and provided, further, the Chair or counsel for the Committee shall first make a good faith effort to poll the members of the Committee concerning the matter at issue, and provided, further, the Chair or counsel for the Committee will use its reasonable best efforts to, within one day after taking such action, give written notice to each of the members of the action taken, the basis for the action and the reason for taking action without a meeting.

Upon request by a member of the Committee, such member's vote on any matter shall be recorded in the minutes of the appropriate meeting.

Executive Session and Meetings

Meetings of the Committee shall be open to all bondholder or indenture trustee creditors of the debtor and other parties invited by the Chairman, provided that the Committee may, by affirmative vote of one-third of the members present, meet in executive session, which shall be open only to members and ex-officio members of the Committee and their representatives (including counsel) and Committee agents.

SUBCOMMITTEES

The Committee shall appoint such subcommittees as it deems appropriate and may delegate to such subcommittees powers and responsibilities so long as any such delegation is approved by a vote of two-thirds of the full Committee.

EXPENSES

Reasonable expenses of the Committee members incurred in connection with Committee business shall be sought to be reimbursed by the debtor. Reasonable expenses shall include travel expenses for meetings for the member and one other agent or representative of or counsel to the member's employer on Committee business, conference telephone calls and such other expenses that the Committee approves.

EX-OFFICIO MEMBER

Any member appointed as an ex-officio member shall have the right to notice and to be present and to speak at meetings but shall not be entitled to make Motions of Seconds, or to vote on any matter before the Committee, or to take any other action.

Although all Committee members acknowledge that they are acting in a fiduciary capacity as defined by law, nothing contained herein shall: (a) prevent any member from (i) exercising or seeking to enforce or protect any of its rights as an individual creditor or other party-in-interest or (ii) taking any actions or enforcing any rights in respect of any security interest that such member may have in the property of the debtors or their estates; or (b) otherwise affect the ability of any member to act in its capacity as an individual creditor or other party-in-interest as it may deem appropriate.

CONFLICTS OF INTEREST

Each Committee member shall disclose any conflict of interest with respect to any matter under consideration by the Committee. The existence of a conflict of interest will be determined by a vote of the Committee upon the advice of counsel. In the event that any matter under consideration by the Committee involves a conflict of interest with respect to any Committee member, such member shall abstain from voting on the matter and, upon request of the Committee, shall be recused from discussions on the matter. In such event, the number of Committee members necessary to obtain a quorum shall be adjusted downward accordingly. Each Committee member shall have an ongoing duty to disclose to the remaining Committee members any actual or potential conflicts of interest. The Committee recognizes and agrees any indenture trustee or trustee for security interest as a member of the Committee serves an important function for the Committee, and there is no conflict for such an indenture trustee or trustee to be a member of the Committee and perform any duties the indenture trustee or trustee may have under its indenture or trust documents.

Confidentiality

Unless the full Committee unanimously agrees otherwise, each Committee member agrees not to disclose or disseminate any material nonpublic information that it receives as a Committee member to any parties other than its agents, directors, officers, representatives, attorneys, advisors, affiliates and employees (collectively, "Related Parties"). Upon request of a Committee member, the Chair or Committee counsel, as applicable, will disclose in general terms the content of any materials to be distributed to the Committee members. Each Committee member then, in its sole discretion, may elect whether or not to receive such information. If a Committee member elects not to receive certain information and that information is pertinent to matters on which the Committee is to vote, such member shall abstain from voting on the matters and shall be recused from discussions on the matters. In such event, the number of Committee members necessary to obtain a quorum shall be adjusted downward accordingly. Except as provided below, in the event that any Committee member (or any entity bound by these confidentiality provisions) is requested or required by any regulatory body or in any judicial or administrative proceeding (by oral questions, interrogatories, requests for information or documents, subpoena, civil investigative demand or similar process) to disclose any material nonpublic information, the member shall use reasonable efforts to notify promptly the debtors, the Committee and their respective counsel of such request or requirement so that the debtor or the Committee may seek an appropriate protective order or waive the compliance provisions of these Bylaws. If, in the absence of a protective order or the receipt of a waiver hereunder, a Committee member is compelled by subpoena or otherwise to disclose the material nonpublic information to a regulatory body or tribunal, that member may disclose such material nonpublic information to such tribunal and shall not be liable for such disclosure. Subject to the foregoing obligation to make reasonable efforts to provide prior notice, a Committee member may disclose material nonpublic information to any regulatory body requiring such disclosure and having jurisdiction over it without first providing notice to the debtor, the Committee or their respective counsel. For purposes of this provision, all materials disseminated to the Committee, all discussions and votes on matters before the Committee and the minutes of all Committee meetings shall be deemed material nonpublic information unless otherwise determined by the Committee or its Chair upon advice of counsel. Each Committee member agrees to take all action required to preserve the attorney-client privilege, the attorney work-product doctrine, the accountant-client privilege and the accountant work-product doctrine applicable to the Committee, Committee counsel and its accountants or financial advisors. The debtors shall be third-party beneficiaries of this section.

AMENDMENTS TO RULES

These rules may be amended only by a vote of a majority of the members of the Committee.

COMMITTEE'S COMMUNICATIONS WITH CREDITORS

Upon authorization by the Committee, written communications with some or all of the creditors of the debtors shall be made on behalf of the Committee by (a) the Chair or (b) Committee counsel at the direction of the Chair. Notwithstanding the preceding sentence, counsel may communicate with creditors of the debtors regarding public matters without the authorization of the Committee or the Chair. Committee members shall be permitted to communicate on their own behalf with other unsecured creditors of the debtors as to any matters other than those matters involving material nonpublic information, as described in these Bylaws. The Committee recognizes that it is the debtors' responsibility, and not the Committee's, to communicate to the debtors' creditors all information that the debtors deem material to their Chapter 11 cases. The Committee recognizes that ___________, as indenture trustee, must keep its holders generally informed on a regular basis of the developments in the case which are not nonpublic and material, and nothing in these Bylaws is intended to limit the indenture trustee in the exercise of its duties. To the extent a holder agrees to become restricted and enters into an appropriate confidentiality and non-disclosure agreement, including, but not limited to, for the purpose of directing and instructing the indenture trustee, the indenture trustee may share material, nonpublic information with such holder.

EXPENSES

Reimbursement of reasonable out-of-picket expenses of the Committee and of Committee members incurred in connection with Committee business shall be sought from the debtors in accordance with applicable provisions of the Bankruptcy Code and orders of the court. Reasonable expenses shall include: (a) costs and expenses for attendance at meetings by the respective representatives or alternate representatives of Committee members, including out-of-pocket expenses incurred for transportation, hotel, food, taxis and related items for not more than two representatives of a member (except that, if the circumstances dictate, the travel expenses of more than two representatives will be reimbursed); and (b) telephone call, facsimile communications, postage and delivery costs associated with Committee business, but shall not include professional fees incurred by individual Committee members in the performance of their duties. Committee members also shall be reimbursed for such other expenses as the Committee, acting by majority vote of the full Committee, may approve and the court shall authorize.

SUBCOMMITTEES

The Committee may establish subcommittees to address particular issues arising in the debtors' Chapter 11 cases upon authorization by the Committee.

ROBERTS' RULE

All matters not covered by these Bylaws shall be governed by Roberts' Rules of Order (current edition).

Appendix XI-B
Form of Proof of Claim

Fill in this information to identify the case:

Debtor 1 Complete in Full

Debtor 2 ____________________
(Spouse, if filing)

United States Bankruptcy Court for the: ________ District of ________

Case number ____________________

Official Form 410

Proof of Claim

04/16

Read the instructions before filling out this form. This form is for making a claim for payment in a bankruptcy case. Do not use this form to make a request for payment of an administrative expense. Make such a request according to 11 U.S.C. § 503.

Filers must leave out or redact information that is entitled to privacy on this form or on any attached documents. Attach redacted copies of any documents that support the claim, such as promissory notes, purchase orders, invoices, itemized statements of running accounts, contracts, judgments, mortgages, and security agreements. **Do not send original documents;** they may be destroyed after scanning. If the documents are not available, explain in an attachment.

A person who files a fraudulent claim could be fined up to $500,000, imprisoned for up to 5 years, or both. 18 U.S.C. §§ 152, 157, and 3571.

Fill in all the information about the claim as of the date the case was filed. That date is on the notice of bankruptcy (Form 309) **that you received.**

Part 1: Identify the Claim

1. **Who is the current creditor?**

   Set forth name of Trustee and issue for whom it is acting
   Name of the current creditor (the person or entity to be paid for this claim)

   Other names the creditor used with the debtor ____________________

2. **Has this claim been acquired from someone else?**

   ☑ No
   ☐ Yes. From whom? ____________________

3. **Where should notices and payments to the creditor be sent?**

   Federal Rule of Bankruptcy Procedure (FRBP) 2002(g)

   Where should notices to the creditor be sent?

   Set forth contact at Trustee
   Name

   Number Street

   City State ZIP Code

   Contact phone ____________________

   Contact email ____________________

   Where should payments to the creditor be sent? (if different)

   Name

   Number Street

   City State ZIP Code

   Contact phone ____________________

   Contact email ____________________

   Uniform claim identifier for electronic payments in chapter 13 (if you use one):

   _

4. **Does this claim amend one already filed?**

   ☑ No
   ☐ Yes. Claim number on court claims registry (if known) ______ Filed on ________ MM / DD / YYYY

5. **Do you know if anyone else has filed a proof of claim for this claim?**

   ☑ No
   ☐ Yes. Who made the earlier filing? ____________________

Part 2: Give Information About the Claim as of the Date the Case Was Filed

6. **Do you have any number you use to identify the debtor?**	❑ No ❑ Yes. Last 4 digits of the debtor's account or any number you use to identify the debtor: ___ ___ ___ ___
7. **How much is the claim?**	$______________ **Does this amount include interest or other charges?** See attached addendum ❑ No ❑ Yes. Attach statement itemizing interest, fees, expenses, or other charges required by Bankruptcy Rule 3001(c)(2)(A).
8. **What is the basis of the claim?**	Examples: Goods sold, money loaned, lease, services performed, personal injury or wrongful death, or credit card. Attach redacted copies of any documents supporting the claim required by Bankruptcy Rule 3001(c). Limit disclosing information that is entitled to privacy, such as health care information. See attached addendum
9. **Is all or part of the claim secured?**	☑ No ❑ Yes. The claim is secured by a lien on property. **Nature of property:** ❑ Real estate. If the claim is secured by the debtor's principal residence, file a *Mortgage Proof of Claim Attachment* (Official Form 410-A) with this *Proof of Claim*. ❑ Motor vehicle ❑ Other. Describe: ______________ **Basis for perfection:** ______________ Attach redacted copies of documents, if any, that show evidence of perfection of a security interest (for example, a mortgage, lien, certificate of title, financing statement, or other document that shows the lien has been filed or recorded.) **Value of property:** $__________ **Amount of the claim that is secured:** $__________ **Amount of the claim that is unsecured:** $__________(The sum of the secured and unsecured amounts should match the amount in line 7.) **Amount necessary to cure any default as of the date of the petition:** $__________ **Annual Interest Rate** (when case was filed)______% ❑ Fixed ❑ Variable
10. **Is this claim based on a lease?**	❑ No ❑ Yes. **Amount necessary to cure any default as of the date of the petition.** $__________
11. **Is this claim subject to a right of setoff?**	❑ No ❑ Yes. Identify the property: ______________

Official Form 410 **Proof of Claim** page 2

12. Is all or part of the claim entitled to priority under 11 U.S.C. § 507(a)?

A claim may be partly priority and partly nonpriority. For example, in some categories, the law limits the amount entitled to priority.

☑ No

☐ Yes. *Check one:*

	Amount entitled to priority
☐ Domestic support obligations (including alimony and child support) under 11 U.S.C. § 507(a)(1)(A) or (a)(1)(B).	$________
☐ Up to $2,850* of deposits toward purchase, lease, or rental of property or services for personal, family, or household use. 11 U.S.C. § 507(a)(7).	$________
☐ Wages, salaries, or commissions (up to $12,850*) earned within 180 days before the bankruptcy petition is filed or the debtor's business ends, whichever is earlier. 11 U.S.C. § 507(a)(4).	$________
☐ Taxes or penalties owed to governmental units. 11 U.S.C. § 507(a)(8).	$________
☐ Contributions to an employee benefit plan. 11 U.S.C. § 507(a)(5).	$________
☐ Other. Specify subsection of 11 U.S.C. § 507(a)(__) that applies.	$________

* Amounts are subject to adjustment on 4/01/19 and every 3 years after that for cases begun on or after the date of adjustment.

Part 3: Sign Below

The person completing this proof of claim must sign and date it. FRBP 9011(b).

If you file this claim electronically, FRBP 5005(a)(2) authorizes courts to establish local rules specifying what a signature is.

A person who files a fraudulent claim could be fined up to $500,000, imprisoned for up to 5 years, or both. 18 U.S.C. §§ 152, 157, and 3571.

Check the appropriate box:

☑ I am the creditor. on behalf of holders

☐ I am the creditor's attorney or authorized agent.

☐ I am the trustee, or the debtor, or their authorized agent. Bankruptcy Rule 3004.

☐ I am a guarantor, surety, endorser, or other codebtor. Bankruptcy Rule 3005.

I understand that an authorized signature on this *Proof of Claim* serves as an acknowledgment that when calculating the amount of the claim, the creditor gave the debtor credit for any payments received toward the debt.

I have examined the information in this *Proof of Claim* and have a reasonable belief that the information is true and correct.

I declare under penalty of perjury that the foregoing is true and correct.

Executed on date ____________
MM / DD / YYYY

____
Signature

Print the name of the person who is completing and signing this claim:

Name ______________________________
First name Middle name Last name

Title ______________________________

Company ______________________________
Identify the corporate servicer as the company if the authorized agent is a servicer.

Address ______________________________
Number Street

____
City State ZIP Code

Contact phone ____________ Email ____________

Print | Save As... | Add Attachment | Reset

Official Form 410 Proof of Claim page 3

Appendix XI-C
Form of Proof of Claim Addendum

IN THE UNITED STATES BANKRUPTCY COURT
FOR THE ______________________________

In Re:)
)
______________________________,) Case No. ______________
)
Debtors.)

ADDENDUM TO
FORM OF PROOF OF CLAIM FILED BY
______________, AS INDENTURE TRUSTEE

The undersigned, who has his/her office at ______________________________, is a ____________________ of ______________________, a national banking association, established and existing pursuant to ______________, with its principal place of business in ______________ at the above-cited address. __________________ is the duly appointed, qualified and acting Indenture Trustee for the ______________ (the "Debentures")* issued pursuant to an indenture dated as of __________________ (the "Indenture") between ______________________________ (the "Debtor") and ________________________ (the "Trustee"). A true and correct copy of the Indenture is attached hereto as Exhibit _____ and incorporated herein. The undersigned is duly authorized to make this Proof of Claim for the Trustee, pursuant to Section _____ of the Indenture.

2.

This claim has not been acquired from someone else. This claim does not amend one that has already been filed. The undersigned is unaware of anyone else who has filed a proof of claim for this claim.

* Form should be modified for notes, bonds, certificates or other evidence of indebtedness or interest or rights under an indenture or trust instrument.

3.

The Debtor, pursuant to the terms of the Indenture, was at the time of the filing of its Petition initiating this case and still is indebted to make payment to the Trustee on behalf of the holders of the Debentures in the sum of at least ____________________ ($________________) plus interest thereafter and interest on all overdue installments of interest to the extent that payment of such interest shall be legally enforceable, plus fees, expenses and advances of the Trustee including attorneys' fees and expenses. There is presently issued and outstanding ____________________ ($________________) in principal amount of the Debentures under the terms of the Indenture. The Trustee files this claim against the Debtor, on behalf of all holders of Debentures issued under the Indenture.

4.

The consideration for said debt is the execution and delivery of the Indenture by the Debtor, and pursuant to said Indenture the issuance and sale of the Debentures, for the benefit of the Debtor and others, and the receipt by the Debtor and certain of its divisions, subsidiaries and affiliates of the proceeds from sale of said Debentures. Events of Default under Section _____ of the Indenture have occurred and continue and exist today uncured by the Debtor. Such defaults include, but are not limited to, the following:

(a) transfer of the proceeds from sale of the Debentures to subsidiaries and affiliates;

(b) transfer of assets, or purported security interests in assets, without fair consideration to certain creditors, impairing the ability of the Debtor and its divisions, subsidiaries and affiliates to reorganize or to obtain additional financing, in derogation and impairment of the rights and interests of the holders of the Debentures, obviating the subordination thereof, at a time when the Debtor was insolvent or was rendered insolvent thereby;

(c) allowing certain persons to exert undue influence and control over the business operations, affairs and decisions of the Debtor and its divisions, subsidiaries and affiliates;

(d) the failure to make the interest payment due on ____________;

(e) the failure to make the required prepayment of principal due on __________;

(f) the filing by the Debtor of the Petition seeking relief under Chapter 11 of the Bankruptcy Code, 11 U.S.C. § 1101 *et seq.*;

(g) the failure to file with the Trustee, as required by Section _____ of the Indenture, copies of certain information, documents and other reports which the Debtor is required to file with the Securities and Exchange Commission (the "Commission") pursuant to the provisions of Section 13 or Section 15d of the Securities Exchange Act of 1934 and the rules and regulations thereunder prescribed by the Commission; and

(h) the failure to comply with the requirements of The Trust Indenture Act of 1939 by virtue of the foregoing.

On _________________, pursuant to Section ____ of the Indenture, Exhibit ____, the Trustee declared the principal of all of the Debentures to be due and payable immediately, thereby accelerating the payment of all principal together with all accrued unpaid interest thereon.

5.

Pursuant to Section ____ of the Indenture, Exhibit ____, the Trustee is expressly authorized to file this Proof of Claim on behalf of all holders of the Debentures without possession or production of any Debentures and for the purposes set forth in that Section of the Indenture which is incorporated herein by reference.

6.

No part of the aforesaid claim has been paid and no cash is held by the Trustee under the Indenture for the aforesaid claim. All of said debt referred to in paragraph 3 above has become due and owing pursuant to the terms of the Indenture.

7.

No judgment has been rendered on this claim.

8.

The amount of all payments on this claim has been credited and deducted for the purpose of making this Proof of Claim.

9.

This claim is not subject to any setoff or counterclaim.

10.

The Trustee holds no security interest and has not received any security for the aforesaid claim.

11.

This Proof of Claim is filed as a general, ____________________ claim which is entitled to the rights of subordination of certain other claims: (a) by contract as set forth in Article ____ of the Indenture, Exhibit ____, and in other written documents and (b) on equitable grounds pursuant to 11 U.S.C. § 510.

12.

The Trustee hereby files this Proof of Claim against the Debtor and each of the other debtors and debtors-in-possession whose names and Chapter 11 case numbers are set forth in the caption hereof (the "Co-Debtors"), and does expressly include a claim against each and every one of the Co-Debtors, and each of their divisions, subsidiaries and affiliates, and those purporting to act on their behalf, for imposition of a continuing security interest in proceeds, constructive trusts, equitable liens, subrogation or any and all of the legal or equitable remedies, rights and interests to which the Trustee or any holder of the Debentures may be entitled by virtue of the use, possession and enjoyment by any of the Co-Debtors or their divisions, subsidiaries or affiliates of any of the proceeds of the Debentures, either directly or indirectly. The Trustee on behalf of itself and the holders of the Debentures expressly reserves its and their rights and claims against each of the Co-Debtors, their divisions, subsidiaries and affiliates and their respective creditors under Section 510 of the Bankruptcy Code, 11 U.S.C. § 510, including claims of equitable subordination and the right and benefit at law or in equity to all the rights and interests under and with respect to the Indenture. The Trustee on behalf of itself and the holders of the Debentures expressly reserves its and their rights to supplement the claims against the Co-Debtors and their divisions, subsidiaries and affiliates after full disclosure of all relevant facts in these bankruptcy proceedings, whether pursuant to Section 1104 or Section 1106 of the Bankruptcy Code, 11 U.S.C. §§ 1104 and 1106, or pursuant to such adversary actions as may be necessary and appropriate. Moreover, this Proof of Claim does expressly include a claim against the Debtor, its divisions, subsidiaries and affiliates, whether as debtors or as debtors-in-possession, and all those purporting to act on their behalf for:

(a) failure to fulfill their contractual and fiduciary obligations to the Trustee and the holders of the Debentures, including breach of implied covenants of good faith and fair dealing, by reason of (among other things):

(i) the transfer of assets, or purported security interests in assets, to certain creditors when insolvent or when such transfer rendered the Debtor and each of the Co-Debtors insolvent; and

(ii) the failure to reorganize their businesses and debts at a time when such reorganization was still possible;

(b) allowing certain persons to exert undue influence and control over the business operations, affairs and decisions of the Debtor and its divisions, subsidiaries and affiliates, and each of the Co-Debtors and their divisions, subsidiaries and affiliates, to the detriment of the Trustee and the holders of the Debentures;

(c) negligently undertaking, authorizing or permitting the Debtor or the Co-Debtors to engage or to continue to engage in businesses known to be unprofitable or not capable of becoming profitable;

(d) making, causing or permitting to be made misleading statements regarding the businesses of the Debtor or any of the Co-Debtors;

(e) failure to take prudent and appropriate action regarding adverse business conditions affecting the business operations of the Debtor or any of the Co-Debtors;

(f) negligently undertaking, authorizing or permitting excessive borrowings by the Debtor, or any of the Co-Debtors, which borrowings were known or should have been known to not be or to likely be sustained or repaid by such persons;

(g) the failure to require adequate financial and accounting controls for the Debtor and the Co-Debtors and permitting misleading or inadequate internal financial and accounting procedures;

(h) failure to oversee properly the use of the proceeds of the Debentures, and improper commingling of cash;

(i) failure to properly disclose all material and relevant facts relating to the financial condition of the Debtor or any of the Co-Debtors;

(j) failure to disclose the relationship between the Debtor, the Co-Debtors and their bank lenders, which would operate to the detriment of the rights and interests of the Trustee and the holders of the Debentures;

(k) the improper and fraudulent acts on behalf of the Debtor or any of the Co-Debtors by certain persons, contrary to the rights and interests and the representations made to the Trustee and the holders of the Debentures;

(l) the failure of the independent accountants for the Debtor or any of the Co-Debtors to disclose the true financial condition of the Debtor or any of the Co-Debtors, and certain improper accounting practices and procedures used by the Debtor or any of the Co-Debtors and such independent accounting firms;

(m) the self-dealing and conflict of interest that certain persons had in connection with the issuance of the Debentures, which would inure to the benefit of certain lending institutions, to the detriment of the holders of the Debentures and the Trustee; and

(n) the improper use, transfer and diversion of the proceeds of the issuance of the Debentures and the assets of the Debtor or any of the Co-Debtors to the detriment of the Trustee and the holders of the Debentures.

Further details concerning these rights, claims and causes of action cannot be given at this time due to the need for a full investigation into the acts, conduct, assets, liabilities and financial condition of the Debtor and each of the Co-Debtors, and due to the privileged and confidential nature of the review by counsel to the Trustee of this matter.

13.

This Proof of Claim is filed under the compulsion of the bar date established in the Debtor's Chapter 11 cases and is filed to protect the Trustee from forfeiture of claims by reason of said bar date. The filing of this Proof of Claim is not intended to be and should not be deemed or construed as (a) an election of a remedy, (b) a consent by the Trustee to the jurisdiction of the Bankruptcy Court or any other court with respect to the proceedings, if any, commenced, in a case against or otherwise involving the Trustee, (c) a consent by the Trustee to trial by jury as to any and all matters so triable herein or in any case, controversy or proceeding related hereto, pursuant to 28 U.S.C. § 157(e) or otherwise, (d) a waiver of the right of the Trustee to a trial by jury in any matter herein or in any case, controversy or proceeding related hereto, (e) a waiver of the right of the Trustee to have final orders in non-core matters entered only after a de novo review by the United States District Court, (f) a waiver of any right of the Trustee to have the reference withdrawn by the United States District Court in any matter subject to mandatory or discretionary withdrawal, (g) a waiver of any past, present or future event of default, (h) a waiver or limitation of any rights of the Trustee, including, without limitation, a waiver of obligations owing to the Trustee, rights, claims, actions, defenses, set-offs or recoupments to which the Trustee is or may be entitled, in law or equity, against the Debtor and/or any subsidiary or affiliate thereof, or any other person, including, without limitation, rights against guarantors, officers or directors, or the right to contest the validity or extent of any liens or security interests, all of which rights, claims, actions, defenses, setoffs or recoupments are expressly reserved by the Trustee or (i) an admission by the Trustee that any property held by the Debtor (or any subsidiary or affiliate thereof) is property of the estate. Under Section ______ of the Indenture, the Trustee, may include in its Proof of Claim a claim for the compensation, expenses, disbursement and advances of the Indenture Trustee and its counsel. The Trustee has incurred fees and expenses prior to ______________ of $______________, all of which has not been paid for by the Debtor. The Trustee has incurred and will continue to incur additional amounts due to the Trustee under the terms of the Indenture for its compensation and expenses as Indenture Trustee, including attorneys' fees and expenses, as to which sums the Trustee is entitled under the expressed terms of the Indenture to payment. The Trustee reserves the right to amend or supplement this Proof of Claim, if the Trustee should deem it necessary and appropriate, given the then-existing posture of this proceeding, for any reason, including an updated statement of the amount then due for such Indenture Trustee's fees and expenses.

________________________, as
Indenture Trustee, as aforesaid
By: ____________________________________
Title: __________________________________

[Date]

This is a claim filed on behalf of the holders of the Debentures in the amount of $___________ plus interest thereon, as aforesaid, plus Indenture Trustee fees and expenses, as aforesaid.

Send All Court Orders and Notices to:

[Name and Address of Attorney for Trustee]

and

[Name and Address of Trustee]

STATE OF ______________)
) SS
COUNTY OF ____________)

____________________________, being duly sworn, deposes and says that:

The Affiant is ______________ of ______________ and has read the foregoing Proof of Claim and the same is true and correct to the best of his or her knowledge, information and belief and he or she is duly authorized to execute such Proof of Claim on behalf of ______________, as Indenture Trustee for the ______________ (the "Debentures").

SUBSCRIBED AND SWORN TO
before me this _____ day of ___________.

____
Notary Public

Appendix XI-D
Advantages and Disadvantages of a Purchase of Assets through a Bankruptcy Proceeding

Advantages	Disadvantages
1. Reduced Liability to Others. Successor liability and product liability eliminated or reduced. Limit successor liability and product liability and warranty claims both through the purchase of assets pursuant to Section 363 of the Bankruptcy Code or through the "purchase" of the Company through funding the Plan of Reorganization.	1. Need for Bankruptcy Exit Plan. A plan of reorganization or liquidation for the Company and remaining assets after sale may require negotiations with certain creditors' groups or conversion to Chapter 7 or dismissal of the case.
2. Fairness Determination. Judicial determination will be made of the fairness of the purchase price and determination of deficiency.	2. Public Securities Laws. If securities are anticipated in a prepackaged plan (*i.e.*, the purchaser purchases the company in part with reorganization securities) there must be compliance with applicable securities laws with respect to the solicitation of consents in advance of filing.
3. Final and Binding Sale. Court approval eliminates second-guessing or claims from shareholder, creditors or unsuccessful lenders.	3. Disclosures. Full disclosure must be made of all material information, including disclosure of any benefits to insiders and fiduciaries.

Advantages	Disadvantages
4. Elimination of Unfavorable Executory Contracts. Unfavorable union contracts, leases or other executory contracts can be rejected and eliminated and the resulting claim would be an unsecured claim against the estate rather than the purchaser.	4. New Players in the Process; Influence of Creditor Committee and U.S. Trustee. The bankruptcy process has the price tag of the judge. Look for a benefit to unsecureds and creditors' committee who want something from the sale and seek a role in the bankruptcy, which may delay sale or increase costs.
5. No Surprise Claims after the Sale, Which Is Free of Liens and Claims. The purchaser should not have to worry about surprise liens and claims after the fact.	5. Inability to Take Shortcuts; Auction Process and Chilling Sale. Some statutory stalking horse bidders do not want a court auction but rather just want approval of the pre-filing sales efforts. Some courts may so proceed, and others may not.
	6. Inherent Delays. Delay with a creditors' committee, the U.S. trustee and a court could cause substantial delay in timing of sale as they investigate or review how the sale effort is conducted.

Appendix XI-E
§ 363 Asset Sale Process – Possible Timeline

30–60 days prior to filing the Petition for Bankruptcy Law Protection under Chapter 11 ("Petition Date")	• Pre-Filing Sales Effort Stalking Horse Bid for all or most of Company's assets at price acceptable to Lenders
Petition Date	• File Petition for Voluntary Proceeding for U.S. Companies • File Motions for Approval of Sale of Assets under Section 363 of the Bankruptcy Code and to Establish Bidding Procedures • File Interim DIP Financing and Cash Collateral Use Motions (tied to budget Approved by Lenders) • File General First Day Orders
1–5 Days from the Petition Date	• Hearing on Interim Order for Use of Cash Collateral • Motion to Establish Bar Date (Expedited Hearing requested) • Have Court set Date for Hearing on Sale Motion and Date for Hearing and Mailing of Bidding Procedures; Mail Notice of Motion for Sale • Debtor to Identify to Court and Lenders Potential Purchasers or Targets and Approve Form of Confidentiality Letter as part of Bidding Procedures
10–20 Days from the Petition Date	• Hearing on Bidding Procedures and Court Order on Sale Bidding Procedures and Approve Confidentiality Letter • Establish Information/Data Room for Potential Purchasers
By 15–25 Days from the Petition Date	• Mailing of Bidding Procedures and Solicitations for Bids to Potential Targets (with Draft Confidentiality Letter) • Objections to Final DIP Order due

By 10–25 Days from the Petition Date	• Objections to Sale Motion due (If Not Resolved at Bidding Procedure Hearing) • Execute Draft Confidentiality Letter with Interested Purchasers • Contact and Negotiation by Broker with Potential Sale Candidates
By 20–30 Days from the Petition Date	• Hearing on Final DIP Financing Order • Hearing on Sale of Assets (if necessary if there is an objection to Bidding Procedures and may be delayed to Sale Approval Hearing) • Debtor and Lenders to receive Qualification (financing) of Bidders who have expressed interest in Bidding • Hearing on Bar Date and Mailing Notices
35–65 Days from the Petition Date	• Bids due on Sale - Debtor in consultation with Lenders regarding right to reject Bids non-conforming with Bidding Purchases and form Contract or negotiate discrepancies - Earnest Money due - Lenders right to reject any and all Bids below cash payout of Loans
By 45–70 Days from the Petition Date	• Auction Sale Date • Court Hearing Approving Auction Sale
By 45–70 Days from the Petition Date	• Entry of Order Approving Sale • File Liquidation Plan and Disclosure Statement for Remaining Assets
By 50–100 Days from the Petition Date	• Closing on Sale of Assets
By 45–60 Days from the Petition Date	• Bar Date (earliest possible date)

By 70–95 Days from the Petition Date	• Objections to Disclosure Statement due (can be expedited if Disclosure Statement was used and is Prepetition Solicitation) • Motion to Estimate Claims or Disallow or Subordinate Claims • Rejection of all Executory Contracts not assumed by Purchasers unless determined to have value
By 75–100 Days from the Petition Date	• Hearing on Disclosure Statement (can be expedited to 30–50 days if there is a Prepetition Solicitation and those material qualify)
By 75–100 Days from the Petition Date	• Objections to Estimation of Claims and Disallowance or Subordination of Claims due
By 120 Days from the Petition Date	• Hearing on Claim Objections
By 105–130 Days from the Petition Date	• Objections to Plan of Liquidation due
By 110–140 Days from the Petition Date	• Hearing on Plan of Liquidation
By 120–160 Days from the Petition Date	• Consummate Plan of Liquidation
By 180 Days from the Petition Date	• Close Case

Appendix XI-F
Selected Plan Provisions

I. DEFINITIONS

As used in this Plan, the following terms shall have the respective meanings specified below, and such meanings shall be equally applicable to the singular and plural forms of the terms defined, unless the context otherwise requires:

Administrative Claim: any cost or expense of administration of the Chapter 11 Case entitled to priority in accordance with the provisions of Sections 503(b) and 507(a)(1) of the Bankruptcy Code, including, without limitation, any actual and necessary expenses of preserving the Debtor's estate and of operating the Debtor's business, including loans or other advances to the Debtor-in-Possession and all Fee Claims, and any fees or charges assessed against the Debtor's estate under Chapter 123 of title 28, United States Code.

Allowed Claim: any Claim (a) proof of which was timely and properly filed or which has been or hereafter is listed by a Debtor on its schedules filed under Section 521(1) of the Bankruptcy Code as liquidated in amount and not disputed or contingent and, in either case, a Claim as to which (i) no objection to the allowance thereof has been timely interposed or (ii) any objection has been determined by a Final Order to the extent such objection is determined in favor of a claimant; (b) based on a Fee Application to the extent such Fee Application is approved by a Final Order; or (c) allowed under this Plan. Unless otherwise specified herein or by order of the Bankruptcy Court, "Allowed Claim" shall not include interest on such Claim for the period from and after the Petition Date.

Ballot Date: the date set by the Bankruptcy Court as the last date for timely submission of a ballot accepting or rejecting this Plan.

Bankruptcy Code: The Bankruptcy Reform Act of 1978, as amended and as applicable to the Chapter 11 Case, as set forth in Section 101 *et seq*. of title 11, United States Code.

Bankruptcy Court: the United States Bankruptcy Court for ____________________ or such other court as may have jurisdiction over the Chapter 11 Case or any relevant proceeding or matter, as applicable.

Bankruptcy Rules: the rules of procedure in bankruptcy cases applicable to cases pending before the Bankruptcy Court, as amended.

Chapter 11 Case: the Chapter 11 case commenced by the Debtor on __________.

Claim: any right to payment, including for interest, from the Debtor or Debtor-in-Possession that arose on or before the Confirmation Date whether or not such right is reduced to judgment, liquidated, unliquidated, fixed, contingent, matured, unmatured, disputed, undisputed, legal, equitable, secured or unsecured; or any right that arose on or before the Consummation Date to an equitable remedy for breach of performance if such breach gives rise to a right of payment from the Debtor, whether or not such right to an equitable remedy is reduced to judgment, fixed, contingent, matured, unmatured, disputed, undisputed, secured or unsecured.

Class: any one of classes ________________ and ________________ described in ________________ of this Plan.

Collateral: property in which the Debtor has an interest that secures, in whole or in part, the payment of a Claim (except pursuant to any lien granted under this Plan).

Confirmation Date: the date of entry of the Confirmation Order in accordance with the provisions of the Bankruptcy Code; provided, however, that if on motion the Confirmation Order or consummation of this Plan is stayed pending appeal, then the Confirmation Date shall be the date of entry of the Final Order vacating such stay or the date on which such stay expires or is no longer in effect.

Confirmation Order: order of the Bankruptcy Court confirming this Plan and approving the transactions contemplated therein.

Consummation Date: the first business day following the date on which the Confirmation Order shall become a Final Order or such other date subsequent to the Confirmation Date as the Trustee and creditors' committee may, in writing, designate; provided, however, that on any such other date no order staying the effectiveness of the Confirmation Order or consummation of this Plan is in effect.

Contested Claim: any Claim as to which the Trustee or any other party in interest has interposed an objection in accordance with the Bankruptcy Code and the Bankruptcy Rules, this Plan or orders of the Bankruptcy Court, which objection has not been withdrawn or determined by a Final Order; provided, however, that any Claim allowed under this Plan shall not be a Contested Claim.

Creditor: any Person that is the holder of a Claim.

Creditors' Committee: the Official Consolidated Unsecured Creditors' Committee appointed in the Chapter 11 Case pursuant to Section 1102 of the Bankruptcy Code and its successor, if any, or such other Person as the creditors' committee may designate to act in its stead, which designation may remain in effect subsequent to the dissolution of the creditors' committee.

*Debenture Claims**: collectively, ____________________ Debenture Claims and ____________________ Debenture Claims.

Debtor: ____________________, a ____________________ corporation.

Debtor-in-Possession: the Debtor, as debtor-in-possession in the Chapter 11 Case.

Deficiency Claim: a Claim of a Creditor against the Debtor equal to the amount by which the aggregate Claims of such Creditor against such Debtor exceed the sum of (a) any setoff rights of the Creditor against the Debtor plus (b) the Net Proceeds realized from the disposition of the Collateral securing such Claim or, if such Collateral is not liquidated to cash, the value of the interest of the Creditor in the Debtor's interest in the Collateral securing such Claim; provided, however, that if the holder of such Claim makes the election provided in Section 1111(b) of the Bankruptcy Code, there shall be no Deficiency Claim in respect of such Claim.

Disallowed Claim: a Claim to the extent that such Claim was disallowed by a Final Order or by written agreement of the holder thereof.

Disclosure Statement: the disclosure statement in respect of this Plan approved by the Bankruptcy Court pursuant to Section 1125 of the Bankruptcy Code.

Effective Date: the date, as soon as practicable but in no event later than ten days after the Consummation Date, on which the distributions required pursuant to this Plan are to be commenced.

___________ *Debenture Claim*: a Claim of __________________ or any of the holders of _____ Debentures arising under, based upon or evidenced by such debentures or the ________ Indenture.

___________ *Debentures*: the ___________ Debentures due ______________ Issued by __________________ pursuant to the ________ Indenture.

Equity Interest: any equity interest in the Debtor represented by Pre-Confirmation Stock.

---

* Form should be modified for notes, bonds, certificates or other evidence of indebtedness or interest or rights under an indenture or trust instrument.

Estimated Claims Order: an order of the Bankruptcy Court that estimates the aggregate amount of Unsecured Claims and Small Claims that are Undetermined Claims to aid in calculating distributions under this Plan.

Fee Applications: applications of Professional Persons under Section 330 or 503 of the Bankruptcy Code for allowance of compensation and reimbursement of expenses in the Chapter 11 Case.

Fee Claim: a Claim under Section 330 or 503 of the Bankruptcy Code for allowance of compensation and reimbursement of expenses in the Chapter 11 Case.

Final Order: an order or a judgment that has not been reversed, stayed, modified or amended and (a) as to which (i) the time to appeal or seek review or rehearing has expired and as to which no appeal or petition for certiorari, review or rehearing is pending, or (ii) if appeal, review, reargument or certiorari of the order has been sought, the order has been affirmed or the request for review, reargument or certiorari has been denied and the time to seek a further appeal, review, reargument or certiorari has expired, and (b) as a result of which such order shall have become final and nonappealable in accordance with applicable law.

Indenture Trustee: collectively or individually, ________________ and ________________.

Indenture Trustee Claim: collectively, the ________________ Claims and ________________ Claims.

___________________: ___________________, as indenture trustee for the ______ Debentures.

___________________ *Claim*: the Claims of ___________________ on behalf of the holders of the _______ Debentures, including any Claims for fees and expenses of ___________________.

______________ *Indenture*: that certain indenture, dated as of _______________, by and between ___________________ and ___________________, as Trustee, as it shall survive after the Effective Date, including Articles ___________________ and ___________________ thereof and the rights and interests reserved in Section _____ hereof.

___________________ *Debenture Claim*: a Claim of ___________________ or any of the holders of the ___________________ Debentures arising under, based upon or evidenced by such debentures or the ___________________ Indenture.

___________________ *Debentures*: the ___________________ Debentures due ___________________ issued by ___________________ pursuant to the ___________________ Indenture.

[*Liquidating Trust*: a Trust to be established pursuant to this Plan and the Liquidating Trust Agreement.]

[*Liquidating Trust Agreement*: the agreement governing the Liquidating Trust.]

[*Liquidating Trustee*: the Person selected by the creditors' committee to administer the Liquidating Trust.]

Person: an individual, a corporation, a partnership, an association, a joint stock company, a joint venture, an estate, a trust, any unincorporated organization, a government or any political subdivision thereof or any other entity.

Petition Date: _______________, 20__.

Plan: this Plan of Reorganization proposed by the Debtor, either in its present form or as it may be amended or modified from time to time.

Post-Confirmation Expenses: all fees and expenses of Professional Persons incurred after the Confirmation Date.

Pre-Confirmation Stock: the shares of common stock and preferred stock, if any, of the Debtor that were issued and outstanding prior to the Effective Date.

Pre-Confirmation Stockholder: a holder of Pre-Confirmation Stock.

Priority Claim: any Claim, other than an Administrative Claim or a Tax Claim, to the extent entitled to priority in payment under Section 507(a) of the Bankruptcy Code.

Professional Persons: Persons retained or to be compensated pursuant to Sections 327, 328, 330, 503(b) and 1103 of the Bankruptcy Code.

Pro Rata: the proportion that the amount of a Claim against the Debtor in a particular Class bears to the aggregate amount of all Claims (including Undetermined Claims until disallowed) against such Debtor in such Class.

Public Debt: collectively, the following types of debt:

(a) the ______ Debentures; or

(b) the ______ Debentures.

Public Debt Claim: any of the following types of Claims:

(a) ______ Claims; or

(b) ______ Claims.

Public Debtholder: any Creditor that is the holder of Public Debt.

Record Date: the date set by the Bankruptcy Court as the date on which ownership of securities of the Debtor shall be fixed for purposes of making distributions under this Plan.

Reorganized Debtor: the Debtor as the same shall be constituted upon the Consummation Date pursuant to this Plan.

____________________: ____________________, as indenture trustee for the ______ Debentures.

____________________ *Claim*: the Claims of ____________________ on behalf of the holders of the ____________________ Debentures, including any Claim for fees and expenses of ____________________.

____________ *Indenture*: that certain indenture, dated as of ____________________, by and between ____________________ and ____________________, as Trustee, as it shall survive after the Effective Date, including Articles ____________ and ____________ thereof and the rights and interests reserved in Section _____ hereof.

Secured Claim: a Claim, exclusive of the Public Debt Claims (to the extent, if any, that such Claims would otherwise be Secured Claims), of a Creditor arising on or before the Petition Date that is secured by a lien on Collateral or that is subject to setoff under Section 553 of the Bankruptcy Code, to the extent of the value of such Creditor's interest in the Debtor's interest in the property, or to the extent of the amount of the setoff, as applicable; provided, however, that if the Creditor makes the election provided in Section 1111(b) of the Bankruptcy Code, the Creditor's Claim shall be a Secured Claim in the full amount of the Creditor's Allowed Claim.

Secured Creditor: any Creditor that is the holder of a Secured Claim.

Small Claim: an unsecured Claim of a Creditor against the Debtor in an aggregate amount, prior to any subdivision or assignment thereof that occurred after the Petition Date, (a) not exceeding $500 or (b) in excess of $500 that is reduced to $500 prior to the Ballot Date by agreement of the holder thereof.

Statutory Lien Claims: Secured Claims, secured by liens, including, without limitation, mechanics' liens, arising by statute rather than by agreement of the parties.

Tax Claim: any Claim that is entitled to priority in payment under Section 507(a)(7) of the Bankruptcy Code.

Trustee: the Person legally appointed by the Bankruptcy Court as trustee for the Debtor.

Undetermined Claim: a Claim, including, without limitation, (a) a Contested Claim, (b) a Claim arising from the rejection of executory contracts or unexpired leases pursuant to this Plan, (c) a Claim that is unliquidated or contingent, (d) a Claim as to which, on or before the later of the Effective Date and ________________, the Trustee has not yet made a determination whether or not to object and (e) a Fee Claim, that is not an Allowed Claim or a Disallowed Claim.

Unsecured Claim: an unsecured Claim, including any Deficiency Claim, that is not (i) a Small Claim, Public Debt Claim or Debenture Claim, (ii) entitled to priority pursuant to the Bankruptcy Code or (iii) subordinated for purposes of distribution to any unsecured Claim pursuant to Section 510(b) or 510(c) of the Bankruptcy Code.

Unsecured Creditor: any Creditor that is the holder of an Unsecured Claim.

II. CLASSIFICATION OF CLAIMS AND EQUITY INTERESTS

Classification: Claims against and Equity Interests in the Debtor shall be classified herein as follows with respect to the Debtor:

(a) *Class I* shall consist of all of the following:

(a) _____ Debenture Claims; and

(b) _____ Debenture Claims.

Resolution of Disputes: Disputes regarding the proper classification of Claims not specifically classified herein shall be resolved pursuant to the procedures established by the Bankruptcy Code, the Bankruptcy Rules, other applicable law, the Bankruptcy Court and this Plan, and such resolution shall not be a condition precedent to confirmation or consummation of this Plan.

III. TREATMENT OF CLAIMS AND EQUITY INTERESTS

In addition to the waiver and release of certain claims provided for elsewhere in this Plan, Claims and Equity Interests shall be treated as follows and all distributions under this Plan shall be free and clear of all liens, claims and encumbrances:

Class I - Public Debt Claims:

Allowance: On the Confirmation Date, (i) all Public Debt Claims shall be Allowed Claims in the amount of the distributions in respect thereof provided for in this Plan and shall be entitled to receive such distributions and (ii) the ________________ Claim and the

__________________ Claim shall, for all purposes under this Plan, including, without limitation, the right to distributions hereunder, be substituted for all Debenture Claims of individual holders of the __________________ Debentures, and the __________________ Debentures, respectively, arising under, based upon or evidenced by any such Debentures.

Distributions: On the Effective Date or as soon as practicable thereafter, Public Debt Claims shall be settled and compromised (except as to any allowance of compensation or reimbursement of expenses under Section 503(b) of the Bankruptcy Code and matters reserved by Section ____ hereof) in full by distributions as follows:

> [All distributions should be listed separately, such as the issuance of stock and warrants or transfers to any liquidating trust or any other distribution fund.]

Allocations of Distributions among Public Debt: In recognition of the compromises and settlements between and among Public Debt embodied in this Plan, the distributions in respect of Public Debt shall be allocated as follows:

> [Specific distributions should be set forth with respect to each of the various Claims, and such Claims should be designated by the Indenture Trustee.]

Manner of Distributions: All distributions provided in this section in respect of Indenture Trustee Claims shall be distributed to the respective Indenture Trustees for application pursuant to the provisions of the respective Indentures and applied first to the payment of fees and expenses properly chargeable thereto as set forth in the respective Indentures and thereafter distributed by the respective Indenture Trustees for the benefit of the respective Indenture Trustees and holders of the __________________ Debentures and the __________________ Debentures Pro Rata within each such Debenture issue. In lieu of distributions made directly to the Indenture Trustees pursuant to the preceding sentence, the respective Indenture Trustees may direct such other distributions as are otherwise consistent with the Plan and the terms of the respective Indentures. At the discretion of the respective Indenture Trustees, certificates of trust may be issued by the respective Indenture Trustees to holders to evidence their rights and interest.

IV. MEANS OF EXECUTION

Vesting and Business Continuity: On the Consummation Date, property of the Debtor shall vest in the Reorganized Debtor free and clear of all liens, claims, charges and interests arising on or before the Consummation Date, except as provided in this Plan or the Confirmation Order. Thereafter, the Reorganized Debtor shall be authorized to continue the business of the Debtor from which it was formed.

Cancellation and Issuance of Stock: On or as soon as practicable after the Effective Date, the following transactions shall occur in the following order:

(a) the cancellation, annulment and extinguishment of all existing Pre-Confirmation Stock;

(b) the issuance, distribution and transfer by the Reorganized Debtor of its stock in accordance with the terms of this Plan.

[Note that this section is to be used only in connection with the issuance of stock.]

Assumption of Liabilities: As of the Confirmation Date, the liability for and obligation to make the distributions required under the Plan, including the payment of Post-Confirmation Expenses, shall be as follows:

(a) the Reorganized Debtor shall have the liability for and obligation to make all distributions of notes, stock and warrants to be issued by the Reorganized Debtor under this Plan.

[All other liabilities should be listed in this section; for instance, if there is a distribution fund it should assume all liability to satisfy its obligations, and if a liquidating trust is used, it should assume the liability for an obligation to make all of its required payments and distributions.]

[The means of execution section of this Plan should also provide for the establishment of any collateral funds, any distribution funds or a liquidating trust; each of those sections should be separately dealt with and should contain sections dealing with its establishment, maintenance, and funding. If any such fund or trust has cash that should be invested, a specific section relating to such investments should be set forth in this Plan.]

Bar Date for Fee Claims: Each Professional Person who asserts a Fee Claim shall be entitled to file a Fee Application not later than _____ days after the Effective Date. Objections to each such Fee Application may be filed on or before the later of _____ days after the Effective Date and _____ days after each such Fee Application is filed.

V. METHODS OF DISTRIBUTION

Estimated Claims Order: On or before the date fixed by the Bankruptcy Court as the date for a hearing on confirmation of the Plan, the Debtor shall make an application to the Bankruptcy Court for the Estimated Claims Order, which will estimate the aggregate amount of Undetermined Claims that are Unsecured Claims (including Deficiency Claims) and Small Claims for purposes of calculating distributions to the Unsecured Creditors under this Plan.

Claims Resolution and Distribution: The Distributions provided for in this Plan shall be made as follows:

[Detailed provisions should be made for the initial distribution for Allowed Claims, reserves for Undetermined Claims, resolution of Undetermined Claims and Final Distributions.]

Additional Provisions Regarding Distribution to Public Debtholders:

(a) *Surrender of Securities*: As a condition to receiving distributions provided for by this Plan in respect of Public Debt Claims, during the period ending on the later of the _____ day after the Effective Date and __________, __________ or any holder of a __________ Debenture or a __________ Debenture must surrender such debenture to the respective Indenture Trustee. All securities surrendered to the Indenture Trustee, shall be marked "Compromised and settled only as provided in Debtor's Plan of Reorganization" and delivered to the Reorganized Debtor. Public Debt Securities shall remain in effect except as compromised and settled herein.

(b) *Settlement and Compromise of Debentures*: On the Effective Date, all outstanding __________ Debentures and __________ Debentures shall be cancelled on the books of the Debtor and become settled and compromised solely as provided herein and with respect to the Debtor, in consideration for the right to participate in distributions provided by this Plan, and all rights, claims and causes of action reserved by this Plan as set forth in Section ____ hereof; provided, however, Public Debtholders and __________ and __________, collectively and individually, do not waive, discharge, relinquish or release any right, claim or cause of action against the Debtor except the right to seek enforcement of such rights, claims or causes of action against the Debtor, so that any Person jointly liable with or derivatively liable through the Debtor shall in no fashion be discharged or in any manner be affected by the waivers, relinquishments and settlements set forth herein. On the Effective Date, as to any Person, the __________ Indenture and the __________ Indenture shall be settled and compromised solely with respect to the Debtor's liability thereunder without effect as to the liability of any such other Person directly or indirectly liable thereunder as an obligor or for any other reason, and with regard to such other Person, the Indenture shall survive with regard to (a) the rights, remedies, causes of action and powers of the Indenture Trustees, (b) the priority and application of any collections and distributions thereunder, (c) the legal relationship between holders of the respective Debentures, the respective Indenture Trustees and all Persons other than the Debtor, and (d) for such other actions as shall be necessary and appropriate to protect and preserve the rights, claims and causes of action of the respective holders and Indenture Trustees under the respective Indenture or pursuant to this Plan. Unless waived by the respective Indenture Trustee, any Person seeking the benefits of being a holder of a _________ Debenture or a _________ Debenture who is unable to surrender the actual debenture to the respective Indenture Trustee, if the respective Indenture Trustee shall so require, shall supply to the respective Indenture Trustee an appropriate indemnity bond acceptable to the Indenture Trustee, holding harmless the Debtor and the respective Indenture Trustee from any damages, liabilities or costs incurred in treating such Person as a holder of such Debenture, together with appropriate evidence satisfactory to the respective Indenture Trustee of the destruction, loss or theft of such Debenture.

(c) *Timing of Distributions*: [The time for various distributions should be set forth with specificity.]

Unclaimed Cash and Securities: If any Person entitled to receive a distribution under this Plan cannot be located at the time such distribution is to be made, then such distribution shall be held in or by [If any funds are used, list those particular funds.] or Reorganized Debtor; provided, however, that distributions in respect of the Indenture Trustee Claims shall be held by the appropriate Indenture Trustee [or the Liquidating Trustee]. If the Person entitled to any such distribution is located on or before the later of one year after the Effective Date or ________ days after its Claim becomes an Allowed Claim, such distribution shall be distributed to such Person. If, however, such Person cannot be located by such later date, then any such distribution, together with any interest or dividends earned thereon, shall be treated as follows:

[List any specific distributions with respect to Secured Claims, Statutory Lien Claims, Administrative Claims, Priority Claims, Tax Claims, Small Claims and Unsecured Claims.]

(a) Distributions for the Public Debtholders shall be divided Pro Rata among the other Public Debtholders holding claims in the same Class as the unlocated Person; provided, however, that distributions in respect of an Indenture Trustee Claim may first be applied by the applicable Indenture Trustee as provided in the applicable Indenture.

[Separate sections of this Plan should contain provisions regarding any notes, stock, warrants or other securities to be issued hereunder. Separate provisions should also be provided with respect to the reconstituted Board of Directors and any amendments necessary to the certificate of incorporation or bylaws of the Debtor in order to implement this Plan. Likewise, this Plan should provide a section that deals with executory contracts and unexpired leases of the Debtor. Such section should provide for assumptions and rejections under this Plan as well as the curing of any defaults under the leases or executory contracts. Such section should provide that any person who is a party to a contract or lease rejected pursuant to this Plan must file a proof of claim within a specified number of days after the Confirmation Date.]

VII. POST-CONSUMMATION SUPERVISION OF THE DEBTOR

[This Plan should provide for the role of the creditors' committee and any role of any Liquidating Trustee provided for herein. Such section might include the following:]

Role of the Liquidating Trustee: On and after the Effective Date, title to the Liquidating Trust shall be transferred to and invested in the Liquidating Trustee for the benefit of Public Debtholders.

(a) *Responsibilities*: The responsibilities of the Liquidating Trustee shall include the following:

(i) maintenance of the Liquidating Trust;

(ii) liquidation to cash of the Intangible Assets;

(iii) calculation and implementation of all distributions from the Liquidating Trust in accordance with this Plan and the Liquidating Trust Agreement;

(iv) periodic reporting to the creditors' committee, the Indenture Trustees and the Reorganized Debtor of the status of the Liquidating Trust and the liquidation of Intangible Assets; and

(v) such other responsibilities and obligations as may be vested in the Liquidating Trustee as he or she may assume pursuant to court order or that are vested in the Liquidating Trustee pursuant to this Plan or the Liquidating Trust Agreement.

(b) *Powers*: The powers of the Liquidating Trustee shall include the following:

(i) the power to withdraw and make payments and distributions from the Liquidating Trust in accordance with this Plan and the Liquidating Trust Agreement;

(ii) the power to employ, retain or replace Professional Persons representing the Liquidating Trustee with respect to his or her responsibilities;

(iii) the power to invest money in the Liquidating Trust in accordance with this Plan; and

(iv) such other powers as may be vested in the Liquidating Trustee, as he or she may assume pursuant to court order or that are vested in the Liquidating Trustee pursuant to this Plan or as may be necessary and proper to carry out the provisions of this Plan.

(c) *Termination*: The duties, powers and responsibilities of the Liquidating Trustee and his or her agents shall terminate in accordance with the terms of the Liquidating Trust Agreement.

VIII. DISCHARGE, SURRENDER AND CANCELLATION OF CLAIMS AND INTERESTS

Discharge of Claims: Except as otherwise provided herein or in the Confirmation Order, the rights afforded in this Plan and the payments and distributions to be made hereunder shall be in complete exchange for, and in full satisfaction, discharge and release of, all existing debts and Claims of any kind, nature or description whatsoever against the Debtor or the Debtor-in-Possession or any of its assets or properties; upon the Consummation Date, all existing Claims against the Debtor or Debtor-in-Possession shall be, and be deemed to be, exchanged, satisfied, discharged and released in full; and all holders of Claims shall be precluded from asserting against the Reorganized Debtor or its assets or properties any other or further Claim based upon any act or omission, transaction or other activity of any kind or nature that occurred prior to the Consummation Date, whether or not such holder filed proof of claim.

Effect of Confirmation Order: Except as provided for in this Plan, the Confirmation Order shall be a judicial determination of discharge of the Debtor from all debts that arose before the Consummation Date and any liability on a Claim that is determined under Section 502 of the Bankruptcy Code as if such Claim had arisen before the Consummation Date, whether or not a proof a claim based on any such date or liability is filed under Section 501 of the Bankruptcy Code and whether or not a Claim based on such debt or liability is allowed under Section 502 of the Bankruptcy Code.

Surrender of Instruments and Release of Liens: Except as otherwise provided in this Plan, each holder of an instrument evidencing a Claim shall surrender such instrument to the appropriate Indenture Trustee [Liquidating Trustee] or Reorganized Debtor, as applicable, and the appropriate Indenture Trustee [Liquidating Trustee] or Reorganized Debtor, as applicable, shall distribute to the holder thereof the distributions provided for in this Plan. No distribution under this Plan shall be made to or on behalf of any holder of any such Claim unless and until such instrument is received or the non-availability of such instrument is established to the satisfaction of the designated distributor and the Reorganized Debtor. Each Creditor who is to receive distributions under this Plan in complete satisfaction of Secured Claim(s) shall not receive such distributions until such Creditor executes a release of such lien(s) (in recordable form, if appropriate) and delivers the same to the Reorganized Debtor. Any such holder that fails to surrender such instrument or satisfactorily explain its non-availability or to execute such release of liens within one year of the Effective Date shall be deemed to have no further Claim and shall not participate in any distribution under this Plan.

Post-Confirmation Effect of Evidences of Claims: Notes, debentures and other evidences of Claims shall, upon the Consummation Date, represent only the right to participate in the distributions contemplated by this Plan or matters reserved by this Plan; provided, however, that the _____ Debentures and the ______ Debentures shall in addition represent all rights, claims and interests that they previously had or that are reserved under this Plan and not specifically settled and compromised by this Plan, including those specified in Section _____ hereof.

Special Provisions Relating to Distributions to Holders of Public Subordinated Debt and Other Public Debt:

(a) As of the close of business on the Record Date for purposes of distribution, the transfer ledger in respect of the Public Debt shall be closed. The Debtor and the respective trustees or agents shall have no obligations to recognize any transfer of Public Debt occurring after the Record Date. The Debtor and the respective trustees or agents shall be entitled instead to recognize and deal for all purposes herein with only those holders of record stated on the transfer ledger maintained by the trustees or agents for the Public Debt as of the close of business on the Record Date.

[Alternative to Manner of Distributions Section]

(b) If the court does not approve payment by the Debtor of any compensation and expense reimbursement claims (including fees and expenses of counsel) made by the respective trustees under the Public Debt Trust Indentures, the trustees have advised that they intend to withhold and liquify a portion of the distribution they receive on behalf of holders of Public Debt under this Plan until their compensation and expense reimbursement claims are satisfied in full, pursuant to a lien for this purpose granted to the Indenture Trustees under Section _____ of the respective Trust Indentures. With respect to all such liens of Indenture Trustees, the Debtor hereby expressly reserves the right to pay the claim of any Indenture Trustee in cash and to withhold from distribution to the constituency on whose behalf the Indenture Trustee has acted, securities equal to the amount of any such cash payment. Consequently, amounts actually received by holders of the Public Debt may be less than the gross distributions provided for under this Plan by the amount of distributions applied by the trustees or agents to their compensation and expense reimbursement claims.

(c) No holder of Public Debt shall be entitled to receive any distribution unless such holder shall have first either (i) surrendered or caused to be surrendered the original Public Debt held by it or (ii) in the event that such holder is unable to surrender his or her original Public Debt because same has been lost, destroyed, stolen or mutilated, (1) furnished such Indenture Trustee with an executed affidavit of loss and indemnity with respect thereto in form customarily utilized for such purposes that is reasonably satisfactory to such Indenture Trustee and to the Reorganized Debtor and (2) provided to such Indenture Trustee a bond in such amount and form as such Indenture Trustee and the Reorganized Debtor shall direct, sufficient to indemnify such Indenture Trustee and the Reorganized Debtor against any claim that may be made against such Indenture Trustee or the Reorganized Debtor on account of the alleged loss, theft or distribution of any such certificate or the distribution of property hereunder. The method and procedure to be followed for surrendering Public Debt certificates and for providing affidavits and bonds shall be prescribed by the Reorganized Debtor upon reasonable notice to holders of the Public Debt. Promptly upon surrender of such instruments, such paying agent shall cancel such Public Debt and deliver such cancelled Public Debt to the Reorganized Debtor or otherwise dispose of such Public Debt in such manner as the Reorganized Debtor may request. The Indenture Trustees shall be compensated by the Reorganized Debtor for services rendered from and after the Confirmation Date in effectuating the surrender and cancellation of certificates as provided under this subsection (c) and in effectuating the distribution contemplated by this Plan to the holders of the Public Debt, including the reasonable compensation, disbursements and expenses of the agents and legal counsel of the trustees or agents, and shall be indemnified by the Reorganized Debtor for any loss, liability or expense incurred by it in connection with the performance of such duties to the same extent and in the same manner as provided in the applicable provisions of the Public Debt trust indentures or agreements.

(d) [Negotiable where applicable.] The distributions to the Public Subordinated Debt Class ______ shall not be subject to levy, garnishment, attachment or other legal process by any other claimant of another class by reason of any claimed contractual subordination rights. The Confirmation Order shall provide that claimants of other classes shall be permanently enjoined from enforcing or seeking any such rights with respect to such distributions to the holders of the Public Subordinated Debt.

Termination of Indenture Trustee's Duties and Release of Trustees and Agents:

(a) On the Effective Date, the Public Debt Trust Indentures shall, except as provided in this Plan, be deemed cancelled, terminated and of no further force or effect. Notwithstanding the foregoing, such cancellation of the Public Debt Trust Indentures shall not impair the rights of holders of the Public Debt to receive distributions on account of such claims pursuant to this Plan, nor shall such cancellation impair the rights of the respective indenture trustees to enforce their liens. The Public Debt shall not be cancelled other than pursuant to Section ____ of this Plan and, until such cancellation, such Public Debt shall be evidence of the entitlement of the holder thereof to receive distributions pursuant to this Plan.

(b) Subsequent to the performance of the indenture trustees or agents required under the provisions of this Plan and Confirmation Order and under the terms of the Public Debt Trust Indentures, the indenture trustees and agents and their successors and assigns shall be relieved of all obligations associated with the Public Debt indentures and agreements.

IX. COMPROMISE AND SETTLEMENT OF CLAIMS

[All claims that are to be compromised and settled should be listed with specificity.]

Compromise and Settlement of Claims against Public Debtholders: Except as provided in Section ____ hereof, as of the Consummation Date, all claims, rights or causes of action of each Debtor, a creditors' committee or any Creditor against the Public Debtholders, collectively or individually, shall be compromised and settled.

Compromise and Settlement of Intercreditor Claims: As of the Consummation Date the following intercreditor claims shall be compromised and settled:

(a) all claims, rights or causes of action of all former, present or future Public Debtholders, Indenture Trustees or their assigns, and former, present or future holders of Equity Interests, collectively or individually, against ____________________, including those for subordination of __________ Claims to the Public Debt Claims, except as follows:

[Specifically list any claims of the holders of the Debentures and the Indenture Trustees that are not being compromised or settled.]

(b) all claims, rights or causes of action of __________, collectively or individually, against the Public Debtholders, collectively or individually, for contractual subordination of the Public Debt Claims to the _________ Claims; provided, however, that the compromise and settlement by the _________ are limited to distributions in respect of Public Debt Claims made pursuant to this Plan; and

(c) all claims, rights or actions of any Public Debtholder against any other Public Debtholder for contractual subordination of any Public Debt Claim to any other Public Debt Claim; provided, however, that the waiver by the holders of the _________ Debentures and _________ and _________ is limited to distributions in respect of Public Debt Claims made pursuant to this Plan.

Notwithstanding the foregoing, Public Debtholders and _________ and _________, collectively and individually, do not waive, relinquish or release any right, claim or cause of action against any Creditor, other than against the ________ as provided in this Section ______ , to the extent that any other such Creditor is jointly liable with or derivatively liable through the Debtor to any Public Debtholder or to ________ or _________, except with regard to any distribution provided to such Creditor by this Plan. In particular, the rights, claims and causes of action of Public Debtholders and _________ and _________ , other than as against ________, as provided in this Section ______ are not waived or limited by this Plan as such claims are asserted in the following actions:

[Specifically list actions in which causes and claims are retained.]

Waiver of Rights Against Third Parties: Except as provided herein, as of the Consummation Date, each Creditor, by virtue of confirmation of this Plan or the acceptance of (a) this Plan by the requisite majority in number and amount of members of the Class in which such Creditor's Claim is classified, (b) this Plan by such Creditor or (c) any distribution under the Plan by such Creditor, waives and relinquishes any and all rights with respect to distributions made or to be made under this Plan to any other Creditor.

Waiver of Rights Against Debtor: Except as provided herein, as of the Consummation Date, each Creditor by virtue of the acceptance of this Plan by the requisite number and amount of members of its Class, the acceptance of this Plan by such Creditor, the acceptance by such Creditor of any payment or consideration given under this Plan, or confirmation of this Plan, shall be deemed to have waived, relinquished and released any and all of its rights and Claims (other than as provided for in this Plan or the Confirmation Order) against the Debtor to the extent provided for in this Plan.

X. Conditions Precedent to Consummation

[The various conditions precedent to the consummation of this Plan should be listed, including that the Confirmation Order shall have become a Final Order.]

XI. PROVISIONS FOR RETENTION OF JURISDICTION BY THE BANKRUPTCY COURT FOR SUPERVISION OF THIS PLAN

Scope of Jurisdiction: The Bankruptcy Court shall retain jurisdiction over the Chapter 11 Case for the following purposes:

(a) determining any and all objections to the allowance of Claims or Interests;

(b) determining any and all Fee Applications and any other fees and expenses authorized to be paid or reimbursed under the Bankruptcy Code;

(c) determining any and all pending applications for the rejection or assumption of executory contracts or for the rejection or assumption and assignment, as the case may be, of leases to which the Debtor is a party or with respect to which it may be liable, and to hear and determine, and if need be to liquidate, any and all Claims arising therefrom;

(d) determining any and all applications, adversary proceedings and contested or litigated matters before the Bankruptcy Court pending on the Confirmation Date;

(e) modifying the Plan or remedying any defect or omission or reconciling any inconsistency in any order of the Bankruptcy Court, including the Confirmation Order, to the extent authorized by the Bankruptcy Code;

(f) determining all controversies, suits and disputes that may arise in connection with the interpretation, enforcement or consummation of this Plan;

(g) implementing this Plan, including, without limitation, entering appropriate orders to protect the Reorganized Debtor from Creditor Actions;

(h) entering an order approving the Debtor's statement of indebtedness;

(i) entering a final decree closing the Chapter 11 Case; and

(j) determining such other matters as may arise in connection with this Plan or the Confirmation Order.

Failure of the Bankruptcy Court to Exercise Jurisdiction: If the Bankruptcy Court abstains from exercising, or declines to exercise, jurisdiction or is otherwise without jurisdiction over any matter arising out of the Chapter 11 Case, including the matters set forth in this Section ____, this

Section shall have no effect upon and shall not control, prohibit or limit the exercise of jurisdiction by any other court having competent jurisdiction with respect to such matter.

XII. AMENDMENT AND INTERPRETATION OF THIS PLAN

Amendment: This Plan may be altered, amended or modified by ___________ before or after the Confirmation Date, in the manner provided for by Section 1127 of the Bankruptcy Code. A holder of a Claim or Interest that has accepted or rejected the Plan shall be deemed to have accepted or rejected, as the case may be, the Plan as modified, unless, within the time fixed by the Bankruptcy Court, such holder changes its previous acceptance or rejection.

Headings: The headings used in this Plan are inserted for convenience only and neither constitute a portion of this Plan nor in any manner affect the provisions or interpretations of this Plan.

Severability: Should any provisions in this Plan be determined to be unenforceable, such determination shall in no way limit or affect the enforceability and operative effect of any other provisions of this Plan.

Successors and Assigns: The rights and obligations of any Person named or referred to in this Plan shall be binding upon, and shall inure to the benefit of, the successors and assigns of such Person.

Internal References: The words "herein," "hereof," "hereto," "hereunder" and other words of similar import refer to this Plan as a whole and not to any particular section, subsection or clause contained in this Plan.

XIII. NOTICES

All notices required to be made in or under this Plan shall be writing and shall be mailed by registered or certified mail, return receipt requested, to ___________.

[A list should then be made of all the appropriate parties to whom notice must be given.]

Appendix XI-G
Form Letter of Transmittal from Holders to Trustee for Receipt of Plan Distribution

LETTER OF TRANSMITTAL FROM HOLDERS TO TRUSTEE

____________________________ **(the "Debentures")**
Trustee

PLEASE READ CAREFULLY THE ACCOMPANYING INSTRUCTIONS (See Reverse Side)

The undersigned hereby surrenders the Debentures described below in order to receive the distributions, pursuant to the terms of the Debtor's Second Amended Joint Plan of Reorganization (the "Plan").

DESCRIPTION OF DEBENTURE(S) (Please Print)		
Print Name and Address and Social Security Number or TIN of Each Registered Holder (Please Fill In)	**Debenture(s) Held (Attach Additional List If Necessary)**	
	Serial Number(s)	**Principal Amount**
	TOTAL	

SUBSTITUTE FORM W-9 **Department of the Treasury Internal Revenue Service**	PART I — PLEASE PROVIDE YOUR TIN IN THE BOX AT RIGHT AND CERTIFY BY SIGNING AND DATING BELOW.	Social Security Number OR Taxpayer Identification No.: ____________________
Payer's Request for Taxpayer Identification Number (TIN)	Part II — For Payees exempt from backup withholding, see the enclosed Guidelines for Certification of Taxpayer Identification Number on Substitute Form W-9.	

Certification — Under penalties of perjury, I certify that:

(1) The number shown on this form is my correct Taxpayer Identification Number (or I am waiting for a number to be issued to me), and

(2) I am not subject to backup withholding because either I have not been notified by the Internal Revenue Service ("IRS") that I am subject to backup withholding as a result of a failure to report all interest or dividends, or the IRS has notified me that I am no longer subject to backup withholding.

Certification Instructions — You must cross out Item (2) above if you have been notified by the IRS that you are subject to backup withholding because of underreporting interest or dividends on your tax return. However, if after being notified by the IRS that you were subject to backup withholding you received another notification from the IRS that you are no longer subject to backup withholding, do not cross out Item (2).

The undersigned hereby represents and warrants that the undersigned has full power and authority to surrender the

Debenture(s) described above and the undersigned has good and unencumbered title thereto, free and clear of all liens, restrictions, charges and encumbrances, and not subject to any adverse claim. The undersigned will, upon request, execute and deliver any additional documents deemed by the Trustee to be necessary or desirable to complete the surrender of such Debenture(s). The undersigned represents and warrants that, in accordance with the order confirming the Plan, only those holders of the Debenture(s) as of __________ (the "Distribution Record Date") shall be entitled to receive distributions under the Plan.

All authority herein conferred or agreed to be conferred shall survive the death or incapacity of the undersigned, and any obligations of the undersigned hereunder shall be binding upon the heirs, executors, administrators, legal and personal representatives, successors and assigns of the undersigned, subject to any contrary provisions set forth in the Plan.

The undersigned will, upon request, execute and deliver any additional documents deemed by the Trustee to be necessary to evidence the ownership of the Certificate by the undersigned.

(1) The undersigned has:

- a. Enclosed all the undersigned's Debenture(s);
- b. Enclosed a properly executed Form W-9 if necessary; and
- b. Completed the Special Delivery Instructions if the address of the undersigned has changed from that shown on the Debenture(s).

(2) In addition to paragraph (1) above, if the person to whom the Plan distribution is to be sent differs from the name shown on the Debenture(s), the undersigned has:

- a. Completed the Special Issuance Instructions box;
- b. Enclosed endorsements, bond powers, etc., with signatures Medallion guaranteed per Instructions 3 and 5, as applicable; and
- c. Completed the steps shown in paragraph (1) above on behalf of such person.

SIGNATURE ____________________ DATE ____________

SPECIAL ISSUANCE INSTRUCTIONS
(See Instruction 3) (Please Print)

To be completed only if the Plan distribution is to be transmitted to a name or names other than the undersigned.

Issue to:
Name(s) ____________________

Address ____________________

____

Tax Identification or Social Security Number:

____

SPECIAL MAILING INSTRUCTIONS
(See Instructions 3 and 4) (Please Print)

To be completed only if the future notices or Plan distribution are to be mailed to an address other than that shown in the "Description of Debenture(s)."

Mail to:
Name ____________________

Address ____________________

____

Signature Guarantee

Required when submitting special issuance instructions. See instructions below. A notary public is *not* acceptable.

FOR USE BY ELIGIBLE FINANCIAL INSTITUTION ONLY. PLACE UNDATED MEDALLION GUARANTY BELOW.

SIGN HERE:

X ______________________________ **Dated:** ______________

X ______________________________ **Dated:** ______________

Signature(s) of Owner(s)

(Must be signed by registered holder(s) exactly as name(s) appear(s) on the Debenture(s) or by persons authorized to become registered holder(s) by documents transmitted herewith. If signatures by attorney, executor, administrator, trustee or guardian or others acting in a fiduciary capacity, please set forth full title and see Instructions 3, 5 and 6.)

SIGNATURE(S) GUARANTEED: (See Instruction 3, 5 and 6.)

____

____

DO NOT WRITE BELOW. FOR USE BY TRUSTEE.

$ Amt. Received	**Entered System & Stops Checked**		**R.S. Req.**	**R.S. Issued**	**Date Mailed**	**Processed By**
	Date	**Initial**				

INSTRUCTIONS

1. Fill in the information describing your Debenture(s) on the front of this Letter of Transmittal and submit it, along with your Debenture(s), to the Trustee at the address indicated on the front of this Letter of Transmittal. Please remember to sign and date the form. If your Debenture(s) are in the possession of your broker, dealer, bank or trust company, you should contact it concerning the surrender of the Debenture(s). All Debentures submitted for distribution are requested to be accompanied by a properly completed Letter of Transmittal. (See front side).

2. If you are the registered holder(s) of the outstanding Debenture(s) surrendered herewith, and the Reorganization Securities are to be issued in the same name as your Debenture(s), the surrendered Debenture(s) need not be endorsed and your signature on the Letter of Transmittal need not be guaranteed.

3. If the Reorganization Securities are to be issued in a name or mailed to an address different from that of the registered holder(s) of the Debenture(s) surrendered herewith, the following is required:

(a) Each of the surrendered Debenture(s) must be duly endorsed by the registered holder in exactly the same way as the name appears on the face thereof without any change or alteration, or must be accompanied by appropriate powers or other proper instruments of assignment.

(b) The signature(s) on the endorsement, or on the instruments of assignment, and on this Letter of Transmittal must be guaranteed by a commercial bank or trust company located or having a correspondent in ____________ or by a member of a national securities exchange or the National Association of Securities Dealers, Inc. (NASD).

(c) Substitute Form W-9: the tendering Debentureholder is required to provide the Trustee with a correct Taxpayer Identification Number (TIN) on Substitute Form W-9. Failure to provide the information on the form may subject the tendering Debentureholder to 20% withholding.

4. If the future notices or Reorganization Securities are to be mailed to an address other than the address of record (the address used for mailing this Letter of Transmittal), please indicate the address to be used in the box entitled "Special Mailing Instructions" and comply with Instruction 3(b) on guaranty of signature.

5. (a) This Letter of Transmittal must be signed and dated by the registered holder(s) of the Debenture(s) surrendered herewith, or other person(s) authorized to act for the registered holder(s), such as a brokerage firm, an investment dealer or a bank or trust company,

in which case evidence of authority to act should be furnished with this Letter of Transmittal and Instructions 3 and 6 will be applicable. The Trustee may, in its discretion, require further evidence of authority of such person(s) to act on behalf of the registered holder(s). If a surrendered Debenture(s) is registered in the name of more than one holder, each person named on the Debenture(s) must sign this Letter of Transmittal.

(b) If the Debenture(s) surrendered herewith are registered in different names, separate Letters of Transmittal are required for each different registration [unless the variations relate to the same person(s) and evidence satisfactory to the Trustee is furnished establishing that the different registrations relate to the same person(s)]. Additional copies of this Letter of Transmittal may be obtained for this purpose from the Trustee.

(c) When this Letter of Transmittal or an endorsement of surrendered Debenture(s) (or the accompanying instrument of assignment) is executed by an officer of a corporation, attorney, executor, administrator, trustee, guardian or others acting in a fiduciary or representative capacity, the person(s) signing must give full title(s) in such capacity and proper evidence, satisfactory to the Trustee, of the appointment and authority of such person(s) to act.

6. The signature(s) of person(s) authorized to act for the registered holder(s) (see Instruction 5) must be guaranteed on the Letter of Transmittal by a commercial bank or trust company located or having a correspondent in ___________ or by a member of a national securities exchange or the NASD. See Instruction 3(b).

7. If your Debenture(s) have been lost, stolen, mutilated or destroyed, please contact the Trustee for instructions as to how to proceed.

8. When mailing Debenture(s) and this Letter of Transmittal to the Trustee, registered mail, properly insured, is recommended since the risk of loss in transit is yours.

9. All inquiries with respect to the surrender of Debenture(s) or for additional copies of this Letter of Transmittal should be made directly to ___________ at the address on the front side of this Letter of Transmittal. Contact ___________ telephone ___________.

10. The Trustee has the absolute right to reject any and all Letters of Transmittal not in proper form and to waive any irregularities or defects in any Letter of Transmittal. All questions with respect to the Letter of Transmittal will be determined by the Trustee, which determination shall be final and binding.

Appendix XI-H
Sources of Indenture Trustee Compensation in Bankruptcy

A.	Contract Claim	→	The basic right to receive payment by contract for the amount owed (postpetition fees may be problematic if unsecured)
	+		
B.	Administrative Claim Sections 503(b)(3), (4) and (5)	→	For "substantial contribution" to the proceedings
	+		
C.	Section 506(b)	→	From secured collateral to the extent value of collateral exceeds principal, interest and expenses
	+		
D.	Indenture Lien* Latch-on Right	→	From distribution to holders to the extent A, B and C are insufficient

* This is in addition to any indemnity received from the holders pursuant to direction and instruction of the holders.

Appendix XI-I
Bankruptcy Timeline

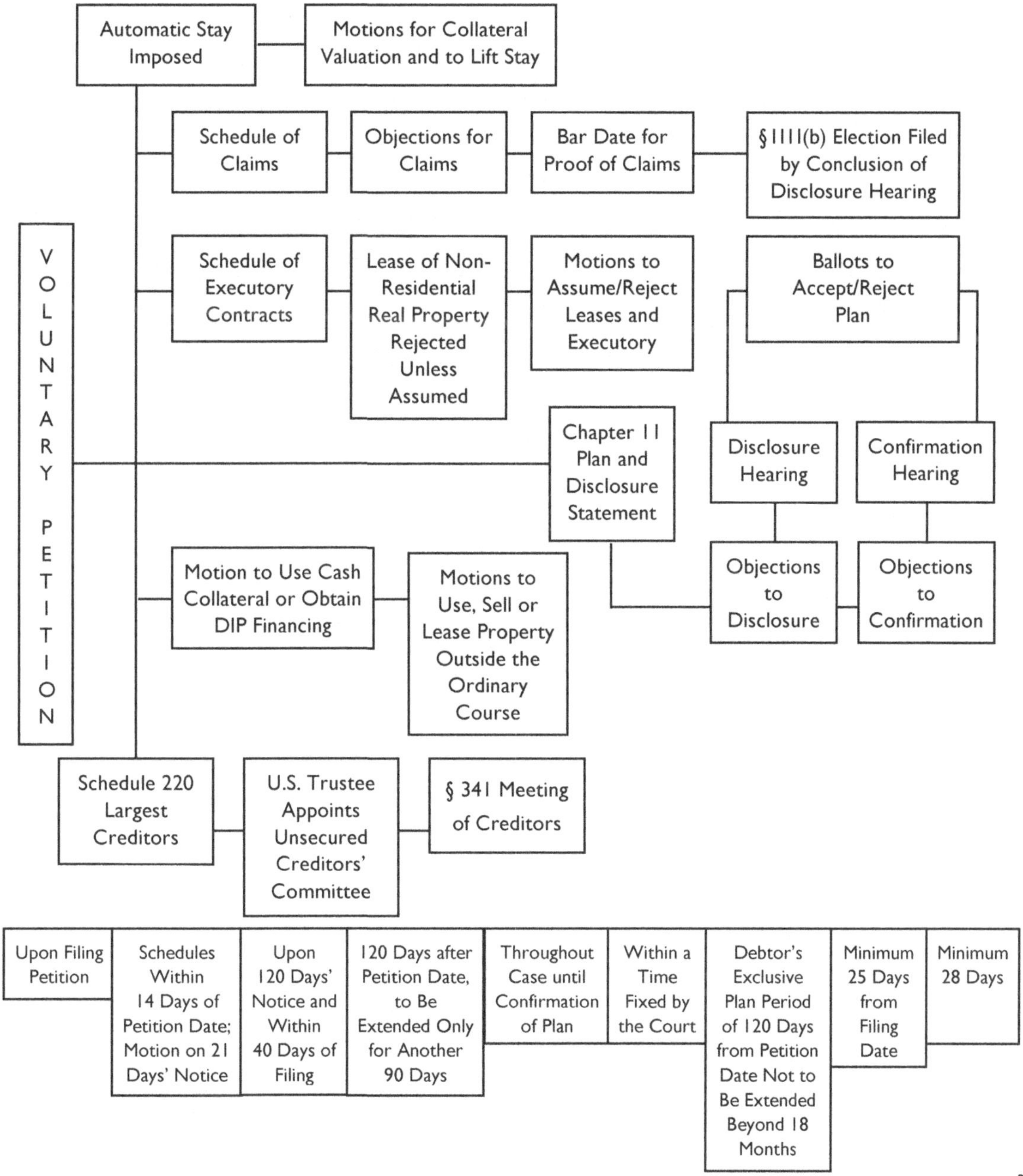

XII. Special Problems of Municipal Default and Bankruptcy

A. Tax Consequences of Tax-Exempt Defaults and Restructuring

The indenture trustee should be generally familiar with the tax consequences of default and bankruptcy on tax-exempt debt and the tax consequences to a bondholder of a default, restructuring or reorganization. Under Section 1001 of the Internal Revenue Code, when a debtor who is obligated to pay $1,000 of principal and $100 of accrued interest is discharged from that obligation by the bondholder in exchange for $500 in property (*e.g.*, cash, new securities), there may be a taxable event and tax consequences to both the bondholder and the debtor. The bondholder may have an immediately recognizable capital loss: the holder has a basis in the obligation which is determined by what the holder originally paid for the investment (*i.e.*, $1,000), and the holder now has received $500 in property and, therefore, has realized a loss. For the bondholder, there are several questions: (1) is the loss recognized for tax purposes, (2) how much is the loss, (3) is there interest income, (4) has there been an exchange of old debt for new debt, and (5) is the interest income still tax-exempt? The answers depend upon the type of property received and whether the exchange constitutes a tax-free recapitalization or a taxable exchange. The loss generally is the difference between the bondholder's adjusted basis in the defaulted obligation and the fair market value of what he receives in satisfaction of his claim. The debtor might like to claim that some part of the $500 payment is a payment of interest which it is entitled to deduct, but generally, it will be unsuccessful in that argument. If the bondholder receives something other than cash, such as new securities, in satisfaction of the old indebtedness, then the questions become: (1) is there an event that is recognized for tax purposes or no such event, so that there is a transfer of the bondholder's basis in the old obligations to the new securities, and (2) what is the fair market value of the new obligations? Tax analysis of these situations depends on all the facts and circumstances, and caution should be the watchword.

A word of warning is in order. The form that a transaction takes is very important for tax purposes. Take, for example, a "refinancing" that is structured by issuing new bonds for cash and using the cash to retire the original bonds, as opposed to a "restructuring" that accomplishes the same result by exchanging a new bond issue for the original issue. Even though the economics of the foregoing transactions show little difference in substance, the tax consequences can be very different depending on the form of the transactions.

The reissuance of defaulted tax-exempt bonds is of great significance in any workout or bankruptcy affecting municipal securities. If the terms of the existing obligation are modified to a significant extent, the modified obligation is treated as reissued. If the obligation is treated as reissued under the reissuance regulations,[410] it is treated as reissued for all purposes under the Internal Revenue Code. Reissuance may trigger very real consequences for the issuer and the bondholder. In particular, the reissuance could trigger a recognition event for the bondholder such as a gain or loss. Typically, the plans filed in bankruptcy cases contain disclaimers as to the tax consequences of consummation of the plan and whether the terms of the plan constitute a significant modification.[411] The indenture trustee should make it clear to the holders that it is not giving any tax advice and that the holders' individual tax advisors should be consulted.

B. No Involuntary Proceedings

As previously stated in the summary of the Bankruptcy Code, there can be no involuntary Chapter 9 proceedings. Not only are involuntary proceedings constitutionally prohibited, but there is no statutory basis for such involuntary action. In order for an entity to proceed under Chapter 9, state law must have specifically authorized it to be a debtor under Chapter 9.[412] Less than half of all states specifically authorize their municipalities to be a debtor in Chapter 9.[413] Twelve states have specifically authorized a municipality to proceed.[414] Two states have specifically prohibited municipalities from filing for relief under the Bankruptcy Code.[415] Another twelve states authorize a filing under certain conditions such as approval of the governor, the treasurer, some legislative committee or authority or use of an additional review process such as the neutral evaluator in California.[416] Three states authorize only a specific municipality or type of municipality to file (*e.g.*, Illinois currently only authorizes the Illinois Power Authority to file under Chapter 9).[417] The remaining twenty-one states have no

---

410 Treas. Reg. § 1.1001-3.

411 *See, e.g.*, Fourth Amended Disclosure Statement for Fourth Amended Plan for Adjustment of Debts of the City of Detroit, *In re City of Detroit, Mich.*, Case No. 13-53846 (Bankr. E.D. Mich. May 5, 2014), ECF No. 4391, p. 189 ("Detroit Disclosure Statement").

412 11 U.S.C. § 101(29).

413 For a detailed description and analysis of the state laws enacted with respect to Chapter 9 see James E. Spiotto, Ann E. Acker, Laura E. Appleby, MUNICIPALITIES IN DISTRESS? HOW STATES AND INVESTORS DEAL WITH LOCAL GOVERNMENT FINANCIAL EMERGENCIES (2d ed. 2016) ("Spiotto").

414 Alabama, Arizona, Arkansas, Idaho, Minnesota, Missouri, Montana, Nebraska, Oklahoma, South Carolina, Texas and Washington specifically authorize municipal bankruptcies. *See, e.g.*, Ala. Code § 11-81-3.

415 Georgia and Iowa prohibit filing. *See, e.g.*, Ga. Code Ann. § 36-80-5.

416 California, Connecticut, Florida, Kentucky, Louisiana, Michigan, New Jersey, New York, North Carolina, Ohio, Pennsylvania, and Rhode Island conditionally authorize municipal bankruptcies.

417 Colorado, Oregon and Illinois authorize only a specific municipality or type of municipality to file.

specific authorization, so their municipalities cannot file Chapter 9.[418] The following chart graphically portrays the authorization status of the states.

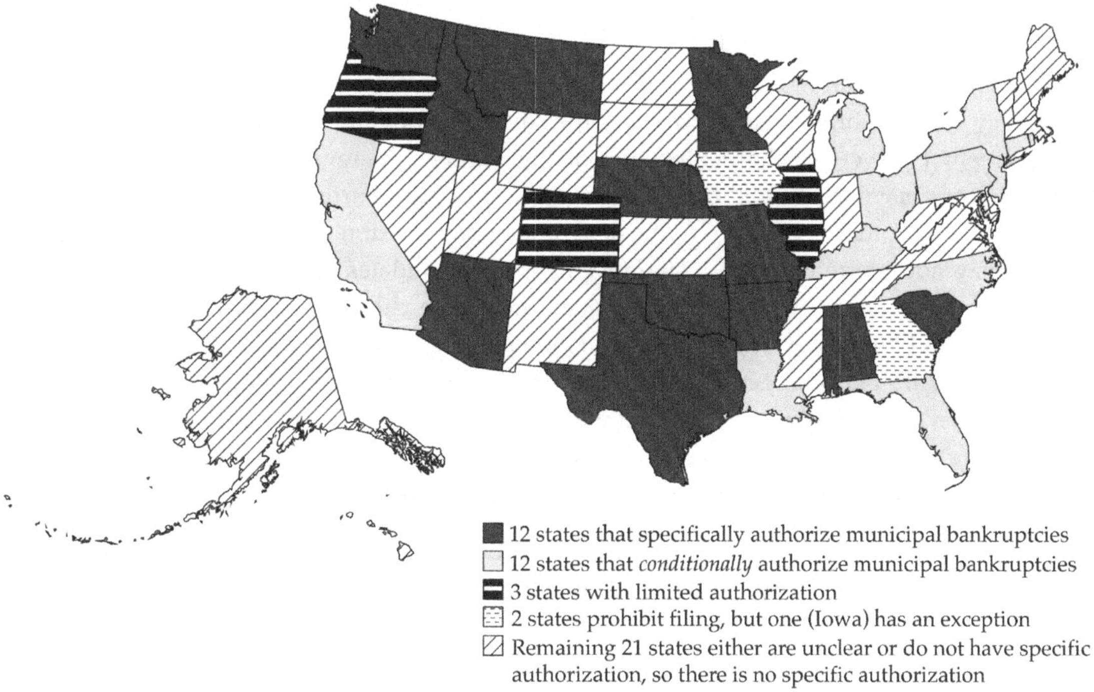

C. Constitutional Limitations

One of the basic principles running through Supreme Court decisions dealing with the issue of municipal debt adjustment is that bankruptcy laws may not infringe upon the sovereign powers of the states. Hence, legislation that permitted involuntary municipal bankruptcy or that interfered with the revenue, property or fiscal or governmental affairs of political subdivisions has been declared unconstitutional. Section 903 of the current Bankruptcy Code provides that it "does not limit or impair the power of a State to control, by legislation or otherwise, a municipality of or in such State in the exercise of the political or governmental powers of such municipality, including expenditures for such exercise." In other words, Section 903 of the Bankruptcy Code reserves to the states and local governmental bodies the power to control governmental functions of political subdivisions. Further, state assistance in municipalities'

418 Alaska, Delaware, Hawaii, Indiana, Kansas, Maine, Maryland, Massachusetts, Mississippi, Nevada, New Hampshire, New Mexico, North Dakota, South Dakota, Tennessee, Utah, Virginia, West Virginia, Wisconsin, Wyoming and Vermont have no specific authorization.

workout of their financial problems, short of the bankruptcy court, is encouraged. The municipality must comply with state law, and a plan of debt adjustment cannot require the municipality to act contrary to state law.

There are additional constitutional concerns that have an impact on municipal default and bankruptcy. Section 904 of the Bankruptcy Code specifically provides that, unless the municipality consents or its plan so provides, the court may not interfere with any of the political or governmental powers of the debtor, any of the property or revenues of the debtor, or the debtor's use or enjoyment of any income-producing property. Further, the municipality cannot consent to anything that is contrary to the state law or constitution. Section 904 makes clear that the court may not interfere with the statutory liens and mandates of the state as to payment of debt, performance related to obligations outstanding or the choices a municipality makes as to what services and benefits it will provide to its inhabitants. It may be difficult for a bankruptcy court that normally plays an active part in the shaping of a corporate reorganization to refrain from passing on requests of taxpayers for lower taxes and more services and competing requests of creditors for higher taxes to pay more debt and to provide fewer services. However difficult it may be, Section 904 of the Bankruptcy Code and the Constitution[419] mandate restraint.

D. What the Indenture Trustee and Bondholders Need to Know about Chapter 9 of the Bankruptcy Code (Municipal Bankruptcy)

Chapter 9 is generally viewed as the remedy of last resort for troubled municipalities. If permitted by its state law, a municipality typically does not seek Chapter 9 relief unless it is in extreme financial distress with no obvious solution. The factors that can lead to such serious financial distress include the decline of urban areas, the decline of industry and related shrinking of the tax base, unaffordable and unsustainable personnel costs and large debt obligations in excess of the ability to pay. Chapter 9, however, is a vehicle not for elimination of debt, but for debt adjustment. The primary purpose of Chapter 9 is to allow the municipal unit to continue operating while it adjusts or refinances creditor claims. An indenture trustee for a debt issue impacted by a Chapter 9 filing should retain experienced counsel as soon as possible to guide the trustee through the process. Holders with large positions in the debt of a Chapter 9 debtor may wish to retain their own counsel. Some of the Chapter 9 issues the indenture trustee and bondholders may face will be highlighted here. A key issue of importance to bondholders will be the priority of the indenture obligations. The following chart summarizes the priorities of creditor payments in Chapter 9.

---

419 In *U.S. v. Bekins*, 304 U.S. 27 (1938), the United States Supreme Court ruled that in implementing any plan of debt adjustment, the municipality must comply with state law. *See also Ashton v. Cameron Cty. Water Improvement Dist. No. 1*, 298 U.S. 513 (1936).

	Type of Claim	Explanation
1.	Obligations secured by a statutory lien to the extent of the pledged revenue collected[ab]	Debt (bonds, warrants, notes, Trans, Rans) issued pursuant to statute that itself imposes a pledge or mandates payment of the debt from a specific revenue source. (There should not be any delay in payments because of automatic stay since the bankruptcy court and municipality have no authority to do otherwise due to the mandate of state law to only use or expend revenues or proceeds for the designated purpose under Section 903 of the Bankruptcy Code, and the municipality cannot act or consent differently since it is unable to do so under state law that controls under Section 904 of the Bankruptcy Code.)
2.	Obligations secured by special revenues (subject to necessary operating expenses of such project or system if applicable) to the extent of the pledged revenue collected.[ab]	Special revenue bonds secured by any of the following: (A) receipts derived from the ownership, operation or disposition of projects or systems of the debtor that are primarily used or intended to be used primarily to provide

a Chapter 9 incorporates Section 506(c) of the Bankruptcy Code, which imposes a surcharge for preserving or disposing of collateral. Because a municipality cannot mortgage city hall or the police headquarters, municipal securities tend to be secured by a pledge of a revenue stream. Hence, it is rare that a surcharge would be imposed. *But see* numbers 3 and 4.

b Chapter 9 incorporates Section 364(d) of the Bankruptcy Code, which permits a debtor to obtain postpetition credit secured by a senior or equal lien on property of the estate that is subject to a lien if the prior lien holder is adequately protected. However, if state law mandates the use of the pledged revenues solely or first to pay the statutory lien or special revenue debt, that mandate of state law cannot be violated and no priming lien or other use of revenues can be authorized. State Law Mandated Payments where the force and effect of the state statutorial or constitutional language mandates that the municipality make the payment of dedicated revenues to the specified debt pursuant to pledged revenues, set-asides, priorities as to the use of revenues or required appropriation shall be treated similar to a statutory lien as set forth below, Sections 903 and 904 of the Bankruptcy Code and the U.S. Supreme Court rulings in *Ashton v. Cameron Cty. Water Improvement Dist. No. 1*, 298 U.S. 513 (1936), and *U.S. v. Bekins*, 304 U.S. 27 (1938).

	Type of Claim	Explanation
	These obligations are often non-recourse and, in the event of default, the bondholders have no claim against non-pledged assets. (Reaffirmed in Jefferson County court ruling and the ultimate treatment of water and sewer revenue bonds in Detroit.)	transportation, utility or other services, including the proceeds of borrowings to finance the projects or systems; (B) special excise taxes imposed on particular activities or transactions; (C) incremental tax receipts from the benefited area in the case of tax-increment financing; (D) other revenues or receipts derived from particular functions of the debtor, whether or not the debtor has other functions; or (E) taxes specially levied to finance one or more projects or systems, excluding receipts from general property, sales or income taxes (other than tax-increment financing) levied to finance the general purposes of the debtor.[c] There should be no delay in payment since automatic stay is lifted under Section 922(d). If the state statute also creates a statutory lien or mandate that the pledged tax revenues can be used only for payment of the debt obligations and for no other purposes before payment in full of the obligation, then there is no reduction for necessary operating expenses — Sections 903, 904 and 928 of the Federal Bankruptcy Code.
3.	Secured lien based on bond resolution or contractual provisions that does not meet test of statutory lien or special revenues to the extent perfected prepetition, subject to the value of prepetition property or proceeds thereof.[c]	Under language of Sections 552(a) and 928, liens on such collateral would not continue postpetition. After giving value to the prepetition lien on property or proceeds, there is an unsecured claim to the extent there is recourse to the municipality or debtor. You may expect the creditor to argue that pursuant to Section 904, the

c A pledge of revenues that is not a statutory lien or special revenue pledge may be attacked as not being a valid continuing postpetition lien under Section 552 of the Bankruptcy Code.

	Type of Claim	Explanation
		court cannot interfere with the property or revenues of the debtor (without the debtor's consent, consistent with state law), and that includes the grant of security to such secured creditor.
4.	Obligations secured by a municipal facility lease financing.	Under Section 929 of the Bankruptcy Code, even if the transaction is styled as a municipal lease, a financing lease will be treated as long-term debt and secured to the extent of the value of the facility.
5.	Administrative expenses (which would include expenses incurred in connection with the Chapter 9 case itself).[d] Chapter 9 incorporates Section 507(a)(2) which, by its terms, provides a priority for administrative expenses allowed under Section 503(b). These would include the expenses of a committee or indenture trustee making a substantial contribution in a Chapter 9 case.	Pursuant to Section 943, all amounts must be disclosed and be reasonable for a plan of adjustment to be confirmed.

d These expenses strictly relate to the costs of the bankruptcy. Because the bankruptcy court cannot interfere with the government and affairs of the municipality, general operating expenses of the municipality after the filing of the Chapter 9 case are not within the control of the court (unless the municipality consents and is not otherwise prohibited under state law from interfering with the payment), are not discharged and will remain liabilities of the municipality after the confirmation of a plan or dismissal of the case.

	Type of Claim	Explanation
6.	Unsecured debt includes:	
	A. Senior unsecured claims with benefit of subordination paid to the extent of available funds (without any obligation to raise taxes), which include any of B, C, D, or E below.	
	B. General obligation bonds.	With a general pledge of "full faith and credit" of the issuing municipality (unlimited or limited) without a dedication of special revenues or a statutory lien. Postpetition, a court may treat general obligation bonds without a statutory lien or special revenues pledge as unsecured debt and permit an adjustment or restructuring of the bonds. Payment on the bonds during the bankruptcy proceeding likely will cease.[e]
	C. Trade.	Vendors, suppliers or contracting parties for goods or services. Payment will likely cease for prepetition goods or services.[f]
	D. Obligations for accrued but unpaid prepetition wages and pensions and other employee benefits.	These do not enjoy any priority, unlike in a Chapter 11 proceeding.[g]

e However, if state law mandates specific appropriation, set-aside or priority of payment of revenue collected, the failure to honor state law may be an obstacle to confirming a plan of debt adjustment since the plan, court and municipality cannot violate state law going forward. *See* Section 903 of the Bankruptcy Code.

f Section 503(b)(9) provides for a priority claim to be paid on confirmation of a plan for the value of goods provided prepetition within 20 days of the petition date.

g Chapter 9 does not incorporate Section 1113 of the Bankruptcy Code, which imposes special provisions for the rejection of collective bargaining agreements (making the standard less restrictive, *i.e.*, "impairs ability to rehabilitate") or Sections 507(a)(4) and (5), which give a priority

	Type of Claim	Explanation
	E. Unsecured portion of secured indebtedness.	
	F. Subordinated unsecured claims.	Any debt subordinated by statute or by contract to other debt would be appropriately subordinated and paid only to the extent senior claims are paid in full. Senior debt would receive combined senior and subordinate *pro rata* distribution (the distribution attributable to the aggregate senior and subordinated unsecured claim) until the senior is paid in full.

"Special Revenues" Pledged to Bondholders[420]

Many municipal bonds are revenue bonds secured by a pledge of revenues derived from a specific project or a special tax levy. In fact, all states recognize some form of revenue bond. As background, in a corporate bankruptcy context, Section 552 of the Bankruptcy Code provides that property acquired by the estate or the debtor after commencement of a case is not subject to any lien resulting from a security agreement entered into by the debtor before the commencement of the case. In a corporate bankruptcy, if a revenue pledge were to exist, such as a lien on inventory or accounts receivable, the pledge likely would not survive the filing of a bankruptcy petition (namely any property or revenue created postpetition, such as inventory manufactured or accounts receivable received from sales of inventory after the filing of the case). In a municipal bankruptcy, however, this is not the case. Specifically, Section 928 of the Bankruptcy Code provides that in the case of "special revenues," the security interest in "special revenues" remains valid and enforceable even though such revenues are received after a Chapter 9 filing. Subsection (b) of Section 928 provides that in the case of project or system financing, the bondholders' lien on "special revenues" is subject to necessary operating expenses of the project or system. Thus, subject to the payment of operating expenses, holders of special revenue bonds would continue to receive payment on those bonds, regardless of the bankruptcy filing.[421]

(before payment of unsecured claims) to wages; salaries; commissions; vacation, severance and sick leave; or contributions to pension plans of currently $12,850 per employee.

420 A detailed discussion of the history and experience in the courts with special revenues appears in Spiotto, ch. VII.

421 *In re Jefferson Cnty., Ala.*, 474 B.R. 228 (Bankr. N.D. Ala. 2012) (discussion of nature of special revenues); *Bank of N.Y. Mellon v. Jefferson Cnty., Ala. (In re Jefferson Cnty., Ala.)*, 482 B.R. 404 (Bankr.

Section 927 is intended to ensure that revenue bonds do not become transformed into general obligation bonds with a call against all the assets of the municipality upon the filing of bankruptcy petition.[422]

In order to avoid the delay in payment caused by the automatic stay of Section 362, subsection 922(d) of the Bankruptcy Code makes the automatic stay provision inapplicable to the payment of pledged special revenues to the holders of municipal indebtedness.[423]

Section 928 of the Bankruptcy Code, along with the definition of special revenues in Section 902(2), protects the lien on revenues. In sum, Congress made clear that revenue bondholders are entitled to receive the revenues pledged to them without any interference and on a timely basis.

Particular attention should be directed to the definition of special revenues, the pledge of which survives bankruptcy.[424] "Special revenues" are defined as:

> (A) receipts derived from the ownership, operation, or disposition of projects or systems of the debtor that are primarily used or intended to be used primarily to provide transportation, utility, or other services, including the proceeds of borrowings to finance the projects or systems;
>
> (B) special excise taxes imposed on particular activities or transactions;
>
> (C) incremental tax receipts from the benefited area in the case of tax-increment financing;
>
> (D) other revenues or receipts derived from particular functions of the debtor, whether or not the debtor has other functions; or
>
> (E) taxes specifically levied to finance one or more projects or systems, excluding receipts from general property, sales, or income taxes (other than tax-increment financing) levied to finance the general purpose of the debtor . . .[425]

N.D. Ala. 2012) (analysis of necessary operating expenses); *In re Sierra Kings Health Care Dist.*, 2010 WL 10018073 (Bankr. E.D. Cal. Sept. 13, 2010).

422 House Report No. 100-1011, 100th Cong. 2d Sess. 7 (1988).

423 *See generally Jefferson Cnty.*, 474 B.R. at 268 ("It is clear from both the House and Senate Reports accompanying the 1988 amendments that eliminating the potential loss of a creditor's lien on revenues was a critical purpose behind the enactment of § 928 and § 922(d).").

424 11 U.S.C. § 902(2).

425 11 U.S.C. § 902.

Examples of the special revenues mentioned in clause (A) are receipts derived from or received in connection with the ownership, financing, operation or disposition of a municipal water, electric or transportation system. An excise tax on hotel and motel rooms or the sale of alcoholic beverages would be a special excise tax under clause (B). "Special excise taxes" are taxes specifically identified and pledged in the bond financing documents and are not generally available to all creditors under state law. General state sales, general income or general property taxes would not be special excise taxes without specific language deemed levied to finance a specific project or system. In a typical tax increment financing referred to in clause (C), public improvements are financed by bonds payable solely from and secured by a lien on incremental tax receipts resulting from increased valuations in the benefited area. Although these receipts may be part of the general tax levy, they are considered to be attributable to the improvements so financed and are not part of the preexisting tax base of the community. Examples of revenues from particular functions under clause (D) would be regulatory fees and stamp taxes imposed for the recording of deeds or any identified function and related revenues identified in the municipality's financing documents, such as tolls or fees related to a particular service or benefit. Under clause (E), an incremental sales or property tax specifically levied to pay indebtedness incurred for a capital improvement and not for the operating expenses or general purposes of the debtor would be considered special revenues. Likewise, any special tax or portion of a general tax specifically levied to pay for a municipal financing should be treated as special revenues.[426]

Statutory Liens Protect Bondholders[427]

In certain situations, even if holding general obligation bonds for which the contractual pledge of a municipality's taxes or revenues generally would terminate on the filing of a municipal bankruptcy petition, a bondholder may continue to receive payment in the wake of a Chapter 9 filing if the underlying statute authorizing the issuance contains a statutory lien, which lien comes into existence by virtue of the statute and arises by force of the statute on specific circumstances or conditions and does not require further action by the municipality.[428] A statutory lien cannot be canceled on the filing of a bankruptcy petition or by the bankruptcy court. This approach was recognized by the district court on appeal in the Orange County bankruptcy. There, the court found that the lien securing tax and revenue anticipation notes pursuant to a California statute authorizing the county to pledge assets to secure notes was a statutory lien. Since the statute, not a security agreement, imposed the pledge, it survived the

---

426 *See Heffernan Memorial Hosp. Dist.*, 202 B.R. 147 (Bankr. S.D. Cal. 1996).

427 A detailed discussion of the nature, scope and treatment of statutory liens appears in Spiotto, ch. VII.

428 *In re Cty. of Orange*, 189 BR. 499 (C.D. Cal. 1995).

filing of a Chapter 9 petition.[429] At least sixteen states recognize some form of a statutory lien in relation to their bond obligations.[430]

The significance of special revenues and statutory liens was illustrated by the case of *Sierra Kings Health Care District,* in which a court order reaffirmed the fact that a Chapter 9 proceeding and any order or plan of debt adjustment cannot interfere with notes, bonds or municipal obligations that are paid from the pledge of taxes or revenues that are special revenues or subject to a statutory lien.[431] Of special significance is the fact that the *Sierra Kings* court confirmed, for the first time, the postpetition effectiveness of a municipality's pledge of *ad valorem* taxes which qualified as both a special revenue pledge and a statutory lien. The Chapter 9 proceeding, orders and plan would not affect the timely payment on these bonds according to their terms. Bankruptcy courts in the confirmed plans for Detroit and Stockton respected statutory liens and special revenues. [432]

The following chart summarizes the intended treatment of bonds and notes, depending on how they are secured, in a Chapter 9 proceeding.

429 *Id.*

430 *See* Spiotto, ch. VIII, 50-State Survey.

431 *In re Sierra Kings Health Care Dist.,* 2010 WL 10018073 (Bankr. E.D. Ca. Sept. 13, 2010); *see also* statutory lien created by CAL. EDUC. CODE § 1521(a) added by Cal. S.B. 222 (ch. 78, Statutes of 2015).

432 In the bankruptcy-like Title III proceeding under PROMESA, 48 U.S.C.A. §2161 *et seq.*, the district court presiding over the Puerto Rico action cautioned that a statute purporting to create a statutory lien must be mandatory in nature and the lien must flow from the actual statute and not from a consensual agreement with the issuer. Opinion and Order Denying Motion for Preliminary Injunction and Motion for Relief from the Automatic Stay. *Peaje Investments LLC v. Puerto Rico Highways and Transportation Authority* (In re the Financial Oversight and Management Board for Puerto Rico, as representatitive of the Commonwealth of Puerto Rico) Case No. 17-151 (D.P.R. September 8, 2017) ECF No. 240.

Summary of Basic Treatment of Bonds and Notes under Chapter 9

Type of Bonds/Notes	Bankruptcy Effects
General Obligation Bonds Without a Specific Pledge	Postpetition, a court may treat general obligation bonds as unsecured debt which does not have a statutory lien or constitutionally mandated payment of dedicated revenues or a pledge of revenues that classifies as special revenues, and the court may order a restructuring of the bonds. Payment on such bonds during the bankruptcy proceeding likely will cease. Prepetition, unlimited general obligation bonds are backed by the unlimited taxing power of the municipality (its "full faith and credit") but no specific pledge of revenue that is a statutory lien or special revenues, and such bonds are historically subject to conditions such as voter authorization, limitations on particular purposes, or debt limitation to a percentage of assessed valuation on the power of municipal entities to incur such debts.
General Obligation Bonds Plus Pledged Revenues or Statutory Lien	Assuming that the general obligation pledge is an actual pledge of specific revenue or to the extent that it may be classified as a statutory lien or constitutionally mandated payment of dedicated revenues, this secured issuance will be respected to the degree it is consistent and authorized under state law. A contractual pledge of revenues that is not a statutory lien or constitutionally mandated payment of dedicated revenues or special revenues may be attacked as not being a valid continuing postpetition lien under Section 552 of the Bankruptcy Code. However, state law mandated payments of revenues whereby the force and effect of language of the state statute or constitutional provision payments related to dedicated revenues, set-asides, priorities or appropriateness are mandated to be made ("State Law Mandated Payments") should be paid postpetition as collected without delay. This would be consistent with Sections 903 and 904 of the Bankruptcy Code because the *Ashton* and *Bekins* cases stand for the proposition that the court may not interfere with the power of a state to control a municipality in exercise of the governmental powers, affairs or revenues of the municipality.

Type of Bonds/Notes	Bankruptcy Effects
Special Revenue Bonds	A pledge of special revenues will survive a bankruptcy filing. Prepetition, a special revenue bond is an obligation to repay solely and only from specific revenues of a municipal enterprise (net of operations and maintenance costs, if applicable) or dedicated funds or tax revenues that are pledged to bondholders. There is no stay during the Chapter 9 proceeding in payment of such special revenues to pay the debt it is pledged to pursuant to the terms of the documents (Section 922(d)). The contemplated remedy for default often focuses on a covenant to charge rates sufficient to amortize the debt and, if necessary, on the appointment of a receiver. Defaulted bondholders are expected to seek mandamus in court to require the municipal borrower to raise its rates or, if necessary, the appointment of a receiver to enforce the rate covenant and prudent operations of the municipal enterprise. To enforce such remedies after the filing of a Chapter 9 case would require the lifting of the automatic stay.
Revenues Subject to Statutory Lien	Assuming the pledge is authorized under state law through a statutory lien, the bankruptcy court should respect that statutory lien. Thus, as long as the revenues are subject to a statutory lien, payments to the bondholders should be protected postpetition and, based on Sections 903 and 904 of the Bankruptcy Code and the *Ashton* and *Bekins* cases, should be paid to the bondholder as mandated by the statute.

General obligation bonds without any pledge of revenues or special statutory or constitutional priority mandated set-aside or mandated appropriation can be treated like any other unsecured claim of vendors, workers or pension; however, in 1968 in Medley, Florida, there was a distinction made to pay bond indebtedness on schedule and to stretch out the payments to other unsecured creditors over a ten-year period since failure to make payment on the bonds might cause the municipality to lose access to the market or to pay a significantly higher price for access that would justify a better treatment for bond indebtedness for the benefit of all.

Payments to Bondholders Are Not Preferences

The Bankruptcy Code also provides assurance to holders of all municipal bond or note obligations that payments received within 90 days of the commencement of a municipal bankruptcy petition are not preferences that may be clawed back. Specifically, Section 926(b) of the Bankruptcy Code provides that a transfer of property of the debtor to or for the benefit of any holder of a bond or note on account of such bond or note may not be avoided under Section 547. While this section refers to "bonds or notes," there is nothing in the legislative history to support the view that this provision is limited only to instruments bearing such titles. The intent appears to be that Section 926(b) should be applicable to all forms of municipal debt and allow such holders to keep such payments where the Bankruptcy Code would otherwise require any payments made within 90 days of a bankruptcy filing to be returned to the estate. This protection should also extend to deposits for the purpose of retiring a bond issue or a defeasance by advance refunding. Special revenues and statutory liens are designed to provide a municipality experiencing financial distress with additional available sources of financing through various options of refinancing or refunding old debt or obtaining additional liquidity with the use of special revenues or statutory liens that are intended to continue to pay and have a continuing lien on taxes collected even if the municipality should authorize filing a Chapter 9 proceeding.

E. Indenture Trustee in Recent Chapter 9 Cases

Whether an indenture trustee will take an activist role in a Chapter 9 case will depend in large part on the wishes of the majority holders of the debt for which the indenture trustee serves. If directed and instructed by the holders, the indenture trustee may raise issues in the case that may result in lengthy litigation. Indenture trustees, sometimes joined by other creditors, have challenged the debtor's eligibility to file the Chapter 9 petition itself.[433] The experience in these cases suggests that, unless strong arguments against the validity of the debtor's filing exist, challenges to eligibility may be expensive and not necessarily fruitful.

On the other hand, the indenture trustee, working with major debtholders, achieved a significant victory in the Jefferson County bankruptcy with respect to the nature and scope of special revenues.[434] Where the debtholder assumes the role of principal negotiator with the debtor, absent some compelling circumstances, the indenture trustee and the holders will be well served by the indenture trustee's cooperation.[435] Another example is the 100 percent recovery for the water and sewer bonds in the Detroit bankruptcy.[436]

---

433 *See In re City of Stockton, Ca.*, 493 B.R. 772 (Bankr. E.D. Ca. 2013); *In re Jefferson Cty., Ala.*, 469 B.R. 92 (Bankr. N.D. Ala. 2012).

434 *In re Jefferson Cty., Ala.*, 474 B.R. 228 (Bankr. N.D. Ala. 2012).

435 *See* Order entered *In re Sierra Kings Health Care Dist.*, 2010 WL 10018073 (Bankr. E.D. Ca. Sept. 13, 2010).

436 *See* Detroit Disclosure Statement.

F. Disclosure of Defaults and Effect on Municipal Credit

1. The New York City Financial Crisis Led to a Rethinking of the Disclosure Obligations with Respect to Municipal Issues

In the spring of 1975, New York City was unable to market its debt because the bond market had discovered that New York had, for more than ten years, been using questionable accounting and borrowing practices to eliminate its annual budget deficits. The banks refused to renew short-term loans that matured or to loan additional cash to the city, and only state cash advances kept the city afloat. The city's spending for operating purposes exceeded operating revenues over several years. The accumulated fund deficit could only be resolved by increasing amounts of short-term borrowing. The city itself had no funds to meet its short-term obligations. The city nearly defaulted on the payment of its notes in October 1975, and it was predicted that a default was likely in December in the absence of federal aid. Although a financial crisis was averted through the use of a *deus ex machina* in the form of the State Municipal Assistance Corporation, which issued securities on behalf of the city, issues were raised as to why the precarious financial situation had not been disclosed in the city's municipal offerings. This crisis ultimately led to the adoption and use of the disclosure guidelines of the Government Finance Officers Association and the establishment of the Municipal Securities Rulemaking Board, which was responsible for developing a system of registration and regulation for dealers engaged in underwriting and trading municipal securities. However, although the 1975 legislation and its progeny require pre- and post-disclosure of material events by the issuer, such legislation was clearly not designed to subject municipal issuers to extensive disclosure requirements similar to those of corporate issuers (10Ks, 10Qs, 8Ks).

2. The Implication of WPPSS

The default by the Washington Public Power Supply System gave rise to litigation of staggering proportion. On September 22, 1988, the SEC issued a report that, while indicating the SEC would take no enforcement action against the participants in the $2.25 billion default, criticized the roles played by WPPSS, lawyers, underwriters, unit investment trusts, and rating agencies in issuing and marketing the bonds to investors. The SEC's findings included assertions that, as WPPSS moved to finance and construct plants, WPPSS withheld information about the financial crisis in projects 4 and 5 that might have warned investors not to buy WPPSS 4 and 5 bonds. The SEC also reported that WPPSS, bond counsel, special counsel, the financial advisor and the consulting engineer failed to seek information about the growing financial catastrophe, and concluded that "they tended to avoid causing full disclosure of negative information in their areas of expertise." Further, on the same date, the SEC voted unanimously to require municipal bond underwriters to account for the accuracy of official statements.

In response to the massive WPPSS default and to dissatisfaction with the level of municipal disclosure, the SEC adopted Rule 15C2-12 under the Securities Exchange Act.[437] The Rule,[438] which went into effect in January 1990, placed obligations on the underwriters of new municipal offerings regarding the official statement. The Rule was amended in November 1994 to require the issuer to provide ongoing disclosure after issuance. While the Rule originally required the distribution of ongoing disclosure to Nationally Recognized Municipal Securities Information Registries ("NRMSIRs"), the Rule was further amended in 2008 to require the disclosure to be provided to the Electronic Municipal Market Access ("EMMA") system, the repository for continuing disclosure filings developed by the Municipal Securities Rulemaking Board ("MSRB").[439] Since the 2010 amendments to the Rule, issuers are required to file event notices with EMMA within no more than ten business days after the occurrence of specified events, including principal and interest defaults; non-monetary, material defaults; and unscheduled draws on debt service reserves and credit enhancements.[440]

While Rule 15c2-12 is directed at the underwriter, the requirement of continuing disclosure is typically satisfied by the execution of a continuing disclosure agreement in which the issuer undertakes the obligation in favor of the bondholders. The indenture trustee should not be responsible, but rather, the municipality or designated representative should have the duty to make disclosure of material events. Sometimes the indenture trustee is a party to the continuing disclosure agreement. Sometimes a disclosure dissemination agreement is entered into by the issuer in which the issuer engages an agent to carry out its disclosure obligations. This agent may be the same financial institution that serves as indenture trustee. Care must be taken

---

437 15 U.S.C. § 78a-11.

438 17 C.F.R. § 240.15c2-12.

439 *See* Securities and Exchange Commission, Release No. 34-59061; File No. SR-MSRB-2008-05 (Dec. 5, 2008).

440 17 CFR 240.15c2-12(b)(5):

- Principal and interest payment delinquencies
- Nonpayment-related defaults
- Unscheduled draws on debt service reserves reflecting financial difficulties
- Substitution of credit or liquidity providers, or their failure to perform
- Adverse tax opinions or events affecting the tax-exempt status of the security
- Modifications to rights of security holders
- Bond calls and tender offers
- Defeasances
- Release, substitution or sale of property securing repayment of the securities
- Rating changes
- Bankruptcy, insolvency or receivership
- Merger, acquisition or sale of all issuer assets
- Appointment of successor trustee

that the terms of any disclosure dissemination agent agreement do not conflict with or expand the indenture trustee's duties under the trust indenture.

G. Limitation of Municipal Default Remedies

Given the difficulties of collecting a money judgment against a municipal body, indenture trustees for holders of defaulted municipal bonds, with no recourse to specific collateral, have few options or remedies.[441] The inherent weakness in the mandamus remedy has been described previously in this book.[442] If there has been an improper expenditure by the municipal body or some other action has been taken that impairs the security for the obligation, injunctive relief may be sought. Moreover, if action is being taken that attacks the essence of the obligation, declaratory action is appropriate to affirm that a binding obligation exists. It may be, given the problems inherent in other forms of relief, that such equitable and declaratory action should be sought before resorting to other remedies. An alternative to litigation and municipal insolvency proceedings is the appointment or use of consultants, financial advisors or financing authorities. The Detroit bankruptcy illustrated the importance of special revenues in the treatment of the water and sewer bonds, which received 100 percent recovery, and the benefit of insurance and statutory lien in the treatment of the unlimited tax general obligation bonds ("ULTGO"), which also received 100 percent recovery, albeit 26¢ payable from bond insurance.[443]

H. Particular Problems of Private Activity Bonds

When the debt is based upon tax-exempt conduit financing for the purpose of financing the project of a private user, there is as an alternative to levying taxes to pay off the indebtedness to the bondholders. Recompense often occurs in the form of rent or mortgage payments made directly or indirectly by the private corporate beneficiary to cover the scheduled debt service on the financing. In such cases, the collateral often takes the form of the guarantee of the corporation and a mortgage or security interest in the collateral, which is financed by tax-exempt bonds.

Remedies available to bondholders in such conduit financings should not be directed against the municipality since the financing is generally non-recourse to the municipality. The government officials or the bondholders (or their representatives) should exercise their remedies against the collateral that is pledged to pay the obligation, namely, the facility that is being financed or the private corporation receiving the benefit. Normally, such remedies will be dependent upon the type of financing that was entered into and the types of remedies provided

---

441 *See* Spiotto, ch. VI, for a more detailed discussion of available remedies.

442 *See* Chapter IX, D, *supra*.

443 *See* Detroit Disclosure Statement.

in the specific documents. Some examples of remedies for conduit municipal financing discussed previously are:

1. A request for foreclosure and sale of the collateral;
2. Nonjudicial sale of collateral;
3. Appointment of a receiver to manage trust property;
4. Suit against the guarantor; and
5. Right to enter and operate trust property.

In the bankruptcy of a private corporation, which received the benefit of tax-exempt financing, a municipality should file a proof of claim on the conduit financing lease or mortgage and cooperate with the bondholders or indenture trustee in obtaining a recovery. Bondholders are generally stayed from exercising any of the remedies in a Chapter 7 or 11 proceeding, absent court approval, and the indenture may clearly place the exercise of remedies in the hands of the indenture trustee. The effect of each putative remedy should be carefully considered. Foreclosure or sale may appear more attractive than a prolonged bankruptcy. However, many conduit-financed facilities are special purpose buildings in areas where sales may not bring the best return. Having competent management for an enterprise is always desirable. Even if a trustee for the bankruptcy estate has not been appointed under Section 1104 of the Bankruptcy Code, a bankruptcy court may determine whether a receiver or a foreclosure is necessary. If a guarantor of a conduit financing is not in bankruptcy, courts generally have held that the automatic stay does not prevent suits against the guarantor where the primary private corporate obligor is in bankruptcy.[444]

Before bondholders or an indenture trustee decides to lift the automatic stay and foreclose, or exercise any other remedy, consideration should be given as to whether there is authorization under the relevant transaction documents to protect the property from unreasonably low bids at the foreclosure sale or to run and operate the facility until it can be sold at an acceptable price.

I. Letters of Credit as Backing for Municipal and Tax-Exempt Conduit Obligations

Letters of credit are not guaranties and are not considered to be guaranties so as to be *ultra vires* for national banks. A letter of credit is considered to be backed by the full faith and credit of a financial institution in the amount set forth therein. In drafting any letter of credit

---

444 *See* Chapter XI, E, *supra*.

transaction, it is important that all documents clearly indicate that the letter of credit is not a guaranty. A letter of credit upon presentment of specified documents and fulfillment of certain conditions is an unqualified obligation to pay.

A letter of credit is an "independent" contract between the issuing bank and the beneficiary (Uniform Commercial Code § 5-114, Official Comment, ¶ 2). As such, if the stated conditions are satisfied, it survives the bankruptcy of the debtor for whom it was issued. Neither the letter of credit nor its proceeds are property of the estate. In issuing the letter of credit, the bank agrees to pay out of its own assets.[445] In the case of conduit financing, the "debtor" for this purpose would be the corporation for whose benefit the municipality issued the bonds. The letter of credit should be drafted so, upon specified default or bankruptcy of the obligor, the indenture trustee may draw thereon without the requirement to give a notice of acceleration or to take further action against the debtor, which may be viewed as a violation of the automatic stay. The language of the draw documents should be simple and, if possible, agreed upon and attached to the indenture in order to avoid later disputes as to form. The principal issue facing the indenture trustee is whether payment under the letter of credit constitutes a transfer of the property of the debtor.

Several cases warrant attention by the indenture trustee. In *Compton v. Blue Quail Energy Inc.*,[446] the trustee in bankruptcy sought to recover a transfer made via a letter of credit to the debtor's supplier, which had unsecured debt on the eve of bankruptcy. The court held that: (1) the letter of credit issuer gave new value for the increased security interest transfer, and the transfer related back to the date the letter of credit issuer filed a final financing statement relating to the security agreement with the debtor, including the future advances clause, so that the increased security interest transfer did not fall within the preference window, for purposes of attempting to avoid preferential transfer; (2) the supplier that was the beneficiary of the letter of credit issued to pay off antecedent unsecured debt received an indirect preference that could be recovered by the trustee; and (3) the supplier had no valid claim against the letter of credit issuer for reimbursement for any amounts the supplier had to pay the trustee under the preference claim. This case, however, can be used to argue that if an indenture trustee allows a letter of credit to lapse and obtains a new letter of credit within the 90-day preference period, then that letter of credit may be a preference because immediately prior to its issuance there was no letter of credit, only antecedent debt.[447] (The aging of a letter of credit obviously is a matter to be

---

445 *In re Page*, 18 B.R. 713 (D.C. 1982) (proceeds of the draw not asset of the estate).

446 831 F.2d 586 (5th Cir. 1988).

447 *See also In re Air Conditioning of Stuart*, 845 F.2d 293 (11th Cir. 1988) (when a bank issued a letter of credit to secure an antecedent debt, debtor's pledge of collateral to secure the letter of credit was a

highlighted and monitored. An evergreen letter of credit, on the other hand, has an expiry date but contains a provision that the expiry date may be automatically extended, often for a one-year period, until the issuing bank informs the beneficiary, usually at least 30 days prior to its nonrenewal.)

In a controversial opinion, one court has held that the agreement between a bank and a debtor that provides for a secured claim to reimburse the bank by the debtor may be an "impermissible preferential treatment" of the unsecured beneficiary by means of the letter of credit.[448]

With respect to payments to be made after commencement of the case, the agreement between the bank and the debtor (which is separate from the "independent" agreement between the bank and the bondholders) may be an executory contract to make a loan, which the trustee in bankruptcy cannot assume.[449] Failure to assume would lead, however, to a damage claim.[450]

In the decision of *Philadelphia Gear Corp. v. Federal Deposit Insurance Corp.*,[451] the court held that, under certain circumstances, a bank's obligation under a letter of credit could be a "deposit" insured by the Federal Deposit Insurance Corporation. In a municipal finance context, this would run afoul of the prohibition against federal guaranties of tax-exempt obligations and could destroy the tax-exempt status of the underlying obligation.

However, the Supreme Court, in a six-to-three decision,[452] reversed the decision of the Tenth Circuit and held that a standby letter of credit backed by a contingent promissory note does not create a deposit and, in light of the fact that such a letter does not entrust any noncontingent assets to the bank, a standby letter of credit backed by a contingent promissory note does not give rise to an insured deposit.

J. Treatment of Lease Obligations

In certain conduit tax-exempt financing and lease financing transactions, the obligation to pay an amount equal to principal and interest on the bonds is contained in a lease obligation

---

voidable preference, as the collateral constitutes property of the debtor's estate). *See* Michael St. Patrick Baxter, *Letters of Credit and the Powerine Preference Trap*, 53 BUS. LAW. 65 (1997).

448 *Matter of Twist Cap, Inc.*, 1 B.R. 284 (D. Fla. 1979). This opinion has been rejected by many courts. *See, e.g., In re M. J. Sales & Distributing Co., Inc.*, 9 BCD 1342 (S.D.N.Y. 1982). However, if the same security is given to the beneficiary of the letter of credit as to the bank, the *Twist Cap* problem should be solved.

449 § 364(c)(2).

450 §§ 365(g) and 502(g).

451 751 F.2d 1131 (10th Cir. 1984), *rev'd* 476 U.S. 426 (1986).

452 476 U.S. 426, 106 S. Ct. 1931, 90 L. Ed. 2d 428 (1986).

from the company obtaining the benefit of the financing. This lease obligation is then normally assigned to the indenture trustee for the benefit of the bondholders. Some corporate debtors have taken the position in bankruptcy that, rather than a claim for principal, interest and expenses, all that remains to the conduit bondholders is a claim for the termination of a lease of real estate under the Bankruptcy Code. Under Section 502(b)(6) of the Bankruptcy Code, a claim arising out of the termination of a lease of real estate is limited to the rent required by such lease, without acceleration, for the greater of one year's rent or 15 percent of the unexpired lease term, not to exceed three years of the remaining term of such lease following the earlier of (i) the date the petition was filed instituting the action, or (ii) the date on which such lessor repossessed or the lessee surrendered the leased property plus any unpaid rent due under such lease without acceleration as of the earlier of such dates. This position, taken by certain corporate debtors, is wrong because the lease in conduit tax-exempt financing, as was noted in the legislative history surrounding Chapter 9 of the Bankruptcy Code, was a "financing lease" and not a lease of real estate.[453] Courts have held that "financing leases" with regard to conduit tax-exempt financing are not subject to the provisions of Section 502(b)(6).[454] As mentioned above, under Section 929 of the Bankruptcy Code, a lease to a municipality will not be treated as an executory contract or unexpired lease solely because it is subject to termination if the debtor fails to appropriate rent. It is, therefore, important from a bondholder's position not only to have the lease obligation from the corporate debtor in a form where it is clear that it is a financing lease, but also to have a guaranty from the corporate debtor for all its obligations to pay principal and interest on the bonds, thereby demonstrating the financing nature of the lease.

The "true lease" controversy took center stage in the United Airlines bankruptcy in which the debtor argued that its leases of several airport facilities financed by tax-exempt special facilities revenue bonds were not obligations under leases pursuant to Section 365 of the Bankruptcy Code but, rather, financing arrangements that could be restructured as part of a plan of reorganization. In three of the four adversary proceedings, the Seventh Circuit Court of Appeals ultimately ruled that the "leasehold-assignment-and-leaseback" arrangements were disguised financings.[455]

---

453 S. Rep. No. 95-989 at 64 (95 Cong., 2d Sess. 1984), *as reprinted* in U.S.C.C.A.N. 5787, 5850.

454 *See In re Winston Mills*, 6 B.R. 587 (Bankr. S.D.N.Y. 1980); *In re Central Foundry Co.*, 48 B.R. 895 (Bankr. N.D. Ala. 1985); *In re Independence Vill., Inc.*, 52 B.R. 715 (Bankr. E.D. Mich. 1985).

455 *See United Airlines, Inc. v. HSBC Bank USA, N.A.*, 416 F.3d 609 (7th Cir. 2005), *cert. denied*, 547 U.S. 1003 (2006) (San Francisco); *United Airlines, Inc. v. Bank of N.Y.*, (7th Cir. 2005) (unpublished order), *cert. denied*, 546 U.S. 508 (2006) (New York); and *United Airlines, Inc. v. U.S. Bank Nat'l Assoc., Inc.*, 447 F.3d 504 (7th Cir. 2006) (Los Angeles). For an extensive discussion of the law regarding airport financing that the case produced see James E. Spiotto, Tax-Exempt Airport Finance: Tales from the Friendly Skies in the Handbook of Municipal Bonds (S. Feldstein & F. Fabozzi eds., John Wiley & Sons, Inc. 2008).

K. Special Requirements of Accepting Municipal Indenture Trusteeship

The trustee should assure itself at closing that it has received and can rely upon all necessary opinions and certificates. These include the opinion of bond counsel, which should be addressed to the trustee, as to the tax-exempt status of the bonds. In addition, the trustee should also be sure that a continuing disclosure agreement for the benefit of the beneficial owners of the bonds has been executed by the issuer. In what hopefully is an aberration, a trial court in the state of Washington held that an indenture trustee should have discovered that certain bonds were invalid and illegal before entering into the agreement.[456]

L. Sensitivity to Role of Bond Insurer

Since the early 1970s, municipal bond insurance has emerged as an important credit enhancement option for municipal bond issues. The attractiveness of municipal bond insurance to cautious investors increased with the massive default of WPPSS. The important role of the bond insurer was evident in the Jefferson County and Detroit bankruptcies, the later case providing 100% recovery to the ULTGO bonds by a 26¢ per dollar payment by the bond insurer.

Bond insurers assume responsibility for the timely payment of principal and interest as it becomes due if the issuer is unable to meet those obligations. Municipal bond insurance also covers sinking fund payments. However, the bond insurer normally does not have an obligation to make full payment of the accelerated principal balance of the bonds upon default. The insurance policy guarantees the timely payment as scheduled over the life of the bonds.

Given the obligations assumed by bond insurers, it is not surprising that they often seek the time and attention of the trustee with respect to monitoring the underlying bond issue. That is understandable because the issuer is the first source of payment of principal and interest on the bonds. Documentation for insured municipal bond issues outlines the relationship between the trustee and the insurer. The trustee will require the consent of the insurer to any amendment of the documents that affects the insurer's rights, the execution of any supplemental indenture or bond ordinance or any significant action by the trustee. It is important for the holders to appreciate that, in the event of an insolvency, the insurer will have the right to vote on behalf of all the holders of insured bonds, absent a default by the bond insurer under the municipal bond

---

456 *Robert Trimble v. Holmes Harbor Sewer Dist. et al.*, Case No. 01-2-00751-8 in the Superior Court for the State of Washington. The court declined to reconsider its ruling despite the declaration on behalf of the Corporate Trust Committee of the American Bankers Association that an indenture trustee is not expected to conduct its own independent investigation into whether an issuer has authority under applicable law to issue the proposed bonds.

insurance policy. Further, upon the occurrence and continuance of an event of default, the insurer will be entitled to control and direct the enforcement of all rights and remedies granted to the bondholders and the right to approve all waivers of events of defaults. Normally, the bond insurer will have its own counsel and thus, while the presence of bond insurance guarantees a payout of the bonds, the trustee will necessarily have to coordinate with and be sensitive to the views of the insurer.

XIII. The Effectiveness of Subordination: Possible Causes of Action and Claims of the Indenture Trustee upon Default

A. Possible Causes of Action of Indenture Trustee Against Other Creditors upon Default

Upon default by or bankruptcy of the issuer, there may be theories or causes of action against other creditors that may assist indenture trustees and debtholders in achieving a recovery. Some of the claims will be discussed below. Of course, the applicability of each of the theories varies from case to case.

1. Equitable Subordination of the Claims of Other Creditors

a. The Doctrine of Equitable Subordination

The equitable subordination of claims is provided for in § 510(c) of the Bankruptcy Code, which provides that:

> Notwithstanding subsections (a) and (b) of this section, after notice and a hearing, the court may —
>
> (1) under principles of equitable subordination, subordinate for purposes of distribution all or part of an allowed claim to all or part of another allowed claim or all or part of an allowed interest to all or part of another allowed interest; or
>
> (2) order that any lien securing such a subordinated claim be transferred to the estate.

The seminal case on equitable subordination is *Benjamin v. Diamond (In re Mobile Steel Co.).*[457] There, the court concluded that three conditions must be met in order to subordinate the claims of one creditor to the claims of another. They are:

(i) The claimant must have engaged in some type of inequitable conduct.

(ii) The misconduct must have resulted in injury to the creditors of the bankrupt or conferred an unfair advantage on the claimant.

---

457 563 F.2d 692 (5th Cir. 1977).

(iii) Equitable subordination of the claim must not be inconsistent with the provisions of the Bankruptcy Act.

Many federal courts have adopted the *Mobile Steel* test.[458] It has been noted that the third prong of the text mandates that the court not alter the priority scheme simply to reach a more equitable result.[459] This is consistent with the holding of the United States Supreme Court[460] that bankruptcy courts may not categorically render priorities in derogation of the Bankruptcy Code. Equitable subordination remains a "drastic" and "unusual" remedy.[461]

b. Frequent Fact Patterns

The most common equitable subordination cases involve bank claims arising in connection with allegations of domination and control of the business of a borrower or debtor on the part of a financial institution. When such allegations are established, the institution, by virtue of exercising control over the debtor, assumes a fiduciary-like duty to other creditors to exercise that control faithfully. In order to equitably subordinate a creditor's claim, the control must be coupled with use of that control to the creditor's advantage and to the other creditor's detriment.[462] Under general principles of corporate law, there are three types of control: voting control, management control and control through financial domination.[463] Each of these types of control has been asserted in equitable subordination cases. It should be noted that some courts have contemplated, and one has held, that control need not be found in order equitably to subordinate bank claims.[464] In so holding, the court stated that:

> The remedy of equitable subordination must remain sufficiently flexible to deal with manifest injustice resulting from violation of the rules of fair play. *See Pepper v. Litton, supra.* To find that control is required in all subordination cases involving the claims of non-insiders would unduly and unnecessarily limit the reach of the equitable subordination doctrine. In the words of the Fifth Circuit in *Matter of Multiponics,* "[w]here ingenuity spawns unprecedented vagaries of unfairness, [the bankruptcy courts] should not

---

458 *See In re Light Squared Inc.,* 511 B.R. 253, 346 (Bankr. S.D.N.Y. 2014).

459 *In re Perry,* 425 B.R. 323 (Bankr. S.D. Tex. 2010).

460 *U.S. v. Noland,* 517 U.S. 535 (1996).

461 *In re Optim Energy, LLC,* No. 14-10262, 2014 WL 1924908 (Bankr. D. Del. May 13, 2014).

462 *In re T.E. Mercer Trucking Co.,* 16 B.R. 176 (Bankr. N.D. Tex. 1981).

463 Douglas-Hamilton, *Creditor Liabilities Resulting from Improper Interference with the Management of a Financially Troubled Debtor,* 31 BUS. LAW. 343 (1975).

464 *Matter of Teltronics Servs., Inc.,* 29 B.R. 139 (Bankr. E.D.N. Y. 1983).

> decline to recognize their marks, nor hesitate to turn the twilight for [the offending claimant] into a new dawn for other creditors."[465]

In *In re Bowman Hardware & Electric Co.*,[466] the bankrupt borrowed money from its lender for a period of ten years prior to its petition. Pursuant to an agreement with the lender, the bankrupt did not reveal the indebtedness on its books to other creditors. In reliance upon the liabilities reflected on the bankrupt's books and upon the debtor's other representations, a creditor extended credit to the debtor. The court found that the agreement between the lender and the bankrupt was, among other things, tantamount to constructive fraud. Although the court determined that the lender had no duty to reveal the true financial position of the bankrupt, once the lender affirmatively deceived the creditor, the lender was estopped from asserting his claim against the creditor who relied upon the deception. The court therefore subordinated the lender's claim in favor of the claim of deceived creditors.[467]

While the doctrine of equitable subordination is flexible, it clearly does not extend to the late filing of a claim. Where an indenture trustee for senior debt filed its proof of claim after a bankruptcy bar date but before any distribution on claims, the senior debt had not waived its contractual subordination rights and the lateness of the trustee did not amount to egregious, inequitable conduct justifying the remedy of equitable subordination.[468]

c. The Effect of Equitable Subordination

The equitable subordination of claims does not disallow the subordinated claim. Rather, it merely readjusts the priority of claims. A subordinated creditor may not take a distribution from the estate until the claims of creditors in whose favor subordination was invoked are paid in full. Additionally, equitable relief is by its very nature remedial rather than penal. Therefore, a

---

465 29 B.R. at 172 (citing *Matter of Multiponics, Inc.*, 622 F.2d 709, 722 (5th Cir. 1980)).

466 67 F.2d 792 (7th Cir. 1933).

467 As part of a plan of reorganization, pursuant to a scheme between management and a group of subordinated debtholders, the subordinated debtholders were issued secured notes enabling them to gain priority over the Internal Revenue Service. The Internal Revenue Service brought an adversary proceeding seeking equitable subordination of the new secured debt. The court granted this relief, holding that the conduct of the debtholders colluding with the debtor's management to facilitate payment on the notes at the expense of the tax claimant with a higher-priority claim was sufficient to warrant equitable subordination. *U.S. v. State St. Bank and Tr. Co.*, 520 B.R. 29 (Bankr. D. Del. 2014). In another case, where a competitor of the debtor, through a special purpose entity, bought debt of the debtor, the court ruled equitable subordination was appropriate. *In re Light Squared Inc.*, *supra* note 458.

468 *In re Franklin Bank Corp.*, 526 B.R. 527 (D. Del. 2014).

claim should be equitably subordinated only to the extent necessary to offset the harm suffered by the debtor and its creditors as a result of the inequitable conduct.[469]

2. Subrogation to Bank Debt

Of the various equitable doctrines, subrogation may be of greatest benefit to indenture trustees and debtholders upon default. The doctrine is designed to deal with those situations in which property obtained by fraud or wrongdoing is used to reduce liabilities, not to create assets on which a constructive trust or equitable lien can attach under normal tracing rules. The doctrine of subrogation does not act to remove property from the estate of a bankrupt.[470] Rather, it affects ownership of property rights prior to bankruptcy. Subrogation is a creature of equity, enforced for the purpose of accomplishing the ends of substantial justice, independent of any contractual obligation between parties.[471] Accordingly, to the extent the facts show that the proceeds of a debt issue discharged other indebtedness of a company (oftentimes bank debt) under circumstances such that it is unjust for the company to retain the benefit of the discharged debt, a court of equity may recreate the obligation discharged in favor of the indenture trustee for the debtholders, as if the discharged debt were still outstanding. Where the discharge of an obligation is not "officious" (unjustified interference with the affairs of another),[472] the person whose property was used is entitled to reimbursement and to the remedy of subrogation to obtain reimbursement.[473] A person is not officious if he is induced to make the payment by fraud.

The doctrine of subrogation has been applied in other instances. For example, in *In re Franklin Savings & Loan Co.*,[474] agents of the bankrupt savings company acquired stock under fraudulent misrepresentations, tendering a note in return. The stock was pledged to the bankrupt's bank, together with other collateral. The bank sold the stock and applied a portion of the proceeds to its debt, returning the excess proceeds and the balance of the collateral to the bankrupt. The district court determined that, at the time the stock was pledged, it was the property of the original owner whose interest therein was subject only to the bank's lien. This

---

469 *Matter of Teltronics Servs., Inc.*, 29 B.R. 139, 168 (Bankr. E.D.N.Y. 1983); *Matter of Mobile Steel Co.* 563 F.2d 692, 701 (5th Cir. 1977); *In re Westgate-Cal. Corp.*, 642 F.2d 1174, 1178 (9th Cir. 1981); *Farmers Bank v. Julian*, 383 F.2d 314, 323 (8th Cir. 1967), *cert. denied*, 389 U.S. 1021 (1967).

470 *Perlman v. Reliance Ins. Co.*, 371 U.S. 132, 135-137 (1962).

471 371 U.S. at 136 n.12.

472 *See* Restatement (Third) of Restitution and Unjust Enrichment ("Restatement of Restitution") S2, Comment (a).

473 Restatement of Restitution § 57.

474 34 F. Supp. 585 (E.D. Tenn. 1940).

gave the original owner of the stock the right to the excess proceeds of the stock's sale, and that owner was subrogated to the right of the bank's lien with respect to the balance of the collateral, and with a general unsecured claim for the balance of its entire claim.

Similarly, in *Pittsburgh-Westmoreland Coal Co. v. Kerr*,[475] the Court of Appeals of New York held that the remedy of subrogation was not limited merely to sureties. The court noted:

> It may be assumed that ordinarily money although obtained by fraud or felony cannot be recovered when it has been paid to the creditors of the party who has thus criminally obtained it even when the only consideration for the payment was the satisfaction of an antecedent debt.
>
> Where, however, a payment with the money of another wrongfully obtained, operates to discharge a lien . . . or a debt that is secured by collateral, or as in this case by the indorsement of another, the debt may in equity be deemed alive for the benefit of the person whose money was so wrongfully used by the debtor and such person may be subrogated to the rights of the one who owned the debt and the debt be deemed transferred and assigned to such person. The rule stated is founded in equity. Because it is equitable it is enforced by the courts at all times unless there are surrounding circumstances and intervening equities that require a different conclusion.[476]

The principle articulated by the *Kerr* court is well settled, and subrogation is available in a wide variety of circumstances in which, at first blush, it might seem to be inapplicable.[477] Even commentators have noted that there is no obvious reason why a subrogation remedy is not applicable when securities are sold by fraud.[478]

The concept of subrogation in favor of co-debtors and others jointly or secondarily liable on the debt, such as a surety, guarantor or co-maker, is embodied in Section 509 of the Bankruptcy Code.[479] In addition, the doctrine of equitable subrogation under state law, which

---

475 220 N.Y. 137, 115 N.E. 465 (N.Y. 1917).

476 115 N.E. at 466–67 (citations omitted) (emphasis added).

477 *See Eastern States Petroleum Co. v. Universal Oil Prods. Co.*, 49 A.2d 612, 616 (Del. Ch. 1946).

478 *See* Slain and Kripke, *The Interface Between Securities Regulation and Bankruptcy — Allocating the Risk of Illegal Securities Issuance Between Securityholders and the Issuer's Creditors*, 48 N.Y. U. L. REV. 261, 276 (1973).

479 *Hamada v. Far East Nat'l Bank*, 291 F.3d 645 (9th Cir. 2002); *In re Chateaugay Corp.*, 89 F.3d 942 (2nd Cir. 1996); *In re Hall*, 477 B.R. 74 (Bankr. N.D. Ill. 2012).

permits a party who satisfied another's obligation to recover from the party primarily liable,[480] also may be available in the bankruptcy content.[481]

3. Imposition of a Constructive Trust on the Proceeds of the Debt

The indenture trustee may also petition the court to impose a constructive trust on the proceeds of the debt for the benefit of the holders. A constructive trust is an equitable remedy whereby the court imposes a fiduciary-like duty upon the holder of property to convey the property to another when, under the circumstances, it would be inequitable for the holder of the property to enjoy the beneficial interest thereof.[482]

The doctrine of constructive trust effectuates the equitable principle that one who would be unjustly enriched if permitted to retain property is under an equitable duty to convey it to the rightful owner.[483] As Judge Cardozo stated in *Beatty v. Guggenheim Exploration Co.*:

> The constructive trust is the formula through which the conscience of equity finds expression. When property has been acquired in such circumstances that the holder of the legal title may not in good conscience retain the beneficial interest, equity converts him into a trustee.[484]

In most cases where a constructive trust is imposed, the result is to restore to the claimant property of which he has been unjustly deprived and to take from the wrongdoer property, the retention of which would result in a corresponding unjust enrichment.[485]

To impose a constructive trust on the proceeds of the debt issue held by other creditors (for example, banks for the benefit of the debtholders), the indenture trustee may pursue either of two avenues. The first is a step-by-step transaction whereby the indenture trustee shows that the initial recipient of the trust *res* (the company) received the proceeds subject to a constructive trust. Then, the indenture trustee traces the trust *res* from the company to the banks. Finally, the

---

480 *In re Air Crash Disaster*, 86 F.3d 498, 549 (6th Cir. 1996); *In re The Celotex Corp.*, 289 B.R. 460 (Bankr. M.D. Fla. 2003).

481 *In re The Medicine Shoppe*, 210 B.R. 310 (Bankr. N.D. Ill. 1997); *In re The Celotex Corp., Id.*

482 *In Re Daves*, 770 F.2d 1363 (5th Cir. 1985); *Harris v. Sentry Title Co.*, 715 F.2d 941 (5th Cir. 1983), *reh'g denied*, 719 F.2d 404, *mandate recalled*, 727 F.2d 1368 (1984), *cert. denied*, 469 U.S. 1037 (1984).

483 Restatement of Restitution § 55.

484 225 N.Y. 380, 122 N.E. 378, 380 (N.Y. 1919).

485 Restatement § 55, Comment d; *Dexia Credit Local v. Rogan*, 629 F.3d 612 (7th Cir. 2010); *Wendell Corp. Trustee v. Thurston*, 680 A.2d 1314 (Conn. 1996); *In re Nat'l Mortg. Equity Corp. Mortg. Pool Certificates Secs. Litig.*, 636 F.Supp.1138 (C.D. Ca. 1986); *Cox v. Wauby*, 433 N.W.2d 716 (Iowa 1988).

indenture trustee establishes that the banks were not bona fide purchasers of the proceeds. When a trustee-beneficiary relationship exists, there is a conclusive presumption in equity that "a trustee dissipates or spends his own funds first, before touching or encroaching upon the trust funds."[486] The court in *Importers' and Traders' National Bank v. Peters* stated that:

> When money held by a person in a fiduciary capacity has been paid or deposited by him in his general account at a bank, the party for whom the money is held can follow it and has a charge on the balance in the banker's hands, and if a person holding money in a fiduciary capacity, pays it to his account at his bankers, and mixes it with his own money and afterwards draws out some by checks . . . the drawer of the checks must be taken to have drawn out his own in preference to the trust money. The rule attributing the first drawing out to the first payments in, does not apply to such a case.[487]

Therefore, the proceeds may be traced, even if the proceeds were commingled with other funds, if the "lowest intermediate balance test" is met. The alternative avenue is to show that the company was nothing more than a straw man in the transaction—a mere conduit in the banks' scheme to defraud the debtholders. Even in the bankruptcy context, the right to a constructive trust turns on whether state law would impress the property with a constructive trust prior to the entry into bankruptcy.[488]

4. Imposition of Equitable Liens on Identifiable Assets

As an alternative and in addition to a constructive trust, the indenture trustee could have claims against the company or other creditors based upon an equitable lien on specific, identifiable assets. Equitable liens are claims against assets imposed by a court of equity to prevent unjust enrichment.[489] As with constructive trusts, the insolvency of the wrongdoer does not affect entitlement to the remedy, and the lien continues on the property unless cut off by a bona fide purchaser.

---

486 *People v. Barrett*, 405 Ill. 188, 90 N.E.2d 94, 98 (1950), *aff'd*, 175 Ind. 161, 92 N.E. 733, 93 N.E. 850. *See also Brown & Williamson Tobacco Corp. v. First Nat'l Bank*, 504 F.2d 998, 1002 (7th Cir. 1974); *Importers' and Traders' Nat'l Bank v. Peters*, 123 N.Y. 272.

487 123 N.Y. at 278-79.

488 *In re Morris*, 260 F.3d 654 (6th Cir. 2001). But see *In re Peregrine*, 487 B.R. 498 (Bankr. N.D. Ill. 2013) (under Illinois law, constructive trust is created when court declares party in possession as the constructive trustee).

489 Restatement of Restitution § 56; *In re Pardee*, 433 B.R. 377 (Bankr. N.D. Okla. 2010).

The basis for establishing an equitable lien is the same as the basis for establishing a constructive trust. The importance of equitable liens arises after the proceeds of the debt are traced to specific, tangible or intangible assets. If the indenture trustee can trace the proceeds to specific assets, then the indenture trustee can use the principle of equitable liens to establish priority over other creditors.[490] This is accomplished by giving the holder of the equitable lien a security interest in the identified property.

Where the proceeds of a bond issue were alleged to have been improperly used to defray costs of a different project, the complaint was held to state a claim for an equitable lien on the other plant. The portion of the complaint seeking to impose an equitable lien on the misspent bond proceeds was dismissed since the proceeds had been distributed to third parties. An equitable lien can be established only if there is some property subject to the lien.[491]

5. The Effect of Section 510(b)

a. Section 510(b)

Section 510(b) of the Bankruptcy Code, 11 U.S.C. § 510(b), provides that:

> For the purpose of distribution under this title, a claim arising from rescission of a purchase or sale of a security of the debtor or of an affiliate of the debtor, for damages arising from the purchase or sale of such a security, or for reimbursement or contribution allowed under section 502 on account of such a claim, shall be subordinated to all claims or interests that are senior to or equal the claim or interest represented by such security, except that if such security is common stock, such claim has the same priority as common stock.

As set forth in Section 101(49)(A)(i) of the Bankruptcy Code, the term "security" includes a note. Therefore, on its face, the statute calls for the subordination of debtholders' claims, if they are for rescission or damages. However, other provisions of the Bankruptcy Code and the legislative history of this section indicate that this section may be inapplicable to certain remedies.

---

490 *In re Estate of Wittenberg*, 577 S. W.2d 120 (Mo. App. 1978); *see also Fosdick v. Schall*, 99 U.S. 235 (1878).

491 *Bonneville Power Admin. v. Wash. Public Power Supply Sys.*, 956 F.2d 1497 (9th Cir. 1992). Note, however, that there is substantial case law expressing disfavor with granting equitable liens in bankruptcy, particularly absent fraud. *See* the discussion in *In the Matter of Einoder*, 55 B.R. 319 (Bankr. N.D. Ill. 1985).

b. Legislative History

The remedies of subrogation, constructive trusts and equitable liens would similarly sustain an attack under Section 510(b). The debtholders would not be seeking to establish a claim for "rescission," "damages" or "reimbursement or contribution." The remedies of subrogation, constructive trusts and equitable liens seek to establish claims for the actual dollars received. These are claims to enforce the debt. As the legislative history behind Section 510(b) indicates, the purpose of that section was not to affect the bargained-for priority established in the underlying transaction for the basic claim. The purpose was to prevent subordinated creditors and equityholders from improving their bargained-for position in terms of distribution by asserting claims in addition to their basic debt or equity claim.

As described in the Report of the House Committee on the Judiciary accompanying H.R. 8200, Report No. 95-595, at page 194, 95th Cong. 1st Sess. (1977) ("House Report"):

> A difficult policy question to be resolved in a business bankruptcy concerns the relative status of a security holder who seeks to rescind his purchase of securities or to sue for damages based on such a purchase: Should he be treated as a general unsecured creditor based on his tort claim for rescission, or should his claim be subordinated?

The House Report states that originally, a security holder was precluded from asserting a tort claim for rescission as being on a parity with general creditors. The rationale behind the rule was that the security holder knowingly assumed an equity position different from that of general creditors, and the tort claim for rescission was an effort to bootstrap equity up to the level of general debt.

c. Case Law

In 1937 the Supreme Court ruled that equityholders could assert rescission claims and such claims should be treated *pari passu* with general creditors, thereby improving their relative positive on distribution.[492] Cases decided thereafter treated the rescinding claimant as tantamount to one seeking reclamation, entitled to a secured position in property or its proceeds and thus superior to general unsecured creditors.[493] Thus, a creditor's position in distribution of

---

492 *Oppenheimer v. Harriman Nat'l Bank and Tr.*, 301 U.S. 206 (1937).

493 *In re Rhine*, 241 F. Supp. 86 (D. Colo.), *reh'g denied*, 242 F. Supp. 127 (1965). Subsequently, the language of Section 510(b) was clarified regarding subrogation of a claim based on the purchase or sale of common stock, effectively rejecting the holding in *Rhine*. The section of the Bankruptcy Code subordinates in priority of distribution rescission claims to all claims that are senior to the

assets of a bankrupt could be altered by asserting the tort claim for rescission rather than the bargained-for contract claim.

The resolution under the Bankruptcy Code of the policy question was to treat rescission and damages claims on an appropriate level of distribution in relation to the basic contract claim:

> [S]ubordination varies with the claim or interest involved. *If the security is a debt instrument, the damages or rescission claim will be granted the status of a general unsecured claim.* If the security is an equity security, the damages or rescission claim is subordinated to all creditors and treated the same as the equity security itself.[494]

Thus, the drafters of the Bankruptcy Code recognized the differentiation between types of securities and that debt instruments are not equivalent to an equity security. Therefore, any bargained-for claims in law or in equity of the debtholders should not be equivalent to an equity claim. There is no intention to alter the basic bargained-for priority and, accordingly, such potential claims by debtholders should not be subordinated pursuant to Section 510(b) to make them in effect equal to an equity claim. The application of Section 510(b) results in a security rescission claim or damages on an unsecured debt claim ranking just below the debt claim and above any equity claim in order of distribution in a bankruptcy plan. There is a need to be alert to other means of altering the priority of claims. If debtholders seek to pursue a cause of action for damages for securities fraud, such suit would be outside the bankruptcy proceeding and Section 510(b) should be inapplicable. In addition, there may be liability to the indenture trustee or debtholders for other causes of action as discussed in Chapter XVIII.

B. Enforceability and Scope of Subordination Agreements

1. Enforcement in Bankruptcy

Section 510(a) of the Bankruptcy Code codifies the rule upholding agreements between creditors regarding the order of payments.[495] Section 510(a) of the Bankruptcy Code provides that subordination agreements are enforceable in bankruptcy to the same extent that they are enforceable under applicable non-bankruptcy law. A requirement in a plan enforcing terms of a subordinated indenture *vis-à-vis* "senior debt" and therefore providing no distribution to subordinated debt until senior debt is paid does not run afoul of Section 1129(b) of the

---

claim or interest on which the rescission claims are based. *See In re Commercial Fin. Servs.*, 268 B.R. 579, 593–94 (Bankr. N.D. Okla. 2001).

494 House Report at 359 (emphasis added).

495 *In re Coronet Capital Co.*, 1995 WL 429494 (Bankr. S.D.N.Y. 1995).

Bankruptcy Code's fair and equitable requirement.[496] Applicable non-bankruptcy law is the law of contracts.[497] A subordination agreement is nothing more than a contract by which one party agrees to subordinate his claim against the debtor in favor of the claim of another creditor.[498] The scope of subordination is often found in the transaction's definition of "senior debt," which should encompass the nature of the debt and whether further extensions of credit, amendments or modifications and refinancings are included. The inclusion of interest, fees, premiums, make-wholes and postpetition interest also must be clearly expressed.[499] Where a subordination provision is deemed ambiguous, the court may consider extrinsic evidence. [500]

Further, the subordination language is to be interpreted in accordance with its plain meaning under settled rules of English grammar.[501] Accordingly, fraudulent transfer claims would be deemed "assets of the Company" subject to an indenture's subordination provision, as a contrary interpretation would eviscerate the purpose of the subordination provisions.[502]

The plaintiff in *In re Sepco, Inc.*, a subordinated creditor, raised four state law defenses against the enforcement of the subordination agreement. A review of this case is instructive. The plaintiff alleged that the subordination agreement was unenforceable because it was procured by fraud; that the bank should be estopped from benefitting from its own inequitable conduct; that there was a failure of consideration; and, finally, that the bank would be unjustly enriched if it were allowed to enforce the subordination agreement against the plaintiff. The bankruptcy court concluded that the bank was precluded from enforcing the subordination agreement under each of the four theories advanced by the plaintiff.

a. Fraud

In *Sepco*, the court found that the bank was a party to the subordination agreement, even though it did not sign the document. The bank drafted the document, including the

---

496 *In re Enron Creditors Recovery Corp.*, 380 B.R. 307 (S.D.N.Y. 2008).

497 *In re Best Products Co., Inc.*, 168 B.R. 35 (Bankr. S.D.N.Y. 1994); *In re Lunan Family Restaurants*, 194 B.R. 429 (Bankr. N.D. Ill. 1996).

498 *In re Sepco, Inc.*, 36 B.R. 279 (Bankr. S.D. 1984). More recently, the Seventh Circuit has ruled that secured creditors may agree to swap priorities through the use of a subordination agreement, assuming that the subordinating creditors' security interest is enforceable. *Caterpillar Fin. Servs. Corp. v. Peoples Nat'l Bank*, 710 F.3d 691 (7th Cir. 2013).

499 *See* Reade Ryan, *The Subordinated World of Junk Bonds*, 105 BANKING L.J. 4 (1988). The unique priority issues raised by securitization transactions will be discussed separately in Chapter XVI.

500 *See MP Silicones*, 874 F.3d 787 (2nd Cir. 2017), where the court cited SEC filings and other public statements before bankruptcy where the debtor said the debt was subordinated.

501 *In re Enron, supra* note 496.

502 *In re Tribune Co.*, 464 B.R. 208 (Bankr. D. Del. 2011).

subordination clause, and was instrumental in getting the creditor to sign the agreement based upon representations that the creditor would be paid from bank funds whereas, in reality, no such payments were intended to be made until the bank loan was paid in full. The court found that this suppression of the truth by one having knowledge of the facts, and the making of a promise without any intention of honoring it, constituted fraud.

b. Estoppel

The facts that give rise to invocation of equitable estoppel are the same as those for fraud. In *Sepco*, the bank concealed and misrepresented facts with the intent to invoke reliance by the creditor. If it could be shown by a creditor that, due to the bank's misrepresentation, he loaned money to the debtor, and that loan was now subject to the subordination provision, the bank may be estopped from invoking the terms of the subordination agreement.

c. Lack of Consideration

In *Sepco*, the subordination agreement was signed after the creditor had loaned the money to the debtor and had a lien priority. In that case, there was a total failure of consideration which prohibited enforcement of the contract. Usually, the subordination provision will be contained in the agreement between the debtor and the debtholders, causing this defense to fail.

d. Unjust Enrichment

The *Sepco* court found that it would be inequitable to allow the bank to retain the benefit of the subordination agreement without first paying the creditor the assured funds that had induced the creditor to sign the subordination agreement. The bank was not allowed to enforce the clause against the creditor, because the bank would be unjustly enriched by retaining the benefit. The facts of each individual situation will mandate whether or not equity will imply an obligation on the defendant to transfer title of the property to the plaintiff.

2. Scope of Subordination—Subordination to Trade Debt

Frequently, debtholders do not agree to subordinate themselves to trade creditors. This is common in subordinated debentures. It is clear that the terms of the subordination agreement control, which means that the words should be given their meaning as an ordinary, average or reasonable person would understand them.[503] The court in *In re Pine Lake Village Apartment Co.*,[504] ruled that the applicable language did not subordinate the mortgagee's principal indebtedness to the claims of trade creditors. The terms of the subordination agreement

---

503 *Matter of Eaton Factors Co., Inc.*, 3 B.R. 20 (Bankr. S.D.N.Y. 1980).

504 19 B.R. 819 (Bankr. S.D.N.Y. 1982).

controlled the subordination, and that contract did not include subordination to trade creditors. As discussed below, the term "money borrowed" clearly eliminated trade creditors from the definition of "senior indebtedness."

3. "Money Borrowed"

The term "money borrowed" has been defined by in *In re Discon Corporation*.[505] The court in that case was faced with a situation in which the term "money borrowed" appeared in a prospectus and an indenture. The court stated as follows:

> There remains the problem of what was meant by "money borrowed"? The debentures are subordinate to "indebtedness for money borrowed," . . . "Borrow" is defined by Webster as "to receive temporarily from another, implying or expressing the intention either of returning the thing received or giving its equivalent to the lender." Webster's New Third Int'l. Dictionary, Unabridged (1967). "Money borrowed," therefore cannot be defined to include money *owed for goods purchased*, except where the indenture has included the same within its definition of indebtedness (amounts due under rental or lease contracts of personalty or realty). It cannot be determined from the record before the Court which, if any, of the creditors would be superior to the debentures within the terms of the indenture. Apparently not all creditors may claim a superior position. However, it is clear that in view of the subordination agreement, the unsecured creditors may not be treated on a parity one with the other, for it would not be in the "best interests of creditors."[506]

Since a trade creditor is a creditor for goods and services, the term "money borrowed" makes it apparent that the debt is not subordinated to such trade creditors.

4. Postpetition Interest

Both the Bankruptcy Act (11 U.S.C. § 63(a)) and the subsequently enacted Bankruptcy Code (11 U.S.C. § 502(b)(2)) generally disallow the payment of postpetition interest to unsecured creditors. This general rule is subject to a properly drafted subordination agreement that provides that junior creditors are not to be paid until senior debt is paid in full, including with postpetition interest. The issue of whether the subordination agreement includes interest that accrues postpetition has been litigated frequently. Prior to the effective date of the Bankruptcy Code in October 1979, a number of cases held that the subordination provision in the agreement

---

505 346 F. Supp. 839 (S.D. Fla. 1971).

506 346 F. Supp. at 844–45.

had to provide *explicitly* for a senior creditor's right to postpetition interest.[507] This became known as the "Rule of Explicitness." The Bankruptcy Code included a provision regarding the effectiveness of contractual subordination that had not been part of the prior Bankruptcy Act: "A subordination agreement is enforceable in a case under this title to the same extent that such agreement is enforceable under applicable nonbankruptcy law."[508] Bankruptcy courts then considered whether the Rule of Explicitness survived the adoption of the Bankruptcy Code, with varying results. The Eleventh Circuit, faced with an agreement subject to New York law, certified the question[509] to the New York Court of Appeals. The New York court responded that it recognized the Rule of Explicitness and stated it would "require specific language in a subordination agreement to alert a junior creditor to its assumption of the risk and burden of allowing the payment of a senior creditor's postpetition interest demand."[510] While the First Circuit held the Rule of Explicitness had been distinguished in "its classic form,"[511] following a trial on the merits, the court held that the language of the indenture was not clear enough. Specifically, the court held, following an evidentiary hearing on the surrounding circumstances, that "interest due or to become due" did not evidence an intent to subordinate to the payment of postpetition interest.[512] A subsequent decision from the bankruptcy court in the Southern District of New York advised that the Rule of Explicitness should be followed.[513] The court in the Bank of New England case cited as an example of clarity as to the right to postpetition interest the language in Section 11.03 of the 1983 version of the American Bar Association Model Simplified Indenture.[514] Similarly, the court in *K-V Discovery Solutions* referenced with approval the

---

507 *See Cont'l Ill. Nat'l Bk & Tr. Co. v. First Nat'l City Bank of N.Y.*, 528 F.2d 789 (10th Cir. 1976); *Bankers Life Co. v. Mfrs. Hanover Trust Co.*, 514 F.2d 400 (2d Cir. 1975); *In re Time Sales Fin. Corp.*, 491 F.2d 841 (3d Cir. 1974).

508 11 U.S.C. § 510(a).

509 *In re Southeast Banking Corp.*, 156 F.3d 1114 (11th Cir. 1998).

510 *Matter of Southeast Banking Corp.*, 93 N.Y.2d 178, 186 (1999).

511 *HSBC Bank v. Brock (In re Bank of New England Corp.)*, 364 F.3d 355, 364–65 (1st Cir. 2004).

512 *In re Bank of New England Corp.*, 646 F.3d 90 (1st Cir. 2011) (Rule 510(a) eliminated reliance on Rule of Explicitness but evidence showed parties did not intend to subordinate junior debt to postpetition interest on senior debt). But see *In re Southeast Banking Corp.*, 179 F.3d 1307 (11th Cir. 1999) (Rule of Explicitness actually part of state non-bankruptcy law doctrine and should be applied).

513 *In re K-V Discovery Solutions, Inc. et al. v. Deutsche Bank Tr. Company Americas, et al.*, 496 B.R. 330 (Bankr. S.D.N.Y. 2013).

514 ". . . [H]olders of Senior Debt shall be entitled to receive payment in full in cash of the principal of and interest (including interest accruing after the commencement of any such proceeding)". 646 F.3d 90, 98.

language in the 1999 American Bar Association Model Debenture Indenture.[515] The definition of "senior debt" should make clear whether postpetition interest is to be included as senior debt.

5. Subordination of Series under One Indenture

In the Eastern Airlines bankruptcy, three series of equipment trust certificates were issued under one indenture. The first series of certificates purported to be senior in right. The value of the collateral was more than the outstanding principal amount of the first series certificates but less than the total principal amount of all three series. The collateral trustee sought a declaration directing appropriate distribution to three classes of certificateholders. The court, assuming the applicability of the Rule of Explicitness, held that the first, second and third priority certificateholders were co-owners of one secured claim against the debtor rather than holders of three separate secured claims for purposes of determining whether the first priority creditors were oversecured and, thus, entitled to postpetition interest. The court also held that the first priority certificateholders were not entitled to postpetition interest prior to payment of principal to lower priority certificateholders absent explicit language in the indenture establishing such entitlement.[516] Even in a non-bankruptcy setting, it has been held that the Rule of Explicitness is an interpretive principle of New York state contract law[517] applicable to the competing rights among four layers of senior lenders. Thus, the importance of clearly describing the priority of claims postpetition cannot be overstated.

6. Operation of the X-Clause

Under the typical subordination clause, a junior creditor must pay over any consideration received from the obligor to senior indebtedness until the senior indebtedness is paid. However, in some indentures these clauses contain an exception, known as the "X clause," in the case of a plan of reorganization which, for example, provides that mortgage bonds, preferred stock or similar high-priority-ranking security be issued to the holders of senior debt, and common stock be issued to the debentureholders. The theory is that this kind of distribution

---

515 "The Model Debenture Indenture adopted by the ABA in 1999 contained a similar clause also providing for explicit priority rights to postpetition interest, even though not allowed as a claim in the bankruptcy case. The clause in the Indenture in this case generally follows this standard language to the extent it includes in the definition of Senior Indebtedness) 'all interest accrued subsequent to the commencement of any bankruptcy or similar proceeding, whether or not a claim for postpetition interest is allowable as a claim in any such proceeding . . .'." 496 B.R. 336.

516 *In re Ionosphere Clubs, Inc.*, 134 B.R. 528 (Bankr. S.D.N.Y. 1991) (Rule of Explicitness not satisfied and language of indenture ambiguous).

517 *U.S. Bank Nat'l Assoc. v. T.D. Bank, N.A.*, 569 B.R. 12 (S.D.N.Y. 2017) (the documents, as a whole, put the lenders on clear notice that the repayment of principal could be subordinated to the superior claims for postpetition interest).

gives practical effect to the subordination and therefore turnover is not required. A bankruptcy court's treatment of contractual subordination with an X-clause has taken any number of different forms. These forms have ranged from making the court the sole arbiter, under its equitable powers, in fashioning plan distributions that were fair and reasonable, to entirely excepting junior or subordinated securities distributed under a plan from turnover to senior creditors. In an attempt for subordinated creditors to introduce a greater element of certainty into the treatment of subordination clauses in bankruptcy, subordinated creditors began to contractually bargain for more palatable treatment by including a form of X-clause in the subordination provision. The X-clause generally modified or limited full subordination. A version of the X-clause in an indenture became necessary to market the subordinated securities, especially in the private placement market.[518]

7. The Other Creditors May Agree to Payment of the Subordinated Debt, or the Senior Debtholders May Waive Their Rights to Enforce the Subordination Agreement

Other creditors may agree to allow payment of the subordinated debt prior to payment of senior debt. In such a situation, the senior debtholders may be deemed to have waived their rights under the subordination agreement.

Creditors may be held to have waived their rights stemming from a subordination agreement in which senior creditors acquiesced in the payment of loans to subordinated debtholders.[519]

---

518 See discussion contained *In re Envirodyne Indus., Inc.*, 29 F.3d 301 (7th Cir. 1994). It has been held that, because an X-clause, as a general proposition, creates only limited exceptions to the otherwise applicable subordination provisions, it therefore must be read narrowly, and in harmony with the entire contract. *In re Dura Auto. Sys., Inc.*, 379 B.R. 257 (Bankr. D. Del. 2007). The form of X-clause in the MSI provides as follows:

> "Section 11.13. Exception for Certain Distributions. The rights of holders of Senior Debt under this Article do not extend (a) to any Distribution to the extent applied to the Trustee's rights to compensation, reimbursement of expenses or indemnification or (b) to (i) securities which are subordinated to the securities distributed to the holders of Senior Debt on terms no less favorable to the holders of Senior Debt than the provisions of this Article, or (ii) Distributions under any plan approved by the court in any Proceeding."

519 *In re Credit Indus. Corp.*, 366 F.2d 402 (2d Cir. 1966).

XIV. Workouts – The Indenture Trustee and Bondholder Roles

A. Role of the Indenture Trustee and Bondholders in a Workout

An indenture trustee does not make investment decisions for the holders of securities. Rather, it is the role of the indenture trustee to seek compliance with the terms of the indenture once a default or troubled situation has occurred. When compliance cannot be achieved, the indenture trustee's role is to work with the holders to obtain the best recovery possible for the holders under the circumstances.[520] Likewise, holders of securities issued under an indenture should consider the opportunities to provide direction, instruction and indemnity to the indenture trustee to foster a prompt, reasonable resolution rather than prolonged default with litigation meltdown or a hard-landing bankruptcy. The role of the holders, especially the large and sophisticated holders, is (i) to the degree possible, to provide direction and instruction to the trustee, (ii) to the degree appropriate, to become restricted in trading or to execute a non-disclosure agreement and (iii) to obtain the information necessary, including material non-public information, to determine if an out-of-court workout is possible and the appropriate terms thereof. The inability or refusal of holders to participate in the workout process complicates any workout and reduces the chances of a successful resolution. Further, those holders who do become involved must view their efforts as being for the benefit of all holders and the involved holders should not attempt to pursue terms of a workout that would not be beneficial to all holders of the same issue equally.

The extent of the indenture trustee's involvement in a workout depends upon whether or not the bond issue includes holders who will participate in the workout and give direction to the trustee. The holders of the troubled issue may include institutional, par purchasers who are sophisticated and capable of facilitating a workout. However, the securities may change hands during the workout and the holders may include distressed debt buyers who normally purchase at a discounted price. A workout will require a balancing of the interests between par and discount purchasers. Ideally, a substantial percentage of holders will be willing to play an active role in the workout discussions, which likely will restrict them from trading for a period of time. Such holders can provide input to the indenture trustee through direction, instruction and

---

520 One commentator has contrasted the duty of corporate directors to maximize value with the duty of traditional trustees to preserve the value of trust assets. Steven L. Schwartz, *Bond Defaults and the Dilemma of the Indenture Trustee*, 59 ALA. L. REV. 1037 (2008). The indenture trustee, *sui generis*, upon default, acts as a prudent person under the terms of the indenture. See Chapter I.

indemnity or through general advice on what type of consideration the holders would accept. Many workouts include an ad hoc committee of holders to direct the process. The indenture trustee often welcomes the involvement of such a committee, assuming the committee is not seeking to prejudice the rights of non-represented holders.

In issues where the holders consist of small, unsophisticated holders, however, the indenture trustee's role in a workout may have to be more aggressive in order to protect all bondholders. Frequently, in a defaulted private placement, institutional holders number fewer than 15. They may meet among themselves and provide direction and instruction to the trustee, or they may meet with the obligor separately from the indenture trustee to negotiate a workout. As a result of these differences, dependent upon the size and makeup of the bondholder group, the indenture trustee must decide its actions on a case-by-case basis and adjust its actions accordingly.

B. Why Use a Workout

One could take the position that, upon default, an indenture trustee should proceed with remedies without consideration of refinancing, debt restructuring or other non-remedial resolutions. In this view, the indenture trustee has no choice— either the obligor pays, or the obligor is sued for the full amount of the securities. If the result of this strategy is a bankruptcy filing by the obligor, so be it. This procedure would unquestionably be simpler, but the results would not always be beneficial to the holders. It will sometimes be to the holders' advantage to attempt a workout, when recovery from the exercise of remedies does not appear substantial, or if it appears the significant expense of bankruptcy and the loss of value therefrom can be avoided. The holders may want the obligor to remain in business.

Financial workouts and accommodations can provide better economic results for the holders and the indenture trustee for a number of reasons. Bankruptcy involves much uncertainty. Workouts have been embraced out of concern over the cost and uncertainty of litigation and bankruptcy. When an obligor and an indenture trustee articulate their views and those views disagree, the ensuing litigation can be expensive, time consuming and unproductive. Professional fees in large bankruptcy cases can range in the millions, dependent upon the size of the company (in the Lehman bankruptcy, professional fees were in the billions). As court costs increase, another, less expensive way, which is less detrimental to ongoing business and financial relationships, has been sought. The production of documents, e-discovery and pleadings with few tangible results in litigation and bankruptcy have led businesses, governmental bodies, indenture trustees and bondholders to the same conclusion: workouts are worth exploring and, in the appropriate circumstance, can be beneficial.

At the start of a workout, all parties should proceed with a realistic appraisal of what can be achieved and of both the benefits and the detriments of a workout. The benefits include the possibility of a cheaper, quicker, more efficient more and controlled resolution of the problem without the negative publicity and turmoil associated with litigation and bankruptcy. Still, workouts are risky. Everyone must agree to hold their peace, not institute litigation, not step out of rank and not file a petition for bankruptcy. There may be irreconcilable differences over certain issues, which must be isolated or left for another day. Some parties may be unable to be controlled. There generally is no effective means by which to bind 100 percent of public debt to a settlement other than through a consensual workout or by a settlement approved by a court as reasonable, fair and binding upon all. The alternatives to workouts (litigation, foreclosure, bankruptcy and lender liability lawsuits) are themselves obstacles to a successful workout. In a successful workout, participants either deal with these issues or find mechanisms by which to avoid them.

It is imperative that bondholders organize as soon as they detect a problem and the possible development of a workout situation. Delay only weakens the bondholders' position. Financial institutions will doubtless have been monitoring the situation for some time. Information and knowledge about the obligor's operations create negotiating leverage when a default arises and restructuring moves onto the fast track. As bondholders attempt to organize, and management continues to fumble, losses are mounting, equity is eroding and valuable assets are up for sale to support underperforming units.

C. Legal Issues Implicated by a Workout

While certain private placements may contain provisions regarding amendments to the terms of the documents by a majority of the holders, indentures issued pursuant to the Trust Indenture Act and other indentures adopting the structure of the act are subject to the provisions contained in TIA Section 316(b). Section 316(b) provides that the right of any holder to receive principal and interest cannot be impaired without the holder's consent. While the formal bankruptcy process eliminates this standard and substitutes its own test to bind members of a class,[521] an out-of-court restructuring must deal with the terms of Section 316(b). Thus, as will be discussed in Chapter XIV below, a successful workout often takes the form of an exchange offer (perhaps including exit consents), a prepackaged plan of reorganization or a Section 3(a)(10) proceeding. It must be kept in mind that if the subject of the workout is debt issued in Europe,

521 11 U.S.C. § 1126(c).

the indenture or loan agreement typically contains collective action clauses whereby a super-majority of creditors of that debt can bind all and drag non-consenting holders along.[522]

D. Phases of Workouts

1. Phase I: The Gathering Storm

The first phase of any workout is early detection. To prevent the often debilitating cost of litigation and bankruptcy, it is important to spot at an early stage the deteriorating financial condition of the borrower. There are some noteworthy signs of financial difficulties: cash-flow problems, reduced sales volume, decline in markets, lower bond ratings, defaults in debt covenants, declining gross margins, deteriorating operating income masked by income from extraordinary transactions, increased credit lines, increased credit inquiries, disproportionate ratio of debt to income or equity, increased capital expenditures, increased stretching of trade payables, increases in accounts receivable, failure to make tax payments, unexplained resignation of officers and directors, decline in debt service coverage, sales of profitable businesses, non-rational mergers and acquisitions, delay in receipt of audited financials, large sales of stock by officers and directors, circular borrowing, trade requiring COD or letter of credit treatment, catastrophic losses that cannot be compensated through operating profit, change in market through regulatory restrictions or prohibitions, significant litigation or unsatisfied large judgments, or problems with other creditors.

Many of these signals of financial distress have their basis in lack of managerial direction. Thus, it is important in any workout to determine at the earliest possible stage whether management is credible and, more importantly, able to perform in a way that facilitates the workout. Problems with managerial direction can be identified by review of the following factors: (1) breakdown of informational channels; (2) displayed inability or unwillingness to perceive remedies for troubled situations; (3) inability to bring sufficient resources to bear to correct the problems in a timely fashion; (4) refusal to act due to business-related factors; and (5) failure to accomplish workouts due to perceived lack of confidence of creditors in management or of management in creditors. If, in considering a workout, the indenture trustee or bondholders note that there is a lack of managerial direction, it is likely that a workout will not succeed unless the management is changed. However, given serious questions of lender liability raised by any attempt to remove management, the indenture trustee or bondholders should not be a part of such effort. Nevertheless, the indenture trustee and bondholders must be able to

---

522 The concept is part of PROMESA, The Puerto Rico Oversight, Management, and Economic Stability Act, P.L. 114-187, 114th Cong., 2d Sess. (June 30, 2016), and Title VI thereof, but a court hearing on the fairness and reasonableness is required. This is similar to a Section 3(a)(10) proceeding discussed in Chapter XV. *See also* Spiotto at 14.

identify the early warning signals of financial distress and, upon identification of financial distress, determine whether or not the company has the ability and willingness to successfully proceed with a workout. In an ideal situation, the indenture trustee will be acting with input from a significant group of holders.

2. Phase II: Stop the Bleeding

The second phase of a workout is the prompt identification of the sources of the problem and the initiation of contact with the obligor. At the beginning of the workout, the parties should consider the execution of a pre-workout agreement confirming that discussions shall not be binding unless memorialized in a document duly executed and delivered in accordance with the terms of the indenture. It is important in this stage that the indenture trustee become advised, either through professionals who are independent of the obligor or through independent professionals retained by the indenture trustee, of the causes of the distressed financial condition. In the best case, the professionals will be acceptable to a majority of the holders. It makes no sense to restructure the debt obligations, and accept a reduced debt service requirement, if the underlying cause for the financial difficulties has not been resolved. The areas of the obligor's operations that are significant bleeders must be identified and the problem addressed before a workout can be finalized. It is crucial at this stage to collect and analyze the information regarding the financial condition and operation of the debtor.

More likely than not, information obtained from the obligor at this time will be confidential, non-public information. The indenture trustee and bondholders receiving this information will typically be required to execute confidentiality letters or non-disclosure agreements to prevent the disclosure of such information while discussions are ongoing to see if the situation can be remedied. This results in those bondholders being restricted from buying or selling the securities. Frequently, the confidentiality agreement is of a limited duration and may contain provisions requiring the obligor to release the confidential information to the public under certain circumstances, thereby burning off the restricted status of the holders. If at all possible, the indenture trustee should be directed by the majority of holders to enter into such an agreement. Any forbearance or standstill agreement must recognize that, pursuant to Section 316(b) of the TIA, there can be no agreement impairing an individual holder's right to payment when due without its consent (subject to a bankruptcy proceeding or Section 3(a)(10) exchange, to be discussed in the next chapter). Of course, Section 316(a)(2) of the TIA allows the holders of 75 percent of the indenture securities to consent to the postponement of any interest payment for a period of three years. The indenture trustee is to disregard directions from known insider parties regarding this interest payment postponement.

The indenture trustee in Phase II, through appropriate professional assistance and hopefully with the input and direction of holders, must make the following analysis: (a) assess short-term and long-term cash requirements; (b) understand the company's business plans and strategic direction; (c) identify losing operations and cash users; (d) identify successful operations and cash providers; (e) identify key personnel with the knowledge of business operations; and (f) develop a plan to stop the bleeding (such as sell cash users, enhance operation of cash producers, restructure business operations, reduction of expenses). This analysis will enable the indenture trustee and holders to determine whether or not the business entity has any chance of success in a financial workout. The indenture trustee should be assisted in this analysis by independent and qualified advisers and experts whose opinion the indenture trustee may in good faith rely upon.[523]

It is also important at this stage for the indenture trustee and holders to set specific standards or conditions to ensure that the workout is accomplishing its objective. These standards or conditions should be structured in such a way that any significant variation from projections would allow the indenture trustee, holders and other creditors to seek appropriate remedies rather than continue with a doomed workout scenario. The use of outside directors and independent experts, who are detached from past failures, is crucial to the workout's success.

3. Phase III: Marshalling of Assets and Information

Once the bleeding has been stopped, the indenture trustee must make a determination of the secured and unsecured debt of the company. The valuation of assets is crucial to determining the ability of the company to handle future debt. Also, a determination of what assets are encumbered, as compared to those that are unencumbered, will provide a basis for determining what collateral or working capital will be available for use in the workout. There should be a determination of the sustainability and affordability of the debt obligations of a reorganized company and sufficient liquidity for the company to be able to withstand the inevitable economic downturns in the business cycle. All this should be wrapped up in an objective feasibility determination by an independent financial advisor.

a. Analysis of Debt

The indenture trustee, ideally in conjunction with the holders, should review all debt of the obligor. Such review may include: (1) the determination of any setoffs or reduction of that debt; (2) the identification of any insider transactions and whether any cause of action exists; and

---

523 Prior to default, under Section 315(a)(2) of the TIA, the indenture trustee may rely upon the statements in opinions or certificates complying with the terms of the indenture. Post-default, seeking out the advice and opinions of experts should be evidence of the prudence of the indenture trustee.

(3) an analysis of whether the debt owed to a creditor may be equitably subordinated by virtue of inequitable conduct with regard to the debtor or other creditors.

b. Valuations of Assets

The indenture trustee should consider retaining the services of an independent appraiser to value the physical assets of the debtor. There are many theories of appraisal: going concern, replacement and liquidation values. Perhaps the most important figure to keep in mind is the liquidation value, as the holders should never accept any debt restructuring that gives them less than they could receive in liquidation. Consideration should be given to having such appraiser and other experts retained by counsel to protect the privileged nature of the information.

c. Marshalling of Assets

It is important to determine what assets exist and how they can best be used by the debtor and creditors. In that regard, the use of accountants and other advisors would provide independent, credible input in connection with this matter. If necessary, the indenture trustee and holders should consider retaining their own accounting or business consulting advisors. To reduce costs, it will be helpful if the indenture trustee and holders can coordinate such retention.

Any discussion of marshalling of assets would be incomplete without discussing the dynamic tension between unsecured and secured creditors. Issues such as the validity of the liens of the secured creditors, whether or not the liens were obtained contemporaneously with funds being lent and whether there was simultaneous and adequate consideration must be addressed by the indenture trustee and holders. In addition, any inequitable conduct by secured lenders may cause unsecured creditors to consider possible causes of action against such secured creditors. See Appendix XIV-A, Checklist of Information Necessary for Indenture Trustee and Holders to Develop a Workout Strategy.

4. Phase IV: Workout Techniques and Gaining the Edge

Once the indenture trustee and holders have stopped the bleeding, have marshalled the assets and understand the facts necessary for an appropriate structure, the indenture trustee and holders may then proceed with developing a workout plan. Normally, the obligor and its consultants will place on the table a proposed plan or structure. This is the point where the challenge and, frankly, the fun begins. While legal positions and existing rights are important, an effective workout requires skilled negotiation. The workout process is actually 90 percent negotiation and 10 percent perseverance. The edge is gained by obtaining all possible facts and having nearly as much meaningful information about the financial affairs of the obligor as its chief financial officer has. Structuring a workout involves balancing interests of the secured and unsecured creditors and, to a lesser degree, the interests of equityholders. The development of the plan must involve all parties sharing the pain (based on their respective priorities and the added benefits to all of a consensual resolution), as opposed to providing benefits to a select few.

a. Sharing the Pain

The indenture trustee should work with the holders to prevent the pain of any debt restructuring being visited on the bondholders more than on other creditors. Accordingly, the indenture trustee in cooperation with the holders should conduct an analysis of the following considerations:

(1) Identification of the priorities of debt.

- Secured, unsecured and subordinated.
- Off-balance-sheet obligations (*e.g.*, rents, pensions, post-retirement benefits).

(2) Compromise of claims and subordination.

- Which claims will be reduced, set off?
- Any counterclaims?
- What claims will be diminished given subordination, and who will benefit from that subordination?

(3) Senior versus junior creditor problems.

- Is subordination effective?
- To what degree should it be given effect in a workout?
- Is subordination only to be effective in liquidation?

(4) What is the relationship with trade debt and bank debt?

- Will they participate in providing trade credit and bank financing after the workout?
- It is important that such matters be resolved and assurances obtained by the indenture trustee and the public debt so that the restructuring will be successful.

(5) What is the relationship among public debtholders?

- Are they institutional? Distressed buyers?
- Are there small, unsophisticated holders?

- What effect does the constituency of public debt have on the consideration that should be received in the workout?
- What relationship will public debt have with bank and trade creditors?

(6) Methods of sharing the pain.

- Pro rata—everyone receives the same, based upon the amount of the debt.
- Trace cash or benefits to the source and value—if you have provided cash for more valuable operations, you will receive a larger piece of consideration, while those who funded the losers will receive less.
- Dilution can occur with consolidation of operations or companies whereby some creditors of better, more financially sound companies will suffer more pain than creditors of companies that have been the real losers will.

(7) It is important in any discussion of sharing the pain that the indenture trustee and holders understand the goals and desires of trade creditors, management, bank debt, and shareholders. The indenture trustee and holders may attempt to discuss how to maximize the return for the public debtholders by meeting some of the goals and desires of others.

(8) Discussion of a debt restructuring will involve dealing with any tax benefits. However, in connection with sharing the pain, the public debtholders who are asked to give up something in a debt restructuring must also be able to obtain upside potential.

b. Further Considerations in Negotiating a Workout

The indenture trustee, in participating with holders in negotiating the equitable sharing of pain in a workout, should consider the following to bring about a successful result:

(1) What is the ability of the debtor to obtain refinancing? Are trade debt and bank debt available?

(2) Is the debt restructuring being validated by an independent advisor as to its feasibility and, if appropriate, is there an opinion of an investment banker or other independent professional as to the fairness of any exchange for public debtholders?

(3) What tax benefits will inure to the benefit of public debtholders and creditors, or are such benefits being retained solely for the current equityholders?

(4) Is there a standstill agreement between the debtor and creditors, or a moratorium agreement? Is it appropriately limited in time and does it contain appropriate termination events?

(5) Is there a pre-workout agreement with strong non-waiver language? (It can be part of standstill agreement.)

(6) What assurances do creditors' groups have that the workout will continue to be negotiated without the outbreak of litigation or bankruptcy?

(7) What sales of assets have occurred and what are planned in the future? As an operating entity, will the company be able to survive, given such sale of assets?

(8) Is the remaining core business of sufficient size to service the debt?

(9) Will the debtor sign an acknowledgment of debt and consent to judgment, which documents would allow the indenture trustee to obtain a judgment without the worry of defenses and delay if the workout is not successful?

(10) Does the obligor plan on sales of stock or equity participation?

(11) Is there any possibility of raising capital through the sale of ownership or equity interest?

(12) What change of management is being considered?

(13) If no change of management is to be made, what assurances do the indenture trustee and the public debtholders have that past management will be capable of bringing about the successful reorganization?

(14) What use is being made of consultants?

(15) Is there an advisory or oversight committee of creditors to monitor progress?

(16) Have realistic goals and objective standards been placed in order to measure the progress of the workout?

(17) Have negotiations between the creditors' groups been allowed?

(18) Has each creditors' group been able to discuss with other creditors, as opposed to the obligor, what they are receiving under the proposed workout and their view of the feasibility of any type of workout?

(19) What guarantees from third parties (parents, affiliates, equity owners) will be obtained in order to ensure such parties' continuing cooperation and support?

(20) What assurances have been received from trade creditors as to the continued availability of trade credit?

(21) Have trade creditors required letters of credit, COD or other restrictive forms of payment that would hinder, if not be fatal to, the workout?

(22) What effort has been made to determine whether or not the company can be sold and, if it were sold, what would be benefit to the creditors of such sale?

(23) What proposed changes in the debtor's covenants, modification of the indenture or use of supplemental indentures are being considered?

(24) Is the proposed debt restructuring to be done as a prepackaged plan where consents to the debt restructuring will be obtained from two-thirds of the holders and, if necessary, the obligor will go into bankruptcy to consummate the debt restructuring?

(25) Are exit consents being contemplated by the obligor and, if so, what is the impact to holders not consenting?

(26) What acceptance of past defaults under the indenture must be allowed?

(27) What curing of past defaults will be obtained?

(28) What documentation is necessary for the workout?

(29) Are the terms and conditions adequate?

E. Dangers to Be Avoided in a Workout

From the perspective of the indenture trustee, there are a number of legal problems and considerations surrounding a workout. Obviously, an indenture trustee and the holders want to avoid the dilemma of their involvement in a workout being such that it would cause the indenture trustee or the holders to be charged as "control persons" or "insiders." The indenture trustee is not the appropriate party to solicit approval of new management or a workout from its holders. Rather, the trustee's role is to inform the holders of recommended actions of any proposals received from the obligor.

In any workout in which collateral is to be received, there is always the question of whether such collateral or new securities could be considered a preference in the event of a bankruptcy and, further, whether such security interests will be properly perfected. It is important that a determination be made that any collateral received in a workout is not a fraudulent conveyance. Specifically, it must be established that the transfer of the property of the debtor was not made while the debtor was insolvent, without adequate consideration. Thus, the method, timing and perfection of collateral are important and must be agreed upon as part of the workout. There could be an opinion of an investment banker or financial advisors as to solvency and adequate consideration given as part of the restructuring and such should be addressed to or usable in litigation by the indenture trustee and holders. In addition, other creditors' groups should not receive collateral and have it perfected prior to the time when the indenture trustee receives its collateral.

The release of any collateral by the indenture trustee must be consistent with the requirements of Section 314 of the TIA, as well as the terms of the indenture. Absent the approval of all holders, collateral cannot be released unless a court of competent jurisdiction has approved such release.

Equitable subordination, equitable liens and constructive trusts are theories that readjust the priorities among creditors. These theories can be used by an indenture trustee or holders against other creditors. Similarly, these theories can be used against the indenture trustee. Every effort must be made to prevent such claims being asserted against the indenture trustee and, therefore, public debtholders.

It is possible to have third parties hold and protect the collateral while a workout is being discussed. Receiverships can be obtained by petitioning a court and demonstrating that there has been a wasting of assets, that the collateral is not being properly protected and that there is no equity in the obligor. A problem with the appointment of a receiver is that often a court requires the posting of a bond, and the indenture trustee is usually not in a position to post such bond.

F. Structuring a Workout to Protect the Indenture Trustee and Holders

In order to structure a successful workout, it is important, as noted above, for the indenture trustee, in connection with financial advisors and the debtholders, to determine the nature and scope of the financial difficulties. In this regard, an indenture trustee and the debtholders should recommend a structure to the workout approach. In structuring the workout, the indenture trustee should consider the following factors:

1. Provide an objective standard of performance in order to judge the scope of the problem (budget versus actual financial performance reviewed during the workout from month to month, etc.).

2. The obligor should first attempt resolutions that are relatively easy and inexpensive to implement (*e.g.*, top-level diagnostics to review business plans). If the obligor cannot implement these simple plans, it is unlikely that the larger workout scenario will be accomplished.

3. Set realistic goals and time schedules using master calendars and action plans.

4. Provide a basis for comparison with other companies in similar businesses.

There are a number of ways in which a creditor can enhance its position in a workout. For example, the indenture trustee and debtholders should consider suggesting the following: (1) obtaining collateral as part of the negotiations of the workout; (2) using acknowledgment of debt and consent to judgment, as previously discussed; (3) reducing the exposure by having some preference-proofed paydown of the debt or grant of collateral during the time of negotiating the workout; (4) discussing what type of credit enhancement may be available as part of the workout; (5) using guarantees from third parties, equityholders, parents or affiliates of the obligor; (6) receiving third-party collateral, *i.e.*, collateral that comes from solvent parents, subsidiaries, affiliates or equityholders; and (7) determining if refinancing may be available whereby the public debtholders will be taken out either in whole or in part.

Defensive litigation by the indenture trustee, ideally at the direction of a majority of holders, may be necessary for (1) the preservation of assets and, specifically, to prevent such assets from being transferred to third parties without proper consideration; and (2) the protection of the obligor's business relationships. Such litigation, even during the workout, may be a source of recovery from third parties. Attached as Appendix XIV-B is a checklist of considerations for the indenture trustee and holders facing a workout situation, and Appendix XIV-C is a list of special problems to be considered. At times, the company and the indenture trustee and holders may agree that the best workout strategy is a sale of the assets of the company. Attached as Appendix XIV-D is a checklist of issues for the indenture trustee and holders to consider when deciding on a sale strategy.

G. Monitoring the Workout

In any successful workout, it is important to set up objective standards or milestones to ensure a periodic review of the continued success of the workout. While the indenture trustee's role is normally to monitor compliance with the terms of the indenture, it is helpful to have consultants, such as the company's auditors or the accountants to a group of creditors, provide periodic reports to the indenture trustee and holders as to compliance with specific terms and objectives of the workout. In addition, the documents evidencing the terms of the workout can provide for appropriate certification by accountants as to whether the company has met the established goals of the workout plan.

It is important that performance standards and objective criteria be established in order to determine the success of a workout. If a workout is not accomplishing its desired effect, the indenture trustee, public debtholders and others should be able to take appropriate action.

While there has been little said as to possible liability of public debtholders, certain creditors may be liable if they attempt to delay bankruptcy and litigation through the use of purported workout discussions which, in reality, are merely an attempt to provide those creditors with enough time to avoid preference problems. Any use of a workout as a technique entered into in bad faith in order to increase one's benefits to the detriment of other creditors would not only be actionable but, more likely than not, would be deemed to be a fraudulent conveyance. The statute of limitations for fraudulent conveyance is longer than that for preference.

H. Tax Implications to a Workout

Because the structure of the workout can have significant tax implications for the obligor and for the debtholders, it is prudent for the indenture trustee to enlist the assistance of accountants independent from the obligor to review any proposed workout for tax minefields. At the very least, holders should be adequately advised to consult their own advisors to the tax considerations.

Appendix XIV-A
Checklist of Information Necessary for Indenture Trustee and Holders to Develop a Workout Strategy

I. General Corporation Context Information

- corporate organization charts
- articles of incorporation and bylaws
- corporate minute books
- joint venture and partnership agreements
- stockholder lists
- a summary of locations where the company is qualified to do business as a foreign corporation
- management organization charts

II. Information on Capitalization Structure and Liabilities

A. Equity Securities/Private Ownership Interest

All agreements and supporting documentation describing each issue of equity security of the company, including:

- warrant agreements
- stock option agreements
- stock voting agreements
- offering memorandum or prospectus

B. Debt Securities

All agreements and supporting documentation describing each issue of debt securities, including:

- indentures, as amended and supplemented
- subordination agreements

- guarantees
- security agreements to collateralize the issue
- offering memorandum or prospectus

C. Bank Debt

All agreements for bank debt and supporting documentation describing each credit facility, including:

- waivers and amendments
- security agreements and mortgages, along with filing or recording information
- borrowing base certificates, if applicable
- guarantees
- subordination agreements
- interest rate protection agreements and devices (*e.g.*, futures contracts)
- foreign exchange contracts, swap agreements and derivatives

D. Other Debts, Liabilities and Obligations

This information will include:

- a list of all liabilities, including contingent liabilities and off-balance-sheet liabilities
- a summary of the terms of trade debt and an aging of trade payables
- a copy of all agreements (other than specific invoices) to purchase
- a copy of all mortgages, purchase money agreements and other debt instruments
- a copy of all leases, both financial and operating, and all other executory contracts
- a copy of all consulting contracts
- a copy of all employment contracts
- a copy of all collective bargaining agreements
- a copy of each pension or profit-sharing plan and other retirement or employee benefit programs
- a summary of all insurance coverages, with copies of all policies

- a copy of all broker contracts and arrangements and statement of position and all future contracts for goods or commodities
- a copy of all agreements to fix or hedge the costs of goods, including futures and options contracts
- a current report on environmental matters (including actual or potential liability)
- a list of all pending or threatened litigation, including arbitration matters, along with a synopsis of the likelihood of success on each matter and an analysis of the potential amount of any adverse adjudication tested against the limits of insurance coverage

III. Information on Assets

A schedule of all assets, including their (a) locations; (b) gross valuations at both fair market value and liquidation value; and (c) net valuations after considering liens and encumbrances, along with supplemental data including:

- accounts receivable agings, charge-off history and policies to manage late payment and uncollectible accounts
- depreciation policies and schedules
- a summary of all officer, director and employee loans and guarantees
- a schedule of net operating loss carryforwards and all tax-sharing agreements
- a summary of all claims and causes of action undertaken by the company or any of its subsidiaries as plaintiff, along with an analysis of the amount and timing of probable recoveries
- all intellectual property agreements (licenses, trademarks or patent or filings) and documents, along with a schedule of projected revenues therefrom
- identification of all underperforming assets
- a list of all bank accounts and a summary of the company's and its subsidiaries' cash management system and procedures
- a list of all assets and business segments acquired in last five years with specific identification of assets or business acquired, purchase price, valuation of assets or business at the time of acquisition and now and whether each business has since operated at a profit or loss
- going-concern and liquidation valuation of the company and its subsidiaries continued and for the company and each of its subsidiaries

IV. Information about the Company's Business

A. Historical Information

- annual reports to shareholders
- proxy statements
- prospectuses
- consulting studies
- internal control and management reports
- audit letters from the company's independent accountants

B. Competitive Information

- market share statistics
- projections for industry growth
- peer group analysis
- analysis of economic cycles and trends

C. Business Plan

The company's strategy to effect a turnaround should address critical issues for operating the business, including information about:

- profit-improvement programs
- revenue enhancers
- justification of new businesses
- summaries of historical data and trends
- unprofitable operations and cash bleeders to be discontinued
- customer relations problems and key employee morale
- capital expenditures
- marketing considerations
- overhead and expense allocations
- inventory controls and management

V. Financial Information and Projections

Financial projections should be prepared under various scenarios, using worst-case, most-likely and optimistic assumptions. Financial information should include:

- historical statements of cash flow, balance sheets and income statements, presented on both a consolidating and consolidated basis
- projected statements of cash flow, balance sheets and income statements, presented on both a consolidating and consolidated basis for the period of the debt restructuring
- analyses explaining the historical results and assumptions supporting the projections
- a capital expenditures budget

Appendix XIV-B
Checklist of Considerations for Workout

The indenture trustee, ideally pursuant to the directions by or in coordination with the debtholders, should consider the following checklist in pursuing the roles of indenture trustee and holders, respectively, in a workout:

(1) Time is of the essence.

- Review documents.
- Make sure of the perfection of security interests.
- Insure a clear paper trail of the workout effort.
- Never put in writing that which you do not want read to a judge or jury.

(2) Investigate the nature and extent of the defaults under the indenture and under other credit instruments.

(3) Review and determine the available remedies and considerations available in a financial workout. Identify the bleeding operations and assess whether the bleeding can be stopped and what the true value of the company is on a restructured basis.

(4) Communicate with other creditors.

- Use caution to avoid making overly pessimistic or overly optimistic statements to the holders or other creditors' groups.
- Remember that creditors may be viewed as a deep pocket as to any damages suffered from statements made.
- Determine whether or not other creditors believe that a workout is possible, and whether such creditors are cooperating with the debtor.

(5) Consider the formation of an ad hoc bondholder committee or other creditors' groups to negotiate the workout plan.

- Identify the major creditors.
- Identify those holders who can help effectuate a workout (normally, large institutional holders who agree to be restricted and, sometimes, distressed buyers or smaller holders who may be interested in being part of those negotiations).

(6) Marshall the assets and information.

(7) Develop a plan that shares the pain resulting from the workout.

Appendix XIV-C
Special Problems Connected with Workout Proposals

The following is a list of some of the types of problems and issues involved in a structuring of a workout proposal:

(1) The methods to be used to determine the actual debt and the actual value of security held by secured creditors, and what equity exists in such collateral

(2) The techniques to be used to transform an affiliate, insider or control person debt into equity in order to effect a debt restructuring

(3) Possible causes of action by the company and its creditors against errant officers and directors for mismanagement and fraud, claims against director and officer insurance carriers, claim procedures, and possible theories and lawsuits—such claims and causes of action may very well be a significant source of recovery and provide needed cash and working capital

(4) Whether creditors should allow the use of corporate assets to fund officer and director indemnity claims in pending security fraud lawsuits

(5) Possible strategies and defenses to disruptive litigation:

- Foreclosure suits brought by secured creditors
- Security fraud actions brought by public debtholders and stockholders
- Suits for collection of debt brought by trade creditors and other unsecured creditors
- Antitrust and takeover suits

(6) The methods to be used to sell assets

(7) Possible use of tender offers and exchange offers as a means of obtaining consent of public debtholders to a workout

(8) The effectiveness of any subordination agreement

(9) The effect of bankruptcy on creditors' rights and, specifically, whether the workout is binding on the creditors in bankruptcy

Appendix XIV-D
Preliminary Checklist of Issues for Indenture Trustee and Holders

I. Analysis of Assets and Liabilities

A. Assets and Liabilities

1. Liabilities

(a) Off-balance-sheet liabilities

(b) PBGC liabilities

(c) ERISA issues

(d) Environmental claim

(e) Tax claim (FICA) and individual income tax obligations

(f) Other liabilities (including payments to management, letters of credit supporting contracts and insurance)

(g) Capital lease obligations

(h) Sale and servicing agreements and potential liability and availability of parts

2. Assets

(a) Any assets not subject to collateral

(b) Guaranty

(c) Intercompany receivables

B. Valuation of Assets

1. Going concern

2. Liquidation

3. Company by company

C. Analysis of compliance with documentation

D. Lien and perfection analysis

1. Any additional collateral capable of being obtained

2. Any cleanup necessary to documentation or perfection

3. All documents and evidence of perfection signed and appropriately filed?

E. Insurance policies

F. Deposit account control agreements

G. Servicing agreements and ability to continue service

II. Issues on Liquidity and Cash Flow Needs

A. What are cash flow needs weekly for the next three weeks, the next three months and on a rolling 12-month basis?

B. When, if ever, will the company be net cash flow positive before debt service?

1. What costs can be reduced or eliminated?

C. Budget for operation

D. Quick sources of cash

1. Accelerated collections of accounts receiveable

2. Accelerated sale of equipment and servicing

E. Other sources of financing or cash

F. Any repayment of management bonuses or professional payments or equity of infusion by new owner?

G. Management contracts: return of prior bonus payment, disclosure of all contracts

III. Issues on DIP Forbearance financing

A. Budget and amount needed and terms and pricing

B. Additional collateral and adequate protection

1. Tax refunds, if any

2. Intangibles

3. Claims against third parties, if any
4. Avoidance actions
5. Directors and officers insurance policy
6. Additional collateral
7. Any valuable servicing or sale contracts

C. Venue of UCC foreclosure sale or bankruptcy

D. Timing of filing and issues on maximizing value

IV. UCC Foreclosure Sale or Bankruptcy Filing Issues

A. Preference for Section 363 sale in bankruptcy and possible dip financing unless borrower can demonstrate actual and significant benefits to UCC sale over and above Section 363 sale

B. First-day orders

1. Interim DIP financing/use of cash collateral
   (a) Validation of liens
   (b) Additional collateral
   (c) Section 506(c) waiver
   (d) Avoidance actions pledged
2. Cash management order
3. Companies that will file for bankruptcy
4. What company or operations to be left out of filing and why?
5. Professionals to be retained for the company
6. Sales process milestones as part of DIP credit agreement or final order

C. Creditors' committee and administrative costs

D. Sale of assets

1. Ability to sell parts as operating group (Section 363 sales or sales out of bankruptcy, UCC foreclosure sale)
2. An ability to sell debtors as a whole

3. Method of sale: investment banker

4. Customer-servicing issues and effect on sales process

E. Soft landing vs. hard landing

1. Basic game plan for UCC foreclosure sale or bankruptcy

2. Whether sale acceptable to holders without UCC foreclosure sale or Section 363 sale possible

3. Is this a liquidating Chapter 11?

4. Potential recovery

(1) Credit bid reservation

(2) Peg bid so that any bids must exceed a set price determined by independent expert or a court

5. Transfer of real estate leases, servicing contracts, distribution contracts

6. Transfer tax issues

V. Timetable

A. Company's timetable for filing and sale, if deemed appropriate

B. Company's proposal for interim forbearance financing and/or continued operations and necessity of any interim or DIP financing above use of cash collateral

C. Meeting and presentation by borrower

D. Analysis of benefits and detriments of UCC foreclosure sale and bankruptcy sale efforts

E. Other sources of recovery

XV. Structuring the Workout: Exchange Offer with Prepackaged Plan, Section 3(a)(10)

A. Exchange Offer Basics for the Indenture Trustee and Debtholders

When an obligor on a debt offering proposes an exchange offer, the indenture trustee and debtholders should quickly consult with counsel to assist in reviewing the situation. Nevertheless, it is helpful to be generally familiar with the forms an exchange may take. When an obligor is struggling with liquidity issues but wants to avoid the great expense of a free-fall bankruptcy, it may consider reducing debt by means of an exchange offer. The issuer may offer to exchange new debt securities for its outstanding debt. These new securities may bear a reduced interest rate, include a stretch-out of the maturity date or modify the terms of the existing securities. An exchange offer is subject to the anti-fraud provisions of the Securities Act and Rule 10b-5 of the Securities Exchange Act. Because the offer and issuance of the securities pursuant to the exchange offer are deemed to be an issuance of new securities, the registration provisions of the Securities Act apply. Accordingly, the indenture trustee and debtholders likely will be faced with one of the following types of transactions:

1. A Registered Exchange Offer

This is probably the most costly approach to an out-of-court restructuring. The obligor files an S-4 registration statement with the SEC with respect to the new securities being offered.[524] The SEC typically takes over a month to provide comments to which the obligor must respond.

a. Exit Consents

The exchange offer may include the use of exit consents. Exit consents involve a situation where an obligor, in seeking to obtain the consent of holders to an exchange offer or other transaction, such as the significant reduction of covenants contained in the indenture, offers to exchange or purchase a certain amount of its debt securities, for a specified price or other security, often at below the price or value set to redeem the bonds provided that the selling holders consent to the removal from the indenture of the specified covenants. Through this purchase, a percentage of the holders will consent to the removal of the covenants at issue from the indenture. The exit consent, *i.e.*, the consent given by those holders who are selling their securities, is then used by the company to modify the indenture. The remaining holders, who

---

524 Securities Act § 5, 15 U.S.C. § 77e.

have not consented to the modifications of the indenture, are left with an indenture significantly weaker than that originally bargained for. Depending upon the financial condition of the obligor, such action may very well be the topic of litigation or, at the very least, serious discussions between the holders and the obligor. The use of exit consents has been approved by one court.[525]

b. Combination with Prepackaged Plan of Reorganization

Exchange offers may include a prepackaged plan provision. The holder agrees that, in voting in favor of the exchange offer, the holder will be deemed to have voted for the same economic treatment in a plan of reorganization. Section 1126(b) of the Bankruptcy Code provides that a pre-bankruptcy acceptance can count toward the requirements of Chapter 11 if it is solicited in accordance with applicable non-bankruptcy law.[526] In order for a class of creditors to accept a plan of reorganization, two-thirds in principal amount outstanding of the indebtedness, or one-half in number of holders voting, are required to vote in favor of the proposed treatment. An obligor may determine this standard is achievable. In the early days of the utilization of the prepackaged plan process, there were issues as to whether the record owner or beneficial owners of debt securities were the proper parties to vote for the prepackaged plan.[527]

2. Section 3(a)(9)

An exchange offer pursuant to Section 3(a)(9) of the Securities Act is based upon an exemption from registration requirements of the act. However, the conditions for the exemption

---

525 *See Katz v. Oak Indus.*, 508 A.2d 873 (Del. Ct. 1986) (upheld exit consent as not "wrongfully coercive)". *See also Gradient OC Master, Ltd. v. NBC Universal, Inc.*, 930 A.2d 104 (Del. Ch. 2007). *See* Discussion in *Roe*, "The Voting Prohibition in Bond Workouts," 97 YALE L.J. 232, 248 (1987), where the author speculated that an appellate court might hold that exit consents, if they devalue the target bonds, destroy the individual bondholder's freedom to choose to retain the original bond. According to the author, future courts may hold that the lack of real choice so undermines the policy of individual consent embodied in Section 316(b) of the TIA that recapitalization by use of such consents must be prohibited. *See* English case, *Assénagon Asset Mgmt. S.A. v. Irish Bank Resolution Corp.* [2012] EWHC 2090 (ch) (27 July 2010) (exit consents an abuse of the purposes for which bondholder majorities are given power to bind minorities) (Eng.). *But see Kass v. Eastern Air Lines, Inc.*, 1986 WL 13008 (Del. Ct. 1986) (*Katz* rule applied since "sweetener" offered to all bondholders); Keegan S. Drake, *The Fall and Rise of the Exit Consent*, 63 DUKE L.J. 1589 (2014).

526 *See* Jason A. Cohen, Melissa Jacoby, Jane Sullivan, *Soliciting Bondholders Pre-Petition: Understanding the Basics*, 22 AM. BANKR. INST. J. 28 (2004); *see* General Order M-454 of the United States Bankruptcy Court for the Southern District of New York, *In re Amended Procedure Guidelines for Prepackaged Chapter 11 Cases* (June 28, 2013) ("Guidelines").

527 *See, e.g., In re The Southland Corp.*, 124 B.R. 211 (N.D. Tex. 1991). Now balloting typically is structured so that the beneficial holders submit individual ballots to their nominees who are or who act for the registered holders, who in turn submit master ballots to the debtor. *See Guidelines*, Ex. C.

imposed by Section 3(a)(9) make it less than attractive in many situations: (i) the issuer of the securities must be the same, (ii) there can be no additional consideration from the security holder except the security to be exchanged, (iii) the offer is directed exclusively to the existing security holders and (iv) no commission or remuneration accompanies from the exchange. Thus, although the delay and expense of registration are avoided, particularly the restriction or the issues of the new security and inability to compensate the party who solicits the exchange can be problematic.

3. Private Exchange Offer—Private Placement Exemption

Another exemption to the registration requirements of the Securities Act is Section 4(a)(2) of the Securities Act: a non-public offering. The offerees must be sophisticated investors with access to the information that registration under the Securities Act would provide.[528] No general solicitation is permitted, but bankers may be paid to solicit the beneficial holders of the securities to be exchanged. The new securities will be restricted. Exit consents frequently are part of the exchange.

4. Section 3(a)(10) Exemption

An additional exemption from registration is offered by Section 3(a)(10) of the Securities Act, which applies to court-approved settlements.

Section 3(a)(10) of the Act exempts from registration:

> Except with respect to a security exchanged in a case under title 11, any security which is issued in exchange for one or more bona fide outstanding securities [or] claims . . . , where the terms and conditions of such issuance and exchange are approved, after a hearing upon the fairness of such terms and conditions at which all persons to whom it is proposed to issue securities in such exchange shall have the right to appear, by any court, or by any official or agency of the United States, or by any State or Territorial banking or insurance commission or other governmental authority expressly authorized by law to grant such approval . . . .[529]

---

528 *SEC v. Ralston Purina Co.*, 346 U.S. 119 (1953).

529 15 U.S.C. § 77c (a)(10).

The SEC has promulgated a number of requirements for Section 3(a)(10) to be effective:[530]

- The securities must be issued in exchange for securities, claims or property interests, not cash;
- A court or authorized governmental entity must approve the fairness of the terms and conditions of the exchange;
- The reviewing court or authorized governmental entity must (i) find that the terms and conditions of the exchange are fair to those to whom the securities will be issued; and (ii) be properly advised that the issuer will be relying on the court's findings to issue securities;
- The reviewing court or authorized governmental entity must hold a hearing before approving the fairness of the terms and conditions of the transaction;
- A governmental entity must be expressly authorized by law to hold the hearing;
- The fairness hearing must be open to everyone to whom securities would be issued in the proposed exchange;
- Adequate notice must be given to all those persons; and
- There cannot be any improper impediments to the appearance by those persons at the hearing.

B. The Role of the Indenture Trustee and the Holders in the Exchange Offer or Debt Restructuring

The indenture trustee is not the party that will make the investment decision as to whether any proposal to alter or amend the basic terms of the security should be accepted. The indenture trustee does not vote on behalf of the holders, but rather the holders themselves must vote to accept or reject a restructuring as part of a bankruptcy plan or out-of-court approach. In connection with any debt restructuring or exchange offer, it is the holders who must make their own individual investment decisions as to whether such restructuring or exchange offer is fair, reasonable and appropriate. However, in a court proceeding, the indenture trustee may settle a dispute that, under certain circumstances, with adequate notice, will bind the holders.

---

530 Securities and Exchange Commission, Division of Corporate Finance: Revised Staff Legal Bulletin No. 3 (CF), Oct. 20, 1999.

The indenture trustee's role is to make sure that, based upon the facts known by the indenture trustee, an exchange offer or a debt restructuring presented to the holders is not woefully inadequate or unreasonable and does not fail to disclose a material fact. For example, a number of years ago, an indenture trustee, upon default of notes issued by a retirement center, obtained additional collateral and a mortgage interest in property located next to the retirement center. While the indenture trustee was attempting to negotiate a resolution to the default, which contemplated a new party coming in to purchase the facility and pay off the notes in full, a not-for-profit entity offered the noteholders 60 cents on the dollar in exchange for their notes. The exchange offer made no reference to the on-going negotiations or the fact that, in the trustee's opinion, the noteholders would ultimately receive 100 cents on the dollar based on their claims and collateral interest. Upon learning of the exchange offer, the indenture trustee sought a court determination of the fairness of the exchange offer and whether it violated any state or federal securities laws. The court hearing the matter not only enjoined the exchange offer, but approved a sale of the facility which provided the indenture trustee with payment in full of all principal, interest and expenses due under the indenture.[531]

This example illustrates the role of the indenture trustee in the exchange offer. The indenture trustee should make sure that notice and communication of the exchange offer are reasonable and complete. Again, it should be stressed that the indenture trustee is not the appropriate party to make an investment decision for the holders. However, when the indenture trustee knows that the exchange offer fails to disclose a material fact or is woefully inadequate, unless the indenture trustee takes some action, the holders may not be fully informed and cannot make their own investment decision. At that time, the indenture trustee may bring these matters to the attention of either a court of competent jurisdiction for a determination of the fairness of the exchange offer or the regulators of state or federal securities laws to see if any action ought to be taken. A note of caution, however: the indenture trustee should not become involved in solicitations or communication battles between the obligor and the holders.

Sometimes the indenture trustee cannot avoid disputes between the obligor and the bondholders over the terms of an exchange offer. The most dramatic example of a trustee being caught in the cross fire has been the dispute between Argentina and 9 percent of its bondholders that raged for over a decade.[532]

---

531 *Harris Tr. and Sav. Bank v. Covenant Living Centers-North, Inc.*, Case No. 80 C 1194 (N.D. Ill. Mar. 31, 1980) (order approving settlement).

532 *See, e.g., NML Capital, Ltd., et al. v. The Republic of Argentina*, 727 F.3d 230 (2d Cir. 2013).

C. Communication to Holders Regarding Exchange Offer

The indenture trustee should not view its role as one of direct involvement in an exchange offer. An exchange offer is simply an offer by the obligor to exchange the present securities held by the holders for either new securities or new securities and cash. If the exchange offer involves an offer to over 30 holders, such an offering must either be registered under the applicable state and federal securities laws or be qualified for an exemption from registration under these laws. As noted above, an offering made to a small group of holders in a private placement (35 or fewer) would qualify for an exemption from registration under Section 4(a)(2) of the Securities Act as a transaction by an issuer not involving any public offering. Under Section 3(a)(9) of the Securities Act, an exchange by an issuer with only its existing security holders is exempt where no commission or other remuneration is paid or given directly or indirectly for soliciting such exchange. Under Section 3(a)(10) of the Securities Act, an exchange for one or more of the bona fide outstanding securities, claims or property interests, or an exchange partly for property and partly for cash, is exempt, where the terms and conditions of issuance and exchange are approved after a fairness hearing.

Given the fact that any communication to the holders of the exchange offer will be pursuant to either a registration statement or an exemption to the obligor under the Securities Act, the basic communication of the exchange offer should be made by the obligor to the holders. The indenture trustee should not be a direct party to the communication. Obviously, the indenture trustee normally provides the obligor with a list of the names and addresses of the registered holders. In addition, the indenture trustee can mail an exchange offer to the holders, including known beneficial holders, as a service to the obligor, but at no time should the exchange offer be characterized as a part of any communication by the indenture trustee to the holders.

At times, issuers may attempt to solicit consents of the holders to a supplemental indenture. Such a solicitation is not an exchange offer, since no new security is being offered, and thus there can be no violation of the federal securities law.[533] With the exception of raising objections to the proposed supplemental indenture, either first to the obligor or then to a court of competent jurisdiction, the indenture trustee has no direct role. As referred to above, the efficacy of exit consents agreeing to strip covenants from the indenture is controversial, and the indenture trustee should always attempt to obtain appropriate opinions in connection with supplemental indentures as to the validity of any exit consents.

---

533 *See Sharon Steel Corp. v. Chase Manhattan Bank*, 521 F. Supp. 104 (S.D.N.Y. 1981), *aff'd*, 691 F.2d 1039 (2d Cir. 1982), *cert. denied*, 460 U.S. 1012 (1983).

The obligor has a duty to give reasonable notice to the holders in connection with a request for action such as an exchange offer. The SEC normally requires at least 20 days' notice.[534] The courts generally have protected the holders' expectation of reasonable notice and have implied a covenant of fair dealing between the obligor and the holders in various transactions.[535] The trustee has no duty to advise the holders as to the fairness of the exchange offer or to alert the holders of their rights under the indenture unless there is a provision in the indenture to that effect.[536] If the terms of the exchange offer do not violate any of the terms of the indenture, the holders' rights are not abridged.[537] However, where an exchange offer is not 100 percent successful, the indenture trustee for the non-exchanging holders may seek a declaratory judgment or injunctive relief to prevent any injustice caused by the exchange. If the exchange offer does not result in the exchange of all of the securities, the indenture trustee continues as indenture trustee for the remaining holders.

D. Analysis of Good Faith Obligations

As suggested above, the obligor making the exchange offer owes an implied duty of good faith and fair dealing to the holders. This duty not only extends to giving reasonable notice and disclosing all material facts, but also includes not pursuing an offer or transaction that clearly is contrary to the best interests of the holders. The best example of a breach of this duty is the exchange offer referred to above. There, the obligor knew that the holders would receive 100 cents on the dollar but attempted to take advantage of a possible lack of knowledge on the holders' part by offering 60 cents on the dollar.

The indenture trustee has no duty to pass on the fairness or appropriateness of the exchange. However, the indenture trustee may, upon learning certain facts concerning the exchange offer, object if the offer is grossly inadequate or if it unjustifiably impairs the bondholders' claims. This is similar to the indenture trustee's right to object to a plan of reorganization in bankruptcy.

---

534 *Van Gemert v. Boeing Co.*, 520 F.2d 1373 (2d Cir. 1975), *cert. denied*, 423 U.S. 947 (1975); Exchange Act Rule 14e-1 through 14e-8, 17 CFR §§ 240.14 e-1 *et seq*.

535 *Pittsburgh Terminal Corp. v. Baltimore & Ohio R.R. Co.*, 680 F.2d 933 (3d Cir.), *cert. denied*, 459 U.S. 1056 (1982); *but see Lorenz v. CSX Corp.*, 1 F.3d 1406 (3d Cir. 1993) (finding no breach of implied covenant in failure to provide notice where notice rights were not included in indenture).

536 *See Broad v. Rockwell Int'l Corp.*, 642 F.2d 929 (5th Cir. 1981), *cert. denied*, 454 U.S. 965 (1981); *Browning Debenture Holders' Comm. v. DASA Corp.*, 560 F.2d 1078 (2d Cir. 1977).

537 *See Brucker v. Thyssen-Bornemisza Europe, N. V.*, 424 F. Supp. 679 (S.D.N.Y. 1976), *aff'd*, 559 F.2d 1202 (1976); *Prescott, Ball & Turben v. LTV Corp.*, 531 F. Supp. 213 (S.D.N.Y. 1981).

E. Who Is the Watchdog?

The indenture trustee has the duty, upon default, to take such actions as a prudent person would take in connection with his or her own affairs. If there is a default existing at the time of the exchange offer, the indenture trustee must carefully consider whether the exchange offer is consistent with the indenture trustee's exercise of rights and remedies under the indenture. The indenture trustee should not allow an exchange offer to deprive the bondholders of the benefit of remedies that the indenture trustee has been attempting to bring about. However, if there is no default, the indenture trustee may have no reason to question or doubt the statements made by the obligor. In the case of no default, the exchange should be carefully reviewed by the holders in order to determine whether it meets with their individual investment positions.

An exchange offer, whether made when an indenture is in default or not, is clearly subject to the anti-fraud provisions of the Securities Exchange Act. Any failure of the obligor to live up to its obligation to completely and adequately provide all material and relevant information with respect to the exchange may subject the obligor to legal actions by both the holders and state or federal securities commissions.

F. When to Object, If Ever?

The indenture trustee should consider objecting to an exchange offer only when it knows with a reasonable certitude that the actions taken by the obligor in presenting the exchange offer to the holders are grossly unreasonable under the circumstances, and that the consideration offered is woefully inadequate. If at all possible, input from the holders should be sought. While the indenture trustee should not substitute its judgment for the investment decisions of the holders, the indenture trustee may object to a woefully inadequate exchange offer by instituting a proceeding in state or federal court to determine its fairness or to determine whether the exchange offer violates any of the anti-fraud or other provisions of federal or state securities laws. Such an action should be taken by an indenture trustee only after it has received advice of counsel and has been counseled that no other method is available to resolve the difficulties the indenture trustee perceives in the exchange. For the most part, obligors should be able to present their exchange offers without any fear of being second-guessed by the indenture trustee, and the indenture trustee should be able to assume that any exchange offers presented by the obligor are reasonable and fair. It is, and should be, only the extraordinary case in which an indenture trustee need raise an objection. In the default situation, an exchange offer should be more carefully reviewed because of the indenture trustee's higher standard of care and the rights and remedies with which the indenture trustee is entrusted.

G. Why a Prepackaged Plan

Exchange offers can be successful in many instances in restructuring the debt of a troubled company. However, holdouts, non-tendering holders who retain the original securities and benefit from the financial concessions made by other tendering holders, can be a problem. As a consequence, exchange offers typically are conditioned upon a very high level of acceptance, often as high as 85–95 percent of the outstanding principal amount. Therefore, a relatively small group of security holders can serve to block the success of an exchange offer. An approach to this threat is a combination exchange offer/prepackaged plan solicitation. In this way, if the high level of acceptance required by the exchange offer is not met, assumedly at least 66-2/3 percent in dollar-amount voting and majority of holders of claims voting will have consented to the prepackaged plan. The company is then able to go forward with a plan of reorganization in the bankruptcy that will bind all the securityholders, including the holdouts.

Prepackaged plans have other advantages as well. Too many securityholders have either read of or experienced the difficulties of complex free-fall bankruptcies where administrative expenses deplete essentially all of the available cash of the bankrupt entity and where the long and arduous nature of the bankruptcy process significantly impairs the value of the claims of the creditors. In addition, the management of a bankrupt entity often conveys to its creditors throughout the proceeding that its business prospects have been adversely affected by the bankruptcy proceeding itself. Thus, competitors of companies in free-fall bankruptcies capitalize on the bankruptcy of a market competitor to attract new business, to keep customers away from the bankrupt entities and to lure customers away from the bankrupt entities. Finally, there is uncertainty in bankruptcy: a creditor does not know whether its claim or interest will be properly treated in the bankruptcy proceeding. Accordingly, creditors oftentimes will either make a concession or take a softer position in the negotiation of a prepackaged plan in order to avoid the uncertainty of a free-fall bankruptcy.

Section 1126(b) of the Bankruptcy Code provides an expedited process by which a debtor may propose and confirm a Chapter 11 plan. Under this provision, a prospective debtor may solicit consents for a proposed plan from its major creditor constituencies and thereafter file a petition under Chapter 11. After filing under Chapter 11, the debtor schedules a single bankruptcy court hearing to pass on the adequacy of its prepetition disclosure materials and confirmation of its proposed plan. A "prepackaged" bankruptcy reorganization is one method of binding all of the security holders to a restructuring.

A summary of the steps involved in a prepackaged reorganization includes:

1. A plan is negotiated with major creditor constituencies;

2. A proposed plan, disclosure statement and voting ballot to solicit creditors' votes are prepared and disseminated;

3. All parties with impaired interests under the reorganization plan are entitled to vote. The debtor must receive votes of at least two-thirds in amount and more than one-half in number of each class of claims voting to accept the plan. Only claims actually voted are computed in determining creditor acceptance;

4. The bankruptcy petition under Chapter 11 is filed, together with the prepackaged plan and creditor acceptances thereof; and

5. The bankruptcy court holds a hearing to consider whether the prepetition disclosure materials meet the requirements for adequate disclosure as set forth in the Bankruptcy Code and any applicable rules of the SEC. If disclosure is found adequate, the debtor presents a certification of creditor acceptances and the court considers whether the proposed plan can be confirmed under the requirements of the Bankruptcy Code.

H. Procedural Issues Related to Prepackaged Plans That the Indenture Trustee and Holders Should Be Generally Aware Of

1. Disclosure

The indenture trustee should review the disclosure document for the adequacy of the information contained therein. Holders should also do the same. Above all, the disclosure document given to any impaired creditor to vote on a prepackaged plan should be as accurate and truthful as conceivably possible. All communication should be forthright with no material fact left undisclosed. The disclosure statement should include such items as compensation of officers and directors, the proposed treatment for each class of claims and interests, possible insider relationships, payments to banks or other secured creditors, treatment of preferences and fraudulent conveyances, tax considerations for the company and holders, and any other possible claims. While the disclosure documentation for a prepackaged plan should be thorough, it should also be, to the degree possible, short and concise.

Under Section 1126(b) of the Bankruptcy Code, the solicitation of a consent for acceptance or rejection should be in compliance with applicable non-bankruptcy law, rules and regulations governing the adequacy of disclosure in connection with such solicitation. If non-bankruptcy law relating to such a solicitation does not exist, then the disclosure must provide adequate information as defined in Section 1125(a) of the Bankruptcy Code. In essence, adequate information is that information of a kind and in sufficient detail, as far as practical in light of the nature and history of the debtor and the condition of the debtor's books and records, that would enable a hypothetical reasonable investor, typical of the holders of claims or interests in the relevant class, to make an informed judgment about the plan. Adequate information must also include a discussion of the federal and state tax consequences of the plan to the debtor and any successor. Adequate information need not include such information about any other possible or proposed plan. Disclosure must be complete and in compliance with applicable law. In reviewing whether a disclosure statement provides adequate information, a court will consider the complexity of a case and the costs and benefits of providing additional information.

2. Form of the Ballot

In general, the form of the ballot should comply with the official form of the ballot provided for in the Bankruptcy Rules and should be clear and easily understood. However, as the factors in a prepackaged plan grow in complexity, so does the size and intricacy of the ballot. For example, in some cases, certain creditors may be asked to release claims or, if the exchange is successful, to consent to an exchange of debt for equity as opposed to a prepackaged plan. But above all, efforts should be made to comply with the official form of ballot. There should be separate boxes for acceptance and rejection.

3. Time for Voting

Sufficient time should be given for the recipient of the disclosure documents to review them, consider them and respond. Generally speaking, a time period between 20 and 30 days would be optimal. Although some prepackaged plans have been confirmed in as little as ten days, and others between 15 and 20 days currently, a 21- to 30-day time period appears to be more reasonable given the consideration of SEC rules and regulations, general mailing procedures and the need for sufficient time to review the disclosure documents. Bankruptcy Rule 3018(b) specifically provides that acceptances or rejections of the plan may be voided if the court finds that an unreasonably short time period was prescribed for a creditor or equity security holder to accept or reject the plan. Additionally, the solicitation must be in compliance with Section 1126(b) as noted above. All creditors of the affected class who are voting and all holders of equity security interests should receive a copy of the disclosure documents and the ballot. The Bankruptcy Court for the Southern District of New York, the venue for many prepackaged plans, has adopted a set of procedural rules regarding such cases, including voting-period guidelines.[538] Attached as Appendix XV-A is a Timeline of Events for a Prepackaged Plan. Attached as Appendix XV-B is a Timeline of Events for a Registered Exchange Offer with a Prepackaged Plan Alternative.

---

538 *See* Guidelines, available at www.nysb.uscourts.gov/court-info/local-rules-and-orders/general-orders.

4. Support of Holders

Hopefully, an organized debtholder group representing a significant percentage of the outstanding securities will take a position on the prepackaged plan. These holders can direct and instruct the trustee as to action to be taken in the case.

I. Standard for the Section 3(a)(10) Fairness Hearing

1. A Federal District Court Is a Proper Forum

As previously mentioned, a Section 3(a)(10) exemption has been utilized to effect debt restructurings, and since the restructuring may affect principal, interest and the nature of the collateral, Section 3(a)(10) provides a mechanism to respond to the requirements of TIA Section 316(b). Following a determination of fairness, the new securities issued in exchange for outstanding securities are exempt from registration under Section 3(a)(10). It is clear that a federal district court of proper jurisdiction may hold a hearing to determine fairness.[539] However, it has been held that a proceeding in Argentina for approval of an exchange did not meet the test.[540]

2. The Fairness Determination

There is no statutory definition of "fairness" as used in Section 3(a)(10). The staff of the SEC typically does not pass on the question of fairness in a no-action letter, and very few courts have examined the concept in the context of Section 3(a)(10). One commentator, however, suggests that the standard should remain flexible, concluding that:

> [it] may well be reasonable and desirable in that section 3(a)(10) is potentially available with respect to very different kinds of transactions and the fairness of the terms and conditions of any one of those transactions will ultimately depend on the particular facts and circumstances surrounding the proposed issuance of the securities sought to be exempted from registration. In the light of the broad availability of the Exchange Exemption, it is further arguable that no single definition of the term 'fairness' would be practicable.[541]

---

539 *See, e.g., Metlyn Realty Corp. v. Esmark, Inc.*, 763 F.2d 826 (7th Cir. 1985); *SEC v. Blinder Robinson & Co.*, 511 F. Supp. 799 (D. Colo. 1981); *Blexnak v. C.G.S. Scientific Corp.*, 387 F. Supp. 1184 (E.D. Pa. 1974); *SEC v. Texas Int'l Corp.*, 498 F. Supp. 1231 (N.D. Ill. 1980); *Merger Mines Corp. v. Grismer*, 137 F.2d 335 (9th Cir. 1943); *LIN Broadcasting Corp.*, SEC No-Action Letters, [1972–73 Transfer Binder] Fed. Sec. L. Rep. (CCH) ¶ 79, 154 (Nov. 8, 1972); *VTR Inc.*, SEC No-Action Letter, [1971–72 Transfer Binder] Fed. Sec. L. Rep. (CCH) ¶ 78, 518 (Oct. 8, 1971).

540 *In re Bd. of Dir. of Multicanal S.A.*, 314 B.R. 486 (Bankr. S.D.N.Y. 2004).

541 Barbara A. Ash, *Reorganizatiosn and Other Exchanges under Section 3(a)(10) of the Securities Act of 1933*, 75 NW. U.L. REV. 1, 17–18 (1980).

3. Discussion of Fairness Cases

In *Metlyn Realty Corp. v. Esmark, Inc.*,[542] the defendant made a tender offer to purchase outstanding shares of a target corporation. The target's shareholders brought several class action suits alleging various violations of the anti-fraud provisions of the securities laws in the tender offer. A settlement was reached which involved an exchange of the defendant's shares for shares of the target company held by the plaintiff class. The court ordered that notice of the settlement and of the hearing be given to all class members. Investors holding approximately one-half of the 1.5 million outstanding shares objected to the settlement. After a hearing as to the fairness of the settlement, the trial court approved the settlement and exempted the securities from registration.

Few published opinions on Section 3(a)(10) discuss the actual mechanics of a fairness hearing. *SEC v. Blinder Robinson* is one of the few cases that consider the fairness of an exchange of new securities for outstanding securities in the context of Section 3(a)(10).[543] In *Blinder Robinson*, the court considered the fairness of a settlement agreement involving the offer of common stock and promissory notes to shareholders and former shareholders in exchange for a release of claims. In its determination of fairness, the court specifically noted that it was not faced with a situation in which the securities involved were exchanged as part of a class action settlement. As a result, the court found that it was not required to measure the adequacy of the relief obtained by comparing the value of the securities to be issued with the claims of loss as required under Rule 23(e). The court held that the factors to be considered in a Section 3(a)(10) fairness analysis include:

1. the recommendations of counsel;
2. the scope of the discovery record as an indicator of the adequacy of the investigation into the facts;
3. the apparent alternatives to the settlement;
4. the nature and volume of responses from those receiving notice of the hearing; and
5. the opportunity for direct participation in the process of obtaining full disclosure.

Applying the above factors, the court found the exchange in question to be fair under Section 3(a)(10) and the securities to be issued and therefore exempt from the registration

542 763 F.2d 826 (7th Cir. 1985).

543 511 F. Supp. 801 (D. Colo. 1981).

requirements of the act. Important to the court's decision were: (1) the arm's-length nature of the negotiations leading to the settlement agreement; (2) that the alternative to the settlement would require the liquidation of the business entity involved, and the result would be only a partial recovery; (3) that of approximately 11,000 mailed notices of the fairness hearing, only 15 responses were received; and (4) that there had been a full and fair opportunity for all affected persons to participate directly in the process of obtaining full disclosure of the matters involved in the settlement. The court also found that its decision was consistent with the purpose of the Securities Act, which was to protect investors by promoting full disclosure of the information necessary to the making of informed investment decisions. The court stated that:

> The fairness hearing here has been the functional equivalent of the full disclosure which would be provided on an appropriate prospectus and registration statement.[544]

Subsequently, the court in the *Macleod-Stedman* case[545] approved a determination of fairness with respect to the issuance of debt and equity securities to settle a default with an indenture trustee for mortgage notes. The court noted that the use of Section 3(a)(10) was particularly appropriate since the section was intended primarily to offer financially troubled corporations an alternative to the burdens of registration. The court supported its finding of fairness based upon a consideration of the value of the settlement compared to the possible results of litigation.[546] In that case, the noteholder group directed and instructed the indenture trustee to join the agreement of settlement and commence the litigation in conjunction with the noteholders.[547] The indenture trustee complied with the direction.

4. Other Section 3(a)(10) Cases

It is not unusual for a Section 3(a)(10) proceeding to be brought as a class action to bind all debtholders. This was the procedure pursued in the previously discussed *Macleod-Stedman* case as well as the *LaBarge* and *Las Colinas* cases.[548] In *Macleod-Stedman*, the request for class

---

544 *Id.* at 802.

545 *Cont'l Assurance v. Macleod-Stedman*, 694 F. Supp. 449 (N.D. Ill. 1988).

546 *Id.* at 468.

547 *Id.* at 454.

548 Class action settlements in effect binding all bondholders to the terms of a workout were approved in *MBank Dallas et al. v. V. LaBarge, Inc.*, 86 C 9583 (N.D. Ill. Dec. 29, 1986) and *Kemper Inv'rs Life Ins. Co. v. Las Colinas Corp.*, 88 C 9162 (N.D. Ill. June 27, 1989); *Allstate Life Ins. Co., et al. v. Lincoln Prop. Assoc. Ltd. et al.*, 1 1CV-93-0547 (M.D. Pa. Nov. 24, 1993). Although not a Section 10(b)(5) case, in the WPPSS case, the Ninth Circuit approved the settlement with the issuer and participant utilities entered into by the indenture trustee and bondholder class over the objections of a group of bondholders. *Class Plaintiffs v. City of Seattle*, 955 F.2d 1268 (9th Cir. 1992). *See also Cont'l Assurance*

certification ultimately was withdrawn when there was 100 percent participation in the restructuring agreement. Mandatory class actions were certified in the other two cases. Settlements continue to be approved utilizing Section 3(a)(10), including approving exchanges of debt for membership interests[549] and stock.[550]

J. The Impact of Section 316(b) on Debt Restructurings

Section 316(b) of the TIA[551] provides in relevant part:

> Notwithstanding any other provision of the indenture to be qualified, the right of any holder of any indenture security to receive payment of the principal of and interest on such indenture security, on or after the respective due dates expressed in such indenture security, or to institute suit for the enforcement of any such payment on or after such respective dates, shall not be impaired or affected without the consent of such holder ...

Congress had several purposes in enacting Section 316(b). The first purpose was to assure the negotiability of indenture securities by making certain the promise to pay was unconditional.[552] Another purpose was to assure that any debt restructuring was subject to judicial scrutiny.

A number of commentators have decried the negative impact Section 316(b) has on out-of-court reorganizations.[553] Moreover, several recent lower court decisions dealing with debt restructurings have suggested that some courts may apply an expansive reading to Section 316(b) so that it is a broad protection against restructurings rather than a narrow protection against majority amendment of core terms. Several district court cases have held that Section 316(b) of the TIA, which protects a bondholder's right to payment of principal and interest and thus prohibits majority bondholders from agreeing to modify payment terms, precluded out-of-court restructurings. One district court case, commonly known as *Marblegate I*, involved an out-of-court restructuring of debt through an intercompany sale of assets foreclosed by secured creditors and

---

Co. v. Macleod-Stedman, Inc., 694 F. Supp. 449 (N.D. Ill. 1988) and *IDS Life Ins. et al. v. Darling-Delaware Co., Inc. et al.*, 91 C 5166 (N.D. Ill. Nov. 24, 1993). *But see Cont'l Bank & Tr. Co. v. First Nat'l Petroleum Tr.*, 67 F. Supp. 859 (D.R.I. 1946).

549 *SEC v. Founding Partners Capital Mgmt.*, 2014 WL 2993780 (M.D. Fla. July 3, 2014).

550 *Oceana Capital Grp. Ltd. v. Red Giant Entm't, Inc.*, 150 F. Supp. 3d 1219 (D. Nev. 2015); *Chapel Investments, Inc. v. Cherubim Interests, Inc.*, 177 F. Supp. 3d 981 (N.D. Tex. 2016).

551 15 U.S.C. § 77 ppp.

552 American Bar Foundation Commentaries on Model Debenture Indenture Provisions, 1967, p. 234.

553 *See, e.g.*, Mark J. Roe, *The Voting Prohibition in Bond Workouts*, 97 YALE L.J. 232 (1987).

the release by secured creditors of the parent's guarantee of unsecured notes,[554] and the other case involved the removal of the parent company's guarantees on the corporate notes.[555] These rulings, which upheld minority holder objections to these deal modifications, could complicate future workouts, including exchange offers, and lead to a resort to bankruptcy court. This result is contrary to that anticipated in sovereign-debt restructurings in Europe where collective-action clauses that impose super-majority (66-2/3 or 75 percent) vote provisions are required,[556] and to the result that is reflected in PROMESA with its qualifying modification of debt if supported by two-thirds of the relevant debt pool, albeit subject to court approval.[557]

However, a decision by the Second Circuit in *Marblegate* vacated and remanded the orders of the District Court in *Marblegate I* referred to in the previous paragraph, which held that the restructuring violated Section 316(b).[558] The Court of Appeals held that this payment protection provision in the TIA applies only to formal amendments to legally enforceable obligations to pay contained in indentures. According to the Second Circuit, Section 316(b) prohibits non-consensual amendments of core payment terms (that is, the amount of principal and interest owed, and the date of maturity).[559] The *legal* right to payment cannot be altered. This is not the same as prohibiting the practical ability to resume payment. The court found that the transaction involving the intercompany sale of assets and release of a guarantee did not amend any terms of the indenture, nor did it prevent any noteholder from initiating suit to collect payments due on the dates specified by the indenture. As a result, Section 316(b) was not violated.

Interestingly, the Second Circuit in *Marblegate* noted that, consistent with its interpretation, Section 316(b) bars a "collective action clause."[560] The National Bankruptcy

---

554 *Marblegate Asset Mgmt. v. Educ. Mgmt. Corp.*, 75 F. Supp. 3d 592 (S.D.N.Y. 2014) ("Marblegate I"); *Marblegate Asset Mgmt., LLC v. Educ. Mgmt. Corp.*, 111 F. Supp. 3d 542 (S.D.N.Y. 2015) ("Marblegate II").

555 *MeehanCombs Glob. Credit Opportunities Fund, LP v. Caesars Entm't Corp.*, 80 F. Supp. 3d 507 (S.D.N.Y. 2015); *see also BOKF, N.A. v. Caesars Entm't Corp.*, 144 F. Supp. 3d 459 (S.D.N.Y. 2015). *But see Waxman v. Cliffs Nat. Res. Inc.*, 222 F. Supp. 3d 281 (S.D.N.Y. 2016).

556 *See* Christian Hoffman, *Sovereign Debt Restructuring in Europe Under the New Model Collective Action Clauses*, 49 TEX. INT'L L.J. 385 (2014); George W. Shuster, *The Trust Indenture Act and International Debt Restructurings*, 14 AM. BANK. INT. L. REV. 431 (2006).

557 The Puerto Rico Oversight, Management, and Economic Stability Act, P.L. 114-187, 114th Cong., 2d Sess. (June 30, 2016), Title VI.

558 *Marblegate Asset Mgmt., LLC v. Educ. Mgmt. Fin. Corp.*, 846 F.3d 1 (2d Cir. 2017).

559 *Id.* at 7. *See also Alyece Cummings, et al. v. Chesapeake EnergyCorp., et al.*, Case No. CIV-16-00647 (W.D. Okla. Feb. 8, 2017), ECF No. 62.

560 *Id.*, citing, *e.g.*, *NML Capital, Ltd. v. Republic of Argentina*, 699 F.3d 246, 253 (2d Cir. 2012).

Conference has proposed an amendment to the Bankruptcy Code targeting the application of 316(b) to debt restructurings. Rather than suggesting the use of collective action clauses where there are no statutory safeguards or limitations on the power of the super-majority, the Conference recommends the addition of a new Chapter 16 to the Bankruptcy Code. This would add a streamlined procedure that would permit a court to impose on all members of an affected class a debt modification approved by two-thirds or 75 percent in amount of the class. There would be no numerosity requirement, and other requirements of Chapter 11 would remain inapplicable.[561] Whether this proposal gains traction remains to be seen.

It is anticipated that, as the courts of appeal examine whether Section 316(b) protects more than a holder's legal right to payment, the scope of the protection will become clearer. However, even at this juncture, the ability to restructure debt through a prepackaged plan or Section 3(a)(10) proceeding should continue.

1. Section 316(b) Has Been Held Inapplicable in a Bankruptcy Proceeding

Even TIA-qualified indentures are subject to modification under the bankruptcy laws. Justice Sotomayor, when she was a judge of the Second Circuit, held in a 2008 case:

> The Trust Indenture Act protects the holder of a bond issued under a qualified indenture from majority-imposed impairment of its rights. It provides that "the right of any holder of any indenture security to receive payment of the principal of and interest on such indenture security . . . shall not be impaired or affected without the consent of such holder." 15 U.S.C. § 77ppp(b). As Argo acknowledges in its brief, however, "[o]f course, the TIA cannot prevent the reorganization of a debtor under U.S. bankruptcy laws." Indeed, "[i]t is self-evident that Section 316(b) could not have been intended to impair the capacity of a debtor and its creditors to restructure debt in the context of bankruptcy," and "[t]he cases have uniformly recognized that reorganization proceedings in Chapter 11 are not within the purview of TIA Section 316(b)." *In re Delta Air Lines, Inc.*, 370 B.R. 537, 550 (Bankr. S.D.N.Y. 2007) *aff'd* 374 B.R. 516 (S.D.N.Y. 2007); *see also In re Bd. of Dirs. of Multicanal S.A.*, 307 B.R. 384, 388 (Bankr. S.D.N.Y. 2004) (*"Multicanal I"*) (observing that a creditor "conceded, as it must, that the rights of holders to principal and interest on

561 The full proposal is available at blogs.harvard.edu/bankruptcyroundtable/2016/02/09/national-bankruptcy-conference-proposed-amendments-to-bankruptcy-code-to-facilitate-restructuring-of-bond-and-credit-agreements-to-bankruptcy-code-to-faciliate-restructuring-of-bond-and-credit-agreement-debt/.

> bonds issued under a TIA-qualified indenture can be impaired by bankruptcy proceedings").[562]

Thus, there should be no question but that an exchange offer coupled with a prepackaged plan is not subject to attack under Section 316(b) of the TIA.

2. The Same Rationale Should Make Section 316(b) of the TIA Inapplicable to Bar a Court-Approved Restructuring Pursuant to Section 3(a)(10) of the Securities Act

Interestingly, among the cases relied upon by the Second Circuit in ruling that the TIA did not bar a bankruptcy court debt restructuring were two cases brought pursuant to Section 3(a)(10). In the *Delta* decision, the bankruptcy court judge found that non-impairment language (such as that found in Section 3(a)(10)) did not apply in case of default:

> In default situations where contractual rights are already impaired by exogenous events, non-impairment clauses are moot and the Trustee's power to sue and settle subject to direction by a majority in amount or a specified minimum percentage will be sustained over the objection of a minority or individual. *See MBank Dallas v. LaBarge, Inc.*, Case No. 86 C 9583 (N.D. Ill. 1986) and *Kemper Investors Life Ins. Co. v. Las Colinas Corp.*, Case No. 88 C 9152 (N.D. Ill. 1989). *See also Beal Savings Bank v. Sommer*, 8 N.Y.3d 318, 333-36, 865 N.E.2d 1210, 834 N.Y.S.2d 44 (2007); *First National Bank of Louisville v. Continental Illinois National Bank and Trust Co.*, 933 F.2d 466, 470 (7th Cir. 1991); *Friedman v. Chesapeake & Ohio Ry. Co.*, 261 F. Supp. 728 (S.D.N.Y. 1966); *aff'd* 395 F.2d 663 (2d Cir. 1968), *cert. denied*, 393 U.S. 1016, 89 S. Ct. 619, 21 L. Ed. 2d 561 (1969); *Home Mortgage Co. v. Ramsey*, 49 F.2d 738 (4th Cir. 1931); *Quirke v. St. Louis-San Francisco R.R. Co.*, 277 F.2d 705 (8th Cir. 1960); Restatement (Second) of Trusts § 192 (1959); *Palmer v. Bankers' Trust Co.*, 12 F.2d 747, 754 (8th Cir. 1926).[563]

Both *La Barge and Las Colinas* were brought as Section 3(a)(10) debt restructurings. The findings of fact and conclusions of law in both cases found that the lawsuits in essence were for enforcement of the right to receive payment of principal and interest on the relevant debt securities so that the holders were not deprived of their right to sue for payment of principal and interest within the

562 *In re Bd. of Directors of Telecom Argentina, S.A.*, 528 F.3d 162 (2nd Cir. 2008).

563 *In re Delta Air Lines, Inc.*, 370 B.R. 537, 550 (Bankr. S.D.N.Y. 2007), *aff'd*, 374 B.R. 516 (S.D.N.Y. 2007).

meaning of Section 316(b) of the TIA.[564] In another Section 3(a)(10) class action case, where first mortgage bonds were restructured, the court held the requirements of Section 316(b) were satisfied.[565] Thus, there is ample support for concluding that Section 3(a)(10) is a useful alternative to the time and expense of a bankruptcy filing.[566]

---

564 *MBank Dallas v. La Barge, Inc.*, Case No. 86 C 9583, Findings of Fact, Conclusions of Law and Order at 19–20, § P (N.D. Ill. Dec. 29, 1986) and *Kemper Inv'rs Life Ins. Co. v. Las Colinas Corp.*, Case No. 88 C 9152, Findings of Fact, Conclusions of Law and Order at 19–20, § I (N.D. Ill. June 27, 1989).

565 *Allstate Life Ins. Co., et al. v. Lincoln Prop. Assocs. Ltd., et al.*, 1:CV-93-0547, Order Approving Proposed Settlement at 14, § 45 (M.D. Pa. 1993).

566 *See also Class Plaintiffs v. City of Seattle*, 955 F.2d 1268 (9th Cir. 1992), discussed in detail in Chapter IX.

Appendix XV-A
Timeline of Events for a Prepackaged Plan

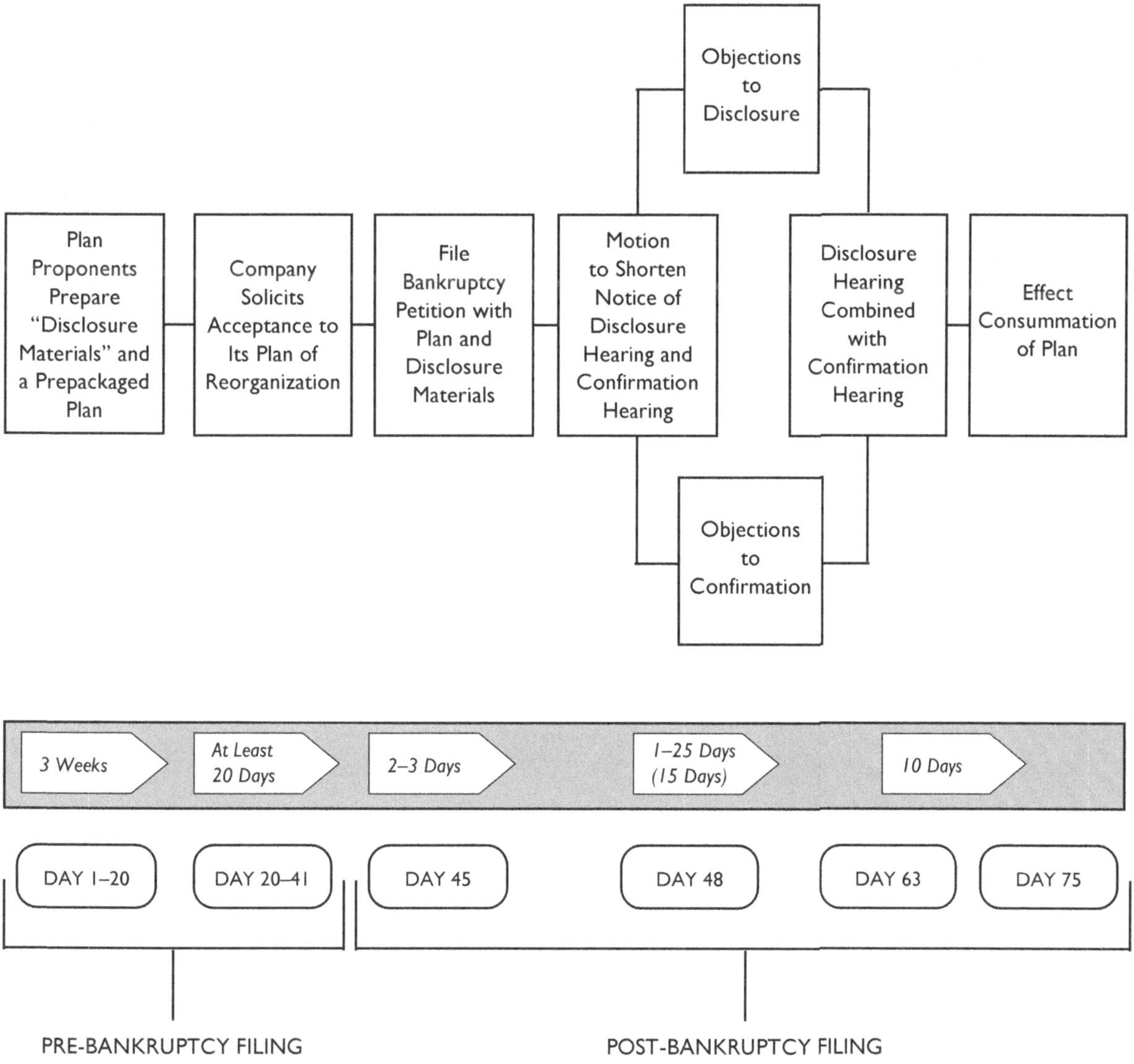

Appendix XV-B
Timeline of Events for a Registered Exchange Offer with a Prepackaged Plan Alternative

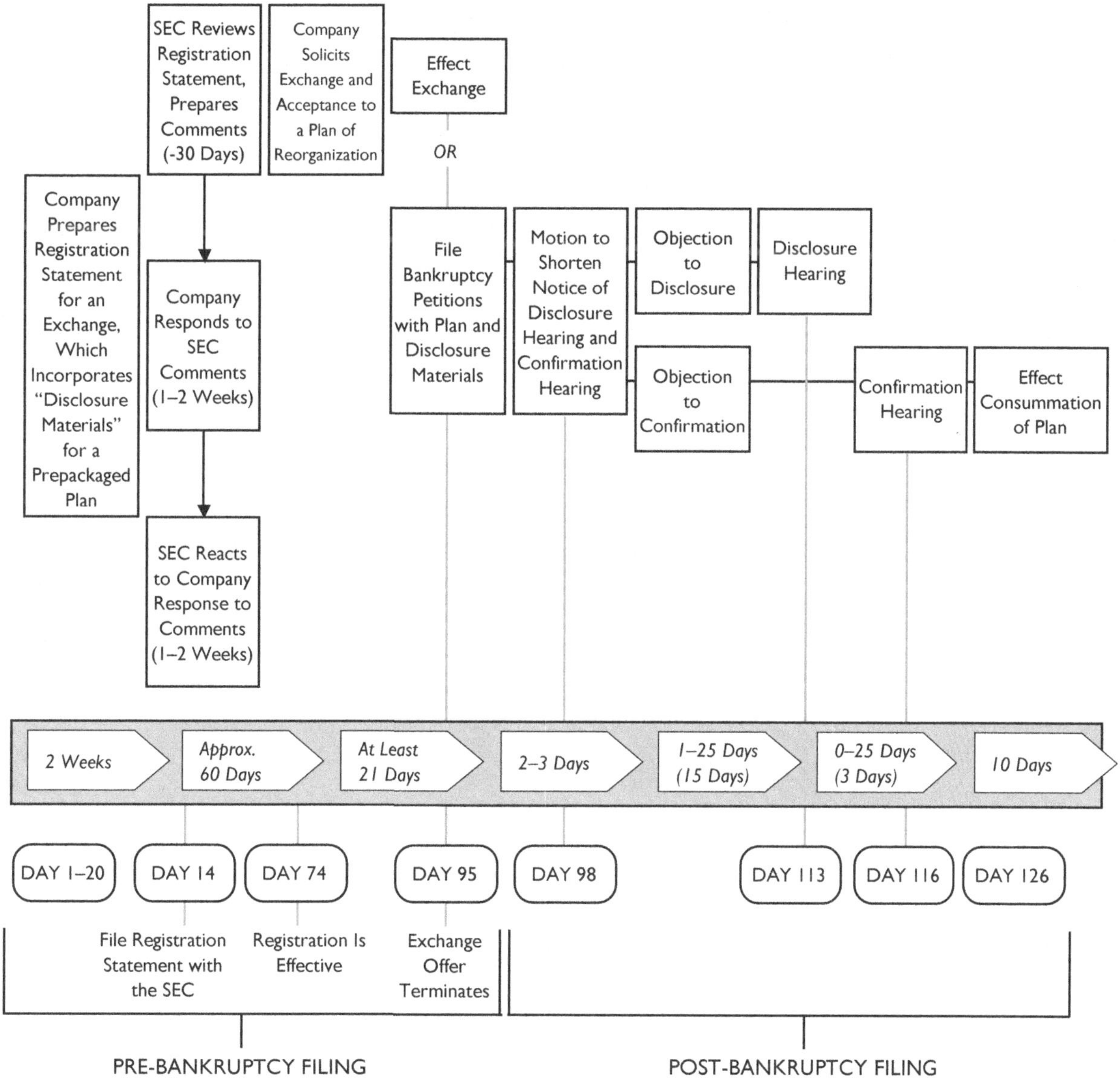

XVI. Securitization Transactions: Different Roles, Different Rights

A. Introduction

The advent of asset-backed securities transactions has led to a unique form of corporate trusteeship. In a typical securitization transaction, a *special purpose entity* ("SPV") issues securities that are secured and paid from payment streams (receivables) on a pool or pools of collateral consisting of various types of financial assets, including residential mortgages, automobile or student loans, consumer receivables and credit card receivables. The *seller, originator or depositor* assembles the financial assets to be sold and deposited with the SPV. The SPV may issue debt securities ("notes") pursuant to an indenture or equity or equity-like securities ("certificates") pursuant to a pooling and servicing agreement ("PSA"). The structure thus may involve (1) a Delaware statutory trust or another limited-purpose entity, organized by the sponsor, which purchases the assets with the proceeds of its notes or other debt securities and pledges such assets to secure the debt instruments or (2) a trustee who receives the assets in exchange for pass-through certificates evidencing beneficial ownership interests in such assets.[567] Asset-backed securities frequently are issued in multiple tranches, each of which may have a different risk characteristic and credit rating. They are payable from pools of receivables as described above. The sole source of payment on the securities is the cash flow generated by the assets in the pool. Attached as Appendix XVI-A is a chart diagramming the structure of a typical residential mortgage-backed securitization with a pooling and servicing agreement, and Appendix XVI-B is a chart diagramming the structure of a typical asset-backed securities indenture structure. These structures introduce the servicer as a party with significant responsibilities. The corporate trust community quite properly has resisted efforts to create obligations of trustees in asset-backed securitizations that are greater than those contractually undertaken.[568] Accordingly, an understanding of the nature of those obligations is important to all concerned.

The securitization transaction typically provides for a *servicer or master servicer* to administer the financial assets, including processing collections, issuing reports to the trustee, documenting loan-level detail and, where necessary, foreclosing upon and maintaining the trust property. Should the servicer be unable to perform under the transaction documents, the trustee

567 *See* The American Bankers Association, Corporate Trust Committee, *The Trustee's Role in Asset-Backed Securities*, www.aba.com/aba/documents/press/RoleoftheTrusteeinAsset-BackedSecurities July2010.pdf, pp. 4–5.

568 *Id.* at 1, 10-12.

may appoint a successor servicer and, in some cases, may become the successor servicer. The *securitization trustee* has specific additional duties, which may include acting as paying agent, asset custodian, investor of funds, recipient of servicer reports, monitor of the servicer reports to the extent prescribed, backup servicer and distributor of reports to investors. The trustee is the party to notify holders and to exercise remedies in the event of default as directed by the requisite holders of the certificates or debt securities even if the transaction documents place the duty to report defaults to the trustee in the hands of the servicer. The seller or depositor usually makes representations and warranties that run to the trustee regarding the nature of the financial assets. These may include the underwriting standards and characteristics of the assets, including the qualities of the underlying obligor. The documents usually give the trustee the authority to enforce breaches of representations and warranties. Generally, the documents indicate the sole remedy is repurchase or substitution in the event of material non-compliance with the specified representations and warranties. If repurchase is not possible, damages may be sought. Further, in the case of securitizations backed by short-term assets, the documents also may define certain triggers or events that lead to amortization of the debt earlier than scheduled.

B. Role of the Securitization Trustee

The structure of the securitization is premised on the sponsor and investor recognizing that the trustee holds the assets owned by the trust in its representative capacity for the benefit of the holders, with the servicer being the party making decisions on the servicing of those assets. Prior to default, the trustee should simply comply with the language of the indenture or PSA. This limited role at this stage has led some to suggest that the term "trustee" is a misnomer.

As a general rule, prior to the occurrence of a servicer event of default, the securitization trustee's duties are non-discretionary and are limited to those specifically set forth in the operative agreement. The indenture or PSA sets forth a limited role for the trustee. However, upon an event of default, which can include the failure of the servicer to remit required payments to the trustee or the insolvency of the servicer, the duties of the trustee under the agreement typically rise to the level of the prudent person. The bankruptcy of the seller/originator will require the trustee to represent the interests of the investors consistent with the terms of the documents. A key task will be monitoring and objecting to any challenge to or interference with the securitization, including the performance of the servicer. While the trustee is not liable for the quality of the underlying assets, the trustee may need to appoint a successor servicer upon the poor performance or default of the servicer. The trustee may need to hire an expert to review or audit the servicer's performance. The expert should consider the matters set forth in Appendix XVI-C, the Servicer Basic Performance Review Checklist and Appendix XVI-D, a Checklist of Potential Servicer Defaults. While some transactions include a "hot" backup servicer that has in its possession relevant documents and is ready to step in upon a default by the original servicer, other deals are structured with a "cold" backup servicer. In such cases, the trustee must appoint a successor servicer or the trustee itself may be required under the documents to assume this function for a time. A protocol governing the transition of the portfolio to a successor servicer could be included in the PSA or indenture to assure a smooth transition. Absent the inclusion of the protocol in the transaction documents, the protocol can be negotiated prepetition before a bankruptcy of the servicer, if possible. (See Appendix XVI-E, a Model Transition of Servicing Protocol.) The benefit of prepetition negotiation and agreement is that the form and content of necessary and appropriate orders and motions to be entered in the bankruptcy will have been agreed upon in advance of the proceedings, allowing the debtor and the trustee to place before the court agreed-upon servicing and transition procedures geared to maintaining the value of the portfolio at the earliest date possible. The ability to reach a prepetition agreement will provide a safety net and protection to the trustee, certificateholders and servicer. There are a myriad of reasons why a prepetition arrangement may not be able to be worked out in advance—there may be insufficient time to negotiate such an agreement, or the servicers may be unwilling to negotiate with the trustee with respect to the terms of such an arrangement. Use of a protocol approved by the court in previous servicer bankruptcies should be considered.

In any event, the postpetition protocol will have to be approved by the bankruptcy court. Issues of servicing and transition protocols have been confronted and approved in a number of bankruptcies.[569] (See, *e.g.*, the basic form of Transition of Servicing Protocol, Appendix XVI-E.) The seriousness of the successor servicer requirement became painfully apparent during the spate of mortgage servicer bankruptcies that sprang from the subprime crisis. In particular, the obligation to make servicer advances of delinquent payments or repurchases of receivables that violate the representations and warranties, complicates the successor servicer role. Attached as Appendix XVI-F is a Checklist of Basic Bankruptcy Considerations in the Event of a Filing by the Servicer.

The use of the term "trustee" to describe the role under a PSA truly is a misnomer since the trustee is not a traditional common-law fiduciary with the attendant duties of care and loyalty. Further, securitization transactions are often structured to be private placements exempt from the registration requirements of the Securities Act and, as a result, the related indentures

---

569 Two examples are *In re Conseco, Inc.*, Case No. 02-B-49672, in the Northern District of Illinois, and *In re DVI, Inc.*, Case No. 03-12658, in the District of Delaware. There have been other cases where transition protocols were addressed and determined by court order: *In re CFS*, Case No. 98-05162-R in the Bankruptcy Court for the Northern District of Oklahoma; *In re Credit Trust*, Case No. 00-5-7812-JA, in the Bankruptcy Court for the District of Maryland, Baltimore Division; and *In re Ameriserve*, Case No. 00-358 (PJW), in the Bankruptcy Court for the District of Delaware.

would not be required to be qualified under the TIA.[570] Certificates issued under a PSA have traditionally been characterized as equity securities such that qualification under the TIA would also not be required. There has, however, been extensive litigation in the Southern District of New York challenging this characterization and seeming to apply the Trust Indenture Act and its mandatory provisions to residential mortgage-backed securities governed by PSAs.[571] Generally, the application of the TIA to RMBS structured pursuant to PSAs and similar transactions would result in substantial disadvantages since the requirements of the TIA would be impossible for the trustee to enforce or obtain registered information and filings given the structure and nature of the transaction. This is not surprising since, in reality, the TIA was never intended to apply to such transactions. At least in the Second Circuit, that issue has been resolved by the decision of the Court of Appeals that the certificates issued under the relevant PSAs are exempt under the TIA.[572] This holding is consistent with the position articulated by the SEC.[573] However, where the transaction is governed not by a PSA but under an indenture (often a Delaware statutory trust), and the structure is not a private placement, the TIA may apply.[574]

C. Considerations for the Trustee and the Holders

Because the nature of the securitization transaction essentially limits the issuer, sponsor and seller from the day-to-day operations of the trust, the trustee has a number of contractual duties, and it is helpful for the trustee's role to be staffed by experienced personnel. The duties of

---

570 Section 304(a) of the TIA sets forth the scope of the statute and the exemptions from qualification. Section 304(a) exempts from the TIA securities exempt under Section 3(a) of the Securities Act, which include certain types of securities such as securities under indentures that limit the aggregate amount outstanding to $10 million principal . Section 304(a) exempts from the provisions of Sections 304 and 306 of the TIA transactions exempt under Section 4 of the Securities Act, including Section 4(a)(2), transactions by an issuer not involving any public offering.

571 *Compare Policemen's Annuity & Benefit Fund v. Bank of America, N.A.*, 943 F. Supp. 2d 428 (S.D.N.Y. 2013) (TIA applies), with *Okla. Police Pension & Ret. Sys. v. U.S. Bank Nat'l Ass'n*, 291 F.R.D. 47 (S.D.N.Y. 2013) (TIA does not apply) (cases later abrogated by *Ret. Bd. of the Policemen's Annuity and Benefit Fund of the City of Chicago v. Bank of N.Y. Mellon*, 775 F.3d 154 (2d Cir. 2014) (TIA does not apply)).

572 *Retirement Bd. of the Policemen's Annuity and Benefit Fund of the City of Chicago v. Bank of N.Y. Mellon*, 775 F.3d 154 (2d Cir. 2014), *cert. denied*, 1365 Ct. 796 (2016) (under § 77ddd the TIA does not apply to "any certificate of interest or participation in two or more securities having substantially different rights and privileges").

573 SEC Division of Corporate Finance, Manual of Publicly Available Telephone Interpretations: Trust Indenture Act of 1939 at 2–3 (July 1997), http://www.sec.gov./interps/telephone/cftelinterps_tia.pdf.

574 *Fixed Income Shares v. Citibank N.A.*, 130 F. Supp. 3d 842 (S.D.N.Y. 2015) (indentures specifically incorporated provisions of the TIA and complaint alleging violation of the TIA with respect to RMBS trustee performance under indentures survived motion to dismiss).

the trustee and the institution's ability to satisfy them should be carefully considered before the trusteeship is accepted. Care must be taken that the assignment of the securitized assets to the trustee is established by the securitization documents. Any related security interest in the assets should also be properly documented. The structure of the transaction likely will depend upon the timely receipt of servicer reports and cash flow, and the trustee should have the key dates and steps to be taken clearly calendared. Current technology to mechanize duties where possible should be embraced. Importantly, the form and content of the required servicer reports should be understood and carefully monitored through the use of a computerized tickler system. The holders will be less confused by the transaction if they are generally familiar with the respective duties of the servicer and trustee.

D. Regulation AB and the Securitization Trustee

In December of 2004, the Securities and Exchange Commission adopted the first set of regulations directed specifically at the issuance of publicly registered asset-backed securities ("ABS"). In particular, Regulation AB establishes disclosure requirements regarding the securitization participants, including the trustee, and a description of its duties with respect to the assets. Item 1109 of the Regulation sets forth the information the ABS prospectus must contain with respect to the trustee:

"Provide the following information for each trustee:

(a) State the trustee's name and describe the trustee's form of organization.

(b) Describe to what extent the trustee has had prior experience serving as a trustee for asset-backed securities transactions involving similar pool assets, if applicable.

(c) Describe the trustee's duties and responsibilities regarding the asset-backed securities under the governing documents and under applicable law. In addition, describe any actions required by the trustee, including whether notices are required to investors, rating agencies or other third parties, upon an event of default, potential event of default (and how defined) or other breach of a transaction covenant and any required percentage of a class or classes of asset-backed securities that is needed to require the trustee to take action.

(d) Describe any limitations on the trustee's liability under the transaction agreements regarding the asset-backed securities transaction.

(e) Describe any indemnification provisions that entitle the trustee to be indemnified from the cash flow that otherwise would be used to pay the asset-backed securities.

(f) Describe any contractual provisions or understandings regarding the trustee's removal, replacement or resignation, as well as how the expenses associated with changing from one trustee to another trustee will be paid.

Instruction to Item 1109. If multiple trustees are involved in the transaction, provide a description of the roles and responsibilities of each trustee."[575]

The disclosure typically is drafted by issuer's counsel. Ongoing trustee disclosure requirements include material litigation against the trustee[576] and material affiliations between the trustee and parties to the transaction.[577]

In 2014, following the adoption of the Dodd-Frank Act,[578] the SEC adopted Regulation ABII, which introduced a number of additional reforms for the offerings of ABS.[579]

---

575 17 CFR § 229.1109.

576 17 CFR § 229.1117.

577 17 CFR § 229.1119.

578 Dodd-Frank Wall Street Reform and Consumer Protection Act, Pub. L. 111-203, 124 Stat. 1376 (2010).

579 SECURITIES AND EXCHANGE COMMISSION, ASSET-BACKED SECURITY DISCLOSURE AND REGULATION, Release Nos. 33-9638, 34-72982; available at http://www.sec.gov/rules/final/2014/33-9638.pdf. Among the rules adopted is amended Rule 17g-5 under the Securities Exchange Act of 1934 that addresses the SEC's position that being paid by the sponsor, issuer or underwriter to issue or maintain a credit rating on asset-backed securities creates a conflict of interest for rating agencies and that this conflict is particularly acute because arrangers of asset-backed securities transactions provide repeat business to the rating agencies. The rule imposes a number of disclosure and conflict-of-interest requirements on nationally recognized statistical rating organizations ("NRSROs"). To manage the conflict of interest, the amended rule is designed to encourage the issuance of unsolicited ratings by non-hired NRSROs by requiring each hired NRSRO to disclose to all other NRSROs that the arranger is in the process of determining an initial credit rating and obtain a representation from each arranger that the arranger will make the information it provides to the hired NRSRO available at the same time to non-hired NRSROs. Rule 17g-7, to implement the requirements of Section 943 of the Dodd-Frank Act, requires that rating agency reports on asset-backed securities report on the representations and warranties and enforcement mechanisms in the transaction documents. The report is to describe how the provisions differ from the same type of provisions in issuances of similar securities. Rule 15Ga-1 requires securitizers of asset-backed securities to make periodic disclosures of all fulfilled and unfulfilled asset repurchase requests.

Of particular interest to trustees, certificateholders and debtholders is the requirement that the transaction documents designate an "asset representations reviewer." According to the SEC, the amendment was in response to concerns about the effectiveness of contractual provisions related to representations and warranties:

> "we are requiring ... that the relevant transaction agreements include provisions providing for a review of the underlying assets for compliance with the representations and warranties upon the occurrence of certain post-securitization trigger events. The rule is designed to address comments received related to the triggers and potential costs, while at the same time balance the need for stronger mechanisms to enforce underlying contract terms. Under the final rule, the agreements must require a review, at a minimum, upon the occurrence of a two-pronged trigger. The first prong of the trigger is the occurrence of a specified percentage of delinquencies in the pool. If the delinquency trigger is met, the second prong of the trigger is the direction of investors by vote. The report of the reviewer's findings and conclusions for all assets reviewed will be required to be provided to the trustee in order for the trustee to determine whether a repurchase request would be appropriate under the terms of the transaction agreements, and a summary of the report must be included on the Form 10-D. We believe that this shelf requirement will address investors' concerns about the enforceability of the representations and warranties and also will incentivize the obligated parties to better consider the disclosure, characteristics, and quality of the assets in the pool."[580]

The amendments also focused on a better method of addressing in a timely manner potential breaches of the representations and warranties.

> "We are requiring that the underlying transaction agreements include a provision providing that, if an asset subject to a repurchase request is not repurchased by the end of a 180-day period beginning when notice is received, then the party submitting such repurchase request would have the right to refer the matter, at its discretion, to either mediation or third-party arbitration. Under the final rule, the dispute resolution provision is a separate and distinct shelf eligibility requirement; investors will be able to take advantage of the

580 *Id.* at pp. 25–26.

dispute resolution provision regardless of whether they had utilized the asset review process."[581]

Further, the issue of facilitating the ability of investors to communicate with one another was addressed.

> "Without an effective means for investors to communicate with each other, investors have told us that they are unable to utilize the contractual rights provided in the underlying transaction agreements. To address this concern, we are requiring as proposed that the underlying transaction agreements must include a provision to require that a request by an investor to communicate with other investors be included in ongoing distribution reports filed on Form 10-D."[582]

These changes were effective November 23, 2015.[583]

E. The Relationship Between the Trustee and the Servicer

At the time of acceptance of the transaction, the proposed trustee should consider whether the bank has relationships with the originator, sponsor and servicer that could create a conflict in the event of a default. The subprime crisis demonstrated the perils to trustees caused by servicer difficulties. With this experience, trustees are increasingly sensitive to the warning signs that the servicer may be in trouble, including the triggering of performance criteria; delayed, inaccurate or restated servicer reports; unexplained lower collections; a ratings downgrade of the servicer; defaults in servicing, including failure to make servicing advances; and amortization events.

These warning signs should cause the trustee to determine if the primary servicer is healthy enough to continue in this role. Considerations include whether the servicer is able to retain key employees, whether the servicer is in bankruptcy, the status of debtor-in-possession financing, and whether the servicer can be rehabilitated or must be replaced. The seamless

---

581 *Id.* at pp. 26–27.

582 *Id.* at 27.

583 Among the requirements that may burden the trustee is the delivery of the platform assessment (item 1122) that must be submitted annually by all transaction parties who perform servicing functions and should disclose instances of material non-compliance. Further, the trustee may desire to remind or provide an update as to fulfilled and unfulfilled requests to the issuer with regard to the issuer's compliance with disclosures regarding asset purchase requests referred to in instructions to paragraph (A)(1)(iv) under Securities Exchange Rule 15Ga-1 adopted to implement Section 943 of Dodd-Frank.

replacement of the servicer is a goal that trustees have sought to achieve in servicer bankruptcies. Prior to filing necessary proofs of claim and considering third-party actions to protect investors, trustees were faced with the transition of servicing. Transition protocols evolved that included:

- Procedures to transfer servicing of the assets and the timing and implementation of a cut-off date;
- Assurances of electronic and physical transfer of information;
- Staffing and knowledge transfer;
- Cooperation by the old servicer by, among other things, identifying demand deposit accounts ("DDA") and transferring ACH authorization for receivables, lockboxes and the right to receive payment from payment systems;
- Transfer of checks, payments and mail after a designated cut-off date;
- Adequate notification to parties about the transfer of servicing to a new servicer, with contact information of the new servicer;
- Transfer of data on collections and assignment of collection efforts;
- Ability to obtain cooperation of the old servicer regarding questions concerning accounts and servicing accounting; and[584]
- Notices to payors regarding the transfer.

The successful transition of servicing also can be impacted by issues regarding the need to review servicing fees that can affect cash flows. In the *Conseco* case previously referred to, the court increased the servicing fee because the waterfall in the agreements provided that the servicing fee was paid last and so the servicer had little incentive to act. In bankruptcy, the court approved an increased servicing fee in exchange for granting the trustee a replacement lien on the servicing platform. Turning the servicer into a profitable enterprise allowed the servicing platform to be sold to a solvent entity and enhanced the value of the certificates.

Obviously, the existence of a clear backup servicing plan is a huge advantage to the trustee and certificateholders or debtholders. The principal lesson learned from the servicer bankruptcies is the benefit to having a protocol built into the transaction for transition of servicing caused by the inability of the servicer to act. This plan should include the ability to negotiate an increase in servicer fees after transition. Consistent with the protocols developed in

---

584 Attached as Appendix XVI-E is a form of protocol approved by a number of courts with respect to the transition of servicing in the event of a bankruptcy filing. Appendix XVI-G is a servicing transition protocol useful when the platform is to be sold to a new purchaser, and documents the representations and warranties by the purchaser to the trustee.

the bankruptcy cases, the built-in protocol would provide a smooth transition of servicing to a successor servicer and maintain access and the rights for the successor servicer to the same telephone lines and numbers. All hard copies of documents would be transferred, as would all written notices and computer-stored information. The same computer technology, licensing of the right to use technology and programming, the same lockbox for mail, the same bank accounts and access and use of the office would remain in force for a transition period so that the trustee or successor servicer, to the extent possible, maintains the flow of funds and the ability to pay the securities.

F. Bankruptcy and the Trustee

The bankruptcy of the seller or the servicer presents unique challenges to the trustee. As previously noted, Appendix XVI-F is a checklist of basic considerations in the event of a possible servicer bankruptcy. The premise of the securitization vehicle is that the deposit of financial assets by the seller or depositor into an SPV is a true sale, that the SPV will be unaffected by the bankruptcy of the sellers or depositors and that the assets of the securitization will not be property of the estate in a seller or depositor bankruptcy. Legal opinions directed to the securitization trustee to this effect are delivered in connection with the closing.[585]

Nevertheless, the bankruptcy of the seller or depositor will require a new level of vigilance by the trustee. Various parties may challenge the true-sale nature of the transaction and seek to bring the assets of the securitization into the estate of the debtor. It may be argued that the securitization transaction was actually a secured loan so that future financial assets should be available to the estate and that the terms of the securitization can be impaired by a plan of reorganization. The battle on the issue may take place in the early days of the case when debtor-in-possession lenders attempt to secure their postpetition lending with assets of the securitization.[586] Obviously, unless the certificateholders or debtholders are taking the laboring oar, this dispute will require the trustee to be assisted by experienced counsel. The representations and legal opinions received at closing should provide ample evidence to establish

---

585 Nevertheless, there are examples where Chapter 11 cases for SPVs have not been dismissed as bad-faith filings or the SPV has not been unauthorized as a bankruptcy-remote entity. See *In re Zais Inv. Grade Ltd. VII*, 455 B.R. 839 (Bankr. N.J. 2011); *In re: Paradigm Elizabeth, LLC, Debtor*, 2015 WL 435067 (D.N.J. Feb. 2, 2015).

586 In *Gen. Growth Props., Inc.*, 412 B.R. 122 (Bankr. S.D.N.Y. 2009), the debtors obtained the use of funds of the SPV during the course of the bankruptcy but were required to provide adequate protection.

the bankruptcy remoteness of the SPV. Depending upon the circumstances, the trustee itself may proactively seek a determination of the true-sale nature of the transaction.[587]

The bankruptcy of the seller may cause the trustee, ideally in conjunction with the investors and each of their counsel, to determine if the continuation of the securitization is desirable given the quality of the assets. An agreement to continue the securitization, modify the terms of the securitization or terminate the securitization in the bankruptcy context should be documented by court orders. As previously discussed, the insolvency of the servicer requires immediate action by the securitization trustee to determine if the servicer can continue to function, if the terms of the servicing (particularly the fee structure) need to be adjusted or if the servicing function should be transitioned. Court orders detailing these matters also must be obtained.[588] The input of the certificateholders on these issues should be encouraged and welcomed.

The trustee must file proofs of claim in the bankruptcy of either the seller or servicer. Depending upon the number of individual securitization transactions for which the trustee serves, this can be a huge undertaking. In the *Lehman* bankruptcy, some trustees literally filed hundreds of proofs of claim on separate transactions. Counsel must be involved well before the bar date so that the important duty of filing proofs of claim can be fulfilled. The claim against the seller will include a protective claim for the indebtedness should the true-sale argument be unsuccessful and a put-back claim for breaches of representations and warranties regarding the assets. The claim against the servicer will includes breaches of the servicer's performance covenants and of any representations and warranties made by the servicer. Attached as Appendix XVI-H is a form of addendum to proof of claim filed encompassing put-back claims and other claims against the debtor depositor. The certificateholders or debtholders should be notified of any bar date for filing proofs of claim and any claims to be filed by the trustee so that if they believe they have any unique claims, they can submit them on a timely basis.

---

587 Attacks on the true sale must be taken very seriously. In *Paloian v. LaSalle Bank, N.A.*, 619 F.3d 688 (7th Cir. 2010), the court held a trustee could be liable for a fraudulent conveyance of the assets of the SPV as an initial transferee for purposes of Section 550(a) of the Bankruptcy Code.

588 In the case of *Amer. Home Mortg. Holdings, Inc.*, 402 B.R. 87 (Bankr. D. Del. 2009), the court held that the loan sale provisions of the PSA were severable from loan servicing provisions of the same agreement so that the debtor could transfer its rights under servicing provisions as a contract severable from loan sale provisions, free and clear of any repurchase obligation existing under sale provisions.

G. Determination of Representation and Warranty and Fraud Claims

Most securitization transactions involve hundreds of individual underlying financial assets. Under New York law, the elements of a breach of warranty claim generally include the following: (1) plaintiff and defendant entered into a contract (2) containing an express warranty by the defendant with respect to a material fact (3) which warranty was part of the basis of the bargain, (4) the express warranty was breached by the defendant and (5) the plaintiff is entitled to indemnification for resulting damages.[589] Generally, the repurchase provisions are triggered under the typical PSA when the representation or warranty "adversely and materially affects the value of the related mortgage loan." This typically means an increase in the risk of loss with respect to the mortgage loans and/or interests of the certificateholders and does not require a default.[590]

Proving up claims for fraud or breach of representations and warranties on a transaction-by-transaction basis is daunting. Several bankruptcy courts have permitted the estimation of representation and warranty claims for purpose of allowance.[591] In another bankruptcy case, statistical sampling was used to determine the reasonableness of a proposed settlement.[592] However, in the *Lehman* bankruptcy four residential mortgage-backed security trustees, involving a total of approximately 405 RMBS trusts and one million mortgage loans, requested an order increasing the reserve amount on their proofs of claim for put-back liability and scheduling a hearing to estimate and allow their claims.[593] While the RMBS trustees sought a statistical sampling methodology to establish their claims, Lehman Brothers argued for a loan-by-loan claim-reconciliation protocol. The bankruptcy court agreed with Lehman Brothers, holding the claims could readily be determined through mathematics and hence the sampling approach was inappropriate; the court ordered that claims must be asserted on a loan-by-loan

---

589 *Wells Fargo Bank, N.A. v. Bank of Am., N.A.*, 2013 WL 1285289 (S.D.N.Y. Mar. 28, 2013), *vacated on other grounds*, 627 Fed. Appx. 27 (2d Cir. 2015).

590 *MASTR Adjustable Rate Mortgs. Tr. 2006-OA2 v. UBS Real Estate Secs., Inc.*, 2015 WL 764665 (S.D.N.Y. Jan. 9, 2015), *reconsideration denied*, 2015 WL 797972 (S.D.N.Y. Feb. 25, 2015). In a subsequent decision after trial in this case, the court held that if the evidence demonstrates it is more likely than not that a borrower made an intentional misrepresentation, the related breach had an adverse and material effect on the interests of certificateholders. *MASTR Adjustable Rate Mortgs. Tr. 2006-OA2 v. UBS Real Estate Secs.*, Case No. 12-7322 (S.D.N.Y. Sept. 6, 2016) ("Castel September 2016 Order").

591 *In re New Century TRS Holdings*, No. 07-10416 (Bankr. D. Del. Mar. 27, 2009), ECF No. 9355, 9479; *In re Am. Home Mortg. Holdings Inc.*, No. 07-11047 (Bankr. D. Del. Feb. 18, 2009), ECF No. 7029, 7042.

592 *In re Residential Capital, LLC*, No. 12-12020 (Bankr. S.D.N.Y. Dec. 11, 2013), ECF No. 4102, 6030-1, 6065.

593 *In re Lehman Bros. Holdings Inc.*, No. 08-1355 (Bankr. S.D.N.Y. Aug. 22, 2014), ECF No. 46078.

basis.[594] The question of the appropriateness of sampling also arises in representation and warranty cases outside of the bankruptcy arena, with mixed results.[595]

H. Common Issues Relevant to the Trustee Raised in RMBS Litigation

1. Standing to Bring Suit

A frequent issue raised in lawsuits brought by certificateholders is standing to pursue representation and warranty claims directly against the sponsor. Generally, the no-action clause has been enforced against holders and the trustee is deemed the proper party to pursue such claims.[596] Of course, the trustee should be open to hearing the views of certificateholders, while keeping in mind the best interest of all the holders. Again, the coordination of efforts by certificateholders and the securitization trustee normally will facilitate an effective resolution. It should be remembered that the securitization trustee and the certificateholders have the same

---

594 *Id.* at Transcript pp. 107–8 (Bankr. S.D.N.Y. Dec. 10, 2014), ECF No. 49007. Sampling was also rejected in the Castel September 2016 Order, a non-bankruptcy RMBS case.

595 *See, e.g., Assured Guar. Mun. Corp. v. Flagstar Bank, F.S.B.*, 920 F. Supp. 2d 475 (S.D.N.Y. 2013) (sampling a widely used method of proof under New York law; but damages were computed based upon insurer's actual loss. It is important to note that this is a bond insurer representation and warranty case based on an insurance contract and not a trustee representation and warranty claim based on a PSA); *Law Debenture Tr. Co. of N.Y. v. WMC Mortg., LLC*, 2015 WL 9581729 (D. Conn. Dec. 30, 2015) (expert report based on sampling admissable); *Assured Guar. Mun. Corp. v. DB Structured Products, Inc.*, 997 N.Y.S.2d 97 (N.Y. Sup. Ct. 2014) (sampling and expert evidence may be used to calculate damages); *Deutsche Bank Nat'l Tr. Co. v. WMC Mortg. LLC*, 2014 WL 3824333 (D. Conn. Aug. 4, 2014) (while statistical sampling could be an acceptable method of proving liability and damages, whether particular proffered statistical sampling evidence is admissible and persuasive is a different question); *MBIA Ins. Corp. v. Countrywide Home Loans, Inc.*, 958 N.Y.S.2d 647 (N.Y. Sup. Ct. 2010) (court did not endorse the plaintiff's sampling method as better or worse than any other, and plaintiff must show that the sample was statistically significant. Sampling merely a vehicle to present evidence); *Syncora Guarantee Inc. v. EMC Mortg. Corp.*, 2011 WL 1135007 (S.D.N.Y. Mar. 25, 2011) (plaintiff could seek a pool-wide remedy against the defendant based on sampling and extrapolation); *Ret. Bd. of the Policemen's Annuity and Benefit Fund of the City of Chicago v. Bank of N.Y. Mellon*, 775 F.3d 154 (2d Cir. 2014) ("Plaintiffs cite no case in which a single sample of loans taken from hundreds of trusts was used to prove liability with respect to each of those trusts."); *Royal Park Invs. SA/NV v. HSBC Bank USA, Nat'l Ass'n*, 109 F. Supp. 3d 587 (S.D.N.Y. 2015) (at trial or summary judgment, plaintiffs must prove their claims loan by loan and trust by trust). *See also, Blackrock Allocation Target Shares: Series S Portfolio v. Wells Fargo Bank, N.A.*, 2017 WL 3610511 (S.D.N.Y. Aug. 18, 2017) (sampling could not identify breaches that materially affected loan value).

596 *GSAA Home Equity Tr. 2006-2 v. Wells Fargo Bank*, 133 F. Supp. 3d 1203 (D.S.D. 2015); *Federal Housing Fin. Agency v. D.B. Structured Prods., Inc.*, 2014 WL 1384489 (N.Y.S. Ct. 2014); *Ace Secs. Corp. v. DP Structured Prods.*, 977 N.Y.S.2d 229 (App. Div. 2013); *VNB Realty, Inc. v. U.S. Bank, N.A.*, 2014 WL 1628441 (D.N.J. Apr. 23, 2014).

interest in an appropriate resolution of the securitization trust issues. Since certificateholders are viewed by courts as lacking standing to assert trust claims, coordination through direction, instruction and indemnity by the certificateholders to the securitization trustee as to actions to be taken regarding purported claims against the sponsor, including breaches of representations and warranties, should result in an effective, focused resolution in the interest of the securitization trustee and the certificateholders.

2. Specificity of Notice

The specificity of the notice of breach required to be delivered by the trustee has received varying treatment by the courts. A number of courts have held that, at least at the pleading stage, allegations of pervasive breach in a financing are sufficient to trigger the repurchase obligation and the notice by the trustee as to each separate loan is not required[597] where the notice refers to specific allegedly defective loans at least where the notice also demands repurchase of all other defective loans.[598] The matter of proof is, of course, a different issue and raises the acceptability of the sampling technique discussed above. The notion of a "pervasive breach notice" in conjunction with a sampling of loans has been rejected by at least one court as requiring the cure or repurchase of all defective loans.[599]

3. Statute of Limitations

Another frequently litigated issue of interest to trustees is the statute of limitations governing actions for breach of representations and warranties, particularly the issue of when the cause of action accrues. At least as far as New York law is concerned, that matter was determined by the New York Court of Appeals rejecting a subsequent discovery test of accrual and holding that the six-year statute of limitations accrues on the closing date of the mortgage loan purchase agreement when any breach of the representations and warranties contained therein occurred.[600]

---

597 *Assured Guar. Mun. Corp. v. DB Structured Prods., Inc.*, 44 Misc. 3d 1206 (A), 997 N.Y.S.2d 97 (Table), 2014 WL 3282310, 2014 N.Y. slip op. 51043 (U) (N.Y.S. Ct. July 3, 2014); *Deutsche Bank Nat'l Tr. Co. v. Morgan Stanley Mortg. Capital Holdings LLC*, 97 F. Supp. 3d 548 (S.D.N.Y. 2015).

598 *Nomura Asset Acceptance Corp. Alternative Loan Tr. v. Nomura Credit & Capital, Inc.*, 2014 WL 2890341 (N.Y.S. Ct. June 26, 2014); *Morgan Stanley Mortg. Loan Tr. 2006-14SL v. Morgan Stanley Mortg. Capital Holdings LLC*, 2013 WL 4488367 (N.Y.S. Ct. Aug. 16, 2013); *U.S. Bank Nat'l Ass'n v. DLJ Mortg. Capital, Inc.*, 2015 WL 5915285 (N.Y.S. Ct. Oct. 8, 2015).

599 *MASTR Adjustable Rate Mortgs. Tr. v. UBS Real Estate Secs.*, 2015 WL 764665 (S.D.N.Y. Jan. 9, 2015).

600 *Ace Secs. Corp. v. DB Structured Prods., Inc.*, 25 N.Y. 3d 581, 15 N.Y.S.3d 716 (2015); *The Bank of N.Y. Mellon v. WMC Mortg., LLC*, 50 Misc. 3d 229, 2015 N.Y. slip op. 25318 (N.Y.S. Ct. Sept. 18, 2015) (holding that the duty to notify is not an independent cause of action that would be governed by a separate limitations period); *Deutsche Bank Nat'l Tr. Co. v. Quicken Loans*, 810 F.3d 861 (2d Cir. 2015). The question of whether sophisticated parties can agree that no cause of action accrues until specific enumerated events have occurred or whether this is against public policy will be reviewed

4. Repurchase as Sole Remedy

Typically, repurchase is stated to be the sole remedy for breach of representations and warranties. The scope of this concept has been examined frequently by the courts. It has been held by several courts that there can be no money damages for failure to repurchase even if specific performance is unavailable.[601] However, other courts have held that, if a loan cannot be repurchased because it is no longer in the trust, damages equal to the repurchase amount are appropriate or can at least be considered.[602] Direct-loss causation generally is not a required element of a repurchase claim nor must the plaintiff typically show actual pecuniary loss resulting from a breach.[603] Damages generally are measured by the repurchase price calculation in the PSA.[604] The elements of a claim for breach of representations and warranties and the quality of the proof required are the subject of a number of pending lawsuits and the legal issues highlighted above likely will continue to be clarified. Experienced securitization trustee counsel should be able to advise the trustee of the requirements of such litigation.[605]

5. Duties of the Trustee

It is important for certificateholders or debtholders to recognize the limits of the duties of a trustee in a securitization. In terms of allegations against the trustee arising out of a troubled securitization, it has been held that the trustee has no duty to undertake any generalized monitoring of the servicer beyond that specifically set forth in a PSA.[606] Further, whether or not the trustee had a contractual duty to give notice, a party may not insist upon performance of a condition precedent when its non-performance is caused by the party itself.[607] Allegations that a

---

by the New York Court of Appeals (APL-2016-00237) in the appeal of *Deutsche Bank Nat'l Tr. Co. v. Flagstar*, 143 A.D. 15, 36 N.Y.S.3d 135 (2016).

601 *MASTR Asset Backed Secs. Tr. 2006-HE v. WMC Mortg. LLC*, 983 F. Supp. 2d 1104 (D. Minn. 2013); see also *Citigroup Mortg. Loan Tr. v. Citigroup Global Markets Realty Corp.*, 2014 WL 1329165 (S.D.N.Y. Mar. 31, 2014).

602 *Ace Secs. Home Equity Loan Tr. v. DB Structured Prods., Inc.*, 5 F. Supp. 3d 543 (S.D.N.Y. 2014); *Deutsche Bank Nat'l Tr. Co. v. WMC Mortg., LLC*, 2014 WL 1289234 (D. Conn. Mar. 31, 2014); *Nomura Home Equity Loan Inc. v. Nomura Credit & Capital, Inc.*, 133 A.D. 3d 96 (N.Y. 1st Dept. 2015).

603 *Ace Secs. Corp. v. DB Structured Prods., Inc.*, 25 N.Y. 3d 581, 15 N.Y.S. 3d 716 (2015); *Syncora Guar. Inc. v. EMC Mortg. Corp.*, 874 F. Supp. 2d 328 (S.D.N.Y. 2012).

604 *Aurora Comm. Corp. v. Approved Funding Corp.*, 2014 WL 1386633 (S.D.N.Y. Apr. 9, 2014).

605 *U.S. Bank N.A. et al. v. Fed. Home Loan Bank of Boston, et al.*, No. 652382/2014, slip op. (N.Y. Sup. Ct. N.Y. Cty., Aug. 12, 2016) ("J.P. Morgan"); *In the matter of MASTR Asset Backed Secs. Tr. 2006-HE3 and MASTR Asset Backed Secs. Tr. 2007-WMC1*, No. 62-TR-CV-14-59, slip op. (Minn. Sec. J. Dist. July 11, 2016) ("WMC").

606 *Ellington Credit Fund v. Select Portfolio Servicing, Inc.*, 837 F. Supp. 2d 162 (S.D.N.Y. 2011).

607 *Fixed Income Shares v. Citibank N.A.*, 130 F. Supp. 3d 842 (S.D.N.Y. 2015).

trustee had actual knowledge of events of default, which would trigger a heightened standard of care, have survived dismissal at the pleading stage.[608] However, general allegations of breach of fiduciary duty without acknowledging the difference between pre- and post-event of default duties have been found insufficient.[609]

6. Application of Recovery Pursuant to the Waterfall

Typically, the priority of payment provides a road map for the application of payments received by the trustee as a result of recovery or collection actions upon a default. The prudent trustee may consider an interpleader or declaratory judgment action to obtain a court determination where the waterfall provisions are unclear. In addition, any real estate mortgage investment conduit ("REMIC") consequences of a resolution or settlement of claims should be considered.

I. Trustee Settlement of Claims Brought Against Parties to the RMBS Transaction

Although litigation brought by the trustee against parties to a failed securitization transaction can be time consuming and expensive, the trustee's decision to settle such litigation should be informed by recent helpful developments in the case law. The trustee's decision to settle has been held to be discretionary.[610] Typically, the trustee will seek instructions from a court of competent jurisdiction, after providing notice and an opportunity to be heard to holders, to confirm the appropriateness of the exercise of its discretion. The court does not second-guess the decision. Rather, the court only needs to determine whether the trustee acted reasonably, in good faith and within the bounds of its discretion in entering into the settlement agreement (which frequently will require court approval as a condition for its effectiveness).[611]

Courts analyzing the reasonableness of a settling trustee's actions focus on the trustee's reliance on experienced trustee counsel and experienced experts. Under the *Countrywide* rule, the trustee's exercise of discretion can be set aside only if reliance on counsel and the experts' assessment was unreasonable and in bad faith. It is not the task of the court to decide whether it agrees with the trustee's decision.[612]

---

608 *Phoenix Light SF Ltd. v. The Bank of N.Y.*, 2015 WL 5710645 (S.D.N.Y. Sept. 29, 2015) (citing cases).

609 *Millenium Partners, L.P. v. U.S. Bank Nat'l Ass'n*, 2013 WL 1655990 (S.D.N.Y. Apr. 17, 2013), *rehearing denied*, 2015 WL 6454844 (S.D.N.Y. Oct. 26, 2015).

610 *In re Bank of N.Y Mellon*, 127 A.D. 3d 120 (N.Y. App. Div. 2015), *affirming as modified*, 2014 WL 1057187 (N.Y.S.D. 2014) ("Countrywide").

611 *Id.*; *J.P. Morgan.*

612 *Id.*

In *Countrywide,* the court cited the experience of trustee's counsel, the role of respected outside experts to the trustee, including experts on potential damages, and the ability to respond to a judgment and the employ of legal experts regarding the interpretation of the documents.[613] In *J.P. Morgan,* the court referenced the trustee's reliance upon the advice of outside experts, including legal experts on the potential trustee recovery in litigation and economic and valuation experts. Both *Countrywide* and *J.P. Morgan* were brought under New York CPLR Article 77.

In the matter of MASTR Asset Backed Securities Trust 2006-HE3 and MASTR Asset Backed Securities Trust 2007-WMC1,[614] brought pursuant to Minnesota Section 501B.16 for trust instructions, the court, in approving the settlement, relied upon the experience of counsel to the trustee and the detailed report of the expert to the trustee who opined on the applicable legal issues, including prior rulings in the case, challenges and expenses related to elements of proof if the case went to full litigation; the ability under the facts to pierce the corporate veil of the sponsor; the ability to pay comparable settlements, not as a mathematical formula but as a reflection of reasonableness; and reasonable settlement range.

The case law thus suggests that a trustee, with experienced trustee counsel and experts, need not risk making a settlement decision on its own but may obtain court approval of its actions. Of course, any direction, instruction and indemnity from holders on the settlement will be of assistance to the trustee, the certificateholders and ultimately the court in determining the proper way to proceed. Further, the court order approving the settlement is binding on all parties to the transaction, including certificateholders who received notice and an opportunity to be heard. Such a court order is especially helpful to certificateholders and the securitization trustee who believe a settlement is in the best interests of the securitization trustee and the certificateholders, but all certificateholders cannot be identified or choose not to direct, instruct or approve of a settlement resolution.

---

613 2014 WL 1057187.

614 WMC.

Appendix XVI-A
Structure of RMBS Securitization Utilizing Pooling and Servicing Agreement

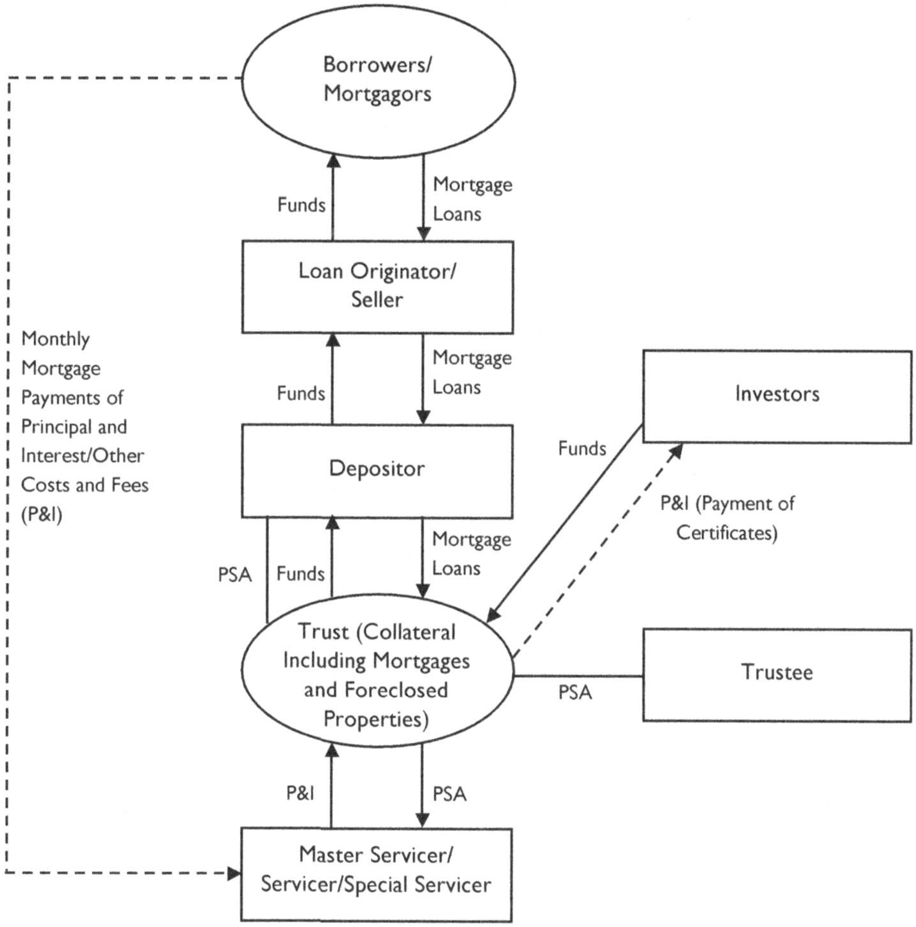

Appendix XVI-B
Structure of ABS Utilizing Indenture

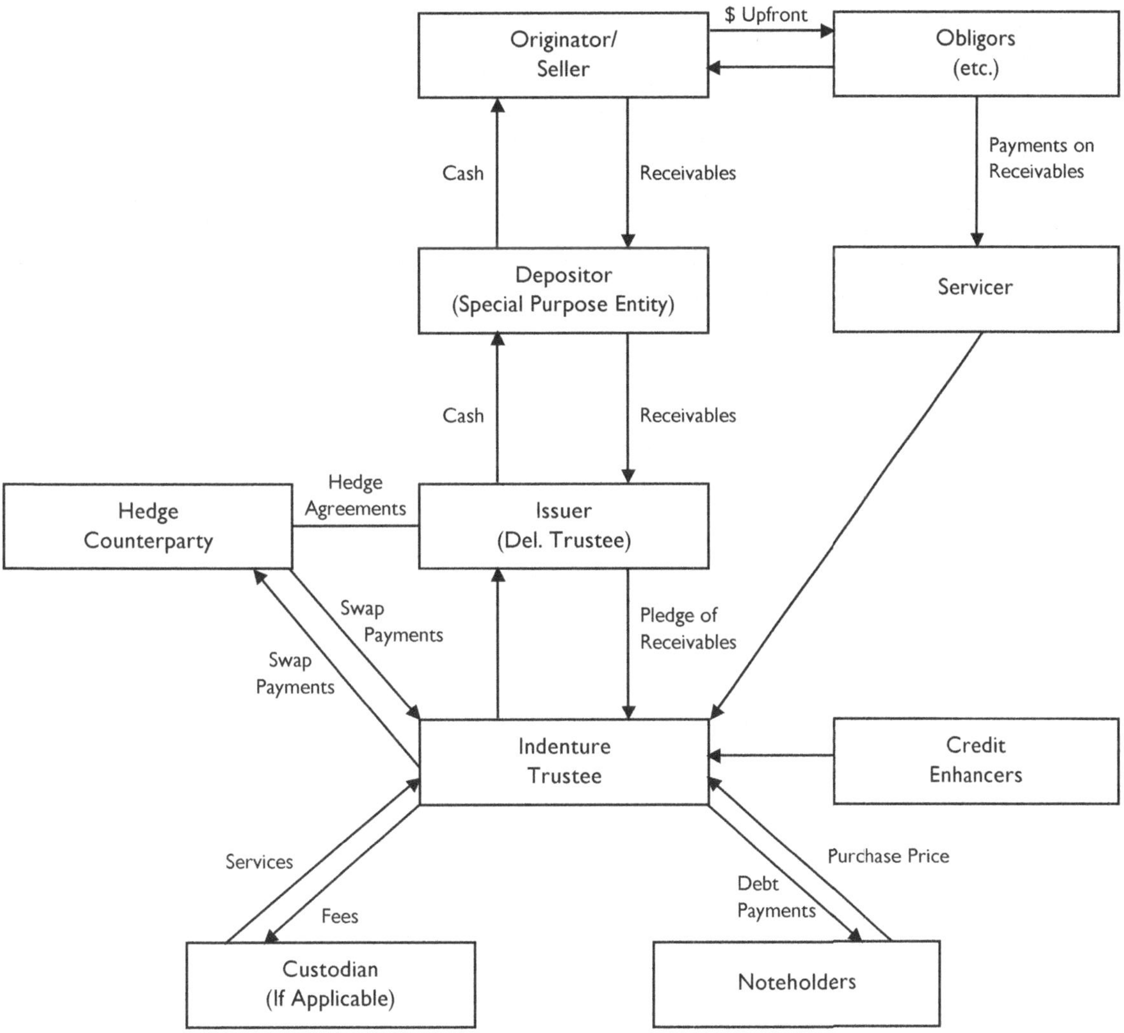

Appendix XVI-C
Servicer Basic Performance Review Checklist

SERVICER BASIC PERFORMANCE REVIEW CHECKLIST

In support of a review of the servicing function by servicers for RMBS-related transactions, the following sets forth below, for discussion purposes, core servicing functions to be reviewed.

- Customer Service—Review Servicer's Procedures, Ability and Frequency To
  - Correspond via mail, email and telephone with obligors
  - Perform:
    - document release and control
    - file storage and imaging
    - ACH maintenance
    - titling
    - relationship with any third-party custodian and compliance with documentation
- Collections—Review Servicer's Ability and Procedures To
  - Identify and implement distinct collection procedures for accounts
    - 0–29 days past due
    - 30–59 days past due
    - 60–89 days past due
    - 90+ days past due
  - Evaluate the effectiveness of, and, as appropriate, grant:
    - extensions
    - modifications
    - forbearances
  - Maximize recoveries utilizing, as appropriate:
    - Banko/Pacer
    - skip tracers or procedures to find "lost" or difficult-to-contract obligors
    - writs of attachment or liens

    - replevins or action to seize property
    - foreclosure
    - force-placed insurance

- Lockbox

    - flow of payment from obligor to lockbox to the collection Account without commingling or third-party ability to interfere
    - any required cash reserve or escrow by lockbox bank—determine amount and ability to increase in distress situation
    - automatic payment systems and electronic transfers such as direct deposits, ACH, quick-pay and other arrangement, and ability to continue and transfer—timeliness of payments/transfers from lockbox to collection account
    - reconciliation of accounts and procedure to correct for mistaken deposit in the wrong lockbox or accounts

- Inventory Control—Review of Non-Performing Loans/Assets, Procedures, Foreclosures and Bid-in of Properties

    - Procedure for:

        - notices of default
        - notices of foreclosure
        - procedure to determine when to bid in and management of real estate owned
        - insurance coverage
        - tax payments
        - sale and market procedures
        - protection of payment

    - Analysis of default, foreclosures and real estate owned

    - Service procedures for foreclosed or to-be-foreclosed property; perform, as appropriate:

        - inspections
        - repair estimates
        - lock change
        - follow-up inspections
        - insurance and guard services

    - identification of staffing and outside service personnel, and assurance of sufficient staffing

  - Identification of sub-servicer and third-party vendors

    - providers, contract terms and nature of services provided
    - vendors, if any, used for deeds-in-lieu, foreclosure, repossession/eviction, repairs and maintenance, guard services and sales and marketing
    - sufficient personnel identified or retained for the respective geographic area to ensure prompt foreclosure, repossession/eviction, repair and maintenance, guard services and sales and marketing given a possible increase in default/foreclosure activity
    - any non-contractual (no written contract) relationships
    - determine frequency of servicers monitoring or auditing of sub-servicer and third-party vendor

  - List of foreclosures, pending litigation and any claims asserted

- Asset Management—Servicer's Procedures Relating To

  - evaluation and approval of liquidations
  - value of collateral
  - development of loss estimates
  - review and approval of liquidation expenses
  - coordination of auctions and package sales
  - approving legal settlements
  - monitoring and assessment of inventory control

- Loan Accounting—Review of Servicer's Procedures and Ability To

  - process payments and payoffs
  - maintain lockboxes
  - perform:

    - billing
    - payment reconciliation

  - resolve credit bureau disputes
  - investigate and pursue collection of nsf checks
  - utilize:

    - speed-pays

    - loss mitigation processing
    - quick-collects
    - direct deposit/automatic withdrawals

  - Exemption from TMP (taxation on mortgage pools)

    - REMIC exception
    - real estate investment trust ("REIT) exception
    - if the equity is in any trust pledged to a lender
    - if a REIT exception is used, how is that exemption assured if there is any equity in the trust that is pledged or subject to a lien

- Advance of Liquidation Expenses to Protect Collateral—Servicer's Procedures and Ability To

  - As determined necessary or appropriate in the exercise of good faith business judgment, advance for

    - taxes
    - insurance
    - cleaning costs
    - auction fees
    - commissions
    - repairs

  - Protect and preserve properties before or after foreclosure

- Administration—Review Procedures and Ability of Servicer To

  - Perform investor trust reporting

  - Maintain and efficiently employ appropriate

    - technology systems
    - facilities
    - telecommunications
    - human resources
    - management, finance and accounting personnel

  - Review disaster recovery plan and procedure

    - hot and cold back-up
    - offsite facilities

    - offsite storage
    - third-party providers

  - Maintain computer and data security

    - programs and procedures to prevent deletion, alteration or addition of electronic data and to assure hard-copy storage
    - program and procedure on preventing hackers and theft of information or data
    - sensitive data loss and reporting procedures

- Review of Servicing Reports and Servicer's Procedures and Ability Relating To

  - compliance with documentation and information requirements
  - notices of exception and issues
  - any failure to timely provide servicer reports
  - provide notice of servicing defaults
  - notice of repurchase events
  - non-compliance notices
  - analysis of performance criteria
  - UCC filings and any lien perfection review

- Transition and Backup Servicer Availability

  - existence of backup servicer and availability to service (hot or cold)
  - backup tapes, availability and storage
  - active monitoring of servicing by backup servicer
  - any agreement on servicing transition protocol (see Appendix XVI-E for general model protocol)
  - review model transition protocol to determine ability of servicer to transition to backup servicer and agreement as to the timing and extent of transition
  - whether or not backup tapes are available to trustee or other parties in interest

- Documentation Review—Servicer's Access to Basic Documents

  - availability of documents—assurance that all documents are available
  - identity of custodians and document exception lists
  - resolution of any documentary exceptions
  - any servicer problem relating to defects or failure to have necessary documents

- Representations and Warranties of the Servicer and Compliance with Documents

    - determine representations and warranties of the servicer and their continued accuracy
    - any required qualifications (FNMA, Freddie Mac, Ginnie Mae or other entities)
    - compliance with all provisions of servicing documents, any issue of non-compliance to be disclosed on the servicer report and appropriate notice to be given
    - any Truth-In-Lending, Fair Debt Collection Act, HAMP, HARP or similar state law / regulations issues or claims from regulators or customers

- Personnel, General Staffing and Funding of Servicing

    - Does servicer currently have sufficient staff to service current transactions, including basic servicing, foreclosure, eviction, repair maintenance, guard service and sale and marketing given potential for increased defaults
    - Do the backup servicers have sufficient staff to service all transactions for which they act as backup servicer including basic servicing, foreclosure, eviction, repair, guard services and sale and marketing
    - What assurance of sufficient capacity to service and being available to service, or should there be an amendment to the servicing agreement to provide:

        - further written assurance
        - lien or pledge on servicing platform
        - option to purchase the servicing platform
        - access agreement to be able to enter into, use and operate the appropriate servicing platform to facilitate a transition

    - Is there sufficient funding of the servicing platform and operations to ensure long-term performance and fulfillment of servicing commitment, including retaining additional staff, facilities and equipment

Appendix XVI-D
Checklist of Potential Servicer Defaults

1. Misallocation of Deposits/Reconciliation Issues

    (a) Failure to make appropriate deposits into the protected account or custodial account, as appropriate

    (b) Failure to make deposits into the servicing accounts

    (c) Failure to timely reconcile servicing accounts

2. Failure to make servicer advances when appropriate.

3. Failure to make appropriate liquidation advances

4. Inappropriate reimbursement of liquidation and servicing advances (*i.e.*, recovery of advances from proceeds or payments on unrelated mortgage loans)

5. Failure to remit insurance payments to appropriate insurer

6. Failure to remit real estate taxes or other taxes to the appropriate tax authority

7. Failure to remit other assessments or fees to appropriate payee (*e.g.*, association dues etc.)

8. Inappropriate crediting of mortgage payments

9. Misappropriation of funds from accounts or lock box for unauthorized purposes (e.g. using trust funds to cover servicer or depositor's obligations)

10. Inappropriate handling of loss mitigation issues (losses as a result of negligence in handling defaults)

11. Any grant of inappropriate modifications to any mortgage loan or mortgage file

12. Failure to perform indemnification obligations

13. Failure to cooperate in servicing transition issues

14. Claims arising out of any violation of law relating to debt collection practices. (any available list of pending cases?)

15. Failure to properly maintain mortgage file and record payments and modification

16. Claims against the servicer by virtue of permitting the assumption of a mortgage by a third party in violation of the standards set forth in the servicing agreement

17. Claims arising out of any consent to a senior lien on the mortgage premises

18. Failure to maintain primary mortgage insurance policies where appropriate

19. Failure to maintain hazard insurance

20. Failure to notify other partners of known document exception that will adversely affect certificateholders' interests, including right to have a timely repurchase of the mortgage loan

21. Failure to maintain fidelity bond

22. Failure to maintain flood insurance (if applicable)

23. Improper allocation of cash in accordance with the terms of the relevant agreements

24. Any other breach of the terms and conditions of the servicing agreement

Appendix XVI-E
Model Transition of Servicing Protocol

MODEL
TRANSITION OF SERVICING PROTOCOL

Transition of Servicing Protocol: Upon the termination of the Original Servicer's[615] management, administrative, servicing and collection functions in accordance with the terms of the Servicing Agreements or hereof, the Original Servicer will assign to the Trustee, or to one or more successor servicers of the Securitization Trusts designated or approved by the Trustee as new servicers of the Assets (collectively, the "Successor Servicers"), all right, title and interest of the Original Servicer in and to all equipment, accounts, records, patents and intellectual property rights that are used or useful in providing the Securitization Services. The Original Servicer will fully cooperate with the Trustee and the Successor Servicers in connection with any transition of servicing to the Successor Servicers, said cooperation to include, without limitation, the following for each Securitization Trust:

a. *Documents.* The Original Servicer will deliver to the Trustee all documents in the possession or under the control of the Original Servicer, its agents or affiliates and relating to the assets and the servicing function, including but not limited to all documents relating to servicing records and files, original credit files, correspondence and all files relating to trailing identification, location and retrieval of trailing documents. Prior to delivery such documents will be held by the Original Servicer in a safe and secure place. Such documents will be delivered to the Trustee electronically, if possible, in a format acceptable to the Trustee and any Successor Servicers on a periodic basis and to the Trustee and the Successor Servicers in an agreed-upon manner. The Original Servicer will cooperate with the Trustee and the Successor Servicer to permit the review and copying of said documents or reproduction of any imaged documents.

b. *Payments Received Prior to the Cutoff Date.* Until instructed otherwise in writing by the Trustee, the Original Servicer will continue to instruct all Obligors to make payments in respect of the Assets in the manner required under the Servicing Agreements. All such payments received by the Original Servicer shall remain assets of the trust; payment being manually held in branches should be forwarded to central lockboxes within 24 hours.

---

615 Terms have the meaning typically utilized in ABS transactions.

c. *Electronic Databases and Files.* The Original Servicer will provide to the Trustee and the Successor Servicer at least thirty (30) business days prior to the Cutoff Date all of the electronic databases of information relating to the Assets (including, but not limited to, the records of payments made), and the Original Servicer will deliver within two (2) business days after the Cutoff Date updated versions of such databases showing information as of the close of business on the Cutoff Date, in format(s) acceptable to the Trustee and the applicable Successor Servicer. The files should include a complete data dictionary and data-formatting standards. In addition to the foregoing, the Original Servicer shall provide a summary database.

d. *Backup of Data.* The Original Servicer will prepare a daily backup of all data relating to the Assets and will store and maintain the backup. Copies of such backup in the format provided to the Successor Servicers will be delivered to the Trustee.

e. *Reconciliation of Financial Information.* If the Cut-Off Date is the last day of a calendar month, the Original Servicer will, for such calendar month, reconcile the financial information in this electronic database of information relating to the Assets to the Monthly Reports for such calendar month for each Securitization Trust. The Original Servicer should also prepare a reconciliation of advances taken from cash already received but not due until future months. If the Cutoff Date is other than the last day of a calendar month, the Original Servicer will assist the Successor Servicers in reconciling the financial information in its electronic database of information relating to the Assets to the Monthly Reports for such calendar month for each Securitization Trust. The Original Servicer shall provide the Trustee and any Successor Servicer with copies of all other reports completed by the Original Servicer in the ordinary course of servicing the Assets. In addition, the Original Servicer will provide any other report reasonably necessary in the transfer of the servicing of the Assets.

f. *Final Report to Credit Bureaus.* The Original Servicer will issue a final report to credit bureaus for the Assets as of the Cutoff Date. The final report will be made by the Original Servicer within fifteen (15) days after the Cutoff Date and will reflect that the Assets have been transferred to the applicable Securitization Trust and Successor Servicer.

g. *Cancellation or Transfer of ACH Authorizations.* The Original Servicer will transfer to the Successor Servicer all ACH authorizations for the Assets three (3) calendar days prior to the Cutoff Date. In the event that such cannot be transferred, the Original Servicer will cancel such ACH authorizations.

h. *Assignment and Transfer of All Payment Systems.* The Original Servicer shall transfer and assign to the Trustee for the benefit of the respective Securitization Trusts or the Trustee's designee (including Successor Servicers) all direct payment systems, checks, remittances, accounts, lockboxes, deposit accounts, ACH or other methods of receipt of payment, including payments received by branch offices, relating to the Securitization Trusts.

i. *Assignment of Mail, Mailboxes and Delivery Systems.* The Original Servicer shall assign to the Trustee or Successor Servicer, as appropriate, all mail, mailboxes and delivery systems used or useful in the servicing of the assets in the Securitization Trusts.

j. *Preparation of Monthly Reports.* The Original Servicer will prepare the Monthly Reports for each Securitization Trust for each calendar month ending on or before the Cutoff Date.

k. *Lockbox Adjustments.* The Original Servicer will cooperate in making any and all lockbox adjustments required for any lockbox accounts relating to the Securitization Trusts and will cooperate in connection with any distributions therefrom.

l. *Collection Efforts.* On and before the Cutoff Date, the Original Servicer will continue to seek collections on the Assets from all Obligors. All efforts to seek collections will be made in accordance with normal credit and collection policies and in compliance with the provisions of the Servicing Agreements, or as otherwise mutually agreed to by the Original Servicer and the Successor Servicers.

m. *Payments after Cutoff Date; Notification of New Payment Address and Procedures.* The Original Servicer will cooperate in the collection and deposit of payments it receives after the Cutoff Date. The Original Servicer will cooperate with the Successor Servicers to notify the Obligors to make payments to an account or lockbox number designated by each Successor Servicer.

n. *Assignment of Mail, Mailboxes and Delivery Systems.* The Original Servicer will assign to the Trustee or the Successor Servicer, as appropriate, all mail, mailboxes and delivery systems used or useful in the servicing of the Assets.

o. *Telephone Numbers.* The Original Servicer will assign to the Trustee (or its designee, including any Successor Servicer) the telephone numbers it uses in the servicing of the Assets for use by the applicable Successor Servicer. In the event the Trustee or the applicable Successor Servicer elects to use new telephone numbers, the Original Servicer will advise Obligors who telephone the Original Servicer of such new number(s). The Trustee and each Successor Servicer will mutually agree with the

Original Servicer as to the manner in which the toll-free telephone numbers utilized by the Original Servicer in its collection efforts will be employed on or before the Cutoff Date, and otherwise cooperate in any telecommunications transitioning issues.

p. *Transfer of Post-Cutoff Date Payments; Power of Attorney.* The Original Servicer will cooperate with the Successor Servicer in the collection and deposit of payments it receives after the Cutoff Date. In connection therewith, the Original Servicer will transfer to the appropriate Successor Servicer, within one (1) business day of receipt, all cash, direct payment, ACH, checks or other payment instruments received from Obligors on or after the Cutoff Date and will provide a power of attorney to the Successor Servicer sufficient to enable the Successor Servicer to negotiate such checks and instruments.

q. *Mail.* The Original Servicer will copy and deliver to the Trustee and the applicable Successor Servicer all correspondence received from or on behalf of Obligors prior to the Cutoff Date. To the extent reasonably available, the Original Servicer will provide to the Trustee or the Successor Servicer copies of bankruptcy notices, cease-and-desist letters and other legal or regulatory notices relating to the Assets or Obligors received prior to the Cutoff Date. Each business day after the Cutoff Date, the Original Servicer will forward to the applicable Successor Servicer by overnight delivery all incoming correspondence relating to Assets received by the Original Servicer after the Cutoff Date.

r. *Servicer Forms.* Within five (5) business days of the Cutoff Date, examples of the form letters sent by the Original Servicer to Obligors (and the schedule and conditions in which such letters are sent) will be provided to the Trustee and the Successor Servicers. To the extent that correspondence from the Original Servicer to the Obligors has been maintained by the Original Servicer, such correspondence will be copied and will be made available to the Trustee and the Successor Servicers.

s. *Delivery of Collateral Documents.* All collateral documents will be delivered to an authorized representative of the Trustee or the Successor Servicers.

t. *Right to Use Intellectual Property; Copies of Software.* The intellectual property and rights to use the intellectual property of others relating to the Securitization Services and any equipment, tools (including behavioral or credit-scoring tools) or software used therein will be transferred and assigned or licensed to the applicable Successor Servicer and the Trustee. The form of any assignment and transfer and any license will be acceptable to counsel for the Trustee.

u. *Goodbye Letter.* On or before the Cutoff Date, the Original Servicer will prepare, execute and deliver to the Obligors, the Successor Servicer and the Trustee a letter from the Original Servicer in a form(s) mutually agreed to with the Trustee and applicable Successor Servicer, advising the Obligors that the Original Servicer is no longer the Servicer for the Assets and that such Successor Servicer is the Servicer as of the Cutoff Date.

v. *Settlement; Pending Litigation.* Prior to the Cutoff Date, the Original Servicer will cooperate to provide each Successor Servicer with a report identifying Assets for which settlements in full are pending or installment arrangements have been entered into as of the close of business on the Cutoff Date. The report relating to Assets for which settlements in full are pending will include information regarding the settlement terms. In addition, prior to the Cutoff Date, the Original Servicer will provide a report identifying pending litigation (including pending Chapter 7 or 13 actions) with respect to the Assets, and the documentation relating to any resolution or settlement thereof, and shall cooperate with the Successor Servicer in substituting such Successor Servicer as a party to any pending litigation.

w. *Cooperation.* The Original Servicer will cooperate with the Trustee and any Successor Servicer in order to attempt an efficient and effective transition of servicing to the Successor Servicer and will meet with representatives of the Successor Servicer and the Trustee to facilitate the transfer of servicing and to provide an explanation of the operations of the servicing and the use and function of information (electronic or otherwise) necessary to service the Assets and to transfer such information. Without limiting the foregoing, the Original Servicer will permit the Trustee and any Successor Servicer to have complete and unfettered access to all facilities (whether owned or leased), books and records, computer systems, data and personnel as will be deemed necessary in the sole discretion of the Trustee or any Successor Servicer to facilitate said transition, and the Original Servicer will instruct all employees, officers, agents, accountants and other relevant parties to provide full cooperation in connection therewith.

x. *Rating Agencies.* The Original Servicer will provide to any rating agency which shall then have outstanding a rating with respect to any certificates issued by any of the Securitization Trusts such information as may be reasonably requested by such rating agency in order for it to assess the appropriate ratings for said certificates.

y. *Avoidance of Damage.* The Original Servicer will endeavor to avoid (1) damage to electronically stored information, documents and records necessary to the servicing of the Assets and avoid theft and loss of the assets generally and (2) the servicing platform and operational ability as transferred to the Successor Servicer under their protocol.

z. *Retention of Employees.* The Original Servicer will endeavor to retain, to the extent possible, those employees it deems appropriate to effectuate the transition of servicing to the Successor Servicers, including mail sorting and computer assistance, phone-call referrals and document retrieval.

Appendix XVI-F
Checklist of Basic Bankruptcy Considerations in the Event of a Filing by the Servicer

I. PRE-BANKRUPTCY ACTIONS

A. Audit of servicer function and actions

- perform audit of servicing function
- review qualifications of servicer and representations and warranties to determine the servicer's ability to continue servicing with adequate staffing and funding
- determine whether governmental agencies have to qualify the servicer
- determine if there is a servicing transition protocol for transition to a successor if the current servicer has not acted for any reason
- identify any sub-servicers

B. Audit of documents

- determine whether the trustee has all transaction documents
- assess whether there any current repurchase or indemnification obligations
- determine waterfall provisions both pre-default and post-default, identifying changes in servicer and trustee payments and reimbursements due to default
- review basic documents to make sure all required actions have been taken

C. Review of servicer defaults

- See Appendix XVI-D

II. POST-BANKRUPTCY ISSUES

A. Is the servicer really insolvent and is it a good-faith filing of bankruptcy?

- possible motion to dismiss based on lack of good faith (rarely granted)

B. Can the servicer in bankruptcy perform its obligations and keep the securitization cash flow separate from other funds in bankruptcy?

- make sure DIP financing orders and cash collateral orders recognize securitization cash flow is *not* property of bankruptcy estate and specifically protect that cash flow from commingling and interference
- object to DIP financing motions or cash collateral motions that do not provide proper protection
- make sure lockbox bank does not require unreasonable holdback on reserve or improper charges
- obtain assurance servicer can perform duties under servicing agreement and timely provide servicer reports and transfer of funds
    - sufficient staffing, experienced personnel and financing

C. If servicer cannot perform or defaults occur in bankruptcy, what can be done?

- motion to require debtor servicer to assume (or reject) servicing contract and, if assumed, provide adequate assurance of future performance (courts early on typically do not require debtor servicer to choose; however, that does not mean the motion should not be made)
- motion to lift stay and take action to remove the servicer (many times this is the heart of the case and will be fought by the debtor and the unsecured creditors)
- stipulation and agreed-upon servicing protocol and transition protocol

D. Can or should the servicer assume or assign all or part of servicing contract?

- cherry-picking servicing contracts should be resisted
- generally assumption is followed by sale and assignment or plan of reorganization

E. Should the servicer be permitted to sell its servicing business? (See Appendix XVI-G, Model Servicing Sale/Purchase Transition Protocol for transaction documentation the trustee may consider)

- What is in it for the trustee, investors and credit enhancer? (Should the sale be objected to?)
- Can the purchasers perform, and do you want them to?

- Who gets the proceeds of sale?

F. Can the servicer be reorganized?

- a prepackaged plan should be agreed to by the trustee, investors, credit enhancer and unsecured creditors prior to filing with agreed-upon result (sale or reorganization)
- always a question of whether it will work and what do investors lose
- remember indemnity, misrepresentation, conversion of funds, negligence and other claims may be predicate for large unsecured claim (who controls the reorganization process—unsecured creditors?) and such claims may have strategic and actual value
- feasibility and consenting class of unsecured claims are required typically (over 50 percent in number and 66-2/3 percent in amount of those voting)
- claims estimation or stipulation or settlement is key to successful resolution
- security fraud claims are subordinated to general unsecured claims in bankruptcy

G. Are there other ways out of bankruptcy?

- the best resolution is settlement and compromise between the servicer and the securitization trustee and investors providing benefit of bargain in servicing and new improved servicer through sale or reorganization
- equity infusion into the servicer is less likely but not impossible
- an increased servicing fee or terms of servicing may be necessary to avoid disaster
- creativity and dedication to the principles of securitization are key

Appendix XVI-G Model Servicing Sale/Purchase Transaction Protocol

MODEL
SERVICING SALE/PURCHASE TRANSACTION PROTOCOL

Upon the consummation of the sale and purchase of servicing of one or more securitization trusts, the Potential Purchaser[616] of the servicing of the respective Securitization Trusts ("Purchaser") shall conduct all management, administrative, servicing and collection functions in accordance with the terms of the Servicing Agreements as supplemented or clarified below. The Purchaser will fully cooperate with the Trustee and any Successor Sub-Servicers in connection with the servicing of the portfolio and in any transition of servicing in accordance with the Transition of Servicing Protocol. (See Appendix XVI-E.) In conducting its servicing activities with respect to a Securitization Trust:

The Purchaser as Successor Servicer. The Purchaser as the Successor Servicer ("Successor Servicer") will be the successor in all respects to the Original Servicer in its capacity as Servicer and in its capacity as Company under the Servicing Agreements and the transactions set forth or provided for in the Servicing Agreements and will be subject to all the responsibilities, duties and liabilities relating thereto placed on the Servicer and the Seller by the terms and provisions in the Servicing Agreements, including, but not limited to, (i) any and all repurchase obligations of the Original Servicer, (ii) the acts and omissions of the Original Servicer occurring prior to the Cutoff Date or for any breach of Original Servicer of any of its obligations contained in the Servicing Agreements or in any related document or agreement, (iii) the obligation of the Seller to pay any Guarantee Payment to the designated Class (to the extent applicable) of Certificateholders and (iv) the responsibility of the Seller to comply with the covenants, representations and warranties related to the Assets set forth in the Servicing Agreements.

Representations, Warranties and Covenants of the Successor Servicer (Purchaser). The Successor Servicer will make to the Trustee, as of the Cutoff Date, each of the representations, warranties and covenants of the Servicer and the Seller set forth in the Servicing Agreements (with such changes as are appropriate based on the type of

616 Terms have the meaning typically utilized in ABS transactions.

organization and jurisdiction of formation of the Successor Servicer). Such representations and warranties will survive after the Cutoff Date, and the Successor Servicer will be liable for breaches of such representations, warranties and covenants as well as for breaches of the representations, warranties and covenants of the Original Servicer prior to the Cutoff Date.

Personnel Requirements. The Successor Servicer (Purchaser) will assign experienced personnel and will maintain sufficient personnel to service the Assets pursuant to the Servicing Agreements in accordance with the second immediately succeeding paragraph.

Hardware Requirements. The Successor Servicer (Purchaser) will keep gateways, hardware, software, systems and the interface used to provide the Securitization Services up to date and otherwise maintain a technology platform that will enable the Successor Servicer to fulfill its obligations at all times under the Servicing Agreements in accordance with the Standard of Care.

Servicer Standard of Care. The Successor Servicer (Purchaser) and all of its employees, officers, directors and agents performing under the Servicing Agreements will exercise that degree of skill and care in accordance with (i) the highest degree of skill and care that the Successor Servicer exercises with respect to similar contracts serviced by the Successor Servicer, (ii) all applicable federal and state laws and regulations and (iii) the express terms of the Servicing Agreements; *provided, however,* that (A) the Successor Servicer shall (x) employ loss mitigation efforts, (y) employ policies with regard to repossessions (and make advances in connection therewith) designed to maximize the value of the collateral and (z) make principal and interest advances to the extent such are reasonably recoverable from cash flow; (B) the degree of skill and care employed will be at least as favorable as (if not better than) the degree of skill and care generally applied by servicers of similar contracts for institutional investors and in no event lower than the standards by which the Original Servicer serviced the Contracts at the time of entering into the Servicing Agreements, and (C) notwithstanding the foregoing, the Successor Servicer will not release or waive the right to collect the unpaid balance on any Contract that is not a defaulted contract. The Successor Servicer will punctually perform all of the Servicer's obligations and agreements under the Servicing Agreements, will maintain all material state and federal licenses and franchises necessary for it to perform its servicing responsibilities under the Servicing Agreements and will not impair the rights of the Trustee or the Certificateholders in any Contracts, payments thereunder or other Assets.

Loss Mitigation. The Servicer will remarket any Assets relating to defaulted contracts in the retail (and not wholesale) market and will provide financing to the buyers of such Assets.

Exercise of Rights and Remedies; Repossession. The Servicer shall employ commercially reasonable policies on the exercise of rights and remedies under the contracts and the repossession of collateral in an effort to maximize the value of the portfolio. The Servicer shall have reasonable policies on the advancement of the costs of exercising rights and remedies.

Payments after Takeover; Notification of New Payment Address and Procedures. The Successor Servicer (Purchaser) will deposit payments from the Obligors on the Assets either to the existing lockboxes or to a new lockbox established by the Successor Servicer. If the Successor Servicer elects to establish a new lockbox, as soon as practicable, but no later than five (5) business days following the conversion of the Assets from the Original Servicer's system to the Successor Servicer's system, the Successor Servicer will notify the Obligors that payments on the Assets should be remitted directly to the new lockbox.

Principal and Interest Advances; Other Advances. The Purchaser shall have reasonable policies and criteria for the principal and interest advances and other advances necessary for the servicing of the Securitization Trust.

Transition. The Successor Servicer (Purchaser) will cooperate with the Trustee and Original Servicer regarding the transition of the Securitization Services, including, but not limited to, cooperating with the transfer of servicing records, lockboxes and other assets of the Original Servicer used to service the Assets.

Telephone Numbers. The Trustee and the Successor Servicer (Purchaser) will mutually agree with the Original Servicer as to the manner in which the toll-free telephone numbers currently used by the Original Servicer in its collection efforts will be employed within ninety (90) calendar days of taking over the servicing of the portfolio.

Hello Letter. On or within one (1) business day after taking over the servicing function, the Successor Servicer (Purchaser) will prepare, execute and deliver to the Obligors a letter from the Successor Servicer, in a form mutually agreed to with the Trustee and Successor Servicer, advising the Obligors that the Original Servicer is no longer the Servicer for the Assets and that the Successor Servicer is the Servicer as of such date.

Appendix XVI-H
Addendum to Proof of Claim Form[617]

1. *Name and Address of Creditor and Basis for Claim.* ________________, a national banking association having a corporate trust office, serves as trustee (the "Trustee") under the Trust Agreement (defined below) in respect of the Trust (defined below) and makes and files this Proof of Claim against ________________ (the "Debtor") pursuant to Section 501 of the United States Bankruptcy Code and Federal Rule of Bankruptcy Procedure 3003.

This Proof of Claim relates to a securitization of commercial mortgage loans. The Trustee is trustee under that certain [Trust Agreement] dated as of [date] by and between ________________, as Depositor, and ________________, as Trustee (the "Trust Agreement"), with respect to the [relevant Trust] (the "Trust") (a bankruptcy-remote mortgage loan securitization trust that holds mortgage loans purchased by the Debtor and sold and/or assigned to the Trust). Under the terms of the Trust Agreement certain commercial mortgage loans were purchased by the Trust using funds obtained from investors through the issuance of certificates.

The [commercial mortgage loans] (the "Mortgage Loans") giving rise to this Proof of Claim were originated by various third parties (collectively, the "Originator") and were purchased by ____________________________ (the "Initial Purchaser") under the terms of a purchase and/or sale and servicing agreement (the "Purchase Agreement"). Thereafter the Initial Purchaser assigned these loans for value to ________________________ (the "Seller"), who thereafter transferred the Mortgage Loans for value to ____________________________ (the "Depositor") under the terms of a Mortgage Loan Sale and Assignment Agreement (the "Mortgage Loan Sale Agreement"). In exchange for the proceeds from the issuance of certificates, the Depositor transferred and conveyed the Mortgage Loans to the Trustee for the benefit of the holders of the certificates pursuant to the terms of the Trust Agreement. In addition to other items of collateral, the Trustee was assigned all of the Depositor's rights under the Mortgage Loan Sale Agreement.

Under the terms of the Trust Agreement and the Mortgage Loan Sale Agreement the Depositor and the Seller made certain representations and warranties with respect to the

617 Proof of Claim Form is Official Bankruptcy Form 410, App. XI-B.

Mortgage Loans to or for the benefit of the Trustee. In the event certain representations and warranties were breached with respect to individual Mortgage Loans, which materially and/or adversely affected the value of such Mortgage Loan, the Depositor and/or the Seller had the obligation to either (a) cure the breach in all material respects, (b) repurchase the Mortgage Loans, or (c) within two years of the Closing Date, substitute a Qualifying Substitute Mortgage Loan for an affected Mortgage Loan. This Proof of Claim is filed as an unsecured and/or administrative expense claim with respect to breaches of these representations and warranties, and alternatively as a secured claim in the event that the securitization transaction is deemed a financing and not a true sale.

On _________________ (the "Petition Date"), _________________ filed its voluntary petition for relief in this court, thus commencing the instant Chapter 11 case. Affiliates of the Debtor, including the Seller, filed voluntary petitions on and after _________________.

2. *Repurchase Obligations.* Pursuant to the Trust Agreement, the Debtor made certain representations, warranties and covenants about the Mortgage Loans that were subsequently acquired by the Trust. If there is a violation of a representation, warranty or covenant with respect to any Mortgage Loan that was sold to the Trust that materially adversely affects the value of such Mortgage Loan or the interest of the Certificateholders therein, the Debtor is obligated to repurchase that Mortgage Loan. As of the date of this Proof of Claim, the Trustee has been advised that the Debtor's representations, warranties and/or covenants with respect to at least ___ Mortgage Loans were incorrect or untrue, which materially and adversely affects the value of such Mortgage Loan and the interest of the Certificateholders therein, and such breaches cannot be or have not been cured. The outstanding principal balance of these Mortgage Loans as of ___________, _________, was approximately $[_________]. To date, the Debtor has not fulfilled its obligation to repurchase these Mortgage Loans. As a result of the Debtor's breach of its representations, warranties and/or covenants in respect of these Mortgage Loans and the Debtor's (and the Seller's) failure to repurchase them, the Trustee hereby asserts a claim against the Debtor in an amount not less than the repurchase price as and when required by the Trust Agreement and/or the Mortgage Loan Sale Agreement. The terms of the Trust Agreement and/or Mortgage Loan Sale Agreement may require other Mortgage Loans be repurchased that the Trustee is not aware of at this time. The Trustee reserves the right to amend its Repurchase Claim in the event it becomes aware of other loans that should likewise be repurchased under the terms of the Trust Agreement and/or Mortgage Loan Sale Agreement. [Annexed hereto as Schedule 1 is a report containing information supporting the liquidated claim amounts described

in the preceding paragraph. The report contains information regarding, among other things, the loan number and the amount of the claim.]

3. *Obligation to Cure Documentary Exceptions.* In addition to the foregoing, the Trustee has identified certain Mortgage Loan files that are missing or contain defective documentation. The Debtor is obligated to correct material defects in the loan files. Attached as Schedule 2 is a list of documentary exceptions relating to Mortgage Loan files in the Trust. It is not certain at this time whether any of these defects in the Mortgage Loan files will give rise to any loss to the Trust, although many if not all of these may impair the value of the respective Mortgage Loan or the interest of the holders of the Certificates therein. As a result, the Trustee asserts a claim up to the full principal amount of these Mortgage Loans as of ___________, ___________, of $_____________. Additional Mortgage Loan files may contain missing or defective documentation that has not been discovered. The Trustee asserts a contingent and unliquidated claim with respect to all undiscovered deficiencies regarding the Mortgage Loan files.

4. *Early Payment Default.* After due inquiry of the Master Servicer, the Trustee is not aware of any outstanding Mortgage Loan that is the subject of an early payment default, but reserves the right to assert a claim in the event it ultimately becomes aware of one.

5. *Servicer Claims.* The Trustee asserts a claim against the servicer, to the extent that ______________________ was a servicer for all or some of the Mortgage Loans, for any breaches of any of the agreements, covenants, representations or warranties contained in the servicing agreement. Any continuing failure to service the loans in strict accordance with the terms of the servicing agreement likewise may give rise to administrative expense claims against ______________________, as servicer. Due to the nature of the servicing roles, claims against the servicer may not be discovered by the Trustee for an extended period of time after the breach, and therefore the Trustee continues to investigate whether or not it has any claims with respect to the servicing of the Mortgage Loans.

6. *Custodial Claims.* The Trustee asserts a claim for breaches of any of the obligations contained in any of the Custodial Agreements listed on Exhibit __, which may likewise give rise to administrative expense claims for fees, claims and expenses incurred postpetition.

7. *Indemnification Obligations.* Under the terms of Sections _____ of the Pooling and Servicing Agreement or the Indenture, the Debtor is obligated to indemnify the Trustee for

[detail: ________________________________]. The Trustee is aware of the following claims: ________________________________. Trustee is continuing its investigation with respect to other claims it may have against the Debtor for indemnification obligations.]

8. *Other Claims.* The Trustee asserts an unliquidated contingent claim for the fees, costs and expenses relating to the failure of the Debtor to comply with various administrative obligations under the terms of the Trust Agreement and related documents, including but not limited to obligations relating to the filing of UCCs, preparation and filing of taxes, Issuer Orders, termination obligations and other administrative duties and for the cost of any required transfer of servicing of the Mortgage Loans in the future.

9. *Fees and Expenses and Other Claims.* The Trustee also asserts a claim for trustee's fees, expenses and indemnification claims; for the fees and expenses of the Master Servicer, Custodian, Owner Trustee or Administrator; and for the fees, expenses and indemnification claims incurred by the Trust, including, without limitation, attorneys, and/or agents' fees, all as more fully set forth and described in the Trust Agreement, any indemnification agreement and other related agreements. Further, the Trustee asserts a claim for indemnification on behalf of itself and the Master Servicer, Custodian, Owner Trustee or Administrator, as appropriate, as more fully set forth and described therein. The Trustee reserves the right to amend this Proof of Claim in the future to assert a liquidated claim in connection with fees, expenses and indemnification.

The Trustee also files this claim for taxes due by the Debtor under the relevant agreement and any other obligations, losses, fees or expenses that are unknown to the Trustee at this time, but that may have been incurred by the Trust and are attributable to the Debtor.

10. *Obligations Are Continuing.* The claims set forth herein may have grown and may continue to grow after the Petition Date, to the extent permitted by law.

11. *True Sale.* If the sale of any Mortgage Loans to the Initial Purchaser, any subsequent purchaser or the Trust is determined to be a financing transaction (rather than a true sale), then the Trustee's claim is in the full amount of the principal and interest due on the Certificates of $____________ and secured by collateral set forth in the Granting Clause of the Trust Agreement, including but not limited to the Mortgage Loans. The Trustee also asserts setoff and recoupment rights with respect to any and all funds held by the Trustee, the Servicer or the Master Servicer and Trust Administrator that constitute property of the Debtor (if any), and any

and all other setoff and recoupment rights, all of which the Trustee expressly reserves, and asserts a secured claim on account thereof. The claims asserted in this Proof of Claim are secured to the extent of the value of any security and setoff rights and unsecured for any deficiency. The above-described security interest (to the extent that the sale of any Mortgage Loans to any prior Purchaser or the Trust is determined to be a financing transaction) is perfected by possession and/or control of the above-mentioned property, as applicable.

12. *Date Debt Was Incurred.* The claims set forth herein relate to a securitization transaction commonly known as entered into on or about ______________________________.

13. *If Court Judgment Was Obtained.* To the best of the Trustee's knowledge, no judgment has been rendered with respect to this claim.

14. *Classification of Claim.* The claim is filed as an unsecured claim or as a secured claim as aforesaid. In addition, the Trustee may have postpetition administrative expense claims against the Debtor. While the Trustee is not asserting these claims herein, as the sole purpose of this Proof of Claim is to assert its prepetition claims against the Debtor, by filing this Proof of Claim, the Trustee does not waive any of its postpetition claims against the Debtor, and expressly reserves all of its rights in connection with such claims.

15. *Documents on Which This Claim Is Based.* The documents supporting this Claim include the Trust Agreement and the Mortgage Loan Sale Agreement. These documents are voluminous and are available upon request.

16. *Credits and Setoffs.* Except as provided above, to the knowledge of the undersigned, the claims are not subject to any setoff or counterclaim. The amount of all payments made prior to the Petition Date has been credited and deducted for the purpose of making this Proof of Claim, but no other payments have been credited or deducted.

17. *Reservation of Rights.* This Proof of Claim is filed under the compulsion of the bar date established in the Debtor's Chapter 11 case and is filed to protect the Trustee from forfeiture of claims by reason of said bar date. The filing of this Proof of Claim is not intended to be and should not be deemed or construed as (a) an election of a remedy, (b) a consent by the Trustee to the jurisdiction of the bankruptcy court or any other court with respect to the proceedings, if any, commenced, in any case against or otherwise involving the Trustee, (c) a consent by the Trustee to trial by jury as to any and all matters so triable herein or in any case, controversy or proceeding related hereto, pursuant to 28 U.S.C. § 157(e) or otherwise, (d) a waiver of the right of

the Trustee to a trial by jury in any matter herein or in any case, controversy or proceeding related hereto, (e) a waiver of the right of the Trustee to have final orders in non-core matters entered only after a de novo review by the United States District Court, (f) a waiver of any right of the Trustee to have the reference withdrawn by the United States District Court in any matter subject to mandatory or discretionary withdrawal, (g) a waiver of any past, present or future event of default in regard to the Trust Agreement, the Mortgage Loan Sale Agreement or otherwise, (h) a waiver or limitation of any rights of the Trustee, including, without limitation, a waiver of obligations owing to the Trustee, rights, claims, actions, defenses, setoffs or recoupments to which the Trustee is or may be entitled under the Trust Agreement, Mortgage Loan Sale Agreement or otherwise, in law or equity, against the Debtor and/or any subsidiary or affiliate thereof, or any other person, including, without limitation, rights against guarantors, officers or directors, or the right to contest the validity or extent of any liens or security interests purported to be equal, senior or inferior to any right, lien or security interest of the Trustee, all of which rights, claims, actions, defenses, setoffs or recoupments are expressly reserved by the Trustee or (i) an admission by the Trustee that any property held by the Debtor (or any subsidiary or affiliate thereof) is property of the estate.

Nothing contained herein shall limit or prejudice the right of the Trustee to file additional claims with respect to any other liability or debt of the Debtor to the Trustee.

To the extent the Debtor has not rejected any particular agreement that constitutes an executory contract, the Trustee reserves its right to amend, supplement or add to this claim to include any rejection damage claim.

18. *Notices.* All notices relating to this proof of claim should be sent to: ____________.

SCHEDULE 1

Information Supporting Repurchase Claims

SCHEDULE 2

Documentary Exceptions

SCHEDULE 3

Custodial Agreements

XVII. The Trustee and Derivatives Transactions

A. Introduction

As the financial transactions for which institutions serve as trustee become more complex, the trustee increasingly must deal with derivatives, securities contracts and other sophisticated financial products as part of its duties. A classic definition of a derivative is a financial instrument that derives its value from an interest rate, exchange rate, equity security, fixed income security, commodity or index or any other underlying asset.[618] Its value is determined by fluctuations in the underlying asset. As a consequence, when a distressed transaction includes a swap, repurchase agreement, financial contract or similar agreement, a trustee often is required to take action to enforce the agreement on an expedited basis. While the prudent trustee will review the agreement and proposed course of conduct with experienced counsel, and consider good faith input from holders, this chapter will highlight some of the issues presented.[619]

B. Commonly Encountered Derivatives

There are certain forms of derivatives that an indenture trustee is likely to find in its portfolio for administration. Because of their special treatment in the case of bankruptcy, it is helpful to identify them. A *repurchase agreement*, often termed a repo, is an agreement that provides for the transfer of one or more certificates of deposit, mortgage-related securities, mortgage loans, eligible bankers acceptances, qualified foreign governmental securities or securities that are direct obligations of or fully guaranteed by the United States with a simultaneous agreement to transfer the same at a date certain, not later than one year after such transfer, or on demand against the transfer of funds. More simply put, a repurchase agreement is a transaction whereby one party transfers a security to another in exchange for funds along with

---

618 Sylvie A. Durham, *Derivatives Deskbook* § 1:2 (2d ed. 2014) ("Durham").

619 Although beyond the scope of this book, it is important to note that the Wall Street Reform and Consumer Protection Act, commonly known as the Dodd-Frank Act, regulates derivatives use in the United States. Dodd-Frank authorizes the CFTC and the SEC to regulate derivatives dealers and improve derivatives market transparency and pricing through regulation. To that end, derivatives users (and their trustees) may be required to undertake certain actions to assure that their derivatives transactions are Dodd-Frank compliant. Further, if the transaction involves a foreign bank, the European Market Infrastructure Regulation ("EMIR") may be an issue.

a simultaneous agreement by the transferee to give back the security upon repayment of the funds.[620]

A *swap agreement* involves the consent of the parties to to "swap" cash flows over a stated period of time on a hypothetical principal known as the "notional amount."[621] Parties can swap payments based upon a number of indices including interest rates, currency rates and security or commodity prices.[622] The definition of swap agreement in the United States Bankruptcy Code contains a detailed list of the types of transactions included within the terms as used therein.[623] One type of swap is the controversial *credit default swap* whereby the credit exposure of bonds or other fixed income products is transferred to another party. The buyer of the swap makes payments to the seller of the swap. However, if the debt issuer defaults, the seller of the swap pays the buyer the premium and interest payments due until maturity.[624]

A *forward contract* is a contract, other than a commodity contract, for the purchase or sale of a commodity or similar interest that is presently or in the future becomes the subject of dealing in the forward contract trade with a maturity date more than two days after the date of the contract.[625] As in the case of the swap agreement, there is a detailed definition of forward contract in the United States Bankruptcy Code.[626]

An *option* is a contract that gives the buyer of the option the right, but not the obligation, to buy (call) or sell (put) an underlying asset or financial instrument at a specified strike price on a specified date or during a certain period of time.

These types of contracts receive special protection under the Bankruptcy Code, as do commodity contracts,[627] securities contracts[628] and master netting agreements[629] ("Protected Transactions"). Specifically, *ipso facto* clauses contained in such contracts are enforceable in bankruptcy; the automatic stay imposed by Section 362 of the Bankruptcy Code does not prevent

---

620 11 U.S.C. § 101(47); *In re HomeBanc Mortg. Corp.*, 2014 WL 1268677 (D. Del. Mar. 27, 2014); *Bevill Bresler & Schulman Asset Mgmt. Corp. v. Spencer Sav. And Loan Ass'n*, 878 F. 2d 742 (3d Cir. 1989); *see also In re: Homebanc Mortgage Corp.*, 573 B.R. 495 (Bankr. D. Del. 2017).

621 *BKB Props., LLC v. SunTrust Bank*, 453 Fed. Appx. 582 (6th Cir. 2011).

622 *Thrifty Oil Co. v. Bank of Am. Nat'l Tr. and Sav. Ass'n*, 322 F.3d 1039 (9th Cir. 2003).

623 11 U.S.C. § 101(53B).

624 Durham at § 1.2.3.

625 *In re Mirant Corp.*, 310 B.R. 548 (Bankr. N.D. Tex. 2004).

626 11 U.S.C. § 101(25).

627 11 U.S.C. § 761(4).

628 11 U.S.C. § 741(7).

629 11 U.S.C. § 101(38A).

the enforcement of rights to close-out, setoff or foreclosure on collateral (accelerate, terminate or liquidate); and certain provisions to avoid prepetition transfers are not applicable. These are known as *safe harbors*.

C. Bankruptcy Protections for Derivatives and Certain Other Financial Products

1. *Ipso Facto* Clauses

As a general rule, the Bankruptcy Code provides that an executory contract or unexpired lease may not be terminated or modified solely because of a provision in the contract or lease that is conditioned on the commencement of a bankruptcy case.[630] However, in the case of Protected Transactions, *ipso facto* clauses are enforceable and a party's contractual right to accelerate, terminate or liquidate a Protected Transaction due to an *ipso facto* clause cannot be stayed, avoided or otherwise limited by any provision of the Bankruptcy Code.[631]

2. The Automatic Stay

While the Bankruptcy Code, specifically Section 362 thereof, operates as a stay of actions against the debtor, its estate or its property, in the case of Protected Transactions, there are broad exceptions.[632] As a result, a party to a swap agreement, repurchase agreement, forward contract, commodity (futures) contract, security contract or master netting agreement may exercise any contractual right under a security agreement or other credit enhancement related to the transaction or to offset or net out any termination value, payment amount or other transfer obligation related to the transaction without violating the automatic stay.[633] Trustees should be aware that these rights may also be affected by a contractual stay. Over 270 entities, including the largest global banks and their subsidiaries, are parties to the International Swaps and Derivatives Association, Inc. ("ISDA") Resolution Stay Protocol.[634] The Protocol provides for contractual

---

630 11 U.S.C. § 365(e)(1).

631 Swap Agreement (11 U.S.C. § 560); Repurchase Agreements (11 U.S.C. § 559); Commodities or Forward Contracts (11 U.S.C. § 556); Securities Contracts (11 U.S.C. § 555); and Master Netting Agreements (11 U.S.C. § 561). See also *In re Tribune Co. Fraudulent Conveyance Litig.*, 499 B.R. 310 (S.D.N.Y. 2013), *aff'd*, 818 F.3d 98 (2d Cir. 2016); *Lehman Bros. Special Financing v. Bank of America, et al.*, 553 B.R. 476 (Bankr. S.D.N.Y. 2016).

632 11 U.S.C. § 362(b)(6), (7), (17) or (27); 11 U.S.C. § 362(0); 11 U.S.C. § 560.

633 But contractual rights that are merely ancillary or incidental to an *ipso facto* clause may not be enforceable. See *In re Calpine Corp.*, 2009 WL 1578282 (Bankr. S.D.N.Y. 2009) (provision regarding timetable for raising any dispute with respect to termination payment not enforceable as part of safe harbor). But see *In re Lehman Bros. Holdings, Inc.*, 502 B.R. 383 (Bankr. S.D.N.Y. 2013) (right of non-defaulting party to rely upon contractual norms for disposing of collateral is an integrated aspect of what it means to cause the liquidation of a swap agreement).

634 http://www.isda.org.

amendments that include short-term stay mechanisms. Additionally, European Union banks are required to include in their agreements that the counterparty agrees to Article 55 of the European Union Bank Recovery and Resolution Directive ("BRRD") and European Union contractual stays and acceptance of the bail-in powers of the BRRD.

3. The Avoidance Provisions of the Bankruptcy Code

A debtor's right to exercise avoidance powers with respect to Protected Transactions is limited. Under the provisions of the Bankruptcy Code, certain pre-bankruptcy transactions that are deemed to result in unfair treatment to other creditors may be set aside. Thus, the debtor may avoid a preference: a transfer of an interest of the debtor in property made to or for the benefit of a creditor, for or on account of an antecedent debt, made while the debtor was insolvent and within 90 days before the bankruptcy filing (one year if the creditor is an insider), that resulted in the creditor receiving a greater distribution than it otherwise would have in a Chapter 7 distribution.[635] In addition, generally, if two years prior to bankruptcy the debtor sells assets for insufficient value (constructive fraudulent transfer)[636] or with an actual intent to defraud a creditor,[637] those transactions can be set aside. However, where Protected Transactions are concerned, transactions are exempt from avoidance as constructive fraudulent transfers and preferences or the fixing of statutory liens on the debtor's property.[638]

4. Setoff

While the Bankruptcy Code does not, as a general rule, prohibit the setoff of a mutual debt, such setoff is prohibited in the case of payments transferred to the creditor within 90 days or credits incurred for the purpose of obtaining a right of setoff.[639] However, the setoff of certain amounts related to Protected Transactions is permitted notwithstanding the prohibitions.[640]

5. Significance for Trustees

The special treatment accorded Protected Transactions, while ultimately a possible aid in increasing the recovery to holders, means that the early days of a bankruptcy can be an intense period for the trustee. Derivative products will need to be quickly examined and terminated if in the best interest of the holders, termination amounts will need to be calculated and setoffs will

---

635 11 U.S.C. § 547.

636 11 U.S.C. § 548(A)(i)(b).

637 11 U.S.C. § 548(A)(i)(a).

638 11 U.S.C. §§ 546(e), 546(f), 546(g) and 546(j).

639 11 U.S.C. § 553(a)(2) and (3).

640 11 U.S.C. § 553(a)(2)(B), (a)(3)(C) and (b)(1).

need to be exercised. Depending upon the complexity of a derivatives transaction, it may not be abundantly clear to a trustee whether a derivatives contract is "in the money" or "out of the money," so if the trustee has the right to terminate a derivatives contract upon default, it may wish to seek the help of an advisor.[641] Files with such Protected Transactions should be flagged so that the trustee is sensitive to the need for special and expedited treatment of these aspects of the matter in the event of insolvency. As always, experienced counsel should be consulted.[642] While it has been held that a trustee under a credit default swap transaction has no free-floating fiduciary duties to advance a counterparty's economic interests in any manner other than with respect to the narrowly circumscribed responsibilities identified in the trust agreement,[643] those responsibilities should be anticipated.

D. The ISDA Master Agreement

Over-the-counter derivatives, which will be the type a trustee is likely to encounter, are traded between two parties, as opposed to exchange-traded derivatives. In an effort to standardize contract terms so that each transaction did not need to be separately negotiated, ISDA developed the ISDA Master Agreement, a type of umbrella contract, which outlines the terms applied to an over-the-counter derivatives transaction. The two versions of the agreement currently in use are the 1992 ISDA Master Agreement[644] and the 2002 ISDA Master Agreement. Copies of the agreements are available on the ISDA website.[645] The agreements provide uniform terms with respect to events of default and termination events and the mechanics of termination, including the calculation of the termination payment. The parties to such an agreement also agree to the terms of a schedule that documents certain elections available under the master agreement and allows for the parties to add to and revise the provisions of the form master agreement. An accompanying credit support annex, which is a type of security agreement, sets forth any agreement with respect to the posting of collateral. This credit support annex may also be found on the ISDA website. The new ISDA Credit Support Index adds additional requirements for

---

641 Some transactions designate someone other than the trustee to make the economic decisions with respect to a swap. Any such designee should not be affiliated with the trustee's swap counterparty.

642 The safe harbor granted to Protected Transactions has at times been controversial. The American Bankruptcy Institute Commission to Study the Reform of Chapter 11 has challenged the effectiveness of such provisions to promote stability in the market and has recommended the amendment and limitation of certain of these provisions. *See* "American Bankruptcy Institute Commission to Study the Reform of Chapter 11: 2012–2014 Final Report and Recommendations," AM. BANKR. INST. L. REV., Winter 2015, at 102–121.

643 *CFIP Master Fund, Ltd. v. Citibank N.A. et al.*, 738 F. Supp. 2d 450 (S.D.N.Y. 2010).

644 The 1992 ISDA Master Agreement comes in two versions: multicurrency – cross border and local currency – single jurisdiction.

645 www.ISDA.org.

posting collateral and clearing of transactions to be consistent with Dodd-Frank and other post-financial crisis regulations. While the trustee will want to have the forms of master agreement and credit support annex and the ISDA user's guides at hand, the prudent trustee will have access to the actual executed agreements and counsel experienced in dealing with the master agreements, especially if there is an event of default or termination event. The calculation of early termination amounts should not be assigned to the inexperienced. In the case of the 1992 ISDA master agreement, the schedule will indicate which of two measures is to be used to calculate the early termination amount: loss, which is based upon the actual loss suffered, or market quotation, which is based upon the market quotation derived as soon as possible from four reference market makers to determine the economic equivalent of compliance with the transaction.[646] The early termination amount under the 2002 ISDA master agreement requires the calculation of the close-out amount pursuant to the close-out methodology that is part of the agreement and includes the concept of set-off. Whether the 1992 or 2002 ISDA master agreement is at issue, unless the trust officer is well versed in the intricacies of the methodology, the trustee should enlist the assistance of experienced advisors in calculating and documenting the early termination amounts.

A filing by the counterparty under the United States Bankruptcy Code is an event of default under both the 1992 and 2002 ISDA master agreements. Parties have the option at the outset of the transaction to treat a bankruptcy event of default as an automatic termination event by so providing in the schedule. If the automatic termination event is not selected, the non-defaulting party must deliver a notice of early termination. In both instances, the calculation of the early termination amount must be provided shortly thereafter. Depending upon the choices made at the time the master agreement and schedules are prepared, the close-out netting process may be applicable where the value of more than one contract is netted and set off. Expert assistance in preparation of the notice, the calculation (including any netting) and the delivery of required documents should be obtained. This is particularly true if the trustee will need to defend the calculation or explain it to a court, counterparty or others. In addition, the calculation will be necessary for the proof of claim the indenture trustee will file in the bankruptcy court. A form proof of claim addendum for a swap transaction is attached as Appendix XVII-A.

---

646 The parties to a 1992 ISDA Master Agreement also elect between two payment methods: First Method, which allows the non-defaulting party to "walk away" from making any termination payments to the defaulting party, or Second Method, which requires full two-way termination payments by the parties. Market convention invariably is to elect the Second Method.

E. Is the Transaction One That Has the Benefit of the Safe Harbors?

A protected transaction that has the benefit of the safe harbor provisions presents opportunities and challenges to the trustee in the event of a bankruptcy. The safe harbor provisions mean that the trustee can move forward to exercise remedies without the strictures of the automatic stay even if the only default is the bankruptcy filing and without concern for any avoidance actions or limitations on setoffs.[647] The primary challenge is the expectation that the trustee will move rapidly to enforce the rights under the transaction. Accordingly, the threshold issue of the nature of the transaction may, at times, need to be considered by the trustee in consultation with counsel. The applicability of the safe harbors may not be readily apparent.[648] However, when the question has been presented, a court has determined that an agreement to deliver natural gas is a commodity forward agreement and thus within the swap agreement defense to an avoidance proceeding,[649] that contracts providing for the sale and repurchase of mortgage loans were repurchase agreements within the meaning of the Bankruptcy Code but the portions of the contracts providing for the *servicing* of mortgage loans were severable and not subject to the safe harbors,[650] and that an agreement under which a party acquired subordinated notes that were interests in mortgage loans qualified as a securities contract under the Bankruptcy Code.[651] Thus, if the trustee is advised that there is a legitimate issue as to the applicability of a safe harbor to a transaction, a declaratory judgment to determine the coverage is obviously preferable to waiver of such argument.[652]

---

647 While the trustee should be entitled to the benefits of the safe harbors, note that in the Lehman bankruptcy discussed in Part G, Lehman argued that the trustee was not a swap counterparty in a transaction involving notes issued by an SPV. The bankruptcy court ruled against Lehman. *In re Lehman Bros. Holdings*, 553 B.R. 476 (Bankr. S.D.N.Y. 2016).

648 *See, e.g., Mich. State Housing Dev. Auth. v. Lehman Bros. Derivative Prods. Inc. et al.*, 502 B.R. 383 (Bankr. S.D.N.Y. 2013) (agreed method of liquidating swap agreement in event a party elects to terminate based on the other party's bankruptcy filing enforceable).

649 *In re Nat'l Gas Distributors, LLC v. U.S.A.*, 415 B.R. 209 (Bankr. E.D.N.C. 2009).

650 *In re Am. Home Mortg., Inc.*, 379 B.R. 503 (Bankr. D. Del. 2008); *Calyon N.Y. Branch v. Am. Home Mortg. Corp.*, 383 B.R. 585 (Bankr. D. Del. 2008).

651 *In re Am. Home Mortg., Holdings, Inc. v. Lehman Bros. Inc.*, 388 B.R. 69 (Bankr. D. Del. 2008). *See also In re MCK Millennium Centre Parking, LLC*, 532 B.R. 716 (Bankr. N.D. Ill. 2015).

652 *In re MBS Mgmt. Servs., Inc.*, there are other exceptions to the debtor's avoidance powers, including settlement payments. 690 F.3d 352 (5th Cir. 2012). Consideration by the trustee of all exceptions is appropriate. At the time of publication, the United States Supreme Court was reviewing the issue of whether Section 546(e) of the Bankruptcy Code protects securities transactions only when a financial institution is the buyer or seller, or whether the provision applies when the institution acts merely as a conduit for the money, *FTI Consulting v. Merit Mgmt. Grp.*, 830 F.3d 690 (7th Cir. 2016), cert. granted 137 S. Ct. 2092 (U.S. May 1, 2017).

F. Are There Triangular Setoff Issues Involved?

Section 553 of the Bankruptcy Code, under certain circumstances, allows a creditor to offset a mutual debt owed by the creditor to the debtor against a claim of the creditor against the debtor if those claims are valid and enforceable. The Bankruptcy Code's mutuality provision is meant to protect against "triangular" setoffs. A triangular setoff occurs when entity A attempts to offset its obligation to the debtor (B) against the debtor's obligation to entity C. Two entities, even if related, cannot aggregate their debts and claims against a debtor for setoff purposes.[653] If a Protected Transaction is involved, some have asserted that the safe harbors eliminate the Section 553 mutuality requirement. The acceptance of such a rule obviously would expand the trustee's analysis of its options in the event of a derivatives bankruptcy. However, that theory has been rejected in favor of the rule that the safe harbor exceptions do not eliminate the mutuality requirement for setoff.[654]

G. The Lehman Bankruptcy, Derivatives and the Trustee

As of the commencement of the bankruptcy in the early hours of Monday, September 15, 2008, Lehman Brothers Holdings Inc. ("LBHI") and certain of its direct and indirect subsidiaries ("Lehman") were parties to approximately 1.2 million derivative transactions, with approximately 6,500 counterparties.[655]

LBHI sponsored various collateralized debt obligations, securitizations and other similar transactions that included swap agreements to which Lehman Brothers Special Financing ("LBSF") was a party. The issuer of the notes would enter into swap agreements with LBSF in which a security interest would be assigned to the indenture trustee for the benefit of the noteholders or certificateholders. Additionally, LBHI was a credit support provider for many of the swap agreements. The transaction documents often had a payment waterfall that indicated that LBSF, for any early termination payment related to a swap agreement, would have a payment priority unless it was a defaulting party, in which case it had a lower priority, the flip clause. While certain of the derivatives automatically were terminated by their terms, many were terminated by the giving of notice by the non-Lehman party. Other counterparties chose not to

---

653 *In re Semcrude*, 399 B.R. 388 (Bankr. D. Del. 2009), citing *Westinghouse Credit Corp. v. D'Urso*, 278 F.3d 138 (2d Cir. 2002), *aff'd*, 428 B.R. 590 (D. Del. 2010) (party seeking relief from automatic stay not entitled to this remedy; mutuality cannot be suffered by multi-party agreement contemplating a triangular setoff).

654 *In re Am. Home Mortg., Inc.*, 501 B.R. 44 (Bankr. D. Del. 2013).

655 DEBTORS' DISCLOSURE STATEMENT FOR THIRD AMENDED JOINT CHAPTER 11 PLAN OF LEHMAN BROTHERS HOLDINGS INC. AND ITS AFFILIATED DEBTORS PURSUANT TO SECTION 1125 OF THE BANKRUPTCY CODE, *In re Lehman Bros. Holdings Inc. et al.*, No. 08-13555 (Bankr. S.D.N.Y Sep. 1, 2011), ECF No. 19629 ("Debtors' Disclosure Statement") at 33.

terminate if the termination would have resulted in a net payment to the debtors.[656] The counterparties for the terminated derivatives struggled to develop early termination calculations based upon market quotations, given the chaos in the market where market quotations were difficult to obtain.[657] The calculation of loss was similarly challenging. If there was a credit support annex, the non-defaulting party had to net out collateral from the termination payment and set off amounts owed between the parties. The counterparties' calculations were provided to Lehman first in the calculation of the early termination amount and in proofs of claim required by the September 22, 2009 bar date.[658] Further, a detailed questionnaire was required to be completed by parties filing claims based upon derivatives contracts, which required extensive information regarding valuation methodology, including quotations received from market makers and any replacement transactions. Many of the claimants were trustees who had literally hundreds of transactions impacted by these requirements. The development of working groups within the trustee's institution and in coordination with counsel enhanced the ability to comply with the onerous requirement. The corporate trust departments of a number of institutions worked to present a united front in raising issues with respect to the feasibility of the procedures Lehman required.[659]

The bankruptcy court granted Lehman's motion to permit the assumption and assignment to third parties without the consent of the counterparty of derivatives contracts that had not been terminated.[660] Subsequently, the debtors obtained the approval of their motion[661] to establish a protocol for the assumption and assignment of derivatives agreements if such was

---

656 DEBTORS' MOTION FOR AN ORDER PURSUANT TO SECTIONS 105 AND 365 OF THE BANKRUPTCY CODE TO ESTABLISH PROCEDURES FOR THE SETTLEMENT OR ASSUMPTION AND ASSIGNMENT OF PREPETITION DERIVATIVE CONTRACTS, *In re Lehman Bros. Holdings, Inc.*, No. 08-13555 (Bankr. S.D.N.Y. Nov. 13, 2008); ECF No. 1498. The debtors state that of approximately 930,000 derivatives transactions, approximately 733,000 had been terminated. This was five weeks after the petition date.

657 The Bankruptcy Code and case law support the use of alternative methods of valuation where market quotations are unavailable or the results are suspect. The 1992 ISDA also states that if a commercially reasonable result is not obtained using market quotations, then the loss method is used.

658 DEBTORS' DISCLOSURE STATEMENT at 46.

659 This type of cooperation among trustees is permissible under the rule of the *United Airlines* and *Sharon Steel* cases. See Chapter XIX *infra*.

660 DEBTORS' MOTION FOR AN ORDER PURSUANT TO SECTIONS 105 AND 365 OF THE BANKRUPTCY CODE TO ESTABLISH PROCEDURES FOR THE SETTLEMENT OR ASSUMPTION AND ASSIGNMENT OF PREPETITION DERIVATIVE CONTRACTS, *In re Lehman Bros. Holdings Inc., et al.*, No. 08-13555 (Bankr. S.D.N.Y. Nov. 13, 2008), ECF No. 1498.

661 DEBTORS' MOTION FOR AN ORDER APPROVING CONSENSUAL ASSUMPTION AND ASSIGNMENT OF PREPETITION DERIVATIVE CONTRACTS, *In re Lehman Bros. Holdings Inc.*, No. 08-13555 (Bankr. S.D.N.Y. Jan. 16, 2009), ECF No. 2561.

in accordance either with the terms of the contract or with the consent of the counterparty. These procedures required great diligence by trustees to monitor and respond to transactions affected. Resolving the claims represented by terminated derivatives was difficult since, in order to settle, Lehman required the reconciliation of the universe of all trades with the counterparty and the valuation of each transaction under the derivatives contract.[662] Lehman's procedures for alternative dispute resolution were no less onerous and expensive for trustees without any assurance that the derivatives claim would be resolved.[663] At the same time, the ability of indenture trustees named to the committee of unsecured creditors in Lehman to have the legal fees paid by the estate as an administrative expense because of such membership was held by the district court to be prohibited absent the finding of a substantial contribution to the reorganization.[664]

H. Lehman Decisions Limiting Protections to Non-Defaulting Counterparty

A number of decisions in the Lehman bankruptcy have the effect of limiting the protections available to the trustee as the non-defaulting party:

- Cases limiting the scope of the safe harbor provisions.
    - A "flip clause" that modifies the priority of payment so that a swap counterparty's right to be paid is subordinated in the event of default following a counterparty bankruptcy is an unenforceable *ipso facto* provision because it did not relate to the liquidation, termination or acceleration of a qualifying financial contract.[665] In the summer of 2016, however, the Lehman bankruptcy court, Judge Shelley C. Chapman presiding, ruled to the contrary, holding that the "flip clauses" in swap agreements were protected by the Bankruptcy Code's safe harbor provided by 11 U.S.C. § 560. Judge Chapman noted that since *Ballyrock,*

---

662 DEBTORS' DISCLOSURE STATEMENT at 33.

663 MOTION PURSUANT TO SECTION 105(A) OF THE BANKRUPTCY CODE AND GENERAL ORDER M-143 FOR AUTHORIZATION TO IMPLEMENT ALTERNATIVE DISPUTE RESOLUTION PROCEDURES FOR AFFIRMATIVE CLAIMS OF DEBTORS UNDER DERIVATIVE CONTRACTS, *In re Lehman Bros. Holdings Inc.,* No. 08-13555 (Bankr. S.D.N.Y. July 20, 2009), ECF No. 4453.

664 *Davis v. Elliott Mgmt. Corp. (In re Lehman Bros. Holdings Inc.)*, 508 B.R. 283 (S.D.N.Y. 2014).

665 *Lehman Bros. Special Fin. Inc. v. Ballyrock ABS CDO 2007-1 Ltd. and Wells Fargo Bank, N.A.*, 452 BR 31 (Bankr. S.D.N.Y. 2011) (Judge James Peck). *Contra,* the decision by the United Kingdom Supreme Court, *Belmont Park Invs. Pty Ltd. v. BNY Corp. Tr. Servs. Ltd. and Lehman Special Fin. Inc.* [2011] UKSC 38, July 27, 2011.

the Second Circuit had instructed that the safe harbor provisions demand a broad interpretation.[666]

- Ruling that a provision in a synthetic CDO transaction, including a related swap agreement, which specified the parties' relative priorities in the event of a bankruptcy default, was unenforceable.[667]
- Terms of Section 2(a)(iii) of ISDA Master Agreement that excused counterparty from making payment to the bankruptcy counterparty were unenforceable. Further, the counterparty waived its right to terminate the swap by waiting a year to do so.[668]
- Safe harbor provisions did not do away with the requirement of mutuality for setoff.[669]
- Swap could not be set off against an unrelated pool of collateral.[670]

Attached as Appendix XVII-B is an outline of lessons learned from the Lehman and other recent bankruptcy cases as of the date of publication.

---

666 *Lehman Bros. Special Fin. Inc. v. Bank of Am. Nat'l Ass'n*, 553 B.R. 476 (Bankr. S.D.N.Y. 2016). The case involved an adversary proceeding brought by LBSF arising out of the transactions whereby LBSF, as the credit default swap counterparty, and the noteholders held competing interests in collateral securing an issuer's obligation to LBSF under a credit default swap and a noteholder under a credit-linked synthetic portfolio note. The transactions included priority-of-payment provisions that entitled the relevant noteholders under certain circumstances to receive distributions from the liquidation of collateral ahead of LBSF. LBSF sued the trustees and noteholders to obtain a declaratory judgment that the so-called priority-of-payment provisions are unenforceable *ipso facto* clauses and to avoid distributions made to noteholders pursuant to these provisions. The bankruptcy court's decision that safe harbor provisions are applicable in bankruptcy to flip clauses could lead the way to broader enforcement of safe harbor provisions for Protected Transactions.

667 *Lehman Bros. Special Fin., Inc. v. BNY Corp. Tr. Servs. Ltd.*, 422 B.R. 407 (Bankr. S.D.N.Y. 2010); but see *Mich. State Hous. Dev. Auth. v. Lehman Bros. Deriv. Prod. Inc.*, 502 B.R. 383 (Bankr. S.D.N.Y. 2013), holding that parties' agreed-upon methodology for liquidating collateral (the calculation method was altered based upon the bankruptcy filing) was within safe harbor.

668 *Metavante Transcript, In re Lehman Bros. Holdings, Inc.*, No. 08-13555 (Bankr. S.D.N.Y. Sept. 15, 2009), ECF No. 5261.

669 *Swedbank AB (PUBL) v. Lehman Bros. Holdings, Inc. and Official Comm. of Unsecured Creditors*, 433 B.R. 101 (Bankr. S.D.N.Y. 2010), *aff'd*, 445 B.R. 130 (S.D.N.Y. 2011). See also *In re Lehman Bros. Inc.*, 458 B.R. 134 (Bankr. S.D.N.Y. 2011).

670 *Bank of Am., N.A. v. Lehman Bros. Holdings, Inc.*, 439 B.R. 811 (Bankr. S.D.N.Y. 2010).

Appendix XVII-A
Addendum to Proof of Claim of Trustee*

ADDENDUM TO PROOF OF CLAIM OF TRUSTEE

Name of Claimant. This claim is made on behalf of ____________________, as trustee (the "Trustee"), for ____________________ (the "Trust") against ____________________ under the terms of a swap agreement ("Swap Agreement") (a) issued under the terms of that certain ISDA Master Agreement dated as of ____________________ between ____________________and the Trust, the Schedule to Master Agreement of equal date, and the Confirmation (the "CDS Transaction"). The CDS Transaction was issued in connection with the Series Trust Agreement dated as of ____________________ by and between ____________________, as Trustee, and ____________________, as supplemented by those certain Standard Terms for Trust Agreements of equal date (collectively the "Trust Agreements").

The undersigned is duly authorized and empowered to make this claim on behalf of ____________________, as Trustee.

Name and Address Where Notices Should Be Sent.

Send all court orders, notices and payment to:

With copies of all court orders and notices to:

1. *Amount of Claim as of Date Case Filed.* As of the Petition Date, the Debtor was obligated to the Trust for all amounts that may become due under the CDS Transaction. As of the Early Termination Date, the amount due and owing by Debtor under the terms of the CDS

* To be appended to Official Form No. 410, an example of which is set forth in Appendix XI-B.

Transaction as more fully set forth in the Statement of Calculation is USD $______________ plus interest at the Default Rate thereon until paid. This amount does not reflect fees and expenses of the Trust (including but not limited to internal fees of ____________ and attorneys' fees) in connection with protecting its rights and otherwise enforcing the terms of the CDS Transaction pursuant to Section 11 of the Master Agreement, and ________ reserves the right to amend this amount to include any other fees and expenses at any time hereafter. This is a claim based on a Derivatives Contract.

2. *Basis for Claim.* _________________, as Trustee, and Debtor are parties to a prepetition swap transaction entered into in connection with that certain Series Trust Agreement and the related Standard Terms for Trust Agreements dated as of __________________ between _________________, as Depositor, and the Trustee. The Swap Counterparties are the Trust and _________________. Upon the occurrence of the Event of Default under the Master Agreement, the Trustee had the right to and did designate _________________ as the Early Termination Date under the Master Agreement ("Notice of Early Termination"). Thereafter, on _________________, Trustee provided _________________ with the Statement of Calculation of the amount due by _________________ to the Trust under the Master Agreement ("Statement of Calculation"). In addition to the amount set forth in the Statement of Calculation, _________________ is also liable for interest on that amount payable in the Termination Currency from and including the Early Termination Date to but excluding the date such amount is paid at the Default Rate in accordance with clause 6(d)(ii) of the Master Agreement.

In addition, the Trustee is entitled to its fees, costs and expenses in connection with the enforcement and protection of its rights.

3. *Classification of Claim.* This claim is an unliquidated general unsecured claim and therefore is not secured by a lien on any property of the Debtor.

4. *Date Debt Was Incurred.* The claims set forth herein relate to the CDS Transaction entered into on or about _________________.

5. *If Court Judgment Was Obtained.* To the best of the Trustee's knowledge, no judgment has been rendered with respect to this claim.

6. *Priority Status of Claim.* This claim, to the extent not discharged from the proceeds of the Underlying Securities, is not entitled to priority under 11 U.S.C. § 507(a).

7. *Credits.* No funds have been paid from the Debtor to ____________________ from the Petition Date to the date this claim is signed.

8. *Supporting Documents.* Documents on which this claim is founded include, but are not limited to, the Master Agreement as amended by the Amendments dated as of ________________; the Credit Support Annex, dated as of ________________; the Notice of Early Termination; and the Statement of Calculation. There may be additional documents in the possession or under the control of the Debtor which may further support this claim. ________________ reserves the right to support its claim with any such additional documents. Upon information and belief, documents in support of this claim are available to, and in the possession of, the Debtors. Copies of certain of the documents have been submitted with the Statement of Calculation. Copies of other documents are available upon request.

9. *Reservation of Rights with Respect to Executory Contracts.* To the extent the Debtor has not rejected any particular agreement that constitutes an executory contract, no claim is due in connection with any damages or claims relating thereto, and therefore the Trustee reserves its right to amend, supplement or add to this claim to include any rejection damage claim.

10. *Reservation of Rights.* The Trust Agreement constitutes a swap agreement under the Bankruptcy Code and therefore ________________ is entitled to the safe harbor provisions under, but not limited to, Sections 560, 546(g), 362(b)(17) and 561 thereof (the "Safe Harbor Provisions"). The Trustee expressly reserves all of its rights, remedies, liens, interests, priorities, protections and claims with respect to the Safe Harbor Provisions.

________________ asserts that any funds, property or collateral held by the Trust or certain funds or property held by the Debtor relating to the transaction is not property of the Estate but is property of the Trust or other parties having a beneficial interest therein and that the possession or assertion of rights over such funds, property or collateral by the Debtor does not transform such funds, property or collateral into property of the Estate and therefore the Debtor has no legitimate legal right to hold or to prevent the transfer of such funds, property or collateral or the proceeds thereof to third parties under the terms of the relevant documents.

________________, as Trustee, expressly reserves any rights, remedies, liens, interests, priorities, protections and claims which it may have against ________________, or the other debtors and other parties under the Bankruptcy Code. ________________, as Trustee, reserves the right to amend, restate and supplement this Proof of Claim or to file additional Proofs of Claim or further pleadings for additional claims against ________________ and its related entities should _________________, as Trustee, deem it appropriate. _________________, as Trustee, reserves all rights and claims accruing to it, including, but not limited to, its rights (a) against all other creditors, (b) to update total exposure estimates of liquidated and unliquidated claims, (c) request payment of administrative expenses (whether in respect of claims asserted herein or otherwise), or (d) amend, update, supplement or modify as it believes is appropriate including, but not limited to, fees, expenses and interest.

This claim is filed under the compulsion of the bar date established in this case and is filed to protect _________________, as Trustee, from forfeiture of claims by reason of said bar date. The filing of this claim is not intended to be and should not be deemed or construed as (a) an election of a remedy, (b) a consent by _________________, as Trustee, to the jurisdiction of the bankruptcy court or any other court with respect to the proceedings, if any, commenced, in any case against or otherwise involving _________________, as Trustee, (c) a consent by _________________, as Trustee, to trial by jury as to any and all matters so triable herein or in any case, controversy or proceedings related hereto, pursuant to 28 U.S.C. § 157(e) or otherwise, (d) a waiver of the right of _________________, as Trustee, to a trial by jury in any matter herein or in any case, controversy or proceeding related hereto, (e) a waiver of the right of _________________, as Trustee, to have final orders in non-core matters entered only after *de novo* review by the United States District Court, (f) a waiver of any right of _________________, as Trustee, to have the reference withdrawn by the United States District Court in any matter subject to mandatory or discretionary withdrawal, (g) a waiver of any past, present or future event of default, (h) a waiver or limitation of any rights of _________________, as Trustee, including, without limitation, a waiver of obligations owing to _________________, as Trustee, or of rights, claims, actions, defenses, setoffs or recoupments to which _________________, as Trustee, is or may be entitled under the relevant documents or otherwise, in law or equity, against _________________ and/or any subsidiary or affiliate thereof, or any other person, including, without limitation, rights against guarantors, officers or directors, or the right to contest the validity or extent of any liens or security interests purported to be equal, senior or inferior to any right, lien or security interest of _________________, as Trustee, all of which rights, claims, actions, defenses, setoffs or recoupments are expressly reserved by _________________, as Trustee, (i) an admission by _________________, as Trustee, that any property held by _________________ (or any subsidiary or affiliate thereof) is property of the Estate, or (j) a waiver of any right to recharacterize any of the claims set forth herein as administrative claims.

[Remainder of Page Intentionally Left Blank]

Appendix XVII-B Outline of Lessons Learned in the *Lehman* and Other Recent Bankruptcy Proceedings

1. Even Though Too Big to Fail, Still Make Sure You Have All the Trustee Protections

Despite what you may hear or read in the press, you can't assume that any entity will never have financial difficulty or is too big to fail. Trust documents ought to be written in a manner that appropriately considers the risk of financial difficulties of all parties to the transaction. Regardless of size of the issuer or the parties involved, adequate and full protection for the trustee and assurance that the trustee will be fully compensated from the trust or the holders must be included.

2. There Should Always Be Funds Available to Pay Trust and Trustee Costs – The Extraordinary Expenses Problem

In the *Lehman* proceeding, there were three types of problematical provisions relating to the recovery of fees and expenses by the indenture trustee. These provisions were likely "required" by the rating agencies to insure cash flow went to the holders and/or by the sponsor to make sure that the rating agencies have "control" over any restructuring of the transaction. A particular problem occurs when it is the sponsor who has financial difficulties. Problematical provisions include:

a. Caps on Fees

In *Lehman*, there were provisions capping the amount of overall administrative fees and expenses. These caps proved woefully insufficient in light of the default. Further, while the trustee's fees were higher in priority on the list, those lower on the list in the priority of administrative fees included those connected with the issuer who, if not paid, would give notice of resignation, thereby orphaning the transaction. Resignations in some instances may cause an issuer not to be in good standing in the jurisdiction of its creation.

b. Payment of Fees and Expenses by a Third Party

In *Lehman*, this third party was generally Lehman Brothers Inc. Because a third party was responsible for fees, there was no provision for the payment of fees in the waterfall. Even if a third party is responsible, fees should be able to be taken from the waterfall at a high priority if they are not timely paid, or there should be a reserve account to pay fees and expenses from a secured funded account.

c. No Extraordinary Expenses

Some documents provide that no extraordinary fees and expenses shall be payable. At least in the context of a given transaction, no upfront fee is sufficient to pay expenses upon a default. Again, all fees should be at the top of the waterfall or covered by secured escrow.

d. Extraordinary Expenses with Holder Consent

Some transactions permit the payment of extraordinary fees and expenses but only with consent of 100 percent of the holders. How many times do you know all of the holders, and what is the likelihood that, even if you are able to identify them, they will all consent?

3. Avoid Definitional Problems – Maintain a Way Out

In *Lehman*, there were many transactions that defined a service provider as a particular entity. For example, a series indenture might define the "Market Agent" as Lehman Brothers Inc., without reference to a successor or providing for a successor to be appointed by the trustee or a court of competent jurisdiction, or without having a successor already designated.

4. Better Safe Than Sorry – in Bankruptcy Be Cautious

Even when you believe you know the law, be cautious in any bankruptcy proceeding. In the *Lehman* case, the court went against market expectations on a number of occasions. Some big examples include:

a. Change in the Priority If a Counterparty Is in Default but Not If It Is Just a Debtor

In the *Lehman* bankruptcy, many transactions included a waterfall provision (which was referenced and included in the swap agreement as well) that provided for the payment of a termination fee to the Lehman counterparty higher in the waterfall (ahead of the noteholders) unless the counterparty was in default. If the Lehman counterparty was in default, the termination payment would be paid lower in the waterfall (often meaning, as a practical matter, no termination payment would be made). Against industry expectations, the court initially found a change in the priority of payment caused as a result of the filing of a bankruptcy by a credit support party (not even the counterparty) to be an unenforceable *ipso facto* clause. (Later, Judge Chapman ruled to the contrary.)

i. *Distributions Made in Reliance upon Perceived Law.* As a result of the industry expectations (and no law at the time to the contrary), distributions were made in some cases based upon the priority of payments contained in the documents.

ii. *Available Defenses.* There may be available defenses in this type of situation, particularly given the standard of care provisions of the indentures.

b. *Metavante* – Non-Debtor Counterparty Must Pay Even When Debtor Does Not

The *Lehman* court found that, notwithstanding the fact that the debtor counterparty had not agreed to assume a swap agreement, non-debtor counterparties were required to continue to abide by the terms of the swap agreement. In many cases, this meant the non-defaulting non-debtor counterparties had to continue to make net payments to a debtor under an interest rate swap with no guarantee that, if rates went the other way, the debtor would likewise be required to pay.

c. Provisions Providing for No Termination Payment upon Default or Other Penalty/Forfeiture Provisions May Be Rewritten

There is an unreported case from the *Drexel* bankruptcy proceeding that finds enforceable a provision where a defaulting debtor counterparty is placed in a different, less advantageous position under the terms of the documents due to a bankruptcy filing, such as a change in the waterfall, so that no termination payment is required to be made. There has been a lot of academic discussion to the effect that this constitutes an unenforceable penalty provision. Beware of holders that ask you to strictly enforce penalty provisions with an issuer in bankruptcy, because the perceived result may change with court's decision.

5. Think before Acting on Swap Terminations

Be thoughtful prior to terminating swaps, because a termination likely will have ramifications throughout the transaction and may impair principal. In some Lehman transactions, interest rates were such that, at the time of termination, a substantial termination payment would be due Lehman as counterparty (in many cases these termination payments were not subordinated). While there are underlying assets to cover the termination payment, such use of the underlying assets may result in the impairment of principal. This may, or may not, matter to holders.

6. Who Calculates the Loss? Swap Termination Payments

To the extent that the trustee is a counterparty to a swap transaction, there ought to be a mechanism or an identified third party that will calculate and prosecute or otherwise handle a termination payment that might be due, including but not limited to meaningful provisions for the payment thereof. Calculation of loss under a default swap may be more than difficult for the trustee unless someone is designated to do it who is not the debtor and a source of compensation is provided.

7. The Problem of the "Floating Controlling Class"

In recent transactions, draftsmen have attempted to match the tranche of securities that has the right to give the trustee instructions and directions with the class at risk. Oftentimes this is done on the basis of valuing the collateral and, based on the valuation, the tranche at risk is the tranche that controls decision making. This creates a problem, however, when values of the collateral change. The trustee may be instructed under the terms of the indenture to proceed with one course of action, only to have that course of action change midstream as a result of a change in valuation. it is easier in a default situation if the controlling tranche is fixed and definite.

8. Beware of Super-majority Requirements

In some cases, a super-majority vote is required to take certain types of action. These super-majority provisions may require 90 percent or more of holders of all certificates or notes, even if many of the tranches are clearly out of the money. While these provisions attempt to insure that the rights of all holders are not unduly trampled upon, they create a very real problem of stagnation. If after thirty (30) days of a default there is no direction, the trustee should be able to rely on direction and indemnity from those holders who choose to give an indemnity and direction so long as the direction exceeds a nominal amount of the principal amount outstanding (5 percent to 10 percent).

9. Coordinating Between Liquidity Providers, Credit Enhancers and Issuers and Their Liens and Their Rights to Receive Payment from the First Dollar of Recovery Versus the Need for the Trustee and Holders to Maximize the Value

Liquidity providers and credit enhancers sometime require that the first dollars back in recovery should be used to pay them rather than be used to pay for costs to maintain or to protect the mortgaged property or to take rights and remedies to maximize the value of the trust estate. There needs to be some rationalization of the liquidity provider's top priority with the actual needs of the trust and trustee to preserve the liquidity provider's rights and interests.

10. The Collapsing or Nonexistent Issue with the Bank as Collateral Agent or Trustee

Collateral agent transactions whereby the bank holds collateral as trustee for a structured financing may create obligations without appropriate protections and rights. A number of structured transactions provided for a trustee or collateral agent to hold the collateral and only to take actions at the direction of the requisite number of holders. The issuer promptly thereafter goes out of business, collapses or abandons the trust or LLC without an operating parent. There are no reports, tax information or information flow from the nonexistent issuer or sponsor. It should be made clear that the collateral agent is not a trustee and the trustee is not the issuer or responsible for deal information. The collateral agent has no fiduciary duties and, absent direction, cannot take any action and cannot be held liable for not taking any action except if such action is necessary to protect its rights and interests or to preserve and protect its possession or lien on the collateral. The trustee protects the trust and its rights and interests but should not without proper authorization provide deal information.

11. Who's on First and Who's on Second — Intercreditor Issues

Trustees in structured financings where there are first liens and second liens or senior and subordinated positions should make sure that the intercreditor relationship is crystal clear so that the trustee is not blamed for the inefficiencies in sorting out where the rights of the first lien holder begin, where the rights of the second lien holder begin and what rights the second lien holder has or does not have in relationship to the first.

12. Stripping Assets or Cash from SPVs

Documents governing a trust or any SPV should make clear that it is a separate legal entity with restrictions on using its assets or the proceeds thereof for any reason other than to benefit the trust, the purpose of the trust and the parties thereto. It is important to distinguish between the sponsor's interest and the issuer's interest in connection with the financing and that of the trust and the bankruptcy of a sponsor, issuer or parent should not lead to the bankruptcy of another (especially if the trust or SPV is not and could not be insolvent), or the use of the trust assets for the benefit of a sponsor or issuer to the detriment of the holders and the purposes of the trust.

13. Coordination with Holders

In a transaction in which there are certificateholders or investors, clear communication to them by the trustee of the complexity of and likely delays in resolving the transaction will be helpful. Further, to the extent they offer constructive cooperation, all will benefit. To the degree that holders can organize and promptly give direction, and indemnity to the trustee for any close-out, set off or foreclosure of collateral (acceleration, termination, liquidation or other disposition), this will facilitate the timing of action by the trustee to the benefit of all concerned.

XVIII. Other Causes of Action by the Indenture Trustee

A. Consideration of Other Non-Contractual Causes of Action That May Be Available to the Indenture Trustee

Upon default, the indenture trustee first considers the exercise of remedies under the language of the indenture. In addition to initiating a lawsuit under the indenture to collect the amount of principal and interest due under the indenture securities, to enforce the security provided under the transaction documents, including foreclosure, or the additional traditional remedies discussed in Chapter IX, the indenture trustee should examine the circumstances and the language of the indenture. Depending on the facts that have given rise to the default and the scope of the remedy section of the indenture, the trustee, ideally in consultation with the holders, may consider whether additional causes of action should be contemplated. It should be noted that there is not unanimity on this issue. While the ability of the indenture trustee to maintain such causes of action will depend upon the facts of the case and the language of the indenture, among the possible claims to be asserted are: (1) breach of contract, especially against any guarantor, (2) breach of implied covenant of good faith and fair dealing, (3) tortious interference with contractual relations, (4) common law fraud or misrepresentation, (5) securities fraud, (6) negligence, (7) claims against officers and directors or other third parties, (8) unjust enrichment and (9) fraudulent conveyance. Counsel should be consulted as to whether any of these causes of action are available. Some indenture trustees and their advisors are of the view that the indenture trustee acts at its peril to pursue remedies other than a suit to collect the indebtedness. However, others take the position that, when faced with egregious debtor or third-party behavior, it is in the best interests of the holders and the indenture trustee itself to be as proactive as possible. (See Chapter XIII regarding actions for subordination, equitable subordination, constructive trust, equitable lien and unjust enrichment). The direction, instruction and indemnity by the requisite percentage of holders are, if possible, advisable before proceeding with any non-contract actions so that the holders and the trustee are not working at cross-purposes. The holders should appreciate that the trustee seeking direction on the initiation of litigation is exhibiting not lack of backbone but prudence in making sure the trustee does not take action the holders do not desire. Likewise, given the no-action clause, actions with respect to the indenture are first to be considered by the trustee, and holders cannot proceed independently to take action on breaches of covenants, representations and warranties under the indenture (except for failure to pay principal or interest) without first requesting the trustee to take the action (see Chapter IX on no-action clause). On the other hand, non-contract causes of action may be pursued by holders independently, but there may be increased benefits and efficiency by pursuing them through the trustee.

While the language of every indenture is to some degree unique, it is interesting to review the approaches taken by various industry groups in suggesting model indenture remedy provisions. For example, the language in the Revised Model Simplified Indenture published by the American Bar Association in 2000 is not particularly expansive.[671] On the other hand, the 2000 Form Indenture of the National Association of Bond Lawyers ("NABL"), typically

---

671 Section 6.03 — Other Remedies. "If an Event of Default occurs and is continuing, the Trustee may pursue any available remedy to collect the payment of principal or interest on the Securities or to enforce the performance of any provision of the Securities on this Indenture. The Trustee may maintain a proceeding even if it does not possess any of the Securities or does not produce any of them in the proceeding. A delay or omission by the Trustee or any Securityholder in exercising any right or remedy accruing upon an Event of Default shall not impair the right or remedy or constitute a waiver of or acquiescence in the Event of Default. All remedies are cumulative to the extent permitted by law." In the Note accompanying the ABA Revised Model Simplified Indenture, it is commented:

> 2. *Fraud Claims*. The Indenture does not empower the Trustee to pursue claims which may be available to purchasers or sellers of Securities under state or federal securities laws or the common law for misrepresentations inducing them to purchase or hold the securities. *See* Central Bank of Denver, N.A. v. Deloitte & Touche, 928 P.2d 754, 758 (Colo. Ct. App. 1996); *cf.* Continental Bank, N.A. v. Caton, 1990 Fed. Sec. L. Rep (CCH) P95,623, at 97,922 (D. Kan. Aug. 6, 1990); *In re* Washington Pub. Power Supply Sys. Sec. Litig., 623 F. Supp. 1466, 1483-84 (W.D. Wash. 1985), *aff'd*, 823 F.2d 1349 (9th Cir. 1987). The Trustee's role is to enforce the rights arising under the Indenture and the Securities against the Company for the equal benefit of all Securityholders. For various reasons pursuing fraud claims may create a conflict for the Trustee in fulfilling that role. Fraud claims may be held by persons no longer holders of Securities who sold their Securities after the fraud was discovered as well as by persons who continue to hold Securities. Securityholders may have different rights depending on when they purchased their Securities and the extent to which they can prove reliance on the fraud. Recoveries by holders of fraud claims may prejudice collections by current holders. Lastly, securities fraud claims may be subordinated to the claims upon the Securities of current holders under Section 510(b) of the Bankruptcy Code, thereby potentially raising adverse interests between fraud claimants and current Holders as to the desirability of or distributions in Proceedings. If a Trustee has the right to assert these claims against the Company and others such as the Company's accountants and investment bankers, it would also have to consider the extent to which it has an obligation to investigate whether such claims may exist. Existing procedures where such claims are pursued by individual or class actions by the injured parties do not appear to require changes to Indentures to change the party responsibility for pursuing such claims. *See also* Note 1 to Section 6.06.

applicable to conduit financing, gives to the indenture trustee pursuant to Section 7.03 the power to:

> proceed to protect and enforce its rights and the rights of the holders of the Bonds under this Indenture by a suit or suits in equity or at law, either for the specific performance of any covenant or agreement contained in this Indenture or in the Loan Documents or in aid of the execution of any power herein or therein granted, or for the enforcement of any other appropriate legal or equitable remedy, and the Trustee in reliance upon the advice of Counsel may deem most effective to protect and enforce any of the rights or interests of the holders of the Bonds under the Bonds or this Indenture.

Further, in the Commentary to the Form Indenture, NABL also suggests language that can be included to specifically authorize the indenture trustee to file securities actions on behalf of bondholders.[672]

In certain situations, a straightforward suit to collect the amount due under the indenture may not be deemed to be the most effective means of recovery for the bondholders. In such situation, the indenture trustee and its counsel should review the facts of the case, the language of the indenture and the law in the applicable circuit or state to determine the practicality of pursuing additional causes of action.[673] Another important consideration is whether there are funds available to support such additional litigation, which can be extremely expensive. It will be important to discuss the funding of such litigation with major bondholders and ideally to obtain the agreement of and a direction, instruction and indemnity from such bondholders recognizing the indenture trustee's first right of recovery for costs expended.

The coordination between holders and the trustee can be key to a successful prosecution of a cause of action for recovery, especially for complex and expensive litigation. There are

---

672 "The trustee is authorized to file securities and lawsuits on behalf of Bondholders if such filing is deemed appropriate within the Trustee's sole discretion."; and "The Committee considered the inclusion of a provision which would specifically authorize the trustee to file securities actions on behalf of Bondholders." It is by no means certain, however, that the trustee must or should have the right so to act. See the Note to Section 6.03 of the ABA Model Simplified Indenture, which does not permit such suits. An informed decision regarding inclusion of such a provision should be made by the trustee, based upon the advice of counsel. Of particular interest to the trustee in such cases will be other relationships the trustee has to the participants in the transaction and the availability of resources to finance any such litigation, including funds held under the indenture.

673 Clearly the indenture trustee will always be open to interpleader or declaratory judgment actions where necessary to determine the rights of the holders. *See U.S. Tr. Co. of N.Y. v. Alpert*, 10 F. Supp. 2d 290 (S.D.N.Y. 1998).

numerous examples of holder groups and trustees cooperating in litigation that is known to be challenging cases involving protecting and preserving collateral in aircraft and railcar financing bankruptcies, contested exchange offers that are perceived by holders to be unfair and in violation of their rights, complex structured financings including derivatives and pooled investment vehicles that where collateral or rights of holders are being wrongfully impaired are best dealt with by coordination of the holders directing, instructing and indemnifying the trustee to take action that is mutually agreed to be necessary. Indemnifications can take many different forms and, given the probability of recovery, can be structured as a backup source of covering the expenses of the effort if not successful for any advances made. Holders have been creative and constructive with the trustee to provide assurance to the trustee that its costs and expenses will be paid, such as specifically agreeing and confirming that any advances made by holders or the trustee to pay for the costs and expenses of the recovery action would first be paid from the recovery before any other payments. This allows holders to advance funds to cover expenses, sometimes with an interest rate similar to that of the security.

B. Early Cases Considering the Power of the Trustee to Bring Additional Causes of Action

One of the first cases in which a court discussed the ability of an indenture trustee to involve itself in securities litigation was the Equity Funding litigation.[674] In that case, the indenture trustee, Chemical Bank, objected to the fund allocation in the multi-district litigation, alleging that the amount to be distributed to debentureholders was insufficient. The obligor on the debt securities had been dismissed from the multi-district securities litigation and the settlement involved third parties. Citing the language of Section 317 of the Trust Indenture Act, which authorized the indenture trustee to institute proceedings "relative to the obligor upon the indenture securities," the court held the indenture trustee had no standing to object to the fund allocation in the securities fraud case.

The Equity Funding case was distinguished by the District Court in the Washington Public Power Supply System Securities, or WPPSS, litigation.[675] Further, the court seized upon

---

674 *In re Equity Funding Corp. of Am. Secs. Litig.*, 603 F.2d 1353 (9th Cir. 1979).

675 "The holding in *In re Equity Funding Corporation of American Securities Litigation*, 603 F.2d 1353 (9th Cir. 1979) does not compel a different conclusion. Although Chemical Bank, as indenture trustee, was denied standing in that case to appeal the reorganization plan, Chemical Bank was in a very different posture with respect to that securities litigation than it is in the present securities litigation. In the earlier litigation Chemical Bank had not sought to represent the debentureholders in the securities litigation, it did not have express authorization to represent debentureholders, and it was a defendant in the initial complaint, 'putting a sufficient taint on Chemical Bank's standing to represent debentureholders in the securities litigation in any capacity . . .' 603 F.2d at 1361–62, n. 10. Here, none of those factors are present." 623 F. Supp. at 1484, N. 9.

the broad language of the indenture[676] to rule that Chemical Bank, the indenture trustee, had standing to bring both security law and tort claims against numerous third parties in a representative capacity. The court also referred to the fact that the indenture trustee had authorization to represent the holders of the bonds. In fact, there was unique cooperation between the indenture trustee and bondholders on the WPPSS litigation, with the indenture trustee aiding class counsel for the bondholders to advance certain of the costs of the case and working in tandem to prosecute the litigation.[677]

C. Subsequent Litigation

Cases following the *Equity Funding* and *WPPSS* decisions tend to rely on one or the other of the rulings to justify the result. In *National City Bank v. Coopers & Lybrand,* 409 N.W.2d 862 (Minn. App. 1987), the court cited *Equity Funding* for the proposition that each such case must be decided based on the language of the indenture. In the *Coopers & Lybrand* dispute, the powers in the indenture were limited to those necessary to enforce the obligations running to the noteholders "on the notes" or under the indenture. According to the Minnesota court, the indenture trustee had no power to assert individual tort claims on behalf of noteholders against third persons that were totally extraneous to the rights and obligations created by the notes and the indenture agreements. As a result, the court dismissed the trustee's lawsuit against the accountants for the issuer. In *Continental Bank N.A. v. Caton,* 1990 U.S. Dist. Lexis 11624 (D.C. Kan. 1990), the indenture trustee sued the underwriter for securities fraud. In dismissing the lawsuit against the underwriter, the court focused on the limited indenture language which, according to the court, distinguished the situation from the *WPPSS* case. The court noted that language giving the trustee the unrestricted authority to enforce any legal or equitable rights of the bondholders was not contained in the agreement at issue.[678]

---

676 The bond trustee shall "be entitled and empowered to proceed forthwith to institute such suits, actions and proceedings at law or in equity for the collection of all sums due in connection with the Bonds and to protect and enforce its rights and the rights of the holders of the Bonds under the Resolution . . . in the enforcement of any other legal or equitable right as the Bond Fund Trustee, being advised by counsel, shall deem most effectual to enforce any of its rights or the rights of the holders of the Bonds . . . ." Similarly, in the summer of 2016, the trustee to certain bonds issued by the University of Puerto Rico filed a complaint against the commonwealth, the commonwealth's governor and the university's president seeking, among other things, relief from the PROMESA stay, declaratory judgment that section 201 of the Moratorium Act is invalid pursuant to the Takings Clause and Contracts Clause of the United States Constitution, and an injunction compelling the defendants to comply with the trust agreement governing such bonds. *U.S. Bank Tr., N.A. v. Garcia-Padilla et al.,* No. 16-02510-FAB (D. P.R. Aug. 19, 2016).

677 *See also* prior discussion of WPPSS in Chapter XII at F-2.

678 *See also Premier Bk. v. Tierney,* 114 F. Supp. 2d 87 (W.D. Mo. 2000) (trustee lacks standing to sue director in tort on behalf of bondholders).

Other cases have taken more expansive views of the ability of the indenture trustee to sue. In *Continental Bank N.A. v. Ludlow*, 777 F. Supp. 92 (D. Mass 1991), the indenture trustee pursued a number of causes of action including declaratory judgment that the agreements with certain Vermont villages were valid and asserting breach of contract against the villages, promissory estoppel, waiver and unjust enrichment. The court relied upon the *WPPSS* decision, asserting that the indenture trustee was broadly empowered by the language of the indenture to bring claims and consequently had proper standing as the legitimate contractual representative of the bondholders.[679] Suing to remedy the diversion of trust property or transfer of corporate assets would seem to be appropriate for the trustee under certain circumstances. In *Citibank (Arizona) v. Miller & Schroeder Financial, Inc.*, the trustee sued the issuer, the developer and the general partner of the developer, the remarketer and its counsel for claims of common law fraud, unjust enrichment and money had and received to recover funds allegedly wrongfully paid out.[680] In upholding the ability of the trustee to pursue these claims to recover funds, the court held that the trustee's power does not end until it accounts for all sums payable. In this case, the bank was asserting claims on its own behalf as trustee and not necessarily for the benefit of third-party bondholders that had been paid. Nevertheless, some subsequent decisions have denied the ability of the indenture trustee to sue third-party accountants in tort, to pursue tort claims against directors and to assert securities fraud and common law fraud against underwriters.[681] These cases all turn on the language of the indentures concluding that the language in question is more restrictive than that in *WPPSS*.

In *Cortlandt Street Recovery Corp. v. Hellas Telecommunications*,[682] the indenture trustee sued third parties based upon a fraudulent conveyance theory, "private equity" defendants and their principals who were not issuers or guarantors of payment in kind notes, arising from the transfer of the proceeds of the notes. The defendants moved to dismiss the complaint, asserting such lawsuit was beyond the scope of the trustee's limited authority. The indenture language was similar to that in *Regions Bank* and *Caton*: "If an Event of Default occurs and is continuing, the Trustee may pursue any available remedy to collect the payment of principal, premium, if any, and interest on the notes or to enforce the performance of any provision of the Notes or this

679 "The Bond Trustee may . . . take such steps and institute such suits, actions or proceedings . . . for the protection and enforcement of the rights of the holders of bonds and the coupons appurtenant thereto, to collect any amount due and owing . . . or by injunction, mandamus or other appropriate proceeding in law or in equity to obtain other appropriate relief."

680 812 P.2d 996 (Ariz. App. 1991).

681 *Central Bank of Denver N.A. v. Deloitte & Touche*, 928 P. 2d 754 (Colo. App. 1996); *Premier Bank v. Tierney*, 114 F. Supp. 2d 877 (D. Mo. 2000); *Regions Bank v. Blount Parrish & Co., Inc.*, 2001 WL 726989 (N.D. Ill. June 27, 2001).

682 996 N.Y.S.2d 476 (Sup. Ct. N.Y. Co. 2014).

Indenture." Citing *Regions* and distinguishing the facts from *WPPSS*, the court held that the indenture did not confer broad authority on the indenture trustee to institute all actions to enforce the rights of the bondholders, but rather limited the authority of the trustee to commence actions for "payment on the notes" or "to enforce the performance of any provision of the Notes or this Indenture." According to the court, the fraudulent conveyance claims could have been brought before the default in payment of the notes and were completely separate. The court rejected the indenture trustee's claim that it was authorized to pursue the fraudulent conveyance claims.[683] However, the Supreme Court of New York, Appellate Division, modified the order of the trial court holding that the indenture conferred standing to pursue not only breach of contract claims, but also fraudulent conveyance, unlawful corporate distribution and unjust enrichment claims. The appellate court found the trustee was not seeking recovery for particular injuries unique to individual noteholders.[684]

D. Relation to No-Action Rule

An interesting approach to the issue of the breadth of the trustee's power to initiate litigation was adopted by the Court of Chancery in Delaware.[685] The court analyzed the scope of the trustee's litigation power in conjunction with the scope of the no-action clause.[686] The court concluded that the no-action clause in question prevented the holders of the bonds from proceeding to sue for breach of fiduciary duty, constructive trust and fraud and actual fraud against the issuer and related entities. As a consequence, the court reasoned that the trustee had standing to pursue those claims. The court concluded that those claims were essentially remedies with respect to the indenture or the notes and, if the trustee was not authorized to bring such claims, no one would have the power to assert such causes of action. The court distinguished the *Regions Bank* case, noting that the court there, while holding the indenture trustee could not bring the non-contractual claims, held that the noteholders could bring the claims.

In *Cortlandt*, discussed previously, the indenture trustee, in attempting to justify its standing to bring the fraudulent conveyance claims, argued that a Delaware court had held that fraudulent conveyance claims were covered by the "no action clause" that applied to any remedy with respect to "this Indenture or the Securities."[687] In other words, the trustee argued the holders could not pursue the claims. The *Cortlandt* court in response cited a New York case that concluded a no-action clause that only referenced the "indenture" and not the "securities" (as in

---

683 *Id.* at 495.

684 *Cortlandt St. Recovery Corp. v. Hellas Telecommunications*, 37 N.Y.S. 3d 505 (Sup. Ct. N.Y.A.D. 2016).

685 *U.S. Bank N.A. v. U.S. Timberlands Klamath Falls, L.L.C.*, 864 A.2d. 930 (Del. Ch. 2004).

686 *See* discussion in Chapter IX.

687 996 N.Y.S.2d at 496 citing *Feldbaum v. McCrory Corp.*, 1992 WL 119095 (Del. Ch. June 21, 1992).

Cortlandt) was ineffective to preclude a holder from bringing a fraudulent conveyance suit. That same decision suggested that a trustee could bring a fraudulent conveyance lawsuit if authorized to do so by the requisite percentage of securityholders.[688]

E. The Indenture Trustee's Dilemma

When faced with a default, the indenture trustee desires to act prudently but does not want to over-step its authority. Further, the indenture trustee may have no trust funds at its disposal to defray litigation costs. In deciding whether to institute third party, including officer and director litigation, or security fraud litigation, the indenture trustee should review the language of the indenture and, if possible, consult with bondholders to determine their desires and whether they will provide a direction in furtherance of their wishes. It has been held that the indenture trustee has no duty to inform the holders of possible securities law violations.[689] Nevertheless, should the indenture trustee conclude that no third-party action is appropriate, it is advisable to inform holders, for example, that the indenture trustee will not be filing a securities fraud action, the relevant statute of limitations and that the holders should consult their own advisors.

---

688 *Quadrant Structured Prods. Co., Ltd. v. Vertin*, 23 N.Y.3d 549, 992 N.Y.S.2d 687 (2014).

689 *Lorenz v. CSX Corp.*, 736 F. Supp. 650 (W.D. Pa. 1990).

XIX. Theories of Liability That Have Been Raised Against the Indenture Trustee

A. Introduction

Unfortunately, when a transaction goes into default, there will be some parties who will seek to recover from solvent entities regardless of their level of involvement or responsibility for the events that led to the default. Increasingly, in class action lawsuits arising out of bond defaults, all participants in the transaction are named as defendants, including the indenture trustee. Further, some issuers and underwriters may attempt a divide-and-conquer strategy with the holders and the indenture trustee. By alleging misconduct by the trustee, the parties who brought the transaction to market may seek to drive a wedge between the holders and the trustee. Obviously, a we/they dichotomy with the trustee is not in the holders' best interest. In rare situations, the trustee or its officers or employees may be the subject of an action by the Securities and Exchange Commission. In this chapter, some of the claims more commonly brought against the indenture trustee will be discussed. The purpose of this discussion is not to keep trust officers awake at night, but to familiarize them with the type of assertions that have been and can be made. Plaintiffs suing indenture trustees have not met with much success, but they have had enough success to keep everyone attentive. Claims leveled against the securitization arising from RMBS transactions are discussed in a previous chapter.[690]

B. Breach of the Trust Indenture Act

A number of courts have held that a private right of action exists under the TIA and have permitted individual bondholders to proceed against the indenture trustee on the theory that the indenture trustee breached its duty thereunder to the ultimate harm of the bondholders.[691] Claims against indenture trustees under the TIA are often brought in situations where the commercial lending relationship of the bank with the obligor created a conflict of interest, and the bondholders assert that the bank favored itself as bank rather than protecting the rights of the bondholders. In this regard, claims for violation of the sharing provisions of Section 311 of the

690 *See* Chapter XVI.

691 *See, e.g., Morris v. Cantor*, 390 F. Supp. 817 (S.D.N.Y. 1975); *Zeffiro v. First Pa. Banking & Tr. Co.*, 623 F.2d 290 (1980), *cert. denied*, 456 U.S. 1005 (1982); *LNC Invs., Inc. v. First Fidelity Bank, N.A.*, 935 F. Supp. 1333 (S.D.N.Y. 1996); *Fixed Income Shares v. Citibank N.A.*, 2015 WL 5244707 (S.D.N.Y. Sept. 8, 2015).

TIA have been asserted, often by successor trustees, against prior trustees.[692] It has been held, however, that a claim under the Trust Indenture Act is not automatically assigned to a subsequent purchaser.[693]

C. Breach of Fiduciary Duty

As outlined in detail in Chapter I, after default, the indenture trustee is a limited fiduciary as that role is generally understood under state trust law. While it is not unusual to see complaints alleging fiduciary duties on the part of the trustee prior to default, hopefully the precedents set forth in Chapter I will permit the indenture trustee to limit such claims to its activities post-default.[694] In the case of *In re New York City Housing Development Corp. Bond Redemption Litigation*,[695] the court declined to dismiss one claim of breach of fiduciary duty. At issue in that case was whether or not a default had in fact occurred. The holders asserted a breach of fiduciary duty because of the failure of the trustee to take action on what the holders contended was a default. The court found that it could not determine as a matter of law whether a default in fact existed and that issue had to be litigated. The court did, however, dismiss a claim for breach of fiduciary duty for failure to give 45 days' notice of a proposed redemption when the indenture specifically gave the indenture trustee the discretion to shorten the notice period.[696] Of

---

692 *See, e.g., U.S. Tr. Co. of N.Y. v. First Nat'l City Bank*, 394 N.Y.S.2d 653 (N.Y. App. Div. 1977), *aff'd*, 410 N.Y.S.2d 580 (1977).

693 *Bluebird Partners, L.P. v. First Fidelity Bank, N.A., New Jersey*, 85 F.3d 970 (2d Cir. 1996).

694 *See, e.g., Groseclose v. Merchants Nat'l Bank & Tr. Co.*, 71 Misc. 2d 111, 335 N.Y.S.2d 652 (N.Y. Sup. Ct. 1972). The distinction will not always prevent suits against the indenture trustee. Prior to the Title III filing, the indenture trustee for the Puerto Rico COFINA Bonds was the target of several lawsuits claiming breach of fiduciary duty. *See, e.g., Ambac Assurance Corp. v. The Bank of N.Y. Mellon*, Case No. 652356/2017 (N.Y. Sup. Ct. May 2, 2017); Robert Slavin, *Cofina Holders Sue Bond Trustee Bank of New York Mellon*, THE BOND BUYER (Apr. 23, 2017), www.bondbuyer.com/news/cofina-holders-sue-bond-trustee.

695 No. 86 Civ. 3274 (S.D.N.Y. May 11, 1987).

696 *See also Meckel v. Cont'l Res. Co.*, 586 F. Supp. 407 (S.D.N.Y. 1984), *aff'd*, 758 F.2d 811 (2d Cir. 1985). *Meckel* involved the registered holder of the debentures bringing action against the issuer and indenture trustee of the debentures, based on a claim that there had been inadequate notice of redemption. The District Court, in granting summary judgment, stated that case law supports the proposition that an indenture trustee's obligations can extend no further than those contained in the indenture. The court found that the plaintiff had neither offered any evidence nor made any allegations that indicated the trustee failed to fulfill its obligations under the indenture when the trustee produced proof of mailing. *See also Elliott Assocs. v. J. Henry Schroder Bank and Tr. Co.*, 655 F. Supp. 1281 (S.D.N.Y. 1987), *aff'd*, 838 F.2d 66 (2d Cir. 1988); *see also AG Capital Funding Partners, L.P. v. State St. Bank and Tr. Co.*, 11 N.Y.3d 146 (2008) (alleged breach of ministerial functions prior to an event of default does not give rise to breach of fiduciary duty); *Abbate v. Wells Fargo Bank, N.A.*, 2011 WL 9698215 (C.D. Cal. Nov. 17, 2011).

course, if a provision of the indenture has been violated by the indenture trustee, a claim for breach of contract would arise. Consistent with the unique nature of the duties of an indenture trustee as compared to those of a typical fiduciary, it has been held that an indenture trustee's fiduciary duties may be limited to those stated in the trust indenture where the language of the instrument clearly expresses such an intent and the surrounding circumstances support that interpretation.[697] Conversely, where the indenture provided that the indenture trustee had a duty to examine the note issuer's certificates stating that it was in compliance with its obligations under the indenture, and the indenture trustee failed to fulfill this duty, the indenture trustee was found to have breached its fiduciary duty.[698] Some cases, however, hold that breach of contract claims may not simply be restated as tort claims. Accordingly, while fiduciary duty claims alleging breach of the duty of care set forth in the agreement should be dismissed as duplicative,[699] claims alleging violation of the duties of independence were not duplicative.[700]

D. Negligence Claims

Section 315(d)(1) of the TIA requires that indentures to be qualified shall not contain any provision relieving the indenture trustee from liability for its own negligent action, its own negligent failure to act or its own misconduct, except that the indenture shall be deemed to contain provisions that the indenture trustee shall not be liable except for the performance of duties specifically set forth in the indenture.

---

697 *Eldred v. Merchants Nat'l Bank*, 468 N.W.2d 221 (Iowa 1991). *See also Page Mill Asset Mgmt. v. Credit Suisse First Boston Corp.*, 2000 WL 877004 (S.D.N.Y. June 30, 2000) (an indenture trustee breaches its fiduciary duty when it fails to abide by the indenture); *Raymond James & Assocs. v. The Bank of N.Y. Tr. Co.*, 2008 WL 4279629 (M.D. Fla. Sept. 18, 2008); *Am. Cont'l Corp./Lincoln Savs. and Loan Secs. Litig.*, 794 F. Supp. 1424 (D. Ariz. 1992) (failure to do independent credit analysis pre-acceptance not breach of fiduciary duty); *E.F. Hutton Southwest Props. II, Ltd.*, 953 F.2d 963 (5th Cir. 1992) (fiduciary duty to invest funds at least open to question); *BNP Paribas v. Bank of Am., N.A.*, 778 F. Supp. 2d 375 (S.D.N.Y. 2011) (alleged transfer of funds from collateral improper purpose stated claim for breach of contract and breach of fiduciary duty).

698 *In re Bankers Tr. Co. (Semi-Tech)*, 450 F.3d 121 (2d Cir. 2006 (holding, however, that only nominal damages were appropriate since the breach was not the cause of the noteholders' loss); *BNP Paribas Mortg. Corp. v. Bank of Am., N.A.*, 778 F. Supp. 2d 375 (S.D.N.Y. 2011) (allegation of failure to notify holders of insolvency of issuer stated claim for breach of fiduciary duty); *Gresser v. Wells Fargo Bank, N.A.*, 2012 NL 5250553 (D. Md. Oct. 22, 2012). *See also Becker v. The Bank of N.Y. Mellon Tr. Co. N.A.*, 2016 WL 1178072 (E.D. Pa. Mar. 23, 2016) (claim that trustee breached fiduciary duty by failing to maintain perfected security interest survived a motion for summary judgment).

699 *Abbate v. Wells Fargo Bank, N.A.*, 2011 WL 9698215 (C.D. Ca. Nov. 17, 2011).

700 *Fixed Income Shares v. Citibank N.A.*, 2015 WL 5244707 (S.D.N.Y. Sept. 8, 2015).

Thus, where the alleged actions of the indenture trustee did not violate the terms of the indenture, a claim alleging negligence should be dismissed.[701] Further, on the question of what the terms of the indenture require, the indenture trustee can rely on the advice of counsel.[702] Where facts are in dispute, the issue can become more complicated. Hence, where a question existed as to whether the indenture trustee required "reasonable detail" in required written requisitions for payment and whether such conduct was the cause of the bondholders' loss, summary judgment in favor of the indenture trustee on negligence and fiduciary duty claims was reversed on appeal.[703] In a highly controversial case arising out of the Continental Airlines bankruptcy, a debtholder sued the collateral trustee and certain series trustees for breach of contract, breach of fiduciary duty, negligence and malpractice, claiming they failed to take necessary action to protect the value of collateral[704] after the airline filed for bankruptcy. Almost 13 years after the alleged wrongful act took place, a $54 million jury verdict against the collateral trustee was upheld by a New York Appellate Court.[705] Where it was alleged the corporation responsible for eight tax-exempt bond issues for healthcare facilities directed and commingled funds for private profit, all the parties to the transaction were the subject of a wide-ranging class action lawsuit, including the underwriter and the indenture trustee.[706] It was alleged that the trustee failed to insist on observance of legal transfer and recordation at the bond closing and failed to require accurate and prompt accounting of revenues and expenditures as mandated by the indenture. Although the court dismissed counts against the indenture trustee for violations of Illinois securities law, conspiracy to defraud, common law fraud and fraudulent concealment and

---

701 *Elliott Assocs. v. J. Henry Schroder Bank and Tr. Co.*, 655 F. Supp. at 1289. In *Becker v. Bank of N.Y. Mellon Tr. Co., N.A.*, 2016 WL 1178072 (E.D. Pa. Mar. 23, 2016), the court refused to dismiss a complaint alleging the indenture trustee was negligent and breached its fiduciary and contractual duties to revenue bondholders by failing to maintain a perfected security interest in the collateral, which resulted in a lower recovery in bankruptcy. The case is troublesome for a number of reasons, including the application of a fiduciary duty and traditional trust law to the indenture trustee prior to an event of default and lack of deference to the indenture language seeming to place the responsibility for perfection on the authority.

702 *E.F. Hutton Southwest Props. v. Union Planters Nat'l Bank*, 953 F.2d at 973.

703 *Shawmut Bank, N.A. v. Kress Assocs.*, 33 F.3d 1477 (9th Cir. 1994); *see also Dell'Oca v. The Bank of N.Y. Tr. Co.*, 159 Cal. App. 4th 531, 71 Cal. Rptr. 3d 737 (2008); *In re Medical Capital Secs. Litig.*, 2014 WL 1344969 (C.D. Cal. 2013).

704 In an unprecedented decision, the bankruptcy court had held that the failure to combine a motion for adequate protection with a motion to lift the automatic stay precluded the granting of adequate protection. *In re Cont'l Airlines*, 154 B.R. 176 (Bankr. D. Del. 1993). The Third Circuit declined to address the issue insofar as a reorganization had been substantially consummated. *In re Cont'l Airlines*, 91 F.3d 553 (3d Cir. 1996).

705 *Bluebird Partners, L.P. v. First Fidelity Bank, N.A.*, 11 A.D.3d 232, 784 N.Y.S.2d 479 (2004).

706 *Al Kellerman, et al. v. Marion Bass Secs. Corp.*, Case No. 01-L-99457 (Circuit Ct., 3d Judicial Circuit, Madison Cty., Ill., Oct. 17, 2016).

found that the indentures did not state that the indenture trustee owed a duty to investigate or report to the bondholders, the indenture trustee ultimately settled the negligence count that included a contribution by the trustee of $6,500,000.[707]

E. Claims Challenging Actions of the Indenture Trustee and Holders

While unusual, notices of default delivered by the indenture trustee with the assent of the holders have been met with lawsuits challenging such action. This is particularly true where the default is based upon financial covenants that can be subject to interpretation. An issuer brought suit against noteholders and indenture trustees related to the contribution of stock from a "restricted subsidiary" to an "unrestricted subsidiary" under various debt documents. The holders had contended that the contribution violated certain covenants of the indentures, and notices of default were issued. After a bench trial, the Texas trial court entered a declaratory judgment holding that the contribution did not violate the terms of the indenture. Rather, the court permanently rescinded the notices of default and enjoined the defendants from further issuing or threatening to issue notices of default as a result of the contribution.[708] Thereafter, the company filed an action against the indenture trustees for a declaration that the company was not obligated to grant a "springing lien" to certain holders of the notes.[709] Thus, a declaratory judgment can be utilized by an obligor against the indenture trustee and holders as an offensive strategy to at least postpone the results of challenges within its capital structure.

F. Other Theories

Certain theories that the indenture trustee can assert against participants in the transaction, discussed in prior chapters, such as unjust enrichment or tortious interference with contract, can be asserted against the indenture trustee if the facts warrant it. In particular, misleading statements regarding the status of the issue post-closing could subject the trustee to liability. However, many of these theories are fatally flawed when brought against indenture trustees, in that they fail to take into account the nature of the duties and responsibilities of the indenture trustee.

---

707 Class Act Settlement Agreement, *William Tennison, et al. v. Marion Bass Secs. Corp., et al.*, Case No. 01-000457 (Circuit Ct., 3d Judicial Circuit, Madison Cty., Ill. Oct. 17, 2016), as approved by the Order and Final Judgment dated Feb. 21, 2017.

708 Stephanie Gleason, "iHeart Media Wins Legal Fight," THE WALL STREET JOURNAL, May 24, 2016, http://www.wsj.com/articles/iheartmedia-wins-legal-fight.-1464111631.

709 Thereafter, the company determined not to repay certain "legacy notes" that purportedly would have triggered the "springing lien." Press Release of iHeart Media, Inc., Dec. 13, 2016, iheartmedia.com/press/iheartmedia-inc-announces-decision-regarding-its-50-50-senior-notes-due-2016.aspx.

One of the most unusual claims asserted against indenture trustees arose in the United Airlines bankruptcy. In that case, the indenture trustees for most of the airline's aircraft financing transactions, pursuant to direction and instruction from their respective holders, coordinated their strategy to counter United's efforts to reduce the below market value consideration paid for aircraft by means of a Dutch auction. The trustees' strategy included exercising their rights under Section 1110 of the Bankruptcy Code to reclaim their aircraft and sell them for market prices. United sued the indenture trustees, alleging the concerted action violated the Sherman Act anti-trust law. The Seventh Circuit Court of Appeals held that United's antitrust claim was "thin to the point of invisibility."[710] The court relied in part on the Second Circuit holding in the *Sharon Steel* case,[711] in which the court noted that coordinated activity by indenture trustees who were faced with a common breach of similar indenture agreements by a liquidating debtor corporation did not violate the antitrust laws. The United Airlines bankruptcy court's analysis that the Seventh Circuit language regarding the antitrust law was simply *dicta* was met with a mandamus order by the Seventh Circuit. The Seventh Circuit declared that the rejection of United's antitrust theory was an independent basis for its earlier ruling.[712]

G. Litigation Process and the Indenture Trustee Creating a Litigation Reserve from Trust Funds

Depending upon the language of the indenture, certain costs of litigation against the indenture trustee may be paid from trust funds. This issue was litigated in the *Bluebird* case[713] previously referred to. The Bank of New York was the successor collateral trustee for a trust, under which the indenture allowed the indenture trustee to reserve funds in its possession "sufficient to pay reasonably anticipated fees and expenses." The indenture also provided that, in the event of a default, the collateral trustee would be indemnified for all expenses incurred in performing its duties. In December 1995, about five years after Continental's bankruptcy filing, the trust had held approximately $34 million, of which $25.6 million had been held in a litigation reserve to indemnify the banks and law firms sued by Bluebird. The court found that the collateral trustee had an obligation to create and maintain the litigation reserve, and that its priority was to pay the reasonable expenses of the collateral trustee and series trustees, including attorneys' fees. The court further found that the collateral trustee acted in accordance with the "prudent man" standard in the amount of money that it set aside.

---

710 *United Airlines, Inc. v. U.S. Bank N.A.*, 406 F.3D 918 (7th Cir. 2005).

711 *Sharon Steel Corp. v. Chase Manhattan Bank, N.A.*, 691 F.2d 1039 (2d Cir. 1982).

712 *United Airlines, Inc. v. U.S. Bank N.A.*, 409 F.3d 812 (7th Cir. 2005).

713 *Bluebird Partners, L.P. v. The Bank of N.Y., et al.*, 2010 N.Y. Misc. LEXIS 2503, 2010 N.Y. slip. op. 31407 (S. Ct. N.Y. Co. June 7, 2010).

H. Automatic Assignability of Claims Against the Indenture Trustee

As previously noted, claims under the Trust Indenture Act must be expressly assigned[714] despite the existence of the New York General Obligation Law that automatically assigns common law claims against an indenture trustee as part of a transfer of the bond.[715] Where the General Obligation Law does apply to transfer state law claims, the transferee need not show its own injury.[716] Even if New York is the governing law of the indenture, discovery may be necessary to determine the law governing the transfer based upon conflict of law principles.[717] The language of the frequently used LSTA Purchase and Sale Agreement purports to be governed by New York law. In that document, transferred rights language with respect to claims is quite broad.[718] However, where the foreign transferees of residential mortgage-backed securities issued under German law attempted to sue the trustee for breach of contractual, fiduciary and statutory duties, they could not take advantage of the General Obligation Law and were held to lack standing.[719]

I. Action Against Indenture Trustee by Securities and Exchange Commission

In some situations, the Securities and Exchange Commission may pursue a claim against the indenture trustee, alleging the indenture trustee assisted the obligor in the violation of the securities laws by concealing problems and red flags from bondholders.[720] Fortunately, actions of this type against indenture trustees by the SEC are rare; however, they are not unheard of. An example of the type of fact pattern that leads the SEC to take action illustrates why such cases are not the norm. A bank, acting through a senior vice president, served as indenture trustee for 39 conduit municipal bond and private placement offerings to build, purchase and renovate senior living facilities brought to the bank and controlled by an Atlanta businessman. Despite clear language in the indentures, the indenture trustee chose not to inform bondholders of the failure to replenish numerous draws on the debt service reserve funds (with a cumulative deficiency of nearly $3.5 million) or the failure to file required annual financial statements for 20 bond

---

714 Sarah Reid and Robert Schumahker, *"Automatic Assignability of Claims: The Tension Between Federal and New York State Law,"* 125 BANKING L.J 725 (2008).

715 New York General Obligations Law § 13-197.

716 *Bluebird Partners, L.P. v. First Fidelity Bank, N.A.*, 97 N.Y.2d 456, 767 N.E.2d 672 (2002).

717 *Racepoint Partners LLC v. J.P. Morgan Chase Bank*, 2006 WL 304416 (S.D.N.Y. Oct. 26, 2006); *Excelsior Fund, Inc. v. J.P. Morgan Chase Bank, N.A.*, 2007 WL 950134 (S.D.N.Y. Mar. 28, 2007).

718 The Loan Syndication and Trading Associates Purchase and Sale Agreement for Distressed Trader, LSTA Standard Terms and Conditions, Apr. 24, 2014.

719 *Phoenix Light SF Ltd. et al. v. U.S. Bank et al.*, 2015 WL 2359358 (S.D.N.Y. May 18, 2015).

720 *See* Jack Casey, *Trustee Agrees to $1.6M Settlement in Brogdon-Related Case*, THE BOND BUYER, Sept. 9, 2016.

offerings. These failures in many instances should have resulted in defaults under the indenture. Rather, the concealment permitted additional bond offerings to go forward. The SEC said the trustee failed in its role as gatekeeper to stand up for the bondholders and notify them about material problems with the bonds, but instead chose to protect the fees it collected from these deals. The parent of the indenture trustee agreed to settle the charges, to disgorge more than $984,000 in fees and to pay a penalty of $600,000 and interest of more than $83,500.[721] The SEC also filed a civil action against a former senior vice president individually,[722] who agreed to a ban from acting as an indenture trustee for municipal bonds in the future as well as a $55,000 payment.[723]

---

721 Press Release, U.S. Securities and Exchange Commission, Litigation Release No. 23640, Sep. 12, 2016.

722 *Securities and Exchange Commission v. Marrien Neilson*, Case No. 16-cv-5475 (D.N.J., Sep. 9, 2016), ECF No. 1.

723 Final Judgment as to Defendant Marrien Neilson, *d.* (Mar. 3, 2017), ECF No. 13.

Made in United States
North Haven, CT
10 November 2026

22096545R00293